French
Women
Poets
of Nine
Centuries

THE DISTAFF & THE PEN

Selected and Translated by NORMAN R. SHAPIRO

Introductions by ROBERTA L. KRUEGER,

CATHERINE LAFARGE, & CATHERINE PERRY

Foreword by ROSANNA WARREN

THE JOHNS HOPKINS UNIVERSITY PRESS   Baltimore

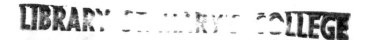

French Women Poets *of* Nine Centuries

Publication of this book has been supported by a grant from the Thomas and Catharine McMahon Fund of Wesleyan University, established through the generosity of the late Joseph McMahon.

The Johns Hopkins University Press
2715 North Charles Street
Baltimore, Maryland 21218-4363
www.press.jhu.edu

Library of Congress Cataloging-in-Publication Data
French women poets of nine centuries : the distaff and the pen /
selected and translated by Norman R. Shapiro ; introductions by
Roberta L. Krueger, Catherine Lafarge, and Catherine Perry ; foreword
by Rosanna Warren.
     p. cm.
    English and French.
    Includes bibliographical references and indexes.
    ISBN-13: 978-0-8018-8804-5 (hardcover : alk. paper)
    ISBN-10: 0-8018-8804-2 (hardcover : alk. paper)
    1. French poetry—Women authors—Translations into English.
2. French poetry—Translations into English. I. Shapiro, Norman R.
    PQ1167.N56 2008
    841.008'09287—dc22   2007032474

A catalog record for this book is available from the British Library.

Page 1183 is an extension of this copyright page.

Special discounts are available for bulk purchases of this book.
For more information, please contact Special Sales at 410-516-6936
or specialsales@press.jhu.edu.

The Johns Hopkins University Press uses environmentally friendly
book materials, including recycled text paper that is composed of at
least 30 percent post-consumer waste, whenever possible. All of our
book papers are acid-free, and our jackets and covers are printed on
paper with recycled content.

In loving memory of my mother,
the first woman poet I knew

Qu'une femme auteur est à plaindre!
Au diable soit le sot métier!
Qu'elle se fasse aimer ou craindre,
Chacun veut la déprécier...
Un raisonneur, qui chez lui brille,
L'accable de ses lourds propos
Et la renvoie à son aiguille,
Après quinze ans d'heureux travaux...

Poor woman writer! Devil take
Her foolish craft! Should she desire
To stir love, fear, for art's own sake,
Everyone seeks to vilify her...
Despite long years of noble endeavor,
A philosophe, true salon wit,
Heaps scorn upon her, and—ah, clever!—
Tells her to go back home and knit...

—from Constance-Marie de Théïs,
    princesse de Salm-Dyck, *Poésies* (1811)

The poet and playwright Constance-Marie de Théïs, princesse de
Salm-Dyck (1767–1845), was the victim of two unhappy marriages,
the first to a Monsieur Pipelet de Leury, and the second to a German
botanist, Prince Joseph Salm-Reifferscheidt-Dyck. Imbued with the
zeal for women's rights inherited from the French Revolution, Théïs
entertained many prominent women (and men) of letters and the arts
in her Paris salon. She is best remembered for her characteristic *Epïtre
aux femmes* (Letter to Women) (1797; reprinted, 1811), a vigorous, witty
condemnation of male faults, flaws, and excesses.

Contents

Foreword

Eight hundred years of poetry by French women: Norman Shapiro has set himself a task of phantasmagorical ventriloquism. From Marie de France through Albertine Sarrazin, who died in 1967, wending his way through the centuries, he has pulled fifty-six poets out of hiding or demi-obscurity and devised an array of voices for poems of dizzying variety. As his introduction makes clear, he had multiple challenges to face: not only the artistic task of finding English forms for French lays, sonnets, rhyming couplets, odes, epigrams, elegies and free verse, but the treasure hunt to find the poems to translate. Some of these poets, like Marie de France, Christine de Pizan, Louise Labé, Marceline Desbordes-Valmore, and Anna de Noailles, already had established reputations (in the case of Labé, perhaps too established); but many of the other poets Shapiro has gathered here had become invisible and inaudible, and not the least of his triumphs has been the act of assembling the texts. In doing so, introducing each writer with her mini-biography, he has implicitly rewritten French literary history.

The new line-up has produced, for this reader at least, violently contradictory responses. On the one hand, I find myself moved and fascinated by the new density Shapiro has given to the sense of French literary culture over the centuries. The stories of these women's lives twine together in one large, complex story of the efforts of one half of French humanity to express itself in writing. The effort crosses boundaries of class, language, and even country: the writers may be queens, like Marguerite de Navarre, or the daughters of chambermaids, like Marie-Catherine Desjardins de Villedieu; they may write in Occitan, like Castelloza; or they may be Belgian, like Marie Nizet and Liliane Wouters. Some lived in centuries, like the eighteenth, when a salon system encouraged talented, privileged women to write and perform; others had to endure extraordinary hardship to seize the power to write. And for none of them, even in the twentieth century, could it have been easy. The narratives are often gripping in themselves. I have long thought that someone should make a film out of the life of Marceline Desbordes-Valmore, from the violence of the Revolution that threw her family into turmoil in her childhood; through her misadventures, in adolescence, with her mother seeking support in Guadeloupe during a plague and a slave revolt; through her life as a professional actress and the multiple griefs for lost lovers and children that marked her life. And her story is by no means the most dramatic; Elizabeth-Sophie Chéron, a painter and musician as well as a poet, was supporting her family by the age of sixteen; Louise Michel was a famous revolutionary; Natalie Barney was a spectacular lesbian révoltée; Albertine Sarrazin was a petty criminal who spent her life in and out of jail.

To dwell on the life stories, however, is to fall into the old trap of critics considering the writings of French women. The lives have often stood in for the writing. And here Norman Shapiro's devotion as a translator clears the view, directing our attention, again and again, to the details of verse forms he is trying to reproduce, to the syllable counts, the rhyme patterns, the vocalic play, the puns. By his art, he makes us attend to *their* art. And that is where one's responses may veer in wildly different directions. I confess, mine do. For in spite of the strong showing by a number of these poets—the sturdy vigor of Marie de France, the elegance of the poems signed by Louise Labé (whether she was a fiction of Maurice Scève's or not), the dramatic immediacy of Desbordes-Valmore—the larger picture may strike some readers as depressing. And that too tells us something. Century after century, a good number of the women poets lament love and claim the province of the heart and breathless sensiblity in diction that never breaks beyond the conventions of their time. My heart is wrung, in poetic sympathy, impatience, and protest, to see Victoire Babois (1760–1839) addressing women, "Your hearts are the rich sources of / Treasures of happiness and love" ("To My Niece Madame B***"); or to see Louise Colet, a smart woman who could have known better, write, "The breath of woe blows barren my distress" ("Sonnet"). As late as the twentieth century Anna de Noailles starts a poem, "O melancholic soul of mine!" and Liliane Wouters describes "Love that I flee yet yearn for, Love sublime" ("Beaches, seaweed, what can you know of me"). With few exceptions, the twentieth-century poets in this collection seem not to have absorbed anything from Rimbaud or Apollinaire or any other poet of ferocious and original power.

Are women afraid of power? This anthology forces one to rethink the very notion of poetic power. While I am not willing to give up the touchstones of strength I have spent my life studying and trying to steal—from Villon, Ronsard, Racine, Chénier, Nerval, Baudelaire, Mallarmé, let us say—this anthology prompts one to search for more varied forms of power. And they are here. They are in Pernette de Guillet's lively phrases: "That in my soul, and with a joy untold, / I see what my mere eyes might not behold" ("Epigrammes," VIII). They are in Madeleine de l'Aubespine's chic Renaissance sonnets, which hold their own with Ronsard: "Let fire weigh heavy and the earth weigh light" ("Sonnets d'amour," III). They are in the salon wit of Marie-Catherine Desjardins de Villedieu's fables: "He sets about cupidifying..." ("The Monkey Who Played Cupid") and in Fanny de Beauharnais's affectations of triviality: "And, with a bit of persiflage, / However weighty your *message*, / Reply with banter, jibe, and jape!" ("To Men").

One traditional response of women, over the ages, to the assertion of male superiority, has been a superficial agreement with that arrangement and a strategic confession of weakness, as camouflage. So we find Jeanne d'Albret (1528–1572) coyly describing, in a sonnet to Du Bellay, her "Paper, too rough, and ink, too thick; my quill, / Too heavy, and my hand as well; words, crude." Gabrielle de Coignard (1550?–1586?) turns the trope of incapacity to theological purpose in "Oh lord God, guide my heart . . . / No art have I, nor grace, nor eloquence / Worthy to raise your holy name on high." Beauharnais, two hundred years later, entitled a collection preemptively, *Mélanges des poesies fugitives et de prose sans conséquence.* Rosemonde Gérard, wife of Edmond de Rostand, portrays herself as an ignoramus in her anthology of French women's poetry in 1948: "Nothing, in fact, is what she knows— / Well, a few things, but almost none." And Liliane Wouters, in a contemporary poem called "Breath," addresses—with what layers of irony!—"Humble little breath of mine."

And yet this volume provides an extraordinary show of force. Some of the poems take on, openly, the theme of the difficulty of writing as a woman. Catherine des Roches (1542–1587), in "To My Distaff," asserts, "My hand holds both the spindle and the pen." Louise Colet shows immense dignity as well as wisdom in her poem about work: looking beyond romance, she addresses work: "by your lights / I live my life: you quell my passion-fires, / Bridle my dreams, rein in my vain desires." One of the most surprising presences is Louise Michel, the revolutionary. Her political energy spills over into poems of jolting vitality, a great relief in the wash of Decadent and Symbolist velleities surrounding her: "What will you do, Fate, with my giant dream?" ("What do you with the daisy, winds of night?").

It is a brilliant stroke to conclude the book with Albertine Sarrazin. This troubled young woman, dead at the age of thirty, an illegitimate child born in Algeria and brought up (miserably) in France, a veteran of reform schools and prisons, breaks upon the scene with startling power. In her presence, poetic niceties fall. The charms, the musings, the hushes, the lulls give way. She is no genius, but she has seen the world freshly and invented a language for her seeing: it is not hand-me-down. "The sun would bleed me nonstop no reprieve," starts one of her poems, already in high gear. One of her poems from the Fresnes prison concludes: "no more / To count the steps from cell to cell" ("For months I've heard the nightfalls rumbling"). In an eerie way, those steps from cell to cell might be imagined as the steps of her sister poets, over the centuries, imprisoned in worlds shaped by men's power, men's laws, men's words. Norman Shapiro's remarkable book gives us a view of that vast prison, and of the liberties individual women managed to craft for themselves within it. Another generation of women poets has succeeded Sarrazin, and they are the richer for her thefts. But that is another story.

Rosanna Warren

Translator's Preface

I recall the times when, as a budding piano prodigy at age six or seven, instead of practicing, I would sit musing over the names of the composers on the back of the sheet music, imagining how to wrap my tongue around them. The French and Italian ones were easy—Debussy and Scarlatti presented no problem—but the plethora of Slavic ones was always a challenge: Rachmaninoff, Moussorgsky, Scriabine . . . and, heaven help us, Leschetizky! The American names, in comparison, were rather banal. No one with a name as easy to pronounce as "MacDowell" could have a flowing beard and diabolical, flashing eyes.

One composer in particular—with a name that seemed the essence of banality—intrigued me. How could "Mrs. H. H. A. Beach" possibly have been a composer? The name conjured up a squat, stolid hausfrau, with her apron and rolling pin. Clearly, her fingers would have been too pudgy to negotiate the dynamic arpeggios or delicate trills that I was supposed to be practicing. (I had no idea, then, that in her later career she came back into possession of her own name, and that, indeed, Amy Cheney Beach was, in her day, a piano virtuoso—virtuosa?—and a very respectable composer.)

Now, I knew even as a child that there were such creatures as women composers. Any young piano student has sooner or later played "The Scarf Dance" of Cécile Chaminade. And, a few years later, I had even come to know that the name Schumann, though most likely referring to Robert, could also conceivably mean Clara. There was even talk that Mendelssohn had had a sister . . . But why so few? Under what rock were they all hiding? Women, I realized even at that tender age, were roughly half the human species. And it certainly couldn't be that they just didn't study the piano. Almost all the other students who, like me, played at Miss Wolk's yearly recital were girls, after all. The same was probably true for other instruments also. (Well, maybe not the ponderous tuba and double bass, or the gymnastic drums, but those had to be exceptions.) So, if they played all the instruments, how come so few women had composed music for them?

It was some time later, studying French literature, that I was struck by a similar scarcity of women poets. True, English and American letters boasted a few prominent ones. But French? I had a faint knowledge of Marie de France from a survey course, tucked in between the *Chanson de Roland* and Chrestien de Troyes. And several other names lingered in the recesses of my brain, more perhaps, for their mellifluousness—Lucie Delarue-Mardrus, Marceline Desbordes-Valmore, the countess Anna de Noailles—than for their actual *œuvres*, which certainly were not on the required reading list for general exams.

And then there was that Louise Labé that everyone in the Renaissance course had begun talking about, and whom some had actually read. But half the race of poets? Hardly!

This paucity, it seemed to me, could not really be explained only by the traditional division of labor—say what you will—between man, the breadwinner, and woman, the housewife. One didn't have to choose either the distaff or the pen to the complete exclusion of the other. Writing is not an all-or-nothing occupation. It is not like being the CEO of a corporation, a high-powered attorney, or a test pilot. It is quite possible to be a devoted wife and mother and still be a poet. One needs only some familiarity with literary tradition and something to write with. And, of course, something to say, with the linguistic acumen to say it attractively. Talent, in other words. But surely those gifts were not the province of the male alone; and, if husbandship and fatherhood needn't prevent their development, why should motherhood do so? Furthermore, that would not even be an issue for all those women who did not become wives or mothers at all.

Literary trends of recent decades made it ever more pertinent to consider the question. Without taking up sociological cudgels or digging up paving stones to hurl at the barricades, a serious student of French poetry might well continue to ask, a little bemused: "So? Where are all the women?" And I did. Not to conform to an ideological, politically correct modishness that might too easily skew the data and lead us to extol works whose only value lay in the mere fact of their existence, but in the hope of uncovering texts of literary interest. (One thinks, analogously, of the many medieval manuscripts that provided nineteenth-century German scholars with doctoral dissertations and that rarely, if ever, were concerned with matters of artistic merit, but that were valued for the mere fact that they had managed to survive the rigors of time, decay, monastery burnings, and such.)

Hence this collection. As a literary translator I am always on the lookout for worthy things to translate, whether previous English versions exist or not. That's one of the joys of translating: no matter how many other hands and minds have reworked a text, there is always room for more. Indeed, as Borges has maintained, the more translations there are of a work, the better we "understand" it, so long as they all remain as rigorously faithful to the original as they can. But just what is that much-vaunted fidelity, and how does the translator go about observing it?

Fidelity in translation isn't like fidelity in marriage: there are many ways to be a faithful translator, and, arguably, only one way to be a faithful spouse. No two translators will come up with precisely the same version, yet both can be faithful to the original despite using many different words to express its sense and that indefinable quality we call its "tone." Clearly, there is no single "correct" translation, only a multiplicity of proximate approaches, each one producing a self-contained version of the original: a new work, in fact—a collaboration, I like to think—that is intimately related to the original, and that needs it in order to exist, but that could still stand on its own artistically if need be.

The translator has to be faithful to the tone as well as to the message. It is much trickier than just finding the meanings of all the words. That's the simple part. While the extremes are easy enough to avoid—who would translate a Ronsard sonnet, say, into hip-hop, except to be funny?—it takes care and a good ear to decide if such and such a word or expression sticks out like a sore thumb in an otherwise unified and convincing linguistic landscape. Would a Cervantes surrogate ever say, "Okay," for example?

As I have often had occasion to observe in the past, the fidelity question is especially controversial in translating formal verse. Some insist that only the literal meaning of a poem need be dealt with, and that rhyme and meter serve only to muddy the waters and are best avoided. For them, ambiguities, wordplay, subtleties of sound, and the like can be glossed in footnotes. Others insist that, if the poet uses such devices they are an intrinsic part of the poem, and the translator should do so too, as long as they don't create a straitjacket of artificiality, and as long as nothing—or, as little as possible—is sacrificed to them. Either camp will find its champions and adepts. It will be clear to which of the two I belong.

Several years ago, in keeping with my foregoing ruminations, I decided to compile a collection of French women poets, assuming that the major figures, whose work I already knew, plus a few others whose names were familiar, would yield up a number of worthy examples and form a pleasant little volume. So much for preliminary resolutions! The more I dug, the more I discovered. And the more I discovered, the more I admired. Reveling in revelation, I gradually expanded my sights. The "pleasant little volume" grew into the present result: not spurred on by any ideological or proselytizing fury, but guided by the desire to bring to light—in faithful English versions—a variety of texts whose very existence was, in large measure, unsuspected even by specialists. Even as I say this, however, I have a slight blush of *mauvaise foi*, since, like any translator, I confront my tasks with a certain self-serving pleasure: the joy of meeting and surmounting the challenges that every work presents; a pleasure that transcends all the disinterested scholarly and missionary zeal that would, no doubt, provide a more idealistic excuse.

Be that as it may, and my own motivations aside, as more and more challenges presented themselves I watched the collection grow well beyond the bounds I had first envisioned. As it is, even this rather mammoth collection could have been greatly expanded, especially with the poems of more recent writers, easier to come by—notwithstanding the vexatious problem of rights and permissions endemic to modern works—than those of earlier centuries. And it might have been expanded even more, also, had I not decided, as a matter of principle, to include only complete poems and to avoid the frequent and frustrating anthology technique of excerpting from longer ones. But it would have been inappropriate to ignore the sacrosanct French virtue of *mesure*, after all, and to let it "just grow," without imposing some reasonable and practical dimensions. And so I resisted the temptation to unbalance the collection still more with additional worthy twentieth-century texts, most of which, in free verse, present a translator with challenges of their own, different from those of more formal verse but no less demanding.

My quest for the French Woman Poet has led me into many byways, not all of which I felt justified in exploring and exploiting. (For which, my thanks, somewhat convolutedly arrived at, to Amy Cheney [a.k.a. Mrs. H. H. A.] Beach.) Suffice it to say that I have learned far more from this project than I knew when I began it. I hope my readers will be able to say the same.

Cambridge, Massachusetts

Note

Given the variable spellings, genders, accent marks, and grammatical constructions of early French through the eighteenth century, readers may mistake fidelity for error. Accents have been omitted throughout on French capitals—except in titles set in small capitals—the capitalization of some titles has been emended for consistent overall style, and the use of quotation marks has been Americanized where necessary, but I have otherwise reproduced the texts as published, correcting only occasional and unquestionable misprints.

Acknowledgments

An anthology like this—any anthology, in fact—is usually the product of many contributors. The editor-compiler either assigns the texts to a variety of invitees or selects from pre-existing materials, then comes around later to supply notes, pull everything together, and write an introduction. (And, of course, acknowledgments . . .) On the contrary, when I explain to any who ask that all the present 700-odd translations are my own, they usually tend to gasp. I have to admit that, on reflection, now that the project is complete—as complete as it will be, that is—I am even a little awed myself. Not only because of the quantity of texts that I eventually and quite unexpectedly found myself including, original intentions notwithstanding, but also because of the chronological and individual stylistic variety imposed *ipso facto* by a span of nine centuries. I hardly need reiterate that translations of a Marie de France, a Louise Labé, an Anna de Noailles, a Lise Deharme (*inter alia*—or *alias,* under the circumstances) demand differences of lexicon, form, and that impalpable but essential ingredient, tone.

But though the translations are all of my own doing, many are the hands, heads, and indeed hearts that have participated in putting them together between covers, and it is a pleasure to acknowledge my indebtedness to the institutions and individuals that have willingly offered much help. Of the former, my university, Wesleyan, has provided valuable financial assistance; and its Olin Library has been able to secure hard-to-find volumes without which several of the poets represented would have remained no more than shadowy names. The staffs of Harvard's Widener and Houghton Rare Book libraries, in the persons, notably, of Mary Smith and Joseph Bourneuf, have been equally appreciated, as have, for less strictly academic reasons, the facilities and personnel of that university's Adams House. It is there that, as Writer-in-Residence, I have been able to work in an atmosphere of intellectual and social—not to mention dietetic—nourishment. My gratitude to the Doctors Judy and Sean Palfrey, its masters, for their hospitality, and to Victoria (Vicky, Vicki, or Viqui) Macy for helping to keep the cogs turning. No less, to the ever cheerful staff of the dining hall, where, at the strategic corner table, most of these translations were written. Likewise, to the amiable crew of Peet's Coffee and Tea, in Harvard Square, who, punctuating my long proofreading chores, helped keep me amply coffee'd and tea'd.

Of the many special individuals whom I am happy to recognize, Evelyn Singer Simha has once again, as with all my endeavors, been a devoted friend, whose encouragement, as boundless as her literary good sense and uncompromising aesthetic taste, has been nothing short of indispensable. So too the frequently called-upon Caldwell Titcomb, seemingly inexhaustible fount of the essential fact and the pertinent reference. To both these good friends my sincerest thanks.

I have been particularly fortunate in having the services of three fine research assistants—Daniela Cammack, Sophie Hermann, and Rachel Hoffman—who never buckled under the burden of frequent assignments, frantic e-mails, and dire deadlines. My thanks to these Three Graces for their hard work and good humor. Likewise to Mike Weidman, much-needed cyberguru, who did not let himself get ruffled by my own computer near-illiteracy. He, Todd Houle, of Wesleyan's computer services, and the ever-obliging expert extraordinaire French Wall, eased me into the twenty-first century, thus completing the mission of dear friend Franklin Smith, who had already tugged me, "kicking and screaming," into the twentieth by convincing me to give up the goose quill for the keyboard.

Many other friends, colleagues, and correspondents, in academe and the publishing industry, and around their edges, have assisted in a variety of ways, big and small. To Kathleen Stefanowicz and Katherine Wolfe, my appreciation for frequently and generously working their interlibrary-loan magic; to Paul-Jean Cahen, Françoise Jurion-De Waha, Catherine Ostrow, and Dominique Rabourdin, my gratitude for *services exceptionnels,* as well as to Bob Gorman, Lynn Coe, and Catherine Muyl, for attempting to untangle the snarls of copyright law for me; to Marie-Claire Barnet, Bruno Batreau, Marie-Christine Bertoldo, Carrol Coates, Faustina Fiore, Marie-Thérèse Kaspar, Joyce Lowrie, Aurélie Nibodeau-Gouteredonde, Catherine Poisson, Jeff Rider, and Daniel Rogov, my thanks for a variety of helpful solutions, suggestions, and courtesies, as well as to Sylvia and Allan Kliman for much good cheer, and to Louisa Solano, the *doyenne* of Boston and Cambridge poetry, for her valued insights. Not least, by any means, a hearty *moltes gràcies* for the numerous chores always smilingly carried out by the selfless Rosalind Eastaway, along with Linda Cummings and their student assistants Lauren Pruneski and Katie Horowitz.

I wish to single out also, for their gracious permissions, the following: Eliane Barnich-Kegels, daughter of Anne-Marie Kegels; Jean Faury, director of the Fédération des Sociétés Intellectuelles du Tarn; Lise Jamati, granddaughter of Cécile Périn; and Jacques De Decker, secretary of the Belgian Académie Royale de Langue et de Littérature Françaises.

My very special thanks to the four collaborators whose contributions have enriched this collection: Rosanna Warren, Roberta Krueger, Catherine Lafarge, and Catherine Perry. The reader will value their graceful erudition as much as do I. The collaboration of my patient and knowledgeable editor, Michael Lonegro, and the skills of my meticulous copyeditor Peter Dreyer, as well as those of Courtney Bond and Thomas Broughton-Willett, all backstage actors essential to the enterprise, though unperceived by the reader, are no less warmly appreciated and most gratefully recognized.

I

The
Middle Ages
& the
Renaissance

The Middle Ages and the Renaissance

FROM MARIE DE FRANCE TO MARIE DE ROMIEU

Introduction by Roberta L. Krueger

From the Middle Ages through the Renaissance, during five centuries when the poetic *moi* was in most cases the creation of a man, and when male authors throughout Europe shaped poetic conventions to reflect their concerns, French women poets were exceptional in many ways.[1] In the Middle Ages, the vast majority of both women and men were unable to read or write. As literacy expanded steadily from the twelfth to the sixteenth century, however, it was not uncommon for young women from elite courts and households to read as well as their brothers. Yet girls' formal education lagged far behind that of boys throughout the medieval and early modern period, and women's learning and literary activities were areas of controversy, if not of suspicion and prohibition.[2] Women were enjoined to wield the distaff, or spindle—which symbolized their domestic responsibilities—rather than to employ the pen. Some moralists felt that women should learn to read so that they could better instruct their own children and absorb pious works during their leisure hours. But women's writing was often viewed either as a dangerous path toward autonomy and secret communication with lovers or as simply unnecessary, since women's intellectual or artistic aspirations were not valued in themselves. During the Renaissance, even when exchanging verse between elite men and women flourished as a mode of sociability and some humanists encouraged women's education, women's access to culture remained problematic. Women who wrote—especially those who circulated their writings beyond family members and transmitted their works in copied manuscripts or published books—often did so against tremendous odds. Given such restrictions, it is all the more remarkable that women writers of the Middle Ages and the Renaissance have left an exceptionally influential and diverse body of works, a corpus that is particularly rich in French.[3]

The poems in this section were produced over a period of five centuries and within a broad geographical area, as European society experienced both steady change and tumultuous events: the gradual demise of feudalism and the centralization of the monarchy; the flowering of culture in elite courts; the Black Death; the Hundred Years' War; the growth of urban middle classes; the advent of printing; and the Protestant Reformation and ensuing religious struggles, to name a few milestones. If women were the "fourth estate" during the medieval period, and if common women fared no better in terms of legal and political rights during the Renaissance, women's contributions were no less vital to domestic and town economies throughout this period. Individual women wielded

3

power and influence as queens, regents, wives managing estates in their husbands' absence, widows governing lands and households, patronesses at court, organizers of salons, and, no less, as mothers who shaped their families' destinies. The women whose works are translated in these pages also empowered themselves in their writing, expressing their trials and accomplishments, their fears and desires in verse. The poems' generic, thematic, and stylistic variety attests to the vitality of poetic writing by French women from the time that the first vernacular works were recited and circulated in manuscripts to the early years of printed books. As literacy for men and women expanded, and as modes of transmission were transformed, French women's poetry, if less frequent and voluminous than men's, continued to expand its boundaries, moving from convents and royal courts to households of the lesser nobility and urban upper middle-class salons, from manuscript to print.

CONTEXTS, FORMS, THEMES: DIVERSITY AND COMPLEXITY

These poets flourished within particular historical and cultural contexts that help to explain the rich tapestry of their works. The first poems were popular and classical tales transplanted to aristocratic soil. Marie de France recast Breton *lais* and Latin fables into *romanz* (vernacular French) in octosyllabic couplets written for oral transmission, probably at the court of Henry II Plantagenet, whose queen was the influential patron Eleanor of Aquitaine. Na Castelloza, the "dark lady" of song, composed her lyrics in the *langue d'oc*, Old Provençal or Occitan, in the world of the troubadours and feudal lords of southern France. Christine de Pizan, the highly literate daughter of an Italian astrologer appointed to the court of Charles V, a self-taught scholar and poet, wrote for the family of Charles VI and for the dukes of Burgundy. A towering figure of Renaissance letters, Marguerite de Navarre, sister of King François I of France and wife of Henri d'Albret, king of Navarre, in her second marriage, used her position of privilege to defend humanistic writers and reformist theologians and was patron to poets and polemicists. Among her extensive writings—and in striking contrast to the worldly *Heptaméron*—she penned numerous devotional poems and verse epistles, including letters exchanged with her daughter, Jeanne d'Albret, mother of Henri de Navarre, the future Henri IV of France.

Renaissance women's poetry was no longer restricted to royal or noble courts. The advent of printing expanded the possibilities for readers and authors alike. Pernette du Guillet, of aristocratic or high bourgeois birth, and Louise Labé, daughter of a rope maker or rope merchant, helped to shape the charmed literary life of Lyon during the 1540s through the 1560s, when the vogue for Neoplatonist and Petrarchan love lyrics was at its height. Each woman left a collection of poems that is modest in output but finely and distinctively wrought. In another provincial city, Poitiers, Madeleine des Roches and her daughter, Catherine des Roches, succeeded during the mid-sixteenth century in establishing their own literary salon and in publishing a body of poetry astonishing for its quantity, its diverse form and subject matter, and its dynamic sociability. During the same period, writing in the convent of Poissy for her sisters in Christ, the nun Anne de Marquets transformed the conventions of the love lyric to express a very different feminine sensibility in religious sonnets that were published posthumously. Widowed with two daughters after only three years of marriage, Gabrielle de Coignard wrote her remarkable spiritual poetry in isolation, recording an intimate spiritual quest that reflects, among other sources, the influence of Ronsard, whose death she commemorated with an elegant sonnet. Ronsard also inspired the more worldly compositions of a contemporary woman who calls herself his poetic "daughter," identified by some critics as Madeleine de l'Aubespine, and who was evidently a woman of high birth and literary accomplishment. The final figure of our medieval and Renaissance female poets, Marie de Romieu, embodies the expansion of women's literacy within this period and the continual diversity of women's writing. Marie wrote, not as a queen, cloistered nun, privileged aristocrat, or wealthy bourgeoise, but as a common laywoman, the daughter of a provincial baker.

As this brief overview suggests, women's poetry flourished in royal and ducal courts, convents, and bourgeois households throughout France. Poems were produced for wealthy patrons, for sister nuns, and for family members and friends, in manuscripts that could be presented to a king or circulated privately; in early printed books published with the author's supervision; or in private manuscripts published only posthumously. The works translated here include verse narratives (*lais* and fables) in octosyllabic couplets; the fixed forms of Provençal lyric and courtly love poetry; Petrarchan *canzonieri* or sonnet sequences; didactic epigrams; allegorical narratives; religious sonnets and odes; occasional poetry; and verse epistles. The verse's subject matter encompasses both private and public concerns, sacred and profane. These poems not only explore love in its many modes—passionate, familial, and divine. They also counsel family members and others about proper behavior; offer advice to rulers; express appreciation for services; lament sickness and loss; request material assistance; examine philosophical and moral problems; construct verbal puzzles for the reader's amusement; and record meditations of the soul seeking God.

POETIC INNOVATIONS / VEXED REPUTATIONS

If women's extant writings comprised only a fraction of those by men that have been preserved, the women's work often strikes out in new ways, with surprising innovations. Marie de France's collection is the first extant vernacular collection of Aesopic fables. Her witty verse inaugurated in the vernacular a literary tradition still immensely popular in France, where schoolchildren regularly memorize La Fontaine, and where Robert Wilson's ingenious 2003 production *Les Fables de La Fontaine*, repeated in subsequent seasons, has delighted theatergoers at the Comédie-Française. Christine de Pizan, best known for her staunch defense of women and attack on misogyny, inaugurated one of the earliest literary debates in France, the *querelle de la Rose*. Inasmuch as she supported her mother and three children after her husband's death by composing courtly poems and didactic treatises for wealthy patrons, Christine has been considered France's first professional woman of letters.

Many of these early writers blazed new trails or crafted poetic monuments. Marguerite de Navarre was one of the earliest French poets to use terza rima, in a poem she wrote to mourn her niece.[4] Her verse allegory *Prisons de la vie humaine* has been acclaimed as a masterpiece of spiritual autobiography.[5] Louise Labé was a pioneer in the composition of the sonnet sequence. Anne de Marquets penned a collection of spiritual sonnets that have been called "far more advanced, in terms of the application of systematic devotional practice to poetry, than anything written in the 1570s and 1580s."[6]

The list of poetic "firsts" and milestones continues with the dames des Roches, who organized an important literary salon and were the first women to publish their correspondence, which included poetry. Marie de Romieu's verse defense of women, published by her brother without her knowledge, has been described as initiating among early modern women a vogue for composing and publishing attacks against misogyny in literature.[7]

These impressive poetic accomplishments have not always been recognized and praised as such, however. During the nineteenth and much of the twentieth century, it was not uncommon to question whether some of these poems were written by a woman; to disparage the mediocre quality of work, if female authorship were conceded; or to focus on the poet's imagined love life rather than on the verse itself. It has thus been charged that the verses in the few extant manuscripts signed by "Marie" de France were not produced by a single author, or that they were produced by a male cleric adopting a feminine voice;[8] that Christine de Pizan was, in the opinion of an eminent French scholar, an "insufferable bluestocking";[9] that Louise Labé was a courtesan;[10] that Marguerite de Navarre did not write the *Heptaméron;*[11] that Marie de Romieu's poems were in fact written by her brother,[12] and so forth.

Indeed, the authorship of at least one other early French female poet has recently come into question. In a controversial study, the French scholar Mireille Huchon published the findings of an extensive investigation into the circumstances surrounding the publication of texts attributed to Louise Labé, claiming that Labé's collected works—as well as, perhaps, the poems of Pernette du Guillet—were written by a coterie of male poets, with Maurice Scève at the helm.[13] Although Labé scholars have not yet marshaled a full response, there have already been counterarguments to Huchon's claims, including the suggestion that Labé's work was a literary collaboration, rather than a total fiction.[14] In the pages that follow, I shall remind readers of Huchon's hypothesis as appropriate, but my own analysis will continue to foreground the interpretations, equally plausible in my view, of those scholars who have attended to the poems' female voice. As the latest controversy shows, French women's poetry remains a contested domain of vexed reputations well into the twenty-first century.

Whether for reasons of neglect or outright dismissal, many of the poems included in these pages were known only by scholars until recently. As literary anthologies and popular editions ignored women's poetry, much premodern French poetry by female authors could be read only in research libraries or rare book rooms.

Medieval and early modern women's historiography underwent a major revolution in the second half of the twentieth century. Women's social, legal, political, economic, and literary histories were reclaimed in a wealth of editions, histories, biographies, and critical studies that have brought the buried treasures of these remarkable writers into the light they so well deserve. With a sense of urgency and excitement, medieval and Renaissance scholars have uncovered hundreds of poems, narratives, letters, and memoirs by dozens of woman writers who had been marginalized or remained unknown in literary studies. Many poems in this section are translated from recent editions of works that had languished in manuscript form or as early editions in rare book archives for centuries.[15] Some of them have been translated into English for the first time here.[16]

THE AUTHORS AND THEIR TEXTS

Arranged in approximate chronological order under their authors' names and presented with their texts in Anglo-Norman, Provençal, Middle French, or Renaissance French, these elegant translations open a long-closed window on the past for anglophone readers. The anthology's handsome printed format may obscure the very different conditions of transmission and reception of these early poems, the fragmentary nature of the literary documents, and the often marginal status of their authors, about whom we often know very little. Marie de France's works were composed to be performed before a courtly public. No extant manuscript contains her entire works; only one manuscript contains all the *Lais* and the *Fables*. The *trobairitz* lyrics were probably sung with musical accompaniment (although there is only one extant melody accompanying *trobairitz* verse).[17] There are roughly 2,500 Occitan lyric poems by around 400 named male troubadours conserved in the *chansonniers*. Twenty names of female troubadours, or *trobairitz*, survive, and scholars continue to debate the extent of the modest corpus of their poetry (around 35 poems).[18] Only recently has a case been made for the existence of women poets, female *trouvères*, in northern France.[19]

Little is known about most poets, male or female, in the twelfth and thirteenth centuries, when works were gathered in manuscript compendia of diverse authors and genres and when literary biographies, such as the Provençal *vidas* and *razos*, tended to be highly fictionalized. It is not until the later Middle Ages that we have firm historical evidence about the lives of women authors who signed and actively sought publication of the works, sometimes in the midst of considerable controversy. The mystic Marguerite Porete (whose verse is not included here) was burned at the stake in 1310 for refusing to recant her remarkable *Mirouer des simples âmes*, a blend of mystical prose and poetry.[20] Christine de Pizan's complaints about the antifeminist timbre of the *Roman de la rose* provoked a lively debate among her contemporaries. We know that Christine de Pizan personally supervised the production and illumination of her manuscripts, which she presented to Queen Isabelle de Bavière, among other notables. Her works circulated in multiple manuscripts and were published in printed editions throughout the Renaissance; several were translated into English and one into Portuguese.[21] Yet later generations considered Christine a minor figure in literary history until a major effort by twentieth-century scholars, many of them women, prepared new editions of many (not yet all) of her works and revived her reputation as poet, moralist, and eloquent champion of female honor.[22]

In the manner of Christine, several women poets cultivated a public persona and used poetry as a vehicle for social engagement and the promotion of female virtue. When Louise Labé published her sonnets (either on her own, or in collaboration, as noted above), she dedicated the volume to a well-known woman of Lyon, Clémence de Bourges, thus increasing Louise's own respectability.[23] Although Christine de Pizan had staunchly defended female intellect and praised the cultural contributions of women in the past (among them the ancient Greek poet Sappho),[24] she stopped short of advocating that other women follow her exceptional path as an autodidact and author. Louise went further, urging her sister Lyonnaises to lay down the distaff and take up the pen, not only so that their learning and intelligence would prompt men to exercise greater virtue, but also so that they could find joy in learning and in writing for themselves.[25]

For Madeleine des Roches and her daughter Catherine, poetry and sociability, artistic endeavors and gallantry, were intertwined. They not only exchanged verse orally with visitors to their prosperous household in Poitiers; they also actively sought the publication of their work. Catherine eloquently argued that women's writing and the domestic sphere could be harmoniously reconciled. The des Roches's writings embrace, rather than shun, the pains and struggles of women's daily lives (see Catherine des Roches's "A ma quenoille" ["To My Distaff"]). Yet their poetry reaches well beyond the quotidian. The mother/daughter dyad not only published a famous exchange of poems between hosts and guests about a flea on Catherine's bosom, they also wrote verse to offer advice to the king's family; to seek indemnity for property destroyed during the civil war ("Au roy"); to defend women's honor; and to offer moral instruction (as in Catherine's translation of Pythagoras's *Vers dorez*). As we have seen, they also published their correspondence. They were among the first bourgeois women in France to promote their own social reputation so self-consciously and so successfully in the newly emerging urban salon through writing.[26]

Other works in these pages are far more private; some remain shrouded in mystery. Pernette du Guillet's lovely epigrams remained in manuscript form on scattered scraps of paper. In his dedicatory letter to the "Dames lyonnoizes," the editor, Antoine du Moulin, explains that a "petit amas de rymes" (little collection of rhymes) was brought to him for publication by Pernette du Guillet's husband, who had found them "parmy ses brouillars en assés povre ordre" (among her drafts in a rather disorderly state) after his wife's death.[27] Most critics concur that the source of the poet's inspiration, the figure named "Jour" (Day) in her "Epigrammes," was Maurice Scève, author of a sequence of dizains, or ten-line poems, *Délie: Objet de plus haulte vertu,* in which Du Guillet is represented as Diana and as the distant moon. Nothing is known of Scève's and Du Guillet's affair, which seems to have been chaste, perhaps fueled by no more than their brilliant verbal exchange. As we have said, one critic suggests that Scève may have played a more active role than has been suspected in bringing Pernette du Guillet's verse to light.[28] Yet whatever the circumstances of their publication, centuries later, Pernette du Guillet's poems stand on their own, offering a distinctive response to Neoplatonic conventions (as will be discussed further below).

Many other poems in this section were also published posthumously. Anne de Marquets's majestic *Sonets spirituels* probably circulated in manuscript form within the convent of Poissy for the spiritual guidance and inspiration of the sisters. The poems did not appear in print until seventeen years after her death. Gabrielle de Coignard's daughters published her powerful *Œuvres chrétiennes* only after their mother's passing.

Given the controversy that surrounded much religious writing during this period, the discretion of devotional poets is understandable. For a woman to speak directly to God or interpret the Scriptures could be construed as dangerously presumptuous. Branded a heretic for allegedly indulging in such practices, Marguerite Porete paid with her life, as we have seen. Anne de Marquets defended herself in print against a Protestant critic who accused her of putting God's words into human utterance. (Unlike Marguerite Porete, however, Anne de Marquets seems to have been encouraged by Catholic officials to defend her orthodoxy by publishing her first work, her *Sonets, prieres et devises.*)[29] Even the king's sister, Marguerite de Navarre, saw one of her initial writings, the *Miroir de l'âme pécheresse,* condemned by the Sorbonne for its reformist tendencies.[30]

The ban against the *Miroir* was soon lifted, and Marguerite published other works during her lifetime. But in her last years, during the bitter religious wars and especially after her beloved brother's death, she penned monumental tomes in private. Her greatest works, including the *Heptaméron*, were published post-humously. Some of Marguerite's most important devotional poetry lay in oblivion, in manuscript form, until its serendipitous discovery by a scholar in the 1890s.[31] Abel Lefranc recounts his "surprise" and "emotion" on realizing that BN fr 24298 contained Marguerite's last works, whose fate he describes in dramatic terms: "No hand seems to have turned these ever-so-precious pages since the day when Jeanne d'Albret closed the manuscript away in an iron box, fastened with solid locks, wishing to protect it from indiscrete eyes, with scruples that are easily understandable" (translation mine).[32] The project of publishing a critical edition of Marguerite's complete works that will assemble her extensive corpus of poetry, prose, theater, and correspondence has only recently been undertaken.[33]

Madeleine de l'Aubespine's poems went unpublished for centuries after her death and remain an enigma. In 1926, Roger Sorg culled poems written in a woman's voice from a manuscript in the Bibliothèque nationale, BN fr 1718, where they appear intermittently within 135 folios containing scores of other poems, many of them by Philippe Desportes; Sorg published the female-voiced poems in a handsome volume, to produce a *canzoniere*-like sequence, which he attributed to Madeleine de l'Aubespine.[34] No such name appeared in the manuscript, however, and the attribution was contested shortly after the appearance of Sorg's edition.[35] Scholars have recently shored up evidence in favor of Madeleine de l'Aubespine's authorship; a critical edition and a bilingual edition are in preparation.[36]

Through new editions, ongoing critical investigations, and translations such as the current volume, female voices from the past, unearthed from "precious pages," will come to the attention of new audiences, readers never intended or imagined by the original authors. If some scholars doubt the existence of "real" women behind some of these texts, others will argue that women's cultural participation was vibrant throughout the Middle Ages and the Renaissance; that women were not only patrons but also authors; and that the poetic exchange between male and female voices that is so richly inscribed in early verse—from troubadour poetry to the intriguing BN fr 1718—might very well emanate from historic women and men in poetic dialogue.

READING THE WOMAN'S VOICE: CRITICAL PERSPECTIVES

To tune one's ear to the female voices of medieval and Renaissance women's female poetry is to enter these poems on their own terms, to attend to their unique rhetorical flourishes, their particular tone and voicing, their repetitions and silences. In the Prologue to her *Lais,* Marie says she will not do as her contemporaries have done by translating Latin texts; she will instead write down oral tales from the Breton tradition.[37] The stories she offers, among them "The

Nightingale" and "The Woodbine," creatively transform motifs from classical literature and from Breton fairy tales to imagine the lives of single and married women struggling to reconcile love with social obligations. When Marie recasts Latin sources in the *Fables* and in *Saint Patrick's Purgatory* (her last work), her translations are once again transformative.[38] She adds new tales to the *Fables*, focuses on the trials of female animals, and offers numerous ambiguous endings (as in "The Man and His Quarrelsome Wife").[39] Throughout the *Lais* and the *Fables*, Marie highlights the struggle of women as readers, writers, and teachers. She ends "The Nightingale" with a scene of dolorous creation, for example. The lady embroiders the story of her thwarted love and wraps it around the nightingale her husband has killed, conveying the bird in a relic to her lover. The *Fables* conclude with the ironic tale of a stubborn hen who continues to scratch at dirt rather than accept the superior nourishment a wise woman has offered. This is a rather disquieting image of the moralist's relationship to her audience. Marie's artfully composed poems draw our attention to women's precarious social condition and to their struggles as storytellers, artists, and teachers.

Marie's tripartite corpus signals three broad and often intersecting registers in which medieval and Renaissance poets composed their verse. The courtly mode of the *Lais,* which focus on amorous relations, is revisited in the lyrics of the *trobairitz* and female *trouvères;* in Christine de Pizan's ballades and rondeaux; in the rhymes and sonnets of Pernette du Guillet and Louise Labé and in numerous other love poems. The didactic mode of the *Fables* is pursued by Christine de Pizan in the *Enseignemens moraux* (as well as in many other works not translated here); by Catherine des Roches in the "Imitation de la mère de Salomon à la roine mère du roy," and in her translation of the *Vers dorez* and *Enigmes* attributed to Pythagoras; and by Marie de Romieu in her moral epigrams (e.g., "To a Scandalmonger"). The religious register of the *Espurgatoire,* which explores the soul's spiritual discovery, is recast within the devotional verse of Marguerite de Navarre, Jeanne d'Albret, Anne de Marquets, and Gabrielle de Coignard.

The poetic conventions of these registers—lyric, didactic, and devotional— were largely determined by the male authors who dominated the literary landscape. What is significant about medieval and early modern French women's poetry is not only that the works of female poets have survived in such quantity and diversity. It is also that their feminine voices succeed—in spite of frequent professions of modesty and insufficiency—in forcefully reshaping masculine poetic traditions. Although the clerical tradition enjoined women to be silent and all but the most enlightened humanists disparaged women's writing, many female authors wielded the pen to inscribe a distinctive feminine perspective and to claim a new authority.

The dilemma of the female persona occurs most acutely in the lyric tradition, where the figure of a male poet who adores a beautiful lady and laments her distance or cruel indifference appears in hundreds of poems, from the earliest medieval troubadours to the Neoplatonic and Petrarchan lover-poets of the Renaissance. As male poets explore their love in myriad inventions and demonstrated their poetic mastery through meter, rhyme, image, and poetic ornament, they often seem more intent on vaunting their poetic talents than on engaging in an actual relationship with a living, breathing lady. The lady of the troubadour tradition is generally silent on her pedestal, the object of the poet's discourse; poetic conventions cast her as an unattainable "other." Similarly, the ideal lady of Neoplatonic poetry exists in an abstract realm, and the Petrarchan *domna* is both silent and distant, often cruelly so. For a woman to sing of her own desire or to tell her side of the story is, in itself, an act that breaks the mold, a move that obliges the female poet to reshape poetic conventions in her own way.

Many troubadour poets deploy highly figurative language and construct the poem as a hermetic object. In contrast, the lexicon and devices of the *trobairitz* are noted for their relative simplicity and frankness. Na Castelloza appeals very directly to her lover, employing the language of feudal obligations to underscore his infidelity and her steadfastness and suffering ("Cansos"). At the end of the Middle Ages, Christine de Pizan is well versed in the forms of court poetry—ballades, virelays, and rondeaux. But her longer sequences, such as the *Cent ballades d'amant et de dame,* contain an implicit criticism of "courtly" love as constructed by men. Christine reminds her readers on many occasions that adulterous or unchaste love is as harmful to a woman's honor as it is gratifying to the ego of the man.[40] In one of her debate poems, Christine ironically asks where the tombs may be of all the men who claim to have died for love.[41] Christine also expands the subject matter of lyric poetry to include verse that celebrates married love. Some of Christine's most moving verses are those mourning the loss of her husband, who died when she was only twenty-five years old. Christine's broad learning, her defense of women's dignity, her refashioning of classical culture, her critical views of courtly love, and her attempt as a female author to seek consolation for life's vicissitudes through her writing in many ways presage the literary projects of later female humanists.

Marguerite de Navarre, who may have known Christine's work, left a major literary corpus, in which profane love is viewed skeptically and where love lyrics are the exception rather than the rule. Like the sagacious, spiritually inclined Oysille in the *Heptaméron,* Marguerite the poet celebrates the fulfillment of divine love rather than the allure—and all too often the dangerous trap—of corporeal passions.

Whether or not the Renaissance poets of Lyon, Pernette du Guillet and Louise Labé, read or heard the lyric poetry of the *trobairitz* or Christine de Pizan, in their own verse, they continued to approach the conventions of male poetry obliquely, to refashion the discourse of love in their own register, and to express their passion directly, eschewing highly figurative or decorative language.[42] Writing in the bustling cultural center of Lyon, removed from the more restrictive atmosphere of Paris, both women refashioned the poetic conventions of their male contemporaries. For most critics (with the reservations noted above), Pernette du Guillet's poems respond to those of Maurice Scève, whose *Délie* extols the beauty of a lady figured alternately as the chaste huntress Diana or the cold moon, whose distance he laments. Scève's Délie is a silent beauty. In Du Guillet's *Rymes*, the lady speaks back with a critical difference. Du Guillet's poems are less rhetorically dense and emotionally convoluted than those of Scève, yet a variety of rhyme schemes and metrical forms belie their apparent simplicity and convey the poet's forceful originality.[43] The sixty epigrams include both *huitaines* and *dizaines;* there are also ten songs, five elegies, and two letters. Du Guillet's lady refuses to be cast into the mold Scève creates for her or to imitate his way of loving.[44] Rather than being distant and cold, she is direct and emotionally expressive. Instead of describing her torment at the absence of physical union, she seeks solace in mutual understanding and speaks serenely and simply of her *contentement*.[45] Pernette's "ring" poem, "If you wish not to prize so much this ring" ("Epigrammes," X), exemplifies her direct emotional appeal. Scholars have demonstrated that the poem responds to a poem in which Scève speaks ruefully to a ring recently bestowed by his lady and accuses the ring of attempting to imprison him.[46] By contrast, Du Guillet addresses not the object but her lover, drawing his attention to the woman who gives the gift. Her love is as steadfast and durable as the diamond. Du Guillet's elegant recasting of the ring conceit can be said to "correct" the bitter complaint of the Neoplatonic lover. In Scève's reply, his next ring poem, the speaker drops his grievance and describes the ring as a relic of his lady's positive qualities, her *foy chaste* (chaste faith), although he continues to speak indirectly to the lady through the ring.[47] Du Guillet's elegant "ring" poem thus responds to a male writer's fantasies of femininity and subtly redefines love in the woman's terms.

Pernette du Guillet herself never published her poetry, although it may have circulated privately during her lifetime. Her poems may shrewdly portray a feminine persona, but she does not sound a feminist call to arms. Yet her editor, Antoine de Moulin, saw the appeal that her poems might hold for women readers, for he calls on the *dames lyonnaises* to follow in her footsteps.[48] Ten years after the publication of Du Guillet's *Rymes*, perhaps inspired by the example of her predecessor, a well-read female member of the city's intelligentsia published *Les œuvres de Louise Labé Lionnoise*, containing an allegorical debate poem, three elegies, and a Petrarchan sonnet sequence of twenty-four masterful poems, as well as a series of poems by men in praise of the author. Unlike Du Guillet, Labé sought her own royal permission and published her poems herself (as many scholars have argued). She penned her own dedicatory preface to Clémence de Bourges, a notable aristocratic lady, and exhorts female readers fortunate enough to escape the repressive laws of men to elevate their spirits above "leurs quenoilles et fuseaus" (distaffs and spindles) and actively to use their minds; the pleasures of study, she says, "leave happiness [*contentement*] of self" that lasts longer than other forms of pleasure or *volupté* ("Epître dédicatoire"). To reread what one has written is to recall not only the pleasurable moment one has described but also the satisfaction (*contentement*) of writing itself. In her love poetry, the author's pleasure is inseparable from the sufferings of love, which she valorizes in exquisitely sensual verse offering consolation to jilted lovers and joy for all readers.

Labé's love poetry boldly recasts a Petrarchan *canzoniere*, where a disconsolate lover depicts his sufferings in a repertoire of natural and classical images and rhetorical figures—among them oxymoron, antithesis, and paradox—that underscore the pains of love and the lover's solitude. Writing her first sonnet in Italian, she acknowledges her debt to Petrarch and makes her choice of vernacular French for the rest of her verse all the more significant. As many critics have shown, Labé's amorous journey differs significantly from the Italian master's.[49] The Petrarchan poet loves a woman with whom a personal relationship and physical union are impossible; his poetry turns inward. The frank sensuality of Labé's verse (II, VIII); her use of *nous* to evoke the couple and the universal condition of lovers (IV); her appeal to the lover as a person, who may at times speak back (in sonnet XIII, not included here); her recollection of past moments of happiness (XXIII)—these qualities all create what Ann Jones has called "a new kind of erotic imagination . . . a focus on the pleasures of mutuality, even identity between the lovers."[50] In Sonnet XIV, "As long as my eyes yet can shed a tear," Labé delicately reworks the convention of male poets longing to die of lost love and valorizes her own poetic creation. As long as the poet can weep, or sing, or imagine—as long as tears, song, and poetry flow to express love—she seeks to live; only when eyes, voice, and hand falter does the poet desire death. Tears and weeping in Petrarch, Scève, and other male poets often represent the dissolution and figurative death of the speaker faced with loss.[51] For Labé, tears are represented as a productive, transcendent force, the wellspring of poetry. When she addresses the *dames lyonnoizes* in the final sonnet, XXIV, she does not apologize for having known "love's biting pain," but warns her women readers that they may suffer from an even "stranger" passion. Labé portrays love, not as an alienating, solipsistic emotion, but rather as a passionate fusion of body and intellect that all women might one day experience.

The love lyrics of Na Castelloza, Christine de Pizan, Pernette du Guillet, and Louise Labé represent the genre of early women's poetry most accessible in recent editions and best known by modern readers.[52] But rhymed verse could and did convey far more than amorous yearnings. As one of the worldly arts learned by women and men of privilege, poetry was an expression of refined sociability, practiced in elite households as sophisticated communication and entertainment. Witty epigrams and elegant verse epistles offering thanks, consolation, or advice added distinction to courts and salons. Poetry could also be an eloquent vehicle for moral instruction or a terrain for spiritual inquiry and devotional practice. The varied selection of poems by Marguerite de Navarre and her daughter Jeanne d'Albret illustrate the elastic quality of verse to celebrate many occasions. We read a prayer for the king's health ("God, save the king"); a prayer for the Eucharist ("Ere I partake of you"); a meditation on earthly temporality and God's eternity ("Time past I bemoan, once gone"); a letter composed during pregnancy, when physical discomfort impedes writing ("Dear heart, my heavy belly will not let"); praise for a famous poet's eloquence ("The ancients, in uncommon glorydom" and "Paper, too rough, and ink, too thick; my quill"); an epistle to a mother from a devoted daughter lamenting their separation ("Madame to the Queen").

Readers today may be surprised by the prevalence of religious poetry in these pages. During the heady years of the Protestant Reformation, the Counter-Reformation, and bitter religious wars, matters of faith were of urgent importance. The printing industry, by now a flourishing technology, aided the production of texts of all kinds. As both Protestants and Catholics sought to establish new devotional practices among the faithful, religious writings proliferated. Literate women were a receptive audience for religious teachings; their piety, their active support of priests and theologians, and their writings helped to foster spiritual communities on both sides of the aisle.

Spirituality was central to the work of Marguerite de Navarre, sister of François I and one of the great figures of the period of evangelical humanism (roughly the first half of the sixteenth century). Although she is best known today for the *Heptaméron,* her clever, proto-feminist recasting of Boccaccio's bawdy *Decameron,* Marguerite's most extensive writings were devotional, expressions of a soul burdened by her sins, grieving over personal losses, and seeking God's grace. In one of her earliest poems, the *Dialogue en forme de vision nocturne* (1524), the poet engages in an exchange of religious reflections with her departed niece Charlotte, who died of rubella at the age of eight;[53] the soul of the deceased child offers consolation and spiritual counsel. In the *Prisons,* written in the last months of her life, Marguerite encounters the follies of earthly love, ambition, and science and seeks consolation in her faith for the death of four loved ones—mother-in-law, husband, mother, and brother.[54] Marguerite de Navarre never consciously discarded the teachings of Catholicism or adopted Calvinist theology, yet she was receptive to new ideas about divine grace and human redemption and, like many Reformers, she sought a more direct relationship with God. Her forty-seven *Chansons spirituelles,* of which three are translated here, are graceful expressions of Marguerite's spiritual quest and religious convictions.[55] Many of the *chansons* are *contrefacta,* imitations of popular songs that recast their melodies and verses into pious prayers and meditations.

The transposition of secular verse to the spiritual realm is most remarkable in the *Sonets spirituels* of the Dominican nun Anne de Marquets and the *Œuvres chrétiennes* of Gabrielle de Coignard. The former's most significant work consists of 480 sonnets organized around the liturgical year and feast days of saints, foremost among them Mary. These must have circulated among her sisters at the convent of Poissy during Anne's lifetime; they were printed only after her death in 1605 at the instigation of Marie de Fortia, a former student. Anne had defended her writings against a Protestant critic after the Colloque of Poissy and generally supported Counter-Reformation theology. Yet even as her poetry rehearses doctrinal themes, it is far from dogmatic. The poet frequently speaks of her feminine community of nuns as *nous* to reflect on their religious practice (e.g., on the significance of fasting in Sonnet CV) and on their personal foibles. Her poem on the birth of the Virgin (CCCLI) is a striking transformation of Renaissance poetic themes. In poems such as Ronsard's celebrated "Ode à Cassandre" or his "Sonnet à Marie," the rose, beloved by the poet, is a fragile beauty that symbolizes a mortal lady's fading charms or her tragic death. By contrast, Anne's rose represents the life-giving forces of the Virgin. Her rare beauty causes a smitten God to rain heavenly liquid, creating within her a honey more delicious than nectar or ambrosia (food of Olympian gods) that nurtures all of humanity. Ronsard had praised Anne's earlier work in a sonnet that celebrates her as a *nouvelle fleur* whose odor and color surpass those of roses, carnations, and lilies.[56] He would no doubt have admired her delicate regeneration of the Rose. "Comme la rose naist d'une branche espineuse" transforms the sensuality of many Renaissance sonnets into divine love that nourishes the faithful for eternity, both "en la terre et au ciel" (on earth and in heaven).

Gabrielle de Coignard also fuses the sacred and the profane in her poetry. Like Anne de Marquets, she wrote privately within an enclosed world. She was confined not by the walls of a convent but by the domestic space of the household. Widowed after only three years of marriage, and with two young daughters in her charge, Gabrielle de Coignard recorded her quest for spiritual consolation in the face of despair (as in Sonnet XI). Her *Œuvres chrétiennes,* composed of 129 *Sonnets spirituels* accompanied by equally substantial *Vers chrétiens,* have been described as a spiritual autobiography and intimate confession.[57] Yet even as they portray the poet's evident religious fervor, they also explore the delights of well-turned verse. Coignard was well acquainted with the poetry of her contemporaries, whose aesthetic qualities she both admires and shuns, just as she celebrates and shuns other worldly pleasures. Her father had been master of the *Jeux floraux,* an annual poetry contest in Toulouse, where Coignard may have first witnessed the allure and perils of poetic fame. In Sonnets I and II, the poet rejects "pagan" sources and classical themes, earthly glory and the "pagan Muse." She declares herself a Christian who "burns" with a divine flame and submits to the shadow of the cross. She clearly rejects the poetic "gloire" that was so avidly self-fashioned by Pléiade poets; pride in her own virtuosity would constitute a sin. Yet her final sonnet (CXXIX) pays homage to Ronsard, whose spirit infuses the collection. The tension between worldly delights and spiritual truths throughout the *Sonnets spirituels* endows these poems with a complexity that rivals that of the great Renaissance *canzonieri*. Although Coignard rejects complex rhetorical flourishes and seeks a simple, sober style befitting her faith,[58] her verse often evokes with elegance the world's natural beauty. Sometimes she struggles against the world, as in Sonnet XL, where the "flowering gaiety" of fields fails to ease her distress at her sins. But at other times the natural splendors portrayed in her verse lead poet and reader to a higher order; in Sonnet XLV, a brilliant moon and serene sky reveal "Heaven's peace profound."

Long neglected by scholars, the spiritual writings of Marguerite de Navarre, Anne de Marquets, and Gabrielle de Coignard deserve consideration as major literary accomplishments. Indeed, as Gary Ferguson maintains, the works of Marquets and Coignard, published at the end of the century, seem to have helped create a new tone in religious discourse, what he terms the "feminization of devotion," by infusing works with "sweet style" and tender sentiments.[59]

The queen of Navarre, the Dominican nun, and the widowed mother, writing privately of their spiritual struggles, sought to transcend earthly language and to find *gloire* in heaven, not on earth. In another vein, Madeleine and Catherine des Roches, mother and daughter, actively cultivated worldly fame and enhanced their social position through their verse and prose. They created a lively literary salon in their home in Poitiers during the 1570s and 1580s and published three weighty collaborative tomes during their lifetimes. Their collective *œuvre* offers intimate glimpses of a remarkable mother-daughter relationship, founded on strong emotional and intellectual bonds. Madeleine nurtured and praised the literary talents of her only surviving child. Catherine rewarded her mother's efforts by pursuing learning and writing at the expense of marriage and a family of her own. The conflict between "distaff and pen"—between women's domestic duties and women's learning—invoked by Christine de Pizan, Louise Labé, and other women of the period is central to the Des Roches's poetry. Madeleine proclaims the "desire to write rather than spin" (Sonnet VIII). She composes poetry, not only to lament her fate as a widow beset with domestic responsibilities, legal entanglements, and physical ailments, but also to improve her condition—as in her appeal to compensate her for property losses suffered during the siege of Poitiers ("Au roy"). Protected from the full force of domestic woes by her mother, Catherine embraced her literary destiny with greater confidence and ambition. In "To My Distaff," the speaker boldly reconciles the tensions inherent in women's social condition by upholding both distaff *and* pen, traditional feminine roles and humanistic learning. With admirable command of a variety of genres, Madeleine and Catherine des Roches cultivate family relationships and friendships, warn about the dangers of love for women, advise on matters of state, defend their family interests, and depict charming vignettes of daily life (as in the poem lamenting a lost lace collar). Catherine also frequently plays the role of instructor, counseling a general public of readers on the conduct of life (as in her *Vers dorez* and *Enigmes.*)

Throughout the medieval and early modern period, moralists exploited the pleasing qualities of verse to offer moral instruction and political advice in a palatable, memorable form. From the clever couplets of Marie de France's *Fables* to the simple, yet pithy rhymes of Christine de Pizan's *Enseignemens moraux* and Catherine's more complex quatrains translated in *rimes embrassées*, cleverly turned lines would have captured the attention of young readers and were easily repeated by tutors or parents. Rhymed verses aided memorization and retention of moral precepts. Much of the poets' commonsense advice rings true today. The rule behind "At table sit in modest wise / And dress yourself in proper guise" (Christine de Pizan, *Enseignemens moraux*) still holds, whether at family table or state dinners. The sentiment behind Catherine des Roches's counsel to "Live your life decently, without excess" has been repeated by preachers, parents, and financial advisers throughout the ages. In a sharper vein, Marie de Romieu's "To a Scandalmonger" and "To One Disparaged" express personal indignation at individual foibles using the familiar *tu*. Her unflattering descriptions of the gossip and the drunkard portray types recognizable today, and the solution remains unchanged: "Therefore, mind your manners, and / Learn to let less wine content you." Given women's primary role as teachers within their families and as arbiters of social behavior in early French history, it is not surprising that they should have contributed significantly to didactic literature, both in prose and verse.

The work of Marie de Romieu, the last poet in this section, attests to the continuing vitality and variety of women's verse and emblematizes in many ways the struggles and accomplishments of her foremothers. Marie, of modest birth, enjoyed none of the privileges of the nobility or urban *haute bourgeoisie*. Her father was a baker in a provincial town. Her family background exemplifies rising literacy among the merchant and artisan class. Her brother, a lawyer, used his writings—and, even more significantly, hers—to advance his interests among the elite. In 1581, he dedicated his sister's *Premières œuvres* to Marguerite de Lorraine, the queen's sister, on the occasion of Marguerite's wedding. Despite Marie's evident poetic accomplishment (now widely accepted as her own), her relationship to learning was vexed. Not only does she allegedly not know that her brother Jacques published her work without her knowledge; she also asserts that he made disparaging comments about women, which prompted her own verse polemic "Brief discours: Que l'excellence de la femme surpasse celle de l'homme" (1581), on the superiority of women. Revising earlier Italian and French tracts, Marie paints fuller portraits of historical female heroines than do her sources and offers a witty, acerbic critique of the love talk men use to deceive women.[60] Whether or not she had read Christine de Pizan, she attacks misogynistic arguments with a verve and precision that Christine would have admired. Her other, shorter poems (of which a representative sampling are translated here), skillfully explore a range of themes and verse forms. Her clever enigma portraying the cat's cruel chase of the mouse may be more than a playful game. It is perhaps significant that *souris* (mouse) is a feminine noun in French and that Marie portrays the animal as the innocent victim of a callous beast, who would destroy her children as well. The poet's sympathy for the female victim echoes the compassionate portrait of Marie de France's female animals in the *Fables*. This Marie's collection also includes encomia to various notables, didactic lessons (as we have seen), and Petrarchan sonnets. That a provincial baker's daughter intones her distinctive voice in the "high" form of verse polemic as skillfully as she does in a popular puzzle says much about the appeal of poetry in its many guises to women across the ranks.

As the poems and translations in this section so eloquently demonstrate, the course of medieval and Renaissance women's verse is one of continual poetic activity in a range of contexts, from the solitude of the convent to the public forum of the court or the more intimate stage of the urban salon or private correspondence. These women's diverse writings testify to the depth of women's learning—despite continual social disapproval—and to their authors' mastery of poetic conventions. Through their creative revision of genres dominated by male writers and thinkers, medieval and Renaissance women writers infused new life into love lyrics, religious poetry, letters, and didactic treatises and developed them as channels for women's personal expression and for their social advancement. Whether these women writers actively sought *gloire* or whether they honed their skills in private, whether their works were published to instant acclaim or brought to light more indirectly, their poetic accomplishments conferred dignity on female eloquence and shaped the intellectual history of France and the course of French poetry in significant ways. Even if their writings might take centuries to be published in their entirety, these early French women poets inaugurated rich traditions of women's writing and laid the cornerstones for the female literary communities that would be inherited and transformed by their spiritual daughters and granddaughters.

NOTES

1. I thank Kirk Read for his thoughtful comments on a draft of this essay; any errors are my own.

2. For example, the medieval moralist Philippe de Novare advised that only nuns should learn to read and write, since literacy might encourage lay women to sin; see Philippe de Navarre (*sic*), *Les quatre âges de l'homme*, ed. Marcel de Fréville (Paris: Didot, 1888), pp. 16–17. During the Renaissance, women's education became increasingly contested, with pros and cons debated; see Linda Timmermans, *L'accès des femmes à la cul-*

ture (1598–1715) (Paris: Champion, 1993), pp. 20–52. For an overview of these issues and of the contributions of French women writers during the Middle Ages, see my "Female Voices in Convents, Courts, and Households: The French Middle Ages," in *A History of Women's Writing in France,* ed. Sonya Stephens (Cambridge: Cambridge University Press, 2000), pp. 10–40, and, for the Renaissance, Cathleen Bauschatz, "To Choose Ink and Pen: French Renaissance Women's Writing," ibid., pp. 41–63. Among many studies of women's status and cultural contributions during the Middle Ages and the Renaissance are *The Cultural Patronage of Medieval Women,* ed. June Hall McCash (Athens: University of Georgia Press, 1996); Margaret L. King, *Women of the Renaissance* (Chicago: University of Chicago Press, 1991); Evelyne Berriot-Salvadore, *Les femmes dans la société française de la Renaissance* (Geneva: Droz, 1990); Susan Broomhall, *Women and the Book Trade in Sixteenth-Century France* (Burlington, Vt.: Ashgate Publishing, 2002). See also *A History of Women in the West,* ed. Georges Duby and Michelle Perrot (Cambridge, Mass.: Belknap Press of Harvard University Press, 1992–94), vol. 2, *Silences of the Middle Ages,* ed. and trans. Christiane Klapisch-Zuber, and vol. 3, *Renaissance and Enlightenment Paradoxes,* ed. Natalie Zemon Davis and trans. Arlette Farge.

3. General studies of medieval and Renaissance women writers include Peter Dronke, *Women Writers of the Middle Ages: A Critical Study of Texts from Perpetua (d. 203) to Marguerite Porete (d. 1310)* (Cambridge: Cambridge University Press, 1984); Katharina M. Wilson, *Medieval Women Writers* (Athens: University of Georgia Press, 1984) and *Women Writers of the Renaissance and Reformation* (Athens: University of Georgia Press, 1987); and *The Cambridge Companion to Medieval Women's Writing,* ed. Carolyn Dinshaw and David Wallace (Cambridge: Cambridge University Press, 2003).

4. Marguerite de Navarre, *Dialogue en forme de vision nocturne,* ed. Renja Salminen (Helsinki: Suomalainen Tiedeakatemia, 1985).

5. Marguerite de Navarre, *Les prisons,* ed. Simone Glasson (Geneva: Droz, 1978). For a translation, see Marguerite de Navarre, *Les prisons,* trans. Claire Wade Lynch (New York: Peter Lang, 1989).

6. Terence C. Cave, *Devotional Poetry in France, c. 1570–1613* (Cambridge: Cambridge University Press, 1969), p. 86.

7. Anne R. Larsen, "Paradox and the Praise of Women: From Ortensio Lando and Charles Estienne to Marie de Romieu," *Sixteenth Century Journal* 28, 3 (1997): 762.

8. Most critics do not subscribe to this view; for discussion of the debate about Marie's female authorship and an argument for her feminine poetics, see Michelle A. Freeman, "Marie de France's Poetics of Silence: The Implications for a Feminine *Translatio,*" *PMLA* 99 (1984): 860–83.

9. In a derogatory remark that has become emblematic of earlier scholars' misogynistic dismissal of female authors, Gustave Lanson in his *Histoire de la littérature française* (1895) described Christine as "the first in that line of insufferable bluestockings, whose indefatigable facility was equaled only by her universal mediocrity"; cited and translated by Charity Cannon Willard, *Christine de Pizan: Her Life and Works* (New York: Persea Books, 1984), p. 222.

10. Most famously, Calvin called her a *meretrix*, or prostitute. For an account and critique of these views, see Cathy Yandell, "Louise Labé's Transgressions," in *High Anxiety: Masculinity in Crisis in Early Modern France*, ed. Kathleen P. Long (Kirksville, Mo.: Truman State University Press), pp. 1–17.

11. As noted by Bauschatz, "To Choose Ink and Pen," p. 46.

12. Marie's modern editor examines and refutes this claim. See Marie de Romieu, *Les premières œuvres poétiques*, ed. André Winandy (Geneva: Droz, 1972), pp. viii–xii.

13. Huchon does not doubt that Louise Labé herself existed but maintains that she was a prostitute who did not write the works attributed to her. Mireille Huchon, *Louise Labé: Une créature de papier* (Geneva: Droz, 2006). Huchon's hypothesis was hailed as "irrefutable" by Marc Fumaroli, *Le Monde*, May 12, 2006.

14. Edouard Launet, in "Louise Labé, femme trompeuse," *Libération*, June 16, 2006, p. 31, cites François Rigolot, editor of Labé's *Œuvres complètes*, maintaining that "Labé certainly existed as a poet, but that 'her work, in keeping with many works before the advent of solipsistic romanticism, is doubtless the product of a collective undertaking'" (translation mine). Articles about the controversy in the popular and scholarly media are being tracked by SIEFAR, the Société Internationale pour l'Étude des Femmes de l'Ancien Régime, on their web site, www.siefar.org (accessed May 15, 2007).

15. Recent modern editions include Madeleine des Roches and Catherine des Roches, *Les œuvres*, (Geneva: Droz, 1993), *Les secondes œuvres* (Geneva: Droz, 1998), and *Les missives* (Geneva: Droz, 1999), all three ed. Anne R. Larsen; Gabrielle de Coignard, *Œuvres chrétiennes*, ed. Collette H. Winn (Geneva: Droz, 1995); and Anne de Marquets, *Sonets spirituels*, ed. Gary Ferguson (Geneva: Droz, 1997).

16. Notable among other recent translations of poets in this section is the series The Other Voice in Early Modern Europe published by the University of Chicago Press. Bilingual editions of writers translated in this section include Gabrielle de Coignard, *Spiritual Sonnets: A Bilingual Edition*, ed. and trans. Melanie E. Gregg (2003); Louise Labé, *Complete Poetry and Prose: A Bilingual Edition*, trans. Annie Finch, ed. and trans. Deborah Lesko Baker (2006); Madeleine des Roches and Catherine des Roches, *From Mother and Daughter: Poems, Dialogues, and Letters of Les Dames des Roches*, ed. and trans. Anne R. Larsen (2006); and Madeline de l'Aubespine, *Selected Poems and Translations: A Bilingual Edition*, ed. and trans. Anna Klosowska (forthcoming in 2007). This essay was written without the benefit of these editions and their excellent introductory material.

17. The melody, extant in one manuscript, accompanies the contessa da Dia's "A chanter m'er de so q'ieu no volria" (I must sing of what I'd rather not), not included here; see *Songs of the Women Troubadours*, ed. and trans. Matilda Tomaryn Bruckner, Laurie Shepard, and Sarah White (New York: Garland, 1995), pp. 6–9.

18. For an edition, introduction and bibliography, see *Songs of the Women Troubadours*, ed. and trans. Bruckner et al.

19. *Songs of the Women Trouvères*, ed. and trans. Eglal Doss-Quinby, Joan Tasker Grimbert, Wendy Pfeffer, and Elizabeth Aubrey (New Haven, Conn.: Yale University Press, 2001).

20. Marguerite Porete, *Le mirouer des simples âmes*, ed. Romana Guarnieri (Turnholt: Brepols, 1986), ed. and trans. Ellen Babinsky as *The Mirror of Simple Souls* (New York: Paulist Press, 1993).

21. For an overview of the publication of de Pizan's works in France and England throughout the Renaissance, see Willard, *Christine de Pizan*, pp. 211–13.

22. Recent editions include Christine de Pizan, *Le livre de l'advision Cristine*, ed. Christine Reno and Liliane Dulac (Paris: Champion, 2001); *Le chemin de longue étude*, ed. Andrea Tarnowski (Paris: Librairie générale française, 2000); *Epistre Othea*, ed. Gabriella Parusa (Geneva: Droz, 1999); *Le livre du corps de policie*, ed. Angus J. Kennedy (Paris: Champion, 1998); *The Love Debate Poems of Christine de Pizan*, ed. Barbara K. Altmann (Gainesville: University Press of Florida, 1998); and *La città delle dame*, trans. Patrizia Caraffi, ed. Earl Jeffrey Richards (Milan: Luni, 1998).

23. Louise Labé, "Epître dédicatoire, à M.C.D.B.L.," in *Œuvres complètes*, ed. François Rigolot (Paris: Flammarion), pp. 41–43.

24. Christine de Pizan, *The Book of the City of Ladies*, trans. Earl Jeffrey Richards (New York: Persea, 1982), see pp. 67–68 and passim.

25. Labé, "Epître dédicatoire," p. 42. Huchon has suggested that this letter may have been written by Claude de Taillemont, author of a similar passage in praise of women's learning. But the defense of women's intellectual capacities is not original with Taillemont; we find the idea also in Christine de Pizan (among others), a woman whose authorship is undisputed. It is certainly conceivable that these words could have been written by a mid-sixteenth-century woman from Lyon.

26. See Anne Larsen, "Introduction" in her edition of Madeleine des Roches and Catherine des Roches, *Œuvres*, pp. 16–47, and George Diller, *Les dames des Roches: Etude sur la vie littéraire à Poitiers dans la deuxième moitié du XVIe siècle* (Paris: Droz, 1936), pp. 54–74.

27. Antoine du Moulin, "Aux dames lyonnoizes" (August 14, 1545), in Pernette du Guillet, *Rymes*, ed. Victor E. Graham (Geneva: Droz, 1968), pp. 1–3.

28. Huchon, *Louise Labé*, pp. 51–69.

29. See the discussion by Gary Ferguson, "Introduction," in de Marquets, *Sonets spirituels*, ed. Ferguson, pp. 21–22, and Gary Ferguson, "Le chapelet et la plume, ou, quand la religieuse se fait écrivain: Le cas du Prieuré de Poissy (1562–1621)," *Nouvelle revue du seizième siècle* 19, 2 (2001): 83–99, esp. 88–92.

30. See Paula Sommers, "The *Mirror* and Its Reflections: Marguerite de Navarre's Biblical Feminism," *Tulsa Studies in Women's Literature* 5, 1 (1986): 29–39. For a summary of the controversy, see Marguerite de Navarre, *Le miroir de l'âme pécheresse de Marguerite de Navarre*, ed. Renja Salminen (Helsinki: Soumalainen Tiedeaketemia, 1979), pp. 21–30.

31. See the description of the discovery of this manuscript by Abel Lefranc, *Les dernières poésies de Marguerite de Navarre* (Paris: Armand Colin, 1896), pp. i–iv.

32. Ibid., p. iv.

33. Thirteen volumes are planned. See the description by the general editor, Nicole Cazauran, in Marguerite de Navarre, *Œuvres complètes*, vol. 1: *"Pater Noster" et "Petit œuvre dévot,"* ed. Sabine Lardon (Paris: Champion, 2001), pp. 7–10.

34. *Les chansons de Callianthe, fille de Ronsard (Madeleine de l'Aubespine, dame de Villeroy)*, ed. Roger Sorg (Paris: Pichon, 1926).

35. See Frédéric Lachèvre, *Poésies de Héliette de Vivonne, attribuées à tort à Madeleine de Laubespine sous le titre "Chansons de Callianthe"* . . . *suivies de douze lettres inédites de Pierre Louÿs non envoyées à leurs destinataires* (Paris: Alph. Margraff, 1932), defending a theory advanced by Louÿs. Whoever the author may be, the alternation of male and female voices within BN MS fr 1718 merits further study.

36. I am grateful to Anna Klosowska for her generous response to my query on the current state of Madeleine de l'Aubespine scholarship. She has prepared a French-English bilingual edition of the poet's works for the University of Chicago's series The Other Voice in Early Modern Europe and is working on a critical edition in the original French.

37. For an overview of Marie's works and of recent critical approaches, see my "Marie de France," in *The Cambridge Companion to Medieval Women's Writing*, ed. Dinshaw and Wallace, pp. 172–83.

38. For a translation of *L'espurgatoire seint Patrice*, a spiritual voyage in verse that is not included here, see Marie de France, *Saint Patrick's Purgatory: A Poem by Marie de France*, trans. Michael J. Curley (Binghamton, N.Y.: Medieval and Renaissance Texts and Studies, 1993).

39. On Marie's transformations in the *Fables*, see, among other studies, Sahar Amer, *Esope au féminin: Marie de France et la politique de l'interculturalité* (Amsterdam: Rodopi, 1999), and Karen Jambeck, "Reclaiming the Woman in the Book: Marie de France and the *Fables*," in *Selected Proceedings of the St. Hilda's Conference, Oxford*, ed. Lesley Smith and Jane H. M. Taylor, vol. 2: *Women, the Book, and the Worldly* (Cambridge: Cambridge University Press, 1995), pp. 119–37.

40. Most notably, in a letter condemning adulterous love written by the chaperone of a young married lady in *Le livre du duc des vrais amans*, trans. Thelma Fenster in *The Book of the Duke of True Lovers* (New York: Persea Books, 1991), pp. 110–20.

41. Christine de Pizan, *Le livre du debat des deux amans*, vv. 987–94, in *Love Debate Poems of Christine de Pizan*, ed. Altmann, p. 108.

42. For a succinct analysis of the way these poets transformed the male poetic conventions of Neoplatonism and Petrarchism, see Ann Rosalind Jones, "Assimilation with a Difference: Renaissance Women Poets and Literary Influence," *Yale French Studies* 62 (1981): 135–53.

43. On Du Guillet's style, see Verdun L. Saulnier, "Etude sur Pernette du Guillet et ses *Rymes*," in *Bibliothèque d'Humanisme et Renaissance*, 4 (Paris: Droz, 1944), pp. 100–107.

44. For comparative analysis of Scève's and du Guillet's poetry, see Jones, "Assimilation with a Difference"; Kenneth Lloyd-Jones, "Writing the Language of Love: Lyonnais Poetry and the Portrayal of Passion," *Romance Languages Annual* 7 (1995): 112–18; Karen Simroth James, "*On vault responce avoir:* Pernette du Guillet's Dialogic Poetics," in *A Dialogue of Voices: Feminist Literary Theory and Bakhtin* (Minneapolis: University of Minnesota Press, 1994), pp. 171–97.

45. As has been emphasized by Jones, "Assimilation with a Difference," p. 141.

46. Maurice Scève, *Délie: Objet de plus haulte vertu*, ed. Eugène Parturier (Paris: Nizet, 1987), dizain 347. On the exchange of ring poems, see Francis T. Bright, "Language as Object: Gift-Giving and Dialogue in Scève and Pernette du Guillet," *MILFC Review: Journal of the Mountain Interstate Foreign Language Conference* 1 (1991): 48–57; and Susan Delaney, "Lyric Dialogue in the 'Ring' Poems of Pernette du Guillet and Maurice Scève," *French Review* 68, 5 (1995): 822–29.

47. Scève, *Délie*, dizain 349 (p. 240).

48. Du Moulin, "Aux dames lyonnoizes," pp. 2–3.

49. Among many readings, see Jones, "Assimilation with a Difference"; Jones, *The Currency of Eros: Women's Love Lyric in Europe 1540–1620* (Bloomington: Indiana University Press, 1990), pp. 155–78; Deborah Lesko Baker, *The Subject of Desire: Petrarchan Poetics and the Female Voice in Louise Labé* (West Lafayette, Ind.: Purdue University Press, 1996); Mary B. Moore, *Desiring Voices: Women Sonneteers and Petrarchism* (Carbondale: Southern Illinois University Press, 2000), pp. 94–124.

50. Jones, *Currency of Eros*, p. 159.

51. My remarks on Labé's tears are indebted to the fine extended analysis of this poem by Deborah Lesko Baker in *Subject of Desire*, pp. 146–53.

52. For example, the works of Labé and Du Guillet are readily available in French in a single volume published more than twenty years ago and still in print. Louise Labé, *Œuvres poétiques précédées des "Rymes" de Pernette du Guillet avec un choix de "Blasons du corps féminin,"* ed. Françoise Charpentier (Paris: Gallimard, 1983).

53. Marguerite de Navarre, *Dialogue en forme de vision nocturne*.

54. See n. 5 above.

55. Marguerite de Navarre, *Chansons spirituelles*, ed. Georges Dottin (Geneva: Droz, 1971).

56. Ronsard's laudatory sonnet introduced Anne de Marquets's first work, her *Sonets, prieres, et devises en forme de pasquins*, first published in 1562. Ronsard's poem was later republished as the introductory sonnet for Marquets's posthumous *Sonets spirituels*, "Sonet de Ronsard à la louange de feue Madame de Marquets"; Anne de Marquets, *Sonets spirituels*, pp. 78–79.

57. Colette H. Winn, "Introduction," to Gabrielle de Coignard, *Œuvres chrétiennes*, p. 26.

58. On Coignard's style, see ibid., pp. 111–19.

59. Gary Ferguson, "The Feminisation of Devotion: Gabrielle de Coignard, Anne de Marquets, and François de Sales," in *Women's Writing in the French Renaissance: Proceedings of the Fifth Cambridge Renaissance Colloquium, 7–9 July 1997*, ed. Philip Ford and Gillan Jondorf (Cambridge: Cambridge French Colloquia, 1999), pp. 187–206.

60. On the originality of Marie's version and its importance as an early female-authored defense of women, see Larsen, "Paradox and the Praise of Women," pp. 759–74.

Marie de France (LATE TWELFTH CENTURY)

Despite a vast bibliography devoted to her, all one can say about Marie de France is that the poet who signed that name flourished in the late twelfth century and apparently composed three works: the *lais*, short verse tales presenting episodes largely of Breton inspiration, with Arthurian elements and with not a little psychological insight, the best known of her works today; a collection of fables, very popular during the Middle Ages and first of a genre that was to enjoy a long life in French letters; and a translation of a Latin monastic text recounting an Irish knight's voyage to Purgatory, the *Espurgatoire Saint Patriz,* the longest of her verse narratives.[1]

It is ironic that Marie, the first identifiable woman writer in French, probably spent most of her life outside of France. Indeed, the appellation "de France" implies this rather clearly: one does not, after all, say where one came from if one is still there. In Marie's case, she tells us simply, in the epilogue to her fables: "MARIE ai nun" (My name is Marie) and, probably referring narrowly to Ile-de-France, the area surrounding Paris, "si sui de France" (I am indeed from France). Modern scholarship suggests that she spent at least her artistic life in Britain, perhaps at the court of the Plantagenet kings Henry II (1154–1189) and Richard I, "the Lion-Hearted" (1189–1199), possibly even in religious orders as abbess of Reading. The same epilogue leads us to believe that she was herself a member of the Norman aristocracy, citing an enigmatic count, one Willame, "le plus vaillant de nul realme" (the noblest in any kingdom) for whom she translated the fables into Old French from an Anglo-Saxon version of a Latin original naively thought to be a translation by the semi-mythical Alfred the Great.[2] All that is incontrovertible is that this shadowy poet was literate in French and Latin, well read in classical authors, and especially familiar with the oral tradition of Breton fairy tales.

Uncertainties about her career notwithstanding, Marie remains—deservedly— one of the most widely studied figures in medieval French literature, both for her fables and, especially, for her *lais*.[3] The twelve fables, translated here from the Warnke edition, are straightforward and rather pithy when compared to what the genre was eventually to become, and are not without their own antique charm and, on occasion, even humor. The two *lais* are typical of her pleasing, few-frills narrative technique, blending objective detail with frequent authorial intervention, and managing considerable stylistic variety within the constraining framework of the traditional medieval octosyllabic couplets.

NOTES

1. See Glyn S. Burgess, *Marie de France: An Analytical Bibliography,* and its *Supplement.* Among the several authoritative editions of her *lais* and fables, see *Die Lais der*

Marie de France, ed. Karl Warnke; *Marie de France: Lais,* ed. Alfred Ewert; and, especially, *Les lais de Marie de France,* ed. and trans. Laurence Harf-Lancner (based on Warnke); *Die Fabeln der Marie de France,* ed. Karl Warnke; *Marie de France: Fables,* ed. Alfred Ewert and Ronald C. Johnson; and, especially, *Les fables,* ed. Charles Brucker. There are also a number of translations into English of both works, in whole and in part, among them, Robert Hanning and Joan Ferrante, *The Lais of Marie de France;* Glyn S. Burgess's volume of the same name; and Harriet Spiegel, *Fables: Marie de France.* For the *Espurgatoire,* see *Espurgatoire seint Patriz,* ed. Yolande de Pontfarcy, and Michael J. Curley's translation, *Saint Patrick's Purgatory: A Poem by Marie de France.* Thomas Atkinson Jenkins has published two editions, the second of which, *L'espurgatoire Seint Patriz de Marie de France,* contains the Latin text as well as the French.

2. It is thought that the ultimate source of many of Marie's fables—at least the first forty—through several lost reworkings, was the Latin prose Aesopica collection known as the *Romulus Nilantii.* See Urban T. Holmes Jr., *A History of Old French Literature from the Origins to 1300,* pp. 207–10; *Marie de France: Fables,* ed. Ewert and Johnson, pp. xi–xii; and, esp., *Les fables,* ed. Brucker, pp. 3–9.

3. Marie has been widely studied and continues to be the subject of books, monographs, and articles, which tend to be concerned more with her language and subject matter than with her style and aesthetic art. There are entries on her in all the relevant major encyclopedias and biographical dictionaries, including the *Encyclopedia of Continental Women Writers,* 2: 779–82; *French Women Writers,* pp. 324–34; *Medieval Women Writers,* pp. 64–89; the *Cambridge Companion to Medieval Women's Writing,* pp. 172–83; and the *Penguin Book of Women Poets,* pp. 91–94. Of the book-length studies devoted to her work, see Richard Baum, *Recherches sur les œuvres attribuées à Marie de France;* R. Howard Bloch, *The Anonymous Marie de France;* Marie-Pierre Le Hir and Dana Strand, *French Cultural Studies: Criticism at the Crossroads;* and, more recently, *In Quest of Marie de France, a Twelfth-Century Poet,* ed. Chantal A. Maréchal.

LAÜSTIC

Une aventure vus dirai
Dunt li Bretun firent un lai.
Laüstic ad nun, ceo m'est vis,
Si l'apelent en lur païs;
Ceo est "russignol" en franceis
E "nihtegale" en dreit engleis.

En Seint Mallo en la cuntree
Ot une vile renumee.
Deus chevaliers ilec maneient
E deus forz maisuns i aveient.
Pur la bunté des deus baruns
Fu de la vile bons li nuns.
Li uns aveit femme espusee,
Sage, curteise a acemee;
A merveille se teneit chiere
Sulunc l'usage e la manere.
Li autres fu un bachelers
Bien coneüz entre ses pers,
De pruësce, de grant valur,
E volentiers feseit honur:
Mut turneot e despendeit
E bien donot ceo qu'il aveit.
La femme sun veisin ama;
Tant la requist, tant la preia
E tant par ot en lui grant bien
Que ele l'ama sur tute rien,
Tant pur le bien qu'ele en oï,
Tant pur ceo qu'il iert pres de li.
Sagement e bien s'entreamerent,
Mut se covrirent e garderent
Qu'il ne feussent aparceüz
Ne desturbez ne mescreüz,
E il le poeient bien fere,
Kar pres esteient lur repere:
Preceines furent lur maisuns
E lur sales e lur dunguns;
N'i aveit bare ne devise
Fors un haut mur de piere bise.

THE NIGHTINGALE

I shall recount a tale for you,
One that the Bretons made into
A *lai*, which in their land they call
"Laüstic," whilst "Le rossignol"
Is how one would in French proclaim it,
And "Nightingale" in English name it.

Not far from Saint-Malo a town
There was, known far and wide: renown
It owed to feats of derring-do
Wrought by two nobles; barons who
Lived by each other, side by side,
In houses strong and fortified.
One had a wife: a lady quite
Well-mannered, elegant, polite
In wondrous wise, as ought one be
In courtliness and dignity.
The other, still a youth, was much
Given to knightly deeds and such
As won him great respect and fame
Amongst his peers, spreading his name
Round and about: in tournament
And joust he spent much time, and spent
Most generously his wealth as well.
Now, it so happened that he fell
In love with her his neighbor had
Taken to wife; and much he bade
Her heed his pleas. And she had heard
Such good of him that she was stirred—
For hard by did he dwell, in fact—
To love him truly. With much tact
And prudence did they ply their love
Lest prying eye catch sight thereof;
And such great secrecy confected
That never would it be suspected:
Easy, indeed, for him and her
Whose houses close together were,
Each with its tower and its hall
Next to the other. And a wall

Des chambres u la dame jut,
Quant a la fenestre s'estut,
Poeit parler a sun ami
De l'autre part, e il a li,
E lur aveirs entrechangier
E par geter e par lancier.
N'unt gueres rien ki lur despleise,
Mut esteient amdui a eise,
Fors tant k'il ne poent venir
Del tut ensemble a lur pleisir,
Kar la dame ert estreit gardee
Quant cil esteit en la cuntree.
Mes de tant aveient retur,
U fust par nuit u fust par jur,
Que ensemble poeient parler.
Nul nes poeit de ceo garder
Que a la fenestre n'i venissent
E iloec ne s'entreveïssent.
Lungement se sunt entreamé,
Tant que ceo vint a un esté,
Que bruil e pré sunt reverdi
E li vergier ierent fluri;
Cil oiselet par grant duçur
Mainent lur joie en sum la flur.
Ki amur ad a sun talent,
N'est merveille s'il i entent!
Del chevalier vus dirai veir:
Il i entent a sun poeir,
E la dame de l'autre part,
E de parler e de regart.
Les nuiz, quant la lune luseit
E ses sires cuché esteit,
De juste lui sovent levot
E de sun mantel se afublot;

Of stone was all there was that stood
Between; and so milady could,
In her bedchamber, standing by
The window, speak; and he, reply.
And likewise trinkets could they pass
* Betwixt, with pleasure; but alas,
For all the joy their love would bring,
Yet were they both long suffering,
Unable to draw near; for she
Was watched and warded jealously
Whenever close was he. But might
They, nonetheless, by day and night,
Avenge their woe with tender speech,
† Window to window, each to each.
No one there was, in short, who knew
Their secret love, nor aught could do,
Therefore, to thwart it, or to mar
The glimpses they would catch, afar,
Each of the other, languishing,
Loving in peace until the spring:
Season when bowers and meadows grow
Green, and when orchards here below
Put forth their blossoms; season when
Birds flit amongst the flowers again
In glee, whilst those naught can prevent
From loving to their hearts' content
Give way to passion, and full well!
As for our knight, now shall I tell,
Truly, how with the lady he
With loving glance and speech made free.
Nightly, when brightly shone the moon
And deep her husband slept, then soon
Milady from her sleep awoke

---

* The precise architectural arrangement—two facing windows? a dividing wall shared
by both dwellings?—is a little confusing. How were the couple able to throw (*geter, lancier*)
things over the wall unless, curiously, there was no roof? The separating wall inevitably
recalls Pyramus and Thisbe, though without the hole that the classical lovers used to com-
municate.

† I accept the reading given by Alexandre Micha in his edition of the *Lais*, p. 225, to
explain how, compounding the confusion, the pair were able actually to see one another.

A la fenestre ester veneit
Pur sun ami qu'ele saveit
Que autreteu vie demenot
E le plus de la nuit veillot.
Delit aveient al veer,
Quant plus ne poeient aver.
Tant i estut, tant i leva,
Que ses sires s'en curuça
E meintefeiz li demanda
Pur quei levot e u ala.
"Sire, la dame li respunt,
Il nen ad joïe en cest mund
Ki n'ot le laüstic chanter.
Pur ceo me vois ici ester.
Tant ducement l'i oi la nuit
Que mut me semble grant deduit;
Tant me delit e tant le voil
Que jeo ne puis dormir de l'oil."
Quant li sires ot que ele dist,
De ire e de maltalent en rist.
De une chose se purpensa:
Le laüstic enginnera.
Il n'ot vallet en sa meisun
Ne face engin, reis u laçun,
Puis les mettent par le vergier.
N'i ot codre ne chastainier
U il ne mettent laz u glu,
Tant que pris l'unt e retenu.
Quant le laüstic eurent pris,
Al seignur fu rendu tut vis.
Mut en fu liez, quant il le tint.
As chambres a la dame vint.
"Dame, fet il, u estes vus?
Venez avant, parlez a nus!
J'ai le laüstic enginnié
Pur quei vus avez tant veillié.
Des or poëz gisir en peis:
Il ne vus esveillerat meis."
Quant la dame l'ad entendu,

And, rising from her bed, would cloak
Herself and to her window go,
Drawn by her love, content to know
That he would be at his; and thus
Would they remain, in amorous
Delight, almost the whole night through,
Pleasuring in the sight they two
Took of each other; for such was
* All they could hope for, and with cause!
But soon the husband, wary growing
Wherefore his lady need be going
Off from her bed, confronted her
And asked her why. Whereat, "Good sir,"
She said, "much does my heart rejoice
To hear the nightingale's sweet voice:
Who knows it not, no joy has he.
Thus do I stand here, eagerly,
Listening to his song, and keep
My watch, for scarcely can I sleep."
Wrathful and wroth, her husband burst
Into an evil laugh, chaffed, cursed,
And formed a plan: the bird, undone,
Would he ensnare, for servant none
Had he but that knew how to set
Many a trap, and lure, and net.
Thus to the orchard went they now
And placed on many a hazel bough
And chestnut branch a snare, enwrapped
In lime: so was the bird entrapped
Alive, whereupon they retrieved it.
Gladly the master thus received it,
Took it to where his lady slept.
"Come look," cried he. "No longer kept
From sleeping shall you be! For I
Have caught your noisy bird! Fie, fie
Upon him! See? Now shall your rest
Be undisturbed!" Angered, distressed
Thereat, she prays the boor if, please,

* Again, I follow Marie's text despite the continuing uncertainties about the logistics
of the situation.

Dolente e cureçuse fu.
A sun seignur l'ad demandé,
E il l'ocist par engresté:
Le col li rumpt a ses deus meins.
De ceo fist il ke trop vileins.
Sur la dame le cors geta,
Si que sun chainse ensanglanta
Un poi desur le piz devant.
De la chambre s'en ist a tant.
La dame prent le cors petit,
Durement plure e si maudit
Ceus ki le laüstic traïrent,
Les engins e les laçuns firent,
Kar mut li unt toleit grant hait.
"Lasse, fet ele, mal m'estait!
Ne purrai mes la nuit lever
Ne aler a la fenestre ester,
U jeo soil mun ami veer.
Une chose sai jeo de veir:
Il quidera ke jeo me feigne;
De ceo m'estuet que cunseil preigne.
Le laüstic li trametrai,
L'aventure li manderai."
En une piece de samit
A or brusdé e tut escrit
Ad l'oiselet envolupé;
Un son vaslet ad apelé,
Sun message li ad chargié,
A sun ami l'ad enveié.
Cil est al chevalier venuz;
De sa dame li dist saluz,
Tut sun message li cunta,
Le laüstic li presenta.
Quant tut li ad dit e mustré
E il l'aveit bien escuté,
De l'aventure esteit dolenz;
Mes ne fu pas vileins ne lenz.
Un vaisselet ad fet forger;
Unques n'i ot fer ne acer,
Tut fu de or fin od bones pieres,
Mut precïuses e mut cheres;

Keep him she may; whence does he seize
The creature, twist its neck betwixt
His fingers, as his wife, transfixed,
Looks on; then flings its body, dead,
Upon her breast, and bloodies red
Her shift therewith, at nipples' height,
And leaves the room, quitting her sight.
She takes the little body, weeping
Many a tear, her curses heaping
On churls who with their net and snare
Have robbed her of her joy; and there
She stood and sobbed: "Alas! Ah me!
Nevermore might I hope to see
My love, or to the window go
By night! And he will think, I know,
That I forswear him and forget him.
Some means must I prepare to let him
Know that it is not so, nay not
A jot! And I must tell him what
Has happened. Thus the nightingale
Send him I shall, nor will he fail
To understand." And thus she laid
The bird within a fine brocade,
Wrapped round, and all her story told,
Sewn on the cloth in thread of gold.
Then did she call a servant, bade
Him take the message that she had
Composed, to him, her love; which then
He did, in much detail. And when
He told him everything that she
Had said to tell, then faithfully
Gave him the nightingale as well.
As for the knight, so foul and fell
The tale he hears, that great is his
Distress; but he much practiced is
In courtliness, and his aplomb
Regains forthwith, though overcome
Is he; and presently he has
A coffer made; but one—not as
One might suspect—of iron wrought
Or steel, but finest gold, with naught

Covercle i ot tres bien asis.
Le laüstic ad dedenz mis,
Puis fist la chasse enseeler.
Tuz jurs l'ad fete od lui porter.

Cele aventure fu cuntee,
Ne pot estre lunges celee.
Un lai en firent li Bretun:
Le Laüstic l'apelë hum.

CHIEVREFOIL

Asez me plest e bien le voil,
Del lai qu'hum nume *Chievrefoil*,
Que la verité vus en cunt
Pur quei fu fet, coment e dunt.

Plusurs le me unt cunté e dit
E jeo l'ai trové en escrit
De Tristram e de la reïne,
De lur amur ki tant fu fine,
Dunt il eurent meinte dolur,
Puis en mururent en un jur.
Li reis Marks esteit curucié,
Vers Tristram sun nevuz irié;
De sa tere le cungea
Pur la reïne qu'il ama.
En sa cuntree en est alez,
En Suhtwales u il fu nez.
Un an demurat tut entier,
Ne pot ariere repeirier;
Mes puis se mist en abandun
De mort e de destructïun.
Ne vus esmerveilliez neënt,
Kar cil ki eime lealment

But precious jewels and gems thereon,
And firmly lidded. Thereupon
He seals the bird within, and never
Parts with the relic, his forever.

Not long this tale lay undisclosed:
The Bretons soon a *lai* composed
Thereon, and named their tender tale
"Laüstic," or "The Nightingale."

---

* THE WOODBINE

Pleased shall I be this tale to tell
One calls "The Woodbine," and full well
And truthfully shall, here and now,
Tell whence it came to pass, and how.

Oftentimes I, indeed, have heard—
And seen as well in written word—
The story of the queen, and of
Sire Tristan, and the tender love
They shared, and of the martyrdom
It wrought, until they died therefrom.
King Marc was wroth and sore distressed
For that his nephew Tristan pressed
His troth upon the queen; and, hence,
Banished him from the country, whence
Into South Wales the young knight fled,
Land where he had been born and bred.
There he remained in sad exile
One whole year long, and all the while
Faced many a peril, risked his life
And limb in exploits danger-rife.
Nor ought you wonder in surprise
Thereat: for who in loyal wise
Suffers love unfulfilled will find

* I have chosen the word "woodbine" over the perhaps more poetic "honeysuckle" to translate the French term because, in English, it is the more venerable of the two, going back to the tenth century.

Mut est dolenz e trespensez
Quant il nen ad ses volentez.
Tristram est dolent e pensis,
Pur ceo s'esmut de sun païs.
En Cornuaille vait tut dreit
La u la reïne maneit.
En la forest tut sul se mist:
Ne voleit pas que hum le veïst.
En la vespree s'en eisseit,
Quant tens de herberger esteit.
Od païsanz, od povre gent,
Perneit la nuit herbergement;
Les noveles lur enquereit
Del rei cum il se cunteneit.
Ceo li diënt qu'il unt oï
Que li barun erent bani,
A Tintagel deivent venir:
Li reis i veolt sa curt tenir;
A Pentecuste i serunt tuit,
Mut i avra joie e deduit,
E la reïnë i sera.
Tristram l'oï, mut se haita:
Ele n'i purrat mie aler
K'il ne la veie trespasser.
Le jur que li rei fu meüz,
Tristram est el bois revenuz.
Sur le chemin quë il saveit
Que la rute passer deveit,
Une codre trencha par mi,
Tute quarreie la fendi.
Quant il ad paré le bastun,
De sun cutel escrit sun nun.
Se la reïne s'aparceit,
Ki mut grant garde s'en perneit—
Autre feiz li fu avenu
Que si l'aveit aperceü—
De sun ami bien conustra
Le bastun, quant el le verra.

* Woeful his heart, unsound his mind.
And so it is with Tristan, who,
Dolorous, bids his home adieu;
Rashly makes off to where abides
The queen, in Cornwall, where he hides
Deep in the woods, alone, well-hid
And safe from view; the which he did
Lest he be caught. By night he would
Seek shelter with the poor, the good
Peasant folk, and would ask them what
News of the king they might have got,
And what his deeds: whereat they said
That he a royal writ had spread
Throughout the kingdom, to command
All of his barons in the land
To come to Tintagel, where he
Would hold court in the company
Of one and all at Whitsuntide,
In glee and gladness; and beside
The king, the queen would come as well.
Whereupon, hearing, Tristan fell
To much rejoicing, for he thought
She could not come but that he ought
Catch sight of her. And when, indeed
Arrived the very day decreed
For the departure, Tristan went
Back to the forest, confident
That, as they would proceed apace,
Certain were they to pass that place.
A hazel branch forthwith he split,
Squaring it smooth, and carved on it
His name, and left it there; because
The queen—who most accustomed was
To stratagems like this—will see,
Surely, the bough, and verily

* My translation makes explicit what *trespensez* merely implies, one of the meanings of the Old French adjective being "brash." The suggestion is that Tristan's emotional state was such that he was not thinking clearly while committing the heroic deeds in question—to which, incidentally, Marie merely alludes, assuming no doubt that they were too well known to require elaboration.

Ceo fu la summe de l'escrit
Qu'il li aveit mandé e dit
Que lunges ot ilec esté
E atendu e surjurné
Pur espïer e pur saver
Coment il la peüst veer,
Kar ne poeit vivre sanz li.
D'euls deus fu il tut autresi
Cume del chievrefoil esteit
Ki a la codre se perneit:
Quant il s'i est laciez e pris
E tut entur le fust s'est mis,
Ensemble poënt bien durer,
Mes ki puis les voelt desevrer,
Li codres muert hastivement
E li chievrefoil ensement.
"Bele amie, si est de nus:
Ne vus sanz mei, ne jeo sanz vus."

La reïne vait chevachant.
Ele esgardat tut un pendant,
Le bastun vit, bien l'aparceut,
Tutes les lettres i conut.
Les chevaliers ki la menoent
E ki ensemble od li erroent
Cumanda tuz a arester:
Descendre voet e resposer.
Cil unt fait sun commandement.
Ele s'en vet luinz de sa gent;
Sa meschine apelat a sei,
Brenguein, ki mut ot bone fei.
Del chemin un poi s'esluina,
Dedenz le bois celui trova
Que plus amot que rien vivant:
Entre eus meinent joie mut grant.
A li parlat tut a leisir
E ele li dit sun pleisir;
Puis li mustra cumfaitement

Know it she will to be, in truth,
Her lover's staff; and then, forsooth,
Will learn that long days has he been
Waiting, yearning to see his queen,
And that, without her, he can never
Hope to live longer, howsoever.
Well will she realize that she
Is like unto the hazel tree;
And he, the woodbine, tender vine
That must, to live, its trunk entwine:
Together can they long survive;
But should one, by and by, contrive
To rip the pair apart, then dies
Straightway the hazel, and likewise
The woodbine twining round about it,
Perishing all too soon without it.
"So, love, live we as well, we two,
* You but with me, I but with you."

At length the queen rode by until
Her horse approached a gentle hill.
Down she looked, and she saw upon
The ground, the branch; and carved thereon
The letters; recognized them; read.
When she was certain what they said
She told the knights escorting her
That she must stop to rest: concur
They did; and she, dismounting, drew
Off a bit from her retinue,
Called for her serving-maid, Branghien—
Most faithful wench—and left her men
Behind whilst with her she went round
Into the forest. There she found
The one she loved beyond all measure,
Bared him her heart, and at their leisure
Much they conversed and reveled, making
Free in their joy, their pleasure taking.
And she told him, as well, how best

* There is much debate as to just how much of the message preceding the final couplet
Marie wants us to believe was actually carved into the branch. See Micha's edition of the
Lais, p. 348. I have tried to let my translation avoid the question.

Del rei avrat acordement,
E que mut li aveit pesé
De ceo qu'il l'ot si cungeé:
Par encusement l'aveit fait.
A tant s'en part, sun ami lait.
Mes quant ceo vint al desevrer,
Dunc comencierent a plurer.
Tristram en Wales s'en rala
Tant que sis uncles le manda.

Pur la joie qu'il ot eüe
De s'amie qu'il ot veüe
E pur ceo k'il aveit escrit
Si cum la reïne l'ot dit,
Pur les paroles remembrer,
Tristram, ki bien saveit harper,
En aveit fet un nuvel lai;
Asez brefment le numerai:
Gotelef l'apelent Engleis,
Chievrefoil le nument Franceis.
Dit vus en ai la verité
Del lai que j'ai ici cunté.

———————

DE RUSTICO ET SCARABAEO

D'un vilein dit ki se giseit
cuntre soleil, si se dormeit.
A denz s'ert mis tuz descoverz,
e sis pertus esteit overz.
Uns escharboz dedenz entra,
e li vileins s'en esveilla.
Grant mal li fist, tant qu'a un mire
l'esteit alez cunter e dire.
Li mires dist qu'il esteit preinz.
Or fu mult pis qu'il ne fu einz;

His fell disgrace might be redressed;
Saying how glum her days and grim
Since first the king had banished him;
Disgrace that had been wrought, said she,
By foul accuser's calumny.
Thereupon does she leave, downhearted,
Quitting her love; and as they parted,
Ending their tryst, much did they fall
To weeping; and Tristan, withal,
Returned to Wales, till the day when
The king would call him back again.

Much pleased that he had seen his love,
For the great joy he felt thereof,
And to keep fresh the message writ,
Just as the queen had heeded it,
Tristan, who harped and sang with skill,
Composed a new *lai*; name it will
I simply: in the English tongue,
* "Goatleaf," or "Chèvrefeuille" among
The French. And thus here have I stated,
Truthfully, what his *lai* related.

THE PEASANT AND THE BEETLE

A loutish lummox lay a-dozing,
Flat on his face, his arse exposing
Unto the sun, with cheeks spread wide;
When lo! a beetle crawled inside
The grandly gaping aperture.
Needless to say, the brutish boor
Awoke at once, in pain, and hied him
Straight to the doctor, who, to chide him,
Told him he must be great with child.
Stupider than before, he smiled

* To the best of my (i.e., the *OED*'s) knowledge, "goatleaf" (Marie's *gotelef*) is not an attested word in English, nor does it appear ever to have been one, being cited in neither the Anglo-Saxon nor Middle English dictionaries I have consulted. I assume *gotelef* to be a nonce-word of Marie's time, or perhaps her own fanciful translation of the two elements of the Old French noun, itself derived from the Latin *caper* (goat) and *folium* (leaf).

kar li vileins bien le creï,
e li fols pueples, ki l'oï,
diënt que c'est signefiance.
En poür sunt e en dutance;
n'i a celui ki bien ne creie
que granz mals avenir lur deie.
Tant est li fols pueples muables,
qu'en veines choses nunverables
unt lur creance e lur espeir.
Le vilein guaitent pur saveir
par unt cil enfes deveit nestre.
Li escharboz par la fenestre,
u il entra, s'en est eissuz:
dunc furent il tuz deceüz.

Par cest essample le vus di:
des nunsachanz est altresi,
ki creient ceo qu'estre ne puet,
u vanitez les trait e muet.

_____

DE RUSTICO STULTE ORANTE

Uns vileins ala al mustier
suventes feiz pur deu preier.
A deu requist qu'il li aidast
e que sa femme cunseillast
e ses enfanz e nului plus;
ceste preiere aveit en us.
Sovent le dist od si halt cri
qu'uns altre vileins l'entendi,
si li respunt hastivement:
"Deus te maldie omnipotent,
ta femme e tes enfanz petiz,
e nuls altre ne seit maldiz!"

Par cest essample vueil retraire:
chescuns deit tel preiere faire,
ki a la gent ne seit nuisable
e ki a deu seit acceptable.

In daft belief, then went to tell
All of his friends, who, daft as well,
Saw in the news a portent grave.
Looking with awe upon the knave,
They sat in wait for Fate to strike.
For that's what fatuous folk are like:
Easily swayed, their minds are not
Immune to trash and tommyrot.
They thrive on foolish folderol.
And so they waited, one and all,
To see just how the babe would come...
At length the beetle, venturesome,
Appearing—much to their chagrin—
Came out the same way he went in.

This moral fable teaches us
That witless folk were ever thus;
Though tall the tale, they're quick to swallow—
Where folly leads, there will they follow!

Fables, XLIII

—————

THE PEASANT AND HIS STUPID PRAYER

A boorish peasant frequently
Prayed God in church, begging that He
Aid him, his wife, his children too,
But no one else. This would he do
Many a time and oft in prayer
So loud that, one day, praying there,
Another peasant hears his pleas,
Turns to the boor and disagrees:
"May you, your wife, and children all
Be cursed by God! May He let fall
Upon you all the very worst,
And may nobody else be cursed!"

I would, with this brief tale, portray
The need for mankind not to pray
In manner hurtful or untoward,
But, rather, pleasing to the Lord.

Fables, LV

Marie de France 45

DE VULPE ET UMBRA LUNAE

D'un gupil dit ki une nuit
esteit alez en sun deduit.
Sur une mare trespassa.
Quant dedenz l'ewe reguarda,
l'umbre de la lune a veü;
mes ne sot mie que ceo fu.
Puis a pensé en sun curage
qu'il ot veü un grant furmage.
L'ewe comença a laper;
tresbien quida en sun penser,
se l'ewe en la mare fust mendre,
que le furmage peüst prendre.
Tant a beü que il creva:
Iluec chaï, puis n'en leva.

Meinz huem espeire, ultre le dreit
e ultre ceo qu'il ne devreit,
aveir tutes ses volentez,
dunt puis est morz e afolez.

DE LUPO ET CORVO

D'un lou cunte ki vit jadis
u uns corbels esteit asis
desur le dos d'une berbiz.
Li lous parla od nobles diz:
"Jeo vei," fet il, "mult grant merveille:
le corp sur le dos d'une oweille.
Siet la u siet, dit ceo que dit,
fet ceo que fet senz cuntredit:
mal ne crient il de nule rien.
Se j'i seïsse, jeo sai bien
que tute genz me huëreient;
de tutes parz m'escriëreient
que jeo la voldreie mangier;
ne m'i larreient aprismier."

THE FOX AND THE MOON'S REFLECTION

A fox, they say, his leisure taking—
Out for the evening, merrymaking—
Started to cross a pond; when lo!
He saw the moon's reflection—though
He had no notion, actually,
What such a curious thing could be.
After a bit of introspection,
It struck the fox that said reflection
Must be a cheese. And so he hung
His head down low, and with his tongue
Began to lap the water, thinking—
While thus he gulped and saw it sinking—
That soon the cheese was his... But first,
He drank, drank, drank... and promptly burst.

How many the men whose aims are such
That they aspire to far too much!
Reaching for goals unwisely cherished,
Many have suffered, many have perished.

Fables, LVIII

THE WOLF AND THE CROW

A wolf, they tell us, gazed in awe
And disbelief, to see a daw
Perching upon a sheep. "Ah me!"
Complained the wolf, bombastically.
A sight to shock the eyes! A crow—
Calmly, politely, poised just so—
Atop a sheep! And look!... Without
The slightest qualm, the merest doubt...
Doing what suits his fancy, freely...
Ah! If *I* chose to sit there, really
I can just hear the hue and cry!
Let me approach him... dare draw nigh...
Folks will expect I must mistreat him.
Worse, they suspect I'm going to eat him!"

Issi est il del tricheür:
en esfrei est e en poür
—sa cunsciënce le reprent—
que tuit cunuissent sun talent.
Forment li peise del leial,
que hum ne tient ses fez a mal.

DE CORVO PENNAS PAVONIS INVENIENTE

D'un corbel cunte ki trova
par un chemin, u il ala,
plumes e pennes d'un poün;
si s'esguarda tut envirun:
plus vil se tint que nul oisel,
pur ceo qu'il ne se vit si bel.
Tutes ses plumes esracha
qu'une sule n'en i laissa:
des pennes al poün s'aturne,
trestut sun cors bien en aürne.
Puis s'asembla od les poüns.
Ne sembla pas lur cumpaignuns:
od les eles le debatirent,
e, se pis porent, pis li firent.
Dunc s'en revolt as cors aler,
si cum einz fist, corp resembler.
Mes il l'unt tut descuneü,
si l'unt chacié e debatu.

Ceo puet hum veeir de plusurs,
ki aveir unt e granz honurs:
uncor voldreient plus cuillir
ceo qu'il ne pueent retenir;
ceo qu'il coveitent n'unt il mie,
e le lur perdent par folie.

Thus does the felon live in fear
Lest all his purposes appear
Base and unworthy, even though
He may behave quite *comme il faut.*
The traitor is his own worst victim:
Conscience will prick him; grief, afflict him.

Fables, LIX

THE CROW WHO FINDS A PEACOCK'S FEATHERS

The tale is told about a crow
Who loped along a road, when lo!
He found before him, on the ground,
A peacock's plumes. Then, looking round,
He mused that he the lowliest was,
Indeed, of all the birds, because
Not pretty was he, not at all.
Thereupon does he pluck, let fall
All of his feathers till not one
Remains in place. When this is done,
Donning the peacock's feathers, he
Goes off in his new finery
To join the peacocks. They, however,
Seeing in him naught whatsoever
Of peacock ilk, pounce, turn on him,
And almost tear him wing from limb.
Now, featherless again, he goes
Once more to dwell among the crows:
They know him not, and so, without
Delay, thrash him and cast him out.
Many's the man who acts like this,
Undone by greed and avarice:

Though wealth is his, and honor, yet
Eager is he still more to get;
But in the end, though he may reap it,
Not long his folly lets him keep it.

Fables, LXVII

DE HOMINE ET BOBUS

Ci nus recunte en ceste fable,
qu'uns vileins traist hors de s'estable
od ses bués le fiens que il firent.
Li buef par tençun l'asaillirent,
si repruverent al vilein
la bone cerveise e le pein,
que par lur travail ot eü;
mes malement lur a rendu:
qu'a grant hunte les demena.
E li vileins lur demanda
que ceo esteit qu'il lur fist faire.
"Le fiens fors de l'estable traire."
Dist li vileins: "Vus le femastes
e la maisun en encumbrastes."
Li buef dïent: "C'est veritez."
Dunc s'est li vileins purpensez,
si lur respunt que hors le traient:
bien est dreiz que la peine en aient.

Issi va del malvais serjant,
ki tutejur va repruchant
sun grant servise a sun seignur:
ne se prent guarde de l'onur
ne del bien ne del gueredun
qu'il a eü en sa maisun.
De ceo qu'il mesfet e mesprent
ne li puet suvenir nïent:
quant sun travail vuelt repruver,
de sun mesfet li deit membrer.

DE APE ET MUSCA

Une musche e une es tencierent
e ensemble se curucierent.
La musche dist que mielz valeit
e qu'en tel liu aler poeit,
u cele ne s'osot veeir:

THE MAN AND THE OXEN

This fable tells a tale about
A peasant who was cleaning out
His stable, with his oxen hauling
Buckets of dung—their own; who, calling
Out to him, loudly criticized
The task he asked of them; advised
Him of the pains that, for his sake,
They had endured; that thus to make
Them do was shameful, surely not
Recompense for the work he got!
"Do what?" the peasant asked. "Why, haul
This blasted dung!" "But after all,"
He answered, "will you not admit it?
Was it not you, my friends, who shit it?"
"True," said the oxen, "true." Whereat
The peasant, giving tit for tat,
Reflects a bit, and then declares
That fit it is the task be theirs.

So too bad servants do we find
Who ever do their lord remind
Of all that they have wrought, with never
A thought of all the good, however—
The honor, praise, and even joy—
That they have had in his employ.
Naught they remember of their flaws
Or everything that wanting was:
Best, when their well-done tasks they tell,
That they recall the ill as well.

Fables, LXXXIV

THE BEE AND THE FLY

A quarrel 'twixt a fly and bee
Arose, in which each angrily
Chided the other. Said the fly
That she was better, by the by,
Because she ventured in her flight

desur le rei poeit seeir;
quan que l'es tut l'an purchaçot
e atraeit e travaillot,
li ert toleit, si ert tuëe
e de sa maisun fors getee.
"Jeo e mes cumpaignes manjuns
de tun miel tant cum nus voluns."
L'es li respunt: "Vus dites veir.
Mes il est legier a saveir
que plus iés vils que jeo ne sui;
kar en tuz lius fez tu ennui.
Sié la u siez, va la u vas,
ja par tun fet honur n'avras;
jeo sui pur le mien fet amee
e mult cherie e bien guardee."

Issi va del natre felun,
quant il a bien en abandun,
vers les meillurs trop se nobleie
e de parole se richeie;
par grant desdein les cuntralie.
Mais se nuls est, ki bien li die
la verité de sun afaire
en pleine curt, le fera taire.

DE MILVO

Uns escufles jut en sun lit;
malades est, si cum il dit.
Uns jais ot sun ni pres de lui,
a qui il fist suvent ennui.
Li escufles se purpensa
que sa mere i enveiera,

Where never a bee would dare alight,
And even sat upon the king!
Whereas the bee, poor busy thing,
Labored all year to suck and gather,
Only to die; for one would rather
Catch her, kill her, and cast her out.
"My friends and I, the while, without
A care, feast to our hearts' content
Upon your honey, pleasure-bent."
Replies the bee: "Yes, surely, what
You say is true, I warrant. But
Easy it is—and no less true—
To see that far more vile are you
Than I; for everywhere you flit,
Abhorrent are you! So, go sit
Wherever you may choose: you never,
Friend, will be honored howsoever;
Whilst I am kept, protected, very
Loved for my labors salutary."

Thus ever acts the rake malicious,
Greedy of gain and avaricious,
Who would in deed and speech presume
To live the noble's life, but whom
One treats with scorn. If none there is
To make him see the truth of his
Base pedigree, then those at court
Will shut him up and cut him short.

Fables, LXXXV

THE KITE

A kite was lying ill abed,
Ailing, or so at least he said.
* Close by a jackdaw had her nest,
Whom, often, he had sore distressed.
At length the kite decides to send
Thither his mother, to commend

*Although the grammatical gender of the word *jais* is masculine, logic, I think, demands that I make the character female.

Marie de France 53

si fera requerre pardun
e que pur lui face oreisun.
"Mere," fet il, "kar i alez!
Qu'il prit pur mei, li requerez!"
"Jeo," fet ele, "cument irai?
Ne sai cument li prierai:
meinte feiz as suillié sun ni
e sur ses oisels esmelti."

Issi est de la fole gent:
la, u il unt mesfet suvent,
vuelent aler merci criër,
ainz qu'il le vueillent amender.

DE HOMINE ET MENSURA

Ci cunte d'un mesureür,
ki terre mesurot un jur.
Durement maldist la mesure;
kar ne pot par nule aventure
od li, ceo dist, dreit mesurer.
La perche dist: "Lai mei ester!
Jeo ne faz par mei nule rien:
tu me getes, ceo veit hum bien.
Mes tu iés pleins de tricherie:
sur mei turnes ta felunie."

Issi funt li nundreiturier:
quant hum aparceit lur mestier,
les altres vuelent enculper
e lur mesfet sur els turner.

DE HOMINE ET UXORE LITIGIOSA

Uns vileins ot femme a espuse,
ki mult esteit cuntrariüse.
Un jur furent ensemble alé
pur els deduire par un pre.

Him to the daw, whose pardon he
Requests, indeed, most earnestly.
"Go to her, please: ask that she say
A prayer for me!" "Ask her to pray?
For you?" replies the mother. "Pshaw!
How would I ask that of a daw
Whose nest you foul and slop upon,
Whose chicks you loose your droppings on!"

Such is how fools will often act,
Who wrong another; for, in fact,
Rather than let their ways be mended,
"Mercy!" they cry from those offended.

Fables, LXXXVI

THE MAN AND THE MEASURING ROD

A man whose trade was to survey
The land performed that task one day.
He cursed the measure that he used:
Try though he might, it quite refused
To gauge the surface properly.
Said the rod: "Yes, of course! Blame me!
Certainly there can be no doubt:
The fault is mine, so throw me out!
What a deceitful hypocrite!
You botch your task: I pay for it."

So those who ill perform and shirk
Their trade: when one inspects their work,
Another's flaws will they bemoan,
For never is the fault their own.

Fables, XC

THE MAN AND HIS QUARRELSOME WIFE

A peasant has a wife who never
With him agrees, but cavils ever.
To take their ease the two have gone
Off to a meadow, whereupon

Li vileins a sa femme dit,
qu'unkes mes de ses uiz ne vit
nul pre falchié si uëlment.
El li respunt hastivement:
"Ainz fu od les forces trenchiez."
Dit li vileins: "Einz fu falchiez."
"Einz est," fet la femme, "tunduz."
Dunc s'est li vileins irascuz.
"Tu iés," fet il, "fole pruvee:
ceste herbe fu od falz colpee.
Mes tu iés si engresse e fole,
qu'avant vuels metre ta parole;
la meie vuels faire remeindre,
par engresté me vuels ateindre."
Li vileins l'a a val getee,
si li a [la] langue colpee.
Puis demande qu'a vis li fu
e qu'ele en aveit entendu,
se li prez fu od falz falchiez
u od forces esteit trenchiez.
La u ele ne pot parler,
od ses deiz li prist a mustrer
que forces l'aveient trenchié
e que falz ne l'ot pas seié.

Par cest essample vuelt mustrer,
bien le puet hum suvent pruver:
se fols parole une folie
e altre vient, ki sens li die,
ne l'en creit pas, einz s'en aïre;
la u il set qu'il en est pire,
vuelt sa mençunge metre avant:
nuls nel fereit de ceo taisant.

The bumpkin tells his wife that he
Never has seen so perfectly
A field put to the scythe as this.
Straightway says she: "You speak amiss:
'Put to the shears,' you mean, monsieur."
The peasant quickly answers her:
"The scythe!" says he; and she, "the shears."
Whereat he wrathful grows; jeers, sneers,
Says she is quite the fool, because
Scythed and not sheared this meadow was.
"Foolish you are, and stubborn too,
To say your say the way you do.
You would, I vow, have me be quiet,
Hush my opinion, or deny it."
So saying he throws her down, plucks out
Her very tongue! Then does the lout
Ask her again if she is so
Certain that shears were used to mow
This meadow! Or will she admit,
Now, that a scythe was used for it!
Speechless, she wags and waves her hands
To prove, with silent reprimands,
That it was shears indeed that cut
The grass, not scythe, no matter what.

This moral tale seeks to disclose
A truth that one already knows:
He whose false, fatuous eloquence
Is contradicted by good sense,
Never believes the truth he hears;
Rather, the more one perseveres,
The angrier he, sure to defend
*   His falsehood to the bitter end.

Fables, xciv

* This fable presents a fascinating ambiguity. If it was clear in Marie's mind which of her two characters she is chastising, her text, unfortunately, does not conclusively reveal her intent. Though the Latin title seems to cast blame for stubbornness on the woman—*litigiosa*—the husband, especially given the violence with which he defends his opinion, is hardly guiltless. The concluding moral appears to mitigate the ambiguity somewhat and throw the burden of blame upon the man, but the gender-neutrality of the third-person pronoun *hums* (one) allows for doubt even here. *Decidat lector.*

DE LEPORE ET CERVO

Uns lievres vit un cerf ester;
ses cornes prist a reguarder,
mult li sembla bele sa teste.
Plus se tint vil que nule beste,
quant altresi n'esteit cornuz
e qu'il esteit si poi creüz.
A la sepande ala parler,
si li cumence a demander,
pur quei ne l'ot si honuré
e de cornes si aürné
cume le cerf, qu'il ot veü.
La deuesse l'a respundu:
"Tais, fols," fet ele, "lai ester:
tu nes purreies guverner."
"Si ferai bien," il li respunt.
Dunc ot cornes el chief a munt.
Mes nes poeit mie porter,
kar ne saveit od tut aler;
car plus aveit qu'il ne deüst
ne qu'a sa grandur n'esteüst.

Par cest essample vuelt mustrer:
li coveitus e li aver
vuelent tuz jurs tant cuveitier,
e si se vuelent eshaleier,
tant enpernent par lur ultrage,
que lur honurs turne a damage.

DE FEMINA ET GALLINA

Une femme se seeit ja
devant sun us, si esguarda,
cume sa geline gratot
e sa viande purchaçot;
mult se travaillot tutejur.
A li parla par grant amur:
"Bele," fet ele, "lai ester
que tu ne vueilles si grater!

THE HARE AND THE STAG

A hare espied a stag close by.
Upon his horns he cast his eye,
Admiring what a comely head
He had, whilst he himself, instead,
Hornless and small, was certainly
As vile a beast as beast could be.
Unto the goddess of the wood
He goes, and asks her why he should
Not likewise honored be, adorned
In stagly guise, so finely horned.
Answers the goddess: "Fool! Why choose
Things you would not know how to use?"
"I would! I would!" replies the hare.
So be it... All at once a pair
Of antlers, rising high, sprout from
His head; but soon, too burdensome
Are they: for now, though he can wear them,
Small as he is, he cannot bear them.

This moral lesson shows that he
Who craves and covets greedily,
And yearns above his state to rise
With honors not his due, defies
Good sense: soon what he coveted
Comes crashing down about his head.

Fables, xcvi

THE WOMAN AND THE HEN

Before her house a woman sat
Watching her hen, who, clawing at
The ground, was searching for her food
In most industrious attitude,
As ever was her wont. With much
Affection, asked the woman—such
Was her surprise: "My sweet, why dig?
I know your appetite is big,

Chescun jur te durrai furment
pleine une grange a tun talent."
La geline li respundi:
"Que diz tu? Va! Qu'ai jeo oï?
Quides tu que j'aim mielz tun ble
que ceo que ai tut tens usé?
Nenil, nenil," fet la geline,
"se devant mei esteit la mine
tuz jurs pleine, pas ne lerreie
ne pur ceo ne me targereie
que ne quesisse tuz jurs plus
sulunc ma nature e mun us."

Par cest essample vuelt mustrer,
que plusurs genz pueent trover
manaie e ceo qu'il unt mestier;
mes il ne pueent pas changier
lur nature ne lur usage;
tuz jurs avive en lur curage.

But I have store enough of feed
To fill you full, and fill your need."
"Come now," the hen replied to her.
"Do you think that I could prefer
The grain you give me to the things
I find in all my foragings?
Nay, nay! This is the way I live,
And always have done. Feed me, give
Me all the grain you will; yes, fill
My bucket to the brim: I still
Will dig for more. For that, madame,
Has always been the way I am."

This fable goes to prove that many
Have all they need, and need not any
More than they have; and yet, how strange:
Never can they their manner change.
Ever are they as they have been:
* Their nature always lives within.

Fables, CII

---

*It is delightfully ironic (even probably intentional?) that, after presenting an entire
collection ostensibly intended to reform mankind's foibles, Marie offers as her parting shot
in these, its final lines—except for a brief but most important epilogue—the observation
that human nature, after all, really cannot be changed.

Castelloza (EARLY THIRTEENTH CENTURY)

Some might justifiably question the inclusion of Na [Lady] Castelloza, in her Provençal (Occitan) designation—in these pages devoted to French women poets. But although medieval Provençal is a language distinct from Old French (and even from the latter-day Provençal of the Midi), one can defend her presence on the grounds that, although linguistically not "French," she nonetheless represents a community of poets from that geographical entity eventually to be known as "France."

One of several dozen female troubadours—*trobairitz*—who flourished in medieval Provence alongside their male counterparts and the best known of whom was Beatriz de Dia, Castelloza has come down to us thanks to a mere three poetic works, originally accompanied by music, which has not fared so well.[1] So little is known of her life that she is often referred to as "the dark lady" of Provençal verse, though many another shadowy *consœur* could well dispute that epithet. Possibly from Auvergne or just as possibly not, she may or may not have been the wife of one Turc de Mairona, descendant of a crusader who, around 1120, had taken the surname of "Turc" in honor of his crusade's happy conclusion.[2]

While generalization from a scant three poems is rather risky business, Castelloza was obviously adept at the technical virtuosity typical of Provençal verse and seems to have been steeped in the tradition of *fin'amors*—that curious paradox of the simultaneous idolization and objectification of woman, known for better or worse as "courtly love"—replete with its common themes of consuming (and, usually, forbidden) passion, its threats, its jealousies, and its eventual solace. And all with a sincerity and freshness that raise her a notch above the banality of many of her conventional colleagues.

The two *cansos* translated here are taken from *Les troubadours cantaliens*, vol. 2. In order to adhere to the formal aspects of rhyme and meter so important in Provençal verse, I have had to stray at times from literal precision in these translations. I have tried, also, with inner rhymes, alliterations, and the like, to suggest at least something of the verbal virtuosity so characteristic of the genre.

NOTES

1. For the texts, see Louis-Félix duc de la Salle de Rochemaure and René Lavaud, *Les troubadours cantaliens*, 2: 496–515. See also, inter alia, Paul Bénétrix, *Les femmes troubadours*, pp. 58–61; Meg Bogin, *The Women Troubadours*, pp. 118–29; Matilda Bruckner, Laurie Shepard, and Sarah White, *Songs of the Women Troubadours*, pp. 14–25, 146–50; and William D. Paden, ed., *The Voice of the Trobairitz: Perspectives on the Women Troubadours*, pp. 95–127.

2. See Bogin, *Women Troubadours*, p. 175.

CANSO

Amics, s'ie-us trobes avinen,
Humil e franc e de'bona merce,
Be-us amera, quan era m'en sove
Que-us trob vas mi mal e fellon e tric;
E fauc chanssos per tal qu'ieu fass' auzir
Vostre bon pretz, don ieu non puosc sofrir
Que no-us fassa lauzar a tota gen,
On plus mi faitz mal et adiramen.

Jamais no-us tenrai per valen
Ni-us amarai de bon cor e de fe,
Tro que veirai si ja-m valria re,
Si-us mostrava cor fellon ni enic;
Non farai ja, car non vuoill poscatz dir
Qu'ieu anc vas vos agues cor de faillir,
Qu'auriatz pois qualque razonamen,
S'ieu fazia vas vos nuill faillimen.

Ieu sai ben qu'a mi estai gen,
Si be-is dizon tuich que mout descove
Que dompna prei a cavallier de se
Ni que-l teigna totz temps tan lonc prezic;
Mas cel qu'o ditz non sap ges ben chausir.
Qu'ieu vuoill proar, enans que-me lais morir,
Qu'el preiar ai un gran revenimen
Quan prec cellui don ai greu pessamen.

Assatz es fols qui m'en repren
De vos amar, pois tan gen mi cove,
E cel qu'o ditz no sap cum s'es de me;
Ni no-us vei ges aras si cum vos vic,
Quan me dissetz que non agues cossir,
Que calqu'ora poiri 'endevenir
Que n'auria enqueras jauzimen:
De sol lo dich n'ai ieu lo cor jauzen.

Tot'autr' amor teing a nien,
E sapchatz ben que mais jois no-m soste
Mas lo vostre, que m'alegr'e-m reve,
On mais eu sent d'afan e de destric;

SONG

Friend, if I found you gracious, fair,
Candid and humble, full of virtuousness,
How I would love you! But, alas, far less
I find you now: so fell, so cruel to me.
Yet do I sing, to let the wide world know
How virtuous you could be; for I would show
That praised would be your virtue everywhere,
Though you bestow me naught but pain and care.

I shall not deem you debonair,
Nor, faithful-hearted, my true love profess
Unless, first, I pronounce how fickle, yes,
How faithless is your heart!... Nay, verily,
Best I think better, lest I too be so
Heartless and faithless unto you—although
So are you unto me!—and lest I bear
Your wrath, should I your slightest wrong declare.

Well do I do; but well aware
Am I that one and all claim we transgress,
Who bare our heart and jabber to excess
Our bane and bale unto our swains. But he
Who judges so, judges us ill; for, no!
Rather than die, I would prove, *à propos*,
That I much comfort feel when, in my prayer,
I pray to him who causes my despair.

Passing daft must one be to dare
Say I ought love you not, nor acquiesce
To love's demands: he knows not my distress,
Nor knows what cheer was mine when I could see
You there before me, telling me that, lo!
Done would my dolor be, undone my woe;
That love for me, once more, might bring you there:
Ah! promise of a joy beyond compare!

All other loves do I foreswear.
None else consoles me in my dire duress,
Nor brings me solace; yours would I possess,
And yours alone, to ease my misery...

E-m cuig ades alegrar e jauzir
De vos, amics, qu'ieu non puosc convertir,
Ni joi non ai, ni socors non aten
Mas sol aitan quan n'aurai en dormen.

   Oimais non sai que-us mi presen,
Que cercat ai et ab mal et ab be
Vostre dur cor, don lo mieus no-is recre;
E no-us o man, qu'ieu mezeissa-us o dic,
Que morai me, si no-m voletz jauzir
De qualque joi; e si-m laissatz morir,
Faretz peccat, e serai n'en tormen,
E seretz ne blasmatz vilanamen.

———————

CANSO

Mout avetz faich long estatge,
Amics, pois de mi-us partitz,
Et es me greu e salvatge,
Quar me juretz e-m plevitz
Que als jorns de vostra vida
Non acsetz dompna mas me;
E si d'autra vos perte,
M'i avetz mort' e trahida,
Qu'avi'en vos m'esperanssa
Que m'amassetz ses doptanssa.

Bels amics, de fin coratge
Vos amei, pois m'abellitz,
E sai que faich ai follatge,
Que plus m'en etz escaritz,
Qu'anc non fis vas vos ganchida;
E si-m fasetz mal per be!
Be' us am e non m'en recre,
Mas tan m'a amors sazida
Qu'ieu non cre que benananssa
Puosc' aver ses vostr' amanssa.

Mout aurai mes mal usatge
A las autras amairitz:
Qu'om sol trametre messatge
E motz triatz e chausitz,

But, friend, I cannot change you; and I go
On yearning, hoping, dreaming of the beau
You will not be! Where is your love? Oh, where
But in my sleep, that love I fain would share?

    I fear I will no better fare,
Nor can, in other wise, my dole express;
For, ceaseless, have I tried, with no success,
Fair means and foul to thwart your cruelty.
This message do I send you—this *canso*—
Writ in my words, my very own. But, oh!
If die I must, yours be the blame! Beware:
Yours, the sin; mine, the woe without repair.

———————

SONG

Friend, long you linger far from me,
And, since you bade me your good-bye,
Dire is my pain, deep my ennui.
By your oath did you swear that I
Would be your only lady: none
But me, for all your lifelong days;
And now your heart that vow betrays.
Slain do I lie, deceived, undone;
For I believed and hoped in you,
That you would love me, loyal, true.

Fair friend, I loved you faithfully
Since first your beauty pleased my eye;
But foolishly I let you see
My sense too clear. Ah me! Awry
Flew our love hence: you fled as one
Who good with naught but ill repays!
And yet my poor heart disobeys,
Still seeks your love, that has begun
To vanish now; and so thereto
Must I, unsolaced, bid adieu.

Ladies in love displeased may be
With me, for I have shown hereby
How much will creatures such as we
Yearn for man's words to satisfy

Et ieu tenc me per garida,
Amics, a la mia fe,
Quan vos prec, qu'aissi-m cove;
Que-l plus pros n'es enriquida
S'a de vos qualqu'aondanssa
De baisar o d'acoindanssa.

Mal aj'ieu, s'anc cor volatge
Vos aic ni-us fui camjairitz!
Ni drutz de negun paratge
Per me non fo encobitz.
Anz sui pensiv'e marrida
Car de m'amor no-us sove,
E si de vos jois no-m ve,
Tost me trobaretz fenida:
Car per pauc de malananssa
Mor dompna, s'om tot no-il lanssa.

Tot lo maltraich e-l dompnatge
Que per vos m'es escaritz
Me-l fai grazir mos linhatge
E sobre totz mos maritz;
E s'anc fetz vas me faillida,
Perdon la-us per bona fe;
E prec que venhatz a me,
Despois quez auretz auzida
Ma chanson, que-us fatz fiansa
Sai trobetz bella semblansa.

Our hearts—well-chosen words, whereon
To dote; and I am one who prays
To be so graced, and thus displays
Keen taste. For, lives there anyone
So fine that your kiss naught would do
To make her finer, nobler too?

Ah, woe! Never have I made free
With fickle love for you—fie, fie!—
Nor beau, although of high degree,
Have I desired by me to lie.
Wistful am I, and woebegone:
You want me not, and naught allays
My lot. If I no hope can raise,
I die: woman cannot live on
In torment. Best her swain eschew
Her love, and leave without ado.

Still, the fell pain and misery
You rain upon me gratify
And fill with pride my family—
Especially my husband, aye!—
So high your rank! And, though you run
From me, and in whatever ways
Earn my displeasure and dispraise,
I pardon you, and pray you shun
Me not... Now is my song sung through.
Come, friend! Be welcomed here anew!

Christine de Pizan (1364?–1430?)

Christine de Pizan—or Pisan, according to those who erroneously thought her family to be from Pisa—was one of medieval France's most accomplished women of letters, and she has been one of the most widely studied in recent years.[1] Venetian by birth, she was the daughter of Tomasso de Pizzano, a scholar from the University of Bologna, and a mother who, it is unrealistically claimed by some, might also have studied there. When her father was named physician and astrologer to Charles V of France, the five-year-old Christine, to the intellectual manner born, found herself surrounded by scholars, books, and ideas, all of which were to leave their mark on her. Married at fifteen to a court secretary ten years her senior, she would lose him suddenly in 1387, and her father three years later. To support her three children and her mother, and to resolve numerous lawsuits left in the wake of her husband's death, Christine undertook a literary career, becoming, it is said, the first European woman to earn her living by her pen, thanks to wealthy patrons. After producing numerous and varied works, disheartened by France's domestic and foreign catastrophes, she retired in 1418 to a convent, where she died a dozen years later, after completing her final poem, *Le ditié de Jehanne d'Arc* (1429).

Bending the meters, traditional and novel, of Old (or, more properly, Middle) French, to a wide variety of inspirations, Christine was equally at home in lyrical pieces, works of philosophical and social speculation, a surprising manual on warfare, the more usual religious devotions, and a genre frequent in the Middle Ages and beyond, the conduct book. The reader will find here characteristic examples of the first and last, more approachable than her often much more demanding lengthier *œuvres*.[2]

Among the latter are several philosophico-amatory treatises, for which Christine de Pizan is perhaps most appreciated, and which champion the cause of her gender in the so-called "Querelle des femmes" (Quarrel concerning women), one of the first of those typical intellectual tug-of-wars that would characterize French literary history. This one pitted the defenders of woman against the misogynistic attacks launched in Jean de Meung's continuation of the allegorical *Roman de la rose* (1275–1280). In her *Epistre au dieu d'amours* (1399), for example, Christine passes in review, in the voice of an outraged Cupid, many reasons why woman is not only not inferior to man but even superior to him. After all, she was fashioned not from base clay, like him, but from a part of God's noble creation itself. Furthermore, a scorn of woman implies disrespect for one's own mother and, indeed, for the Virgin. As for love, if it turns awry, the fault most often lies with faithless man, as Christine would prove by citing the travails of various historical and mythological heroines.[3]

One finds similar reasoning, often deliciously ingenious, in the sequels *Le dit de la rose* (1402) and the prose *Epistres du debat sur le Roman de la rose* (1401–1403), as well as in several other works, the longest and most widely read of which is the utopian dream-vision *Le livre de la cité des dames* (1405), which, when translated in 1982 by Earl Jeffery Richards, helped to revive interest in her career. No less important is her *Livre des trois vertus* (1405), which purports to reveal spiritual, moral, and practical counsel to all classes of women. Less weighty are the 113 quatrains on proper behavior written for the edification of her son, the *Enseignemens moraux* (1400), whose form, by definition, precludes excessive profundity;[4] and less weighty still, her early and later lyrics—virelays, ballades, rondeaux—which added to the already traditional theme of courtly love the sorrows of widowhood, and which range stylistically from the elegantly somber to the almost playfully light-hearted.

The examples in these pages—a variety of lyrics and twenty-nine quatrains from the *Enseignemens moraux*—are taken from *Œuvres poétiques de Christine de Pisan*, edited by Maurice Roy.

NOTES

1. For an authoritative biography of Christine, see Charity Cannon Willard, *Christine de Pizan: Her Life and Works,* and the same author's edition, *The Writings of Christine de Pizan.* For a briefer biographical sketch and selection of texts, see Jeanine Moulin, *Christine de Pisan.* See also the several studies in *The Selected Writings of Christine de Pizan,* ed. Renate Blumenfeld-Kosinski.

2. New books and articles quickly outstrip the bibliographies of studies devoted to her work, but the following are very useful: Edith Yenal, *Christine de Pizan: A Bibliography of Writings by Her and About Her,* and Angus Kennedy, *Christine de Pizan: A Bibliographical Guide.*

3. In regard to this aspect of her work, see esp. Rosalind Brown-Grant, *Christine de Pizan and the Moral Defence of Women: Reading Beyond Gender.*

4. The conduct-book inspiration would be more substantially exploited in her later *Livre des fais et bonnes meurs du sage roy Charles V* (1404), a laudatory biography of the monarch, whose much admired morality was intended to contrast with the licentious lifestyle of her royal contemporary, Charles VI.

Je suis de tout dueil assaillie
Et plus qu'oncques mais maubaillie,
Quant cellui se veult marier
Que j'amoye sanz varier,
Si suis de joye en dueil saillie.

Helas! il m'avoit promis
Que ja ne se marieroit,
Quant tout mon cuer en lui mis,
Et qu'a tousjours tout mien seroit;

Mal eschange m'en a baillie,
Car hors s'est mis de ma baillie;
Une autre veult apparier,
Et encontre moy guerrier;
Puis que s'amour or m'est faillie
Je suis de tout dueil assaillie.

Cellui devient mes anemis
Qui jadis vers moy se tiroit
Comme mes vrais loiaulx amis,
En moy regardant souspiroit.

Or est celle amour tressaillie
En autre, et vers moy deffaillie;
Car ne lui puis, pour tarier,
Sa voulenté contrarier,
Dont d'en morir j'en suis taillie,
Je suis de tout dueil assaillie.

Il a long temps que mon mal comença,
N'oncques despuis ne fina d'empirer
Mon las estat, qui puis ne s'avança,
Que Fortune me voult si atirer
Qu'il me convint de moy tout bien tirer;
Et du grief mal qu'il me fault recevoir
C'est bien raison que me doye doloir.

Plunged am I deep in agony,
Nor was so dark my destiny
As now it is; for he whom I
Loved faithfully weds by and by,
And from my joy springs misery.

Never would he another wed!
Alas! Such was the vow he made:
Mine would he ever be, he said;
I, with my heart, his pledge repaid.

But he has wronged, rejected me,
Casting aside my company;
Now comes another maid to vie
With me and battle me awry;
Since I torn from his love must be,
Plunged am I deep in agony.

Today is he my foe, though we
Together were, and ever nigh;
Ah! Once my loyal lover, he
Would gaze at me with soulful sigh.

Now is that love turned enmity,
And I am lost, alas! too free;
Naught that I do, try though I try,
Will change his mind; and that is why
Well might I die of my ennui:
Plunged am I deep in agony.

"Virelays," ix

Long do I bear the woe I suffer from;
Nor does my sorry state cease now yet more
And worse to grow: for I, instead, become
Victim of Fortune, fell conspirator,
Who would deprive me of all joy; and, for
The foul and rueful ills I suffer thus,
Reason have I to sigh full dolorous.

Christine de Pizan 73

Le dueil que j'ay si me tient de pieça,
Mais tant est grant qu'il me fait desirer
Morir briefment, car trop mal me cassa
Quant ce m'avint qui me fait aïrer;
Ne je ne puis de nul costé virer,
Que je voye riens qui me puist valoir.
C'est bien raison que me doye doloir.

Ce fist meseur qui me desavança,
Et Fortune qui voult tout dessirer
Mon boneür; car depuis lors en ça
Nul bien ne pos par devers moy tirer,
Ne je ne sçay penser ne remirer
Comment je vif; et de tel mal avoir
C'est bien raison que me doye doloir.

———————

FROM *ENSEIGNEMENS MORAUX*

I
Filz, je n'ay mie grant tresor
Pour t'enrichir; pour ce trés or
Aucuns enseignemens noter
Te vueil, si les vueilles noter.

II
Aimes Dieu de toute ta force,
Crains ley et du servir t'efforce,
La sont, se bien les as apris,
Les dix commandemens compris.

IV
Tant t'estudies a enquerre
Que prudence puisses acquerre,
Car celle est des vertus la mere
Qui chace Fortune l'amere.

VI
Se tu veulz en science eslire
Ton estat par les livres lire,
Fays tant, et par suivre l'estude,
Qu'entre les clers ne soyes rude.

Long lasts my mourning and my martyrdom:
But so deep they, that I my days deplore,
And fain would quickly die; for burdensome
Now is the broken life I bear and bore.
Look where I may, no solace see I, nor
Anything worth the fray or worth the fuss:
Reason have I to sigh full dolorous.

Fortune it was, I fear, grievous and glum,
Who, hunting me, tracking me down, so tore
My life to shreds that, sick of heart and numb
Of soul, naught see I but distress in store.
Nor want I more, nor even know why, or
How I can live a life so piteous:
Reason have I to sigh full dolorous.

"Cent balades," VIII

FROM *MORAL TEACHINGS*

I
My son, no wealth have I with which
To favor you and make you rich;
Instead, these lessons I impart,
And pray you take them much to heart.

II
Love God with all your energy,
Fear Him and serve Him faithfully;
If you can learn to live thereby,
Therein the ten commandments lie.

IV
Study your lessons hard and well
So that with prudence you may dwell;
For, mother of all virtues, she
Banishes Fortune's cruelty.

VI
If you the scholar's life would choose
Among the books, you must peruse
And learn them well lest, to be sure,
The clerics think you but a boor.

Christine de Pizan 75

VII

Se tu es noble et veulz les armes
Suivir, il fault que souvent t'armes,
Ou l'en te tendroit pour faillis,
Sans honneur, lasche et deffaillis.

XI

Se tu as maistre, serfs le bien,
Dis bien de lui, garde le sien,
Son secret celes, quoy qu'il face
Soies humble devant sa face.

XII

Trop covoiteux ne soies mie,
Car covoitise est anemie
De charité et de sagece,
Et te gar de fole largece.

XVIII

S'as disciples, ne les reprendre
En trop grant rigueur, se mesprendre
Les vois; pense que foible et vaine
Est la fragilité humaine.

XXIII

Se de marchandise te vifs
Vens et achate a ton advis
Si que ne perdes ou marchié,
Mais ne deçoys nul, c'est pechié.

XXVI

Tiens toy a table honnestement
Et t'abilles de vestement
En tel atour qu'on ne s'en moque,
Car on congnoist l'œuf a la coque.

XXXIV

Pour perte d'amis ou de biens
Ne chées en desespoir et tiens
Qu'assez est poissant Dieu celestre
Pour toy aidier et pour toy paistre.

VII

If you are noble and would lead
A knightly life, you must succeed
Often at arms, else will you be
Thought honorless and cowardly.

XI

If you a master have, I pray
You serve him well, no evil say,
Reveal no secrets, and whatever
Ill he may do, be humble ever.

XII

Covet not: greed is wisdom's foe,
And charity's; but make not so
Free with your generosity
That foolish you be thought to be.

XVIII

If you have students, and if they
Reason awry and go astray,
Be not too harsh, but bear in mind
Fragile indeed is humankind.

XXIII

If you become a merchant, try
To profit when you sell and buy;
But take care lest, therefor, you use
Evil deceit and sinful ruse.

XXVI

At table sit in modest wise
And dress yourself in proper guise
Lest one make fun, for as they tell,
He knows the egg who sees the shell.

XXXIV

When friends and wealth you lose, be not
Quick to despair, lament your lot,
Nor scorn God's power to succor you
Straightway, and fill your belly too.

XXXVIII

Ne croy pas toutes les diffames
Qu'aucuns livres dient des femmes,
Car il est mainte femme bonne,
L'experïence le te donne.

XL

Se tu veulx vivre a Court en paix
Voy et escoute et si te tays,
Ne te courroces de legier,
Dongereux ne soit ton mengier.

LXI

En ta vieillece en nulle guise
De vestement ne te desguise
Ne de mignote cointerie,
Car sourdre en pourroit moquerie.

LXXV

Deshonneur d'autrui ne racontes
Ne voulentiers n'en tiens tes contes,
Ains, s'aultre le dit, fays ent paix,
Se tu puez, ou se non t'en tais.

LXXVII

Se bien veulx et chastement vivre,
De la Rose ne lis le livre
Ne Ovide de l'Art d'amer,
Dont l'exemple fait a blasmer.

LXXXIV

Ne tiens maignée a ton loyer
Si grant que ne puisses paier,
Car souvent par trop gent avoir
On despent la terre et l'avoir.

XXXVIII
Believe not all the calumny
Books heap on women's company:
Many excel; the evidence
Will you find from experience.

XL
If you would live at Court, secure,
Keep eyes, ears open, but be sure
To hush your temper: indiscreet,
You had best watch the things you eat.

LXI
When you have older grown take care
Lest you improper garments wear:
Coquettish garb you must eschew,
Else will one chaff and laugh at you.

LXXV
Tales of another's infamy
Spread not, nor hear them willingly:
Deny them, if you can, among
The tattling ones; else hold your tongue.

LXXVII
If chaste you would be read not those
Books like the one about the Rose
Or Ovid's *Art of Love,* which ample
* Measure provide of bad example.

LXXXIV
Keep not so large a retinue
That you can pay them not; such do
Many, who hire more than they ought,
Ill spend their wealth, and then have naught.

* On the importance of the *Roman de la rose,* see p. 70. As for Ovid's "how-to" poem
on the art of courtship, the *Ars amatoria,* and the subsequent *Remedia amoris* intended
to "cure" the afflicted, their influence in the Middle Ages cannot be overemphasized. For
examples from Old French, see my *The Comedy of Eros: Medieval French Guides to the Art
of Love,* passim.

LXXXVI

Ne raportes parole aucune
De quoy sourdre puisse rancune;
Ton ami rapaise en son yre,
Se tu pues, par doulcement dire.

XCI

Selon ton pouoir vestz ta femme
Honnestement et si soit dame
De l'ostel après toy, non serve,
Fay que ta maignée la serve.

XCIV

Fay toy craindre a ta femme a point
Mais gard bien ne la batre point,
Car la bonne en aroit despis
Et la mauvaise en vauldroit pis.

XCV

Tes filz fay a l'escole aprendre,
Bat les se tu les vois mesprendre,
Tien les subgiez et en cremour
Et leur celes ta grant amour.

XCVI

Tien tes filles trop mieulx vestues
Que bien abuvrées ne peues;
Fay les aprendre bel maintien
Ne point oyseuses ne les tien.

XCIX

Ains que tu parles si t'avise
Que veulz dire et en quel devise,
Tu parleras plus sagement
Devant gent et en jugement.

CII

Gardes bien qu'yvrece ne face
Changier ton parler ne ta face
Ne ton sens, car c'est trop grant honte
Quant vin le sens d'omme surmonte.

LXXXVI

Be not a tattler lest your tale
Cause you a deal of bane and bale;
Rather should you—calm, passionless—
Quell your friend's wrath with gentleness.

XCI

Your wife should be clothed in the best
That you can give her, seemly dressed;
Mistress, not serving-wench, is she:
Served by the servants let her be.

XCIV

Let your wife fear you as she should,
But beat her not; for if you would,
A good one will your conduct curse,
A bad one will grow even worse.

XCV

Be certain that your sons, at school,
Learn well; but if they play the fool,
Threaten and beat them, and conceal
The great love that, indeed, you feel.

XCVI

Your daughters keep in proper dress,
Rather with somewhat more than less;
School them in gracious mien lest they
Idly fritter their time away.

XCIX

Think well what you will say before
You speak, and how to say it; for
Better, thus, is the way you do it,
Sounder the judgment you bring to it.

CII

Let drunkenness your speech not alter,
Nor let it cause your sense to falter,
Or change your face: shame it is when
Wine dulls the sense and humbles men.

CIV

Se Dieu t'a envoyé victoire
En quelque cas belle et nottoire,
Les vaincus trop mal n'atourner,
Tu ne scés ou tu puez tourner.

CV

Se tu scés que l'en te diffamme
Sans cause et que tu ayes blasme
Ne t'en courcer; fay toudis bien,
Car droit vaintra, je te di bien.

CXI

Ne te dampnes pas pour acquerre
A tes enfans avoir et terre;
Fay les aprendre et entroduire
A science ou a mestier duire.

CXII

Bon exemple et bonne doctrine
Oz voulentiers et t'y dottrine,
Car pour neant son oreille euvre
Homs a ouïr sans mettre a œuvre.

CXIII

Ne laisses pas a Dieu servir
Pour ou monde trop t'asservir,
Car biens mondains vont a defin
Et l'ame durera sans fin.

———————

Com turtre suis sanz per toute seulete
Et com brebis sanz pastour esgarée;
Car par la mort fus jadis separée
De mon doulz per, qu'a toute heure regrette.

Il a sept ans que le perdi, lassette,
Mieulx me vaulsist estre lors enterrée!
Com turtre suis sanz per toute seulete.

CIV

If God grants you a victory
Glorious and grand, you must not be
Quick to demean your foe; for who
Can say what fate yet holds for you?

CV

Should one speak ill of you without
Good reason, and your honor flout,
Vent not your wrath; for I contend
Right always conquers in the end.

CXI

Sacrifice not your life and health
To leave your children land and wealth;
More it behooves that they be made
To learn a science or a trade.

CXII

Be sure to listen and pay ample
Heed to good teaching and example:
Useless the lessons that they teach
If one not practice what they preach.

CXIII

Do God's work and forsake it not
For human pleasures misbegot;
Though worldly wealth is constant never,
Endless, the soul will last forever.

———————

Like turtledove without her mate am I,
And like a lamb that, shepherdless, strays here
And there; for death has stolen my compeer,
Whom I lament with endless sob and sigh.

Full seven years without him have gone by;
Rather had I been buried too, I fear!
Like turtledove without her mate am I.

Car depuis lors en dueil et en souffrete
Et en meschief trés grief suis demourée,
Ne n'ay espoir, tant com j'aré durée,
D'avoir soulas qui en joye me mette;
Com turtre suis sans per toute seulete.

———————

Je ne sçay comment je dure;
Car mon dolent cuer font d'yre,
Et plaindre n'oze, ne dire
Ma doulereuse aventure,

Ma dolente vie obscure,
Riens, fors la mort, ne desire;
Je ne scay comment je dure.

Et me fault par couverture
Chanter quant mon cuer souspire,
Et faire semblant de rire;
Mais Dieux scet ce que j'endure;
Je ne sçay comment je dure.

———————

Il me semble qu'il a cent ans
Que mon ami de moy parti!

Il ara quinze jours par temps,
Il me semble qu'il a cent ans!

Ainsi m'a anuié le temps,
Car depuis lors qu'il departi
Il me semble qu'il a cent ans!

For since that moment I in mourning lie,
And life is naught for me but dolor drear;
Nor can I hope whilst on this earthly sphere
Solace or joy to know before I die:
Like turtledove without her mate am I.

"Rondeaux," I

———————

How I live still, I know not:
Sorrowful I grieve, heartsore;
Yet lament I dare not, nor
Tell my sad tale misbegot.

Dark my days and grim my lot:
Death I want and nothing more;
How I live still, I know not.

Feign I must, laugh, sing; ignore
My heart's sighs, no matter what,
Nor reveal my pain one jot:
God knows well my woes galore;
How I live still, I know not.

"Rondeaux," VII

———————

It seems to me a century
Since I am of my love bereft!

Though it will but a fortnight be
It seems to me a century!

So much has time beleaguered me,
That, since the moment when he left,
It seems to me a century!

"Rondeaux," XXIX

Il a au jour d'ui un mois
Que mon ami s'en ala.

Mon cuer remaint morne et cois,
Il a au jour d'ui un mois.

"A Dieu, me dit, je m'en vois";
Ne puis a moy ne parla,
Il a au jour d'ui un mois.

Le plus bel qui soit en France,
Le meilleur et le plus doulx,
Helas! que ne venez vous?

M'amour, ma loial fiance,
Mon dieu terrien sur tous,
Le plus bel qui soit en France.

S'il est en vostre poissance
Pour quoy n'approchiez de nous?
Si verré lors sanz doubtance
Le plus bel qui soit en France.

Amis, venez encore nuit,
Je vous ay aultre fois dit l'eure.

Pour en joye estre a no deduit,
Amis, venez encore nuit.

Car ce qui nous empesche et nuit
N'y est pas, pour ce, sanz demeure,
Amis, venez encore nuit.

One month is it, to the day,
Since my love went out the door.

Grieves my heart in sad dismay:
One month is it, to the day.

Said he: "Now I go my way,"
And to me he spoke no more;
One month is it, to the day.

"Rondeaux," xxx

Far the fairest lad in France,
Much the finest and most dear,
Why, alas, draw you not near?

Loyalest of my gallants,
Earthly god without a peer,
Far the fairest lad in France.

If you have the power, perchance,
Why have you not ventured here?
Let me see, with eager glance,
Far the fairest lad in France.

"Rondeaux," xxxiii

My love, come yet again this night,
At that same hour I said before.

To frolic to our hearts' delight,
My love, come yet again this night.

For aught that interrupt us might
Will be here not; so bide no more:
My love, come yet again this night.

"Rondeaux," li

Christine de Pizan 87

Il me tarde que lundi viengne
Car mon ami doy veoir lors.

A fin qu'entre mes bras le tiengne
Il me tarde que lundi viengne.

Si lui pri qu'il lui en souviengne;
Car pour veoir son gentil corps
Il me tarde que lundi viengne.

Cest anelet que j'ay ou doy
Mon doulz ami le m'a donné.

Souvent nous assemble toudoy
Cest anelet que j'ay ou doy.

Je l'aime bien, faire le doy;
Car pour ma joye est ordené
Cest anelet que j'ay ou doy.

Vous n'y pouez, la place est prise,
Sire, vous perdez vostre peine:
De moy prier c'est chose vaine,
Car un bel et bon m'a acquise.

Et c'est droit qu'un seul me souffise,
Plus n'en vueil, folz est qui s'en peine;
Vous n'y pouez, la place est prise.

Toute m'amour ay en lui mise
Et l'ameray d'amour certaine,
Mais ne m'en tenez a villaine;
Car je vous di qu'en nulle guise
Vous n'y pouez, la place est prise.

Await I Monday eagerly,
For that day shall I see my swain.

That I may clutch him close to me,
Await I Monday eagerly.

I pray that he may mindful be;
To see his comely form again,
Await I Monday eagerly.

"Rondeaux," LII

This ring I on my finger wear,
My dearest love bestowed on me.

Ever it binds us, constant pair,
This ring I on my finger wear.

Love it I must; for I declare
A source of my delight to be
This ring I on my finger wear.

"Rondeaux," LIII

Naught can you do, the fort is won;
Sire, you lay siege to me in vain.
A goodly and a gentle swain
Has won the day; the fray is done.

Nor wish I now still more, nay, none:
Folly it is to yearn for twain;
Naught can you do, the fort is won.

Love him I shall, all others shun,
With perfect love; so would I fain
Insist, and tell you yet again—
Nor think me but a simpleton—
Naught can you do, the fort is won.

"Rondeaux," LX

Amoureux œil,
Plaisant archier.

De toy me dueil,
Amoureux œil.

Car ton accueil
Me vens trop chier,
Amoureux œil.

Ma dame
Secours.

Par m'ame,
Ma dame.

J'enflame
D'amours,
Ma dame.

———————

Amorous eye,
Bowman of love.

You glance, I die,
Amorous eye;

Your grace: too high
The price thereof,
Amorous eye.

"Rondeaux," LXVI

———————

Lady fair
Fire! Fire!

I declare
Lady fair:

I flame, flare
With desire,
Lady fair.

"Rondeaux," LXVII

Marie de Clèves, comtesse d'Orléans (1426–1487)

If Marie de Clèves is represented here by only two short poems, it is not because I would not have happily translated and included others. The two are pleasant examples of the *rondeau* form and suggest a worthy if not spectacular talent. The problem is that, however many more she may have written over her lifetime, these appear to be the only two extant.[1]

Born in 1426, the daughter of Adolf, duc de Clèves, and Marie de Bourgogne, Marie was married at the tender age of fourteen to Charles, duc d'Orléans—for purely political reasons—upon the latter's return after twenty-five years of captivity in England after the battle of Agincourt. Their union produced the future Louis XII, king of France. Following Charles's repatriation, Marie apparently took an active part in the poetic and artistic life of his ducal court, to which he devoted his later years. As one of the most important poets of his age—perhaps exaggeratedly credited with being "the father of the French lyric"—Charles seems to have encouraged his young wife's poetic endeavors. Marie remarried in 1480, some fifteen years after his death, and spent the last seven years of her life in pious works.[2]

NOTES

1. Edith Joyce Benkov's brief encyclopedia article on Marie, stating that "(t)he bulk of her works are rondeaus and ballads centering on love," causes me to wonder to what "bulk" its author is referring. See *Encyclopedia of Continental Women Writers*, p. 258.

2. See also Pierre Champion, *Histoire poétique du XVe siècle*, passim.

RONDEL

En la forest de longue attente
Entrée suis en une sente
Dont oster je ne puis mon cueur,
Pourquoy je viz en grant honneur
Par fortune qui me tourmente.

Souvent Espoir chascun contente
Excepté moy, poure dolente!
Qui nuit et jour suis en doleur.
En la forest de longue attente
Entrée suis en une sente
Dont oster je ne puis mon cueur.

Ay-je donc tort se me garmente
Plus que mille qui soit vivente?
Par Dieu! nennil veu mon maleur,
Car ainsi m'aist mon Créateur
Qu'il n'est paine que je ne sente
En la forest de longue attente.

RONDEAU

* Here, in the Wood of Long Awaiting,
I chose a path—my heart not sating,
Leaving it not, I must confess;
Wherefore I dwell in languorousness,
Mid Fortune's torments unabating.

Hope comforts all, their pain placating,
But mine, 'tis ever aggravating:
I, who live wretched, comfortless!
Here, in the Wood of Long Awaiting,
I chose a path—my heart not sating,
Leaving it not, I must confess.

Thus, more than woman born, berating
Fate for the woe life keeps creating,
Do I err? Nay! Oh, fell distress!
I pray that the Almighty bless
My days, all bane alleviating,
Here, in the Wood of Long Awaiting.

* This *rondeau*, with its allegorical conceit, attracted a number of poets of the period, being apparently the subject of one of the poetic "competitions" so frequent in the late Middle Ages, and so dear to Charles d'Orléans in particular. For the names of the poets in question, Charles d'Orléans and Madame d'Orléans (Marie de Clèves) among them, and a number of examples, see Gaston Raynaud, *Rondeaux et autres poésies du XVe siècle*, pp. 30n2, 30–34, 42–43, 79. The version here, found in several manuscripts, offers a few divergent readings. I reproduce the text from the appendix of *Les poésies du duc Charles d'Orléans*, ed. Aimé Champollion-Figeac, p. 109, with two exceptions: the readings, from other manuscripts, of *langueur* (line 4) and *nulle* (line 13) seem logically preferable to *honneur* and *mille,* and I have seen fit to use them.

L'abit le moine ne fait pas.
Car quelque chière que je face
Mon mal seul tous les autres pace
De ceulx que tant plaignent leur cas.
Souvent en dansant fais maint pas
Que mon cueur près en dueil trespace:
L'abit le moine ne fait pas.

Las! mes yeulx gectent sans compas
Des larmes tant parmy ma face
Dont plusieurs foiz je change place
Alant apart pour crier las!
L'abit le moine ne fait pas.

† Alas, clothes do the man not make.
Far worse my woe than that of those
Who evermore lament their woes,
Whatever mien I choose to take.
Ofttimes I dance, though sore my ache
As, sick to death, my heart's pain grows:
Alas, clothes do the man not make.

Endless, my tears refuse to slake
My grief, and from my eyes there flows
‡ Such dole that, lest it I disclose,
I hide, to let my poor heart break!
Alas, clothes do the man not make.

* Like the previous poem, this *rondeau* also owes its existence to one of Charles d'Orléans's poetic contests. See Albert Pauphilet, *Poètes et romanciers du Moyen Age*, p. 1113. I reproduce the version in *Les poésies du duc Charles d'Orléans*, ed. Aimé Champollion-Figeac.

† Perhaps the proverbial French original, "L'abit le moine ne fait pas" ("Clothes do not make the *monk*"), bespeaks a greater concern with things clerical than its less specific English equivalent, which I use in my version.

‡ My use of the word "dole," with its double meaning of "grief" and "quantity," has created an inadvertent wordplay that the reader should not expect to find in the original.

Marguerite de Navarre (1492–1549)

Although scholarship in recent decades has broadened its opinion of Margueri[e]
de Navarre's place in letters, many students of French literature, and of Renai[s]
sance literature in particular, long appreciated only her role in the developme[nt]
of the novella. The one work that her name was sure to evoke was the *Hept[a]
méron* (1559), her unfinished collection of prose tales modeled on Boccacci[o's]
Decameron and utilizing the same Chaucerian framing fiction: a company [of]
travelers forced by circumstances to pass their time telling daily stories that m[ix]
lusty medieval-inspired narrative with heady philosophical speculation. Thou[gh]
scholars would always pay tribute to her impressive Renaissance erudition, h[er]
religious fervor and evangelical leanings, her sisterly devotion to François I, an[d]
her role as protectress to intellectuals of the period, most gave short shrift—[if]
any shrift at all—to her lyric poetry. And this although lyrics figure prominent[ly]
in her earliest works, from the 1520s, and no less so among her last. Happil[y]
modern scholarship recognizes her importance in areas beyond the prose na[r]
rative.

This noblewoman's gender was no bar to her becoming an icon of her ag[e.]
Daughter of Charles de Valois, comte d'Angoulême, and Louise de Savoie—a[n]
enlightened lady who, widowed in 1498, raised both her and her younger brothe[r,]
later to become François I, in the company of scholars, thinkers, and writers [of]
the day—Marguerite was tutored in languages ancient and modern, philosoph[y,]
theology, and the arts. At seventeen, she was given in a marriage destined to b[e]
childless to the duc d'Alençon, and continued to indulge her intellectual tast[es]
despite the displeasure of her rather priggish spouse. The latter died in 1525 [of]
wounds suffered at the battle of Pavia, during the Italian wars waged against th[e]
emperor Charles V by François, who had ascended the throne ten years earlie[r.]
It was, in fact, Marguerite's diplomatic intercession that won the king's relea[se]
from captivity in Madrid after his defeat.

In 1527, Marguerite married Henri d'Albret, king of Navarre—or what the[re]
was left of it still free of Castilian domination. Her daughter, the pro-Calvini[st]
Jeanne d'Albret, future mother of Henri IV, influenced by Marguerite's mu[l]
tiple talents, would become a poet in her own right (see pp. 158–69 below). A[s]
queen of Navarre, Marguerite was taken with the likes of Rabelais, Calvin, M[a]
rot, and many prominent and controversial figures, both in and out of offici[al]
favor, and she not unexpectedly transformed her court into a center of artist[ic]
and humanistic activity. Though never breaking with the Church, she woul[d,]
on occasion, be at odds with it, especially when her first lengthy work, *Le miro[ir]
de l'âme pécheresse* (1531), was banned by Sorbonne officialdom.[1] Her sympath[y]

for the evangelists persisted, but she was unable to placate her brother, who would soon have enough of rioting and placard posting in the name of religious reform. Devastated by his death in 1547, Marguerite was to survive him for only two more years, spending them in virtual solitude and religious contemplation and composing devotional dramas and lyrics, as well as her longest poem, the mystical *Les prisons*, a kind of spiritual odyssey imbued with Platonic and Christian teachings.[2]

Marguerite's poems translated here—early *rondeaux* and *épistres*, later *chansons*, and her final *dixains* and *épigrammes*—are taken respectively from *Poésies du roi François Ier, de Louise de Savoie, duchesse d'Angoulême, de Marguerite, reine de Navarre* [etc.], ed. Aimé-Louis Champollion-Figeac; her *Chansons spirituelles*, ed. Georges Dottin; and *Les dernières poésies de Marguerite de Navarre*, ed. Abel Lefranc.

NOTES

1. For the most recent translation of *Le miroir*, by Melanie E. Gregg, see *Writings by Pre-Revolutionary French Women*, ed. Anne R. Larsen and Colette H. Winn, 35–61.

2. *Les prisons* exists in two modern translations: one by Hilda Dale and another, bilingual, by Claire Lynch Wade. For a definitive study of Marguerite's life and works, see Patricia F. Cholakian and Rouben C. Cholakian, *Marguerite de Navarre: Mother of the Renaissance*. For more concise essays, see Colette H. Winn's entry in *French Women Writers*, ed. Eva Martin Sartori and Dorothy Wynne Zimmerman, pp. 313–21; and, for specific studies of her poetry, see Paula Sommers, *Celestial Ladders: Readings in Marguerite de Navarre's Poetry of Spiritual Ascent*; Robert D. Cottrell, *The Grammar of Silence: A Reading of Marguerite de Navarre's Poetry*; and Gary Ferguson, *Mirroring Belief: Marguerite de Navarre's Devotional Poetry*. Of the many other studies and journal articles devoted to her work, especially in recent years, few deal specifically with her verse.

RONDEAU

Sur: Domine! salvum fac regem, et exaudi nos in die qua invocaverimus te.

Saulvez le Roy, ô Seigneur gratieux!
Et exaulcez, ce jour, en voz sainctz cyeux,
Nous qui pour luy invocquons vostre grace.
Las! retournez vostre benigne face
Pour essuyer les larmes de noz yeux.

Vous estes seul, par sur tous aultres dieux,
Puissant, piteux, misericordieux:
Monstrez-le-nous bientost, en peu d'espace:
            Saulvez le Roy!

Nous congnoissons que noz maulz vitieux
Meritent bien les tourmens ennuyeux
Que maintenant justice nous pourchasse;
Vostre bonté nostre malice passe:
En ceste foy vous prions pour le myeulx:
            Saulvez le Roy!

RONDEAU

A toy mon Dieu donne mon ame et corps,
Te suppliant de n'estre point records
Des grans péchez que ay pensez, dictz et faictz;
Qui me feront tresbucher soubz le faix,
S'il ne te plaist m'estre misericords.

RONDEAU

*   *On: Domine! salvum fac regem, et exaudi nos in die qua invocaverimus te.*

God, save the king! O Lord, bestow your grace!
Pray hear the pleas that, in this time and place,
We raise unto your heavenly majesty.
Alas! Let shine your face upon us; see
The tears we shed, and cleanse their every trace.

Your powers alone all other gods' efface;
Compassionate and loving, your embrace:
Pray prove it to us, here, now! Let it be!
     God, save the king!

We know that all the vices that debase
Our lives deserve the woes that fall apace
Upon us, at this moment, rightfully.
Greater your good than our iniquity;
In this faith pray we you his ills erase:
     God, save the king!

RONDEAU

In you I place my body and my soul,
My God! Pray be not mindful of the toll
My sins exact, in deed, and word, and thought!
Stagger shall I beneath their weight, distraught,
If you grant not your grace to ease my dole.

* Marguerite's Latin source ("O God! Keep the king safe, and heed us on the day when we shall have prayed to you") will be strikingly familiar to generations of Harvard graduates who have heard it sung since the 1940s in a setting by Gounod as the "Commencement Hymn," with the traditional *regem* (king), appropriately changed to *praesidem nostrum* (our president). Gounod's version of the text, dating back to one used in medieval German coronations—and set by other composers as well, among them Buxtehude—was apparently written as an encomium to Napoleon III, with the phrase altered to *Imperatorem nostrum* (our emperor). See Mason Hammond, "Notes on the Words and Music Used in Harvard's Commencement Ceremonies," *Harvard Library Bulletin* 26, 3 (July 1978): 306–13.

L'ennemy faulx, qui seme tous discords,
Quert me seduire et à cris et à cors,
Pour m'accuser enfin de mes forfaictz:
A toy mon Dieu donne mon ame et corps!

Mais si par luy vices laidz et très ors
Ont de vertu tous mes esperitz mis hors
En les rendant poluz et imparfaictz,
Las! reçoy-moy amendant mes mesfaictz
Et que raison reface mes accords
      A toy.

———————

RONDEAU

Si Dieu le veult, il a toute puissance,
Il voit noz cueurs; il sçait ce que l'on pense.
Riens ne nous fault, si non fermement croyre
Qu'il est tout bon digne d'amour et gloire,
Et en luy seul avoir nostre espérance.

Prenons tous biens de sa main et clémence,
Tous maulx aussi en doulce pacience;
Ainsi aurons de nous mesme victoire
      Si Dieu le veult?

Puysqu'il peult tout ce qu'il veult, sans doubtance,
C'est grand folye de faire résistence
A son vouloir; mais ayons en mémoire
Qu'il veult tout bien, et desirons de boire
Au calice de sa juste ordonnance,
      Si Dieu le veult!

———————

RONDEAU

A tous humains la doulce humanité
De Dieu saulveur et sa benignité
Se sont faict veoir, quand sur nostre desserte,
Par pure grace, a reparé la perte
Que feist Adam à sa postérité.

The Fiend plays out his false, deceitful role!
He would seduce me to his foul control
And loud proclaim the ills my soul has wrought:
In you I place my body and my soul!

But if, with vices vile and black as coal,
He draws my mind from virtue's noble goal,
Corrupts, alas! defiles my every thought,
Pray welcome me and turn my sins to naught:
My God, let reason make my spirit whole
          In you.

RONDEAU

If God so wills, ever His will be done;
He knows our hearts, and sees our thoughts, each one.
Naught need we do but to believe that He
Deserves our love and glorious eulogy;
To trust in Him, but in no other, none.

Whatever good or ill He casts upon
Our days, let us in patience carry on;
Thus shall we, for our pains, know victory,
          If God so wills!

Since He does what He will—doubt not thereon!—
Folly it is His firm intent to shun;
Only for good He works: therefore must we
Drink down His righteous chalice to the lee;
Such be our goal forever and anon,
          If God so wills!

RONDEAU

For humankind, to ease its dire distress,
God, gentle savior, eager to profess
His word, and to bestow His purest grace,
Did, thus, redeem the loss that Adam's race
Would suffer for his sinful, fell excess.

*As throughout medieval French literature, *l'ennemy* here would appear to be an epithet referring specifically to the Devil.

Car Jesus-Christ, Dieu homme en unité,
Nostre salut justice et équité
Du ciel promect la seure voye ouverte
    A tous humains.

En attendant ce bien non mérité,
Prions souvant que sa grand charité
Qu'en sa naissance et mort a recouverte,
Soit seure addresse et guide bien experte,
Pour addresser sa paix et vérité
    A tous humains.

RONDEAU

Avant manger je gemys et souspire,
Craignant, mon Dieu, que mon ame s'empire,
Pour indigne vostre corps recevoir.
Je sçay n'avoir pas bien faict mon devoir:
Dont suis pour vray de tous mauvais le pire.

De tout mal faict, mal penser et mesdire;
De mal vouloir de toute envie et d'ire,
Debvons sur tous noz cueurs vuides avoir,
    Avant manger.

Graces vous rendz, mon Dieu, mon père et Sire,
De telle mort et si cruel martire,
Dont vous a pleu de paier le debvoir;
Congnoissance donnez moy et sçavoir
De mes péchez tous confesser et dire
    Avant manger.

RONDEAU

Ce n'est qu'ung cueur, et ne sera jamais
De vous et moy, ainsi je le promectz,
Quelque chose que vous puisse advenir.
Le sang ne peult au contraire venir
Ny la raison: aussi je m'y soubzmectz.

Jesus, the Christ, born man but God no less,
Promising soul's salvation and redress,
Lays out the path to heaven's holy space
        For humankind.

This boon, though ill deserved, would we possess:
Let us, then, pray Our Lord will acquiesce—
Through birth, death, and rebirth—to guide our pace
To peace and truth, and falseness fain efface,
Unerringly, with loving tenderness
        For humankind.

RONDEAU

Ere I partake of you, O God adored,
I sigh and moan, for fear my soul abhorred
Be not fit to receive your flesh. I know
I have not lived the life I ought; and so,
Of all your sinners, am the most deplored.

My heart must needs be free of all discord,
All base desire, all sinful thoughts untoward:
All ire and contumely must I forego,
        Ere I partake.

I praise you, God, my father and my Lord,
Whose death and martyrdom were the reward
That unto me it pleased you to bestow;
Show me my wicked ways, that, here below,
By my confession, I might stand restored,
        Ere I partake.

RONDEAU

Ours is one heart, and never shall it be
But mine or yours; this do my lips decree,
Whatever be your fortune, bright or blear.
Neither shall blood nor reason interfere:
Such is the power that you hold over me.

Ma voulonté à la vostre remectz;
Parolle et faictz entre voz mains je mectz;
Puisque je veulx vostre ainsi devenir,
   Ce n'est qu'ung cueur!

Ainsi du tout à vous je me commectz,
Qui vostre suis et seray desormais
Mieulx qu'oncques; mais plaise vous souvenir
De nostre accord, pour nous y maintenir
A tousjoursmais: puisqu'en vous me desmectz,
   Ce n'est qu'ung cueur!

———————

ÉPISTRE

Le groz ventre trop pesant et massif
Ne veult souffrir, au vray bon cueur naïf,
Vous obeyr, complaire et satisfaire,
Ce que surtout il desire de faire:
Car s'il cuide prandre la plume en main,
Ung mal de cueur le remect à demain,
Et par doulleur souvent et passion
Il oublye sa bonne invention,
De foiblesse luy donne tel tourment,
Qu'il empesche sens et entendement;
Mais, toutesfois, ne me rend insansible
D'avoir regret à vous dire impossible:
Qui s'augmente tant plus avant je voys,
N'ayant le bien et l'honneur que j'avoys,
Et qui pis est, ne vous faisant service
Fors prier Dieu, voylà tout mon office.

Je ne vous puis au long mander ma vie,
De vous donner tel ennuy n'ay envye;
Mais s'il vous plaist sçavoir quelle je suis,
Comparaison mieulx bailler ne vous puis

I pledge my will to you; for, devotee
In word and deed, yours am I utterly.
To be but yours: this, my one wish sincere;
  Ours is one heart.

Thus I commit myself to you; and we
Shall be as one; complete in harmony,
More than before: more yet than yesteryear.
Forget not what we vow; that now, and here,
And for eternity, we shall agree:
  Ours is one heart.

EPISTLE

* Dear heart, my heavy belly will not let
Me satisfy your wish—to my regret—
Though fain would I comply with what you ask;
But when I take my quill in hand, the task
Begs for delay. Rebuke me not, for then,
Often I find that I must puke: my pen—
So great my torment, and so weak my hand—
Cannot obey my eager mind's command.
But think not that I am not much distressed
That my intent remains thus unexpressed.
Ever grows my regret thereat, most sad
That now the honor and the wealth I had
Are mine no more; and, worst of all, that I
Can nothing do to serve, to satisfy
Your needs, for now my one and only chore
Is to pray God, my Lord, and nothing more.

I would not tell you—long, laboriously—
All that my life has been, for such would be
A tiresome tale; but if it pleases you
To know my fate, naught better might I do

*In *Poésies du roi François Ier* [etc.], Champollion-Figeac suggests that this *épistre*, apparently destined for the king, her brother, dates from the period of her first pregnancy, namely, the year 1527 (ibid., p. 76n).

Que du rochier de Cerès, dont racompte
Eurialo, qui d'asseurer n'a honte
Que par douleur la pierre fut contraincte
A recevoir de leurs larmes l'empraincte.

Ce dur chaillou, monsieur, je vous envoye,
Que j'ay trouvé en ce desert sans voye,
Il suppléra à ma pouvre escripture,
Vous demonstrant quelle est ma pourtraicture.
Par mes larmes sentirez la douleur,
Qui procedant de la triste couleur,
Soustenue par foy et esperance
De recouvrer ce que m'oste l'absence,
Et qui jamais de vostre bonne grace
Jà ne perdra, pour temps qui soit, sa place
Celle qui vit en desir et atente
Vous veoir contant et Madame contante,
Quy est le tout au vray de mon atante.

———————

ÉPISTRE

Si Dieu m'a Christ pour chef donné,
Fault-il que je serve aultre maistre?
S'il m'a le pain vif ordonné,
Fault-il du pain de mort repaistre?
S'il me veult saulver par sa dextre,
Fault-il en mon bras me fier?
S'il est mon salut et mon estre,
Point n'en fault d'aultre ediffier.
S'il est mon seul et seur espoir,
Fault-il avoir aultre esperance?

Than to invoke the rock of Ceres, sung
Long years ago in Euryalus's tongue,
Who, with no shame, assures us that its stone
Bore deep the mark of sorrow's tears long sown.

Therefore, monsieur, this pebble do I send
To take the place of my poor thoughts unpenned,
That I found in this barren, empty waste,
With no escape, that it might paint, dour-faced
And pale, my portrait; let your fingers feel
The woeful torment that my tears reveal;
For naught but faith and hope sustain me now:
The hope that what is gone I shall, somehow,
Regain; and that I nevermore need lose
My place within your gracious heart; I, whose
One wish is that you and Madame might be
Forever blessed with life's felicity.

---

† **EPISTLE**

If God gave me the Christ as lord,
Must I another wait upon?
If bread of life is my reward,
Must I the bread of death feed on?
If my salvation comes anon
From His hand, must I trust my own?
If His is my support, whereon
I lean, so must he be, alone.
If He is my one hope, and sure,
Must I hope on another too?

* Marguerite's reference would seem to be to the young Trojan hero Euryalus, who, with his bosom-companion Nisus, is mentioned in the *Aeneid* (9.179ff.). Though his death, as the result of his rash bravoura, does, indeed, cause many a tear to fall—shed, in fact, by his doting mother—I find no mention in Virgil to Ceres in his exploit, let alone to a tear-moistened rock associated with that goddess.

† This *épistre* occurs in the present form in *Poésies du roi François Ier* [etc.], ed. Champollion-Figeac. A slightly different version, separated into octets and based on another manuscript, is included as no. 33 in Marguerite's *Chansons spirituelles*, ed. Georges Dottin.

S'il est ma force et mon pouvoir
Fault-il prendre ailleurs asseurance?
Et s'il est ma perseverence,
Fault-il louer ma fermetté?
Et pour une belle apparence,
Fault-il laisser la seureté?
Si ma vye est en Jesus-Christ,
Fault-il la croire en ceste cendre?
S'il m'a donné son sainct escript,
Fault-il aultre doctrine prendre?
Si tel maistre me daigne apprendre,
Fault-il a aultre escolle aller?
S'il me faict son vouloir entendre,
Fault-il par crainte le céler?
Si Dieu me nomme son enffant,
Fault-il craindre à l'appeller pere?
Si le monde le me deffend,
Fault-il qu'à son mal j'obtempere?
Si son esprit en moy opère,
Faut-il mon couraige estimer?
Non, mais Dieu, qui partout impère,
Fault en tout veoir, craindre et aimer!

———————

Si quelque injure l'on vous dit,
Endurez le joyeusement;
Et si chacun de vous mesdit,
N'y mettez vostre pensement.
    Ce n'est chose nouvelle
D'ouyr ainsi parler souvent:
Autant en emporte le vent.

Si quelcun parle de la Foy
En la mettant quasi à riens
Au prix des œuvres de la Loy,
Les estimant les plus grans biens,
    Sa doctrine est nouvelle;
Laissez le là, passez avant:
Autant en emporte le vent.

If He is all my strength secure,
Must I seek greater and more true?
And if naught but His will I do,
Must my persistence lauded be?
Would I the falsely fair pursue,
Must I forsake His certainty?
If Christ is all my sense, my wit,
My life, must I prize mortal dust?
If He bestowed the Holy Writ,
Must I some other doctrine trust?
If He deigns teach, wherefore needs must
I seek a better school than His?
If He decrees His will august,
Must I hide what that message is?
If God calls me His child, must I
Fear to accept His fatherhood?
If those of worldly bent deny
Me this, must I comply? And should
He work in me all that is good,
Must I boast as the source thereof?
No! God does all one can and could:
Him alone must we fear and love!

———————

If men offend you in some wise,
Bear the affront light-heartedly;
And, if with calumny and lies,
Let not our thoughts unceasing be.
        Much empty blathering
Prevails; and so, say what they may:
Gone with the wind are such as they.

If they would, rather, Faith discuss,
Claiming it worthless, far below
The ancient Law, insisting, thus,
You prize the latter, best forgo
        Such novel worshiping!
Leave them behind to have their say:
Gone with the wind are such as they.

Et si pour vostre Foy gaster,
Vous vient louer de vos beaux faitz,
En vous disant (pour vous flatter)
Qu'il vous tient du reng des parfaitz,
　　Fuyez parole telle,
Qui ameine orgueil décevant:
Autant en emporte le vent.

Si le monde vous vient tenter
De richesse, honeur et plaisir,
Et le vous vient tous presenter,
N'y mettez ni cœur ni désir;
　　Car chose temporelle
Retourne où estoit paravant:
Autant en emporte le vent.

Si l'on vous dit qu'en autre lieu
L'on puisse trouver réconfort
Et vray salut, qu'en un seul Dieu,
C'est pour mettre vostre âme à mort;
　　Monstrez vous lors rebelle,
Et desmentez le plus sçavant:
Autant en emporte le vent.

Le temps passé je souspire,
Et l'advenir je désire;
Le présent me fasche fort,
Le temps plaisant me fait rire,
Et, fâcheux, cause ma mort.

Le temps faict plaindre en vie[i]llesse
Le doux temps de la jeunesse,
Le temps de contentement
Se passe au temps de tristesse:
Le temps n'arreste ung moment.

If some there be who would destroy
Your Faith, praising your qualities
Of perfect beauty, who employ
Compliments and cajoleries,
     Flee from such flattering;
For they would lead your pride astray:
Gone with the wind are such as they.

If, with temptation's words of gold,
Life promises to heap upon
Your head joys, honors, wealth untold,
Set not your heart's desires thereon:
     Since every worldly thing
Returns to its beginnings, yea,
Gone with the wind are such as they.

If some deny that God alone
Can comfort you and make you whole—
The one source of salvation known—
Death would they deal unto your soul;
     Resist their reasoning:
However wise they seem, say "Nay!"
Gone with the wind are such as they.

Chansons spirituelles, 5

---

* Time past I bemoan, once gone,
And the future crave anon.
Present time my heart dismays,
Pleasant time I smile upon;
Noisome time cuts short my days.

Time makes us sweet youth lament
When, grown old, we see it spent;
Time of happiness and peace
Turns to pain and discontent.
Not one moment does time cease.

* The obvious influence of *Ecclesiastes* 3 throughout this poem and analogues in Ovid's *Metamorphoses* (15.175ff.), the *Roman de la rose* (v. 373ff.), and verses included in the 24th tale of Marguerite's own *Heptaméron* are noted in *Chansons spirituelles,* ed. Dottin, pp. 163–64n.

Le bon temps bien tost se passe
Et le mauvais prend sa plasse.
Le temps apporte santé,
Mais le temps après l'efface
Par maladye à planté.

Le temps apporte richesse,
Le temps l'oste en grant destresse.
Le temps donne pluie et vent,
L'esté et la sécheresse;
L'iver monste bien souvent.

Le temps mect l'homme sur terre,
Le temps par la mort l'enterre,
Le temps faict naistre et mourir,
Le temps apporte la guerre,
Le temps faict la paix fleurir.

Le temps faict beauté plaisante,
Le temps la laideur augmente,
Le temps invente les fardz,
Le temps arrache et si plante,
Le temps invente les artz.

Le temps faict croistre les arbres,
Le temps endurcist les marbres;
Puis le temps vient allumer
Et estaindre candellabres,
Le temps faict luire et fumer.

Le temps est très variable
Et du bien ou mal muable,
Le temps n'arreste ung seul pas;
Le temps ung jour est louable,
Le temps après ne l'est pas.

Par-quoy voiant nostre vie
Par le temps ainsi ravie,
Pour [n'] estre des mal contens,
Arreste cueur et envie
A Celluy qui est sans temps.

Good time passes quickly, flees;
Bad time comes, stays, takes its ease.
Time brings wealth, then turns about
And too quickly rubs it out
With its myriad maladies.

Time brings wealth untold, until
Time removes it, treats us ill.
Time gives us the wind, the rain,
Summer and its drought; then will
Winter's chill come round again.

Time puts man on earth, but oh!
Time soon buries him below:
Time lets man be born and die.
Time spreads war, with all its woe;
Time calms, quells it by and by.

Time makes beauty grow in grace,
Time makes worse the ugly face,
Time paints rouge on pale complexion.
Time sows, reaps, sows on apace;
Time invents the arts' confection.

Time makes trees rise up and sprout,
Hardens marble, strong and stout.
Time makes candelabra bright
Cast their glow, then flicker out:
Time makes flame, and smoke, and light.

Time goes on and changes ever
In its endless course, forever
Flowing; fickle, versatile,
Stopping not, but constant never:
Now for good, and now for ill.

Wherefore, since our life we see
Rife with time's woe, ceaselessly,
Lest you know naught but distress,
Place in Him your heart; for He
Knows not time, but timelessness.

Chansons spirituelles, 35

J'ayme une amye entierement parfaicte,
Tant que j'en sens satisfaict mon desir.
Nature l'a, quant à la beaulté, faicte
Pour à tout œil donner parfaict plaisir;
Grace y a faict son chef d'œuvre a loisir,
Et les vertuz y ont mys leur pouvoir,
Tant que l'ouyr, la hanter et la veoir
Sont seurs tesmoings de sa perfection:
Un mal y a, c'est qu'elle peult avoir
En corps parfaict cœur sans affection.

Puisqu'amour est le Dieu qui faict aymer,
Je le requiers, si au commencement
M'a esté doulx, qu'il ne me soit amer,
Quant il me doit donner contentement.
Qui n'a de luy nul bien, n'a nul torment,
Mais qui a eu le mieulx qu'on peult attaindre,
L'ayant perdu, se doit bien de luy plaindre,
Et desirer n'avoir jamais eu bien.
C'est pis que mort, quant regret [il] fault faindre,
Et en riant dire à tous: "Je n'ay rien."

Or, je l'ay veu, mais c'est bien clairement:
Vous le pouvez maintenant confesser
Ce que m'avez nyé si longuement,
Quand du sçavoir vous ay voulu presser.

* I love a lady perfect every wise,
Who satisfies all my heart's tenderness.
Nature endows her such that, to all eyes,
Great pleasure does she give, perfect no less.
Grace fashioned her its most complete success,
And virtues have their powers on her conferred
So much that, be she seen, approached, or heard,
Her being entire is perfect proof thereof.
One flaw: her body—perfect, in a word—
Harbors a heart that nothing knows of love.

Dernières poésies, "Dixains et épigrammes," LVI

I pray the god—him whose dominion is
To make us love—that, since he treated me,
At first, with gentleness, it be not his
Intent to let my joy now bitter be.
Who never knew his boons lives torment-free;
But who once knew the best of love, then, lo!
Lost it, may rightfully lament that woe
And deem that better were loveless to dwell.
Worse than death is it when one cannot show
One's grief, but, smiling, must say: "All is well."

Dernières poésies, "Dixains et épigrammes," LXV

Now, at last, I perceive the truth: ah, yes!
Clearly I see what you so long denied
Each time I plied you, pled that you confess.
Alas! Less did I learn the more I tried.

*As will be seen from a number of examples in this collection, especially in the tradi-
tional courtly themed poetry of earlier ages, it was not unusual for a female poet to adopt
a male voice for her artistic laments.

Je doy doncq bien ma grand amour cesser,
Non pour aymer ailleurs, car je ne puis,
Mais pour mourir, puisqu'il vous fault laisser,
Veu que de vous le seul amy ne suis.

———————

L'un vit du feu, car tousjours est nourry
D'ardente amour, non moins forte qu'honneste;
L'aultre de l'eau, car il s'en va pery
Par les ruisseaulx qui sortent de sa teste.
Le tiers, à qui toute esperance est preste
De son secours, vit seullement de l'air,
Mais le dernier, qui ne faict que parler
D'aller mourir, vit de la terre obscure:
Je vous requiers, ne me vueillés celer
Lequel de tous plus de douleur endure.

———————

Le temps est bref et ma voulenté grande,
Qui ne me veult permettre le penser;
Ma passion me contrainct et commande,
Selon le temps, le parler compencer.
Jusques icy j'ay crainct de m'advancer,
En attendant un temps de long loisir,
Mais il n'est pas en moy de le choysir;
Parquoy du peu fault que mon prouffist face:
En peu de motz vous diray mon desir,
C'est que je n'ay volunté ne plaisir
Que d'estre seur de vostre bonne grace.

Now needs must I my passion's end declare:
Not to love elsewhere—that could never be!
Rather to die, for you I must foreswear,
* Since other swains you fancy more than me.

Dernières poésies, "Dixains et épigrammes," LXVI

One lives on fire: love's burning flames, that fill
The heart, with strong and honest passion fed.
One lives on water, and perish he will
In streams of tears that trickle from the head.
A third there is, on hope full surfeited,
Who lives, alas, on naught but empty air.
And then, the last one of the four is there,
† Who rants on death, feeds on earth's dreariness:
Be not, I pray, unwilling to declare
Which of them suffers the most fell distress.

Dernières poésies, "Dixains et épigrammes," LXIX

My time grows short, and great my soul's desire—
Too great to turn my mind to lengthy thought;
Wherefore my passion must constrain its fire,
Fashion my speech to time's brief measure wrought.
Till now I kept my silence, thinking naught
Could ever spend the time that lay in store.
Now mine is not to choose, nor time ignore,
But, rather, make the most of its brief space.
This is my wish, in few words: nothing more
I crave today, no pleasure yearn I for,
Save to be sure of your abiding grace.

Dernières poésies, "Dixains et épigrammes," LXXIV

* See p. 117n.
† It will be obvious that Marguerite is playing here, with a rather ingenious twist, on the classical theory of the four elements: earth, air, fire, and water.

Pernette du Guillet (1520?–1545)

Most of what is known of the life of this poet is presented in the first edition of her all-too-brief *œuvre*, cut short as it was by an early death.[1] Two epitaphs appended to that single collection, though offering a few additional details, must be taken with a grain of salt, given the customary adulatory nature of such tributes, colored as they are by recent demise. This is especially true of the epitaph by the eminent Renaissance poet Maurice Scève (ca. 1501–ca. 1560), who had something of a personal axe to grind. As has been virtually proven for the past hundred years, Pernette was the inspiration for his celebrated Petrarchan-style cycle *Délie* (1544). Hermetic as are most of Scève's poems, his admiration and affection for Pernette are clear.[2] No less, conversely—and perhaps even more so—are hers for him, revealed in coy puns and allusions throughout her *Rymes* (1545) (see, e.g., pp. 123–27 below).

A young woman of beauty, musical skill, and—like Christine de Pizan, before her, and Marguerite de Navarre, her contemporary—of considerable linguistic and intellectual talent, Pernette was born in Lyon and became part of that flourishing school of poets, artists, and thinkers that has come to be known as "L'Ecole lyonnaise," and whose outstanding female figure was the poet Louise Labé (see pp. 133–56 below). When Pernette met Scève, its leading light, he was more than twice her age. But neither that nor his apparent ugliness prevented a love that would dominate her brief life and that would find expression in her *Rymes*. Whether it was strictly platonic—and appropriately so, in this center of Neoplatonic debate—one cannot say today. One could not even say with certainty at the time, despite rare rumors to the contrary. There is at least a suggestion in one of her poems that her connubial pleasures with Monsieur du Guillet, whom she had married as a young teenager, left much to be desired, and that her feelings for him were rather slight. (His for her, however, were obviously profound, and such that, on her death, it was he who had her poems assembled into a volume and published.) Then again, the Pernette-Scève "affair" may well have been little more than a literary convention, a forbidden amour in the undying tradition of courtly love, with her husband playing the necessary role o spoilsport.

The past dozen or so years have seen Pernette's stock among scholars rise dramatically.[3] Some might cynically be tempted to attribute this to little more than an increased interest in the feminine muse in general, or to a fascination with gossip surrounding her biography in particular, not to mention the fact o her youth and its promise of an artistic life unfulfilled. I would hope it migh rather be for the very real quality of her inspiration and the artistry of a style, by turns delicate and vigorous, well tuned to its demands.

Reproduced from Victor E. Graham's critical edition of her *Rymes,* the single *chanson* (with its opening-line denial of popular accusations) and the eleven *épigrammes,* deftly handled in their varied lengths and versification, are good examples of Pernette's treatment of the unoriginal subject of love with, however, many an original and attractive touch.

NOTES

1. For bibliographical data, see the introduction to Du Guillet's *Rymes,* ed. Graham, which reprints the texts of the original 1545 edition by Antoine du Moulin; and for a brief but detailed and informative study of her work, its themes, and the feminist (and other) criticism it has produced, see Marian Rothstein's entry in *French Women Writers,* pp. 143–52, as well as the essay by Ann Rosalind Jones in *Women Writers of the Renaissance and Reformation,* pp. 219–31.

2. The thesis was first put forth by Joseph Buche in 1904, in "Pernette du Guillet et la *Délie* de Maurice Scève."

3. In addition to numerous journal articles, see Paul Ardouin's *Pernette du Guillet: L'heureuse renaissante* and id., *Maurice Scève, Pernette du Guillet, Louise Labé: L'amour à Lyon au temps de la Renaissance;* and esp. Verdun L. Saulnier's "Etude sur Pernette du Guillet et ses *Rymes* avec des documents inédits."

Quand vous voyez que l'estincelle
De chaste Amour soubs mon esselle
Vient tous les jours à s'allumer,
Ne me debvez vous bien aymer?
    Quand vous me voyez tousjours celle,
Qui pour vous souffre, et son mal cele,
Me laissant par luy consumer,
Ne me debvez vous bien aymer?
    Quand vous voyez, que pour moins belle
Je ne prens contre vous querelle,
Mais pour mien vous veulx reclamer,
Ne me debvez vous bien aymer?
    Quand pour quelque autre amour nouvelle
Jamais ne vous seray cruelle,
Sans aucune plaincte former,
Ne me debvrez vous bien aymer?
    Quand vous verrez que sans cautelle
Tousjours vous seray esté telle
Que le temps pourra affermer,
Ne me debvrez vous bien aymer?

La nuict estoit pour moy si tresobscure
Que Terre, et Ciel elle m'obscurissoit,
Tant qu'à Midy de discerner figure
N'avois pouvoir, qui fort me marrissoit:
    Mais quand je vis que l'aulbe apparoissoit
En couleurs mille et diverse, et seraine,
Je me trouvay de liesse si pleine
(Voyant desjà la clarté à la ronde)
Que commençay louer à voix haultaine
Celuy qui feit pour moy ce Jour au Monde.

When, every day, the spark of chaste,
* Pure Love betwixt us—arms enlaced—
Flashes anew: when such you see,
Ought you not, then, my lover be?
   When you see how I pine, debased,
By hidden bale and bane laid waste,
Languishing in my misery,
Ought you not, then, my lover be?
   When you see that I have no taste
To carp on one less beauty-graced,
And that I want you all to me,
Ought you not, then, my lover be?
   When I, by some new love embraced,
Never would wish your love replaced,
Lest you lament my cruelty,
Ought you not, then, my lover be?
   When you see time, in fleeting haste,
Prove me to be not many-faced
But true to you eternally,
Ought you not, then, my lover be?

Chansons, II

Dark was my night; so deep, indeed, was it
That Earth and Sky lay hidden, veiled from me:
Noon's vision had I not—nay, not a whit—
Whence great my grief and utter my ennui.
   But when the dawn appeared, and I could see
Its myriad colors cast about, ablaze,
Filled was I with a joy so calm—a-gaze
At its vast-spreading brilliance—that the sight
Moved me at once to sing aloud the praise
† Of him who is my Day, and my World's light.

"Epigrammes," II

* Pernette's text has required a certain amount of interpretation here. In the original,
she speaks of "the spark of chaste Love" flashing *soubs mon esselle,* that is, "under my arm-
pit," suggesting, perhaps, in a not especially poetic manner, the area around the heart.

† There seems little doubt that the inspiration the poet speaks of here and in the epi-
gram following was Maurice Scève; see Graham's edition of Pernette's *Rymes,* p. xivn5.

Jà n'est besoing que plus je me soucie
Si le jour fault, ou que vienne la nuict,
Nuict hyvernale, et sans Lune obscurcie:
Car tout cela certes riens ne me nuit,
Puis que mon Jour par clarté adoulcie
M'esclaire toute, et tant, qu'à la mynuict
En mon esprit me faict appercevoir
Ce que mes yeulx ne sceurent oncques veoir.

Si tu ne veulx l'anneau tant estimer
Que d'un baiser il te soit racheptable,
Tu ne doibs pas, au moins si peu l'aymer,
Qu'il ne te soit, non pour l'or acceptable,
Mais pour la main qui, pour plus rendre estable
Sa foy vers toi, te l'a voulu lyer
D'un Dyamant, où tu peulx desplier
Un cueur taillé en face pardurable,
Pour te monstrer, que ne doibs oublier,
Comme tu fais, la sienne amour durable.

Pour contenter celuy qui me tourmente,
Chercher ne veulx remede à mon tourment:
Car, en mon mal voyant qu'il se contente,
Contente suis de son contentement.

No longer is there any need that I
Mourn for the dying day; nor, come the night,
Moan winter's chill beneath a Moonless sky:
Naught do they harm me; for the tender light
Of him who is my Day shines, by and by,

*   Upon me in the dead of night, so bright
That in my soul, and with a joy untold,
I see what my mere eyes might not behold.

"Epigrammes," VIII

†   If you wish not to prize so much this ring
That it be worth your fond embrace, think it
At least not some mere bauble, worthless thing,
But value it: not for the exquisite
Glitter of gold—indeed, worth not a whit—
But for her hand, where Diamond, glistening,
Bespeaks her faithful heart unwavering;
Each facet bright revealing how unfit
Is it for you to leave her languishing,
Whose love for you is endless, infinite.

"Epigrammes," X

No remedy I seek, in my defense,
For the distress—nay, woe!—he causes me:
Pleasure he takes at my displeasure, whence
Most pleased am I to see how pleased is he.

"Epigrammes," XV

* In following Pernette's rhyme scheme (*ababcc*), I have maintained the same vowel
sound between the first six alternating lines, as does she.

† Graham calls attention to the Petrarchan and Platonic nature of the ring theme, cit-
ing its use by Scève and other poets; see his edition of Pernette's *Rymes*, p. 18n.

Si le servir merite recompense,
Et recompense est la fin du desir,
Tousjours vouldrois servir plus qu'on ne pense,
Pour non venir au bout de mon plaisir.

———

Je ne croy point ce que vous deites:
Que tant de bien me desiriez,
Comme à celle, pour qui vous feites
Ce que pour vous faire debvriez.
    Mais quelle plus estimeriez:
Ou celle qui, d'un cueur tremblant,
N'ose dire ce que vouldriez,
Ou qui le dict d'un faulx semblant?

———

Puis que, de nom et de faict, trop severe
En mon endroict te puis appercevoir,
Ne t'esbahis si point je persevere
A faire tant, par art, et par sçavoir,
Que tu lairras d'aller les autres veoir:
Non que de toy je me voulsisse plaindre,
Comme voulant ta liberté contraindre!
    Mais advis m'est que ton sainct entretien
Ne peult si bien en ces autres empraindre
Tes motz dorez, comme au cueur, qui est tien.

———

Si descharger je veulx ma fantasie
Du mal que j'ay, et qui me presse fort,
On me dira que c'est la jalousie
(Je le sçay bien) qui faict sur moy effort.
Mais qui pourroit estre en propos si fort,

Since serving well one's love deserves a boon,
And since, the boon bestowed, that love grows dim,
Let me serve ill my love, lest, all too soon
Undone, I feel no further lust for him.

"Epigrammes," XXI

Believe you I will not, although
You say you prize me dearly; for
Her you treat as your own, and so,
Say what you will: I set no store.
    Which one would you esteem the more:
One who, a-tremble, tells not what
You wish to hear, too timid; or
One who tells all, yet means it not?

"Epigrammes," XXXI

* Since too severe are you, in name and deed,
Toward me, be not bemused, I pray, if you
Nevertheless no longer feel my need
To do, with art and skill, all I might do
To make you bid all other hearts adieu:
Not that I would reprove you, plaintively,
That you should seek none but my company!
    Rather, I know this heart of mine alone,
More than those others', can imprinted be
With your gold, saintly words: this heart you own.

"Epigrammes," XXXIV

Would I might rid my fancy of the ill
That harries me and, lately, lays me low!
Jealousy is the cause of it: so will
They tell me (though, alas, too well I know!).
Ah, is there one so glib of tongue, and so

---

* As she does frequently, Pernette plays here, in the word *sévère,* on the name of Scève.

Pernette du Guillet 127

Et d'argumentz si vivement pourvueu,
Que ce que j'ay de mes propres yeulx veu
Soit une folle imagination
Il feit accroire à mon sens despourveue?
Il me feroit grand' consolation!

––––––––––

Point ne se fault sur Amour excuser,
Comme croyant qu'il ait forme, et substance
Pour nous pouvoir contraindre et amuser,
Voire forcer à son obeissance:
Mais accuser nostre folle plaisance
Pouvons nous bien, et à la verité,
Par qui un cueur plein de legereté
Se laisse vaincre, ou à gaing, ou à perte,
Esperant plus, que n'aura merité
Son amytié de raison moins experte.

––––––––––

Deux amys, joinctz par estroicte amytié,
Eurent, sans plus, une dissention:
L'un soubstenoit (par raison la moytié)
Que le Thuscan a plus d'affection
L'aultre disoit par resolution
Que le François parle plus proprement.
Pour les vouloir mettre d'appointement,
Je dy: qu'ilz sont tous deux beaux à descrire:
Mais, pour en faire au vray le jugement,
Celuy despeinct ce que cestuy veult dire.

Well-armed of proof as to convince my sense
That this fell woe is but the consequence
Of wild imagination, though behold
I did, with my own eyes, the evidence?
Much would I be by such an one consoled!

"Epigrammes," XXXVI

Cast not the blame for loving upon Love,
As if his were the form and substance whence
Forced are we, blithely, to partake thereof,
Succumbing in our blind obedience;
Rather ought we accuse the diffidence
With which our heart, on pleasure's folly bent,
Yields to Love's power, for good or ill, intent
To hope for more, in its capriciousness—
As wages for our tender efforts spent—
Than friendship, inexpert and reasonless!

"Epigrammes," XLIX

A pair of friends, close as could be, fell out
Over the value of two tongues: the one
(Half of the pair, perforce) had little doubt
That Tuscan was the finest, and that none
Matched it in grace; but, not to be outdone,
The other held for French. When they asked me,
I, for the sake of peace and harmony,
Assured them: "Both are fair, nor one the less."
But if I were to judge more truthfully,
Tuscan makes pale what French can best express.

"Epigrammes," L

* The precise intent of the last line hinges on the meaning of the verb *despeindre*, which, in the Middle Ages and sixteenth Century, had two quite opposite meanings: "to color" and "to discolor, make pale." I opt for the latter, assuming that, although Pernette, like many poets from Lyon at the time, knew (and even wrote in) Italian, she would nevertheless have espoused the linguistic nationalism typical of the Renaissance. In his edition of Pernette's *Rymes*, p. 79n, Graham likens this epigram to a similar work by the poet Jean Lemaire de Belges comparing the merits of French and Italian, also to the advantage of the former.

Pernette du Guillet 129

Toute personne assés Jeune, et moins docte
Qu'il ne fauldroit pour se experimenter,
Par une mode ignorante et sotte
Vouldra tousjours son pareil frequenter:
Mais un cueur hault taschera de hanter
Où il verra sa perfection pleine,
A celle fin, que, pour se contenter,
Tout bien luy soit usure de sa peine.

When one is rather Young and practiced not
In worldly ways, one casts a friendly eye
Upon the misbegotten, simple sot,
And cleaves to him as comrade and ally.
But he of higher, nobler heart will try
Those of more ample knowledge to frequent;
So that his woeful wants may be, thereby,
* Lightened and lessened, to his heart's content.

"Epigrammes," LIII

* On the possible influence here of Plato's dialogue *Lysis* (214a–215c; 216e–216d), translated into French in 1544, see Graham's edition of Pernette's *Rymes*, p. 91.

Pernette du Guillet 131

Louise Labé (1520?–1566)

Very recent scholarship has suggested, to the wide-eyed disbelief of literati, that
the poet admired for centuries as Louise Labé, while no doubt a historic figure,
was a literary fiction, and that her poetry was actually the work of several male
poets—Maurice Scève and others—who, for a variety of reasons, chose to effect
a hoax, or *supercherie,* of a kind not unknown to the kaleidoscopic world of let-
ters. Did they "create" her work out of whole cloth? Did they retouch her own
less-than-worthy efforts? Did they compose some of her pieces and not others?
Will the entire theory eventually be discredited? The truth may never be wholly
known, and the matter will likely cause much future ink to flow in Academe. In-
deed, one has to ask what personal satisfaction perpetrators would derive from
a hoax so well conceived and so convincingly carried out that their talents would
lie unappreciated for centuries, if, in fact, they were ever to come to light at all?
Who can say?[1]

What one can, however, say is that the poetry rightly or wrongly attributed
to Labé—three *élégies,* twenty-four sonnets *à la* Petrarch (the first of which is,
in fact, in Italian), and an amusing prose dialogue between Love and Folly—has
an importance far outweighing its modest quantity. Louise Labé the persona
would, I think, have enjoyed the tongue-in-cheek and rather snide epigraph of
Constance-Marie de Théis that introduces this volume. That importance, ar-
tistically well deserved, was, in her own time, and is, in ours, buttressed by her
supposed role as a feminist model who refused to "go back to her knitting," and,
even more titillatingly, by a free-wheeling life that, though concrete details are
scarce, bred not a little contemporary scandal. (The latter has even given rise to
perhaps ill-founded latter-day suspicions of lesbianism occasioned, no doubt, by
her admiration for the then newly rediscovered Sappho.) Turning the tables on
the courtly tradition, it was she, the purported woman poet, who, in her verse,
yearned for and even lusted after her objectified male, not, as traditionally, vice
versa. It is thought that her "dark gentleman of the sonnets," so to speak, was
the poet Olivier de Magny (1529?–1561?), a friend of the Pléiade poet Joachim du
Bellay and, according to the recent theory, one of the hoaxers. And it is, perhaps,
the vivacity and outspokenness of some of the sonnets allegedly addressed to
him that earned for her the reputation that Calvin acerbically fostered, in a 1560
pamphlet, dubbing her the *plebeia meretrix* (whore of the people), in the minds
and mouths of the good ladies of Lyon.

It was in that bustling intellectual and commercial southern hub of sixteenth-
century France, far enough from Paris to enjoy a quasi-independent life of its

own, that the historic Louise Labé, future poet or not, was born. Various dates are given, but all that can be stated with assurance is that the year fell somewhere between 1516 and 1523.² What is less uncertain is that she spent her entire life there. Daughter of a wealthy rope maker—a *cordier*—she was married to another, much older than herself, and received the sobriquet "La Belle Cordière." As irony would have it, accomplished musician that she was, the nickname was also applicable to the strings—*cordes*—of her lute; and, no less so, I might add, to the proverbial expression "plusieurs cordes à son arc" (many strings to her bow). For her talents, it would seem, whether or not poetry was among them, were many: musical, linguistic, and even physical. Legend—hardly to be believed—has it that she was sufficiently skilled in horse- and swords(wo)manship to disguise herself as a man and even fight against the Spaniards at Perpignan, either for the glory of France, like a latter-day Joan of Arc, or, according to some versions, to seek out her lover.

Perhaps encouraged by the publication of Pernette du Guillet's *Rymes* (see pp. 120–31 above), Labé appears to have solicited and received royal permission to publish her own work in 1555. The collection, whose dedicatory epistle to Clémence de Bourges is often cited as something of a feminist manifesto, included also twenty-four customary works by others in her honor. It would appear that the volume's success was such that it was reprinted three times within a year, and the poet's salon—thanks either to her poetic talents (?) or to her alleged indiscretions, or both—attracted the intelligentsia and artistic lights of Lyon, sadly falling victim only to the politico-religious upheavals that ensued.

The *élégie* and the fifteen sonnets presented here display not only the formal perfection of Labé's—or whoever's—aesthetic, but also the passion that fires and enlivens her verse and that, three centuries later, would cause poet Marceline Desbordes-Valmore (see pp. 568–603 below) to call her "la Nymphe ardente du Rhône" (the Burning Nymph of the Rhône); a poetry typical in its traditional conceits and antitheses in the service of love, both platonic and carnal, but no less strikingly original for all that.³

NOTES

1. For details of the carefully developed hoax theory, see Mireille Huchon, *Louise Labé: Une créature de papier*.

2. See François Rigolot's entry on Labé in *French Women Writers*, p. 262.

3. Not unexpectedly, the Labé corpus has produced a constantly expanding bibliography even prior to the current hoax theory. For the works themselves, one might consult François Rigolot's edition of the *Œuvres complètes* and Edith Farrell and Frederick Farrell Jr.'s edition and translation of the *Complete Works*. Among numerous book-length studies, the reader can scratch the surface with the following cross-section: Albert Champdor, *Louise Labé: Son œuvre et son temps*; *Louise Labé: Les voix du lyrisme*, ed. Guy Demerson;

Keith Cameron, *Louise Labé: Renaissance Poet and Feminist;* Deborah Lesko Baker, *The Subject of Desire: Petrarchan Poetics and the Female Voice in Louise Labé,* especially useful for its bibliography to 1996; Mary B. Moore, *Desiring Voices: Women Sonneteers and Petrarchism;* Mady Dépillier, *Louise Labé: La première féministe;* and Madeleine Lazard, *Louise Labé, Lyonnaise.* Needless to say, all such works and the many others must be viewed in varying degrees through the prism of the present controversy.

D'un tel vouloir le serf point ne desire
la liberté, ou son port le navire,
comme j'atens, helas, de jour en jour
de toy, Ami, le gracieus retour.
Là, j'avois mis le but de ma douleur,
qui fineroit, quand j'aurois ce bon heur
de te revoir; mais de la longue atente,
helas, en vain mon desir se lamente.
Cruel, Cruel, qui te faisoit promettre
ton brief retour en ta première lettre?
As tu si peu de memoire de moy,
que de m'avoir si tot rompu la foy?
Comme ose tu ainsi abuser celle
qui de tout tems t'a esté si fidelle?
Or' que tu es aupres de ce rivage
du Pan Cornu, peut estre ton courage
s'est embrasé d'une nouvelle flame,
en me changeant pour prendre une autre Dame:
ja en oubli, inconstamment est mise
la loyauté que tu m'avois promise.
S'il est ainsi, et que desja la foy
et la bonté se retirent de toy,
il ne me faut emerveiller si ores
toute pitié tu as perdu encores.
O combien ha de pensee et de creinte,
tout aparsoy, l'ame d'Amour ateinte!
Ores je croy, vu notre amour passee,
qu'impossible est, que tu m'aies laissee;
et de nouvel ta foy je me fiance,
et plus qu'humeine estime ta constance.
Tu es, peut estre, en chemin inconnu
outre ton gré malade retenu.
Je croy que non: car tant suis coutumiere
de faire aus Dieus pour ta santé priere
que plus cruels que tigres ils seroient,
quand maladie ils te prochasseroient,
bien que ta fole et volage inconstance
meriteroit avoir quelque soufrance.
Telle est ma foy, qu'elle pourra sufire

The serf craves not his liberty as much,
Alas, nor yearns the boat its port to touch,
As, Friend, do I, with each day passing, burn
For the sweet moment when you will return.
My pain, thought I, would surely finish when
Mine the fair fate to see you once again;
But long I wait, and all in vain my yearning
Seems, as I quite despair of your returning.
Cruel! Cruel! What made you trouble to pretend,
In that one letter that to me you penned,
That briefly would you bide? Think you of me
So little that you break thus, faithlessly,
Your word so soon? How dare you so ill use
One who has not been—nor would ever choose
To be—less than a faithful friend and true?
Now, by the Horned Pan's distant banks, do you
Burn with a new-lit flame I know naught of?
Perhaps another Lady knows the love
You promised once to me; perhaps now she
Enjoys the fruit of your inconstancy.
If this be true, if all your goodness, thus,
And all your faith, must prove so frivolous,
No wonder is it then that you should show
No pity for me now and scorn me so.
Alas! How great the doubt—and fear besides—
That in the very soul of Love abides!
But oh! When on our love I muse, I must
Believe you could not leave me thus: my trust
Grows yet; and I would fain believe you are
Most constant of all human men by far.
Perhaps on some lost byway, lying ill,
Lo! do you now remain against your will.
But no! How could I so suppose? I pray
The Gods so often for your health that they
Would tigers be if, much though I besought
And pled, yet still their ills upon you wrought—
Although, betimes, your faithlessness might be
Deserving of its deal of agony!
My faith alone would keep you safely from

a te garder d'avoir mal et martire.
Celui qui tient au haut Ciel son Empire
ne me sauroit, ce me semble, desdire;
mais quand mes pleurs et larmes entendroit
pour toy prians, son ire il retiendroit.
J'ai de tout tems vescu en son service,
sans me sentir coulpable d'autre vice
que de t'avoir bien souvent en son lieu
d'amour forcé, adoré comme Dieu.
Desja deus fois depuis le promis terme
de ton retour, Phebe ses cornes ferme,
sans que de bonne ou mauvaise fortune
de toy, Ami, j'aye nouvelle aucune.
Si toutefois, pour estre enamouré
en autre lieu, tu as tant demeuré,
si sày je bien que t'amie nouvelle
à peine aura le renom d'estre telle,
soit en beauté, vertu, grace et faconde,
comme plusieurs gens savans par le monde
m'ont fait à tort, ce croy je, estre estimee.
Mais qui pourra garder la renommee?
Non seulement en France suis flatee,
et beaucoup plus, que ne veus, exaltee.
La terre aussi que Calpe et Pyrenee
avec la mer tiennent environnee,
du large Rhin les roulantes areines,
le beau païs auquel or' te promeines
ont entendu (tu me l'as fait à croire)
que gens d'esprit me donnent quelque gloire.
Goute le bien que tant d'hommes desirent,
demeure au but ou tant d'autres aspirent,
et croy qu'ailleurs n'en auras une telle.
Je ne dy pas qu'elle ne soit plus belle,
mais que jamais femme ne t'aymera,

The evil and the pain of martyrdom.
He who rules his Domain from Heaven's height
Would not, I know, oppose me; rather might
My prayers, my tears for you, so copious shed,
Make him withhold his wrath upon your head.
Well have I worshiped him my whole life through;
My only sin: that I have worshiped you,
At times, instead, the more possessed by love.
*   Twice has bright Phoebe joined her horns above,
And filled the space betwixt, grown full thereby,
Since your avowed return; and still have I
No news—nor bad, nor good—of what your fate
Might be. But if you bide because, of late,
You have a new love found, I can declare
And certain be that she cannot compare
In beauty, virtue, grace, glibness of tongue,
To me—or so, at least, one says among
Those who must know, although no doubt they err.
Besides, how long those praises they confer?
Nor is it France alone that spreads my name
And flatters me with ill-deserved acclaim.
So too that land enveloped by two seas,
†   Between Gibraltar and the Pyrenees;
Likewise those Rhenish hillsides, and that fair
Country where now you wander: everywhere
(So have you told me) men of taste and wit
Perceive my worth, commend and honor it.
Thus do I say, waste not your time in vain
Pursuit of other loves, but love again
This treasure many other men desire:
When you have reached the highest, seek no higher!
None will you find, I vow, better than her.
I do not say that none is prettier,
More fair; but one, I fear, will you find never

---

   * In Greek mythology, Phoebe, the moon, is the sister of Phoebus, the sun. The horns in Labé's classically periphrastic allusion are, of course, the cusps of the monthly crescent.

   † The reference in the original is to Calpe, ancient name of one of the two mountains— the other being Abyla—that formed the Pillars of Hercules. In some versions, the two were originally a single mountain that Hercules tore apart; in others, he raised each mountain first and proceeded to pour the sea between them.

ne plus que moy d'honneur te portera.
Maints grans Signeurs à mon amour pretendent,
et à me plaire et servir prets se rendent,
joutes et jeus, maintes belles devises
en ma faveur sont par eus entreprises;
et neanmoins tant peu je m'en soucie,
que seulement ne les en remercie:
tu es tout seul, tout mon mal et mon bien;
avec toy tout, et sans toy je n'ay rien;
et n'ayant rien qui plaise à ma pensee,
de tout plaisir me trouve delaissee,
et pour plaisir, ennui saisir me vient.
Le regretter et plorer me convient,
et sur ce point entre un tel desconfort,
que mile fois je souhaite la mort.
Ainsi, Ami, ton absence lointeine
depuis deus mois me tient en cette peine,
ne vivant pas, mais mourant d'un Amour
lequel m'occit dix mille fois le jour.
Revien donq tot, si tu as quelque envie
de me revoir encor un coup en vie.
Et si la mort avant ton arrivee
ha de mon corps l'aymante ame privee,
au moins un jour vien, habillé de dueil,
environner le tour de mon cercueil.
Que plust à Dieu que lors fussent trouvez
ces quatre vers en blanc marbre engravez:

Par toy, amy, tant vesqui enflammee,
qu'en languissant par feu suis consumee,
qui couve encor sous ma cendre embrazee,
si ne la rens de tes pleurs apaizee.

To love you more than I, search wheresoever,
Or treasure you the more. Many's the lord,
Many the *grands Seigneurs,* who have implored
My love, and who, to please and serve me, wage
Tourney and joust, and for my sake engage
In courtly sport. But I so little care
Therefor—do what they do, dare what they dare—
That not a word of thanks I proffer, for
You are my all, my only: nothing more
Nor less than everything; without you naught
Have I; and, having naught, within my thought
Lies no delight but only emptiness.
Tears and laments betide, and so oppress
And harrow me that, with each sobbing breath,
A thousand times I sigh and yearn for death.
Yes, for two months my woe and misery
Grow as you wander, Friend, far, far from me,
And I, scarce living, die of Love's dismay
That lays me low ten thousand times a day.
Return, then, soon if you still have a will
To see me one more time, and living still.
And if cruel death my body has deprived
Of my soul's love before you have arrived,
I pray, at least, in mourning clothed, one day,
You stroll about my tower-tomb; and may
You find, please God, as gazing then, upon
Its marble white, these lines engraved thereon:

For you, friend, lived I so enflamed by love
That, yearning, now am I consumed thereof,
To ashes turned, fire smouldering still in them
Until your tears weep me a requiem.

Elégies, II

I

Non hauria Ulysse o qualunqu'altro mai
piu accorto fù, da quel divino aspetto
pien die gratie, d'honor et di rispetto
sperato qual i sento affani e guai.

Pur, amor, co i begli occhi tu fatt' hai
tal piaga dentro al mio innocente petto,
di cibo et di calor gia tua ricetto,
che rimedio non v'e si tu nel' dai.

O sorte dura, che mi fa esser quale
punta d'un Scorpio, et domandar riparo
contr' el velen' dall' istesso animale.

Chieggo li sol' ancida questa noia,
non estingua el desir a me si caro,
che mancar non potra ch' i non mi muoia.

II

O beaux yeus bruns, ô regars destournez,
ô chaus soupirs, ô larmes espandues,
ô noires nuits vainement atendues,
ô jours luisans vainement retournez!

O tristes pleins, ô desirs obstinez
ô tems perdu, ô peines despendues,
ô mile morts en mile rets tendues,
ô pires maus contre moi destinez!

O ris, ô front, cheveus, bras, mains et doits!
O lut pleintif, viole, archet et vois!
Tant de flambeaus pour ardre une femmelle!

De toy me plein, que tant de feus portant,
en tant d'endroits d'iceus mon cœur tatant,
n'en est sur toy volé quelque estincelle.

I

Neither Ulysses nor one shrewder might
have foretold what a fell and grievous woe
I suffer for that heavenly face, whence glow
respect and honor, fair-graced in my sight.

Ah, Love! You have, with beauteous eyes—despite
my innocence—ravaged my poor breast so,
in search of warmth and sustenance, that no
cure, save it come from you, can ease my plight.

Cruel fate! The Scorpion's dart has stung me; still
must I entreat the beast, whose poisoned sting
has laid me low, to heal me of my ill.

I beg you thus dispel my woe; but I
pray you not quell thereby my languishing,
for, should I feel it not, I needs must die.

II

O fair brown eyes, looks that aloof remain,
O ardent sighing, tears that flow unpent,
O dark nights, long awaited, vainly spent,
O bright days, vainly coming round again!

O sad lament, yearning that naught can rein,
O time lost, pain dealing its dire torment,
O thousand snares on thousand deaths intent,
O baleful woes: my destiny, my bane!

O smile, O brow, O hair, arms, fingers, hands!
O plaintive lute, voice, bow, viol! Flaming brands
to kindle woman's flesh! Ah! how I rue

all those fair fires of yours, that my heart plies,
and tries to test, to taste—here, there—yet flies
no single spark, not one, from mine to you.

O longs desirs, ô esperances vaines,
tristes soupirs et larmes coutumieres
a engendrer de moy maintes rivieres,
dont mes deus yeus sont sources et fontaines!

O cruautez, ô durtez inhumaines,
piteus regars des celestes lumieres,
du cœur transi ô passions premieres,
estimez vous croitre encore mes peines?

Qu'encor Amour sur moy son arc essaie,
que nouveaus feus me gette et nouveaus dars,
qu'il se despite, et pis qu'il pourra face:

Car je suis tant navree en toutes pars,
que plus en moy une nouvelle plaie,
pour m'empirer ne pourroit trouver place.

IV

Depuis qu'Amour cruel empoisonna
premierement de son feu ma poitrine,
tousjours brulay de sa fureur divine,
qui un seul jour mon cœur n'abandonna.

Quelque travail, dont assez me donna,
quelque menasse et procheine ruïne,
quelque penser de mort qui tout termine,
de rien mon cœur ardent ne s'estonna.

Tant plus qu'Amour nous vient fort assaillir,
plus il nous fait nos forces recueillir
et tousjours frais en ses combats fait estre.

Mais ce n'est pas qu'en rien nous favorise,
cil qui les Dieus et les hommes mesprise,
mais pour plus fort contre les fors paroître.

III

O yearnings unrequited, miseries;
O springs of tears, welling mid sobs and sighs,
flowing in torrents streaming from my eyes!
Limitless founts and endless sources, these!

O callous, harsh, inhuman cruelties!
Pitiful glances cast from star-lit skies!
O heart benumbed, yet still in love's first guise!
Think you that you can whet my agonies?

Let Cupid aim his bow at me again;
let him shoot arrows, darts of fire, anew;
let him, in wrath, loose all he has in store.

For, cut so to the quick am I, pierced through,
that he would wreak new wounds on me in vain:
no room have I to suffer now still more.

IV

Ever since Love first cruelly plied my breast
with passion's fiery poison here below,
burned have I with that god's mad fire, with no
surcease to ease my heart: not one day's rest.

Whatever the travails upon me pressed,
whatever threats or bale he might bestow,
whatever thoughts of death—all-ending woe!—
my burning heart, unwondering, acquiesced.

The more Love seeks to harry us, the more
he makes us even stronger than before,
and keeps us ever fresh in combat's throes.

Yet it is not for reasons generous
that he, scornful of Gods and men, serves us,
but to prove stronger than his strongest foes.

V

Clere Venus, qui erres par les Cieus,
entens ma voix qui en pleins chantera,
tant que ta face au haut du Ciel luira,
son long travail et souci ennuieus.

Mon œil veillant s'atendrira bien mieus,
et plus de pleurs te voyant getera
mieus mon lit mol de larmes baignera,
de ses travaux voyant témoins tes yeux.

Donq des humains sont les lassez esprits
de dous repos et de sommeil espris.
J'endure mal tant que le Soleil luit.

Et quand je suis quasi toute cassee,
et que me suis mise en mon lit lassee,
crier me faut mon mal toute la nuit.

VII

On voit mourir toute chose animee,
lors que du corps l'ame subtile part:
je suis le corps, toy la meilleure part.
Ou es tu donq, ô ame bien aymee?

Ne me laissez par si long tems pâmee,
pour me sauver apres viendrois trop tard.
Las, ne mets point ton corps en ce hazart:
rens lui sa part et moitié estimee.

Mais fais, Ami, que ne soit dangereuse
cette rencontre et revuë amoureuse,
l'acompagnant, non de severité,

non de rigueur: mais de grace amiable,
qui doucement me rende ta beauté,
jadis cruelle, à présent favorable.

V

Bright Venus, you who wander through the Skies,
hear the laments my voice will raise before
your shining face on high; for I, heartsore
with long travail, would have you heed my sighs.

Best I remain awake: the more my eyes
bewail my bane before your face, and pour
their bitter tears on my soft bed, the more
you see my bale, and watch me agonize.

The human spirit, bowed beneath its woes,
eagerly yearns for sleep and sweet repose.
Ill do I bear the Sun's clear-shining light.

And when full spent am I and near outspun,
and I am lying in my bed, undone,
then must I cry my pain all through the night.

VII

All that draws breath must die; the soul, astray,
flies from the body, quits the human state:
the body, I; you, its most perfect mate.
Where are you, soul belovèd? Tell me, pray.

Leave me not long a-swoon, for well you may,
coming to succor me, arrive too late.
* Let not this body—yours—suffer that fate,
but give it back its better half straightway.

Yet, Friend, let danger not accompany
that sweet reunion; let love, rather, be
its boon companion, neither pitiless

nor harsh; but gracious, and of gentle air,
to grant me once again your loveliness,
and all its erstwhile cruelty forswear.

* The confusion as to whose body and soul are whose is resolved if one assumes that,
when the poet refers to *ton* (your) *corps*, the implication is that, though her own, that body
belongs, indeed, to him.

Louise Labé 147

Je vis, je meurs: je me brule et me noye.
J'ay chaut estreme en endurant froidure;
la vie m'est et trop molle et trop dure;
j'ay grans ennuis entremeslez de joye.

Tout à un coup je ris et je larmoye,
et en plaisir maint grief tourment j'endure;
mon bien s'en va, et à jamais il dure;
tout en un coup je seiche et je verdoye.

Ainsi Amour inconstamment me meine;
et quand je pense avoir plus de douleur,
sans y penser je me treuve hors de peine.

Puis quand je croy ma joye estre certeine,
et estre au haut de mon desiré heur,
il me remet en mon premier malheur.

IX

Tout aussi tot que je commence à prendre
dens le mol lit le repos desiré,
mon triste esprit hors de moy retiré
s'en va vers toy incontinent se rendre.

Lors m'est avis que dedens mon sein tendre
je tiens le bien, ou j'ay tant aspiré,
et pour lequel j'ay si haut souspiré,
que de sanglots ay souvent cuidé fendre.

O dous sommeil, ô nuit à moy heureuse!
Plaisant repos, plein de tranquillité,
continuez toutes les nuiz mon songe;

et si jamais ma povre ame amoureuse
ne doit avoir de bien en verité,
faites au moins qu'elle en ait en mensonge.

I live, I die; I burn, yet do I drown.
In sweltering heat and freezing cold I dwell;
gentle and mild my life, yet harsh and fell;
great joys have I, yet torments weigh me down.

I laugh and smile, yet do I weep and frown.
Pleasure and pain at once abound, pell-mell;
good fortune flies, yet ever lasts as well;
I blossom, green, yet do I wither, brown.

Thus fickle Love does ill his will with me:
oft, when I sense, at hand, dole and duress,
freed in a trice am I of my ennui.

Then, when I think no happier might I be—
when I have reached the height of joyousness—
he casts me down again, to dark distress.

IX

No sooner do I, yearning, take my rest,
lying in my soft bed at eventide,
than straightway flies my spirit, sad, to bide
with you, wrenched from my body, love-possessed.

Then does it seem that, to my bosom pressed,
mine is the boon that I have longed for, cried
aloud for, often and again, and sighed
sobs that I feared might burst my tender breast.

O gentle sleep! O peaceful night! Pray, ever
grant me the tranquil joy of sweet repose:
night after night, let me dream in this wise;

and if my poor soul, love-beset, must never
enjoy, in truth, that boon that love bestows,
let it, at least, enjoy its endless lies.

XI

O dous regars, ô yeus pleins de beauté,
petits jardins, pleins de fleurs amoureuses
ou sont d'Amour les flesches dangereuses,
tant à vous voir mon œil s'est arresté!

O cœur felon, ô rude cruauté,
tant tu me tiens de façons rigoureuses,
tant j'ay coulé de larmes langoureuses,
sentant l'ardeur de mon cœur tourmenté!

Donques, mes yeus, tant de plaisir avez,
tant de bons tours par ses yeus recevez;
mais toy, mon cœur, plus les vois s'y complaire,

plus tu languiz, plus en as de souci,
or devinez si je suis aise aussi,
sentant mon œil estre à mon cœur contraire.

XIV

Tant que mes yeus pourront larmes espandre,
a l'heur passé avec toy regretter,
et qu'aus sanglots et soupirs resister
pourra ma voix, et un peu faire entendre;

tant que ma main pourra les cordes tendre
du mignart Lut, pour tes graces chanter;
tant que l'esprit se voudra contenter
de ne vouloir rien fors que toy comprendre,

je ne souhaite encore point mourir.
Mais quand mes yeus je sentiray tarir,
ma voix cassee, et ma main impuissante,

et mon esprit en ce mortel sejour
ne pouvant plus montrer signe d'amante,
priray la Mort noircir mon plus cler jour.

XI

O tender glances! Eyes of beauty wrought:
gardens filled with the flowers of love, but where
Love's arrows lurk and threaten: for I dare
let my eyes gaze on you more than I ought!

O heart untrue! Behold how I lie caught
in your cruel grasp, in your perfidious snare,
weeping my tears of anguish and despair
at my heart's passion, burning, sore distraught!

And so, O eyes of mine, much do you prize
those glances that you cherish, from his eyes;
but you, my heart, despise their coquetries,

ever to suffer, long and languorous.
Imagine, then, how I must feel if, thus,
my eyes and heart must live as enemies.

XIV

As long as my eyes yet can shed a tear
whilst I mourn for our joy, now long since spent,
and my voice can forgo the sad lament
of sigh and moan, still singing, weak but clear;

as long as my hand yet can persevere
to pluck your praises to my Lute's content,
and my mind, yet unwilling to relent,
is filled with naught but you, still holds you dear;

then no desire at all have I to die.
But when, one day, I feel my eyes grow dry,
when hoarse my voice, trembling my hand; and when

my mind, in this drear life, no longer might
show you the slightest sign of love: ah, then
shall I pray Death make dark my day's fair light.

XVII

Je fuis la vile, et temples, et tous lieus,
esquels prenant plaisir à t'ouir pleindre
tu peus, et non sans force, me contreindre
de te donner ce qu'estimois le mieus.

Masques, tournois, jeus me sont ennuieus,
et rien sans toy de beau ne me puis peindre,
tant que tachant à ce desir esteindre,
et un nouvel objet faire à mes yeux,

et des pensers amoureus me distraire,
des bois espais sui le plus solitaire.
Mais j'aperçoy, ayant erré maint tour,

que si je veus de toy estre delivre
il me convient hors de moymesme vivre,
ou fais encor que loin sois en sejour.

XIX

Diane estant en l'espesseur d'un bois,
apres avoir mainte beste assenee,
prenoit le frais, de Nynfes couronnee.
J'allois resvant comme fay maintefois,

sans y penser, quand j'ouy une vois
qui m'apela, disant, Nynfe estonnee,
que ne t'es tu vers Diane tournee?
Et me voyant sans arc et sans carquois:

Qu'as tu trouvé, ô compagne, en ta voye
qui de ton arc et flesches ait fait proye?
Je m'animay, respons je, à un passant,

et lui getay en vain toutes mes flesches
et l'arc apres; mais lui les ramassant
et les tirant me fit cent et cent bresches.

XVII

City and temples, every place I flee
where you might master me and, by the by,
I might be pleased, hearing your plaintive sigh,
to give you what you once deemed best in me.

Games, tourneys, masques fill me with fell ennui:
naught, save for you, can pleasure my mind's eye;
thus, if I would my yearning quell, and try
to find some other object fair to see,

pondering not my thoughts of love now flown,
I wander roundabout the woods, alone.
But when, alas, my errant course is through,

I find that, would I cast off the chagrin
you cause me, I must quit my very skin,
or flee as far as far I might from you.

XIX

Deep in the wood, where she was wont to go,
surrounded by her Nymphs, Diana went
a-stroll, fresh from the hunt. I, ever bent
upon my wanderings, strolled as well, when, lo!

musing, I heard a voice, calling me, so:
"Brash Nymph! Why stray you, thus, impertinent,
far from Diana's side?" And, discontent,
seeing me quiverless, without a bow:

"Tell me, what ever did you come upon,
to lose your bow and spend your arrows on?"
"A passer-by," said I, "who stirred my heart:

I loosed my arrows at him, all in vain,
and even flung my bow! Wherewith, the swain
pierced me a myriad times, dart after dart."

XXI

Quelle grandeur rend l'homme venerable?
Quelle grosseur? quel poil? quelle couleur?
Qui est des yeus le plus emmieleur?
Qui fait plus tot une playe incurable?

Quel chant est plus à l'homme convenable?
Qui plus penetre en chantant sa douleur?
Qui un dous lut fait encore meilleur?
Quel naturel est le plus amiable?

Je ne voudrois le dire, assurément
ayant Amour forcé mon jugement;
mais je say bien et de tant je m'assure,

que tout le beau que lon pourroit choisir,
et que tout l'art qui ayde la Nature,
ne me sauroient accroitre mon desir.

XXIII

Las! que me sert, que si parfaitement
louas jadis et ma tresse doree,
et de mes yeus la beauté comparee
à deus Soleils, dont Amour finement

tira les trets causes de ton tourment?
Ou estes vous, pleurs de peu de duree?
et mort par qui devoit estre honorée
ta ferme amour et iteré serment?

Donques c'estoit le but de ta malice
de m'asservir sous ombre de service?
Pardonne moy, Amy, à cette fois,

estant outree et de despit et d'ire;
mais je m'assur', quelque part que tu sois,
qu'autant que moy tu soufres de martire.

XXI

What height is mete for man to be adored?
What girth? What hair? What color of the skin?
What gives the eyes the honeyed glance therein?
What keeps a wound unhealed, flesh unrestored?

What air most pleases man with fair accord?
What delves, with song, deepmost in his chagrin?
What tunes a lute better than it had been?
What gentle mood is its own sweet reward?

I would not my opinion tell, for Love
assuredly has forced my thoughts thereof;
still am I sure, and take full well as true,

that all the beauty one goes gleaning for,
and all the art that favors Nature too,
are not enough to make me yearn the more.

XXIII

Alas! What profits me to recollect
with what finesse you praised my golden hair;
my eyes, whose beauty you would fain compare
to two Suns, whence god Cupid's darts, direct

and deadly, pierced you with their fell effect?
Where, now, those tears that dried too soon? And where,
that death you called upon, that you would swear
might prove the measure of your love abject?

So? Was your purpose not but to beguile,
to bend my will, to feign with ruse and wile?
Pardon, my Friend! Though, bitter and enraged,

I loathe your name, wherever you may be,
at least a little is my wrath assuaged
to hope that woe plagues you as much as me.

Louise Labé 155

XXIV

Ne reprenez, Dames, si j'ay aymé,
si j'ay senti mile torches ardentes,
mile travaus, mile douleurs mordantes.
Si en pleurant j'ay mon tems consumé,

las que mon nom n'en soit par vous blamé.
Si j'ay failli, les peines sont presentes,
n'aigrissez point leurs pointes violentes,
mais estimez qu'Amour, à point nommé,

sans votre ardeur d'un Vulcan excuser,
sans la beauté d'Adonis acuser,
pourra, s'il veut, plus vous rendre amoureuses,

en ayant moins que moi d'ocasion,
et plus d'estrange et forte passion.
Et gardez vous d'estre plus malheureuses.

XXIV

Ladies, I beg you think of me no ill
that I have loved, and known love's biting pain,
its myriad burning brands, its bitter bane.
If I, alas, have wept my tearful fill,

condemn me not; though I have sinned, yet still
sin's woes abide with me, never they wane:
thus spare me, pray, the barbs of your disdain;
and keep in mind that Cupid, if he will—

though less your lust than Vulcan's heat, and though
less than Adonis's grace lay you low—
can, nonetheless, beset your heart with love:

stranger, betimes, than mine, that passion-fire.
Whilst less than I you languish with desire,
take care lest, more than I, you smart thereof.

Jeanne d'Albret (1528–1572)

No less a literary personage than Joachim du Bellay admired Jeanne d'Albret the poet, though whether sincerely or sycophantically is hard to say, given that the lady in question was also queen of Navarre and daughter of the celebrated Marguerite (see pp. 98–119 above). Nor can we appreciate for ourselves the quality of most of her verse, unfortunately lost to us long since. What survives is to be found in a contemporary collection of Du Bellay's works—sonnets thanking him for his high opinion—and in a poetic exchange between her and her mother: epistles that reflect both the tensions and differences, political and religious, that separated them, as well as the deep affection that these two royal ladies felt for each other.[1] Product and victim of the wars of religion that divided and ravaged sixteenth-century France, Jeanne d'Albret shared her mother's generous sympathies for the reformers but went one step farther, actually passionately embracing their theology.

Jeanne d'Albret was born in 1528, the only surviving child of Marguerite de Navarre (who long mourned the death of an infant son, Jean) and was raised in the intellectual environment that one would expect of her eminent mother. When she was thirteen, her uncle, King François I, had her married to the duc de Clèves. The (supposedly) unconsummated union, which ended in annulment, was followed by another marriage, in 1548, which, though of her own choosing over parental objection, was also not without its problems. Evidently, however, it was not unconsummated, five or six children—sources differ—being the result. Antoine de Bourbon, duc de Vendôme, in direct line to the throne of France, was not only unfaithful as a spouse—progeny notwithstanding—but, even more damning from Jeanne's point of view, unfaithful to the religious reformism in which the couple had been involved.

Becoming queen of Navarre in 1555 upon her father's death, Jeanne was eventually able, as sole monarch on Antoine's demise several years later, to establish Calvinism as her little domain's official religion. And that, in spite of threats of excommunication and even an unsuccessful plot by Felipe II of Spain to have her kidnapped and condemned by the Inquisition. The marriage of her one surviving son, the future Henri IV, a Protestant, to Marguerite de Valois, a Catholic, was an attempt to establish peace between the warring factions; a peace soon to be shattered by the Saint Bartholomew massacre and a continued period of hostility in the name and barbaric defense of God. Jeanne died in 1572, two months before the wedding and the carnage that ensued.[2]

Far more devoted to matters of faith than to matters of poetry, Jeanne d'Albret was, judging by her surviving works, no less a technically proficient poet, if not a spectacularly original one. The four sonnets to Du Bellay and the two epistles to her mother in the following pages show her to be capable of both a vigor and grace that a more tranquil life might have allowed to flower.

NOTES

1. Jeanne d'Albret's sonnets were originally published in *Œuvres françoises de Joachim du Bellay, gentilhomme angevin* and are included in *Mémoires et poésies de Jeanne d'Albret*, ed. Alphonse de Ruble. A few *épistres* to her mother, Marguerite de Navarre, figure with the latter's own *épistres* to Jeanne in *Les dernières poésies de Marguerite de Navarre*, ed. Abel Lefranc.

2. For biographies of Jeanne d'Albret, see Nancy Lyman Roelker's definitive *Queen of Navarre: Jeanne d'Albret (1528–1572)*; and, more recently, David Bryson, *Queen Jeanne and the Promised Land: Dynasty, Homeland, Religion and Violence in 16th-Century France.*

Que mériter on ne puisse l'honneur
Qu'avez escript, je n'en suis ignorante:
Et si ne suis pour cela moins contente,
Que ce n'est moy à qui appartient l'heur.

Je cognois bien le pris et la valeur
De ma louange, et cela ne me tente
D'en croire plus que ce qui se présente,
Et n'en sera de gloire enflé mon cœur.

Mais qu'un Bellay ait daigné de l'escrire,
Honte je n'ay à vous et chacun dire
Que je me tiens plus contente du tiers,

Plus satisfaite, et encor glorieuse,
Sans mériter me trouver si heureuse,
Qu'on puisse trouver mon nom en voz papiers.

De leurs grands faicts les rares anciens
Sont maintenant contents et glorieux,
Ayant trouvé poètes curieux
Les faire vivre, et pour tels je les tiens.

Mais j'ose dire, et cela je maintiens,
Qu'encor'ils ont un regret ennuieux,
Dont ils seront sur moy-mesme envieux,
En gémissant aux Champs Elyséens:

C'est qu'ils voudroient, pour certain je le sçay,
Revivre ici et avoir un Bellay,
Ou qu'un Bellay de leur temps eust été.

Car ce qui n'est sçavez si dextrement
Feindre et parer, que trop plus aisément
Le bien du bien seroit par vous chanté.

Only too well I know that I do not
Merit the praise with which you write of me.
Yet, forasmuch, not displeased can I be
That mine, indeed, is such a happy lot.

I know the value of such praise begot,
But tempted not am I in it to see
More than a generous deal of flattery,
Nor will my heart be swelled one whit, one jot.

Still, without shame, I hasten to admit
That, since a Du Bellay has written it,
Happy am I, in such an one delighting—

Though little be my worth!—here to confess
That I exult therein, glory no less,
To see my name thus mentioned in your writing.

"Réponse de la royne aux louanges de Du Bellay," I,
in Œuvres françoises de Joachim du Bellay

The ancients, in uncommon glorydom,
Take pride in fame reborn; for they have found
Poets to plumb their great feats, laurel-crowned,
And I delight to see them proud become.

But, I would warrant, still they glower, glum
With dour regret, however much-renowned,
Jealous of me, lamenting, envy-frowned,
Despite their place in the Elysium.

For this I know: doubtless would they, today,
Be born anew, to have a Du Bellay,
Else wish that he had lived when they were young.

So skillful is your pen's imagining,
So artfully you paint the past you sing,
That in your best wise would their best be sung.

"Réponse de la royne aux louanges de Du Bellay," II,
in Œuvres françoises de Joachim du Bellay

Le papier gros, et l'encre trop espesse,
La plume lourde, et la main bien pesante,
Stile qui point l'oreille ne contente,
Faible argument, et mots pleins de rudesse,

Monstrent assez mon ignorance expresse,
Et si n'en suis moins hardie et ardente
Mes vers semer, si subjet se présente.
Et qui pis est, en cela je m'adresse

A vous, qui pour plus aigres les gouster,
En les mestant avecques des meilleurs,
Faistes les miens et vostres escouter.

Telle se voit différence aux couleurs:
Le blanc au gris sçait bien son lustre oster.
C'est l'heur de vous, et ce sont mes malheurs.

Le temps, les ans, d'armes me serviront
Pour pouvoir vaincre une jeune ignorance,
Et dessues moy à moy-mesme puissance
A l'advenir peult-être donneront.

Mais quand cent ans sur mon chef doubleront,
Si le hault ciel un tel aage m'advance,
Gloire j'auray d'heureuse récompense,
Si puis attaindre à celles qui seront

Par leur chef-d'œuvre en los toujours vivantes.
Mais tel cuyder seroit trop plein d'audace;
Bien suffira si, près leurs excellentes

Vertus, je puis trouver petite place:
Encor je sens mes forces languissantes
Pour espérer du ciel tel heur et grâce.

Paper, too rough, and ink, too thick; my quill,
Too heavy, and my hand as well; words, crude;
Style, harsh, the essence of ineptitude,
Rude on the ear; argument, proffered ill;

All proving that most paltry is my skill.
And yet, no less am I of eager mood,
Nor is my passion to write verse subdued
When fit the subject. More unseemly still,

I send you it! So much the worse for me:
When one hears yours, then mine, what can mine do?
Next to the best, it suffers bitterly.

And so it is with shades and colors too:
Pure white shows how lackluster gray can be.
Woeful for me, most fortunate for you.

"Réponse de la royne aux louanges de Du Bellay," III,
in *Œuvres françoises de Joachim du Bellay*

As the years pass in time's unending queue,
Arm me they shall against simplicity
Of callow youth, and grant perhaps to me
Each day the power to rule my life anew.

But if I lived one hundred years or two,
Should heaven bless my head so generously,
The only glory I would seek would be
That I might equal those fine women who

Live on in praises to their talents paid.
Ah! But such thought is most vainglorious:
Quite enough will it be if, undismayed,

I crouch beside their virtues! Yearning thus,
I feel my strength to wane, my force to fade,
In hopes that heaven be so magnanimous.

"Réponse de la royne aux louanges de Du Bellay," IV,
in *Œuvres françoises de Joachim du Bellay*

Mes yeulx, craignant trop de larmes respandre,
Ont bien osé sur ma bouche entreprandre,
Luy deffendant le pleurer et l'adieu,
Se departant du tant regretté lieu.
Mais maintenant que l'œil est appaisé,
Assurez-vous estre fort mal aisé
Garder les mains pour mon c[u]eur satisfaire,
Lequel ne peult de ce mal se deffaire,
Sans ung adieu et piteuse harengue,
Là où la main me servira de langue,
Pour declairer la douleur trop amere
Que sent la fille à l'adieu de la mere,
Perdant du tout de parler la puissance,
Tant empesché par trop grande abondance
De pleurs, touz prestz des yeulx dehors sortir.
A quoy, helas! je n'osay consentir,
Craignant de vous la desolation,
Disant l'adieu de separation.
Or vous supplie avoir pour agreable
Que cest adieu à la langue importable
Vous puissiez lire et non pas escoutter.
O dur morceau malaisé à gouster
A vous et moy! Que l'amour maternelle,
Qui sans finer me sera si cruelle,
Ne peult ce mot de triste adieu soufrir!
Je ne vous puis, Madame, rien offrir:
Je suis à vous et en vostre puissance,
Asseurez-vous que ceste obeissance,
Que je vous doibz, si bien observeray
Que mon debvoir en cela je feray.
Vous suppliant très humblement, Madame,
Pour la santé de mon corps et mon ame,
M'entretenir en vostre bonne grace;
Car, m'asseurant y avoir bonne place,
Malheur ny mal je ne puis recepvoir,
Sinon celluy que j'ay pour ne vous veoir.

MADAME TO THE QUEEN

My eyes, fearing too many a tear to shed,
Dared to enjoin my lips—grief-surfeited—
To weep, or bid good-bye, as I commence
From this belovèd place to venture hence.
But now—my eyes, assuaged—you may be sure
That I cannot, in my discomfiture,
Prevent my hand from doing what it will
To quell my heart's distress by dint of quill,
Rather than mournful tongue's long-drawn adieu,
Letting the hand do what the tongue would do
Were it, indeed, but able to express
A daughter's deal of bitter dolefulness
At mother's sad "farewell," unable, she,
To speak at all, as tears well copiously,
About to flow. Alas! I would not thus
Dare to subject you to so dolorous
A woe as to give ear to that dour word:
"Adieu!" And so I pray, rather than heard,
That it, instead, be read, difficult though
It be for both of us to swallow! No,
A mother's endless love, that cannot bear
That sad "adieu," will drive me to despair,
Since leave I must! Naught have I to allay
Your pain, save the assurance that obey
I shall your every wish, and that, Madame,
Your duteous subject—as is meet—I am,
And shall forever be: in humble wise
I pray that I be worthy in your eyes,
Else would my body and my very soul
Agonize in duress; no bale, no dole
Can you impart me, save the dreary lot
Not to be near you, and to see you not.

---

* These lines and many of the following would seem to allude to Marguerite's bitter
dissatisfaction with her daughter's marriage to the duc de Clèves, which was annulled by
Pope Paul III in 1545, four years before Marguerite's death (see p. 158 above).

Or, entendez, Madame, ung grant tourment
Que j'ay senty en ce departement,
Car deux amours qui ne me furent qu'une,
Je sens en deux, dont l'une m'importune
En me voullant presenter passience,
Me promectant l'agreable plaisance
Et le plaisir de reveoir ung mary.
Mais quoy! mon cueur encores trop ma[r]ry
Ne la veult poinct avoir ne recepvoir,
Car ceste amour du naturel debvoir
Je sens si fort, que si l'autre j'accepte
Aucune fois, soudain je la rejecte.
Tantost, je sens mon œil pleurer puis rire,
Mais la fin [n']est tousjours de ce martire,
Qui durera, sans prandre fin ne cesse,
Jusques à tant que je reprenne adresse
Pour retourner vers vous en dilligence.
Lors, obliant la trop facheuse absence,
Je recepvray la joye et le plaisir
Et joyray de mon parfaict desir
D'ensemble veoir pere, mere et mary.
Lors cessera mon cueur d'estre mar[r]y.
Donc attendant ceste heureuse journée
Je languiray de mal environnée,
Ayant toujours de vous reveoir envie,
Suppliant Dieu vous conserver la vie.

———————

AUTRE DE MADAME LA PRINCESSE À LA ROYNE

A ce matin, Madame, j'ay receu
En grand plaisir votre epistre bien leue,
Mais me faisant souvenir de l'adieu.
A tous ennuys certes j'ay donné lieu,
Et si le ciel retarde de pleuvoir,
Pour ne me veoir aux yeulx la larme avoir,
Je vous diray pourquoy cela advint:
C'est qu'à l'adieu d'un "Dieu gard" me souvint
Qui recrea mes pleurs, mais non obstant
N'effaça pas en mon cueur mal contant
Ce dur ennuy qu'à present me tourmente.

And so, Madame, I would you lend an ear
To the great torment that I feel—now, here—
As I depart: for, twofold loves have I,
Grown one; the first urges me not to fly,
Assuring me that, waiting patiently,
The pleasure shall be mine once more to see
My husband by and by. But ah! My heart
Is much distressèd, and I would have no part
Of such; for nature's duty to my mother
Demands that if, instead, I prize the other,
I spurn the great love that I feel for her.
Naught can I do: weep, laugh, proceed, demur...
My suffering, I fear—harsh martyrdom—
Will last until I find a way to come
Hastening homeward to your side again.
Forgetting my most painful absence then,
I shall enjoy, combined, the company
Of mother, father—my dear family—
And husband mine as well; then will I feel
A heart no longer full of woe, but weal.
Yet till that blessèd, happy time has found me,
Languish I must amidst the bane around me,
Yearning once more to see you, with one prayer:
That God protect and keep you in His care.

Dernières poésies de Marguerite de Navarre, "Epistres," III

ANOTHER FROM THE PRINCESS TO THE QUEEN

Madame, I read with loving care today
The letter that you penned; and I must say
That, though it pleased me much, nevertheless,
The thought of your farewell brought such distress
That, whilst no tears fall raining from the sky,
Whilst yet unweeping and still dry of eye,
I shall explain: that sad farewell it was,
Whose "godspeed," recollected, was the cause
Of many a tear, but not enough—ah, no!—
To soothe my heart and wash it of its woe.
Last evening I recalled again, downhearted,

Et en tant que [je] vous trouvay absente,
Hier au soir, je me mis à me plaindre;
Lors Dieu voullut astres et ciel contraindre
Vous declairer mon mal dur à porter;
Le vent cueillit, pour vous les transporter,
Les hau[lt]x souspirs de mon deuil importable.
Voila comment j'euz le ciel favorable,
Ayant voullu le vent prompt et leger,
En me servant, vous estre messager,
Faisant oyr mes plainctz à vostre oreille,
Où me contrainct ma douleur non pareille.
Or, craignant trop que ma longue escripture
Vous feist sentir de nouveau la poin[c]ture
De vostre ennuy, si fort à supporter,
Je prie à Dieu qui nous peult conforter
Me faire veoir vostre centiesme année.
En attendant ceste heureuse journée,
Que le "Dieu gard" me fera autant rire
Que cest adieu m'a causé de martire,
Je vous supplie estre de moy contente
Et me tenir la plus obeissante
Fille, qui fut et qui jamais sera,
Tant [qu']en ce corps l'ame demeurera.

How thus you took your leave of me, and started,
Sadly, once more to voice my drear complaining;
Whereupon, God—the sky and stars ordaining
To prove to you how much my torments weighed
Heavily on me—seized the wind, and bade
It waft unto your ear my doleful sighs,
Impossible to bear. So did the skies
Impart my message, blowing on the light
And fleeting wind—swift messenger—my plight
Unparalleled, that you might hear it. Now,
I fear lest overlong I write, and vow
I would not have you suffer yet the smart
Of woe so grievous to your aching heart,
Praying that God, who ever comforts us,
Reward you with a lifetime generous
Unto a hundred years! May that I see
With my own eyes, and may your "godspeed" be
As happy, waiting for that day to come,
As sad the "farewell" of my martyrdom.
Meanwhile I trust that I can give to you
Much joy: I, loving daughter, faithful, who
Ever obeyed, obeys, and ever will,
So long as breath of life stirs in me still.

Dernières poésies de Marguerite de Navarre, "Epistres," IV

Madeleine des Roches (1520?–1587)
Catherine des Roches (1542?–1587)

Marguerite de Navarre and Jeanne d'Albret are not the only poetic mother-daughter duo in this collection. Madeleine and Catherine des Roches claim the same honor, though quite different from their predecessors, in that they were sentimentally and artistically much closer to each other. Except for a reputed early volume of poems by Madeleine, now lost, they were, in fact, published in tandem both in their own day and in the three critical editions in which modern scholarship has reproduced them: *Les œuvres, Les secondes œuvres,* and *Les missives.*[1] While the last is a collection of letters—said to be the first personal correspondence between two women published in France—the first two present the body of the respective poetry of the Des Roches; odes, sonnets, epistles especially—often poems of circumstance—as well as a prose dialogue of Catherine's in defense of women and the pains (and pleasures) that they cause their men.

Les secondes œuvres contain, in addition to poetic works of similar inspiration, Catherine's transcription of Erasmus's Pythagorean *Vers dorés* and *Enigmes,* in quatrains reminiscent of the medieval courtesy book, but with particularly elevated moral messages. In the same volume, quite at the other end of the respectability spectrum, is her celebrated poem "La puce." For those who might view the sixteenth century as starchy or humorless, it should be noted that it is for these almost one hundred octosyllabic couplets on the peregrinations of a flea that Catherine was especially famous in her time. The Des Roches, prominent ladies of their native Poitiers, were accustomed to holding a literary salon whose fame had spread even to Paris, and which was frequented by the intelligentsia of the thriving intellectual and artistic center that Poitiers had become. On one occasion, the jurist Etienne Pasquier apparently noticed a flea venturing about on Catherine's bosom. The daring insect would be immortalized not only by the usually staid humanist but also by Catherine herself, giving rise to a veritable genre of flea verses composed in a variety of languages.[2]

Biographical dates and other data for the two ladies are a bit murky. The date often given for Madeleine's birth, 1530, would have made her a child bride in 1539 and a child mother if Catherine's birth date of 1542 is correct. More credible is the date 1520 given by others. The date of both ladies' demise, however, is as well-documented as those of their births are questionable: they died on the same day in 1587, apparently of the plague. In their time between, their lives were devoted to one another, to their writing, and to the salon society of their native city. Both were women of considerable humanistic erudition, and both defended women's right to lead a life of the mind, though not at the expense of traditional womanly pursuits, which they defended as well. Twice a widow, Madeleine found much inspiration in her personal griefs and travails—among them the loss of two young children—as well as in the political unrest of the age. Never married, Catherine, on the other hand, without avoiding personal concerns in her verse, turned also to subjects of more universal scope.[3]

The following translations—sonnets, odes, epistles, et al.—present a sampling of the product of this fascinating symbiosis, rare in the history of letters.

NOTES

1. Anne R. Larsen has published detailed editions of all three, the originals of which date, respectively, from 1578, 1583, and 1586.

2. See the four volumes of *La puce de Madame des Roches*.

3. For biographical studies and literary detail see, inter alia, Anne R. Larsen, ed. and trans., *From Mother and Daughter: Poems, Letters, and Dialogues of Les Dames des Roches*; the introduction to Larsen's edition of *Les œuvres*; George Diller, *Les dames des Roches: Etude sur la vie littéraire à Poitiers dans la deuxième moitié du XVIe siècle*; Ann Rosalind Jones, *The Currency of Eros: Women's Love Lyrics in Europe, 1540–1620*, pp. 52–78; Evelyne Beriot-Salvadore, *Les femmes dans la société française de la Renaissance*, pp. 456–61 and passim; *Writings by Pre-Revolutionary French Women*, ed. Anne R. Larsen and Colette H. Winn, pp. 151–69; and Diane Landry, *Le dialogue chez Louise Labé et Catherine des Roches*.

Quelqu'un mieux fortuné dira de ma complainte,
Mes douloureux soupirs, et mon gemissement:
"Cette-cy n'eut jamais que mal-contentement;
On ne voit que rigueur dessus sa charte peinte.

Est-ce une histoire vraie, ou une fable feinte,
Se veut-elle exercer sur un triste argument?"
La perte du repos me faict plus de tourment
Cent et cent mille fois que je ne fay de plainte.

Par le repos perdu j'ay la raison blessée,
J'ay le discours rompu, la memoire offencée;
L'aprehension faict mon cerveau distiller.

Le feu de mon esprit perd sa douce lumiere,
Et ne me reste plus de ma forme premiere
Sinon que j'ayme mieux escrire que filer.

O Prince, aymé de Dieu, quittez-vous nostre terre?
Laissez-vous ce grand Roy, vostre frere germain,
Ores que Dieu et luy, et vostre heureuse main,
Avez tiré la paix du ventre de la guerre?

Avez-vous tant à cœur la barbare Angleterre,
Vous qui estes clement, courtois, doux, et humain,
Vous qui estes l'apuy du sainct siege Romain,
De l'Eglise de Dieu, de la foy de sainct Pierre?

Monsieur, l'Anglois s'est veu le meurdrier de ses Rois,
Contempteur du vray Dieu, ennemy de ses loix,
Et fleau capital du repos de la France.

Someone more blessed might ask, of my woe-spent
And doleful sighs, my mournful moans: "Did she
Never know joy, poor soul? In misery,
Did the stars trace her days in long descent?

Is it the truth? Or would she, pity-bent,
Merely rehearse a sad soliloquy?"
Nights without sleep torment and torture me
Ten thousand times more than I dare lament.

Sleepless nights blunt my reasoning; my head
Remembers little; tongue's fair skill has fled;
Fear shrinks my mind from what it once had been.

Dulled of its fire, my spirit fails to flare.
And of my former self, nothing is there
But my desire to write rather than spin.

Les œuvres, "Sonnets I–XXXVI," VIII

---

† O Prince, of God beloved, can it be true?
You leave your brother—him, your country's king—
Now that he, God, and your own laboring
Have wrenched peace from war's womb, now born anew?

Love you so well barbaric England? You,
So courtly, gentle, versed in everything?
You, pillar of the Roman church, who bring
Strength to Saint Peter's faith, and cleave thereto?

The Englishman, sire, is a regicide;
He has the true God's laws despised, decried,
And to fair France brought naught but wickedness.

---

* Given the context, I assume *charte,* rather ambiguous in the original, to have an astrological meaning.

† According to Anne R. Larsen in her edition of *Les œuvres,* p. 130, the poem is addressed to François d'Alençon, duc d'Anjou, younger brother of Henri III, who, in 1579, left for England with the soon-aborted intention of marrying Queen Elizabeth.

Madeleine des Roches 173

Au moins, souvenez-vous que leur dernier seigneur
Par un semblable nœud, n'esprouvant que mal-heur,
Detestoit le païs, le peuple, et l'alliance.

Veux-tu sçavoir passant, quel a esté mon estre?
Sçaches que la nature, et fortune, et les Cieux,
Noble, riche, et sçavant autrefois m'ont fait naistre,
Me rendant possesseur de leurs dons precieux.

Apres avoir vescu d'une loüable vie,
Je fus pris d'un catere, et maintenant le sort
Des Parques me guerit de ceste maladie:
Je mourois en ma vie, et je vis en ma mort.

Je fus trente ans Breton; vingt et huict mon espouse
Me retint dans Poëtiers lié de chaste amour.
Mon ame devant Dieu maintenant se repose,
Et mon corps en ce lieu attend le dernier jour.

Mon corps n'est pas tout seul souz ceste froide tombe;
Le cœur de ma compaigne y gist avec le mien.
Jamais de son esprit nostre amitié ne tombe;
La mort ne trenche point un si ferme lien.

O Dieu, dont la vertu dedans le Ciel enclose
Enclost mesme le Ciel; vueillez que ma moitié
Toutes ses actions heureusement dispose,
Honorant pour jamais nostre saincte amitié.

* Remember, pray, that their most recent lord
Tied such a knot as well, but soon deplored
The land, his union, and their race no less.

Les œuvres, "Sonnets I–XXXVI," XI

---

† EPITAPH OF THE LATE MAÎTRE FRANÇOIS ÉBOISSARD,
SEIGNEUR DE LA VILLÉE, HER HUSBAND

Would you know, traveler, what I used to be?
Know then that nature, fortune, Heaven above,
Bestowing learning, wealth, nobility,
Had granted me the precious gifts thereof.

After an admirable life, I was
By the palsy laid low, but then was I
Cured of my ill by The Fates' mortal laws:
I died in life, but in death living lie.

Thirty years I a Breton was, whereon
The chaste love of my wife, in Poitiers
Kept me for twenty-eight. God now looks on
My body's rest, as I wait Judgment Day.

But I lie not alone here, cold entombed;
My wife's heart lies with mine. For her love never
Can be undone, or to oblivion doomed:
Death is too weak to rend our bonds a-sever.

O God, whose virtue, in the Heavens enclosed,
Encloses Heaven itself, pray let my wife,
To honest actions evermore disposed,
Honor our sacred love all through her life.

* The reference is to the Spanish king Felipe II (1527–1598), who married Mary I of England. See Larsen, p. 131. The English alliance ended with Mary's death in 1558.

† After the death of her first husband, André Fradonnet, Madeleine Neveu—the name Des Roches came from a family property—married François Eboissard, a lawyer (hence his title *maistre*), in or around 1550. Eboissard died in 1578.

AU ROY

Sire, durant l'effort de la guerre civille,
Je plaignois le malheur de nostre pauvre ville:
J'eslevois jusque au ciel ma parole et mes yeux,
Ayant le cueur espoint d'un ennuy soucieux.
Mais helas! cependant que ma triste pensée,
De tant de maux publics griefvement offencée,
Alloit sur les autels, j'apperçeu deux maisons
Que j'avois au faubourg n'estre plus que tisons.
Et si ce n'eust esté que la perte commune
M'estoit cent mille fois plus aspre et importune,
A peine eussé-je pu m'apaiser promptement,
Voyant mon peu de bien se perdre en un moment.
Ces maisons pouvoient bien valoir deux mille livres,
Plus que ne m'ont valu ma plume ny mes livres
Qui seront inutils s'ils n'ont ceste faveur
Que vostre majesté estime leur labeur.
Depuis, j'ay entendu que vostre main Royalle
A ceux qui ont perdu se monstre liberalle,
Et que vostre bonté les veut recompenser.
Voilà l'occasion qui m'a fait avancer,
Sire, pour vous offrir ma treshumble requeste,
Priant le Seigneur Dieu vous couronner la teste
De l'heur de Salomon, comme de ces vertus;
De voir vos ennemis à vos pieds abbatus;
D'acomplir un tres beau et tres long cours de vie
Sans avoir de mourir ny crainte, ny envie;
D'establir pour jamais ce regne ferme et seur,
Et d'y laisser de vous un digne successeur.

TO THE KING

* My lord, throughout the strife of civil war
I mourned the bane that our poor city bore:
Heartsore and sad afflicted, I raised high
My eyes to heaven, my voice unto the sky
In prayer. But alas! Whilst thus undone
By the disaster wrought on everyone,
My houses twain, on city's edge, I learned,
Had been to little more than embers burned.
Were it not that the public bale and ill
Were hundred thousandfold more grievous still,
Seeing my paltry wealth thus, instantly
Destroyed, the woe that had befallen me
Would have been most impossible to bear.
Two thousand pounds, perhaps, were what that pair
Was worth: more, indeed, than my books, my pen,
Which have but little use if you—of men
Most generous!—prize and esteem them not.
Your royal hand, I hear, has eased the lot
Of those who have lost all; thus, deep distressed,
Come I to proffer my humble request,
Praying the Lord make you as virtuous
And wise as Solomon, and ever thus,
To see, cast at your feet, your slain foes lying;
† Neither to wish for death nor to fear dying,
But to reign long and well, and firm of hand,
‡ Leaving a worthy heir to rule the land.

* Apparently this request for help was addressed to Henri III—to no avail, we are told, despite his usual generosity—following the destruction of certain properties of the poet and her daughter during the siege of Poitiers, in 1569. See Larsen, *Les œuvres*, p. 172.

† Larsen notes (ibid., p. 173) that this appears to quote the Latin poet Martial.

‡ Larsen tells us (ibid.) that the royal couple were obsessed with their apparent infertility, but that Madeleine's (and their subjects') pious wish bore no fruit.

O miserable estat ou je me voy posée,
Dont j'ay tousjours au cueur un amer souvenir
Qui me fait le cerveau fontaine devenir,
Dont l'humeur par les yeux n'est jamais espuisée.

Si je sens quelquefois ma peine reposée,
C'est un presage seur du malheur advenir;
Et le menteur espoir n'a pu entretenir
La promesse qui m'a longuement abusée.

Ainsi donc le printemps et l'esté de mon aage,
Dont l'autonne cruel despouille le feuillage,
Sans fruit et sans plaisir se passe vainement.

Les tristesses, qui sont dedans mon ame encloses,
Ayant formé de moy mille metamorphoses,
N'ont pourtant transformé mon extreme tourment.

À CATHERINE DES ROCHES

Tout ainsi que l'on voit le maistre de Platon
Recherchant les effets par les premieres causes,
Transformer l'argument en cent Metamorphoses
Par l'anneau de Giges et l'armet de Pluton:

Ainsi tu m'affranchis de la main de Clothon
Par tes vers admirez plus beaux que nulles choses.
Tu faits d'un froid hiver le printemps et les roses:
Et dans tes mots dorez tu change mon leton.

O wretched state wherein I hapless lie,
Heart filled with memory's bitter woe intense
That turns my brain to brimming fountain, whence
From my eyes tears stream endless, never dry.

If, at times, pain seems to release me, I
Know that, alas, it must soon recommence:
Long does hope tell its lies, never relents,
And breaks its every promise by and by.

Thus do my spring and summer, cruelly
Stripped bare now of their withering greenery,
Empty and fruitless, turn to joyless fall.

But the woes that transform me, mournful-souled,
With metamorphoses a thousand-fold,
Cannot transform my autumn grief withal.

Les œuvres, "Sonnets I–XXXVI," II

* **TO CATHERINE DES ROCHES**

   Just as effects' First Causes once were sought
   By Plato's teacher, Master Socrates,
   Transformed in myriad metamorphoses—
† By Gyges' ring and Pluto's helmet wrought—

   So too your verse, fairer by far than aught,
‡ Frees me from Clotho's harsh-spun destinies,
   Makes roses bloom in winter, spring decrees,
§ Turns my brass gold, with moral axioms fraught.

---

   * This adulatory sonnet, although without dedication in the original, was clearly one of four intended for Madeleine's daughter, Catherine des Roches. See *Les missives,* ed. Larsen, p. 120.

   † In Greek mythology, Gyges' ring and Pluto's helmet were both supposed to confer invisibility; see *Les missives,* ed. Larsen, p. 122.

   ‡ Clotho is the Fate who spins the thread of life, measured out by Lachesis and cut by Atropos.

   § A reference to Catherine's adaptations of Erasmus's *Vers dorés* (Golden Verses). See *Les missives,* ed. Larsen, p. 122, and pp. 194–97, below.

Aux hommes bien disans, dont les vertus exquises
S'honorent à l'envy des sciences acquises,
Laisse voir de tes vers la divine clairté.

Voy-tu pas que Phebus les cherit et embrasse?
Calliope, voyant le parfait de leur grace,
Les pend au saint Autel de l'immortalité.

Pour chanter le parfait qui ton ame decore,
Et couronne ton chef des rameaux verdissans,
Faudroit du Dieu luysant la voix et les accens,
Dignes de la vertu qui ton siecle redore.

Tu invoque la Muse, et la Muse t'honore,
Sçachant combien par toy ses effets sont puissans.
Moy, qui defaux d'esprit, de discours et de sens,
Crainds de souiller ton nom que nostre France adore.

Si tu veux qu'envers toy je face mon devoir,
Preste-moy ton esprit, ta grace, et ton sçavoir:
Et lors je chanteray tes supresmes loüanges.

Mon parler, empenné de ta sainte grandeur,
Fera voir de ton los la divine splendeur
A l'Euphrate et au Nil, au Danube et au Gange.

Let men of virtues rare and eloquence,
Laureled with wisdom and intelligence,
Observe your verses' clarity divine.

See you them not in Phoebus's embrace?
* Calliope, viewing their flawless grace,
Hangs them, immortal, from her holy shrine.

Les missives, "Responses," 3

I need—to sing your flawless soul, I fear—
† Radiant Apollo's voice, dear *demoiselle;*
‡ And, to wreathe you with verdure nonpareil,
The golden words wherewith he lights your sphere.

You call upon the Muse; the Muse, sincere,
Pays you her homage, for she knows how well
You serve her. I—dull, witless, truth to tell—
Fear lest I soil your name, that France holds dear.

If you wish that I praise you as one should,
Lend me your talent, spirit, grace; then would
§ I sing your glorious fame, as skyward soars

Your saint-like grandeur; and, in flight, my tongue
Will extol your celestial splendor, sung
By Danube's, Nile's, Euphrates', Ganges' shores.

Les missives, "Responses," 5

---

* Calliope (the name means "Beautiful Voice") is the muse of epic poetry, devoted, appropriately, to Phoebus Apollo, patron of music and poetry. Ironically, she is best known to us today for having given her name to the tootling circus instrument, a far cry from her artistry.

† This sonnet is addressed to Catherine des Roches; see *Les missives,* ed. Larsen, p. 124. The *Dieu luysant* (shining god) is, of course, Apollo, identified by Roman poets with the sun god, whose Greek epithet Phoebus (or, more properly transliterated, Phoibos), comes from the verb *phaō,* to shine.

‡ Though I tend to recoil at it, I am assured by several dictionaries that, French origins notwithstanding, the word "nonpareil" in English does indeed rhyme as used here.

§ For the scrupulous reader who might take me to task for using an enjambment between stanzas, not found in the original, I would point out that, although she does not do so here, Madeleine has no qualms about doing so in several of her other poems.

J'ayme, j'admire, estime, honore et prise
Ce beau desir en ton cueur allumé,
Qui du sçavoir te rend amy aymé,
Favorisant la vertu tant exquise.

J'ay reveré ta Muse bien aprise,
Qui du saint chœur te rend plus estimé,
D'Orphée aussi le lutz mieux animé,
Dont Apollon cede à ton enterprise.

Mais j'ayme plus ta naïve bonté,
Honte modeste et grand onnesteté,
Qui te fait estre à tous yeux agreable.

Le son, la Muse, et le docte parler,
Ainsi qu'un vent s'esvanoüist par l'air,
Et la vertu est à jamais durable.

CATHERINE

À MA QUENOILLE

Quenoille mon souci, je vous promets et jure
De vous aimer tousjours, et jamais ne changer
Vostre honneur domestic pour un bien estranger,
Qui erre inconstamment et fort peu de temps dure.

I honor, love, esteem that fair desire
That lights your heart and makes you yearn to be
Knowledge's friend much loved, and lovingly
Graced no less with its virtue's glorious fire.

Your muse I prize, muse that the heavenly choir
Admires as well, such that Apollo—he
Of Orphic art the god—would fain decree
You to be master of his lute and lyre,

But more I love your modest mien, your shy
And pure simplicity, that every eye
Delights to see, and looks upon with pleasure.

Your muse, your voice, speech learnèd, debonair,
Blow on the wind, then vanish in the air,
But virtue lasts forever, knows no measure.

Les missives, "Responses," 7

TO MY DISTAFF

Distaff my dear, I promise you and swear
Ever to love you, never to replace
Your household honor and your homely grace
With ware unknown, unsure, fickle as air.

* Tempting as it is to think that this sonnet, like several others, was written for the poet's daughter, there is no hint to whom the "response" was addressed. The masculine form *amy* in line 3 would indicate that it was a male.

† The context here makes clear that, unlike its use elsewhere, *Muse* is to be taken as a common, not proper, noun (i.e., inspiration), and I lower case it accordingly.

‡ Apollo, in his role as patron of music and poetry, is generally associated with a lyre. Since it is a lute that is specifically attributed to him here, I compromise by including both.

Vous ayant au costé je suis beaucoup plus seure
Que si encre et papier se venoient aranger
Tout à l'entour de moy; car pour me revanger
Vous pouvez bien plustost repousser une injure.

Mais quenoille m'amie, il ne faut pas pourtant
Que pour vous estimer, et pour vous aimer tant
Je delaisse du tout cest' honneste coustume

D'escrire quelquefois; en escrivant ainsi,
J'escri de voz valeurs, quenoille mon souci,
Ayant dedans la main, le fuzeau, et la plume.

––––––––––

À MES ESCRITS

Je ne pensay jamais que vous eussiez de force
Pour forcer les efforts de l'oubly, ny du temps.
Aussi je vous escry comme par passe-temps,
Fuyant d'oisiveté la vitieuse amorce.

Et pource mes escrits, nul de vous ne s'efforce
De vouloir me laisser, car je le vous deffens.
Où voudriez-vous aller? He mes petits enfans,
Vous estes abillez d'une si foible escorce.

Je croy que vous pensez me faire quelque honneur
Pour m'emporter aussi, envieux du bon-heur
Que deux freres ont eu portent leur mere au temple:

Lors qu'ell' en demanda digne loyer aux Dieux,
Un sommeil eternel leur vint siler les yeux,
Et cela, mes enfans, vous doit servir d'exemple.

More safe I feel to have you by me, there,
Than ink and paper spread! Were it the case
That even might I some fell danger face,
* One who would do me ill ought well beware.

But, distaff mine, sweet friend, think not that I,
Loving you, prizing you, would fain put by
This honest urge I feel, time and again,

To write; for, when I write—as now I do,
† Writing, distaff my dear, in praise of you—
My hand holds both the spindle and the pen.

———————

TO MY WORKS

Never had I a notion that you might
Have might enough, my works, or might possess
The means, to vanquish time's forgetfulness:
‡ To pass time and flee sloth is why I write.

Therefore let none of you seek to take flight
And quit my side—where would you go?—unless
You would transgress my word. For, I confess,
Ill-clad are you, my dears, and thin-skinned quite!

Off, I think, you would bear me, envious
Of brothers twain, who bore their mother, thus
Honored, unto the temple, joyfully:

When she begged that the Gods their worthiest prize
§ Bestow on them, death's sleep sealed tight their eyes!
Let this, my children an example be.

* In this, her best-known and perhaps most discussed poem, Catherine seems to be
suggesting—though less explicitly in the original than in my translation—that, for all its
domestic virtue, the distaff, basically a pointed stick, could make a convenient weapon
should the need arise.

† The reader will appreciate that my seemingly careless repetition of "write" and "writ-
ing" is intentional, as is, no doubt, Catherine's use of *escrire, escrivant,* and *escri.*

‡ Regarding my blatant repetitions of "might" and "time," see the previous poem, note
to line 13, on Catherine's similar wordplay.

§ Larsen explains the allusion in her critical edition of *Les œuvres.* According to Herod-
otus and Plutarch, the mother of Cleobis and Biton prayed the goddess Hera to grant her
sons the greatest possible happiness. Hera's reply was to grant them eternal sleep.

IMITATION DE LA MÈRE DE SALOMON, À LA ROINE MÈRE DU ROY

Quelle chose, mon fils, ma nourriture chere,
Entendras-tu de moy, de moy qui suis ta mere?
Je ne puis te laisser qu'un brief enseignement,
Qui pour ta Royauté servira d'ornement:
Car d'un Prince excellent l'ame prudente et sage
Ayme plus les vertus que son riche heritage.
Doncques, souvienne-toy qu'il faut que les grands Rois
Commandant à leur peuple obeissent aux loix.
Et tiens dedans ta main la balance equitable,
Veu que ton premier jour l'a faict recommendable,
Pource que le soleil la regardoit voisin,
Alors que tu naquis souz un heureux destin.
Mais tu dois commencer d'observer la Justice
En toy-mesme, et tousjours fermer la porte au vice,
Ne laisser point tirer tes desirs par les yeux,
Et ne donner ton bien pour estre vicieux,
Suyvant les faux appas d'une impudique flame
De craincte d'offencer ta legitime femme:
Car se seroit manquer à Dieu, aux loix, à toy,
Et parjurer l'autel de luy faucer la foy;
Qui sent d'un autre feu l'amoureuse scintille
Est en danger d'avoir une espouse sterile,

* **TO THE QUEEN MOTHER, IN IMITATION OF
KING SOLOMON'S MOTHER'S ADVICE**

What would you have me say, dear progeny?
My son, what would you wish to hear from me,
Your mother, who but little can instruct
Your Highness, that with grace you may conduct
The realm's affairs? For, Prince well-met and wise
Will more his virtues than his riches prize.
Remember that great kings, though they command,
Must harken to the laws that rule the land.
Hold in your hand the scales of justice, sign
Celestial, for, by heavenly design,
† You were born with the sun in Libra; thus
Is yours a steadfast fate, and prosperous.
To Justice must you pay respect within
Your heart; never fling wide the door to sin,
Nor ever let your eyes your flesh entice,
Nor spend your wealth in search of worldly vice,
Letting a lustful passion lead you on
To faithless trumpery, lest, thereupon,
You should your lawful wife offend unduly.
Your God would you offend no less, and, truly,
Even yourself, and Law as well: man dooms
‡ His wives, thereby, to barren, fruitless wombs,

---

* The inspiration for this poem, as Larsen indicates (*Les œuvres*, p. 324), is to be found
in the Proverbs of Solomon (31:1–9), in which the mother of Lemuel, an otherwise shad-
owy king of an unidentified country, offers him her advice. (Most scholars, assuming
Lemuel to be a fiction or a linguistic artifact referring to Solomon—the name means "de-
voted to God"—attribute the work to Solomon himself.) Larsen cites a number of other
ancient and medieval works of the same genre, among them the *Enseignemens moraux* of
Christine de Pizan (see pp. 74–82 above). For my translation from Robert de Blois's late
thirteenth-century *Le chastoiement des dames* (Advice to Ladies), see *The Comedy of Eros*,
pp. 63–84. The same medieval author also produced the similar *L'enseignement des princes*
(Advice to Princes) dating from 1280. Catherine's own adaptations of Erasmus (see pp.
194–201 below) partake of the same didactic inspiration.

† This biographical detail is apparently accurate. Henri III, the king in question, was
born in September 1551, under the sign of Libra. See Larsen, pp. 324–25.

‡ I don't know any statistics on adultery and sterility in the Middle Ages, but this super-
stition that the one caused the other probably indicates a prevalence of both.

Et ne voir de longtemps les regards blandissans
Ny les soubsris mignards de ses petits enfans.
Je ne te priray point de te garder de boire
Le breuvage fumeux qui gaste la memoire;
Je sçay que ta raison garde le souvenir
De ce qui est passé, jugeant de l'advenir.
Mais je te priray bien d'ayder à l'innocence
Des pauvres affligez qui n'ont point de deffence.
Je te supplie encor de fuyr prontement
Des propos depravez le traistre enchantement;
Regarde si celuy qui pend à ton oreille
Est digne d'estre ouy en ce qu'il te conseille;
Qui sçait bien gouverner par ordre en sa maison
Il peut bien conseiller un prince avec raison.
Mon fils, tu es des tiens l'espoir et le refuge,
Ils n'ont que Dieu au Ciel, toy en terre pour juge;
Pense avant que dire, et juge sagement
Puisque tout obeit à ton commandement.
Pour nuyre à tes voisins ne dresse point d'armée;
Et que sert-il de voir nostre terre semée
De tant de corps humains? Qui fait guerre à autruy,
Il sent premierement la guerre dedans luy.
Tu ne dois pas pourtant supporter l'insolence
Des hommes corrompus qui sont sous ta puissance;
Sans te monstrer vers eux, ny severe, ny doux,
Il les faut chastier en ton juste courroux;
Un Roy n'est estimé pour estre plus robuste,
Ou plus jeune, ou plus beau, mais pour estre plus juste.
Dieu vueille mon enfant qu'un Laurier verdissant
Entourne pour jamais ton sceptre fleurissant,
Et qu'il soit ceint aussi par les branches d'Olives,
Afin que plusieurs ans paisiblement tu vives.

Never to know the tender blandishments
Of his posterity, year by year hence.
I need not caution you to shun that drinking
That clouds the memory and dulls the thinking.
I know your reason rightly governs you:
Born of the past, it lights the future too.
Yet shall I pray that you be kind to those,
Defenseless in their innocence, whom woes
Falsely afflict; and beg you promptly flee
The lure of treacherous tongues' depravity.
Lend not an ear to such as hang about,
Proffering much advice, unless no doubt
Is there that they be worthy to be heard:
Even a prince may heed the reasoned word
Of one who rules his house in ordered guise.
My son, your subjects turn their hopeful eyes
To you for solace: God in heaven have they,
And you on earth, as judges, to obey
In every wise. Think carefully, therefore,
Before you render judgment. Furthermore,
Raise not an army every time you would
Do harm unto your neighbor; for, what good
Is there, and what can be the earthly boon,
To see our land with broken bodies strewn,
The country round? He who makes war, abhorrent,
Wars much within himself as well, I warrant.
Nevertheless, you must not tolerate
The insolence of those, foes of the state,
Who live lives base, corrupt: be not austere
Nor gentle with them; rather, persevere
To let your worthy wrath put them to rights.
It is not kingly vigor that excites
Mankind's esteem, nor how young, nor how fair
Of feature, but how just! God hear my prayer,
Grant that your scepter ever be entwined
With laurel leaf and olive branch combined,
My son, so that you reign in glorydom,
And live in blessèd peace, long years to come.

À G. P.

Vous dictes que je vends ces vers à leurs hautesses.
Non, je ne les vend point; le present est entier.
Car je proteste Dieu que Princes ny Princesses
Ne m'ont jamais donné la valeur d'un denier.

─────────

MÉDÉE

Fuyez, Dames, fuyez l'amoureuse pointure,
Tirez un doux salut de ma peine tant dure;
Beautez, grandeurs, tresors, herbes, enchantemens,
Ne sçeurent alleger mes ennuieux tourmens;
Je fus Roine, et forçay les estoilles hautaines,
Mais le tyran amour triompha de mes peines,
Et voulant m'affranchir de son cruel esmoy,
Je tuay pere, frere, espoux, enfans, et moy.

─────────

CLITEMNESTRE

Oreste, furieux pour la mort de son pere,
Voulant rougir la terre aux despens de sa mere,
Delaissa promptement l'accoustrement royal
Qui ornoit la beauté de son corps desloyal;

FOR G. P. *

You say I write because Their Highnesses
Pay for my verses. No! God knows, not true!
They are my gifts: Princes nor Princesses
† Have ever paid me even half a *sou!*

‡ MEDEA

Flee, ladies, flee love's passion-pointed sting,
And draw redemption from my suffering:
Beauty, rank, potions, wealth, enchantments—none
Could ease the torments of my soul undone.
I was a queen, the stars obeyed my whim;
But tyrant Love bound me in thrall to him.
Seeking to break my bonds, I killed, pell-mell:
Father, mate, brother, babes . . . Myself as well.

§ CLYTEMNESTRA

Orestes, furious that his sire lay dead,
Wishing his mother's blood to color red
The earth therefor, stripped off the royal dress
That garbed her treacherous body's loveliness;

---

* The addressee of this epigram is unknown, according to Larsen, who discusses it in her edition of *Les missives*, pp. 46–47. She calls attention to a similar denial of financial motivation in Louise Labé's "Elégie III," line 24. See *Les œuvres*, p. 327.

† The original has "la valeur d'un denier," which was, in effect, the twelfth part of a *sou*, but for purposes of translation such exactitude hardly seems necessary.

‡ This epitaph and the three following, on classical female figures, are translated by Catherine from the Italian of Bernardo Accolti (1465–1536). See *Les œuvres*, ed. Larsen, pp. 342–46, where the originals also are given.

§ The adulterous Clytemnestra, with her lover Aegisthus, was responsible for the murder of Orestes' father, Agamemnon, upon his return from the Trojan War.

Quand elle, regardant sa dextre furieuse
Avec le fer trenchant, luy dist en voix piteuse:
Veux-tu frapper mon fils, ou mon sein, ou mon flanc?
De l'un tu pris le laict, et de l'autre le sang.

––––––––––

LUCRÈCE

Le pauvre Colatin, voyant sa triste femme,
Disoit: chere Lucrece, appaise ta douleur,
La coulpe ne tient point à ceste gentille ame;
Si ton corps est pollu tu as un chaste cueur.
Refusant ses raisons, la courageuse Dame
Luy dist, perdant la vie: il faut sauver l'honneur,
Tu m'absous, je me juge à la trenchante lame,
Ne pleure point ma mort, mais pleure ton mal-heur.

––––––––––

NIOBÉ

Je suis Niobé: helas! plaignez mon adventure!
Mon sort est miserable, et digne de pitié.
Sept filles, et sept fils me donna la nature,
J'en perdis en un jour l'une et l'autre moitié.

Whereat, seeing his right hand holding high
The trenchant blade, she asked, with piteous cry:
"Where would you strike? My breast? My womb? Which one?
* One gave you milk, the other, blood, my son."

---

† **LUCRETIA**

Poor Collatinus, to his ravished wife,
Said: "Sweet Lucretia, grieve not. Though despoiled,
Your noble soul deserves nor blame nor strife.
Chaste is your heart though much your flesh be soiled."
She spurned his reasoning and, unafraid,
Dying, replied: "Your pardon, thus, will not
Redeem my honor: I must choose the blade.
Weep not my death, weep but your luckless lot."

NIOBE

Niobe am I: pity my despair
And mourn my misery, my grievous state.
Seven sons, seven daughters did I bear,
And in one day lost all! Disconsolate,

* Catherine's version, with its reference to milk and blood, is rather more graphically anatomical than the original, in which Accolti says simply: "L'un ti nutri, ne l'altro ti portai" (One nourished you, the other bore you).

† According to legend, Lucretia, renowned for her chastity, chose death rather than dishonor after being raped by the son of the Roman king Tarquinius Superbus. Shakespeare immortalized her suicide in *The Rape of Lucrece* (1594):
Poor hand why quiverst thou at this decree?
Honour thyself to rid me of this shame
It was as a result of this regal infamy that the Romans exiled the Tarquins and rejected kingship altogether.

Le marbre est maintenant du marbre sepulture;
Ainsi le veut du Ciel la fiere inimitié;
Je fus Roine, et suis marbre; or dessoubs ceste terre,
Passant, tu n'y verras que la pierre en la pierre.

FROM *VERS DOREZ* DE PYTHAGORE

I

Adorez humblement les grands Dieux Eternelz,
Ensuyvant du pays la forme coutumiere:
Reverez de la Foy la vertu singuliere,
Qui unit les humains avec les immortelz.

III

Laissez-vous attirez aux propos gracieux,
Suyvez l'enseignement d'une sage parole,
Et ne permettez point qu'une cause frivole
Vous rende vos amis prontement odieux.

XII

Vivez honnestement sans superfluité,
Rendez-vous la Fortune heureusement amie,
N'attirez contre vous le venin de l'Envie,
Suyvez de la Vertu le mediocrité

To marble turned, in marble tomb's repair
I lie. Thus hateful Heaven decrees my fate.
Queen was I once, now marble! Passerby,
* Beneath this stone, only a stone am I.

---

† FROM *GOLDEN VERSES* OF PYTHAGORAS

I
Worship the Gods Eternal, loftymost,
Humbly, as in the manner of the land:
Revere Faith's special power that, hand in hand,
Joins humankind with the immortal host.

III
Be drawn to gracious talk, comely, polite;
Follow the teachings wrought of wise advice,
And let no trivial matter, in a trice,
Render good friends unseemly in your sight.

XII
Live your life decently, without excess,
Accept Fate as your comrade, happily;
Attract not poison-venomed Jealousy:
Follow the mean that leads to virtuousness.

* As Ovid recounts in book 6 of the *Metamorphoses*, the overweening maternal pride of Niobe, queen of Thebes and essence of motherhood, offended Hera, who punished her not only by killing all her children but also by turning her to stone. Her fate is immortalized—ironically enough, in stone—in one of the best-known statues of antiquity; and Lord Byron, in *Childe Harold*, uses her as a metaphor for the degradation of latter-day Rome: "The Niobe of nations! There she stands, / Childless and crownless in her voiceless woe; / An empty urn within her withered hands, / Whose holy dust was scattered long ago" (4.79).

† Concerning the general and specific bibliographical and exegetical details of Catherine des Roches's adaptations of Pythagoras's *Golden Verses* and his rather more hermetic *Symbols* (or *Enigmas*), both more than likely by way of Erasmus, see Larsen's introduction to her edition of *Les secondes œuvres*, pp. 26–39, and her authoritative notes to the individual quatrains (pp. 112–42).

XIII

L'on ne se doit jamais promptement avancer
De causer un effet qui apporte dommage;
En tous deportements l'homme prudent et sage
Va prevoyant la fin avant le commancer.

XVIII

L'homme le plus souvent cause de sa douleur,
Se lamente, se deut de ce qui luy est proche,
Ignorant bien et mal tousjours il fait reproche
Aux Astres, les nommant artisans de malheur.

XXII

Inspirez-nous aussi, supréme Deité,
Que nous puissions par vous reconnoistre les choses
Dans les cercles des Cieux songneusement encloses,
Observant en leurs cours un ordre limité.

XXIII

Si ce bien doit venir par revelations,
Il nous faut sobrement abstenir de tout vivre
Dont je deffens l'usage, et rendre plus delivre
Le Cors de ses humeurs, l'Esprit de passions.

XXIV

Comme le feu luysant eslongne le tison
Pour s'eslever en haut, delaissants la depouille
De ce cors imparfait qui nous corront et souille,
Divins, nous laisserons la mortelle prison.

———————

FROM *ÉNIGMES* DU MESME AUTEUR

I

Ne recherchez jamais les chemins frequentez,
Pour vous guider au temple, ains suivez une trace
Qui vous retire loing de la vulgaire place,
Et des profanes lieux impudemment hantez.

XIII

To cause results distressing and chagrining
Let no one be too quick; for circumspect
And sage is he who foresees the effect
Of what he does, indeed, before beginning.

XVIII

Cause of his own misfortunes, yet will man
Reproach the Stars as authors of all ill:
Of good and evil knowing naught, he will
Place all the blame on anything he can.

XXII

Inspire us, O supreme Divinity,
That through you we may learn what lies within
The heavenly orbs, enclosed with care therein,
As we their course observe, fixed, orderly.

XXIII

And if that boon is properly to be
Revealed, then must we from that life abstain,
Wisely, that I decry, and let remain
Flesh cleansed of humors, Spirit passion-free.

XXIV

Like flames leaving behind the firebrands' glow,
Rising aloft, so too, divine, shall we,
Quitting our flesh's foul impurity,
Our bodies' mortal prison leave below.

———————

* **FROM *ENIGMAS* OF THE SAME AUTHOR**

I

When you repair to church, pray you refrain
From treading paths trod by the vulgar masses.
Rather, seek out the worthy road that passes
Far from those places common, base, profane.

* See note, p. 195.

IV

Tout ce que l'on dira des ouvrages parfaitz
De la Divinité, croiez l'aussi de mesme;
L'on ne voit rien de bon, de beau, ny de supréme,
Que Dieu ne soit tosjours cause de tels effaictz.

V

Ne rongnez pas vostre ongle aupres de l'Autel saint,
Mais priez ardamment, ayant une pensée
Craintive poursuivant l'oraison commencée;
Dieu ayme volontiers cetuy-là qui le craint.

VIII

Dieu celeste est sans pair, il n'a point de pareil,
Pource le nombre impair luy est plus agreable
Que ne sera jamais le nombre divisable,
Appartenant aux Dieux qui n'ont point de Soleil.

XI

Ne jettez la viande en un vaisseau polu,
Ne vueillez pas semer une belle sentence
En un esprit gasté de vice et d'ignorance,
Qui est en son erreur folement resolu.

XV

N'essayez d'entailler la figure de Dieu
En Bague, ny joyau, veu qu'il est toute forme;
Vous ne pouvez rien voir à sa grandeur conforme,
Ny renfermer celuy qui renferme tout lieu.

XIX

Ne regardez jamais au dedans du miroir,
Le soir, quand vous avez une foible lumiere.
Vostre œil, perdant des Cieux la clarté coutumiere
Ne juge ce qu'il voit, mais ce qu'il pense voir.

XXIII

Si vous avez des biens, des honneurs, des estatz,
Ayez des heritiers: mais c'est une misere,
Estant pauvre indigent de s'ouïr pere
Par un peuple d'Enfans qui sont noüez si bas.

IV

Harken to talk of God, always agreeing
With praise for the Divinity's perfection:
Naught is most fine, most fair, that, on inspection,
He has, himself, not brought forth into being.

V

Bite not your nails before the holy altar;
Rather, pray keenly, follow ardently
The prayers intoned, and ever fearful be:
God loves who, fearing him, nor flinch nor falter.

VIII

God in his heaven, alone, is one, and thus
Loves numbers indivisible; for he
Favors not that divisibility
Proper to demons in realms tenebrous.

XI

Cast not your meat into a filthy pot,
Nor sow wise counsel in a mind unfit—
Too base and stupid to do aught with it—
That clings to vice and folly, spurns them not.

XV

Try not, in ring or gem, to etch God's face;
Too vast, indeed, is his immensity
To be contained therein: he cannot be
Contained, who holds the world in his embrace.

XIX

Gaze in the mirror not by night; you err
If such you do: when dim the light, your eyes
See, as day's bright rays vanish from the skies,
Not what you are, but what you wish you were.

XXIII

If you have wealth, and rank, and property,
Have heirs; if poor, have none: woeful it is
To hear oneself called "Father mine" by his
Vast host of children chained to misery.

* The sense of this line is clear despite the fact that, in the modern edition at least, it apparently lacks a two-syllable infinitive after *s'ouïr*, possibly *clamer* or *nommer* (to name).

XXXVIII

Quand vous offrez du vin dessus l'Autel des Dieux,
Au moins qu'il ne soit pas d'une vigne sauvage:
Si le Ciel liberal vous donne ce breuvage,
Honorez d'un labeur ce dous present des Cieux.

XL

Ne blamez la Couronne, ains reverez les Roys,
Car ilz sont Lieutenantz du celeste Monarque:
Dieu grave sur leurs fronds sa veritable marque,
Et fait plier leurs cueurs soubz le vent de sa vois.

XLII

Ne vueillez point tuer les innocents poissons
Qui demeurent segretz dans leurs ondes tranquilles,
Ilz ne vont ravageant vos campagnes fertiles,
Ny n'emportent jamais le bien de vos maisons.

XLV

Estant pres de la fin, ne vous estonnez pas,
Attendez constamment le cizeau de la Parque;
Ne craignez point d'entrer dans la fatale Barque,
L'Ame, ny le renom ne sentent le trespas.

PRIÈRE AVANT LE REPAS

Nourrissez-nous des biens que vostre main produit,
O pere Souverain, que cete compaignie
Desirant ardamment vostre grace infinie,
Gouste par vive foy le perdurable fruit.

XXXVIII

At the gods' altar, when you offer wine,
Let it come from a vine well cultivated:
Honor them with your labors, consecrated
In thanks to them for this sweet gift divine.

XL

Rail not against the Crown: kings are God's choice
For his lieutenants; thus he marks their brows
With his sign unmistakable, and bows
Their hearts beneath his mighty breath and voice.

XLII

Kill not the fish, peaceful and innocent,
That, hidden, live beneath the waves; they lay
Not waste your lush and fertile fields, and they
Rob not your houses, rich and opulent.

XLV

Be not undone, sensing your final breath,
* Life's end: let Atropos cut short your thread.
Calmly attend; face not the Styx with dread:
Your soul and your renown know naught of death.

————————

† **PRAYER BEFORE THE MEAL**

Let your hand's bounty feed this company,
O sovereign father, and grant us your favor,
That we, seeking your boundless grace, may savor
Its fruits, in living faith, eternally.

---

* In this last of the *Enigmes*, the classical allusions are particularly in evidence: Atropos, the Fate who cuts the thread of life; the barque of Charon that transported dead souls across the river Styx; and, finally, the Roman concept of *gloria*, the renown that transcends death.

† For references to other Renaissance pre- and post-prandial "grace and thanksgiving" verses in the spirit of this and the following quatrain, see *Secondes œuvres*, ed. Larsen, p. 143n1.

PRIÈRE APRÈS LE REPAS

Dieu, qui fistes pleuvoir sur Israël la mane,
Quand dedans les Desertz il languissoit de fain,
Eslongnez de nos cœurs tout vain desir profane,
Nourrissant nos Esprits par le celeste pain.

SUR LA PERTE D'UN COLLET

Collet, mon cher mignon, que j'ay autant aimé
Comme mes propres yeux, faloit-il que je fisse
De ta perfection si piteux sacrifice?
Faloit-il que par moy tu fusses consommé?

Collet, mon cher mignon, helas! j'ay alumé
Le feu qui t'a brulé, mais ce n'est de malice,
Car reconnoissant bien ton fidelle service,
Je t'ay sur tous colletz cherement estimé.

Collet, mon cher mignon, si tes beautez perdues
Se pouvoyent recouvrer par larmes espandues,
Tu revivrois encor, et la bourrelle main,

Pauvre, qui t'a destruit, te donneroit pour gage
Mon col, ton prisonnier: mais helas! c'est en vain
Que je pleure ta perte, et mon trop grand dommage.

O Belle Main, qui l'arc et les fléches ordonne,
Et les flambeaux ardans de mon cruel Seigneur,
Belle Main dont il prend aide, force, et valleur,
Pour garder son pouvoir, son sceptre, et sa couronne.

PRAYER AFTER THE MEAL

God, who to starving Israel had given
Manna, when she lay lost in desert waste,
Cast from our hearts all vain desire unchaste,
And feed our spirits with the bread of heaven.

ON THE LOSS OF A LACE COLLAR

Lace collar mine, my sweet! O filigree!
You, dearest pet, you, apple of my eye!
Why laid I waste your fair perfection? Why
Had you to be consumed because of me?

Lace collar mine, my sweet! Unthinkingly
I lit the flame that laid you low! Ay, ay!
Of all my collars, you, most staunch ally,
Most honored were, as loved as loved could be.

Lace collar mine, my sweet! If my tears could
Bring back your beauty—fled, alas!—then would
You live anew; and this destructive hand

That did you in, poor dear, would let you take
My neck as hostage! But in vain I stand
Weeping your loss, and—ah!—my fell mistake.

* O beauteous hand that bends my Liege's bow,
That shoots his arrows, brands of flaming fire;
That vests my conquering, crowned and sceptered Sire
With strength to ply his cruel power here below.

* Larsen convincingly suggests (*Secondes œuvres*, p. 347n) that this sonnet is an adaptation of one by the Italian poet Giovanni Mozzarello ("O bella man, che'l fren del carro tieni"). This would help explain the curious gender ambivalence of the possessor of the hand apostrophized by our poet, that of a "cruel Seigneur" but at the same time displaying all the qualities of a traditional lady love.

O delicate Main qui à toute personne
Dérobes doucement l'Esprit, l'Ame, et le Cueur,
Belle Main qui conduis le Char du Dieu vainqueur,
Range ses ailes d'Or et sa trousse luy donne.

O excellente Main de Roses et de Lys,
De nege, yvoire, argent, de perles precieuses,
O Main de quy les doys delicatz et polys

Maintiennent de Venus les pompes glorieuses,
O Main, sans vos atraitz de Graces embellys,
L'on verroit sans éfet toutes Loix Amoureuses.

O dainty hand that gulls all mankind, so
That it may filch Mind, Soul, and Heart entire;
That drives Love's chariot—godling of desire!
Give him his darts, tidy his wings aglow.

O wondrous Hand, of lily and of rose,
Of precious pearl, snow, silver, ivory white;
O Hand, whose fingers, set in tender pose,

Serve Venus in her revels, wrought aright;
* O Hand, without your charms that grace bestows,
Bootless would be Love's laws, and fruitless quite.

* Hard to explain is the sudden shift to the formal *vos* when the intimate second-person
verb forms have been used up to this point. The informal *tes* would not affect the meter.

Catherine des Roches 205

Anne de Marquets (1533?–1588)

The religious lyrics of Sœur Anne de Marquets are at least partially the result of the devastating wars of religion that divided France in the late sixteenth century. An ardent champion of the Catholic cause, she first expressed her devotion in her allegorical *Son(n)ets, prières et devises*, addressed to the ecclesiastics convened at Poissy in 1561 in an attempt to calm the theological waters and published the next year, dedicated to the cardinal of Lorraine. A second edition followed in 1566. Marquets also, in 1568, published a translation of the neo-Latin religious verse of the Italian poet Marc'Antonio Flaminio (1498–1550), who reputedly sacrificed a papal secretaryship at age seventeen by rejecting the homosexual advances of Pope Leo X. "La Belle Religieuse," as she was called, is best known, however, for her *Son(n)ets spirituels*, published posthumously in 1605, from which all the poems given below are taken. Written throughout her life, even during the blindness that struck her in middle age, the 480 sonnets of this collection are arranged in groupings appropriate to the offices of each Sunday and other important dates of the Church calendar. The subjects, taken from the Bible and the Gospels, range from the horrors of hell to the delights of paradise.[1]

Marquets was born in Normandy of a noble family and spent her life, from early childhood until her death in 1588, at the convent of Poissy, near Saint-Germain-en-Laye, in the prestigious Dominican order (probably thanks to family ties), in which she took the veil in 1548 or 1549. Few other concrete facts of her life are known, probably owing to an understandable dearth of recordable events. One event, however, does stand out: namely, her probable meeting with Ronsard and his Pléiade colleague Jean Dorat, a virtual certainty according to one source.[2] Her devotion to "the Prince of Poets" and his influence on her work are clear. It can be seen, in the seven sonnets translated here, that she was most skillful in adapting to the demands of her devotional inspiration the sonnet form that Ronsard had perfected in the service of a more worldly passion.[3]

NOTES

1. For a modern critical edition, see *Anne de Marquets: Sonets spirituels*, ed. Gary Ferguson. The original 1605 edition was titled *Sonets spirituels de feue très-vertueuse et très-docte Dame Sr. Anne de Marquets, Religieuse à Poissy, sur les Dimanches et principales solennitez de l'année*. No less typically verbose are the titles of the two other works not published in modern editions: *Sonets, prières et devises en forme de pasquins pour l'assemblée de messieurs, tenue à Poissy* and *Les divines poésies de Marc-Antoine Flaminius, avec plusieurs Sonnets & Cantiques ou Chansons spirituelles pour louer Dieu*.

2. See *Anne de Marquets: Sonets spirituels*, ed. Ferguson, 22.

3. The following are studies of Marquets's works: Sister Mary Hilarine Seiler, *Anne de Marquets, poétesse religieuse du XVIe siècle*, and Gary Ferguson, *The Feminisation of Devotion: Gabrielle de Coignard, Anne de Marquets, and François de Sales*. See also Léon Feugère's venerable *Les femmes poètes au XVIe siècle*, pp. 63–66, and Terence Cave, *Devotional Poetry in France, c. 1570–1613*, pp. 85–86, 196–97, and passim.

J'admire du grand Dieu l'eternelle puissance
Qui de rien a basti tout ce triple univers,
Et voyant si bel ordre en tant de corps divers,
Je n'admire pas moins sa haute sapience.
Mais j'admire sur tout son extreme clemence
Et sa grande douceur (argument de mes vers),
Que voulant rachepter les meschans et pervers,
Il ait daigné vestir nostre humaine substance.
Hé, que n'ay-je la grace, ayant la volonté,
De rendre dignement par ma Muse chanté
Un mystere si sainct, si haut et admirable!
Pour le moins mon essay sur si digne subject
Sera plaisant à Dieu, et à moy honorable,
Puisque la volonté est prise pour l'effect.

Quand un pauvre captif, accablé de tourment,
Entend dire pour vray qu'un Roy plein de clemence
Viendra de liberté luy donner jouissance,
O que ceste venue il desire ardemment!
Ainsi ce genre humain, sçachant asseurément
Que le grand Roy du Ciel, prenant nostre substance,
Le viendroit delivrer de misere et souffrance,
Sans cesse desiroit ce sainct advenement.
C'est pourquoy si souvent les bons anciens peres
Crioyent: Vien, Seigneur, vien, et ne tarde plus guieres,
Vien rachepter ton peuple et l'oster de prison;
Hé, pleust à ta bonté que les cieux tu rompisses,
Forcé d'extreme amour, et que tu descendisses!
Car ta presence donne à tous maux guerison.

———————

I wonder at great God's eternal might
* That built this threefold universe from naught,
Nor wonder less that His wisdom has wrought
Such diverse things, yet set them all aright.
But most of all I wonder—and delight—
At His compassion, tender, mercy-fraught;
That, deigning to take human form, He sought
To save the wicked (wherefore do I write).
Ah! might my Muse—since well have I the will—
Graciously sing, and more worthily still,
This sacred, lofty, wondrous mystery!
At least my pains, on worthy subject spent,
Will pleasing be to God, and honor me:
The will shall equal the accomplishment!

†   "Pour le premier dimanche de l'Advent," I

———————

Should a poor captive, wracked by torment, learn
That, truly, comes a King, whose clemency
Will grant to him the joys of liberty,
Ah! For that coming how his heart will burn!
In such wise did mankind, unceasing, yearn,
Sure that the King of Heaven, great monarch He,
Would come deliver man from misery,
Taking our form for His holy sojourn.
Thus, often, did the blessèd ones of old
Cry: "Come, Lord! Pray you not your self withhold!
Redeem your people, held in bondage still!
Descend, in your great goodness, from above,
Bursting the bounds of heaven with untold love:
For, by your presence, cure you every ill."

                "Pour le premier dimanche de l'Advent," III

    * I suspect that the *triple univers* of the original refers to the world's supposed composition of earth, air, and water.

    † Marquets provides a number of sonnets for each of the Sundays of Advent: ten for the first, and four each for the second, third, and fourth. See also *Sonets spirituels*, ed. Ferguson, p. 90n.

Au temps que Jesus-Christ voulut prendre naissance,
Cesar Auguste feit un expres mandement
Que la description fut faicte entierement
De tous ceux qui estoyent sous son obeissance:
Signifiant qu'un Roy d'eternelle puissance,
Prenant un corps humain, venoit expressément
Pour enroller les siens, à fin qu'heureusement
De son regne eternel ils eussent jouissance.
Or si à ce grand Roy nous voulons protester
Nostre humble servitude, il luy faut presenter
Le fidelle tribut et du corps et de l'ame:
C'est qu'il faut exercer en bon œuvre le corps,
De vertus orner l'ame, et en jetter dehors
Peché, qui seul la rend mal-heureuse et infame.

Herodes mal-heureux, pourquoy crains-tu si fort
Ce petit Roy nouveau qui ne fait que de naistre,
Et qui ne vient expres passible et mortel estre
Que pour donner à tous salut, ayde et confort?
Tant s'en faut que par guerre et martial effort
Il vueille aux rois oster la couronne et le sceptre,
Qu'il se veult, bien qu'il soit de tous Seigneur et maistre,
Rendre vil et abject, jusqu'à souffrir la mort.
Luy, qui vient pour donner le Royaume celeste,
Voudroit-il usurper le terrestre et mondain?
C'est luy qui nous apprend la vie humble et modeste,
Et qui ha tout orgueil en mespris et desdain:
Ne crains donc qu'en ton regne il te soit successeur,
Mais bien de tes mesfaits le juste punisseur.

When Jesus Christ decided that it was
Time to be born, Caesar Augustus sent
Word that be counted all those resident
In his domain, and subject to his laws:
A King of might eternal was the cause,
Coming, in human form, to choose those meant
Ever to glory in His reign, content
In its perfection, with nor faults nor flaws.
Now, if we wish to prove our fealty,
Humbly, to this great King, surely must we
Faithfully pledge our souls and bodies; thus,
Our bodies must we use for naught but good,
And from our souls, virtue-adorned, we should
Cast out the sin that it finds odious.

"Du jour de Noël," XLI

Poor Herod, why must you be so distressed?
Why fear this infant King, newborn, and who,
Able to suffer death, comes hereunto
Only to soothe and save us, sore oppressed?
So little does He seek, by arms, to wrest
Kings' crowns and scepters, that, though He can do
Anything that He choose, as Lord, know you
That lowly will He die, vile, dispossessed.
Would He who comes heaven's Kingdom to bestow,
Who looks on human pride with contumely,
Teaches a life of humble modesty,
Wish to usurp earth's kingdom here below?
Fear not that He covet your throne's succession,
But that He chasten your every transgression.

"Pour le Jour des Rois," LXIX

* "Le Jour des Rois" (The Day of the Kings) is a common name for the Feast of the
Epiphany, celebrated on January 6.

Le jeusne est tres-utile à macerer le corps,
Mais ne pensons qu'à Dieu il puisse estre agreable,
Si nostre volonté est fiere et indomtable,
Et si nous ne fuyons les noises et discords.
La musique ne plaist que pour les bons accords:
Ayons donc entre nous une paix desirable;
Usons envers autruy de pitié secourable,
Et de cela sur tout soyons tousjours records.
Mesmes pour bien jeusner (qu'à ceste chose on pense),
Ce que nous mangerions, n'estoit ceste abstinence,
Ne doibt estre espargné pour croistre nos moyens,
Mais pour le disperser à ceux qui ont disette:
Qui en use autrement, quoy qu'en avant il mette,
N'a pas esgard à Dieu, mais seulement aux biens.

Puisque nous avons tant de cruels ennemis,
Dont la ruse et l'effort est presque insuperable,
Comme avons-nous le cœur si lasche et miserable
De demeurer tousjours en paresse endormis?
Veu mesme qu'aux vainqueurs le Seigneur a promis,
En son regne eternel, un loyer admirable:
Au contraire, aux enfers, un tourment perdurable
A ceux qui se seront en proye aux vices mis?
De surmonter Sathan que chacun donc s'efforce,
Rejettons de la chair et du monde l'amorce;
Combatons hardiment, armez de vive foy,
D'esperance et d'amour, et ne perdons constance,
Car Dieu ne faudra point de nous faire assistance.
Le soldat prend courage, estant pres de son roy.

Comme la rose naist d'une branche espineuse,
Ainsi ce jour nasquit de Judée une fleur
De si rare beauté, de si grande valeur,
Que la Deité mesme en devint amoureuse.

Fast mortifies the flesh most usefully,
But think we not it pleases God unless
We cleanse our will of pride and stubbornness,
And from discord and strife fail not to flee.
Music is pleasing for its harmony:
Amongst ourselves, then, let us peace possess,
And, to our fellows, charity profess,
Forgetting never that so must it be.
And, to fast well (if we should think thereon),
Our abstinence ought not become, anon,
A means to save our wealth and spend it not,
Which must be given freely to the poor;
Say what he may, who does this not, for sure,
Spurns God and thinks but of his worldly lot.

"Pour le premier jour de quaresme," CV

Since many a cruel enemy have we,
Whose crafty wiles defeat and lay us low,
How can our hearts lie ever idle so,
Lulled in our cravenness and infamy?
When the Lord pledged that the victorious be
Lodged in His glory's endless reign; and, oh!
When Hell's eternal pain He would bestow
On those who yield to vile iniquity?
Thus must we subdue Satan, evil-rife,
And scorn the lure of worldly, fleshly life,
Armed with a living faith, endeavoring,
Boldly, with love and hope, and constant ever;
For God will help us and forsake us never.
Brave grows the soldier standing by his king.

"Pour le premier dimanche de quaresme," CVII

As blooms, upon a thorny branch, the rose,
So, in Judea, was there born this day
A flower of worth and beauty such that, yea,
To crown it with His love the Godhead chose.

Anne de Marquets 213

Par ceste fleur, j'entens la Vierge bien-heureuse,
De laquelle disoit le souverain Seigneur:
Des filles de Sion m'amie est tout l'honneur,
C'est entre les piquants la rose gracieuse.
Sur ceste fleur tomba une liqueur des cieux,
Qui si bien l'arrousa de tout heur et de grace,
Que d'elle en fin sortit un miel delicieux
Qui la douce ambrosie et le nectar surpasse,
Et qui, seul repoussant de tout vice le fiel,
Repaist tous les esleus en la terre et au ciel.

By that flower, I the Virgin blest propose,
Of whom the sovereign Lord was wont to say:
"Of Zion's daughters, none more honored, nay!
 * The rose is she, that midst the brambles grows."
Heaven-sent, a liquor glorified and graced
This bloom, spreading so well its drops divine
That from it honey sprang, of wondrous taste,
Sweeter than nectar and ambrosia fine,
And which, alone, casting out evil's gall,
Nurtures the chosen—heaven's, earth's—one and all.

"Pour la nativité Nostre Dame," CCCLI

---

  * As Gary Ferguson points out in his critical edition of the *Sonets spirituels*, p. 294, quoting from the Catholic liturgy ("Sicut spina rosam: genuit Judea rosam"), the rose has long been symbolic of the Virgin Mary.

Anne de Marquets 215

Madeleine de l'Aubespine (1546–1596)

If Ronsard was admired by his poet contemporaries, male and female, there would seem to be only one of the latter to whom he amply returned the favor. At least, only one with a talent—and we assume it was her talent—that would have earned for her the rank of honorary "adopted daughter," much as Mlle Gournay was "adopted" by Montaigne. Even more warmly admired than was Jeanne d'Albret by Du Bellay (see p. 158 above), it was supposedly the beautiful and witty Madeleine de l'Aubespine who enjoyed that privileged position.

"Would seem," "would have earned," "supposedly"—terms intentionally indecisive because, for a time, there were seemingly good reasons to question the authenticity of her authorship. One such was the fact that, even sporting the master Ronsard's alleged imprimatur, her work was not published in her own time and had to wait four centuries before appearing in print. It was thought, indeed, that only if one accepted the word of the twentieth-century editor Roger Sorg would Madeleine de l'Aubespine be the author of *Les chansons de Callianthe*, composed under a pseudonym (from the Greek meaning "beautiful flower") given to her by the poet Philippe Desportes (1546–1606), her alleged lover, who, again according to Sorg, celebrated her under the pet nom de guerre of Cléonte.[1] Recent research, however, seems to confirm her authorship (see pp. 10, 23n36).

Born in Burgundy, in the town of Villeroy, Madeleine de l'Aubespine, dame de Villeroy, was the wife of Nicolas de Neufville, a distinguished courtier to both Charles IX and Henri III, in whose courts it is assumed that she herself would have served as lady-in-waiting to the unscrupulous Catherine de Médicis, mother of both monarchs and politicking regent during the minority of the first; that her social and intellectual eminence was reflected in one of the earliest salons of the period in Paris, and in her country residence at Conflans, meeting places for the many prominent poets whom she counted among her friends.; and that her own literary abilities first manifested themselves in a translation from Ovid's early *Heroides,* a significant choice considering its feminist leanings: mythological tales of infamous male heroes as retold from the perspective of the women whom they wronged.

While other writings attributable to Madeleine de l'Aubespine continue to surface, the somewhat enigmatic collection, *Les chansons de Callianthe* (whose title was, in fact, an invention of Sorg's) contains a variety of works: among them, two pairs of sonnets from and to Ronsard and Desportes, a poetic debate with the latter, eleven love sonnets and two on devotional themes, and diverse poems of more capricious bent. They show, despite their rather limited num ber, from which I have translated six sonnets and three miscellaneous works, the varied inspiration of which this gracious, graceful, and occasionally even mischievous poet was capable.[2]

NOTES

1. See Roger Sorg's edition, *Les chansons de Callianthe, fille de Ronsard.*

2. For supposed biographical data the introduction to the Sorg edition remains, for perhaps understandable reasons, the only "authoritative" source. There is also a brief but informative entry in the *Bloomsbury Guide to Women's Literature,* pp. 301–2, probably based on the former.

À RONSARD

Tant de flame et d'amour, dont tu vas allumant
La nuict de mes escriptz que ta Muse eternise,
Font que je me tiens chere et me plais et me prise,
Car je ne puis faillir, suyvant ton jugement.

Mon esprit, qui devant se trainoit bassement,
Pretend voller au ciel si tu le favorise.
Donc, ô divin Ronsard, ayde à mon entreprise:
Je sçay bien que sans toy j'ozerois vainement.

Ainsy que Phaeton, d'une audace nouvelle,
Puisque, ô mon Apollon, ta fille je m'apelle,
Je te demande un don, gaige de ton amour:

Monstre moy le chemin et la sente incongnue
Par qui tant de lumiere en la France est venue,
Et qui rend ton renom plus luysant que le jour.

ÉPIGRAMME D'AMOUR SUR SON NOM

Autour d'un aubespin j'escrivis une fois:
Icy croisse la foy et vive la constance.
Peu apres, retournant passer parmy le bois,
J'y recognu soudain une extreme accroissance.

Ha! mon Dieu, dis je lors, voyez la cruauté!
Dans les rudes deserts privés d'humanité,
D'ame et de sentiment, la foy croist d'heure en heure,
Et au cœur des amans ne peut faire demeure!

TO RONSARD

So much the flame of love—wherewith you light
My verses' darkness, hallowed by your Muse—
Fills me with pleasure and my pride renews:
Worthy am I, for you must judge aright.

Heavenward would my spirit take its flight,
Up from its humble depths, if you but choose.
Thus, O divine Ronsard, I beg you not refuse
Your grace, else must I fail, dare though I might.

† Apollo mine, like Phaeton—brash son, he!—
I pray, as one who would your daughter be,
That you grant me a boon to prove your love:

Show me the way, the path unknown, whereby
Such brilliance came to France, to magnify
Your name, more glorious than day's sky above.

---

‡ **AMOROUS EPIGRAM ON HER NAME**

About a hawthorn, once, I chanced to write:
"Let faith grow here, and long thrive constancy."
Soon after, passing by the wood, my sight
Fell on the spot, grown full, uncommonly.

"God!" I exclaimed. "How cruel! What do I find?
In deserts harsh, bereft of humankind,
Sense, and soul, faith grows, ever multiplied,
§ And yet in lovers' hearts cannot abide!"

* The poet's sonnet is her reply to a laudatory sonnet supposedly addressed to her by her idol Ronsard ("Madelene, ostez-moi ce nom de l'Aubespine" [Madeleine, shed that name of "l'Aubespine"]).

† The allusion is to Phaet(h)on, son of Helios, the sun, the latter personified as Phoebus Apollo. Among other mischievous and haughty acts, Phaeton attempted to drive the chariot of the sun, nearly setting fire to the world when the horses bolted, for which he was struck dead by Zeus.

‡ The poet's wordplay arises from the meaning of *l'aubespine* (in modern French, *l'aubépine*), the common name of the hawthorn, from the Latin for "white thorn."

§ The reader will notice that I do not attempt to regularize the rhyme scheme of the two quatrains: *abba/ccdd.*

Resvant parmy ces boys, je voy s'entrebaiser
Deux tourtres que d'amour l'Amour mesme convie.
De leurs mignardz baysers la source est infinie,
Et sans fin leurs plaisirs je voy recommancer.

O bien heureux oyseaux, qui d'ung mesme penser
Contentez voz espritz francs de la tyrannie
Qu'apporte le respect, l'honneur, la jalousie
Et mille aultres soucyz qui me font trespasser,

Vous voletez sans soing, joyeux, de branche en branche,
Esprouvans le bon heur d'une liberté franche,
Et les suefves doulceurs d'une egalle amitié.

Ha, je puisse mourir si je ne vouldroys estre
Avec vous, chers oyseaux, tourterelle champestre,
Pourveu que, comme vous, j'eusse aussi ma moictié!

L'on verra s'arrester le mobile du monde,
Les estoilles marcher parmy le firmament,
Saturne infortuné luire benignement,
Jupiter commander dedans le creux de l'onde:

L'on verra Mars paisible, et la clarté feconde
Du Soleil s'obscurcir sans force et mouvement,
Vénus sans amitié, Stilbon sans changement,
Et la Lune au quarré changer sa forme ronde:

Le feu sera pesant et legere la terre,
L'eau sera chaude et seiche, et dans l'air qui l'enserre
On voira les poissons voller et se nourrir,

Plustost que mon amour, à vous seul destinee,
Se tourne en autre part, car pour vous je fus nee,
Je ne vis que pour vous, pour vous je veulx mourir.

Dreaming amid the woods, I watch as two
Turtledoves coo and kiss, whom, lovingly,
Love himself has called hither, and I see
Their tender pleasures, endless, spring anew.

O happy birds of but one mind—you, who
Surfeit your souls, your spirits, ever free
Of honor's, favor's, envy's tyranny
And myriad other woes that run me through—

Joyous, from branch to branch you flit with never
A care, fly where you will, whithersoever,
Reveling in love's sweet delights as well.

Upon my life, I swear I would be such
A rustic dove, dear birds, if forasmuch
My mate, like yours, ever by me might dwell!

"Sonnets d'amour," II

Let the earth cease its turning, suddenly,
And the fixed stars travel the firmament;
Let somber Saturn shine, benevolent;
Jupiter rule the hosts beneath the sea;

Let Mars turn peaceful; Sun's lush clarity
Turn dim, then dark; grow motionless, outspent;
* Venus, unloving; Mercury, content,
Changeless; Moon square, no more a circle be;

Let fire weigh heavy and the earth weigh light;
Water feel dry and warm; and let the flight
Of fish go coursing, grazing through the sky,

Sooner than might another know my love.
Born was I but to grant you all thereof:
For you alone I live, and for you, die.

"Sonnets d'amour," III

* The epithet "Stilbon," from the Greek *stilbōn*, meaning "glittering," was often applied
to the planet Mercury in classical literature and, thence, in a variety of Renaissance texts.

Madeleine de l'Aubespine 221

Quiconque dict qu'Amour se guarist par l'absence
N'a esprouvé l'effort de son bras tout puissant:
Mon mal en est tesmoing, qui va tousjours croissant,
Plus j'esloigne l'objet de ma douce souffrance.

Mon esprit bien heureux jouist de ta presence,
D'amour mon cher soucy, et mon cueur languissant
Se forge sans cesser un amour renaissant
De tes perfections dont il a souvenance.

Quand tes yeux plains d'amour sont aux miens opposez,
Et que j'oy tes propos si chers et si prisez,
Mes sens, raviz d'amour, perdent la cognoissance.

Mais or que loing de toy je languis sans pitié,
C'est or que je congnois quelle est mon amitié,
Croissant à qui mieux mieux mon mal et ma constance.

Jamais, jamais ne puissiez vous, mon cœur,
De cest ingrat esprouver la feintise.
Plus tost la flame en mon courage esprise
Brule mes os d'eternelle rigueur:

Plus tost l'archer qui causa ma langueur
Change les traictz dont mon ame il maistrise
Aux traictz de mort, qu'ainsi soit ma franchise
Subjecte aux lois d'un parjure trompeur:

Plus tost le feu, l'air, la mer et la terre
Soient conjurez à me faire la guerre,
Et sans cesser croisse mon desconfort,

Que je consente une telle misere.
Pouvant mourir, trop lache est qui prefere
Sa vie esclave à une belle mort!

Whoever claims that absence cures Love's sting
Has never felt that god's might, poised therefor:
Witness my woe, growing apace, the more
I quit the object of my suffering.

My spirit, in your presence reveling,
Cares for your love alone; and I, heartsore,
Forge endless love from your perfections' store,
Born, ever fresh, of my remembering.

When, close to mine, I see your love-filled eyes
And hear your words that I so dearly prize,
I swoon, and, lovesick, lose all quickening.

But distant, now, constant and comfortless,
I see my love in all its languorousness:
And keener still, my pain, my anguishing.

"Sonnets d'amour," VI

Nevermore, never, O my heart, may you
Suffer that thankless wretch's base pretense!
Rather let love's flame, from this moment hence,
Ever my bones consume, burned through and through.

Rather, I pray, let him, that bowman who
So laid me low, transform his arrows, whence
He rules my soul, to deadly instruments,
Lest I a vile deceiver's bidding do:

Rather let fire, and air, and earth, and sea
Conspire together to wage war on me;
Let grow my anguish with my every breath,

Before I would accept such cravenhood.
A coward she, who, although die she could,
Prefers a slave's life to a noble death.

"Sonnets d'amour," XI

DIALOGUE D'UN POURPOINT ET D'UN ROBON QUI JADIS FURENT ROBES

POURPOINT

Seigneur robon faict de nouveau,
Où allez vous si bien en poinct?
Quoy? Vous ne me respondez point?
L'orgueil vous trouble le cerveau.

ROBON

Seigneur, je vous requiers pardon.
L'orgueil l'esprit ne me desrobe,
Mais, pourceque hier j'estois robe,
Je n'entens point bien à robon.

POURPOINT

Que cela ne vous fache point.
Je cours toute telle adventure,
Car je fuz robe de nature,
Et maintenant je suis pourpoint.

ROBON

Ce n'est pas ce qui me martelle.
Pour un coup, c'est peu de danger.
Mais je crains de me voir changer
Tous les jours en forme nouvelle.

POURPOINT

Tes frayeurs ne seront point faulces,
Car, avant qu'il soit longuement,
Je seray hors d'accoustrement,
Et toy tu doubleras des chausses.

ROBON

Nos maulx de pres se vont suivans.
Mais puisqu'il se fault consoler,
Aux aultres nous pourrons parler
Comme les morts font aux vivans.

POURPOINT

Vous qui passez entre telz hommes
Pleurez nostre calamité:
Comme vous, nous avons esté,
Et vous serez comme nous sommes.

DIALOGUE OF A WAISTCOAT AND A MANTLE THAT ONCE WERE GOWNS

WAISTCOAT

"Sire mantle, fashioned now anew,
Whither go you so decorously?
What? Will you not reply to me?
Your pride, methinks, unhinges you."

MANTLE

"Pardon me, sire. Nay, not a jot.
My mind is clear: pride's not the cause.
But yesterday a gown I was,
And, mantle now, I heard you not."

WAISTCOAT

"You need not be distressed thereby;
A like adventure, friend, is mine.
Gown was I born, by fate's design,
And waistcoat now become am I."

MANTLE

"That's not what causes me my pain,
For, but one time, no harm I find.
Yet I fear lest they be inclined,
Each day, to change my shape again."

WAISTCOAT

"Well met your worries, goodness knows:
Soon shall it come to pass that I'll,
Alas, no longer be in style,
And you'll be turned a pair of hose."

MANTLE

"Indeed, we share the same misgiving.
Still, let us ease our own chagrin,
Telling our woes unto our kin
As do the dead unto the living."

WAISTCOAT

"You who clothe humankind, beware.
Weep for our fate calamitous:
We were like you, now look at us;
For fare you shall as now we fare."

CHANSON MISE DU BISCAYEN EN FRANÇOIS

BERGER

Resveillez vous, belle Catin,
Et allons cueillir ce matin
La rose que, pour mon amour,
Vous me promistes l'autre jour.
Vive l'amour, vive ses feux,
C'est mourir de vivre sans eux.

CATIN

Ha! vrayment je vous ayme bien,
Mais pourtant je n'en feray rien,
Car l'on dit que, cueillant la fleur,
Le rosier pert grace et faveur.
Vive l'amour, vive ses feux,
C'est mourir de vivre sans eux.

BERGER

Ouy bien, qui l'en voudroit oster
Et, larron privé, l'emporter.
Mais, belle, mon contentement
C'est de la baiser seulement.
Vive l'amour, vive ses feux,
C'est mourir de vivre sans eux.

CATIN

J'ay peur que soubz ceste raison
Se cache quelque trahison,
Car, aujourd'huy, tous les bergers
Sont menteurs, trompeurs ou legers.
Vive l'amour, vive ses feux,
C'est mourir de vivre sans eux.

SONG DONE INTO FRENCH FROM THE BASQUE

SHEPHERD

†   "Wake up, fair Cath! I pray, awake!
Let us this morning go and take
The rose that, just the other day,
You promised would my love repay.
Let love's fires thrive, and long live love:
Dead is the life bereft thereof!"

CATH

   "Ha! Yes, I love you, but I'll not
Do as you ask; for ill the lot,
They say, the rosebush suffers when
Plucked is the rose: gone her grace then.
Let love's fires thrive, and long live love:
Dead is the life bereft thereof!"

SHEPHERD

   "Indeed, there are some, I admit,
Who would filch and make off with it.
But I, my sweet, would happy be
Merely to kiss it tenderly.
Let love's fires thrive, and long live love:
Dead is the life bereft thereof."

CATH

   "I fear beneath that thought concealed
Some treachery will be revealed;
For every shepherd nowadays
Cheats, lies, and plies his fickle ways.
Let love's fires thrive, and long live love:
Dead is the life bereft thereof!"

---

* I think it is safe to see a bit of playful facetiousness in the attribution to a supposed Basque original.

† "Catin," originally a diminutive of "Catherine," had not yet quite taken on the pejorative connotation of "whore" that the common noun *catin* was eventually to have.

Madeleine de l'Aubespine 227

BERGER

Je jureray par voz beaux yeux,
Et par le pouvoir de mes dieux,
Que jamais je n'auray plaisir
Qu'à contenter vostre desir.
Vive l'amour, vive ses feux,
C'est mourir de vivre sans eux.

CATIN

Pastoureau, c'est trop marchander
Ce qu'on ne doibt point demander:
Je me ris de tous ces débats,
Car, ma fy, vous ne l'aurez pas.
Vive l'amour, vive ses feux,
C'est mourir de vivre sans eux.

SONNET CHRESTIEN

Seigneur, change ma guerre en ta paix eternelle,
Eschaufe les glaçons de mon cœur endurcy,
Et faiz qu'à l'avenir je n'aye autre soucy
Qu'à suivre le sentier où ta bonté m'apelle.

Dompte les passions de mon ame rebelle
Et lave mon esprit de peché tout noircy,
Départs de ta lumiere à mon œil obscurcy,
Et m'apprens les secretz qu'aux esleuz tu revelle.

Sur toy tant seulement mon espoir j'ay fondé.
Si grande est mon erreur, plus grande est ta bonté
Qui ne laisse jamais celluy qui te réclame.

Purge donc mon esprit et le retire à toy,
Luy donnant pour voller les aisles de la foy,
Sans que l'abus du monde arreste plus mon ame.

SHEPHERD

"I swear by your eyes' loveliness,
And by the power my gods possess,
That all delight will I eschew
Except as I might pleasure you.
Let love's fires thrive, and long live love:
Dead is the life bereft thereof!"

CATH

"Enough discussion! Ask no more
What it is wrong to ask me for.
I scoff at you, my shepherd lad,
For, by my faith, I'll not be had!
Let love's fires thrive, and long live love:
Dead is the life bereft thereof!"

CHRISTIAN SONNET

Let my war turn to peace eternal, Lord,
And my heart, hard as ice, melt in your fire;
Let me be moved, henceforth, by one desire:
To heed your call, tread your just path, restored.

Vanquish the passions of my soul's discord;
Purge my mind of transgression, dark and dire;
Accord my eyes your light, unveiled; inspire
In me your grace, secret of heaven's reward.

In you alone my every hope I place:
Great though my wrongs, yet greater still that grace
That fails not who cries unto you her dole.

Redeem my spirit; keep it evermore:
Give it the wings of faith, that it may soar
Aloft, cleansed of life's sins that tempt my soul.

Gabrielle de Coignard (1550?–1586?)

Gabrielle de Coignard is one of those figures whose biography abounds in question marks. The date of her birth is given variously as 1550? and 1558?; and that of her death, anywhere between 1586? and 1594?, those two seeming to be the most often cited. Melanie E. Gregg, who has recently published a free verse translation of her sole collection of poems—the one hundred twenty-nine "Sonnets spirituels" of her *Œuvres chrestiennes*—opts for 1550 and 1586, dates that Colette H. Winn, author of the work's modern critical edition, appears to accept. Since it is known that the original publication—*Œuvres chrestiennes de feue dame Gabrielle de Coignard*—dating from 1594 and 1595, was brought out after her death by her daughters, a death date closer to that occurrence is favored by some.

As is proper, such biographical details clearly take second place to the important fact of her work itself, a rather recent and much appreciated "discovery" of Renaissance literature scarcely known to earlier generations. The few facts we do have inform us that Coignard was born into a wealthy family in Toulouse, was married in 1570 to one Pierre de Mansencal de Miremont, president of the parliamentary court of that city (making rather suspect the birth date of 1558), and that, three years after an especially happy marriage and the birth of two daughters, she was widowed and turned for consolation to poetry, religion, and a combination of the two.[1]

Another (not unusual) fact is Coignard's great admiration for Ronsard—poet-hero to the age—on whose death the final sonnet of her collection was composed (see p. 241n below). Some, indeed, see Ronsard's influence in the fervor and intensity of her sonnets, as well as in frequent appeals to the beauties of the natural landscape. Some also compare her favorably, for the depth of her sincerity, to Louise Labé (see pp. 133–37 above). Questions of influence aside, the nine sonnets translated here display both Coignard's considerable technical skill as a versifier and the gamut of her unhappy inspiration, born of a widow's mourning, a mother's concern, and a tormented soul's mystical yearning for the solace of her faith.

NOTE

1. For such biographical facts as are available, see the following: Jeanine Moulin's brief entry on Coignard in her *La poésie féminine du XIIe au XIXe siècle*, 1: 155–56; Melanie E. Gregg, *Gabrielle de Coignard: Spiritual Sonnets*, pp. 4–7; Colette H. Winn's introduction to her critical edition, pp. 13–22; Glenda Wall's entry in the *Encyclopedia of Continental Women Writers*, 1: 259–60; Léon Feugère, *Les femmes poètes au XVIème siècle*, pp. 35–38; and Terence Cave, *Devotional Poetry in France, c. 1570–1630*, pp. 86–87 and passim. See also Gary Ferguson, *The Feminisation of Devotion*, and André Gendre, *Quête de Dieu et éduction du monde dans les Sonnets spirituels de Gabrielle de Coignard*.

Je n'ay jamais gousté de l'eau de la fontaine,
Que le cheval aeslé fit sortir du rocher.
A ses payennes eaux je ne veux point toucher,
Je cerche autre liqueur pour soulager ma peine.

Du celeste ruisseau de grace souveraine,
Qui peut des alterez la grand soif estancher:
Je desire ardemment me pouvoir approcher,
Pour y laver mon coeur de sa tasche mondaine.

Je ne veux point porter le glorieux laurier,
La couronne de myrte ou celle d'olivier,
Honneurs que l'on reserve aux testes plus insines.

Ayant l'angoisse en l'ame, ayant la larme à l'oeil,
M'irois-je couronnant de ces marques d'orgueil,
Puis que mon Sauveur mesme est couronné d'espines?

Guide mon coeur, donne moy la science,
O Seigneur Dieu, pour chanter sainctement
Ton haut honneur que j'adore humblement,
Recognoissant assez mon impuissance.

Je n'ay nul art, grace, ny eloquence,
Pour ton sainct nom entonner dignement,
Mais ton clair feu de mon entendement
Escartera les ombres d'ignorance.

Never have I drunk from that spring profane
That the winged horse caused from the rock to flow.
I would not touch its pagan waters; no,
I seek a different draught to ease my pain.

Rather would I that heavenly stream attain,
Whose grace the greatest thirst quells here below.
How fervently I yearn thither to go,
To cleanse therein my heart of worldly stain.

I wish no glorious laurel crown to wear,
Nor myrtle wreath, nor olive, in my hair:
Honors that naught but worthier brow gird round.

With anguish in my soul, tear in my eye,
Ought I such marks of pride bear, crowned thereby,
Whilst my dear Savior's head with thorns is crowned?

"Sonnets spirituels," I

O lord God, guide my heart: grant the skill whence
I may, in humble fashion, magnify
Your majesty in sacred song hereby,
Though know I well how deep my impotence.

No art have I, nor grace, nor eloquence
Worthy to raise your holy name on high;
But bright, your fire will light my sense, and I
Shall see its darkling shadows driven hence.

---

* The allusion is to Pegasus, who, with a kick of his hoof, brought forth the fountain Hippocrene on Helicon, the mountain of the Muses. See *Œuvres chrestiennes*, ed. Colette Winn, p. 139.

† As Winn observes (ibid., p. 140), each of the three trees mentioned is symbolic of a particular divinity: the laurel of Apollo, patron of letters and the arts; the myrtle of Venus, goddess of love; and the olive of Minerva, goddess of wisdom.

Gabrielle de Coignard 233

Je ne veux point la Muse des payens,
Qu'elle s'en voise aux esprits qui sont siens,
Je suis Chrestienne et bruslant de ta flamme.

Et reclamant ton nom à haute voix,
Je sacrifie à l'ombre de ta croix,
Mon tout, mon corps, mes escrits, et mon ame.

———————

Le clair soleil par sa chaleur ardente
Fait destiller la neige d'un rocher,
Et je me fons en sentant approcher
Le doux rayon de ta flamme excellente.

Mon oeil devient une source coulante,
Et l'ame à lors commande sur la chair,
Deliberant de jamais ne cercher,
L'occasion à l'offence coulante.

Mais quant ce feu de moy s'en est allé,
Mon pauvre coeur demeure plus gelé
Qu'un jour d'hyver tout blanchissant de glace.

Revien, Seigneur, ne m'abandonne pas,
Si je te pers, las je voy mon trespas,
Car je ne vy qu'aux douceurs de ta grace.

———————

Si ce mien corps estoit de plus forte nature,
Et mes pauvres enfans n'eussent de moy besoing,
Hors des soucis mondains, je m'en irois bien loin
Choisir pour mon logis une forest obscure.

Las! je ne verrois plus aucune creature,
Ayant abandonné de ce monde le soing,
Dans quelque creux rocher je choisirois un coing,
Et les sauvages fruicts seroient ma nourriture.

I wish not for the pagan Muse; indeed,
Let profit it those minds that pay it heed:
Christian, I burn in your flame, glorying;

And, as upon your name aloud I call,
I offer, in your cross's shadow, all
My verse, my flesh, my soul, my everything.

"Sonnets spirituels," II

———————

The sun, upon a cliff its bright rays beaming,
Trickles the melting snow; and so my lot
As well: I too melt when I feel the hot
Gentleness of your flame upon me gleaming.

My weeping eye becomes a brooklet, streaming;
And my soul, vanquishing my flesh, vows not
Again to bend its will—nay, not one jot—
To seek out vice or be full wayward-seeming.

But let your fire desist, leaving me lost,
And cold my heart grows, frozen more than frost
Of frigid winter's day, white as the snows.

Dear Lord, I pray you not abandon me!
Return, else death must be my destiny:
I live but by that gift your grace bestows.

"Sonnets spirituels," IV

———————

If this, my body, could but stronger be,
And my poor children need me not, then lose
Would I all worldly interest, and choose
My dwelling mid the forest's mystery.

I would this world and all its creatures flee,
With all its cares, and find some cave to use
As my abode, some distant refuge, whose
Wild-growing fruits would feed and nourish me.

Gabrielle de Coignard 235

Et là j'admirerois en repos gracieux
Les oeuvres du haut Dieu, l'air, la terre et les cieux,
Les benefices siens sainctement admirables.

Et en pleurs et souspirs requerant son secours,
Je passerois ainsi le reste de mes jours,
Recevant de mon Dieu les graces secourables.

—————

Je beniray tousjours l'an, le jour et le moys,
Le temps et la saison, que la bonté divine
Lança ses doux attraits au fonds de ma poitrine,
Arrachant de mon sein le coeur que je portois.

Un soir il me sembla ainsi que je dormois
Dessous l'obscurité de ma sombre courtine,
Que je me submergeois dedans la mer mutine,
Hallettant à la mort peu à peu je mourois.

J'avois mille regrets de mes fautes commises,
Je promettois à Dieu des sainctes entreprises,
S'il me donnoit loisir de vivre encor un peu.

Je m'esveille en sur-saut, et mon ame advertie
Par ce songe divin de corriger ma vie,
Demande ton secours pour accomplir son voeu.

—————

Amour est un enfant, ce disent les poetes,
Qui a les yeux sillés par un obscur bandeau:
C'est un cruel serpent, un devorant flambeau,
Qui brusle les humains par les flammes secrettes:

Dardant à tous propos des mortelles sagettes,
Il donne en nous flattant la mort et le tombeau,
Il vole dans nos coeurs tout ainsi qu'un oyseau,
C'est un foudre tonnant, racine de tempestes.

There would I contemplate in sweet repose
The holy boons almighty God bestows—
His saintly works: earth, air, the heavenly spaces.

With tears and sighing, weeping, I would spend
My waning days praying that, at the end,
My God redeem me with His saving graces.

"Sonnets spirituels," XI

———————

Ever shall I the year, the month, the day,
The season bless, when God's divine grace streamed
Its charms into this breast of mine, redeemed
And freed it of a heart oft gone astray.

One night, as on my darkened couch I lay
Asleep, beneath my canopy, I dreamed
I sank deep in a stormy sea, and seemed
To feel my gasping breath ebbing away.

Oh, how I grieved for myriad sins committed;
Vowed they would be by holy deeds acquitted,
Would God let me live but a little now.

Startled, I wake: my vision-chastened soul
Yearns to restore my life, to make it whole,
And begs you, Lord, to help it keep its vow.

"Sonnets spirituels," XVII

———————

Love, say the poets, is a little child,
Who wears about his eyes a blindfold band.
Nay! Rather a serpent cruel, a firebrand
Whose furtive flames leave none whole, undefiled.

He shoots his mortal darts, and we, beguiled,
See not the death they deal, as there we stand,
Our hearts his prey: he streaks the heavens spanned,
Bird-like; or, thunderbolt, spawns tempests wild.

Gabrielle de Coignard 237

Chassons donc vistement cest aveugle estranger,
Avant que dans nos coeurs il se puisse loger,
Cherchons cest autre amour qui fait la vertu suivre,

Qui est chaste et parfaict, modeste, et gracieux,
Dardant ses trais dorez de la voute des cieux,
Non pour nous massacrer, mais pour nous faire vivre.

———————

Ni des vers prez les fleurettes riantes,
Ny d'un ruisseau le doux flot argentin,
Ny le long cours d'un fleuve serpentin,
Ny les rameaux des forests verdoyantes,

Ny de Ceres les pleines blondoyantes,
Ny ce beau ciel d'où vient nostre destin,
Ny la fraischeur du soir et du matin,
Ny du printemps les beautez differentes,

Las! ne m'ont point le regret allenty
De mes pechez: je l'ay plus ressenti,
Considerant cest ouvrage admirable

De ce grand Dieu, qui par ses beaux objects,
Fait que mon coeur recognoist ses forfaicts:
Forfaits, l'horreur de mon ame coulpable.

———————

M'esveillant à minuit, dessillant la paupiere,
Je voy tout assoupi au centre du repos,
L'on n'entend plus de bruit, le travail est enclos
Dans l'ombre de la terre, attendant la lumiere.

Let us, then, cast aside this stranger blind—
Lest he, within our hearts, a lodging find—
And seek that other love with virtue rife,

Perfect, and chaste, and gracious without fault,
That flings its golden darts from heaven's vault,
Not to destroy us, but to grant us life.

"Sonnets spirituels," XIX

Neither the green fields' flowering gaiety,
Nor brooklet's calm and gentle silvered swell,
Nor river's course, meandering pell-mell,
Nor forest's branches spread with greenery,

*   Nor the blond Ceres' meadow granary,
Nor sky, whence comes our fate—or fair, or fell—
Nor morning's cool and evening's cool as well,
Nor spring with its beauteous variety,

Can my regrets, my woes, alas, allay,
Ease my distress at my transgressing; yea,
Grieve I the more before this wondrous whole

Of that great God, who, with such loveliness,
Makes clear the sins my heart would fain confess:
My sins, the horror of my guilty soul.

"Sonnets spirituels," XL

Waking at midnight, opening wide my eye,
I see all lying quiet, girt in rest;
Labors, stilled, nestle in earth's shadow-breast,
Silent, and wait for daylight, by and by.

* Despite the injunction in English prosody against rhymes introduced by the same consonant, I take the liberty of rhyming "greenery" with "granary" in an effort to produce something of the effect of the original's ultra-rich rhyming of *verdoyantes* with *blondoyantes.*

Le silence est par tout, la lune est belle et claire,
Le ciel calme et serain, la mer retient ses flots,
Et tout ce qui se voit dedans ce large clos
Est plein de majesté et grace singuliere.

La nuit qui va roulant ses tours continuels,
Represente à nos yeux les siecles eternels,
Le silence profond du Royaume celeste.

En fin le jour, la nuit, la lumiere et l'obscur,
A louer le haut Dieu incitent nostre coeur,
Voyant reluire en tout sa grandeur manifeste.

———————

SUR LA MORT DE RONSARD

Muses, sçavez vous point la piteuse avanture,
Qui a d'un coup mortel affligé l'univers?
Ouy, vous la sçavez, d'un nuage couvers,
Vos beaux yeux vont pleurans ceste mesadvanture.

Vostre Apollon est mort, couvres sa sepulture
De vos cheveux dorez, faictes cent mille vers
A celuy qui premier planta vos lauriers vers,
Et vous faict honorer d'un los qui tousjours dure.

Dieu l'a voulu tirer du cloistre de ce corps,
Sa belle ame a trouvé les celestes accords,
Ayant vollé plus haut que le mont de Parnasse.

Ronsard est immortel en la terre et aux cieux,
Nous heritons icy ses labeurs precieux,
Il possede le ciel voyant Dieu face à face.

All is calm: fair, the brilliant moon; the sky,
Serene, at peace; the sea's waves do their best
To cease; all things, with grace made manifest,
Majestic, in this vast enclosure lie.

Night, as it turns in its continuous
Circlings, rolls on, and seems to paint for us
Time's boundless centuries, Heaven's peace profound.

At day's end, light, and shade, and dark of night
Move us to praise God, as His grandeur, bright,
Glows clearly in all things the wide world round.

"Sonnets spirituels," XLV

---

* ON THE DEATH OF RONSARD

Know you not, Muses, what dismay, what rue
Besets the universe this day, heartsore?
Ah, but you must! Your fair eyes, dimmed, outpour
Their tears to mourn the woe naught will undo.

Dead, your Apollo lies: come, his tomb strew
With your gold locks; intone poems galore
To him who, first, your verdant laurels wore,
And who, with lasting praise, will honor you.

God loosed him from his body's cloister, free:
Now his soul finds celestial harmony,
That soul that higher than Parnassus soared.

Immortal is Ronsard, on earth and heaven:
Ours, here below, his works, preciously given;
His, life eternal, gazing on the Lord.

"Sonnets spirituels," CXXIX

* In her critical edition of Coignard's *Œuvres chrétiennes*, Winn suggests (p. 295n) that this, the final poem of the collection, probably written shortly before the poet's own death in 1586, must date from that year of Ronsard's burial on February 24, two months after his death on December 27 of the preceding year.

Gabrielle de Coignard 241

Marie de Romieu (LATE SIXTEENTH CENTURY)

It can certainly be said of Marie de Romieu, with no offense, that she is a shadowy figure. But the shadow she casts is an intriguing one. Her authorship of a brief poetic encomium on woman's superiority over man—"Brief discours: Que l'excellence de la femme surpasse celle de l'homme," supposedly written in reply to an anti-feminist screed by her brother Jacques—is not beyond doubt. Some have even questioned her very existence, suggesting that Jacques de Romieu himself—the "de" is known to have been an unmerited affectation—was not only the author of the "Brief discours," but the poet's alter ego as well. The modern (1972) edition of André Winandy rejects both hypotheses on the grounds that what is known of Jacques's writing style is inferior to that of his putative sister.[1]

Winandy's volume is a thoroughly annotated reedition of *Les premières œuvres poétiques*, the slim collection in which the "Brief discours" originally appeared in 1581,[2] together with incidental verse in a wide variety of forms, on traditional subjects, and brief occasional pieces flattering assorted authority figures in the poet's native Viviers. They were originally published by her brother, thus further fueling speculation as to her/his identity. Their tone is often rather *précieux*, but not without agreeable flashes of wit here and there.

More salacious is the wit of a courtesy book for ladies—a translation of an Italian work, supposedly by Allessandro Piccolomini—sometimes attributed to the enigmatic Marie thanks to the initials contained in its title: *Instruction pour les jeunes dames, par la mère et la fille d'alliance, par M. D. R.* (1573). Winandy and others, however, consider the attribution unlikely, all things being equal, and suggest that, rather than indicating "Marie de Romieu," the initials might well stand for one of several other authors, among them her possible contemporary Madeleine des Roches (see pp. 170–82 above).

While a number of facts are known about Jacques de Romieu—a lawyer with noble pretensions—Marie's existence being what it is (or is not), tangible biographical details are nonexistent, and the intangible suppositions are suspect. For example, an entry in the *Encyclopedia of Continental Women Writers* suggests "1526?" as a birth date, though with no indication as to how it was arrived at. According to Winandy (p. xviii), this would be a good thirty years too early.

My translations offer a representative sampling of Marie de Romieu's—or whoever's—pleasant and varied muse.

NOTES

1. See *Les premières œuvres poétiques,* pp. vi–xii. Regarding the enigmatic Marie, see also the following: Léon Feugère, *Les femmes poètes au XVIe siecle,* pp. 27–34; Marcel Raymond, *L'influence de Ronsard sur la poésie française (1550–1585),* pp. 201–2; and Auguste Le Sourd, *Recherches sur Jacques et Marie de Romieu, poètes vivarois,* p. 6.

2. Only four copies of the original edition are known to have survived.

QUATRAIN

Le beau nom d'Isabeau ne sonne rien que beau,
Avecques le beau nom Isabeau est fort belle.
La beauté convient bien avec un' Isabeau:
Mais le nom d'Isabeau ne convient mieu qu'en elle.

ÉNIGME

Un habillé de gris va, de nuit et de jour,
Or deçà, or delà, queimander à son tour
Des vivres pour passer la nuit et la journée;
La nuit, quand il n'a peu faire bien sa dinée,
Le jour, quand il se voit hors de bruit escarté.
Il aime mieux la nuit que la belle clarté.
Mais, helas! il n'a pas si tost passé la porte
De son petit convent qu'un ennemy ne sorte,
Tire-laine rusé, ayant guetté long temps
Avant que d'exercer son cruel passe-temps
Contre luy, qui ne veut avoir que la passade
Et appaiser sa faim, sans faire à nul cassade.
Si tost que ce pauvret a de loing apperceu
Son mortel ennemy, se voit mort et deceu.
Une froide sueur luy coule dans les veines,
Et ne sçait comme doit eviter tant de peines,
Contre un si coleré. Or s'eslance deçà,
Et or, viste-courrier, guinde ses pas delà.
Ce galand, qui ne fait autre estat que surprendre
Ses pareils compagnons, sçait comme les faut prendre,
Sçait ses tours et detours, et sçait encor comment

QUATRAIN

Isabelle is a belle, and "Isabelle"
Is a fair name, as fair as fair can be.
Though fair is every Isabelle as well,
* No belle wears "Isabelle" as well as she.

VI

† RIDDLE

Off he goes begging in his costume gray,
Now here, now there, now by night, now by day,
Hunting for food to pass the day, the night;
Night, when he has ill fed his appetite,
Day, when he seeks escape out of the maze
Of noise; and less likes day's bright-shining rays
Than night's dark shade. But ah! no sooner will
He pass the threshold of his domicile,
Than there appears an enemy most hated,
Crass brigand, clever, who has long lain, waited
To strike his blow, as he is wont to do,
Treacherously, against the other, who
Wants but to go his way, find food, and never
Wishes to do the slightest harm whatever.
When out he steps, poor soul, and spies, ahead,
The enemy, he knows as good as dead
‡ Is he! Sweat flows cold in his veins! Aghast,
How shall he ever safely venture past
That painful obstacle that angrily
Awaits him there? And so, hoping to flee,
He tries, fleet-footed, to avoid his foe,

---

* Winandy indicates (p. 51n) that the object of this encomium—reminiscent of the verbal jugglings of the *grands rhétoriqueurs*—is apparently unknown.

† The *énigme*, or riddle poem, was a genre of light verse commonly practiced by early poets, and especially by the *précieux* salon versifiers of the seventeenth century, presenting an ambiguous description for the reader (or listener) to solve.

‡ I have resisted the temptation to correct the poet's curiously faulty anatomy in these lines and faithfully transmit her assumption that sweat flows through the veins.

Marie de Romieu 245

Bien tost il doit souffrir la mort, en payment
De l'avoir rencontré. O sinistre rencontre!
Ce pendant ce chetif devant luy se rencontre
Pensant de se sauver, l'autre le prend soudain
Et met sur son collet sa graffinante main,
Puis se joue de luy et se rit de sa parte.
Mais, s'il a de quelqu'un la face descouverte,
Le r'empoigne soudain, grondant entre ses dents,
N'ayant nulle pitié de ses petits enfants.
Ains, s'il avoit encor toute sa geniture,
Tacheroit d'en finir la semence et nature.
Quand il voit qu'il reprend en soy quelque vigueur,
Alors change son ris en cruelle rigueur:
En pieces le vous met, dechiré le devore,
Tant il est inhumain, Son Seigneur l'en honore,
Le cherit, le caresse et le tient pres de soy,
Qui, soul pour quelque temps, aussi demeure coy.
Vous le voirriez apres qui de sa cornemuse
Semble s'en resjouir, les assistans amuse.
Dy moy doncques, lecteur, qui est ce chetif là,
Dy moy encor qui est celuy qui l'estrangla,
Et je t'estimeray le grand Dieu des Poetes,
Des hommes et des Dieux les communs interpretes.

C'est un Chat, quand il prend une Souris.

Making a sudden dash—now to, now fro,
Now side to side—knowing that by surprise
And feint alone can he and his allies
Be bested; knowing too, only full well,
That fearsome suffering and death most fell
Would be the price that he would have to pay
For his ill-starred encounter! Lackaday!...
The enemy slashes and lashes out,
Seizes him by the neck, gives him a clout,
Laughs, mocks him as he takes a step or two,
Thinking that he can flee. But, *tout à coup,*
The villain, spying someone drawing near,
Grips him again, grunts, growls for all to hear,
Merciless, and utterly disinclined
To pity the poor orphans left behind.
Indeed, were they but all there, on the spot,
He would be quick to finish with the lot
And put an end to his whole line forever!...
One desperate, final, effort... But the clever,
Inhuman foe, now fierce, laughing no more,
Rips him to shreds, devours him; and therefor
Does his lord cherish him, heap on his head
Much love and honor. He, now surfeited,
Will, for a time, in calm tranquillity
Remain, tooting his pipes in seeming glee
As all about enjoy those sounds of his.
Tell me, dear reader, who that poor soul is—
Or was!—and who, the one who slew him so,
And I, upon you shall the name bestow
"God of the Poets," and shall fain profess
That well you know man, and the gods no less.

* A Cat it is, when he a Mouse lays low.

XVI

* I have not seen fit to maintain the same fidelity to the poet by avoiding rhyme in the
final line as she has done. I think the rhyme neatly ties the poem up without doing any
harm to the original.

À UN MAL-DISANT

Qui nous a des enfers chassé ce diable noir,
Aux yeux hideux et creux, tout bouffi d'arrogance,
Qui d'un front ramassé veut vomir sa vengeance,
Sur l'amie des Seurs, des bons le vray manoir?

Va, malin, exercer sur autruy ton vouloir,
Pernicieux meschant, va, que jamais la France
Ne t'enrolle des siens; ainçois que l'oubliance
T'entombe pour jamais dans l'infernal terroir.

Dy moy, quel fauls Demon t'a esmeu à mesdire
Contre celle qui n'a qu'en estime une lyre
Aimée d'un chacun en honneur et renom?

Ha! certes, tu te fauls, tu te fauls, miserable.
N'avois-tu point subject autre plus honorable
Que vouloir estaler par mesdire ton nom?

À DAMOISELLE FRANÇOISE DE PÉRONNE, LA FILLE

Tu es la mesme grace et la science mesme,
Et la mesme beauté dont sommes maintenus;
Par ainsi donc tu es ma Charite quatriesme,
Ma dixiesme des Sœurs et mon autre Venus.

* TO A SCANDALMONGER

Who sent us this black devil, chased from hell,
Sloping of brow, hideous and hollow-eyed,
Who would spew forth his malice, puffed with pride,
On her the Muses love, where virtues dwell?

Go, wretch! On others work your fancy fell!
Begone, churl! Nevermore in France abide.
Rather, the dark, infernal land bestride;
Then be entombed, spurned to a fare-thee-well!

Tell me! What errant Demon goaded you
To slander her whose lyre sings fair and true,
Beloved by all of honor and high station?

You err! Oh, how you err! Can you design
No manner less abject, more decent, swine,
Than, by such lies, to spread your reputation?

XXII

† FOR DEMOISELLE FRANÇOISE DE PÉRONNE, THE DAUGHTER

Knowledge itself, and grace itself, and these
Beauties themselves sustaining us, are you!
Wherefore are you fourth of the Charites,
‡ The tenth Muse, and a second Venus too.

XXIV

* On this curious upbraiding of an anonymous slanderer of an equally anonymous
amie des Seurs ("lady friend of the Muses"), see Winandy, p. 94n.
    † On the problematic identity of the dedicatee, see Winandy, p. 96n.
    ‡ Besides making her a second Venus, the poet associates her heroine with the nine
Muses and the (usually) three "Charites," or Graces—Aglaea (Radiance), Euphrosyne (Joy),
and Thalia (flowering)—generally considered the daughters of Zeus and various mothers,
sung by Hesiod, Pindar, and other classical poets.

Marie de Romieu 249

SONET À MA-DAME DE MILLIEU

Dans ton cœur genereux, ô! si l'on pouvoit lire,
Mon Dieu! que de vertus, ma-dame, on y liroit!
La magnanimité au premier rang iroit,
Comme on voit dans le ciel un clair soleil reluire.

Apres, la pieté, que langue ne peut dire
Ny la bouche exprimer, au ciel t'attireroit,
Et là, comme Deesse, un chacun te feroit,
Honneur du genou droit. Jour n'est que je n'admire

Entre tant de vertus, ton magnanime cœur,
Qui se monstra constant sans semblant de douleur
Au triste departir du cœur qui te voisine.

Là, là je cognuz bien que la divinité,
N'avoit rien de commun avec l'humanité:
Aussi tu es en tout, docte, sage, divine.

POUR UN INJURIÉ

Celuy qui se laisse prendre
A la Bacquique liqueur,
Et qui se laisse surprandre
A sa vineuse douceur,

Ne merite pas de vivre
Parmi les gens de raison;
Ains le malheur le doit suivre
Hors et dedans sa maison,

SONNET FOR MADAME DE MILLIEU

Dear God! What virtues one would recognize,
Madame, could one but read your heart and see,
Foremost of all, your magnanimity,
As one sees, bright, the sun light up the skies.

Next, piety—more than, in any wise,
Tongue can express!—would draw you eagerly
Toward heaven: and, goddess, all would bend the knee
Before you. No day dawns but that I prize—

Virtue of virtues!—your staunch heart, that so
Unflinchingly and nobly bore the woe
† Wrought by a dear heart's sad abandoning.

Ah! Then I knew that human beings, though less
Than gods, can rise, despite their humanness:
Wise, sage are you, divine in everything.

XXXIV

‡ TO ONE DISPARAGED

He who lets the Bacchic brew
Catch him in its liquid snare,
And who, victim thereunto,
Wine's sweet charm cannot forebear,

Truly has no right to dwell
Where well-reasoned men abide;
Rather must woe foul and fell
Follow closely by his side,

* According to Winandy, p. 106, the dedicatee was one Hippolyte Scaravelli, dame de Millieu, widow of the *contrôleur-général* Jean de Chastellier.
† The allusion is to the death of the lady's husband in 1580.
‡ Winandy, p. 113n, indicates that the object of this invective is unknown.

Marie de Romieu 251

Comme toy mange-chevance,
Mange-gain, dissipe-bien,
Prodigue de ta substance
Qui ja desja n'est plus rien.

Toute la plus grande gloire
Que j'entends de toy chanter,
C'est tousjours parler de boire
Et du meilleur te vanter.

Puis, quand du vin la fumée
A esperdu tous tes sens,
C'est puis en la Renommée
De chacun que tu descends.

Appren, appren à bien dire
Et à moderer ton vin,
Si tu ne veux que mon ire
T'aille tourmentant sans fin.

IMITATION D'UN SONET DE PÉTRARQUE

Paix je ne treuve, et ne puis faire guerre;
J'espere et crains; je brusle et je suis glace;
Rien je n'estrains, et tout ce rond j'embrasse;
Je vole au ciel, et si je suis en terre.

Je suis captif, et si rien ne m'enserre;
Enrethé suis, et rien ne m'entre-lace;
Rien je ne veux, et si j'aime la face
De celle là sur toutes qui m'enferre.

Je voy sans yeux, sans cœur me convient vivre;
Le dueil me paist, le plaisir me veut suivre;
Je veux perir, l'aide le cœur m'enflamme;

Autruy me plaist, et moy mesme m'ennuye;
Egalement veux la mort et la vie:
En tel estat je suis pour vous, ma-dame.

As it does with you, my friend—
Wanton wastrel, wealth-bereft—
You who all your substance spend
Till, now, naught of it is left.

When one sings your glories gallant,
There is little one can think
Save that tippling is your talent
And naught but the best you drink.

And, when wine's ill vapors go
Headward, deadening your sense,
Then your Reputation, lo!
Sinks low as a consequence.

Therefore, mind your manners, and
Learn to let less wine content you,
Lest you wish my fury fanned
Evermore to taunt, torment you.

XL

---

* **IMITATION OF A SONNET BY PETRARCH**

No peace I find, nor know war's bale and bane;
I hope and fear; I burn and freeze apace;
Naught I contain, yet all this sphere embrace;
I fly to heaven and yet on earth remain.

A prisoner, I, yet know nor bond nor chain;
Enmeshed, my limbs, yet naught the strands enlace;
Nothing I want, and yet I love the face
Of her who holds me fast, and tight the rein.

With no heart must I live, eyeless I see;
Sorrow feeds on my being, joy follows me;
I want to die, boon sets my heart afire;

I vex myself, another gives me pleasure;
I seek both life and death in equal measure;
Such is the state, madame, your charms inspire.

XXXII

* Petrarch's sonnet in question, rather closely adapted, is number 134 of *Il canzoniere*
("Pace non trovo, e non ho da far guerra").

Marie de Romieu 253

AU SEIGNEUR ÉDOUARD

Mon vers est si petit, ma Muse si petite,
Mon chant si enroué, si peu forte ma vois,
Que d'un grand Edouard entonner le merite
N'appartient seulement qu'aux Princes et aux Roys.

SONET

L'un chantera de Mars la force et le courage,
L'autre lou'ra les Rois, les Princes et Seigneurs
Et l'autre entonnera de Venus les honneurs,
Son œil, son ris, ses traits et son gentil corsage.

L'un voudra s'esgayer (orné d'un beau ramage)
Sus un hymne mondain qui de sa voix les cœurs
Des hommes va charmant; l'autre dira des mœurs.
L'un à mespris aura la loy de mariage;

L'autre d'un vers doré des celestes flambeaux,
Qui de Mars, qui des Rois, qui des humides eaux,
Qui d'amour, qui des cieux, qui dira de sagesse.

Quant à moy, je ne veux desormais que mes vers
Chantent sinon le los de Dieu par l'univers,
Luy offrant tout le fruit de ma tendre jeunesse.

* FOR SEIGNEUR ÉDOUARD

My verse is slight, my Muse is slight no less;
So weak my voice, so hoarse my melody,
That none but prince or king should fain express
The merits of an Edouard great as he.

XLII

SONNET

One will sing great Mars' strength, with courage blessed;
Another will praise kings, lords, princes too;
One will laud Venus, with the glories due
Her glance, smile, visage, and her comely breast.

Some will take joy—melodiously expressed—
Charming our hearts with worldly song; some, who
Would judge us, pass Man's morals in review;
And some their scorn for wedded life attest.

Some, ranting on and on in manner wise
And verses gilded by the torch-lit skies,
Will Mars, kings, oceans, love, and heaven salute.

As for me, I wish that my verse sing naught
But God's praise, for the universe He wrought,
To offer Him all my youth's tender fruit.

XLIII

* According to Winandy (pp. 7, 114), the dedicatee of this typically fulsome encomium is a Burgundian poet and doctor by the name of Jean-Edouard du Monin (1557–1586), who was the author of two prefatory poems to Marie's collection, "A Mademoiselle de Romieu, Sonnet fœminin sur son Discours" and "Ad nobilem heroinam M. de Romieu," though only the first of these actually appears in the edited volume.

II

The Seventeenth & Eighteenth Centuries

The Seventeenth and Eighteenth Centuries

FROM MADELEINE DE SCUDÉRY TO MARIE-MADELEINE JOLIVEAU DE SEGRAIS

Introduction by Catherine Lafarge

Many readers may be familiar with some of the thirteen women poets who have been selected to represent the seventeenth and eighteenth centuries. However, several have remained in the shadows. Sadly, on the whole, they are for the most part known because of their unconventional lives rather than their works, and if their works have been deemed worthy of mention in literary histories, the discussions have tended to focus on their novels rather than their poetry. Moreover, although their names and lives appear in a recent encyclopedia, their works are rarely available in contemporary editions. Since, as a rule, critics have overlooked many authors included in this section, the following pages fill a gap, give examples of their contributions to poetry, and are proof of their talents.

On first impression one is struck by the thirteen poets' differences in social background, religion, education, geographical origin, and economic and civil status. And yet, when one takes a closer look, one sees that they have much in common. They share more than their talent and their determination to have a career in a world that did not make it easy for them to succeed.

Half of them belonged to the aristocracy. The families of Henriette Coligny de La Suze, Fanny de Beauharnais, and Félicité de Genlis had close ties to reigning monarchs. Coligny's ancestor Admiral Gaspard de Coligny (1519–1572) was an advisor to Charles IX and a victim of the Saint Bartholomew's massacre. Beauharnais, the aunt by marriage of Empress Joséphine—Napoleon's first wife—was also the godmother of Joséphine's daughter from her first marriage, Hortense de Beauharnais, who, as the wife of Napoleon's brother Louis, became queen of Holland. Genlis taught the future King Louis-Philippe in her capacity as governor of the children of Louis XVI's cousin, Louis-Philippe-Joseph, duc de Chartres (later duc d'Orléans, and later yet called Philippe Egalité), and his duchess, Marie-Adélaïde.[1] Although the other three aristocrats, Madeleine de Scudéry, Antoinette Deshoulières, and Marie-Aimable de La Férandière, came from less prominent families they found powerful patrons. In the case of Scudéry, the queen of Sweden, Cardinal Mazarin, and Madame de Maintenon, and in that of Deshoulières, the Grand Condé. The third estate is represented by members of the well-to-do bourgeoisie like Catherine Bernard, whose mentor appears to have been Fontenelle and whose protectors were Mesdames de Pontchartrain and de Maintenon; Marie-Madeleine Joliveau de Segrais, whose father was a lawyer; Louise-Geneviève Gillot de Sainctonge; Elisabeth-Sophie Chéron, the daughter of a painter; and Marie-Emilie de Montanclos, who was a protégée of Queen Marie-Antoinette. Marie-Catherine Desjardins de Villedieu's origins were more humble: her mother was a chambermaid in the Rohan family. On the other hand, she found in her mother's employer her first supporter. As for Elisabeth Guibert, nothing much is known about her.

Not surprisingly, three of the poets born in the seventeenth century—Coligny de La Suze, Chéron, and Bernard—were Protestant by birth and converted to Catholicism, the last one shortly before the Revocation of the Edict de Nantes so as not to have to leave France.[2] This religious affiliation is a reminder of a more pluralistic society than the one it would become in the last two decades of the century. It brings to mind that several celebrated male poets, Girard de Saint-Amant, Théophile de Viau, François de Boisrobert, Paul Pellisson, and the grammarian Valentin Conrart, who was the first secretary of the Académie française, were also Protestant and chose to convert to Catholicism rather than go into exile. In the case of our three women poets, the religion of their family almost guaranteed them a cultural and intellectual environment in which their talents would be encouraged to develop more freely than those of their Catholic sisters.

The educations these women received were as different as their circumstances. In both centuries, women's education was lacking. Most upper-class women spent their youth in convents, where they were not always even taught how to read and write—by the end of the eighteenth century, literacy rates averaged 27 percent for women. Thus, when a woman received an education comparable to the one given to a man, it was more the exception than the rule. For every Poullain de La Barre, who called in three treatises for women to have access to the broadest education available,[3] there were many Fénelons who wrote that women's education should be limited to the preparation of their role as Christian wives and mothers.[4] In the eighteenth century, among the philosophes, Condorcet alone argued that women were entitled to an education and called for primary and secondary instruction in public institutions.[5] There is no doubt that education was reserved to a privileged few. While we do not always know what kind of education our thirteen poets received, thanks to their accomplishments, we can assume that they were fortunate enough to have access to some. We know, for instance, that Scudéry was brought up by an uncle who was kind and learned and we can infer that he did not neglect her education. The Parisian Deshoulières's parents saw to it that she received an excellent education. At a young age, she learned Latin, Italian, and Spanish and studied poetry, music, dance, and the philosophy of Descartes and Gassendi. Another Parisian, Chéron, learned drawing from her father and became famous at the tender age of fourteen. She was not only an accomplished painter and engraver but also excelled in music. Later in life, she studied Hebrew in order to write her essays on the psalms. Gillot de Sainctonge translated from the Spanish and the Italian. Bernard grew up in a family belonging to the upper Protestant bourgeoisie of Rouen and benefited from a social and cultural milieu where her intellectual and literary talents flourished. Genlis, who was a virtuoso on the harp, never received a proper education and was essentially self-taught, which is all the more extraordinary since she dedicated her life to the education of her children, both those of the duc d'Orléans and several others she adopted. Finally, Joliveau de Segrais was well-educated and learned Latin, Italian, and English to undertake the education of her children.

If we do not always have precise information on the formative years of our poets, we know more about them as adults. One institution, the salon, played a major role in the development of at least eight of them as poets and writers and helped launched them on the literary scene.

Much has been written on the salon and what it stood for in the social, intellectual and cultural life of Paris during these two centuries.[6] The salons that are still mentioned in today's history books were places where an elite gathered and freely exchanged ideas on literature, politics, and philosophy, and where elegant and witty conversation was the norm. However, much had changed between the heyday of the hôtel de Rambouillet, where the marquise de Rambouillet, Catherine de Vivonne (1588–1665), received the self-styled *précieux* and *bas-bleus,* and the salons of Marie-Thérèse Rodet Geoffrin (1699–1777) and the marquise du Deffand (1687–1780). Whereas in the circles of the seventeenth century, the social and literary elites mingled to talk about literature and hear the latest poem, in those of the eighteenth century, artists, musicians, and, finally, philosophers were added to the mix and greatly contributed to the exchange of ideas. In both centuries, though, it would have been difficult for most of the poets discussed in these pages to find recognition if they had not been first invited to the famous salons of the day or, for a smaller group, if they had not held salons themselves. In their friends, they found a sympathetic public that was responsible for creating a nurturing atmosphere indispensable for the blossoming of their talents. Madame de Genlis is known to have said that no author was ever booed in a salon.

No social and literary circle was more important for the careers of men and women of letters in early seventeenth-century Paris than the salon of the marquise de Rambouillet. As soon as Scudéry arrived in Paris from Rouen to join her brother she was welcomed into this most prestigious circle. The guest list included the poets Jean Chapelain, Vincent Voiture, and Paul Pellisson, Scudéry's faithful admirer, as well as the influential critic Valentin Conrart. Later in the century, both Madame de Sévigné and Madame de Lafayette were guests of the marquise. Scudéry could not have found a better audience before which to show off her talent and pursue her literary education. Not only was the atmosphere congenial, but poetry was also the privileged genre. There she met Henriette de

Coligny de La Suze, another recruit from the provinces. Soon both Scudéry and Coligny had their own salons. Scudéry's was known as "Sappho's Saturdays." In Coligny's salon, one could meet the poets François de Boisrobert, Girard de Saint-Amant, Honorat de Racan, Charles Cotin, and the memorialist Tallemant des Réaux. She corresponded with the critic J.-L. Guez de Balzac and the essayist Charles de Saint-Evremond.

Other members of the nobility or the wealthy bourgeoisie followed in the footsteps of the marquise de Rambouillet. Antoinette Deshoulières made her debut in the salon of the financier Georges Pélissari. She became acquainted with several distinguished representatives of the literary scenes, the poets Isaac de Benserade, Gilles Ménage, and Paul Pellisson, the playwrights Corneille and Philippe Quinault, the author of fairy tales Charles Perrault, and the moralist La Rochefoucauld. Poems were written about her, and she was called the tenth muse, the French Calliope. She was such a celebrated poet that Elisabeth Chéron painted her.

Chéron herself had a salon on the rue de Grenelle. It was the gathering place of many artists and men and women of letters. Madeleine de Scudéry was a frequent visitor and so was Anne Dacier, a translator of Homer and major participant in the Querelle des anciens et des modernes.[7] Marie-Catherine Desjardins became a favorite of the salons of her day, we are told,[8] and Catherine Bernard frequented the salons of mesdames de Montausier, de Bouillon, and de Coulanges.

A salon gave this first group of poets—Scudéry, Coligny, Deshoulières, Desjardins, Chéron, Bernard—a place to meet models and mentors. Thus, being welcomed in a circle was much more than a social activity; it was being given access to a forum where conversations were far-ranging and discussions centered on the latest publications and plays. It was also a place where these women could read their works and were made to feel on an equal footing with men. If their education had been neglected, the salon offered them repeated opportunities to complete it. In addition, several of these women poets were published thanks to the encouragement of the friends they made in the salons.

In the second half of the eighteenth century and after the Revolution, both Fanny de Beauharnais and Félicité de Genlis presided over famous salons. Beauharnais was an ardent advocate of women writers and already a feminist. She found in the poet Claude-Joseph Dorat an ally, a lover, and someone who would introduce her to men of letters and politicians. In her salon, the seeds of what was to become the first National Assembly were planted. Even if it was rumored that Dorat wrote her novels and poems, both Voltaire in his letters and Grimm in the *Correspondance littéraire* praised her writings. She corresponded with Jean Jacques Rousseau, and Buffon was one of her many admirers. She herself was a devoted friend of Louis-Sébastien Mercier and Rétif de La Bretonne. There is little doubt that the men of letters who gathered in her salon approved of her lit erary aspirations. As already stated, Genlis's first claim to fame was her musical talent. She made her debut in the salon of her protector the "tax farmer" Le Riche de La Poupelinière when she was only twelve years old. She sang and played the harp, excelled in it and became a favorite of salon society. Her career started in earnest when she was lady-in-waiting of the duchesse de Chartres—later duchesse d'Orléans—in the Palais-Royal. After being the organizer of the duchesse's salon, she opened her own, in which she received men of letters on Tuesdays and musicians on Saturdays. When she moved to a convent on rue de Bellechasse in 1779, she welcomed writers and artists on Saturdays. Buffon, the critic La Harpe, d'Alembert, and many others were frequent guests. Even the celebrated hostess and patron of the arts Madame du Deffand put in an appearance a few times. Her presence signaled that the baton had been passed to a new generation. Madame Necker, herself the hostess of an influential salon, brought her daughter Madame de Staël.[9] In her long life, Genlis presided over many salons, not only in Paris before and after the Revolution, but also in exile in Hamburg, and the list of her guests would include at one time or another most of the luminaries of Europe. Nevertheless, her sometimes intense social activity not only never prevented her from writing and publishing in several genres and becoming a popular novelist and playwright, but also can be seen as beneficial to her success. Her salon was her study or laboratory, where conversation led to writing. Though poetry was not her major production, she indulged in it and wrote fables, which she considered better suited to education than those of La Fontaine.

The overall picture strongly suggests that behind a façade of social gatherings, most salons hid more serious ambitions for a good number of their habitués. And for the majority of the women whose poems are presented in Part II of this volume, a salon provided an ideal gathering place, where they mixed with contemporary men and women of letters, honed their skills, and found the support and encouragement they needed to achieve their literary goals.

It is also clear that Paris was the center of all intellectual and artistic activities. If only four—Deshoulières, Chéron, Gillot de Sainctonge, Beauharnais—of our poets were Parisians by birth, all the others eventually came to Paris. We do not always know the exact reasons for their move to the capital but can easily guess that life in the provinces did not present them with the opportunities they longed for. Scudéry left Rouen at the mature—for the time—age of thirty; as soon as Coligny separated from her second husband she came to Paris; Villedieu was brought to Paris as an adolescent by her mother; Bernard came in her early twenties; and Joliveau de Segrais as a young bride. The Parisians Deshoulières and Beauharnais, who respectively followed their husbands to Flanders and La Rochelle, left them to return to their birthplaces. This convergence of lives in Paris is another trait these poets have in common.

But there are more similarities. Traditionally male bastions opened—or half-opened—their doors to them. Thanks to her talent as a painter and the sponsorship of Charles Le Brun, Chéron was elected to the Royal Academy of Painting and Sculpture. Scudéry, Deshoulières, and Chéron could also call themselves academicians, having been elected to the Academy of the Ritrovati of Padua. In addition, Deshoulières was a member of the Academy of Arles. Joliveau de Segrais was a member of two Parisian societies, the Société des Belles-lettres and the Athénée des Arts, and of the Sociéte d'Emulation de l'Ain. Recognition came to Scudéry, Deshoulières, Villedieu, Chéron, and Bernard in the form of pensions from Louis XIV; to Guibert, from Louis XV; and to Genlis, from Napoleon I. Although the doors of the Académie française remained closed to women, the all-male institution awarded prizes to two women poets, first, Deshoulières and later, on more than one occasion, Bernard, who was also honored by the Jeux floraux de Toulouse.[10]

To no one's great surprise, these women collected firsts. Coligny de La Suze was the first woman to have a collection of her poems published during her lifetime. Villedieu was the first woman to live by her pen; Chéron, the first woman admitted to the Royal Academy of Painting; Bernard, the first woman playwright to have a full-length play performed at the Comédie-Française; and Deshoulières, the first woman poet to receive a prize from the Académie française. As previously noted, Genlis was governor—not governess—of the children of the duc d'Orléans, another first for a woman. And Joliveau de Segrais was the first woman member of the Sociéte d'Emulation de l'Ain.

Their marital status is worth noting. Scudéry, Bernard, and Guibert never married. Marriage for the others was celebrated at different ages and rarely brought happiness or even contentment. It could be an alliance arranged by the woman's family, sometimes at a very young age: Deshoulières married at thirteen; Beauharnais, at fifteen, to a man twenty-one years her senior. In the case of Coligny, who became a widow in her twenties, remarriage to a man she loathed was forced on her by her mother. She fought for eight years to obtain an annulment. Villedieu waited until she was thirty-seven to marry and soon became a widow. Chéron, single most of her life, married even later—at sixty. Montanclos lost her first husband and remarried, but the couple separated within months of the ceremony. Beauharnais, separated at first from her husband, was widowed when he died on the guillotine. Genlis's husband, who, as a member of the Convention, voted against Louis XVI's death sentence, was also a victim of the Terror. Joliveau de Segrais was widowed at the age of fifty-six. Only Gillot de Sainctonge and La Férandière remained married throughout their lives.

It seems that for most of these women, when it took place, marriage was not an end in itself. As often as not they were not bound by its laws and never hesitated to pursue independent lives. Many were single mothers who took on the responsibility of educating their children alone. Genlis was the most exemplary. Though still married, she was the educator in the family. Deshoulières raised her four children. Her daughter must have learned to admire her mother's gift since it was she who published her works. Montanclos also raised her daughters by herself and had to juggle her private and professional lives. The consequences of these women's independence brought difficult financial situations. We know from poems and letters they wrote that they could not always count on the royal pensions promised to them. Half of them—Scudéry, La Suze, Chéron, Deshoulières, Bernard, Genlis—led impecunious lives and had to work to make ends meet. Chéron, a child prodigy, supported her mother and siblings when she was only sixteen. Genlis, another child prodigy, started supporting herself and her mother at about the same age as Chéron. Except as a young married woman and later as governor of the children of the duc d'Orléans, her financial situation was always precarious. During her exile and after she returned to Paris at the end of the century, she lived by her pen.

These women wore many hats, as their careers as painters, educators, musicians, editors, novelists, playwrights, translators, and, last but not least, poets, illustrate. The spectrum of their activities and the extent of their successes are proof, first, of their talent and, second, of their resourcefulness, courage, and resilience. There is really no need to dwell on what some saw as the scandalous aspects of their lives; there is plenty to admire about these uncommon, modern women.

The fate of poetry differed in the seventeenth century from what it would be in the eighteenth. Considered as one of the noble genres in both centuries, in the age of Louis XIV, it found its greatest practitioners in two playwrights, Corneille and Racine; in the satirist Boileau and the fabulist La Fontaine; and, on the eve of the French Revolution, in the lyric theorist André Chénier. This rather short list should not hide the fact that poetry was the raison d'être of many more writers who received applause and recognition from their contemporaries, and that among them we find not only the names of our thirteen women poets but also that of Voltaire.

From the beginning of the seventeenth century, poetry thrived in the salons. It was without any doubt the literary genre par excellence. As Boileau wrote in *L'art poétique* (1674), "Enfin Malherbe vint" (At long last, Malherbe came), and poetry acquired a spokesman and a reformer who inspired several generations of poets: men like Mathurin Régnier, Racan, de Viau, Saint-Amant, Voiture, and Benserade. The other noticeable change from the preceding century is the link between writers and the ruling classes. Richelieu first and then Mazarin viewed artists as useful to the sovereign and rewarded those who served him well. As for Louis XIV, he went a step further and singled out poets as an integral part of his politics of grandeur. The king was quick to understand how he could take advantage of poets to extol his virtues, victories, and glory. All through his long reign, he searched in vain for a poet capable of writing an epic adequately celebrating his exploits. Given the way he felt about poets, he was appropriately generous to them, as illustrated by the number of royal pensions, gratifications, and court appointments. For instance, in 1677, two poets, Racine and Boileau, were named royal historiographers. Assisted by his minister Colbert and the newly founded Académie française, Louis approved the creation of a prize for the best poetry composed in his honor. As previously noted, both Deshoulières and Bernard were recipients of this award. Moreover, princes of the blood and members of the aristocracy who did not want to be outdone, as well as a new breed of financiers, joined the ranks of patrons. Several of the women poets presented in this anthology were the beneficiaries of this largesse, which was responsible for enhancing their status.

Some literary historians have suggested that the eighteenth century should be called a century without poets.[11] This rather provocative if somewhat untrue label underlines the fact that, although there were many poets, the quantity of their productions never really made up for their lack of quality. And despite attempts to rehabilitate the century, the balance sheet remains disappointing. Voltaire was considered the greatest poet of his day, but his poetry is seldom read now. Chénier alone has received a better treatment from posterity. Also Louis XV and Louis XVI had little interest in supporting artists and especially poets. Of course, writers still found patrons, and salon society continued to exist and to define poetry as a social accomplishment, but the general atmosphere was quite different from the one that had prevailed in the preceding century. After the rather heated debate at the beginning of the century of the Querelle des anciens et des modernes, from which poetry could have benefited but did not, taste shifted toward other artistic forms of expression and above all philosophy. As we shall soon see, this did not mean any radical changes for the poetic output of the six women who represent the eighteenth century in this volume.

In both centuries, poetry came in different guise. First, there was the light and playful poetry popular in the salons, usually linked to the movement known as preciosity. The range of themes was narrow and expressed in madrigals, epigrams, impromptus, songs, bouquets, portraits, and idylls. Second, there were the deferential poems celebrating the actions of the greatest king on earth and by extension his entourage. Third, the influence of La Fontaine was felt in the many fables written by poets trying to cash in on this vogue. Fourth, there was a body of religious poetry. And last, there was a more serious kind of poetry: complaints, reflections, and maxims. Poetry sold well because it continued to be regarded as the noblest branch of rhetoric and the most prestigious form of literary expression. It reached a wide audience in numerous collections by individual poets or groups of poets—the *Parnasse des dames*, the *Almanach de Muses*, the *Parnasse français*, and the *Mercure gallant*, for instance.

Some of the poems written by the thirteen women representing the seventeenth and eighteenth centuries are excellent illustrations of the five categories just mentioned. The anthology gives numerous examples of madrigals. These may be addressed to an admirer, like Scudéry's "A Pelisson," or simply speak of love, like Gillot de Sainctonge's "Le premier plaisir est d'aimer, / Et le second est de charmer / Celle pour qui l'on soupire" (A pleasure, first, it is to love; / Second, to charm the object of / Our sigh and moan). It is elegant flirting in the salon tradition. The tone, sometimes, is more serious, as in the two madrigals in which Scudéry says she would not mind being immortal as long as she were surrounded by her friends (she was in her nineties when she died). On the other hand, Bernard is having fun with a madrigal entitled "Pour un chien de Madame de Coulanges appelé Follet" (For Madame de Coulanges's Dog Follet), in which she plays on the similarity between "Follet" and folly. Epigrams are also a common type of poetry. A good example is the following one by Gillot de Sainctonge: "Iris, cette folle coquette, / Dont les couleurs couchent sur la toilette, / Demandoit à Damon comme il trouvoit son teint: / Ah! reprit-il d'un ton malin, / J'ai toujours laissé l'art pour suivre la nature, / Et jamais je ne fus connoisseur en peinture" (Iris—coquettish ninny, she— / Whose face paints on her dressing table lie, / Asks Damon how he likes her blush. "Since I," / Replies the wag, maliciously, / "Quit art to follow nature, I demur: / Never was I a painting connoisseur!")

Examples of songs—usually set in nature among shepherds—can be found in the poems of Coligny and Deshoulières, and in the following one by Gillot de Sainctonge. "Ne voyons plus ce Berger, / Il pourroit bien m'engager: / Malgré son humeur volage / Je lui trouve des apas; / Et s'il devenoit plus sage, / Je pourrois ne l'être pas" (Let me no more that shepherd see, / Lest he win me quite utterly. / For, though he be a fickle lad, / Yet charming do I find the knave: / Ah! If he better manners had, / Then might I much the worse behave). Bernard's series of bouquets—pieces of gallant inspiration—are another form of light poetry. In the eighteenth century, Montanclos wrote a four-line impromptu on a penalty at cards that was just as carefree as the various types of poetry listed above, and Beauharnais published a quatrain on the fleeting nature of beauty in a collection appropriately called *Mélange de poésies fugitives et de prose sans conséquence*.

La Férandière's "Portrait des maris" illustrates another favorite pastime of salon society. In this particular case, since it deals with marriage, it is appropriately satirical. Not unlike Silvia, the heroine of Marivaux's *Le jeu de l'amour et du hasard,* the poet worries about what happens to a man when he becomes a husband. "Sitôt que du mariage / Le lien sacré l'engage, / Plus de voeux, pas un hommage; / Plaisirs, talens, tout s'enfuit; / En vertu de l'hyménée, / Il vous gronde à la journée, / Bâille toute la soirée, / Et ronfle toute la nuit" (Once the sacred marriage bond / Binds him ever and beyond, / Gone the vows, the tributes fond; / Pleasures, fled; and passion too: / Married now, our popinjay / Scolds and scolds the livelong day, / Yawns the evening hours away, / Snores and snores the whole night through). In a lighter vein is Guibert's self-portrait "Vive jusqu'à l'étourderie, / Folle dans mes discours, mais sage en mes écrits" (Pert, even unto thoughtlessness, / Daft in my talk, but in my writings wise). The tone remains mocking in Beauharnais's "Aux hommes, " and "Portrait des François." Deshoulières's 1674 idyll "Les moutons" deserves special mention, because it brought her fame and also because, in a pastoral and dreamlike setting, the poet paints the happiness of the sheep, which is the envy of every man.

We are told that what Scudéry felt for Louis XIV was real adoration, and that in her eyes he was not Louis *le Grand* but Louis *le plus Grand*. And so she played the role of the semiofficial poet who never missed a chance to celebrate the king, his deeds, and his family. The reader will not only find madrigals of hers praising the king for peace and for the conquest of Luxembourg but also several poems flattering other members of the royal family and thus still paying court to the sovereign. She was commissioned to write a poem "Sur la mort de la reine-mère." The eight-line madrigal in alexandrines was deemed appropriately majestic to warrant being engraved in gold on a portrait of the queen. When Bernard gave up writing for the theater in 1691, she committed herself to poetry for two reasons. The first one was because of the prestige the genre enjoyed, and the second because she was hoping to belong to a group of artists toward whom the king felt particularly benevolent and generous. That same year, she entered one of her poems in the competition set up by the Académie française and was awarded the prize. Two years later, she was once more the one chosen by the academicians to receive the prize. From then on, she never missed an occasion to sing the praises of the king, influential people at court and, last but not least, Madame de Maintenon, the king's morganatic second wife. Although this volume does not give examples of the poems that won prizes, the selection includes six others that will enable readers to decide how good an encomiast she was. The madrigal "A Mignard, sur les portraits de Louis XIV et de Madame de Maintenon" was such a success when it came out that Madame de Coulanges sent it to Madame de Sévigné so that she too could enjoy it. In it, Bernard writes that she has already praised her master a thousand times—one wonders if it is just a figure of speech! As by nature an epigram is meant to be witty, it is interesting that she chose that form to write "A Madame de Maintenon," thus adding an irreverent note to her praises. But paying tribute to a sovereign one admired did not die with Louis XIV. The relationship between Voltaire and Frederick II of Prussia has been thoroughly documented,[12] as has that of Diderot with Catherine II of Russia. Likewise, Montanclos wrote a six-line poem in alexandrines entitled "A Catherine II, impératrice de Russie, après avoir remporté une victoire sur les Turcs" in which the queen becomes a king, a hero and a warrior.

The anthology contains a selection of fables written by four of our poets—Villedieu, La Férandière, Genlis, and Joliveau de Segrais. The first two and the fourth were great admirers of La Fontaine. La Férandière says as much in a self-deprecating and amusing poem entitled "Le bon choix du rat," (The Rat's Wise Choice), in which she imagines that, during the night, a rat has eaten her La Fontaine: "Ciel! ma bonne édition / De mon bien aimé La Fontaine" (Heavens

Perdition! / A rat has nibbled on that fine edition / Of my belovèd La Fontaine!). When she realizes that she made a mistake, she exclaims "Le mal n'est pas grand: / Ce rat d'esprit n'a mangé que les miennes" (The damage is not great: / Mine are the only ones the creature ate!). Since the eight fables by Villedieu appeared in 1670—only two years after the publication of La Fontaine's first book of fables—it proves that she saw it as a challenge. Both women poets tried to emulate the master with varying degrees of success. Villedieu's fables are a bit long, and so the reader often loses interest before reaching the moral expressed in the last lines, and those of La Férandière are missing the picturesque portraits of the animals that are part of La Fontaine's genius. But let's not be too harsh on them and recognize their talent. In "La tourterelle & le ramier" (The Turtledove and the Ringdove), Villedieu describes the ringdove as "Houpé, patu, de beau plumage, / Et quoy que jeune, vieux Routier / Dans l'Art de soulager, les douleurs du veuvage" (Fair of face, / Elegantly and finely feathered, and / Though young, much the experienced hand, / Well-versed in consolation's art, and good / At calming the despair of widowhood). In the first line of "Le sansonnet & le coucou" (The Starling and the Cuckoo), the starling is described as a "Jargonneur signalé" (glib of chatter). In "Le papillon, le freslon, & la chenille" (The Butterfly, the Hornet, and the Caterpillar), the rivalry between the butterfly and the hornet is seen as a bloody combat. The most felicitous portrait may be the one of the monkey who played Cupid "A se cupidonner le Magot se prepare; / Endosse le carquois, s'affuble du bandeau, / En conquerant des cœurs, se rengorge, & se quarre, / Et se mirant dans un ruisseau, / Se prend pour Cupidon, tant il se trouve beau" (Now in the godlet's guise, / He sets about cupidifying... / At length, stopping beside a brook— / Swelling with pride— he goes to look, / And there perceives so fair and fine a sight / That he, indeed, believes he might / Play Love himself). The neologism *cupidonner* is well coined and somewhat jolting in that it refers to a monkey. As for La Férandière, in "Le papillon et la chenille" (The Butterfly and the Caterpillar) or in "L'abeille et le limaçon" (The Bee and the Snail), she captures the lively rhythm of the dialogues between these creatures that gives the fables their charm. In "Le financier et les paysans" (The Financier and the Peasants), she certainly found the perfect name for a financier, "Monsieur Mondor," or "Mr. Mount of Gold"! Genlis, the third author of fables in this anthology, did not share her predecessors' admiration for La Fontaine. As a former friend and disciple of Jean-Jacques Rousseau, she disapproved of the lessons given in the fables. Like Rousseau, she loved to collect plants, so in an attempt to distance herself from her model, she called her collection of eighteen fables *Herbier moral* (Moral Herbarium) and set her stories among plants. On the other hand, Joliveau de Segrais emulated her model, as the examples included in this volume will show. In three of them, one will admire the wit and art of the fabulist who is able to tell a story *and* deliver a moral in six lines—"Les deux charrues" (The Two Ploughshares), four lines—

"La paille et l'ambre" (The Straw and the Amber), and even two—"L'aigle et le ver" (The Eagle and the Worm). This talent has led a modern critic to call her fables "small jewels."[13]

The already multitalented Chéron chose to write in a genre that singles her out among the other poets of this volume, religious poetry. For her paraphrase of the Book of Psalms, she learned Hebrew to better understand the meaning of the original texts. The result is both powerful and graceful. The three psalms in this volume show a poet in full possession of her craft as she depicts first the joy of the Jews when they obtained permission to return to Jerusalem after seventy years of captivity and then their despair at being held captive by the Babylonians.

Notwithstanding the number of madrigals, epigrams, songs, and so on mentioned in the preceding pages, women poets could and did write serious poetry. In her "Plaintes d'une épouse tendre à son mari" (Lament of a Loving Wife to Her Husband), Montanclos conveys the everlasting and painful nature of her love using the vivid image of a wounded doe. Coligny de La Suze in "L'amour raisonnable," discusses the choice of a mistress, how the young wrongly think love to be everlasting, and how friendship always brings happiness, whereas love often brings sorrow. Her elegies were praised by Boileau—a demanding critic—in a letter to Perrault. Villedieu, in "Maximes diverses sur plusieurs sujets," also writes about love and lovers in a perceptive and sincere fashion. However, Deshoulières, in "Réflexions diverses," raises topics of broader human interest, such as death: "Que l'homme connoît peu la mort qu'il apprehende, / Quand il dit qu'elle le surprend! / Elle naît avec lui: sans cesse lui demande / Un tribut dont en vain son orgueil se défend" (How little does man know when, fearing death, / He claims it takes him unawares! / Born with him, as he breathes his life's first breath, / It levies constant tribute, one he dares / In vain refuse); knowledge of oneself: "De ce sublime esprit dont ton orgueil se pique, / Homme, quel usage fais-tu? / Des plantes, des métaux, tu connois la vertu, . . . / Des Astres le pouvoir suprême: / Et sur tant de choses savant, / Tu ne te connois pas toi-meme!" (That mind sublime wherein you take such pride, / O Man: what use make you of it? / You know each plant's, each metal's benefit; . . . / The power of the stars, . . . / In many ways, you are so wise: / And yet your self you scarcely know!); poverty, wisdom, and brevity of life: "Palais, nous durons moins que vous / Quoique des Elemens vous souteniez la guerre, . . . / Un rien peut nous détruire; & l'ouvrage d'un Dieu / Dure moins que celui des hommes!" (Old palaces! Less do we last than you. / Though Nature on you wages war, . . . / How passing odd / That, easily brought down, work of a God, / Less do we last than the mere work of Man!). Deshoulières was, after all, the most admired lyric poet of her generation, and one can see the reason for her fame. She treated grave topics with great sensitivity. Her works were published before she died and reprinted many times in the eighteenth century.

But one type of poetry is in a class by itself and deserves to be mentioned last because it is the most unexpected from the pen of a woman. The reader will enjoy the five drinking songs Gillot de Sainctonge wrote, and will be interested to see, as Shapiro points out, that when the poet is inspired by such a topic, she writes in a masculine voice. To the lover whose mistress has a heart of stone, she/he recommends "Pren la Bouteille pour Maîtresse, / Elle a de plus doux attraits. / Elle ne s'enfuit jamais / Du Beuveur qui la caresse" (Best let the bottle take your mistress's place: / Softer and gentler are her charms, / Nor will she flee a drunkard's arms' / Tender caress and sweet embrace). And in "Hiver bachique" (Bacchic Winter) we are told: "Pour braver les froideurs d'un Hiver rigoureux, . . . / Je cours au glouglou des bouteilles" (To brave the rigors of the winter chill, . . . / I run to make the bottles' gurglings mine.) When called for, the lady did find the right onomatopoeia and wrote something less traditional and affected than poems of love among shepherds.

This is only a beginning, and much remains to be said and done about poetry in the seventeenth and eighteenth centuries—especially poetry written by women. The preceding pages do not mean to be an exhaustive picture of the situation. They try to show that many of these poets were well known for their talents and found success among their contemporaries. The lives they led often challenged the norm, and the métier they chose came with its rewards as well as its price. In any case, whether their poems are light, deferential, religious or serious, whether they wrote fables or drinking songs, they deserve a larger place in our literary histories and a fairer treatment by critics.

NOTES

1. Until the duc d'Orléans promoted Genlis from governess of his daughters to governor of his sons and daughters, the title was only given to men. Sons of noble families were educated by men (governors), and daughters by women (governesses). The controversial appointment was the talk of Paris and Versailles.

2. In 1685, Louis XIV signed an edict that made it illegal to practice Protestantism in France, and thus forced many French into exile.

3. François Poullain de La Barre, *De l'égalité des deux sexes: Discours physique et moral où l'on voit l'importance de se défaire des préjugez* (Paris: J. Du Puis, 1673), *De l'éducation des dames pour la conduite de l'esprit dans les sciences et dans les moeurs* (Paris: J. Du Puis, 1674), and *De l'excellence des hommes contre l'égalité des sexes* (Paris: J. Du Puis, 1675), trans. Vivien Bosley under the title *Three Cartesian Feminist Treatises*, ed. Marcelle Maistre Welch (Chicago: University of Chicago Press, 2002).

4. François de Salignac de La Mothe-Fénelon's *Le traité de l'éducation des filles* (Paris, 1687) forbids the teaching of Italian and Spanish, because it would only lead to the reading of dangerous books and of science, to preserve girls' sense of modesty.

5. In his *Mémoires sur l'instruction publique* (1790), Condorcet also advocates coeducation.

6. Dena Goodman, *The Republic of Letters: A Cultural History of the French Enlightenment* (Ithaca, N.Y.: Cornell University Press, 1994), and Benedetta Cravi, *The Age of Conversation* (New York: New York Review Books, 2005).

7. The Querelle des anciens et des modernes was the name given to the literary quarrel that, between 1687 and 1715, opposed a group of authors—La Fontaine, La Bruyère, Boileau—respectful of tradition represented by antiquity and another group—Perrault, Fontenelle, Houdar de La Motte—who were champions of modernity.

8. Micheline Cuénin, *Roman et société sous Louis XIV: Madame de Villedieu (Marie-Catherine Desjardins, 1640–1683)*, 2 vols. (Paris: Honoré Champion, 1979), 100–101.

9. Suzanne Churchod (1737–1794) married the Swiss financier Jacques Necker (1732–1794), who was Louis XVI's finance minister between 1776 and 1789. Their only daughter, Anne Louise Germaine Necker (1766–1837) became a renowned author under her married name, Madame de Staël.

10. Toulouse claims to have organized the oldest poetry competition in the world in 1324, the Jeux floraux, which became an *académie* under the patronage of Louis XIV in 1694; it honored Chateaubriand and the young Victor Hugo in the nineteenth century.

11. *Histoire littéraire de la France,* ed. Pierre Abraham, Roland Desné, et al. (Paris: Editions sociales, 1969), 3: 433.

12. Every biography of Voltaire devotes a chapter to his tumultuous friendship with Frederick, but two studies focus on it: Christiane Mervaud, *Voltaire et Frédéric II: Une dramaturgie des Lumières, 1736–1778,* Studies on Voltaire and the Eighteenth Century, 234 (Oxford: Voltaire Foundation, 1985), and André Magnan, *Dossier Voltaire en Prusse: 1750–1753,* Studies on Voltaire and the Eighteenth Century, 244 (Oxford: Voltaire Foundation, 1986).

13. Giorgio Puttero, "Une fabuliste au XVIIIe siècle: Adine Joliveau de Segrais," *Reinardus* 17, 1 (2004): 140.

Madeleine de Scudéry (1607–1701)

For anyone familiar with the endless novels of sentimental adventure penned b⸱
Madeleine de Scudéry (or Scudéri) and, to a minor extent, her brother George⸱
(1601–1667), he of "three dramatic unities" fame, the poems presented her⸱
will come as something of a surprise. I say "familiar" because most students o⸱
French literature will know at least the name, though few would claim to havin⸱
really trudged through the ten-volume *Artamène, ou Le grand Cyrus* (1649–1653⸱
or the likewise-lengthed *Clélie: Histoire romaine* (1654–1661), with its celebrate⸱
"Carte de tendre," a map of the various stages of socially acceptable love (se⸱
p. 283n below). And I say "surprised," not only because few know that she eve⸱
wrote verse—though her own generation dubbed her "the new Sappho"—bu⸱
also because many of her poems, so brief that they finish almost before they be⸱
gin, stand out in striking contrast to her rather long-winded prose.

Madeleine de Scudéry was certainly one of the most important and impres⸱
sive women writers of her time and—a happy coincidence when considerin⸱
her novels—one of the longest-lived. Born into a debatably aristocratic famil⸱
she was orphaned early and raised in Rouen. At thirty, she moved to Paris to joi⸱
her brother and soon began frequenting the celebrated salon of the marquise d⸱
Rambouillet. *Ibrahim ou l'illustre Bassa,* a (mere!) four-volume opus, was pub⸱
lished under her brother's name in 1641, and its success prefigured that of he⸱
own next two works. Despite all their enormous popularity, and perhaps to ac⸱
commodate to a changing literary taste, she eventually reined in her inspiratio⸱
with a pair of shorter *nouvelles* and, toward the end of her life, a large numbe⸱
of *Conversations* on a variety of social and sentimental subjects reminiscent o⸱
those discussed by the many characters of her novels: questions of gallantr⸱
platonic love (in and out of wedlock), and all the conceits inherited and devel⸱
oped from the medieval courtly love tradition, and for whose refinement th⸱
post-Fronde generation yearned. In 1653, she started her own salon when tha⸱
of the elegant marquise began to decline in popularity. Among the faithful wa⸱
her "spiritual" lover, the variously spelled Paul Pel(l)is(s)on (see below, p. 283n⸱
Their relationship was supposedly an excellent example of the rarefied, non⸱
carnal ideal of love as put forth in her novels. (If Pellisson was as ugly as he⸱
perhaps facetious madrigal suggests, we can understand why it was not mor⸱
physical.) A royal pension awarded her in 1683 was one of several honors pai⸱
her before her death in 1701 for her contribution to French letters and culture.

Scudéry's prose extravaganzas left their mark on the development of th⸱
novel—not only the novel of adventure, in which her narratives abound, bu⸱
also in the minute dissection of sentiment and its many "psychological" rami⸱

fications through protracted debate similar to salon conversation. Ironically, their excesses are not their least important element, for it was in reaction to them that the novel would, eventually, pare itself down to the more compact dimensions of such works as Madame de Lafayette's *La princesse de Clèves* (1678) and its successors.[1]

Clearly, Scudéry's madrigals, impromptus, and variously inspired quatrains—"occasional" verse in both senses of the term—is of *précieuse* inspiration and also show that, like many artists throughout history, she was not above flattering the wealthy and powerful. Most of her verse is found in disparate volumes, as indicated in the notes to the individual translations.

NOTE

1. Details of Scudéry's life, correspondence, and a selection of poems can be found in Edmé-Jacques-Bénoît Rathery and Boutron, *Mademoiselle de Scudéry, sa vie et sa correspondance, avec un choix de ses poésies*. For biographical details, see Victor Cousin's important *La société française au XVIIe siècle d'après "Le grand Cyrus" de Mlle Scudéry*, and, more recently, Nicole Aronson, *Mademoiselle de Scudéry*; Alain Niderst, *Mademoiselle de Scudéry, Paul Pellisson et leur monde*; and René Godenne, *Les romans de Mademoiselle de Scudéry*, among others. Katharine Ann Jensen's entry in *French Women Writers*, pp. 430–37, contains an informative biographical sketch, and a discussion of her importance as a writer in general and a woman writer in particular.

Iob perdit enfans & troupeaux,
Ce Iob que l'Histoire renomme;
Iob vit flamber tous ses Chasteaux,
Iob souffrit mille & mille maux,
Et les souffrit en galant homme.
Mais estre condamné par vous,
Objet aussi puissant que doux,
Princesse, ornement de la France,
C'est un si grand malheur, que lors qu'il le sçaura,
Malgré toute sa patience,
Ie croy que Iob enragera.

A vous dire la verité,
Le destin de Iob est étrange,
D'estre tousiours persecuté
Tantost par vn Demon, & tantost par vn Ange.

Job lost his flocks, his children—oh!
Poor Job, well known to History;
† Job watched flames ravage his *châteaux,*
Job suffered many a woe on woe,
And suffered them most gallantly.
Ah! But to be condemned by you,
Creature of power, yet gracious too—
Glorious princess fair of France—
Is such a blow that, when he learns of it,
His patience will be flung askance,
And Job, I fear, will have a fit.

Poésies choisies (1653)

To tell the truth, Job's destiny
Is strange, and leaves me much perplexed:
To be the constant victim, he,
‡ First, of the Devil, and of an Angel, next.

Poésies choisies (1653)

* This is one of a plethora of verses occasioned by a celebrated—and typically French—literary quarrel: the one between those of Scudéry's contemporaries who preferred a sonnet on the embodiment of beauty, "A Uranie," by Vincent Voiture (1579–1648), to one on Job by Isaac de Benserade (1613–1691), both typical examples of the exaggerated preciosity of the time. The issue divided literary and social Paris for several years, with *Uranistes* championing their taste, and *Jobelins*, theirs. Anne, duchesse de Longueville (1619–1679) and sister of the Grand Condé, was an ardent anti-*Jobelin*. The present poem and the one following are from a sampling of the poetic results of the quarrel, found in the first and second editions of Scudéry's *Poésies choisies*, published by Charles de Sercy, the so-called Recueil de Sercy. Another brief Job-inspired poem attributed to Scudéry follows these two below.

† I doubt that the poet really believed that Job possessed any *chasteaux*, but I would be loath to replace the notion with a more appropriate one.

‡ I think it safe to assume that, given the context of the preceding poem, the "angel" in question is Madame de Longueville.

Madeleine de Scudéry 277

Contre Job autrefois le démon révolté
Lui ravit ses enfants, ses biens et sa santé;
Mais pour mieux l'éprouver et déchirer son âme,
Savez-vous ce qu'il fit?... Il lui laissa sa femme.

IMPROMPTU À L'HONNEUR DU PRINCE DE CONDÉ, QUI CULTIVOIT DES FLEURS

En voyant les œillets, qu'un illustre guerrier
Arrose d'une main qui gagne des batailles,
Souviens-toi qu'Apollon a bâti des murailles;
Et ne t'étonne pas que Mars soit jardinier.

AU ROI, SUR LA PAIX

Dès que tu fais un pas l'Europe est en alarmes,
      Et contre l'effort de ses armes
      Rien ne pourroit la soutenir;
Mais dans un calme heureux tu gouvernes la terre:
      Quand on peut lancer le tonnerre,
      Qu'il est beau de le retenir.

Satan, provoked at Job, once took his wealth,
Bore off his children, robbed him of his health;
And then, to try him more, poison his life,
* What did he do?... He let him keep his wife.

† IMPROMPTU IN HONOR OF THE PRINCE DE CONDÉ,
WHO WAS RAISING FLOWERS

A warrior, with that conquering hand of his,
Waters his pinks; but that ought not surprise:
Apollo caused many a wall to rise,
So wonder not that Mars a gardener is.

‡ TO THE KING, ON THE PEACE

You need but make a move and Europe quakes,
    Nor is there any help one takes
    To save her from your arms' attack.
But now you rule in peace, earth's wounds are healed:
    When one the lightning bolt can wield,
    How noble it is to hold it back.

Parnasse des dames (1773), "Madrigaux," I

---

* Not having been able to locate the original of this poem, I reproduce the modernized orthography of *Huit siècles de poésie féminine*, ed. Moulin, for the French text.

† This quatrain appears in [Joseph de Laporte], *Histoire littéraire des femmes françoises*, 5 (1769): 285. It is not cited in other sources that include Scudéry's occasional verse. Louis II, prince de Condé (1621–1686), known as the Grand Condé to distinguish him from several others of the same family, notable throughout four centuries of French history, was one of Louis XIV's most celebrated generals and commanded the victorious French forces at the battles of Rocroi, Nordlingen, Fribourg, and others. He fell into temporary disfavor at the time of the Fronde.

‡ The king is, of course, Louis XIV, though it is hard to know precisely to what "peace" the poet is alluding, given the numerous wars that marked his reign both before and after the ministry of Mazarin.

À MONSEIGNEUR LE DAUPHIN
LE JOUR QU'IL REÇUT LE NOM DU ROI

Sentez-vous bien le prix du grand nom qu'on vous donne?
Prince, par mille exploits il faut le mériter;
Tout l'Univers le craint, la gloire l'environne,
Il n'en fut jamais un si pesant à porter.

À L'OCCASION DE LA PRISE DE LUXEMBOURG

A cette ville

Contre Louis vous n'avez pu tenir,
Consolez-vous d'un sort inévitable;
Vous vous trompiez de vous croire imprénable,
Mais en ses mains vous l'allez devenir.

* FOR MONSEIGNEUR LE DAUPHIN ON THE DAY WHEN HE RECEIVED THAT TITLE FROM THE KING

Prize you, Prince, that fine title now bequeathed?
A myriad feats must earn its honor rare:
Feared by the Universe, in glory wreathed,
Never has one been weightier to bear.

Parnasse des dames (1773), "Madrigaux," II

† ON THE OCCASION OF THE TAKING OF LUXEMBOURG

To that city

Unable were you to resist Louis:
You thought you were impregnable, but oh!
How wrong you are to mourn your fate; for, lo!
In his strong hands that is what you shall be.

Parnasse des dames (1773), "Madrigaux," IV

* The reference is to Louis de France (1661–1711), eldest son of Louis XIV, by Maria-Theresa of Austria, and, eventually, father of Felipe IV of Spain and grandfather of Louis XV. Known as the Grand Dauphin and Monseigneur, he was entrusted, in 1688, with nominal command of his father's armies in Germany, actually led by Vauban. But despite an education at the hands of the churchman Bossuet, he lived a rather undistinguished life, one that did not quite fulfill the wishes the poet expressed for him in this brief, traditional encomium.

† The dates of the poet's occasional verse are not always clear. In 1684, Louis XIV seized Luxembourg (which France kept until he was obliged to restore it to Spain by the Treaty of Ryswick in 1697). The reference would be to that campaign, unless it alludes to an earlier incursion into Luxembourg in 1659, when the Peace of the Pyrenees ceded a large portion of the duchy to France.

À PELISSON, BEL-ESPRIT TRÈS-CONNU PAR SES TALENS & SON EXCESSIVE LAIDEUR

Enfin, Acante, il faut se rendre,
Votre esprit a charmé le mien;
Je vous fais Citoyen du *Tendre*,
Mais, de grace, n'en dites rien.

RÉPONSE À UN MADRIGAL, OÙ ON LA TRAITOIT D'IMMORTELLE

Quand l'aveugle destin auroit fait une loi
    Pour me faire vivre sans cesse,
    J'y renoncerois par tendresse,
Si mes amis n'étoient immortels comme moi.

AUTRE RÉPONSE À UN MADRIGAL OÙ ON LA TRAITOIT ENCORE D'IMMORTELLE

    Votre madrigal est joli,
    Il est agréable et poli;
    Vous me louez de bonne grâce:
    Mais pour cette immortalité
    Dont on parle tant au Parnasse,
    Hélas! ce n'est que vanité.

**FOR PELISSON, A FINE WIT WELL KNOWN FOR
HIS TALENTS AND EXCESSIVE UGLINESS**

At length, Acante, I yield: amen.
Your wit prevails, second to none.
† I dub you *Tendre*'s citizen,
But, pray, do not tell anyone!

Parnasse des dames (1773), "Madrigaux," VIII

**REPLY TO A MADRIGAL IN WHICH
SHE WAS TREATED AS IMMORTAL**

If blind fate could enact a law whereby
   I might, myself, immortal be,
   I would reject it, lovingly,
‡ Unless my friends could live as long as I.

Parnasse des dames (1773), "Madrigaux," XIV

**ANOTHER REPLY TO A MADRIGAL IN WHICH
SHE WAS AGAIN TREATED AS IMMORTAL**

The madrigal you sent to me,
Well wrought, was written charmingly.
Most gracious is your praise; but want
I not the gift your lines contain:
That immortality they vaunt
Upon Parnassus! Ah, how vain!

---

* In all likelihood, divergent spelling and pet name notwithstanding, the reference is to Paul Pellisson (1624–1693), defender of Fouquet, historiographer of Louis XIV, and author of a history of the Académie française, of which he was a member.

† Readers familiar with the period will recognize the allusion to Tendre, the allegorical land of love described in the author's lengthy *précieux* novel *Clélie* (1654–1660), and made famous for generations by its map, the *carte de* (or *du*) *Tendre*, locating the various sentimental stages of a lover's quest, roundly ridiculed by Boileau and others.

‡ It must have seemed to many of her contemporaries that the poet, who lived until the age of ninety-four—an unusual age for her period—was, indeed, well on the way to physical immortality at least.

Madeleine de Scudéry 283

Car à la fin, Damon, le plus grand nom s'efface
    Dans la sombre postérité:
Et si le ciel vouloit contenter mon envie
J'en quitterois ma part pour un siècle de vie.

———————

SUR SON PORTRAIT

    Nanteuil, en faisant mon image,
A de son art divin signalé le pouvoir;
      Je hais mes yeux dans mon miroir,
      Je les aime dans son ouvrage.

———————

SUR LA MORT DE LA REINE-MÈRE

Anne, dont les vertus, l'éclat & la grandeur
Ont rempli l'Univers de leur vive splendeur,
Dans la nuit du tombeau conserve encor sa gloire,
Et la France à jamais aimera sa mémoire.
Elle sut mépriser les caprices du sort,
Regarder, sans pâlir, les horreurs de la mort,
Affermir un grand Trône & le quitter sans peine;
Et, pour tout dire enfin: vivre & mourir en Reine.

For, Damon, great though be the name we flaunt,
    It fades in future's dark domain:
With heaven's blessing, my share would I give
Had I, instead, one hundred years to live.

Rathery and Boutron, *Mademoiselle de Scudéry*

ON HER PORTRAIT

*   My portrait by Nanteuil: ah, 'tis
Proof of the power wrought by his art divine:
    I loathe my eyes in mirror mine,
    I love them in this canvas his.

Parnasse des dames (1773), "Madrigaux," xv

---

† ON THE DEATH OF THE QUEEN MOTHER

Anne—she, whose virtues, glorious and grand,
Splendidly all the universe outspanned—
In the tomb's darkness sheds her light the more:
Ever will France her name and fame adore.
Able was she to scorn fate's whim, prevailing
Over death's horrors, never shrinking, paling;
Strengthen the throne; quit it with tranquil mien;
And, be it said, to live and die a queen.

Parnasse des dames (1773), "Madrigaux," xvi

* The reference is to the celebrated painter and engraver Robert Nanteuil (ca. 1623–1678), known for his portraits of famous figures of the time, and especially admired for his lively and lifelike style.

† This poem can be rather accurately dated, given the death of Anne of Austria in 1666. Daughter of Felipe III of Spain, she was born in 1601, was married to Louis XIII, and served as regent during the minority of their son, Louis XIV, from his accession in 1643 until the death of her minister Mazarin in 1661, when Louis assumed personal power.

Henriette de Coligny de La Suze (1618–1673)

Although she did publish a modest volume of poems in 1666,[1] Henriette de Coligny, comtesse de La Suze, would be known to her contemporaries—literarily speaking—for works included in various evanescent collections; some, like *Le Parnasse des dames*, published well into the eighteenth century. (Non-literarily-speaking, she would be known as much, or more, for her personal adventures.) Madrigals, odes, epigrams—such were the usual brief poetic fare that would predominate, though several more substantial elegies, possibly retouched by this or that admirer or lover, received accolades from the likes of that arbiter of classical poetic taste Boileau. Each time one of these collections, especially, would be expanded and republished, it would include more and more of her work until, finally, in 1725, the *Recueil de pièces galantes en prose et en vers des plus beaux esprits du temps*, originally dating from 1663, contained, posthumously, virtually her entire œuvre.

Henriette de Coligny was born to the Protestant Gaspard III de Coligny, maréchal de Châtillon, and Anne de Polignac, and she was thus related to the French royal family. Contemporaries differ as to her physical attributes: some call her a beauty, but others are far less complimentary. Whatever the truth, she was twice married, though neither time because of or in spite of her attractiveness or lack of it, both marriages being arranged. Her first husband, a Scotsman, Thomas Hamilton, third earl of Haddington, died when she was twenty-seven, shortly after she became his wife, and her dominating mother picked her another staunch Calvinist, Gaspard de Champagne, comte de La Suze. Still young and frivolous, the new countess apparently had little affection for her spouse; and when, in 1653, she renounced her religion, the queen of Sweden is said to have quipped that she did so "in order not to be with her husband in this world or the next." At any rate, her conversion to Catholicism alienated her—not unintentionally—from her mate, resulting first in a separation and, finally, in 1661, in a much-publicized official divorce on the grounds of impotence.

By this time, La Suze, quite the social butterfly, had become part of the *précieuse* elite, flitting through the Hôtel de Rambouillet long enough to attract important friendships before starting a salon of her own. Madeleine de Scudéry and her faithful Pellisson were among her most vocal admirers, and it is supposed that their encouragement urged her along her poetic career. The former sang the thinly veiled praises of her *mille charmes* (thousand charms) and *bonté généreuse* (generous kindness) in her *Clélie* (see p. 274 above). A dyed-in-the-wool *précieuse*, La Suze was nonetheless able to appreciate her contemporaries' excesses and to express even some of the most traditional clichés with a delicate freshness and turn of wit that set her apart from most of them.[2]

Among her more striking verses are the ninety-five brief pieces in "L'amour raisonnable," a section of the *Recueil de pièces galantes en prose et en vers*, each of which is preceded, curiously, by a pithy prose reflection. I include twelve of them, along with four other typically pleasant trifles from the same collection. Each of the poems in "L'amour raisonnable" is preceded by a prose preamble, which is usually longer than the poem itself.

NOTES

1. The volume, published by Charles de Sercy, contains eighteen poems previously printed in the same bookseller's "Recueil de Sercy" of 1653.

2. Among the few works of substance devoted to La Suze's life and works, see Emile Magne, *Madame de La Suze et la société précieuse*, and Antoine Adam, *Histoire de la littérature française au XVIIe siècle*, 3: 171–72.

CHANSON

Lors que Tirsis me parut infidelle,
Apres m'auoir promis vn amour eternelle,
Ie fis vœu de hayr vn si leger Amant:
Mais malgré le dépit que cause vn tel outrage,
Ie n'eus pas si tost veu cet ingrat, ce volage,
Que ie me repentis d'auoir fait le serment.

Ie voulois le bannir quand il m'eut offensée,
Mais, helas! il parut à mon ame blessée
Tel que ie l'auois veu quand il sceut m'enflamer,
Quoy que son inconstance eust émeu ma colere,
Qu'est-ce qu'en ce moment mon cœur auroit pû faire,
Si ce n'est s'appaiser, l'écouter, & l'aimer?

CHANSON

Vous ne m'attirez pas par vos attraits charmans,
   Beaux lieux où tant d'heureux amans
   Trouvent de douces avantures:
Ah! je ne songe point à chercher des plaisirs
Et je viens seulement sous vos ombres obscures
Entretenir ma peine, & cacher mes soûpirs.

MADRIGAL

Entre deux beaux objets vostre cœur se partage,
Tous deux, à ce qu'on dit, vous peuuent enflâmer,
Escoutez mon conseil, cessez d'estre volage;
Tirsis, c'est trop de deux quand on veut bien aimer.

SONG

* When Thyrsis pledged me his eternal love,
And proved disloyal in the proof thereof,
I swore to loathe the cad who feigned his troth:
But though his treachery caused me much pain,
No sooner I beheld the fickle swain
Than, straightway, I repented of my oath.

Much grieved, I sought to send him on his way,
But to my wounded soul—alackaday!—
He loomed, quite as he was when the first thrill
Of passion flamed; and though, faithless, he spurred
My rage, helpless thereat, my heart was stirred
To pay him heed, be calmed, and love him still.

SONG

You lure me not with all your charms, O fair,
Delightful groves, sweet landscape, where
So many happy lovers pass
Their frolicsome adventures: in no wise
Seek I your joys; I crave your shades, alas,
But to endure my woe and hide my sighs.

MADRIGAL

Your heart between two creatures fair is split,
Thyrsis, and each is of a beauty such
As to enflame you; heed me, cease to flit
Betwixt: when one would love, two are too much.

---

* The poet's first line is curious for two reasons. First, either by negligence or design (and with no typographical indication), it is decasyllabic, while all those succeeding are alexandrines; and, second, the poet strays from the usual French spelling, "Tircis," of the traditional pastoral name, probably first used by Virgil in his *Eclogues*. Note also the difference between the ortho- and typographical archaisms in this and the following two texts, taken from the 1666 edition of the *Recueil,* and those, far fewer, in the others, taken from the edition of 1725.

MADRIGAL

Qvand vous pristes mon cœur, Amour me fut témoin
Que vous promistes avec soin
De n'abuser iamais d'vne telle victoire,
De m'aimer tendrement & de ne point changer:
Mais vous en perdez la mémoire,
Et vous estes, Tirsis, infidelle & leger.
Pour imiter vostre inconstance,
Ie deurois de mon cœur à iamais vous bannir:
Mais ne craignez point ma vengeance,
Ie me punirois trop en pensant vous punir.

FROM "L'AMOUR RAISONNABLE"

Le nombre des Rivaux ne fait pas le mérite d'une Belle. La plûpart des hommes aiment par caprice, ou suivent leur inclination, sans consulter la raison. Ils s'attachent souvent auprès de ces beautez adroites, à qui mille cœurs ont déjà passé par les mains, & qui ont donné le leur à mille Amans; ou bien ils s'engagent avec ces beautez naissantes, qui n'ont encore rien aimé.

La belle dont le cœur est tout neuf en amour,
Vous fait mal à propos soûpirer plus d'un jour,
A peine vous peut-elle entendre:
Mais n'y soyez point abuzé,
Il est plus facile de prendre
Un cœur tout neuf qu'un cœur usé.

MADRIGAL

You won my heart and swore by Love that you
    Would take great care never to do
Anything to misuse your hold on me:
* To love me ever tenderly; but oh!
    Now you forget, and, fancy-free,
Thyrsis, you are a faithless swain. But though
    I ought to ape your fickleness,
Banish you from my heart—indeed, abhor!—
    Fear not my vengeance: I confess,
Punishing you would punish me the more.

FROM "LOVE WELL-REASONED"

*The number of rivals does not increase a fair lady's worth. Most men love
on a whim, or merely to follow their inclination, without consulting their
reason. They often chase after those scheming beauties through whose hands
a thousand hearts have already passed, and who have given their own to a
thousand lovers; or else they take up with those budding beauties who have
not yet loved at all.*

The belle whose heart discovers love but newly,
May make you sigh day after day, unduly,
    And scarce may hear the sighs you make;
    But be not misled or bemused:
    Easier is it, yet, to take
    A new heart than a heart well used.

IV

* This line in the French, apparently omitted in error from the 1666 edition, is found
in the edition of 1725.

· · · · · · · ·

*Je ne conseillerois jamais d'offrir un cœur à ces belles capricieuses qui ne
font rien par raison; qui depensent sans choix les rigueurs & les graces, &
qui ne considerent ni les soins ni les services d'un amant. On n'est jamais
assuré de leur affection; elles désavoüent un moment après ce qu'elles
ont dit d'obligeant, & on ne sçait de quelle maniere les prendre pour
leur plaire.*

Gardez-vous bien d'aimer une belle inhumaine,
    Capricieuse, fiere & vaine,
    Car vous la perdrez tôt ou tard.
    Son cœur ne s'acquiert qu'avec peine,
    Et se conserve par hazard.

· · · · · · · ·

*Il est difficile de dire de quelle humeur doit être une Maîtresse; les uns aiment
les enjoüées, les autres en veulent aux mélancoliques: la bonne foi ou la
coqueterie se peuvent trouver en ces divers temperammens. C'est à l'Amant
à choisir, ou plûtôt c'est à l'Amour à l'attacher auprès de celle qui lui plaît.
Il ne dépend pas toûjours de nous de disposer de notre cœur.*

Le choix d'une Maîtresse est assez difficile,
Sur tout quand on la veut jeune, belle & civile,
Et dont l'esprit ne soit ni gay ni serieux:
    Mais selon le commun usage,
Si l'enjoüée a l'art de plaire davantage,
    La mélancolique aime mieux.

. . . .

Never should I advise one to offer his heart to those capricious belles who
act not according to reason; who randomly dispense their rigors and their
favors, and who esteem neither the concerns nor the services of a lover.
One can never be certain of their affection; they proffer a compliment and
gainsay it a moment later, and one knows not how to approach them if one
would give them pleasure.

Love not a belle of callous cruelty—
    Vain, proud, capricious—lest you be
    Without her, sooner, later; for
    Her heart is won most painfully,
    And kept by chance, and nothing more.

VI

. . . .

It is difficult to say of what humor a mistress ought be; some men love the
playful ones, others prefer the melancholic: in both of these temperaments
can one find good faith or coquettishness. It is the lover's task to choose; or,
rather, it is the task of Love to draw him to the one that he finds pleasing.
It is not always for ourselves to determine our heart's direction.

Choosing a mistress is not lightly done;
Especially a young, fair, well-bred one,
Not giddy, nor with dark thoughts to beset her:
    In man's experience one sees
That, if the first has greater art to please,
    The melancholic one loves better.

VII

Peu de gens sçavent faire une declaration d'amour de bonne grace, cependant chacun s'en mêle, & croit s'en acquitter heureusement. Il faut bien prendre son tems pour y réüssir. Un Amant qui ne plaît pas alors, court risque de ne plaire jamais. Avant que de vous engager à parler de votre passion, examinez bien les dispositions qu'on a de vous écouter.

Je vous aime sont trois mots
Qu'un Amant dit dès qu'il soûpire;
Mais ce n'est rien que de les dire,
Si l'on ne les dit à propos.

. . . .

C'est une erreur de croire que la hardiesse sied bien aux Amans, lorsque la raison ne la guide pas. L'amour respectueuse est la veritable Amour, & un honnête homme n'en connoît point d'autre.

Auprès de jeunes beautez
Gardez-vous bien d'avoir de ces temeritez
Que le respect a condamnées:
Car un temeraire Amant
Perd souvent dans un moment
Le fruit de plusieurs années.

. . . .

Few men know how to declare their love graciously, although everyone attempts to do so, and believes that he does it well. One must choose the proper moment if one is to succeed thereat. A lover who does not please then runs the risk of never pleasing at all. Before undertaking to declare your passion, study carefully whether one is disposed to hear you out.

* The words "I love you" go for naught—
Three words a lover sighs: but they
Mean nothing, say them how he may—
Unless he says them when he ought.

XI

. . . .

†   *It is a mistake to believe that bold action, unguided by reason, is favorable to lovers. The only true love is respectful love, and a man of gentle breeding knows no other.*

    If young belles you would be pursuing,
Be not too rash or daring, in your wooing,
     With disrespectful act: I fear
     Too often but the merest trice,
     For the rash lover, will suffice
‡   To lose the fruit of many a year.

XX

---

* Less than scrupulous in her syllable count (see p. 289n), the poet, curiously, begins her octosyllables with a seven-syllable line. I see no artistic reason to do likewise.

† The poet here in two sentences sums up the classical concept of "reason" as the essential element in the formation of the *honnête homme,* that icon of seventeenth-century French literature.

‡ As elsewhere, the author is rather cavalier in the syllable-count of her short lines—now seven, now eight—without aiding the reader with the appropriate indents usually found where such variety occurs.

. . . .

On a beau dire à un homme amoureux, qu'il cessera d'aimer, il n'en veut rien croire, & il ose même assûrer qu'il aimera toûjours. C'est répondre un peu legerement de l'avenir, & c'est vouloir ignorer que le tems affoiblit l'amour, & que malaisément on peut disposer pour toûjours de son cœur.

Il est certain qu'un jeune Amant
Croit aimer d'une amour extrême,
Et jure qu'éternellement
Il aimera l'objet qu'il aime;
Mais souvent il n'est plus le même,
Et change presque en un moment.

. . . .

Encore que le cœur d'un Amant soit capable de changer, il faut qu'il soit persuadé que s'il étoit possible, il aimeroit au delà du tombeau; que rien ne peut ébranler sa passion; que le tems ne fera que l'augmenter: & il doit agir comme si son amour ne pouvoit jamais finir.

Un veritable Amant présume d'ordinaire,
    Qu'il doit aimer d'une éternelle amour,
Et quiconque prévoit de n'aimer plus un jour,
S'il n'a cessé d'aimer, est bien près de le faire.

. . . .

Il est à souhaiter qu'un Amant soit toûjours propre, & qu'il ne paroisse jamais en désordre aux yeux de sa Maîtresse, ou du moins que sa negligence ne puisse pas lui déplaire.

    Ne vous piquez point de beauté,
    C'est une trop grande foiblesse,
Soyez pourtant bien mis sans paroître affecté:
    Qui neglige la propreté,
    Semble negliger sa Maîtresse.

. . . .

It is of no use to tell a man in love that he will stop loving; he will have none of it, and he even dares assert that his love will last forever. In so doing, he takes the future upon himself rather lightly and seems to forget that time weakens love and that he cannot always easily direct his heart to do as he desires.

A young beau thinks, undoubtedly,
That, endless, will his passion last,
And swears his love will ever be
Unlimited and unsurpassed;
But often change comes all too fast,
And soon a different beau is he.

XXXVI

. . . .

Although a lover's heart can change, he must be convinced that, were it possible, he would continue to love even beyond the grave; that nothing can shake his passion; that time will only increase it: and he must behave as if it were impossible ever for his love to end.

He who loves truly thinks love lasts until
    Time is no more, eternally;
And he who can, one day, love's end foresee,
If he has not ceased loving yet, soon will.

XXXVII

. . . .

It is desirable that a lover be always clean, and that he never appear disheveled in the eyes of his mistress; or, at least, that his untidiness never cause her displeasure.

Beauty has little power, and best
    You take no pride therein; but you
Should be well-groomed, neat, though not overdressed:
    Spurn not a clean appearance, lest
    It seem you spurn your mistress too.

LXII

. . . .

L'esprit donne cent agreables moyens de gagner le cœur d'une Belle, & la réputation d'homme d'esprit fait souvent une partie de la bonne fortune d'un Amant.

Et par la Prose, & par les Vers,
Votre amour peut avoir mille sujets divers
De se faire connoître:
Faites-les donc servir à votre passion;
Mais gardez-vous bien de paroître
Bel esprit de profession.

. . . .

Un Amant dont la voix est agreable, a l'avantage de ne laisser jamais languir la conversation, & c'est un secours pour ceux qui n'y peuvent toûjours fournir; mais il ne faut pas imiter ceux qui chantent à tout moment, & qui malgré la beauté de leur voix, ne laissent pas à la fin de lasser ceux qui les écoutent.

Bien souvent un cœur amoureux,
Par un air triste & langoureux,
Exprime toute sa tendresse:
Et l'on a vu plus d'une fois
Une ingrate & fiére Maîtresse,
Se rendre aux doux accens d'une charmante voix.

.

. . . .

Wit provides a hundred agreeable ways to win the heart of a belle, and a reputation as a quick-witted gentleman is often one of a lover's most prized advantages.

In prose and verse your pen can find
A thousand ways to show your love; but mind:
      Carefully, cautiously,
Let them abet your passion, foster it;
    But take heed lest you seem to be
    A tiresome wag and would-be wit.

LXVI

. . . .

A lover whose voice is pleasant has the advantage of ever being able to keep a conversation alive, and it is a boon to those who do not always have something to add to it; but one must never imitate those who break into song at every moment, and who, despite the beauty of their voices, do not fail, eventually, to weary those who listen to them.

Often an amorous heart expresses,
Lovingly, all its tendernesses
With sorrowful and languorous air:
And more than once has it been found
That mistress proud, deaf to your prayer,
† Yields to a charming voice's lovely sound.

LXVII

* The poet distinguishes here between the pejorative *bel esprit de profession*—one thinks of a number of foppish examples in Molière—and the complimentary *homme d'esprit.*

† As in a number of La Suze's pieces, this poem seems somewhat to contradict its prose preamble, and the double meaning of *air* (melody, manner) in line 2 of the original makes her precise intent a little ambiguous.

Henriette de Coligny de La Suze 299

. . . .

Un Amant ne doit jamais rien faire qui puisse l'éloigner du cœur de sa Maîtresse, & lorsqu'il a sujet de s'en plaindre, il faut qu'il lui parle en Amant soûmis, & qu'il ne l'irrite jamais.

De craindre qu'une Belle ait lieu de vous blâmer,
Ne vous emportez point quand vous voudrez vous plaindre;
Le propre d'un Amant est de se faire aimer,
   Et non pas de se faire craindre.

. . . .

On se tromperoit de croire que l'Amitié & l'Amour eussent du rapport; leurs droits sont differents, & les moyens dont ils se servent pour parvenir à leur fin, n'ont rien de semblable. L'empire de l'Amour n'a point d'autres bornes que celles de la terre, & il a presque autant de sujets qu'il y a d'hommes. L'empire de l'Amitié est plus borné: s'il a moins de sujet[s], ils sont choisis, et son autorité n'a rien que de doux & de raisonnable.

L'Amour & l'Amitié ne sont jamais semblables,
   Bien qu'elles plaisent toutes deux:
L'Amitié rend toûjours tous les sujets heureux,
   L'Amour en fait de miserables.

. . . .

A lover ought never do anything that might estrange him from the heart of his mistress; and when she gives him reason to complain, he must speak to her as a submissive lover, and never provoke her.

When angered, lest a belle think ill thereof,
Restrain your wrath: a lover, to endear
Himself, must act to earn his mistress' love,
    Rather than act to earn her fear.

LXXIV

. . . .

One would be mistaken to think that love and friendship are closely related; the rights attributed to each are different, and the means that each uses to reach its goal are in no wise the same. The empire of love is bounded only by the ends of the earth, and it contains almost as many subjects as there are men. The empire of friendship is more closely bounded: though it contains fewer subjects, they are more carefully chosen, and its authority over them is ever gentle and reasonable.

*   *

Friendship and love are different as can be;
    Both please as much, nor one the less:
Friendship will always bring us happiness,
    Love often brings us misery.

XCV

* While I try to respect the vagaries of seventeenth-century typography and spelling, I have corrected *sujet* (singular), an obvious misprint in the French text, to *sujets* (plural).

Antoinette Deshoulières (1638?–1694)

Despite the no doubt exaggerated opinion of her friend Voltaire, who claimed to consider her one of the best of the French women poets, Antoinette Deshoulières is little known today. Not so, however, during her own lifetime. Indeed, her numerous examples of light verse—madrigals, ballads, idylls, and such—and of several plays and an opera libretto, would earn her election to the literary Académie d'Arles in 1689 and the Accademia dei Ritroverati in Padua, a pension of 2,000 *livres* from Louis XIV, as well as the acquaintance of the habitués of the Hôtel de Rambouillet, where she counted among her friends such luminaries as the playwrights Corneille and Quinault, the philosopher Bayle, and the popular moralist La Rochefoucauld. Obviously inspired by the latter, she expressed her disillusionment with problems encountered toward the end of her life—ill health and monetary woes—in a brief collection of "Réflexions diverses" dating from 1686, clothing in poetic form a dark cynicism similar to his prose *Maximes* and very different from the frivolity of her earlier works.

Born into a wealthy Parisian family, Antoinette du Ligier de la Garde was the daughter of Melchior de la Garde, *maître d'hôtel* to two queens, Marie de Médicis and Anne d'Autriche, and received an education that included not only the de rigueur foreign languages and a smattering of philosophy but even the rudiments of versification. At the tender age of thirteen, she married Seigneur Deshoulières (or Des Houlières), lieutenant-colonel in one of the Grand Condé's regiments, and followed him when, falling out of favor, he was exiled to Flanders.

It is said that, returning to the salon whirl of the capital, Antoinette Deshoulières spent little time with her husband, preferring the company of her many already distinguished (or soon to become distinguished) colleagues, involving herself in the nasty rivalry between Corneille and Racine in favor of the former and participating as a champion of the "moderns" in the celebrated Querelle des anciens et des modernes. She spent enough time with monsieur, however, to have several children. One of these, a daughter, Antoinette-Thérèse (1662–1718), a would-be poet herself, collected her mother's entire *œuvre* upon the latter's death in 1694, taking advantage of the occasion, not a little self-servingly, to insert a section of her own very traditional works as well, under the title *Poésies de Madame et Mademoiselle Deshoulières.* All the poems by Antoinette Deshoulières printed below are taken from this. A previous collection *Poésies de Madame Deshoulières,* had appeared in 1688. The mother's works were republished several times during the next century, while the daughter's faded out of sight.[1]

In addition to seven examples of her characteristic short forms—among them, her best-known idyll, "Le mouton," dated 1674—the following selection includes also seven of Deshoulières's moralistic "Réflexions diverses."

NOTE

1. Studies of Antoinette Deshoulières are few and far between. There is a typical nineteenth-century appreciation in Sainte-Beuve's *Portraits de femmes,* pp. 358–84, and Maureen E. Mulvihill gives a compact overview in the *Encyclopedia of Continental Women Writers,* 1: 309–10.

Loin de remplir ici d'ennuieux complimens,
  Un inutile & long prélude;
  Sans crainte, sans inquietude,
  Je livre mes amusemens
  A la critique la plus rude.
  Cette espece de fermeté
  Ne vient point de la vanité
Que m'auroient pu donner les plus fameux suffrages:
De plus justes raisons font ma tranquilité.
Du tems qui détruit tout, je crains peu les outrages:
Le grand nom de Louis, mêlé dans mes ouvrages,
Les conduira sans doute à l'immortalité.

MADRIGAL

  Je ne sçaurois passer un jour
Sans me ressouvenir du beau berger que j'aime:
  Quand j'y pense un plaisir extrême
Vient redoubler l'ardeur que j'ay pour son retour.
  Triste devoir dont je n'ose me plaindre
A ce retour, helas! n'aurez-vous rien à craindre?
  Si, pour y penser seulement,
Des plus tendres transports je sens la violence,
  Quand je reverrai mon amant
  Que ne fera point sa presence?

CHANSON

  Pourquoi me reprocher, Silvandre,
Que je vous promets tout pour ne vous rien tenir?
Helas, c'est moins à moi qu'à vous qu'il s'en faut prendre!
Pour remplir vos desirs, j'attens un moment tendre:
  Que ne le faites-vous venir?

PREFACE

I shall not fill with florid compliment
    A prelude tiresome to excess;
    With no fear, no uneasiness,
    I give my trifles, confident,
    To critics rude and mannerless.
    No vain resolve have I to be
    Favored by words of flattery,
Pronounced by famous connoisseurs of verses;
Something more worthy calms and comforts me.
Little fear I time's all-destroying curses:
The name LOUIS, which my works intersperses,
Will lead the way to immortality.

MADRIGAL

    No day I spend but that I burn
For that fair shepherd whom I love; for, when
    I think of him, ah! what bliss then
Doubles my yearning for his quick return!
Sad duty mine, no plaints from me you hear;
But when return he does, needs must you fear:
    For, if naught but his thought can fill
My heart with tenderest passion, ardently,
    When I my lover see, what will
    His sight, alas, not do to me?

SONG

    Why blame you me, Sylvander? Yes,
I promise everything, but naught you get!
Alas! You are at fault, and I far less.
To yield to you I wait your tenderness:
    Why have I had none from you yet?

Antoinette Deshoulières 305

LES MOUTONS: IDYLLE

Helas, petits Moutons, que vous êtes heureux,
Vous paissez dans nos champs sans souci, sans alarmes
       Aussi-tôt aimez qu'amoureux!
On ne vous force point à répandre des larmes;
Vous ne formez jamais d'inutiles desirs.
Dans vos tranquilles cœurs l'amour suit la nature,
Sans ressentir les maux vous avez ses plaisirs,
L'ambition, l'honneur, l'interêt, l'imposture,
       Qui font tant de maux parmi nous,
       Ne se rencontrent point chez vous.
Cependant nous avons la raison pour partage,
       Et vous en ignorez l'usage.
Innocens animaux n'en soyez point jaloux
       Ce n'est pas un grand avantage.
Cette fiere raison dont on fait tant de bruit
Contre les passions n'est pas un sûr remede.
Un peu de vin la trouble, un enfant la séduit.
Et déchirer un cœur qui l'appelle à son aide,
       Est tout l'effet qu'elle produit.
       Toûjours impuissante & severe
Elle s'oppose à tout, & ne surmonte rien.
       Sous la garde de votre chien,
Vous devez beaucoup moins redouter la colere
       Des loups cruels & ravissans,
Que sous l'autorité d'une telle chimere
       Nous ne devons craindre nos sens.
Ne vaudroit-il pas mieux vivre comme vous faites
       Dans une douce oisiveté?
Ne vaudroit-il pas mieux être comme vous êtes
       Dans une heureuse obscurité,
       Que d'avoir sans tranquilité
       Des richesses, de la naissance,
       De l'esprit & de la beauté?
Ces prétendus trésors dont on fait vanité
       Valent moins que votre indolence.
Ils nous livrent sans cesse à des soins criminels:
       Par eux plus d'un remords nous ronge:
       Nous voulons les rendre éternels,
Sans songer qu'eux & nous passerons comme un songe.

THE SHEEP: IDYLL

Ah, little sheep, how happy you must be!
So loved, so loving, and without a care,
    You graze our fields in peace, fear-free,
With never a tear; nor know you the despair
Of vain desires: with tranquil hearts you do,
    Simply, what nature asks of you,
Reaping love's joys and untouched by its woes.
    Ambition, pride, sham-full pretense,
    Self-interest, and all of those
Evils of ours are not your lot, whilst sense
And reason have we for our legacy:
    Virtues whose use you know naught of!
Innocent beasts, envy us not. Though we
    Boast of our reason endlessly,
Most useless is it in the face of love:
A sip of wine throws it in disarray.
Even a little child leads it astray,
Seduces it; and when a heart cries out,
Seeking its help, no change can it effect,
    No succor can it bring about.
Rather, the heart lies ever more abject,
Asunder rent: severe but powerless,
Reason opposes all our foolishness,
    But never gets the best of it.
Less need you fear the wolves' ravenous jaws,
    Nor to their angry claws submit—
Protected by your hound—than we have cause
    To fear our senses, in the thrall
Of that chimera, reason. All in all,
Were it not better for us if we would
    Live as do you, idle, content?
Were it not better for us if we could,
    Like you, avoid life's turbulent
    Activity, unknown, in sweet,
    Modest obscurity complete,
    Rather than, with no peace of mind,
Possess birth, wealth, beauty, and wit combined?
    These treasures, prized, are far less meet
    For us than is that leisure-life

Antoinette Deshoulières 307

Il n'est dans ce vaste Univers
Rien d'assuré, rien de solide;
Des choses d'ici bas la fortune decide
Selon ses caprices divers:
Tout l'effort de notre prudence
Ne peut nous dérober au moindre de ses coups.
Paissez moutons, paissez sans regle, & sans science:
Malgré la trompeuse apparence
Vous êtes plus heureux & plus sages que nous.

CHANSON

A La Cour
Aimer est un badinage,
Et l'amour
N'est dangereux qu'au Village;
Un Berger,
Si sa Bergere n'est tendre,
Sait se pendre,
Mais il ne sauroit changer.
Et parmi nous quand les belles
Sont legeres ou cruelles,
Loin d'en mourir de dépit,
On en rit,
Et l'on change aussi-tôt qu'elles.

Of yours, untroubled, pleasure-rife.
Worse yet, those virtues urge us on
To sinful thoughts and actions, whereupon
Deep the remorse that gnaws our hearts: we try
To make them last forever, never thinking
    That they, like us, die in a winking,
Much like a dream, quick to pass by and by.
Nothing in this vast universe retains
Its form unchanged; what happens here below
Fate deigns decree at whim; and all the pains
    Our reason's wisdom plies, have no
Effect, withal, against its slightest blow.
    Graze, sheep! Graze ignorant and free!
Think what we will, the fact remains, just so:
More happy are you—and more wise!—than we.

----

* **SONG**

    At the Court,
Love is but an idle sport,
    And it will
Only in the country kill:
    Shepherd boy
Might, when lass gives him no joy,
    End his days
Sooner than his loving ways.
But *chez nous*, when belles betray—
Cruel and fickle-hearted!—nay,
Lovers die not of their plight:
    With delight
They change loves as quick as they.

* Given the freedom of the original—no obvious poetic form—I have taken the liberty of altering the rhyme scheme while remaining faithful to the meter.

CHANSON

Je croyois que la colere
Avoit dégagé mon cœur:
Mais à la moindre douceur
J'ai bien connu le contraire.
Helas! un fidelle Amant,
Se propose vainement
De n'aimer plus ce qu'il aime.
S'il se mutine aisément,
Il s'appaise tout de même.

CHANSON

 Revenez charmante verdure,
Faites regner l'ombrage, & l'amour dans nos bois:
 A quoi s'amuse la nature,
Tout est encor glacé dans le plus beau des mois?
Si je viens vous presser de couvrir ce bocage,
Ce n'est que pour cacher aux regards des jaloux
Les pleurs que je répans pour un Berger volage.
Ah! je n'aurai jamais d'autre besoin de vous?

Que l'homme connoît peu la mort qu'il apprehende,
 Quand il dit qu'elle le surprend!
Elle naît avec lui: sans cesse lui demande
Un tribut dont en vain son orgueil se défend.
Il commence à mourir long-tems avant qu'il meure:
Il périt en détail imperceptiblement.
Le nom de mort qu'on donne à notre dernière heure
 N'en est que l'accomplissement.

SONG

Anger—or so had I thought—
Made my heart its bondage quit:
But his slightest favor wrought
Taught me quite the opposite.
Ah! The faithful lover tries—
All in vain!—in every wise,
Not to love where love he found.
If with ease he turns and flies,
Just as quickly he comes round.

SONG

    Come back, spring greenery, I pray!
With shadowing boughs, with love our woodland fill:
    What is this game nature would play?
This, the year's fairest month, lies frozen still?
If thus I beg you wide your leaves to spread,
It is to hide from others' jealous view
The tears a fickle shepherd makes me shed.
    Ah! Must this be all I can ask of you?

How little does man know when, fearing death,
    He claims it takes him unawares!
Born with him, as he breathes his life's first breath,
It levies constant tribute, one he dares
In vain refuse; for, long before he dies,
Little by little, does sly death commence:
That name of "death" that we give our demise
    Is but the final consequence.

"Réflexions diverses," I

Antoinette Deshoulières 311

Etres inanimez, rebut de la nature,
    Ah! que vous faites d'envieux!
Le tems loin de vous faire injure,
Ne vous rend que plus précieux.
On cherche avec ardeur une Médaille antique:
D'un Buste, d'un Tableau le tems hausse le prix,
Le voyageur s'arrête à voir l'affreux débris
D'un Cirque, d'un Tombeau, d'un Temple magnifique,
Et pour notre vieillesse on n'a que du mépris!

De ce sublime esprit dont ton orgueil se pique,
    Homme, quel usage fais-tu?
Des plantes, des métaux, tu connois la vertu,
Des differens pays les mœurs, la politique,
La cause des frimats, de la foudre, du vent,
    Des Astres le pouvoir suprême:
    Et sur tant de choses savant,
    Tu ne te connois pas toi-meme!

La pauvreté fait peur, mais elle a ses plaisirs.
Je sai bien qu'elle éloigne aussi-tôt qu'elle arrive,
La volupté, l'éclat, & cette foule oisive
Dont les jeux, les festins remplissent les desirs.
Cependant, quoiqu'elle ait de honteux & de rude
Pour ceux qu'à des revers la fortune a soumis,
Au moins dans leurs malheurs ont-ils la certitude
    De n'avoir que de vrais amis.

You lifeless things, nature's most lowly! Why
   Make you so many envious!
   Time, far from treating you awry,
   Renders you precious, dear to us.
To find some ancient coin we quest and fret;
Time will a bust's, a painting's worth adorn;
The traveler halts to prize the vile, time-worn
Ruins of theaters, temples, tombs: and yet,
Our own old age we treat with naught but scorn!

"Réflexions diverses," ii

That mind sublime wherein you take such pride,
   O Man: what use make you of it?
You know each plant's, each metal's benefit;
Each people's ways, with whom each is allied,
The power of the stars, and why the skies
   Bring lightning, winds, and winter snow.
   In many ways, you are so wise:
   And yet your self you scarcely know!

"Réflexions diverses," iii

Fearsome is poverty; and yet it brings
Its boons: let it but show its face, and lo!
Gone, dazzling feasts, and games, and fleshly things
That idlers covetous desire; and, though
Dismal and dire their woe's discomfiture,
Happy are those whom fate casts down in need:
At least in their distress they can be sure
   The friends they keep are friends indeed.

"Réflexions diverses," iv

Antoinette Deshoulières 313

Pourquoi s'applaudir d'être belle?
Quelle erreur fait compter la beauté pour un bien?
A l'examiner il n'est rien
Qui cause tant de chagrin qu'elle.
Je sai que sur les cœurs ses droits sont absolus,
Que tant qu'on est belle on fait naître
Des desirs, des transports, & des soins assidus:
Mais on a peu de tems à l'être,
Et long-tems à ne l'être plus.

On croit être devenu sage,
Quand après avoir vû plus de cinquante fois
Tomber le renaissant feuillage,
On quitte des plaisirs le dangereux usage:
On s'abuse. D'un libre choix
Un tel retour n'est point l'ouvrage;
Et ce n'est que l'orgueil dont l'homme est revêtu,
Qui tirant de tout avantage,
Donne au secours de la vertu
Ce qu'on doit au secours de l'âge.

Palais, nous durons moins que vous
Quoique des Elemens vous souteniez la guerre,
Et quoique du sein de la terre
Nous soyons tirez comme vous,
Frêles machines que nous sommes,
A peine passons-nous d'un siecle le milieu!
Un rien peut nous détruire; & l'ouvrage d'un Dieu
Dure moins que celui des hommes!

Why should a woman gloat if she
Has beauty? No boon is it to be fair!
    Upon reflection, naught is there
    That causes so much misery.
True, hearts cannot resist it, not a jot;
    And while her beauty lasts, we see it
Spawn kind attentions, yearnings, passions hot.
    But one has little time to be it,
    And so much time to be it not.

"Réflexions diverses," v

We feel so wise when—after all
The times we see (full fifty times and more)
    Spring's bloomed rebirth give way to fall—
We quit base pleasures' fleshly folderol!
    How wrong we are! If we deplore
    Deeds of our youth, deeds that appall,
Repel us now, we do so not by choice:
    Though pride, which holds our souls in thrall,
    Tells us in virtue to rejoice,
    Naught but age saves our souls withal.

"Réflexions diverses," IX

Old palaces! Less do we last than you.
    Though Nature on you wages war,
And though, like you, the earth our being bore:
    For, we of clay are fashioned too.
    But frail machines are we: we span
Scarce half a century! How passing odd
That, easily brought down, work of a God,
Less do we last than the mere work of Man!

"Réflexions diverses," XII

Marie-Catherine Desjardins de Villedieu (1640?–1683)

One of the more colorful, controversial, and, on occasion, scandalous figures of seventeenth-century French literature, Marie-Catherine Desjardins[1] deserves far more recognition than she has received. Of humble birth—daughter of a chambermaid to the duchesse Anne de Montbazon—she was obliged to live by her wits and her pen, and did both with not a little éclat, producing, besides a quantity of occasional verse, a number of pastoral novels, and even several tragedies and tragicomedies. Brought to Paris as an adolescent by her mother, in the wake of severe marital problems, she began writing and publishing poetry as early as 1658. But it was her unorthodox social life and the free spirit that characterized it that quickly made her one of the salon favorites of the age. That spirit is exemplified in the aristocratic name by which she is best known—Madame de Villedieu—and the manner in which she took it. As the common-law wife of a military man, one Antoine de Villedieu, she persisted in maintaining it throughout their tempestuous on-again, off-again relationship—whose on-again moments do not seem to have prevented other escapades—and kept it even after the lieutenant's official marriage to another in 1667 and his death in battle soon after.

At age thirty-seven, establishing herself on the literary scene with her poems, plays, and especially her novels, Madame de Villedieu married an aristocrat, Claude-Nicolas Chaste—a name whose irony was not lost on her sardonic contemporaries—by whom she had a son. Her husband was to die a few years later, apparently precipitating a taming of her passions and a religious conversion of sorts, as well as a growing addiction to alcohol, which would hasten her own demise, if some reports are to be believed.[2]

Of more that passing interest is the collection of Madame de Villedieu's *Fables, ou Histoires allégoriques*, which, profiting from her continuing popularity, she had published in 1670. That volume, dedicated to Louis XIV himself, who had granted her a generous pension the previous year, contains eight lengthy animal fables very similar in subject, dramatis personae, style, and detail to those that La Fontaine, in his first six books, had published only two years before. It was that similarity that prompted one later critic to put forward the elaborate thesis that the not-yet-famous fabulist was, in effect, Madame de Villedieu's lover, and that the eight fables in question were really his, published under her name—with the collusion, and perhaps at the instigation of their common publisher, Claude Barbin—to take advantage of her social and literary prominence. The thesis, though eventually discredited, remains a telling tribute, however farfetched, to the prestige of this singular *courtisane de lettres*.

Translated here are the eight fables in question, as well as eight of her rather cynical "Maximes diverses sur plusieurs sujets differens" and a madrigal, the latter all taken from the third volume of *Œuvres meslées par Madame de Villedieu.*

NOTES

1. The name "Hortense," which modern observers frequently add to her name, is apparently spurious.

2. Numerous studies chronicle Madame de Villedieu's life and works. Among those of general interest, see Bruce Morrissette, *The Life and Works of Marie-Catherine Desjardins;* Micheline Cuénin, *Madame de Villedieu (Marie-Catherine Desjardins, 1640–1683);* Arthur Flannigan Saint-Aubin, *The Disorders of Love: Madame de Villedieu;* and Roxanne Decker Lalande, *A Labor of Love: Critical Reflections on the Writings of Marie-Catherine Desjardins (Mme de Villedieu).* Regarding the discredited attribution of her fables to La Fontaine, see Auguste-Louis Ménard, *La Fontaine et Mme de Villedieu, etc.* Katharine Ann Jensen has provided an excellent detailed biographical study and critical observations, with an emphasis on her novels, in her entry in *French Women Writers,* pp. 503–11.

LA TOURTERELLE & LE RAMIER

Qu'on ne me parle plus d'Amour, ny de Plaisirs,
    Disoit un jour la triste Tourterelle,
Consacrez-vous mon Ame, à d'eternels soûpirs:
    J'ay perdu mon Amant fidelle.
  Arbres, Ruisseaux, Gazons delicieux,
    Vous n'avez plus de charmes pour mes yeux,
    Mon Amant a cessé de vivre.
Qu'attendons-nous mon cœur? Hâtons-nous de le suivre.
  Comme on l'eust dit, autresfois on l'eust fait.
Quand nos Peres vouloient peindre un Amour parfait,
    La Tourterelle en estoit le symbole,
Elle suivoit toûjours son Amant au trépas,
    Mais la mode change icy-bas,
    De cette constance frivole.
  Le Desespoir a perdu son credit,
    Et Tourterelle se console,
S'il faut tenir pour vray, ce que ma Fable en dit.
    Elle pretend, que cette Desolée,
A sa juste douleur, voulant estre immolée,
Choisit un vieux Palais, vray sejour de Hiboux;
    Où sans chercher aucune nourriture,
Un prompt trépas estoit, son espoir le plus doux;
    Mais qui ne sçait, qu'en toute conjoncture,
    La Providence est plus sage que nous?
    Dans cette demeure sauvage,
    Habitoit un jeune Ramier.
    Houpé, patu, de beau plumage,
    Et quoy que jeune, vieux Routier
Dans l'Art de soulager, les douleurs du veuvage.
Pour nostre Tourterelle, il mit courtoisement,
    Ses plus beaux secrets en usage.
    La Pauvrette, au commencement,
    Loin de prester l'oreille à son langage,
    Ne vouloit pas, se montrer seulement:
Mais le Ramier, parlant de deffunt son Amant,
    Insensiblement il l'engage,
    A recevoir son compliment.

THE TURTLEDOVE AND THE RINGDOVE

* "Let no one speak of joy or love
To me again," said the sad turtledove
   One day. "And you, my soul, I pray you
Give yourself up to sighs eternal, for
My faithful lover have I lost: no more,
O trees, O brooks, O pleasant greenswards, may you
Delight my eye; my lover's life is fled.
Why tarry you, my heart? Best I were dead
As well! Come, let us follow him!" In days
   Gone by, no sooner was that said
Than it was done. For, in deeds amorous,
The turtledove was symbol of perfection;
And, should her lover die, such her dejection
That she would follow to the grave. For us
Such constancy—a trifle frivolous—
Is out of style: no longer is despair
   Much à la mode; and if my tale
Is true, our turtledove, for all her air
Of deep despondency and dark travail,
Will, at length, be consoled. It tells that she,
Disconsolate, desired only to be
Sacrificed to her grief. And so she chooses
A palace, old and owl-frequented; loses
   All thought of food, yearns but to perish.
But who knows not that, though some hopes we cherish,
Fate is far wiser than ourselves? In that
   Most inauspicious habitat,
   There dwelt another dove, of race
Almost the same: a ringdove, fair of face,
Elegantly and finely feathered, and,
   Though young, much the experienced hand,
Well-versed in consolation's art, and good
At calming the despair of widowhood.
He practiced all the tricks at his command,
   Gallantly, gently as he could,

* Throughout this and the author's succeeding texts, I have reproduced all the redundant commas and other punctuational oddities—and occasional inconsistencies—found in her originals.

Marie-Catherine Desjardins de Villedieu 319

Ce compliment fut d'une grande force,
Il disoit du deffunt, toute sorte de bien,
Ne blâmoit la Veuve de rien;
Bref, c'estoit une douce amorce,
Pour attirer un plus long entretien.
Voilà donc la belle Affligée,
En tendres propos engagée:
Elle tombe sur le discours,
De l'histoire de ses Amours:
Dépeint, non sans cris, & sans larmes,
Du pauvre Trépassé, les vertus et les charmes:
Et ne croyant par là, que flater sa douleur,
Elle apprit au Ramier, le chemin de son cœur.
Par ce que le Deffunt avoit fait pour luy plaire,
Il comprit ce qu'il faloit faire.
Il estoit copiste entendu,
Il sçeut si dextrement, imiter son modelle,
Que dans peu nostre Tourterelle,
Crût retrouver en luy, ce qu'elle avoit perdu.

LE SINGE CUPIDON

Vn vieux Singe des plus adrois,
Ayant veu l'Amour plusieurs fois,
Décocher ses fléches mortelles,
Sur les cœurs de maintes Cruelles;
Comme luy, voulut estre Archer,
Et fléches d'Amour décocher.
Il eust donné leçon d'adresse,
A tout maistre en tours de souplesse.
Il prend si bien son temps, choisit si bien son lieu,
Qu'il détrousse le petit Dieu.
Enrichy d'un butin si rare,
A se cupidonner le Magot se prepare;
Endosse le carquois, s'affuble du bandeau,
En conquerant des cœurs, se rengorge, & se quarre,
Et se mirant dans un ruisseau,
Se prend pour Cupidon, tant il se trouve beau.
Ces Animaux pour l'ordinaire,

Upon the turtledove. Now, she, at first,
    Stayed out of sight, turned a deaf ear
And spurned him quite, until his tongue rehearsed
The virtues of her erstwhile cavalier,
       And subtly interspersed
Sweet words for her as well. (Hers was "the very
Model of widow's conduct exemplary,"
    And such...) Well, nibbling on the bait,
She finds herself in lengthy conversation,
With many a tear and many a lamentation,
Chatting of her amour, and of her late
Love's qualities, thereby revealing how
His charms had made her his, and by what art:
Thinking to find relief, she shows him now
The very road whereby to win her heart.
    Doing all that the late lamented
Himself had done, our plagiarist presented
So fine a copy that our dove, star-crossed,
Found in him once again the love she lost.

Fables, I

THE MONKEY WHO PLAYED CUPID

    A shrewd old monkey, deft and sly,
Often would watch as Cupid would let fly
    Those barbs of his—love-dealing darts,
To prick so many heartless damsels' hearts—
And thought that surely he could wield as well
    The bended bow. Now, truth to tell,
    So artful was the ape that he
Could teach the masters of skulduggery:
Lying in wait for Cupid, to undo him,
He chose the proper place and moment; whence
    The little god had no defense,
But had to yield his bow and arrow to him.
    Enriched by such a priceless prize,
    Quiver behind and blindfold tying
About his face, now in the godlet's guise,
    He sets about cupidifying...
    At length, stopping beside a brook—

Marie-Catherine Desjardins de Villedieu 321

Naissent sçavans, en l'art de contrefaire,
Et dans le langage commun,
Singe, & Copiste ce n'est qu'un.
Celuy-cy donc campé dans un boccage,
Attend une Nymphe au passage,
Et comme souvent le hazard,
Aux blessures du cœur a la meilleure part,
Nostre Archer d'espece nouvelle
Atteint droit au cœur de la Belle.
Iamais la Nymphe avant ce jour,
N'avoit senty les fléches de l'amour.
Si cette blessure cruelle,
Fut un cas surprenant pour elle;
I'en fais Iuge le jeune cœur,
Atteint de pareille douleur.
Iour, & nuict, la nouvelle Amante
Soûpire, se plaint, se tourmente,
Sans sçavoir ce qu'elle sentoit,
Ny pourquoy tant se lamentoit.
Maistre Magot darde-sagette,
Qui mieux instruit du mal de la Pauvrette,
S'applaudissoit de sa dexterité,
Se voyant la Divinité,
Pour qui se preparoit l'amoureux Sacrifice,
Se tenoit fier comme un Narcisse.
Quand la Belle par ses soûpirs,
Exprimoit ses tendres desirs;
Que de ses yeux, la langueur indiscrette,
A son cœur servoit d'interprete,
Peu s'en faloit, qu'en ce moment,
L'indigne Auteur de son tourment,
Ne se crust ce qu'il feignoit d'estre.
Il eust avec l'amour disputé d'agrément,
Tant l'orgueil nous fait méconnoistre.
Mais on voit ordinairement,
Que la Gloire sans fondement,
Est chimerique, & peu durable.
Du carquois dérobé, le Maistre redoutable,
Cherchoit plein de ressentiment,
Le sacrilege Auteur, d'un fait si punissable.
Le sort le guida sur le lieu,
Où le Magot pare des dépoüilles du Dieu,

Swelling with pride—he goes to look,
And there perceives so fair and fine a sight
That he, indeed, believes he might
Play Love himself. (For monkeys are such mimes
That, in the common speech, at times,
We say "to ape" and mean "to imitate.")
This beast of ours, at any rate,
Among the bushes takes his stance,
Stalking a passing nymph. The counterfeit,
Unwonted bowman shoots... By sheerest chance—
For so it is with love—the sprite is hit,
Square in the breast. Nor had she ever,
Until that day, suffered the merest whit
From Cupid's dart; nay, none whatever.
Imagine her surprise: like many a young
And callow heart, to be so cruelly stung!
By day, by night, Love's newest devotee
Sighs, beats her bosom, sobs and cries,
With never a notion, not the least surmise
Of what the reason for her woes might be.
Sir Ape the Archer knows, for sure,
The cause of her discomfiture.
Thanking his godly skill for her new passion,
Proudly the would-be Cupid waited,
Pleased with himself, Narcissus-fashion,
And watched it flourish unabated.
With sighs aplenty our poor nymph expressed
The tender yearning burning in her breast.
And when her eyes, with languid indiscretion,
Eloquent in their mute confession,
Revealed her heartsick melancholy,
The wretched author of her woe—Oh, Folly!—
All but believed himself, forsooth,
To be the one he feigned, and fairer truly.
(So much does pride distract us from the truth.
But glory that we claim unduly
Is vain illusion, quick to dim.)
Quiver-bereft, but filled with righteous wrath,
The god decides to search the wood for him.
Fate leads him on the proper path:
There sits the ape, still at his vile charade,
Reveling in the amorous homage paid

Recevoit l'amoureux hommage
Qu'on devoit à son Equipage.
Si Cupidon fut offensé;
Qu'un Magot pour luy se fist prendre,
Et comme tel fust encensé,
Il est aisé de le comprendre.
"Quoy?" dit-il, "ce ridé Museau,
A la faveur de mon Bandeau,
Chez les Mortels remplit ma Place?"
A ces mots Messire l'Amour,
Détrousse le Singe à son tour,
Montre a nud sa laide grimace,
Et tirant la Nymphe d'erreur,
Fit naistre un plus beau feu, dans son aveugle cœur.

Ainsi l'ame préoccupée,
Et par l'apparence trompée,
Eleve aux hommes des Autels,
Qui ne sont deus qu'aux Immortels.
Le bandeau de l'Amour, fait des Metamorphoses
Des plus desagreables choses;
Mais quand un retour de raison,
Peut enfin trouver sa saison,
Ou qu'un Amour, d'une plus pure essence,
A nos cœurs prevenus, fait sentir sa puissance,
Combien trouvons-nous odieux
Ce qu'avoient admiré nos yeux?

LA CIGALE, LE HANNETON, & L'ESCARBOT

La Cigale, & le Hanneton,
Contracterent jadis un mariage ensemble;
Et comme pour un jour, dit-on,
Tout Hymen à l'Amour ressemble,
Le leur eut d'abord la beauté
Qui suit tousiours la nouveauté.
L'Epoux trouvoit l'Epouse belle,

His godly trappings. Is it any wonder
        That Cupid takes offense, by thunder!
To see himself by monkey imitated
        And his impostor adulated?
"What?" he exclaims. "That dunderhead! That lout!
An ape, to play at Love? to mimic me,
        Hiding his grizzled, wrinkled snout
Behind my blindfold? And shamefacedly!
 *   Ye gods, what fools these mortals be!"
That said, he said no more, but ripped the ape's
Disguise away, and left the jackanapes
        To leer his naked leer, stripped bare,
From top to bottom, front to derrière.
        Whereupon mistress nymph discovers
That there can be more gallant, gracious lovers!

Too often, in the blindness of the mind,
        Gulled by appearance, we erect
        Gods' altars to mere mortal kind:
Love's blindness makes us less than circumspect,
Transforming ugly cause to fair effect.
But when, in time, our reason, once again
        Returns to grace our wit; or when
New love—of purer essence, therewithal—
        Seizes and holds our hearts in thrall;
Then do we see how hateful was the prize
That once we longed for with adoring eyes.

Fables, ii

THE CICADA, THE MAYBUG, AND THE DUNGBEETLE

Years past, the maybug and cicada wed;
        And since, as is so often said,
The joys of wedded life last but a day,
They lived in beauteous bliss at first, the way
One does when love is new: he finds her fair;
        She finds him dashing, debonair...
        Ecstasy! Passion! Naught know they

* The perspicacious reader will, of course, appreciate that this somewhat deformed
Shakespearean reminiscence does not occur in the original.

Comme elle le trouvoit charmant,
Ce n'estoit que transport, & que ravissement,
Ils se juroient une ardeur eternelle,
Et croyoient tenir leur serment.
Mais tels sermens se tiennent rarement,
Ce premier jour qu'un long usage,
A fait nommer communément,
Le seul heureux du Mariage,
Estoit à peine encor passé;
Que le nouveau Couple lassé
De si longue Paix domestique,
En interrompit la pratique.
Le Hanneton alloit souvent
Voir une Guespe sa voisine:
Dame Cigale en eut le vent,
Pour moins Epouse se mutine.
Elle entre en feminin courroux,
Accuse le coquet Epoux,
De fausser la Foy conjugale.
Hanneton de s'enfuïr aux cris de la Cigale;
Elle, de redoubler ses cris;
Luy, de l'accuser de manie,
Adieu l'amour & les soûris,
Au triste Hymen ils faussent compagnie.
Le Hanneton, morne & transsi,
Connoissant, mais trop tard, les soucis du ménage,
Va consulter sur son soucy,
Un Escarbot du voisinage.
Cet animal n'avoit point son pareil,
Il décidoit de tout en *Auditeur de Rote*,
Et toute la Gent Escarbote
N'agissoit que par son conseil.
Compere, dit-il au Mary,
Ce sont suites de l'Hymenée,
Vous n'estes pas le seul Epoux marty
Qui déplore sa destinée.
Nous autres petits Escarbots,
En de pareilles conjonctures,

But these! And so, of course, they swear
Their burning love eternal, sure
Never to let their hearts abjure
Their oath. But such vows kept are rare;
And scarcely was the first day done—
That first day of their wedded life,
That, true to common wisdom, is the one
And only happy day 'twixt man and wife—
Than the new couple, tiring, quite,
Of conjugal tranquillity,
Tempered its oh-so-dull ennui.
Often our maybug fly-by-night
Would go to pay a friendly visit
To a wasp damosel nearby.
Now, it is not unusual, is it?
For wives, on hearing such, to fly
Into a female rage; which is
Precisely what that spouse of his,
On learning of his escapade,
Did to monsieur, and promptly made
The most vociferous accusations
Against his matrimonial violations.
Monsieur flies off before her cries, accusing
Madame, in turn—alas!—of losing
Her mind, whereat her cries redoubled,
Trebled! Adieu their wedded bliss,
All smiles! For, the result of this
Dispute was that our husband, sorely troubled,
Learning, too late, how wedlock goes amiss,
Consults a beetle of the dungheap breed,
Church arbiter plenipotentiary
In sacred matters, legendary
Among dungbeetledom, whom all agreed
To be the ultimate authority.
    "My friend," he tells the maybug, "be
    Advised, yours is the normal state
    Of those who marry: you are not
The only martyred spouse to moan his fate.

* The allusion is to the Sacred Roman Rota, whose twelve judges (*auditeurs de rote* in French) constitute a court of final appeal in ecclesiastical matters, especially those dealing with marital problems.

Marie-Catherine Desjardins de Villedieu 327

Entendons dire de bons mots
A Mesdames les creatures.
Quand pour divertir son chagrin,
Un homme vient à son voisin,
Faire en se promenant secrette confidence,
Luy conter ses douleurs, & ses soupçons jaloux,
Dieu sçait si pour avoir des témoins tels que nous,
Il en dit moins tout ce qu'il pense.
Ecoutez, ce que l'autre jour
J'entendois raconter à Seigneur d'apparence:
J'épousay, disoit-il, une veuve de France,
Des premieres de cette Cour:
Soit que pour témoigner un amour plus parfait,
Elle crust à propos de paroistre jalouse,
Ou qu'elle le fust en effet,
Tousiours quelque soupçon tourmentoit mon Epouse;
Je n'avois plus un moment de repos,
Sur la moindre visite, ou le moindre propos,
Nostre Jalouse avoit un reproche à me faire;
Un Amant me tira d'affaire.
Il nâquit certaine amitié
Dans le cœur de nostre Moitié,
Plus fine d'un carac que l'estime ordinaire;
Depuis ce jour, tout fut calme chez moy,
Je fus respecté comme un Roy;
On ne songeoit plus qu'à me plaire.

Compere Hanneton, poursuivit l'Escarbot,
Si tu sçais le secret d'entendre à demy-mot,
Fais ton profit de l'avis salutaire.
Laisse gronder ta femme tout le jour,
Ou si tu veux la faire taire,
Permets-luy de faire l'amour.
Dame trop prude, & beaucoup de raison,
Est un assortiment fort difficile à faire;
Et pour la paix de la Maison,
Un peu d'intrigue, est un mal necessaire.

We beetles hear their tales, the lot
Of them, and juicy morsels, too!
When husband visits friend next door,
In confidence, to spout and spew
His jealousies, console his woes, outpour
His griefs, God knows, he is no less inclined,
With us as witnesses, to speak his mind.
In fact... Why, just the other day
I heard a fine *seigneur* having his say.
'I wed a widow,' so he said, 'from France,
One of the foremost ladies of that court;
But, true or false, my dear consort
Decided that it would enhance
Her love if she could but make clear that she
Was much beset by jealousy,
Real or contrived. And so, wherever
I went, whatever I might say, she never
Failed to reproach, to harry me
With accusation most unnecessary,
Until, at length, a young voluptuary—
A lover, if you will—proved my salvation.
For in milady's heart a fondness grew,
A trifle weightier than mere admiration,
Indeed! And, from that day, we two
Lived on in peace. I reigned, king-like, respected;
Her only wish, to do as I directed.'

"Friend maybug, can you take a hint? If so,"
Continued our dungbeetle, "you will find
A profitable quid pro quo behind
The tale he told. Let your wife go
And scold her fill, day out day in. Or, better,
If you would keep her still, then let her
Go get herself a lover. (I doubt whether
Good sense and prudish woman dwell together!)
If household peace and calm are what you will,
A little intrigue is a welcome ill."

Fables, III

LE SANSONNET & LE COUCOU

Vn Sansonnet, Jargonneur signalé,
De captif qu'il estoit, devenu volontaire,
De desirs amoureux se trouva régalé:
C'est de l'indépendance, une suite ordinaire.
Il dresse son petit Grabat
Dans un Buisson de Noble-Epine.
Vn Coucou fameux scelerat,
Qui, comme chacun sçait, ne vit que de rapine,
Qui va de Nid en Nid croquant les œufs d'autruy
Et les remplaçant d'œufs de luy,
Au Nid du Sansonnet, traduisit son lignage.
Nostre amy Jargonneur, ignoroit cet usage;
Il fut dés sa jeunesse élevé parmy nous,
Et vivoit, par hazard, en honneste ménage,
Où l'on ne parloit point des ruses des Coucous.
Frere le Rossignol, disoit-il en luy-mesme,
Couvant les nouveaux Œufs avec un soin extrême,
Vous vous vantez d'estre le Roy des Bois;
Mais si jamais ma Famille est éclose,
Ha! Foy de Sansonnet, c'est bien à cette fois,
Que vous aurez la gorge close.
Dans vostre Art de rossignoler,
Vous donnez des leçons, à tout ce que nous sommes;
Mais, mes petits sçauront parler,
Comme parlent Messieurs les hommes.

Ces petits long-temps attendus,
Et de tout mal-heur deffendus,
Il plût à l'Eternel de donner la lumiere
A nos Sansonnets pretendus.
Maistre Oyseleur, d'espece singuliere,
Se promet d'exercer son Mestier doctement.
Le Plumage coucou, blessoit un peu sa veuë,
Mais il esperoit en la meuë;
Les Peres, comme on sçait, se flattent aisément.
Le voilà donc, tenant Ecole de ramage,
Il n'est dictons, ou quolibets,
Qu'apprennent tels Oyseaux en cage,
Qu'il ne siffle aux Coucous, reputez Sansonnets.

THE STARLING AND THE CUCKOO

A starling—glib of chatter, as one knows—
Erstwhile a captive, gains his freedom, whence,
Prickled by passion (common consequence
    Of independence!) straightway goes
Off to a hawthorn bush, there to set out
    His modest nest. A cuckoo too
There is, one of that race of blackguards who
    Live but by theft, flying about
From nest to nest: so fell and fulsome is
    Their villainy that each makes free,
Glutting on others' eggs and placing his
Where theirs had been. Thus does ours wantonly
Bring to the starling's nest his unhatched brood.
Our chatterer, raised up since youth with us,
The human breed, has not heard one allude
    To cuckoos' loathsome habits, thus
Knows nothing of such nasty cuckoo ruses.
"Ah, brother nightingale," the starling muses,
Sitting upon the eggs with care. "You boast
That you are king of all the woods, unmatched.
Well, if this family of mine is hatched,
Then, starling's honor, shall you hear the most
Wonderful sounds, and you will forthwith shut
    Your bill, hush still your throat, and strut
No more; you, who regale us endlessly
With the fine art of nightingalery!
For I, who have frequented Man, will teach
    My young to chirp in human speech!"

    Long were the little ones awaited,
    Safe from harm's ever-present reach,
Until, their egghood being consummated,
It pleased the Maker to bring to the light
Our would-be starlings; which he did. Wherewith
The magister—rare bird—viewing his kith
(So he assumes), pledges as best he might
    To ply his skill. Though just a bit
Put off by cuckoo's plumage, he was sure
    That, once his fledglings molted, it

Parlez, leur disoit-il, parlez l'humain langage,
    C'est le plus éloquent de tous,
    Coucou, répondent les Coucous,
    Il n'en peut tirer autre chose,
    Quoy qu'il entonne, ou qu'il propose,
    Coucous ne disent que Coucou:
    Le Sansonnet pensa devenir fou.
Depuis quand, disoit-il, cette Metamorphose?
Comment œufs de Coucou sont-ils sortis de moy?
Du temps que j'augmentay l'espece volatille,
Tout Oyseau n'engendroit qu'Oyseau semblable à soy:
C'est depuis que j'habite en humaine famille,
Que la Nature a fait cette nouvelle Loy.
Mais quoy? reprenoit-il, dans cette Loy nouvelle,
La Nature se trompe, ou n'est pas naturelle.
Pourquoy moy Sansonnet engendrer des Coucous?
Pourquoy couver des œufs, qui ne sont point à nous?

Pourquoy?... Sans doute il eust poussé loin le murmure;
    Mais un Milan passant par là,
    Quoy? luy dit-il, ce n'est que pour cela
Que tu vas de POVRQVOY fatiguant la Nature?
Hé! mon amy ton mal est devenu commun,
Parmy les Animaux, je n'en connois aucun
Qui ne puisse s'attendre à pareille aventure.

Would turn to starling's feathers, far more fit
    For such as his progeniture.
Fathers believe the best!... And so our poor
Gulled bird, deceived paterfamilias,
Proceeds to school the birdlings, holding class
In warbling skill, attempting to impart—
With every quip and dictum caged birds learn—
Unto the pseudo-starlings, mankind's art,
"Most eloquent!" But when it comes their turn,
"Speak!" he commands. And "Cuckoo" they reply.
    No other sound from them he draws.
For "Cuckoo" is, and "Cuckoo" ever was,
The only sound a cuckoo makes. "Why? Why?"
    Wonders the starling, near gone mad.
"How can this be? How muddled up is this?
How to explain this metamorphosis ?
    Cuckoos? Cuckoos?... Zounds and egad!
    How could I father such as these?
Ever since I was born, bird fathers bird
In his own image, with his qualities
And not another's! Ah! Upon my word,
Only since I frequent Man and his kind
Has Nature changed her law!" So he opined,
And he went on to add: "Nature has erred.
How comes it that, a starling, I begat
Cuckoos, of all things? Why? Why have I sat,
Waiting and waiting? By what foul design
Have I hatched eggs that are not even mine?"

Why? How?... He might have wondered longer yet
Had not a kite come passing by. He sighs:
"You browbeat Nature with your 'hows' and 'whys,'
But common is your woe. When beasts beget
    Their young, no male can ever be
Sure to have spawned his female's progeny."

Fables, IV

Vn vieux Freslon depuis long-temps
Avoit fait des desseins sur une Tubereuse;
Un Papillon, nouveau fils du Printemps,
Traversoit en secret, sa fortune amoureuse.
De grand murmure, & de sanglant combat,
Se vit alors la prochaine apparence,
C'est tousiours de la concurrence,
Que naissent le bruit & l'éclat.
A maintenir leurs droits, les Rivaux s'appresterent.
Pere Freslon de bourdonner,
Papillon de papillonner
Tant volerent, tant bourdonnerent,
Qu'enfin l'Amour ils obligerent,
A juger de leur different.
Il cite devant luy le Couple concourant,
Leur ordonne à tous deux, d'exposer l'aventure:
Jamais sans doute avent ce jour,
Ils ne s'estoient trouvez en telle conjoncture;
Mais tout parle dans la Nature,
Quand il s'agit d'obeyr à l'Amour.
Je suis, dit le premier, un Freslon qu'on estime
Pour son labeur et pour son rang.
D'un essain renommé le Prince legitime
Me reconnoist pour estre de son Sang:
Cette Tubereuse naissante,
Par sa jeunesse florissante,
A sceu meriter mon ardeur;
Depuis le jour qu'elle est éclose,
Je voltige sans cesse autour de cette Fleur,
Et quitte pour la voir, Lys, Anemone, & Rose,
Qui tenoient de ma part, ces soins à grand honneur.
Ce foible Papillon, cette fragile engeance,
Qui parmy nous s'ose à peine enrôler,
Sans redouter l'effet de ma vengeance

THE BUTTERFLY, THE HORNET, AND THE CATERPILLAR

A hornet, long of years, once had designs
    Upon an amarillis fair;
A butterfly, newborn of spring, opines
That he would be the better of the pair
    To woo the belle. So, then and there,
A blustering, bloody combat seems to be
The probable eventuality.
For ever must such amorous competition
Spawn a bombastic, bellicose condition...
    The foes make ready for the fray:
    Old Hornet buzzes fiercely as
Young Butterfly keeps fluttering away:
So fierce their buzz and flutter, that one has,
    At length, to bring their suit before
The god of Love, who tells each warrior
To plead his case. Until that day, no doubt,
Neither had been obliged to talk about
Himself; but talk they did, for nothing or
    No one, in nature, flouts the word
    Of Love! The first one to be heard—
The hornet—states: "Hornet am I, esteemed
For both my labors and my lineage, sprung
From swarm renowned the garden round, and deemed,
Yea, by the Prince himself, to be among
    Those of blood royal! Well, this young,
Fair flower, scarce bloomed in all her beauty tender,
Is worthy of the ardor that I render
Unto her; and I fly about her, quitting
The rose, the lily, the anemone—
All of them, blooms who found it most befitting
    That I should honor them! Now he,
This fragile butterfly of base degree
And lowly race, who barely dares to show
His face, now flitting, fearless, to and fro,
Follows my trail, unmindful of my just

---

* While "tuberose" would be a more precise rendering of the French, I have opted for the more poetic (and less metrically flexible) "amarillis"; both flowers are of the same botanical family.

Marie-Catherine Desjardins de Villedieu 335

Sur mes traces semble voler.
Si pour travailler à ma tasche,
Je donne à mes desirs, un moment de relasche,
Ou vais succer d'un fruit le naissant vermillon,
Quand ie viens reparer prés de ma Tubereuse,
Une absence si douloureuse,
J'y retrouve tousiours l'assidu Papillon:
Faut-il qu'un Freslon de ma sorte,
Chery de Flore, envié des Zephirs,
Souffre qu'un Papillon apporte
Un obstacle secret à ses tendres desirs?
Qu'il ose impunément luy disputer la place,
Exciter sa colere, & ses soupçons jaloux,
Ay-je tord de vouloir reprimer cette audace?
Grand Dieu, je m'en rapporte à vous.

C'est, dit le Papillon, avoir mauvaise grace,
Et faire à ce Dieu mal sa Cour,
Que d'exposer son travail & sa Race,
Quand il s'agit des faveurs de l'Amour.
Moy Papillon, je ne me vente
Ny d'ancestres fameux, ny d'exploits importans;
Mais ma parure est éclatante,
Et j'en change tous les Printems.
A la saison que les Roses nouvelles
Estalent à mes yeux leurs beautez naturelles,
Si je me trouve épris de leurs jeunes appas,
Je ne prends point mon vol vers elles,
Que l'éclat qui sort de mes aîles
Ne m'ait devancé de cent pas.
J'ay du brillant, de la jeunesse,
De l'enjoument, & de la propreté.
Je suis leger, je le confesse,
Mais je rends grace au Ciel de ma legereté,
Lors que Papillonnant, de fleurette en fleurette,
Indifferemment ie muguette
Tout ce qui paroist à mes yeux,
Cette inconstance est souvent une adresse
Pour inspirer à la Fleur ma Maistresse
Le desir de m'arrester mieux.
Si d'un illustre Sang ta vanité se louë,
En humble Papillon j'avouë

And swift revenge! And if I must
Quell my desires, to tend my work and go
Sip the vermilion juice of some new berry,
When I return, after my temporary,
Distressing absence, he, the butterfly,
Is ever there, pressing his quest! Must I,
    Hornet, of worth extraordinary,
I, whom the Zephyrs envy, and whom she,
The goddess Flora, treasures lovingly,
Must such a one as I allow a mere
    Butterfly thus to interfere,
    Furtively, with my tender passion?
When he dares try—audacious cavalier!—
To take my place in such unseemly fashion,
Raising my fell suspicion, do I err,
With jealous wrath, to curb him? I defer,
    Good god, to your august decision."

"It seems to me," the butterfly replies,
Properly, but not quite without derision,
    "A trifle tasteless to apprise
This god of matters such as work and race.
My ancestry, I fear, is commonplace,
And I perform no worthy deeds; and yet,
Most splendid is my elegant toilette;
Radiant of hue, a new one every spring.
And in the season when the blossoming
Roses spread their young grace before my gaze,
    When I am lured to their displays
Of beauty, I no sooner shall take wing
Than my own brilliance much precedes my flight.
For, in my youth's enthusiasm, bright
I shine with dazzling splendor and éclat!
    I may be light of body, yes,
But I thank heaven for all that weightlessness
    That lets me flitter... flutter... Ah!
Flower to flower!... Such is my stratagem;
For when, capricious, I go wooing them
With faithless fickleness, the one I love
Desires me all the more! If race, whereof
    You boast, and rank are yours, I do
Confess in all humility hereby

Marie-Catherine Desjardins de Villedieu 337

De ne meriter pas cét honneur comme toy;
     Mais pour finir la dispute amoureuse,
          Demandons à la Tubereuse,
Lequel luy plaist le plus, du Freslon, ou de moy.

          Malgré le royal Parentage,
     Le Papillon auroit eu l'avantage,
          Si la Fleur eust reglé son sort:
     Il estoit jeune, il estoit agreable;
Mais pendant que tous deux redoubloient leur effort,
     Pour obtenir un Arrest favorable,
          Une Chenille impitoyable
Achevoit sourdement de les mettre d'accord.

Ainsi voit-on finir parmy les creatures,
          Maintes & maintes avantures;
On entre en concurrence, & de feux, & de soins,
          On se dispute, on se querelle,
Pendant que le Rival qu'on redoute le moins,
          Triomphe en secret de la Belle;
Et laissant aux Muguets, le murmure & l'éclat,
S'enrichit du butin, sans aller au combat.

LE CHAT & LE GRILLON

Que l'homme se sert mal de son raisonnement!
          Qu'injuste fut la Loy suprême
Qui soûmit l'Animal impitoyablement
A tel qui ne sçait pas se gouverner luy-mesme,
Et qui tout Animal instruit facilement.
          Ainsi s'exhaloit en murmure,
          Certain Grillon seditieux,
Qui bien-tost eust changé l'ordre de la Nature,
Si Grillons décidoient dans le Conseil des Dieux.

That you deserve your honors more than I.
As for our suit, let me propose to you
    That we allow our flower to be
The judge of whom she favors: you or me."

Butterfly would have won the day, of course,
Despite our Hornet's regal pedigree,
Had the two rivals had the chance, perforce,
To let the flower decide: his youth, his air
Would have prevailed forsooth. But while the pair
Argued their cases with much eagerness,
    Amid the bicker and the brawl,
* A stealthy caterpillar, pitiless,
    Solved their dispute for good and all.

Thus, many a time and oft, has it ensued,
When competition, fierce and fiery, flares
Betwixt two rivals: in suchlike affairs
Men fume and fret; but how does it conclude?
While one and two dispute the belle, a third,
    Of whom they had not even heard,
Spirits her off and leaves our beaus, bereft,
    To flit about—dejected, quite—
With nothing but their fuss and fury left:
The other wins the prize without a fight.

Fables, v

THE CAT AND THE CRICKET

"How ill Man uses reason! How unjust,
    That law supreme, that glorious plan
    That told us animals we must
    Bend to the will, the power of Man,
Who cannot rule himself, and who, in fact,
    Learns from us beasts how best to act..."
So chirped a cricket of seditious leaning,
Who would have remade Nature, by all odds,
If crickets sat in council with the gods.

  * Though not clearly stated, the suggestion seems to be that the "pitiless" caterpillar
mooted the dispute, not by winning the flower romantically, but by doing what caterpillars
do best: destroying it. My translation attempts to preserve that vagueness.

C'est bien à toy, mon cher, à faire le Critique,
    Interrompit un vieux Matou,
Qu'un peu de cendre chaude attiroit prés du trou
    De notre Grillon Satirique.
Encore si c'estoit quelque Chat comme moy,
    Qui blamât la suprême Loy,
Je luy pardonnerois de se donner carriere.
Matou courant de nuict, de Goutiere, en Goutiere,
Peut se formaliser d'avoir l'homme pour Roy.
Il luy voit en secret, commettre tant de crimes,
    Suivre tant de folles maximes.
Icy fait le lutin, le frenetique Epoux,
    Croyant que grilles & verroux
    Rendent une Epouse fidelle,
Pendant que le Galant qui luy tient en cervelle,
    Doit aux seuls soupçons du jaloux,
    Toutes les faveurs de la Belle.
Là, garde le Mulet quelque credule Amant,
    Comptant pour un Siecle un moment,
Pensant que sa Philis le compte à sa maniere,
Et l'égale en desirs comme en fidelité.
Que s'il pouvoit en Chat passer par la Chattiere,
Seroit bien-tost guery de sa credulité.
    Es-tu témoin des serenades,
    Et des nocturnes promenades,
Où s'occupent souvent les plus sages mondains?
Passes-tu quelquesfois sur les toits les plus saints,
D'où lorgnant par un trou, le rusé Solitaire,
J'ay veu l'hypocrisie, à tel degré monter,
    Que moy, Matou, je n'ose raconter,
Ce que tel qu'on croit Saint, n'a pas honte de faire?
Chacun sçait ce qu'il sçait, reprit d'un ton chagrin,
Le Grillon mal content de son petit destin:
Si tu vois le Bigot démentir sa grimasse,
Je voy peut-estre plus, sans partir de ma place.
    J'entends souvent le Magistrat

"My friend, if I perceive your meaning,"
Cut in an old puss, tempted by the few
Last glowing embers to repair thereto,
Close by our caustic cricket's hole, "at least
    Were it some knowledgeable beast—
    Some cat, like me—who jibed about
That 'law supreme,' I should have heard him out.
For, we who scuttle on Man's roofs by night,
    Gutter to gutter... Well we might
Complain of his dominion over us.
We see his many secret sins; we see
The foolishness of the philosophy
He follows. Here, a frantic spouse—the dolt!—
    Who thinks that gate, and lock, and bolt
Will guarantee his wife's fidelity;
Whilst the young swain who covets her in mind
Owes all the favors of the belle confined
    To jealous husband's fell suspicion.
There, on his mule, a patient lover, waiting
    To consummate his amorous mission,
    Counting the minutes, calculating
Each one a century, anticipating,
And certain that his Phyllis counts no less,
    And yearns for him as much! Ah yes,
Could he but squeeze in through the pussy-door
He would be cured of such foolhardiness,
    And be so gullible no more!
Are you a witness to those serenades,
Those strolls nocturnal that the worthiest
    And wisest ply to woo their maids?
Do you scamper along those saintliest
Of rooftops, peeping through a hole to spy
* Monkish hypocrisy, so foul that I,
Tough old puss though I be, dare not relate it?"
"Each knows what each can know," quick to reply,
Says Cricket, rankling at his paltry state. "It

* In the original, the reference to religious hypocrisy is in the form of a specific barb aimed at the "Solitaires" of the celebrated Port-Royal abbey, which had become a stronghold of Jansenism. Though playing an important role in the intellectual and literary life of the period, its members were a not infrequent target of ridicule. For a typical example, see La Fontaine, "Le rat qui s'est retiré du monde" (*Fables* 7.3).

Marie-Catherine Desjardins de Villedieu 341

De son Foyer prendre des Villes,
Le Cavalier parler, de matieres civiles,
   Et le Bourgeois, trancher du Potentat.
Tel qui ne peut trouver, de party pour sa fille,
De tout le genre humain, fait le Chef de Famille.
Et croit estre nommé de Dieu pour le pourvoir;
Il donne celuy-cy de puissance absoluë,
A telle que peut-estre, il n'aura jamais veuë,
   Et qu'il ne devra jamais voir.
   Que diray-je de la licence
   Que se donne leur médisance?
Est-il rien de sacré pour ces Prophanes-là;
   Un de ces soirs j'entendois dire...
   A cet endroit de la Satyre,
   Le patron de cafe appella;
Sa voix pour nos censeurs, fut pis qu'un coup de foudre.
Matou ne fit qu'un saut, jusques au trou du Chat,
Et Grillon se croyant desia reduit en poudre,
Rentra plus mort que vif dans son sombre grabat.

L'AGNEAU & SES FRÈRES

Autrefois nâquit un Agneau,
Plus digne d'estre Louveteau,
Que d'avoir Moutonne origine.
Il crioit sans cesse famine,
A tous les Agneaux du troupeaux.

May be you see the zealot, false of face,
    But I, from this, my humble place,
See more. I hear the magistrate ofttime
Take towns entire; the petty knight discuss
Matters of state; the bourgeois odious
    And base, aspire to power sublime;
The father who finds no one who will wed
His daughter take it on himself instead
To find a mate for all humanity,
As if endowed by God's divine decree,
Bestowing this one, that, on maid he never
Has seen or known, and, likely, will not ever!
What shall I say about the infamy
Of their malicious tongues? Is nothing holy—
    Nothing?—to these debased and lowly
Souls?... Let me tell you what I heard one night..."
    At that point in their obloquies
    The innkeep's voice boomed out, and these
Courageous censors scurried off in fright:
Old Puss, back to his hole in but one leap,
    And Cricket, less alive than dead,
Fearing lest he become a powdered heap,
Back to his darkly dismal, somber bed.

Fables, VI

THE LAMB AND HIS BROTHERS

A lamb there was, born years ago,
Who more the wolf cub seemed to be
Than one of sheepdom's pedigree.
To all the flock he wailed his woe,
    Starving—or so he claimed—for he
Sucked at an udder all but dry. And so

* The original *patron de cafe* poses a cultural more than a translational problem. Etymological dictionaries indicate that the first French establishment serving the newly introduced coffee was opened in Marseille in 1654, and the first one in Paris, not until 1672 or thereabouts, two years after the publication of Madame de Villedieu's collection. It is hard to know exactly how she envisioned the *cafe* referred to (and which, curiously, she spells without its usual accented *é*, thus making it a monosyllable for metrical purposes). My solution is something of a compromise.

Sa Mere, disoit-il, estoit presque tarie,
  Il remplissoit d'un plaintif bêlement,
    Pâturages, & Bergerie,
    Et voyez la friponnerie!
Sa Mere avoit du laict, plus que suffisamment;
Mais outre qu'il estoit d'un naturel gourmand,
Il s'estoit apperceu que Bergers & Bergeres,
De Bestail bien nourry font tousiours plus de cas,
  Que de Bestail qui ne profite pas.
Le voilà donc gueusant du laict, à tous ses freres.
    Hé! leur disoit-il, par pitié
    Souffrez que ie tette vos Meres,
Elles ont trop de laict pour vous de la moitié:
Et moy pauvre Agnelet, natif de mesme Estable,
  Qui nuict & jour, tire la mienne en vain,
    Je serois desia mort de faim,
Si ie n'avois trouvé quelqu'Agneau secourable.
    Jamais la feinte, avant ce jour,
Chez les simples Agneaux, ne fut mise en pratique,
Ceux-cy croyant aux dits, du rusé famelique,
Luy cedoient bonnement, leur place tour à tour.
Il profite à gogo de cette complaisance,
    Il croist, il devient grasselet,
Au lieu que les Agneaux, qu'il tenoit au filet,
    Jeûnant de son trop d'abondance,
    Auprés de luy ne sembloient qu'avortons.
    Arrive un Marchand de Moutons.
  On luy fait voir la Peuplade nouvelle,
    A peine il jette l'œil sur elle,
Qu'il croit que les Sorciers, ont maudit le Troupeau;
Où mene-t'on, dit-il, ces pauvres Brebis paistre?
    Leurs petits n'ont que les os & la peau.
Gardez-les pour peupler, Monsieur, dit-il au Maistre,
    Car de les vendre en cet estat,
Vous n'en tirerez pas seulement une obole.
    En prononçant cette parole
    Il mit la main sur nostre Scelerat.
    Ho, ho, dit-il, je taste un drôle,
    Qui s'est sauvé du Magique attentat.

The pastures and the pen resounded
With many a bleating cry. But most unfounded
Were his laments, fruit of the rogue's deceit!
    In fact, his mother's milk abounded!
    But he, a glutton at the teat,
    Had noticed, too, all the attention
Lavished by shepherds and their shepherdesses
On those well fed, with naught but condescension
For those too gaunt. Thus, begging, he addresses
His mutton ilk: "Ah! Pity, pity! Heed
    My prayer, O brothers! Let me share
Your mothers' milk. For much more than you need
Have they, whilst I, your stable-kin, despair
And suck in vain, poor lamblet that I am,
By night, by day! Alas, had I not been
Succored already by one kindly lamb,
I should have died." Unused to guile and sham,
    Our innocents are taken in
    By his ignoble infamy,
    And yield their places, one by one,
Beneath the dugs maternal, graciously;
Whereat, glutting with greed second to none,
Exploiting their simplicity, he grows
Plumper and plumper, whilst the others—those
    Caught in his wiles and going without,
As copiously he sups—seem, next to him,
Mere runts, of scrawny size and scraggy limb...
In time a mutton merchant thereabout,
    Looking for lamb to buy, came round;
But scarcely had he laid an eye upon
The flock, than he believed it hexed, spellbound
By wizards who had placed some curse thereon.
"Where do they take these ewes to graze, I wonder!
    Their lambs are wizened skin and bones!
    Better," he tells the one who owns
The flock, "to let them grow a deal rotunder!
For, wretches that they are, I promise you,
    They will not fetch a single sou."
No sooner said than, suddenly, "By thunder!"
He shouts, as on our villain lamb he lays
His hand. "Aha! What's this? This one, I vow,
    Escaped the magic spell somehow!

Marie-Catherine Desjardins de Villedieu 345

Il l'achepte, on luy livre, il fait le meilleur plat,
De la prochaine Hostellerie,
Pendant que les Agneaux, qu'il a mis aux abois,
Bondissent sur l'herbe fleurie,
Ou ruminent en paix à l'ombrage des bois.

Ie n'expliqueray point ma Fable.
Tout convoiteux du bien d'autruy,
Tout Parasite insatiable,
Bref, tout humain, du siecle d'aujourd'hui,
Qui d'estre mon Agneau, se sentira capable,
Sçaura bien que je parle à luy.

L'YRONDELLE & L'OYSEAU DE PARADIS

L'Yrondelle, craignant, le froid de nos quartiers,
S'en alloit faire un tour, jusqu'aupres de Carthage.
L'Oyseau de Paradis, se trouve à son passage,
Voyageurs, comme on sçait, confinent volontiers.
Les voila donc jasant, d'un climat & d'un autre,
L'Yrondelle ventoit, les raretez du nôtre,
Et l'Oyseau, les beautez du sien:
Elle prit goust à l'entretien.
Elle se connoissoit, pour n'estre qu'Yrondelle,
Et sçavoit que l'oyseau, n'est pas oyseau pour elle;
Mais contre ce qui plaist, on ne prend loy de rien.
L'Oyseau de Paradis, est charmant au possible,
Et nostre voyageuse, a le cœur susceptible.
Elle niche souvent, en tel Palais de Cour,
Où l'on n'habite point, sans connoistre l'amour:
Elle admire, tantost, le bec, & le ramage,
D'autresfois, le rare plumage,
De l'hoste à ses yeux si charmant;
Et sans considerer, dans son emportement,
Que le celeste Oyseau, n'habite que la nuë
Et qu'il vit de l'air seulement,
La voilà d'abord resoluë,

And so he buys him, dearly pays,
And takes him to the nearby inn, where he
Graces the tables of the hostelry.
Meanwhile, the victims of his flim-flam crass
Gambol in peace, and graze upon the grass
Amid the shades and flowers of the wood.

My moral will be understood,
Nor need it be explained, alas!
All those who covet others' wealth, who prey
Like parasites; in short, all who, today,
Would use the lamb's fell stratagem,
Will know the fable is for them.

Fables, VII

THE SWALLOW AND THE BIRD OF PARADISE

A swallow, fearful of our climes' cold weather,
Winging her way toward Carthage, southward flies,
And meets, en route, a bird of paradise.
Now, as you know, travelers, when thrown together,
Willingly share each others' company.
And so our pair, in pleasant colloquy,
Go jabbering on this and that,
Chatting, each one, about their habitat—
Climate and such—the swallow, eagerly
Boasting how passing odd ours is;
The other, how delectable is his.
The former took much joy therein,
Yet knew that, a mere swallow, she would err
To think that such a bird could be for her.
But one who scorns what pleases cannot win.
Powerless is our heroine,
Her heart touched by his charms. Often she nests
In this palace or that: lifeless the breasts
That feel not love and adoration
In such a royal place! Bestowing on
His song, his plumage rare, his beak—upon
His being entire—her utter adulation,
She quite forgets, so turbulent
Her passion, that this heavenly one

A ne le perdre plus de veuë.
Cependant la faim la pressoit,
Dame Nature patissoit,
Et l'on sçait que cette Commere,
Ne se repaist point de chimere.

Tant d'amour qu'on voudra, tant de charmans appas,
　　Il faut toûjours manger, & boire,
Et c'est un incident, necessaire à l'histoire,
　　Que de prendre au leger repas.
　　Que faire donc dans cette conjoncture?
Faut-il se revolter, contre Dame Nature?
　　Ou faut-il se rendre à ses coups,
　　Jeunes Amans, ma Fable parle à vous.
　　Quelle que soit l'ardeur qui vous transporte
Sur un peu de prudence, appuyez vostre amour,
Les plaisirs les plus grands, sont sujets au retour,
Et la necessité demeure la plus forte.

———————

SUR L'INGRATITUDE DES AMANS DU SIÈCLE

　　Qui veut trouver un remede suprême
　　Contre l'ennuy, d'un long engagement,
　　　　N'a qu'à montrer à son Amant,
　　　　Qu'il est autant aimé, qu'il aime.
　　　　La tiedeur irrite ses feux,
D'un desir sans effet, on en voit cent renaître:
　　　　Mais si-tost qu'il se croit heureux,
　　　　Il sent qu'il se lasse de l'estre.

Lives in the very firmament,
And feeds on air; and she decides
To follow him, no matter what betides,
Fly where he may, whithersoever...
Her plans soon go awry, however:
For hunger soon betrays our swallow,
As, where Dame Nature beckons, she must follow.

Love all you will, and hold charm's pleasures fast.
Still, as my fable tries to show,
You must have food and drink—although
It might be but a light repast.
Should we rebel against Dame Nature then?
Or should we do as she would have us do?
My tale, young lovers, is addressed to you.
However strong your passions when
You love, however hotly they transport you,
Be prudent; for necessity remains
Above them all: for all your pains,
The greatest pleasures can turn round and thwart you.

Fables, VIII

ON THE INGRATITUDE OF THIS AGE'S LOVERS

She who would find the supreme remedy
Against the boredom of a long affair,
Need do no more than to declare
Her lover loved as much as she.
A tepid ardor spurs his fires:
From one fruitless desire a hundred grow;
But when he thinks himself her beau,
No more he loves, and promptly tires.

"Maximes diverses," I

SUR LE VICE DE L'HABITUDE

L'age entreprend en vain, de rendre un Vieillard prude,
    Qui s'enflâma, peut s'enflâmer,
    L'Amour est un mal d'habitude,
Plus on aime, dit-on, plus on voudroit aimer.

QU'IL NE FAUT POINT ALLER DIRECTEMENT CONTRE L'INCLINATION D'UNE DAME

    Pour n'estre point Pilote temeraire,
Il faut selon les vents, mettre sa barque en mer:
        L'Amant qui n'est pas seur de plaire,
        Rarement se laisse charmer.
        Il faut éviter quand on aime,
        Les perils d'un cœur égaré,
        Le prudent laboureur ne seme,
        Que dans le champ bien preparé,

SUR CE QUE LES PEINES QU'ON SOUFFRE EN ALLANT À UN RENDEZ-VOUS, NE SONT COMPTÉES POUR RIEN DÉS QU'ON Y ARRIVE

Il n'est temps si facheux, ni froid si redoutable,
Qui ne cede aux ardeurs d'une maîtresse aimable:
En vain pour moderer les transports d'un Amant,
        La Saison la plus rigoureuse
Le prendroit pour l'objet de son dereglement.
Dés que l'amour travaille à son soulagement,
        Un instant d'heure bien-heureuse
        Repare un siecle de tourment.

ON THE VICE OF HABIT

Age cannot make an old man lose his lust;
Who flamed with passion once can do so still.
    Love is a habit that bodes ill:
The more one loves, the more, they say, one must.

"Maximes diverses," II

THAT ONE MUST NOT GO FORWARD
AGAINST A LADY'S INCLINATION

Lest one be thought a helmsman rash, one must,
    Before embarking, test the wind;
So too the Lover, if he cannot trust
His charms, should he press on, will be chagrined.
    In love one ought be sure to shun
    The perils of a heart misled;
    The prudent ploughman is the one
Who tends his field before the seed is spread.

"Maximes diverses," V

ON HOW ONE FORGETS THE DIFFICULTIES
ENCOUNTERED ON THE WAY TO A TRYST
ONCE ONE HAS ARRIVED

However rude the weather, there is none
So frigid that, when all is said and done,
It yields not to sweet mistress's warm passion.
    Let winter howl in foulest fashion
To cool a lover's ecstasies: ah no!
In vain it wreaks its wildest devastation:
    One moment of love's consolation
    Repairs a century of woe.

"Maximes diverses," VI

Marie-Catherine Desjardins de Villedieu 351

QUE D'ORDINAIRE LES ENFANS TIENNENT DE LEUR PÈRE & DE LEUR MÈRE

L'Art d'aimer est un doux talent,
Hereditaire en certaines familles,
Et meres ayant eu le cœur tendre & galant,
Font rarement severes filles.

QU'IL NE FAUT DONNER AUX AGENS DE L'AMOUR QU'UN POUVOIR LIMITÉ

En Amour il est dangereux
De donner un pouvoir trop ample,
Et d'Agents agissants pour eux,
On fourniroit plus d'un exemple.
Si le pouvoir n'est limité,
Souvent le trop d'authorité
Rend permis tout ce qu'on desire
Contre soy mesme on ne prend loy de rien,
Et l'Electeur qui peut s'élire,
Prononce rarement d'autre nom que le sien.

QU'ON SURMONTE MIEUX L'AMOUR PAR LA FUITTE QUE PAR LES COMBATS

Au moment que l'Amour se montre,
S'il se fait contre luy quelque coup important,
C'est en évitant sa rencontre,
Et non pas en le combattant.

THAT CHILDREN USUALLY TAKE AFTER
THEIR FATHER AND MOTHER

The art of loving is a talent sweet,
    Passed down in certain families,
And mothers, kind of heart, gallant, discreet,
Seldom make daughters with harsh qualities.

"Maximes diverses," VIII

THAT ONE SHOULD GIVE INTERMEDIARIES
IN LOVE VERY LIMITED POWER

    In love it is a danger great
    Excessive power to delegate:
    Many examples could attest
    To those who serve their interest
    Instead of ours. In point of fact,
Those whom we grant authority to act
In our behalf will, often, thereunto,
Accept no limit to the liberty
They take to see their own ambitions through;
And the elector who will shamelessly
    Vote for himself, unlikely is
Ever to speak another's name but his.

"Maximes diverses," X

THAT ONE CONQUERS LOVE BY FLEEING
RATHER THAN BY FIGHTING IT

When love declares itself, if we would show
Our power to prevail, it is more fit
    That we resist by shunning it,
Not by combatting, and thus lay it low.

"Maximes diverses," XIV

Marie-Catherine Desjardins de Villedieu 353

CONTRE LES VIEUX AMANS QUI ENTREPRENNENT DE PLAIRE À DE JEUNES DAMES

Quand vieux Seigneur entreprend jeune Dame,
Il ne fait qu'aplanir les chemins de son âme,
    Pour un plus jeune qui le suit.
Par ses sçavans conseils, ses ruses, son addresse,
    Il va semant les germes de tendresse,
    Dont un autre cueille le fruict.

MADRIGAL

    En vain tu veux me secourir,
    Raison, je ne veux pas guerir,
    De ces maux mon cœur est complice.
Cessez de tourmenter mes esprits abbatus,
Faux honneur, faux devoir: si l'amour est un vice,
C'est un vice plus beau que toutes les vertus.

AGAINST OLD LOVERS WHO UNDERTAKE
TO PLEASE YOUNG LADIES

An aging sire who woos a demoiselle
Merely makes way for younger swain than he
To follow in his path, and woo as well.
    With counsel sage, ruse, *jeux d'esprit,*
    He sows love's seeds; but vain his suit:
Another will come by and pluck the fruit.

"Maximes diverses," xx

MADRIGAL

Reason, in vain you seek to succor me:
    I wish no cure; for, of all those
    Ills that I suffer, all my woes,
My heart is an accomplice, willingly.
False honor and false duty, cease, I pray,
Troubling my wits, scarce clinging to their tether:
If loving is a vice, as some will say,
'Tis fairer than all virtues put together.

Marie-Catherine Desjardins de Villedieu 355

Elisabeth-Sophie Chéron (1648–1711)

Woman of talents artistic, musical, and poetic, and accomplished in all of them, Elisabeth-Sophie Chéron, Parisian born and bred, was called upon at the age of sixteen to help support a family virtually abandoned by her father, a painter of enamel miniatures. It was perhaps because of his influence and teaching that she developed her ability as a portrait painter and was ultimately commissioned to do the portraits of the mother superior of the abbey of Jouarre, the princesses d'Epinay, and others. Thanks to her warm welcome among the good sisters—if not simply to a desire to avoid impending persecution—she was to abjure her family's Protestant faith, unlike her brother, who fled to England after the revocation of the Edict of Nantes. It was for her excellence as a portraitist that she was elected to the Académie royale de peinture et de sculpture in 1672, presenting for her candidacy a self-portrait and sponsored by the eminent painter Charles Le Brun.

Equally gifted with literary ability, Elisabeth-Sophie Chéron apparently penned a humorous work, *Les cerises renversées,* which has escaped my investigation; but it was particularly to her *Essay de Pseaumes et cantiques, mis en vers,* with engravings by her brother Louis, that she turned her poetic inspiration in 1694, and for which—still a reformist at heart—she studied Hebrew in an effort to penetrate as deeply as possible the sense of the original text. Considering that she was the beneficiary of a pension bestowed by Louis XIV, it is not unlikely that the work's anonymous dedication to "Monsieur ***" may well refer to the king himself. Be that as it may, the resulting psalms and hymns, in the lingering spirit of Marot's *Psaumes* a century and a half earlier, and of her contemporary Racine's *Cantiques spirituels,* are vigorous, strikingly dramatic renditions, which, thanks to her skillful versification and judicious use of varying meters, avoid a monotony all too often found in such devotional works. It was this collection that earned her election, in 1699, to the Accademia dei Ritrovati of Padua, where the name "Erato" was bestowed on her after the Muse of lyric poetry, when she took her place among her eight sister Muses, limited in number to the nine of classical mythology.

Elisabeth-Sophie Chéron was married at the age of sixty to one Jacques Le Hay, whose name she subsequently added to her own. Noticeably lacking are substantial works devoted to her literary *œuvre,* of which my translations offer three characteristic examples.

Lætatus sum in his quæ dicta sunt mihi, &c.

Ce Pseaume fut fait lorsque les Juifs eurent obtenu de Cyrus la permission
de retourner à Jerusalem aprés 70 ans de captivité

Quel transport imprevû s'empare de mon ame!
Seroit-il vray qu'encor je verrois de mes yeux
La celebre maison du Dieu que je reclame?
Je reverrois Sion, le bien de nos Ayeux.
Jerusalem séjour où regnoit la concorde,
Où l'on vit triompher la justice & la paix,
    Le Tout-puissant par sa misericorde
    Te rendroit-il à nos souhaits?
Que je sens vivement cette heureuse nouvelle
Encor j'adoreray dans ce lieu glorieux,
Où mille nations offrent au Dieu des Cieux
    Avec la victime mortelle
    Le sacrifice precieux
    D'une ame & sincere & fidelle.
Dans l'attente du jour qui fait nôtre bon-heur
    Nos cœurs exempts d'ingratitude
Sans cesse beniront notre liberateur,
    Il rompt les fers de nôtre servitude;
    Que favorisé du Seigneur,
Ses jours soient couronnez & de gloire & d'honneur.
Et toy Jerusalem, ô nôtre Cité sainte,
Que les graces du Ciel se répandent sur toy,
Goute la douce paix qui regne en ton enceinte,
Que mes freres unis puissent joüir sans crainte
Des biens que le Seigneur leur partage avec moy.

Lætatus sum in his quæ sunt mihi, &c.

*This Psalm was composed after the Jews had obtained permission
from Cyrus to return to Jerusalem after seventy years of captivity.*

Ah! What joy unexpected grips my soul!
Can it be that, once more, my eyes will see
The temple of that God whom I extol?
What? Might our Fathers' precious Zion be
Spread out anew before my gaze? And you,
Jerusalem, where harmony once reigned
  In peace and justice: will you, too,
  By the Almighty's grace reclaimed,
Be ours again? I shudder with delight
To hear the news! For I shall worship there,
In glory, where a myriad peoples' prayer
  Rises unto God's heavenly height
  In sacrifice, there to unite
  Victim and faithful soul, and bear
Them both before Him... As we wait that day
  Of bliss, our grateful hearts will bless,
Unceasing, him who liberates us; yea,
Smashes our chains and frees us from duress.
  May the Lord smile on him, and may
His days be crowned with glory limitless.
May heaven its mercy spread on you as well,
Jerusalem, O city blessed, wherein
I pray peace ever reign; there let us dwell
United: may the Lord of Israel
His boons bestow on us and all our kin.

---

* This psalm bears the same number in the Vulgate but is numbered 122 in the King James version. It is generally accepted that the *Psalms*, traditionally attributed to David, were composed by more than one hand and at more than one time, the final collection dating from about 150 B.C.E. This would help account for the apparently anachronistic reference to Cyrus—unmentioned by name in the psalm—though it was he, in fact, who, centuries after David's death (ca. 972 B.C.E.) did allow the Jews to return to Jerusalem after the Babylonian Captivity, 538 B.C.E.

Elisabeth-Sophie Chéron 359

PSEAUME CXXIX

De profundis clamavi, &c.

Ce Pseaume fut composé par quelque Israëlite dans les fers des Babyloniens

Du profond abîme où je suis,
Seigneur, entens ma voix, exauce ma priere,
Soit que le jour commence ou perde sa lumiere,
Je ne vois point de bornes à mes cruels ennuis.

Tu connois les douleurs dont mon ame est atteinte,
Seigneur, preste l'oreille à mes tristes clameurs,
Ne me rebute point, favorise ma plainte,
Efface les pechez qui font couler mes pleurs.

Si tu mets nos forfaits dans ta juste balance,
Si tu veux nous juger au poids de l'équité,
O mon Dieu, qui pourra soutenir ta presence?
Qui pourra nous sauver de nôtre iniquité?

J'espere cependant qu'à mes larmes propice
Tu me pardonneras en faveur de ta loy;
Un cœur contrit, Seigneur, doit s'assurer en toy,
Si ta misericorde égale ta justice.

Helas! C'est sur toy seul que fonde son espoir,
Israël opprimé d'une injuste puissance:
Tant que durent les jours, de l'aube jusqu'au soir,
Ton peuple dans les fers implore ta clemence.

Ne le méprise point ce peuple infortuné,
A ses pressans regrets ne sois pas inflexible,
Ah! si de toy, Seigneur, il est abandonné,
Rien ne le peut sauver, sa perte est infaillible.

De profundis clamavi, &c.

This psalm was composed by one of the Israelites in the chains of the Babylonians

From my abyss, I pray you might
Pay heed, O Lord, unto my plaintive plea:
Neither at dawn nor dusk can my eyes see
An end, alas, to this, my ruthless plight.

You know my soul, O Lord, with anguish rent:
Listen, I pray you, to my cries of woe;
Reject me not, but, moved by my lament,
Wipe clean the sins that cause my tears to flow.

If you weigh our transgressions in just wise
And judge us, God, as we deserve, no less,
Who will withstand your presence? Who will rise
To save us from our wretched sinfulness?

Yet, Lord, I hope that, in propitious fashion,
Touched by my tears, your law might pardon me:
A heart contrite ought win your sympathy
If you but temper justice with compassion.

In chains, and crushed beneath a power unjust,
Your people—Israel—cries out to you
For mercy; you, in whom she puts her trust
Year after year, and all the long day through.

Leave not your people to her woeful state;
Give ear to her regrets and spurn them not!
You alone, Lord, can save her from her fate,
Else must destruction surely be her lot.

*This psalm is numbered 130 in the King James version. As with the preceding and fol-
lowing poems, its interpretation in terms of the Babylonian Captivity is an understandable
anachronism that may or may not be justified.

Elisabeth-Sophie Chéron 361

PSEAUME CXXXVI

Super flumina Babylonis, &c.

Ce Pseaume fut composé par quelque prophète dans les premiers tems
de la captivité de Babylone

Assis sur l'orgueilleuse rive
Où Babylone regne & voit couler nos pleurs,
Captifs nous déplorions tes funestes malheurs,
    Triste Sion, miserable captive:
Nos harpes, nos hautbois aux saules suspendus
      Muets n'étoient plus entendus:
En vain nos durs vainqueurs enflez de leur victoire
Se flatoient d'en oüir les agreables sons,
Chantez-nous, disoient-ils, ces celebres chansons
Qui de vôtre Sion jadis vantent la gloire.

Helas! leur disions-nous, par ces cruels mépris,
Pourquoy renouveller nos douleurs assoupies?
Ces cantiques si saints les avons-nous appris
Pour estre prophanez en des terres impies?
Déplorable Sion, si jamais l'avenir
De tes cruels malheurs m'ôte le souvenir,
Que sur nos luths sacrez mes doigts s'appesantissent,
Que la langue me reste attachée au palais,
    O Jerusalem, si jamais
Sur ces bords étrangers tes concerts retentissent.

O, Seigneur! souviens-toy que les enfans d'Edom,
Au jour de ta colere exerçans leur furie,
Jusques dans le lieu saint blasphemant ton saint Nom,
Crioient, exterminez, desolez leur patrie:
Sous ces fameuses tours, sous ces murs démolis
Que tous ces habitans restent ensevelis,

362 *Elisabeth-Sophie Chéron*

PSALM CXXXVI

Super flumina Babylonis, &c.

This Psalm was composed by one of the Prophets in the first days
of the Babylonian Captivity.

O captive Zion, prisoner pent,
We sat by Babylon's imperious shore
And, captives we, sighed for your griefs galore
Amid our flooding tears, unspent.
Our pipes, our harps from willow boughs were hung,
    Stilled, and our songs remained unsung:
In vain our conquerors, flushed with victory,
Wishing to hear their notes melodious,
Cruelly commanded: "Sing those songs for us
That praised your Zion's glorious destiny!"

"Alas," we answered, "why must you renew
The woe that we have taught our souls to bear?
Think you we learned those sacred hymns, to share
Them with vile foreign infidels like you?"
Pitiful Zion! If the future ever
Lets me forget your doleful pains, then, never
Let these, my fingers, pluck the blessèd lute;
May my tongue cleave unto my palate, and
    Jerusalem, in alien land,
Be your celestial concerts aver mute.

Forget not, Lord, the sons of Edom's race,
Who, loosing all their fury on your day
Of wrath, shouting, heaped all their fell disgrace
Upon your holy house and name: "Go, lay
Waste to their fatherland! Let all who dwell
Beneath these famous towers, destroyed pell-mell,

---

* This psalm, among the more famous, is numbered 137 in the King James version.
    † The poet provides a note in which she explains that Edom—land of the Idumaeans—
was named for Jacob's brother, believed to be their founder. The history of the Edomites
included their alliance with Nebuchadnezzar, when the Babylonians destroyed Jerusalem in
586 B.C.E. For the genealogy of Edom, also known as Esau, see Gen. 36:1–19.

Qu'en des fleuves de sang se changent leurs rivieres;
Que leurs Autels soient abatus,
Et que Jerusalem ne se remarque plus
Que par de vastes cimetieres.

Toy qui nous fais gemir sous le poids de tes fers,
Babylone superbe en ta rage cruelle,
Qui pourra nous vanger de tant de maux souffers?
Qui prendra contre toy nôtre juste querelle?
Qu'il soit remply de biens, qu'il soit comblé d'honneur
Celuy qu'a choisi le Seigneur,
Pour livrer à son bras tes villes embrasées,
Qu'il arrache tes fils de leur sein maternel,
Que versant leur sang criminel,
Tes pierres en soient arrosées.

Ever lie buried; let their streams flow red
  With blood; their altars be cast down;
And may Jerusalem know no renown
  But for the vast fields of her dead!"

O you, proud Babylon, whose haughty rage
Makes us, beneath your weighty chains, cry out!
Who will avenge us; who, our ills assuage?
Who will defend our just cause? Who will flout
Your wrath? Let one, so chosen by the Lord,
  Honored with many a rich reward,
Bring him your cities' ashes! Let him tear,
From mothers' bosoms wrenched, your progeny;
  And may their sinful blood flow free,
  To drench your pavements everywhere!

Louise-Geneviève Gillot de Sainctonge (1650–1718)

It is primarily as an author of opera libretti in verse that Madame de Sainctonge—née Louise-Geneviève Gillot de Beaucour—was known to her contemporaries. Born in Paris, she became the wife of a lawyer in the parlement and saw her two five-act works, *Didon* and *Circé*, performed at the Académie royale between 1693 and 1704, with music composed by the erratic Henri (or Henry) Desmarets (Demarest? Desmaretz? Desmarais?), and subsequently published. Another opera, *Histoire secrète de Dom Antoine, roi du Portugal*, is of interest in that she claimed that it was based on events in the life of her grandfather, Gomez de Vasconcelles, and the part he played in the tribulations of the said king, as chronicled in family papers that she fortuitously discovered. Sainctonge also translated the pastoral novel *La Diana enamorada* of the sixteenth-century Spanish poet Jorge de Montemayor, as well as Ariosto's *Orlando furioso*, from which one can infer, at least, that she was rather well educated.

It can also be inferred from her occasional verse—a mixture of pastoral cliché with flashes of suggestiveness—that she was no bluenose. (Indeed, how many other female poets of the time wrote drinking songs?) Originally published in 1696 in her *Poésies galantes*, her witty and often unfeminine verse—in the traditional sense, that is—was republished in an expanded two-volume edition as *Poésies diverses de Madame de Sainctonge*, which included also two verse comedies: the five-act *Griselde ou la princesse de Salluste*, and the one-act *L'intrigue des concerts*, both performed in Dijon in 1714, five years before her death in Paris. It seems reasonable to assume that the salon society of the capital would have been greatly entertained and titillated by her capricious talents.[1]

The following twenty-one varied examples of her art—brief madrigals, epigrams, *chansons*, and several drinking songs that may well have shocked her contemporaries, as well as two somewhat longer but no less charming *contes*—are taken from her *Poésies diverses*.

NOTE

1. For one of the few accounts of Sainctonge's life and works, see Fortunée Briquet's *Dictionnaire historique, littéraire et biographique des Françaises et des étrangères naturalisées* [etc.], pp. 298–99. Other time-honored biographical dictionaries make brief and uninformative passing references to her.

CHANSON

Je trouvai l'autre jour le Berger qui m'engage,
    Endormi prés de ce ruisseau,
En badinant je lui jettai de l'eau
        Sur le visage;
Il s'éveilla, je courus me cacher,
    Croyant qu'il viendroit me le rendre;
    Mais, hélas! ce Berger peu tendre
Ne prit pas seulement le soin de me chercher.

ÉPIGRAMME

        Damon me disoit l'autre jour,
Qu'il feroit par ses Vers la fortune à la Cour,
Qu'il seroit de Louis, bien-tôt Pensionnaire:
        Il est vrai, lui dis-je à mon tour,
        Que ce GRAND ROI pourroit bien faire
Ce que jadis César fit en pareille affaire.

Un Poëte indigent & fort méchant rimeur,
Voulant de ce Héros célebrer la valeur,
Esperant quelque fruit de sa fade Poësie:
        De César il eut pension;
        Mais ce fut à condition
        Qu'il ne rimeroit de sa vie.

CHANSON

Ne voyons plus ce Berger,
Il pourroit bien m'engager:
Malgré son humeur volage
Je lui trouve des apas;
Et s'il devenoit plus sage,
Je pourrois ne l'être pas.

SONG

I found my shepherd love the other day
    Sleeping beside the brook and threw
Water about his face, as one might do
        In gentle play.
He woke... I ran to hide, thinking that he
    Would doubtless pay me back in kind;
But, ah! He did not even have a mind—
Hard-hearted swain!—to come and look for me.

EPIGRAM

    Damon told me the other day
That he, at court, was going to make his way
Thanks to his verses; that the great Louis
    Would pension him. "Ah! What you say,"
    Said I, "might come to pass, and he
Might do as Caesar did, similarly:

"A wretched versifier, light of purse,
Wanted to sing that hero in his verse,
* Hoping to reap fruit from his vapid pen.
    Caesar rewarded his ambition,
    But did so only on condition
†   That never would he try to rhyme again."

SONG

Let me no more that shepherd see,
Lest he win me quite utterly.
For, though he be a fickle lad,
Yet charming do I find the knave:
Ah! If he better manners had,
Then might I much the worse behave.

    * I reproduce the original as published, though the poet must certainly have intended the word *fade* to be truncated as *fad'*, in order to preserve the twelve-syllable alexandrine.
    † Some readers will appreciate that the poet is indulging here in anachronistic metaphor, since Latin poetry did not use rhyme until well past the time of Caesar.

Louise-Geneviève Gillot de Sainctonge 369

MADRIGAL

Le premier plaisir est d'aimer,
Et le second est de charmer
   Celle pour qui l'on soupire;
Mais le plus touchant des plaisirs,
Lors qu'on répond à nos désirs,
   Est de le dire.

MADRIGAL

Souvent de trop douces chaînes,
Font relâcher bien des cœurs;
Ils se lassent moins des peines
Que des plus tendres faveurs.

ÉPIGRAMME

   Midas, tu ne t'y prends pas bien
   Lors qu'aux Poëtes tu veux nuire:
Contre leurs Vers ne fais plus de satyre,
     Ce n'est pas le vrai moyen:
     Pour décrier un Ouvrage,
     Il ne faut que ton suffrage.

MADRIGAL

*Sur un bel enfant qui n'avoit qu'un œil, & dont la mère, qui étoit très belle,
avoit aussi le même défaut*

Tu ne viens, bel Enfant, que de paroître au jour,
Tu ne sçais pas encore le prix de la lumière:
Fais present de ton œil à ta charmante Mere,
Elle sera Vénus, & tu seras l'Amour.

MADRIGAL

A pleasure, first, it is to love;
Second, to charm the object of
   Our sigh and moan.
But when *her* love responds to *his,*
The most heartwarming pleasure is
   To make it known.

MADRIGAL

Sweet, love's chains; and oft, thereto,
Hearts will offer less resistance
Than to tenderest boons they do,
That fatigue with their persistence.

EPIGRAM

   Midas, when it is your intent
   To damn our poets' work, and flout them,
Rather than pen satires and such about them,
   Your efforts can be better spent:
   For, if you would a work belittle,
   You need but praise it, jot and tittle.

MADRIGAL

*On a beautiful child who had but one eye, & whose mother, who was
very beautiful, had the same defect*

You know not yet what joy it is to see,
Sweet babe scarce born. Give, then, your beauteous mother
That eye of yours: for, should she have another,
Fair Venus, she, and you blind Love would be.

CONTE

Un jeune Cavalier, plus vif qu'on ne peut croire,
    Fait pour les jeux & les ris,
Fourni de bonnes dents, cela sert à l'histoire,
    Etoit un jour prés de Cloris:
    Il lui dit d'un air agréable,
    Qu'elle est une Dame à manger,
Qu'en la mordant du moins il veut se soulager.
    Votre machoire est redoutable,
    Dit-elle, pour d'autres que moi,
    Je suis trop ferme & trop doduë
    Pour être pincée ou morduë;
Malgré vous & vos dents je ne sens nul effroi.
    A ce défi de la Belle,
Il se jette à ses pieds, & se penchant sur elle,
Il la mord à travers sa jupe de velours:
Contre de telles dents il n'est aucun secours;
    Elle en ressent une atteinte cruelle,
    Elle crie, elle est en courroux;
A notre Cavalier ses cris paroissent doux:
    Je sens, dit-il naître mon esperance,
Je vois que l'on n'a pas toujours la fermeté
    Dont on s'étoit vanté.
Je pourrai mordre un jour sur votre indifference.

ÉPIGRAMME

Grégoire, ce fameux & grand Prédicateur,
Causoit avec Martin, sur la belle maniere
Qu'en chaire il faut avoir pour toucher & pour plaire.
    Ce dernier, moins bon Orateur,
    Prit la liberté de lui dire
    Que dans le monde on trouvoit à redire
    Qu'il n'avoit pas des airs assez flateurs,
Et qu'il faisoit la moüe à tous ses Auditeurs;

A knight, all jest and jibe and sport,
Young, brisk beyond belief, endowed as well
    With good strong teeth—which will import
In this, the tale I am about to tell—
    Was standing by Chloris one day.
    He tells her in the nicest way
That she would be a Lady fit to eat;
    That he, to quell his appetite
And ease his eagerness, would find it meet
    To take at least a lusty bite.
    Says she: "Your jaw, I must confess,
Might frighten others, but myself far less.
Too plump and firm of flesh am I to fear
    Lest bitten, plucked, or pinched I be
By such as you!" Whereat, our cavalier,
    Challenged, bends down and, eagerly,
Bites through her velvet skirt. Ah, misery!
Angry, in pain, she shrieks. Alas, there is
    No proof against those teeth of his.
Yet, to his ear, her cries are sweet. "I sense
Hope rising in my heart," says he. "For you
    Boast of a corpulent defense;
    But wrong you are, and some day hence,
Nibble shall I on your indifference too!"

EPIGRAM

Two preachers, chatting—one, the great Grégoire,
Martin, the other—argued on the matter
Of pleasant, moving pulpit-mien. The latter—
    The lesser of the pair by far
    In talents oratorical,
Boldly, in manner categorical,
Informed the former that one found his air
Bothersome; that, indeed, one could not bear

Nous sommes donc, lui répliqua Grégoire,
Fort differens sur ce fait,
Je fais la möüe à tout mon Auditoire,
Et tout le vôtre vous la fait.

ÉPIGRAMME

Iris, cette folle coquette,
Dont les couleurs couchent sur la toilette,
Demandoit à Damon comme il trouvoit son teint:
Ah! reprit-il d'un ton malin,
J'ai toujours laissé l'art pour suivre la nature,
Et jamais je ne fus connoisseur en peinture.

HIVER

Nos bois les plus charmans sont changez en déserts,
L'Hiver y fait regner l'horreur & le silence,
Les vents affreux s'élévent dans les airs,
Tout céde à leur violence;
Mais mon cœur n'est plus agité,
J'ai brisé pour jamais une chaîne cruelle,
Les douceurs de la liberté
Valent bien les douceurs de la Saison nouvelle.

CHANSON

Un je vous aime
D'un fidéle Berger, n'est pas sans agrément:
Mais c'est un plaisir extrême
D'entendre d'un nouvel Amant
Un je vous aime.

To watch him. Said Grégoire: "How different, we!
I grimace at my listeners. Yes, I do.
    Whilst all of yours, you must agree,
        Grimace at you."

EPIGRAM

    Iris—coquettish ninny, she—
Whose face paints on her dressing table lie,
Asks Damon how he likes her blush. "Since I,"
    Replies the wag, maliciously,
"Quit art to follow nature, I demur:
Never was I a painting connoisseur!"

WINTER

Our loveliest woods, stripped bare, are deserts turned,
And winter's silent horror reigns: the air,
    With frightful bellows, tempest-churned,
Blows everything before it, everywhere,
Save for my heart; nay, trammeled it lies not:
Love's shackles have I cast off, shattering;
    And joy, of freedom thus begot,
Is worth more than the sweetest joys of spring.

SONG

        An "I love you"
From faithful shepherd's lips may bring good cheer:
    But from the lips of lover new,
    Ah! What a joy it is to hear
        An "I love you."

MADRIGAL

Un aimable Berger m'aime avec violence,
    Son ardeur fait tous mes plaisirs:
Je le flate souvent d'une douce esperance,
Mais ja me garde bien de remplir ses désirs:
Il n'auroit plus pour moi que de l'indifference,
    S'il joüissoit du bonheur qu'il attend;
      Chaque pas d'un amour content
      Méne un Amant à l'inconstance.

CHANSON À BOIRE

Amour, avec de fortes armes
Tu livres la guerre à nos cœurs;
Mais pour triompher des Beuveurs,
Il ne faut que montrer tes charmes:
Fais-nous bon quartier, Dieu charmant,
Nous te céderons la victoire,
Si tu nous permets en aimant,
De chanter, de rire & de boire.

CHANSON À BOIRE

    Ah que je te plains, pauvre Amant,
D'aimer une Beauté dont le cœur est de roche!
    Elle fuit si-tôt qu'on l'aproche,
   C'est de Tantale éprouver le tourment:
    Pren la Bouteille pour Maîtresse,
      Elle a de plus doux attraits,
      Elle ne s'enfuit jamais
      Du Beuveur qui la caresse.

MADRIGAL

A shepherd loves me in most violent fashion,
    And pleased am I to have his love;
But though I let him hope to ply his passion,
Yet never does he gain the fruits thereof.
Surely would he treat me indifferently
If lustful joys he seeks not be denied:
No step a lover takes, once satisfied,
    But leads him to inconstancy.

* DRINKING SONG

God Cupid, with strong weapons you
Wage war upon our hearts, although
To lay a proper drunkard low
You need but show your charms thereto:
Desist, Love—charming god thereof—
Then shall we let you win the day,
If you allow us, whilst we love,
To laugh and sing and drink away.

DRINKING SONG

    I pity you, poor lover, who
Love a belle with a heart of stone; for thus,
    As you draw near, she flies from you,
Leaves you to bear the woes of Tantalus!
Best let the bottle take your mistress's place:
    Softer and gentler are her charms,
    Nor will she flee a drunkard's arms'
Tender caress and sweet embrace.

* Curiously, Madame de Sainctonge's collection seems to indicate an unusual fond-
ness for drinking songs, most of which are written, like a number of her other traditional
lyrics, in a masculine voice. The several in this samplng are not especially gender-specific,
though one would be hard put to imagine them expressed by the elegant salon ladies of
the period.

Louise-Geneviève Gillot de Sainctonge 377

CHANSON À BOIRE

Quand on a passé son Printems
L'Amour n'a plus que des peines;
Gardons-nous bien dans l'Hiver de nos ans,
De porter d'amoureuses chaînes:
Suivons Bacchus, il est toujours charmant;
A tout âge, en tout tems, sa liqueur nous enchante;
Un vieux Beuveur rit & chante,
Et l'on se rit d'un vieil Amant.

CHANSON

Vous cachez avec soin vos peines,
Bergers qui n'êtes pas contens,
Et vous ne dites vos tourmens
Qu'aux bois, aux rochers, aux fontaines;
Que n'êtes-vous aussi discrets
Quand on a soulagé vôtre amoureux martyre;
Si vous ne le disiez qu'aux ruisseaux, aux forêts,
On vous permettroit de le dire.

LA VEUVE DUPÉE

Certaine Veuve aux vieux ducats,
A pas lents & tortus, fournissant sa carriére,
Ne plus ne moins qu'une canne-petiére,
Prit de l'amour pour certain jeune Gas;
De l'épouser elle fit la folie.
Le soir venu, grande étoit son envie
De se gaudir avec son jeune Epoux,
Ja s'en faisoit un friand avant-goût;
Mais las, point ne joüa de chance:
Le Jouvenceau lui dit d'un ton mocqueur,
Point avec vous je n'aurai d'acointance,
Je suis par trop méchant coucheur,
Et qui plus est, je ronfle à faire peur.
Comme le chêne à la campagne
Est abattu par l'Aquilon fougueux,

DRINKING SONG

When past one's springtime, love appears
With naught but pains:
Best we take care lest, in our winter years,
We wear its chains.
Rather, we ought Bacchus's charms chase after;
At any age, sublime his brew one quaffs:
A drunkard, old, still sings and laughs,
But let an old man love, and oh, the laughter!

SONG

Shepherd lads, you who, malcontent
In love, tormented, take great care
To hide your woes, and to lament
To naught but Nature your despair—
When once we yield, and quell your passions, please,
Can you not be discreet as well about it?
If you told but the brooks, the rocks, the trees,
We would mind little how you shout it.

THE WIDOW DUPED

A widow elderly and rich—a mass
Of aging ducats had the crone in store!—
Halt, and with tortuous gait, nor less nor more
Than an old bustard waddling on the grass,
Fell in love with a lad. Foolhardy, she
Became his wife. Her amorous fantasy,
Alas, come night, came not to pass, although
Much had she lusted for the youth.
"My pet," said he, "if you would know
The truth, methinks I must, forsooth,
Confess that never will I do with you
All of the pleasures I would like to do:
I fear most bad in bed I am!
What's more—and worse!—I snore, madame,
Enough to frighten any wife to death!

Louise-Geneviève Gillot de Sainctonge 379

Je ferois choir du lit ma gentille Compagne
Avec mon soufle impétueux.
J'en aurois grande fâcherie,
Par respect je ne veux troubler votre repos,
Je vous laisse en la compagnie
Du paisible Dieu des Pavots.
La pauvrette, fort ébahie
De ce burlesque compliment,
Pleura, dit-on, amérement;
Mais point ne changea sa planette;
Il lui fallut coucher seulette,
Sans avoir à son mal aucun alégement.

Veuves qui reprenez un Maître,
Lorsque sur vôtre front le tems
Par maints sillons grave vos ans,
Bien voyez que l'Himen est traître:
C'est navrer vôtre cœur d'ennuis
De vous remettre en sa puissance:
La Vieille au Jouvenceau donne en vain sa chevance,
Elle a toujours de veuves nuits.

––––––––––

MADRIGAL

D'un tendre amour on n'est jamais le maître,
On ne peut le cacher aux regards curieux:
Un veritable Amant a toujours dans les yeux
Je ne sçai quoi qui le fait trop connoître.

––––––––––

CHANSON À BOIRE

Fuyons l'Amour, c'est un Normand,
Il m'a promis cent fois de finir mon martyre;
Il prend plaisir à se dédire,
Il ne compte pour rien de faire un faux serment:
Fuyons l'Amour, c'est un Normand.

Just as the oak tree in the wood
   Is felled by North Wind's furious breath,
So do I fear, fair lady, lest I should
   Blow you quite out of bed; which could
Cause me much grief. And so, to let you sleep,
   I leave you here and pray the mild
   God of the poppies come and keep
   You company..." She, unbeguiled,
   But awed by his droll flattery,
   Wept, so they say, most bitterly;
Left not the planet; but, unsatisfied,
Slept all alone, with no one by her side.

   Widows, who take a second master
When age furrows your brow, you court disaster!
   Marriage will play the traitor now.
   And, if before its power you bow,
   Ah! How your heart will know chagrin!
Our beldame bought her lad, but fruitlessly:
   Lonely her nights will ever be,
   And widowed, just as she had been.

––––––––––

MADRIGAL

He who feels tender love cannot conceal it,
Nor keep it safe from gaze that probes and pries:
Something there is in a true Lover's eyes
   That simply cannot help reveal it.

––––––––––

DRINKING SONG

*   Let's flee from Love: a Norman he.
Ever he vows to solace my affliction,
   Then revels in his contradiction.
He has no qualms to swear disloyally:
   Let's flee from Love: a Norman he.

* The Normans have long had a reputation in France for shrewdness. The poet seems
to feel that this quality extends to untrustworthiness as well.

Suivons le Dieu de la Tonne,
Tout ce qu'il promet il le donne,
Il va combler nos vœux avec son jus charmant:
Fuyons l'Amour, c'est un Normand.

HIVER BACHIQUE

Pour braver les froideurs d'un Hiver rigoureux,
L'Amour & le Dieu de la Treille,
Viennent m'offrir le secours de leurs feux;
Ah, c'est assez de l'un des deux!
Je cours au glouglou des bouteilles;
Il vaut mieux s'échauffer au cercle de Bacchus,
Qu'au flambeau du Fils de Vénus.

Rather, let's serve the Spirit of the Cask;
 He promises, gives what we ask,
And grants our wishes with fair eau-de-vie:
 Let's flee from Love: a Norman he.

BACCHIC WINTER

To brave the rigors of the winter chill,
 Love and the god who rules the vine
Offer their fires and bid me take my fill.
One will suffice; I need not both. Thus will
I run to make the bottles' gurglings mine:
Warmer the heat of Bacchus and his band
 Than Venus's son's firebrand.

Catherine Bernard (1663?–1712)

Those specialists who know the name of Catherine Bernard today remember her, essentially, for two plays: *Laodamie, reine d'Epire* (1689) and *Brutus* (1690), the latter pitting a father's love against a patriot's duty. Both tragedies were performed with considerable success by the Comédiens du Roi at the Théâtre-Français, enjoying a very honorable number of performances: twenty-two and twenty-five, respectively. The latter of the two earned her even more fame—or notoriety—after her death, as subject of a long-lasting controversy typical of French literary history.

It would be suggested in the 1730s that much of Bernard's theater had not, indeed, been her own, but was the work of her mentor and supposed cousin, the philosopher Fontenelle. (She was also thought to be the niece of Corneille, whose influence on the conflict in *Brutus* is not hard to detect.) Her own champions countered by insisting that not only was *Brutus* entirely of her own inspiration, but also that her play had actually furnished Voltaire with many passages for his 1730 tragedy of the same name. Voltaire, understandably piqued, insisted that Bernard's play was, in fact, the work of Fontenelle altogether. And so the battle raged.

Be these posthumous claims and counterclaims as they may, it was not primarily as a playwright but rather as a poet that Bernard was especially admired by her contemporaries. Born in Rouen—1662 and 1663 are the dates usually given, the latter being the more likely—Bernard left her bourgeois Protestant milieu for Paris sometime before 1685, converting to the Catholic faith only days before the revocation of the Edict of Nantes. It was there that she frequented the salons of such elite ladies as the duchesse de Montausier, the duchesse de Bouillon, Madame de Coulanges, and the social butterfly-cum-poet Antoinette Deshoulières (see pp. 302–15 above), cultivating the friendship (and enjoying the largesse) of her courtly protectress, the ever-generous Madame la Chancelière de Pontchartrain, who supposedly persuaded her to turn from theater to poetry. In that elegant society, encouraged by its adepts, Bernard was to compose the respectable if not voluminous body of verse that would three times win for her the poetry prize of the Académie française (in 1691, 1693, and 1697) as well as the laurels of the Jeux floraux de Toulouse (in 1696, 1697, and 1698). It would also earn her a royal pension of 200 écus from Louis XIV, who was apparently appropriately flattered by her frequent poetic praise.

Growing more and more devout, and less and less socially visible, Bernard stopped publishing by 1698. She died in Paris, virtually unknown, on September 6, 1712, leaving, in addition to her two plays and a variety of largely occaɔnal and gallant verse, a few early short novels, and a pair of versions of the ɪrsery tale *Riquet à la houppe,* as well as other disparate works variously (and ɪbiously) attributed to her.[1]

NOTE

1. Besides a number of recent dissertations and several articles devoted to her, the ɪgle indispensable study of Catherine Bernard is Franco Piva's two-volume edition of ɪr complete *Œuvres.*

POUR LA PENSION À MADEMOISELLE DE SCUDÉRY: MADRIGAL

La Fortune aujourd'hui se remet en crédit.
　　　On en avait toujours médit;
Souvent au vrai mérite elle faisait outrage;
Mais enfin ils ont fait une étroite union:
D'illustres mains devaient accomplir cet ouvrage:
Louis en est l'auteur, Sapho l'occasion.

À MIGNARD, SUR LES PORTRAITS DE LOUIS XIV
ET DE MADAME DE MAINTENON: MADRIGAL

Oui, votre art, je l'avoue, est au-dessus du mien.
J'ai loué mille fois notre invincible Maître;
Mais vous en deux portraits, vous le faites connaître.
　　　L'on voit aisément dans le sien
　　　Sa bonté, son cœur magnanime;
Dans l'autre on voit son goût à placer son estime.
　　　Ah! Mignard que vous louez bien!

À MADAME DE MAINTENON: ÉPIGRAMME

　　On ne sait si vous êtes reine,
　　Incomparable Maintenon;
　　Mais que vous le soyez ou non,
　　C'est une chose fort certaine,
　　Qu'il est beau d'en faire douter,
D'en fuir le rang, l'honneur, et de le mériter.

* **MADRIGAL ON MADEMOISELLE DE SCUDÉRY'S PENSION**

Fortune, this day, earns back her fair renown.
    For long was she cursed and cast down;
Often, indeed, she gave worth foul offense.
Now, joined at last, their tight embrace gives pause:
Illustrious hands wrought this beneficence;
LOUIS's they are; our Sappho is the cause.

† **MADRIGAL FOR MIGNARD ON HIS PORTRAITS
OF LOUIS XIV AND MADAME DE MAINTENON**

Your art is well above my own, by far.
A thousand times I praise our mighty Master;
But in two portraits you do better, faster.
    In his, you clearly paint, Mignard,
    His generous heart, of goodness graced;
In hers, your skill shines forth his flawless taste.
    Mignard! How deft with praise you are!

‡ **EPIGRAM FOR MADAME DE MAINTENON**

    Fair, peerless Maintenon, madame,
    Be you the queen or be you not,
    Of one thing still most sure I am;
    The doubt thereof is well begot:
You shun the rank and scorn the courtliness,
    And much deserve them nonetheless.

---

* For the details surrounding this first work attributable to Catherine Bernard, dating from 1683 and celebrating a pension of 2,000 *livres* granted by Louis XIV to Madeleine de Scudéry (see pp. 274–85 above), see Bernard's *Œuvres*, ed. Piva, 2: 404–5. Scudéry, the admired "Sapho" of the last line, though an octogenarian at the time, was still a prominent figure in Paris salon society. Bernard was later to write a lament on her death in 1704 at age 94 in "Ne pleurons plus de Sapho le trépas" (Let Us No More Mourn Sappho's Death [not translated here]).

† In 1694, the baroque artist Pierre Mignard (1612–1695) had painted two well-known royal portraits, one of Louis XIV, which has since disappeared, and the other of the king's mistress (and eventually wife) Madame de Maintenon, currently in the Louvre.

‡ After the death of the queen, Anne d'Autriche, in 1683, Madame de Maintenon's status as Louis's legal spouse, though generally well known, was for a long time kept officially secret.

AU R.P. DE LA RUE, JÉSUITE, SUR L'ORAISON FUNÈBRE DE MONSIEUR LE DUC DE LUXEMBOURG: MADRIGAL

Tu rends les morts immortels
En traçant leurs vertus au pied de nos autels;
Contre l'oubli des temps tu fournis un asile;
Si le grand Alexandre encor voyait le jour,
Il ne pleurerait plus sur le tombeau d'Achille,
Mais sur celui de Luxembourg.

SUR LE ROI D'ESPAGNE: MADRIGAL

Que vois-je? Quel éclat soudain?
Quelle divinité brille aux yeux de la France?
C'est la Fortune qui s'avance
Avec vingt sceptres à la main.

A ce pompeux aspect, loin que Louis s'empresse
D'accepter ces dons précieux,
Il songe à consulter l'équitable déesse
Qui porte un bandeau sur les yeux.

A ses Conseils elle préside,
La Fortune en attend la loi.
C'est la Justice qui décide,
Et sa voix seule fait un roi.

Peuples qui remplissez l'un et l'autre hémisphère,
Jouissez du bonheur qui vous est présenté:
Philippe a de Louis le noble caractère.
Si vous connaissez bien votre félicité,
Vous n'avez plus de vœux à faire.

**MADRIGAL FOR REVEREND FATHER DE LA RUE, S.J.,
ON HIS FUNERAL ORATION FOR THE DUC DE LUXEMBOURG**

Immortal life you give our dead,
Tracing their virtues by our altars spread,
Preserving them in memory's safekeeping;
If Alexander lived today, for sure,
Not on Achilles' grave would he be weeping,
But on that of our Luxembourg.

MADRIGAL ON THE KING OF SPAIN

What sudden splendor greets my eye?
What brilliance shines in France's godly glances?
Fortune it is who now advances
With twenty scepters brandished high.

Louis does not, awed by this solemn sight,
Covet these gifts preciously bought,
And would consult the goddess recondite
Whose banded eyes, indeed, see naught;

At all his Councils she presides,
Fortune waits on her sanctioning;
Justice herself alone decides:
Only her voice proclaims a king.

O nations who people each hemisphere,
Enjoy your vouchsafed gift of happiness:
Philippe has all Louis's august *noblesse.*
And if you know your joy, be of good cheer:
No wishes more need you express.

---

* The Jesuit dedicatee of this "madrigal"—a curious genre for a rather lugubrious event—was Charles de la Rue (1643–1725), who pronounced the funeral oration in question in 1695 for François Henry, seigneur de Bouteville, comte de Montmorency, duc de Luxembourg, and maréchal de France from 1675 until his sudden death (Bernard, *Œuvres,* ed. Piva, 2: 418–19).

† On the political circumstances leading to the proclamation of Louis's grandson Philippe d'Anjou as king of Spain after the Treaty of Ryswick, see Bernard, *Œuvres,* ed. Piva, 2: 455–57.

POUR UN CHIEN DE MADAME DE COULANGES APPELÉ FOLLET: MADRIGAL

Vous êtes, Dame, un peu bien sage
Pour un chien aussi grand follet;
Mais il s'est montré fou complet,
Et vous l'en aimez davantage.

Je ne saurais dire pourquoi:
Ce faible est le défaut de la plus accomplie.
On veut être sage pour soi,
Mais dans ce que l'on aime, on veut de la folie.

SUR LA CONVALESCENCE DE MADAME LA DUCHESSE D'ORLÉANS

La fièvre avide de ravage,
Lasse de porter son flambeau
Chez la gent de moyen étage,
Voulut se faire un sort plus beau.
La voilà qui songe à paraître
Dans les palais, et dans les cours,
Et veut se faire reconnaître
Comme arbitre des plus beaux jours.
Elle arrive chez vous ardente, opiniâtre,
Enflamme votre sang de son feu le plus vif.
Pouvait-elle choisir un plus fameux théâtre
Pour rendre à ses exploits l'univers attentif?
Tel un grec d'indigne mémoire
Par un temple fameux de sa main consumé,
A ses propres dépens se plaça dans l'Histoire,
Content d'être odieux pourvu qu'il fût nommé,
Esculape au récit de vos douleurs mortelles,

MADRIGAL FOR MADAME DE COULANGES'S
DOG FOLLET

Madame, you use your wisdom for
A dog, Follet by name, dumb cur,
Than which there is none daffier,
And yet you love him all the more.

I could not tell you why this trait
Flaws wisdom's foremost women-devotees:
Wise for themselves, they advocate,
In what they love, a touch of folly please!

† ON THE CONVALESCENCE OF
MADAME LA DUCHESSE D'ORLÉANS

Fever, with burning zeal, grew tired
Of ravaging, with flaming brand,
The common folk, and so desired
To find herself a fate more grand.
Thus does she fancy to appear
In court and palace, seeking ways
To be acknowledged, far and near,
Arbiter of life's fairest days.
Headstrong, she burns a path to your front door,
Enflames your blood with her ardentmost fire.
Could she select a more noble décor
To play before the universe entire?
‡   Much like a certain odious Greek
Who burned a famous temple to the ground,
Happy if History would merely speak
His name (though ill!), the doctors hastened round,
Learning of your deathly discomfiture—

* Regarding Mme de Coulanges, whose dog is immortalized in this badinage-cum-quasi-philosophical reflection, see p. 384.
† The identity of the duchess in question and the nature of her illness remain uncertain; see Bernard, *Œuvres*, ed. Piva, 2: 502–3.
‡ The "odious Greek" is Herostratos, who sought to immortalize himself by burning down the Artemision at Ephesos.

Vous offrit ses savants secours;
Mais votre bon génie, encor plus sûr contre elles,
Voulut seul prendre soin de vos précieux jours.
Peut-être eût fait en vain sur vous tous ses efforts.
    Votre esprit est pour votre corps
    Le seul remède spécifique.
A ce génie heureux qui vous redonne à nous,
    Que sans cesse l'on sacrifie.
Agréez les autels pour votre bon génie,
    Si vous n'en voulez pas pour vous.

MADRIGAL

Quand le sage Damon dit que d'un trait mortel
L'Amour blesse les cœurs, sans qu'ils osent se plaindre,
    Que c'est un dieu traître et cruel,
    L'Amour pour moi n'est point à craindre.
Mais quand le jeune Athis me vient dire à son tour:
"Ce Dieu n'est qu'un enfant doux, caressant, aimable,
    Plus beau mille fois que le jour,"
    Que je le trouve redoutable!

SUR UN OUBLI

Il est vrai, l'autre jour j'ai pu vous oublier;
Cependant mon ardeur n'en est pas moins constante;
Et ces fleurs, que ma main aujourd'hui vous présente,
    Doivent nous réconcilier.
    Traitez ma mémoire d'ingrate,
    Je la livre à votre rigueur:
    Mais permettez que je me flatte,
    Que vous jugiez mieux de mon cœur.

Babbling new Aesculapii!—
Hied themselves by with many a learnèd cure.
But your strong body, answering "Fie, fie!"
Alone doctored your precious life: success
Is yours; their therapeutic efforts would
    Have done, I fear, but little good.
    Your spirit quelled fleshly duress.
Accept our altars, sacrifice-bedecked,
    Raised to your body's steadfast soul
That has returned you to us, hale and whole;
    Altars you would, yourself, reject.

---

* MADRIGAL

When Damon, in his wisdom, says that Love—
God cruel and traitorous—casts deadly darts
    Into our uncomplaining hearts,
    Myself, I have no fear thereof.
But when, in turn, young Athis comes to say:
"That god is but a stripling, sweet and mild,
    A thousand times more fair than day,"
    Then how I fear that tender child!

---

† ON A LAPSE OF MEMORY

True, I forgot you just the other day;
But, for all that, my flame burns no less true;
May the blooms that my hand now offers you,
    See our contention wiped away.
    The villain is my memory,
    Treat it as roughly as you deem
    You ought; but let my heart yet be
    Worthy, I pray, of your esteem.

* This madrigal, with its Damon and Athis—typical *précieux* nomenclature—and "re-
fined expression of the psychology of love" (Bernard, *Œuvres*, ed. Piva, 2: 509), is said to
have enjoyed a good deal of popularity throughout the eighteenth century.

    † This and the following brief poems are from a group of so-called "bouquets," a term
the author applies to pieces of gallant inspiration.

BOUQUET

Volez, tendres Zéphirs; que votre douce haleine
Au milieu de l'été ramène le printemps;
      Faites éclore dans nos champs,
      Des fleurs dignes de ma Climène.
Quoi? vous ne voulez pas répondre à mes désirs?
Eh bien, à vos refus, il faut que mes soupirs
Se plaignent tendrement des maux qu'elle me cause;
Et puisque cette ingrate a refusé mon cœur,
Je veux, par le secours d'une métamorphose,
Que pour la mieux tromper, il se transforme en fleur.

BOUQUET

Non, je ne veux pas vous offrir
De ces dons inconstants de Flore,
Que le même jour voit éclore,
Et le même jour voit mourir.
Le bouquet que je vous apprête,
Est plus digne de votre tête.
Le Parnasse en est le jardin;
La durée en est éternelle:
Rien ne convient mieux à mon zèle;
Daignez l'accepter de ma main.

BOUQUET

      Pour solenniser votre fête
Je dois, au lieu de Flore, implorer Apollon;
Je ne sais point de fleurs dignes de votre tête,
      Hors celles du sacré vallon.

BOUQUET

Fly, tender Zephyrs. Let spring, once again,
Waft on your gentle breath midst summer's heat;
    Make our fields bud with blooms replete
*   Deserving of my fair Climène.
What? You would not give ear unto my prayer?
Alas, my sighs, rebuffed, needs must despair;
For her hard heart deals such a share of woe,
That I must moan her thankless cruelty.
Oh, might I be transformed and straightway be
† Turned to a flower, better to trick her so.

BOUQUET

No, I am loath to offer you
Those fickle boons of Flora born
That one sees blossom forth at morn
Only to die when day is through.
The blooms that I proffer you now
Are fitter far to grace your brow.
Parnassus' soil is whence they spring;
Eternal is the life they live:
No fairer tribute can I give;
Pray deign accept my offering.

BOUQUET

    To celebrate with solemn vow
Your *fête*, not Flora I invoke; instead,
Apollo must I call to grace your head
    With flowers most worthy of your brow,

* As frequently seen in other examples, the apostrophe to a lady love, here under the very conventional name of "Climène," is no more than a topos of the gallant tradition.

† The poet is referring here to the ruse employed by Pluto, who sprang forth from the narcissus to carry off Proserpina as she was admiring it while gathering lilies with her mother, Ceres. Ironically, of course, the flower had, itself, been created by the well-known metamorphosis by which Narcissus, loveliest of young men, in his vanity, had also been transformed.

Mille dons que sur moi vos mains daignent répandre,
Demandent un juste retour;
Et ce serait mal vous les rendre,
Que vous donner des fleurs qui ne durent qu'un jour.
Non, ce n'est pas là votre affaire;
Dans les présents qu'on veut vous faire,
Il faut plus de solidité.
Mais sais-je bien à quoi je pense,
Quand je veux en agir avec tant d'équité?
Les bienfaits sur mon cœur n'ont que trop de puissance,
Et votre générosité
Alarme ma reconnaissance:
Je crains de la porter trop loin.
Il m'en coûtera cher, s'il faut que je m'acquitte;
Hélas! vous n'avez pas besoin
D'être si généreux avec tant de mérite.

BOUQUET

Quoi? vous ne voulez pas que j'acquitte mes dettes,
Cruel créancier que vous êtes?
J'avais pris soin d'intéresser
Apollon à vous satisfaire;
Mais avec vous on a beau faire,
C'est toujours à recommencer.
Ah! si de vos bienfaits rien ne tarit la source,
Quelle sera donc ma ressource?
Quand ce serait argent comptant
Que tout ce qu'Apollon m'inspire,
A la fin vous en ferez tant,
Que je ne saurai plus que dire.
Ainsi, quels que soient mes efforts,
Je mourrai votre redevable
Puisque vous savez rendre Apollon insolvable,
Au milieu de tous ses trésors.

Sprung from his sacred vale: your kind hands lay
    A thousand gifts outspread on me,
    And it were an indignity
To proffer thanks with blooms that live one day.
    No, such indeed is not your due;
    The gifts that one must offer you
    Must longer last. But what think I,
    Truly, if I would fain react
To your abundant gifts with measured tact?
The boons you cast upon my heart defy
    My will to thank you; for, in fact,
    They wrench my gratitude awry.
    I fear lest it cost me too much
And that my thanks be far too profligate:
    Alas! You need not give with such
A lavish hand, you whose worth is so great.

BOUQUET

What, heartless creditor? You would I not
    Repay my debts? How cruel my lot!
    I sought Apollo's interest
    In your behalf—alas, in vain,
    For naught—and must begin again:
    He paid no heed to my request.
Ah! Should the well of your boons not run dry,
    What other recourse shall I try?
    Were it but lucre that Apollo
    Inspires in me, your gifts are such—
    Lavishly given—that it would follow,
    No more need I say forasmuch.
    And so, despite my eager measures,
    Dead, I shall yet your debtor be,
Since you confound that god to penury,
    Surrounded though with earthly treasures.

Elisabeth Guibert (1725–1787)

It is likely that, at least in the eyes of her contemporaries, Elisabeth Guibert did not deserve the obscurity into which she has since fallen. Granted a pension by Louis XV, she must have been rather highly thought of, given that monarch's lack of enthusiasm for the arts in general and letters in particular. It was probably for the royal court that she composed two comedies—*La coquette corrigée* (1764) and *Les filles à marier* (1768)—and two more serious dramas—*Les Philéniens, ou Le patriotisme* (1765) and *Le sommeil d'Amythe* (1768). Having published, in 1764, a collection of *Poésies diverses,* she appeared before the public primarily for her occasional verse, which was subsequently sprinkled through the pages of the *Almanach des Muses* between 1766 and 1769. While her madrigals and similar trifles are typical eighteenth-century poetic pirouettings around clichés of love, friendship, coquettishness, and betrayal, they are not lacking in a kind of pert quirkiness that distinguishes them from the effete offerings of so much preromantic poetry. Her self-portrait (p. 404–5 below) is a particularly charming example.

Other than her dates and her birthplace—Versailles—few facts seem to be known about Elisabeth Guibert. She is mentioned briefly in two contemporary biographical dictionaries, but with few concrete details.[1] My notes in the following pages indicate the provenance of the eleven poems translated here.

NOTE

1. See Joseph-Marie Quérard, *La France littéraire,* 3: 517; and Nicolas Le Moyne Des Essarts, *Les siècles littéraires de la France,* 3: 369–70. For sparse data, see also Earl Jeffrey Richards's entry in the *Encyclopedia of Continental Women Writers,* p. 501, and the brief entry in the *Bloomsbury Guide to Women's Literature,* p. 606. In addition, Joseph de Laporte devotes one of his *lettres* (XXXVI), in his *Histoire littéraire des femmes françoises, ou lettres historiques et critiques* (5: 169–77) to a brief appreciation and a sampling of her texts (see p. 401n below), including a brief scene from one of her plays, the one-act verse comedy *Les filles à marier.*

L'HOMME HEUREUX POSSIBLE

La vie est un instant; il en faut profiter;
Rejetter avec soin tout préjugé nuisible,
Croire un Dieu bienfaisant, croire un ami possible,
Et connoître le prix du bonheur d'exister;
Caresser la folie, estimer la sagesse,
Aimer un seul objet, en être un peu jaloux,
Être toujours fidele, & jamais n'être époux,
Effleurer les talens, les aimer sans foiblesse,
Paroître indifférent sur le mépris des sots,
Avoir le cœur ouvert sur ses propres défauts,
Etre content de soi, mais sans trop le paroître;
Enfin se croire heureux, c'est le moyen de l'être.

MADRIGAL

Heureux talent des vers, agréable manie,
   vous remplissez le vuide de ma vie:
   je ne tiens rien, ni ne veux rien de vous:
les dieux, en vous bornant, ont su me satisfaire;
   vous me servez à plaire,
& ne suffisez pas pour faire des jaloux.

THE HAPPIEST POSSIBLE MAN

Life's but an instant, best you use it well:
Trust in God's mercy, and in friendship too;
Know that mere living is a boon; eschew
All baleful thought, misjudgment foul or fell;
Hold wisdom in esteem, but be not loath
To dally, too, with folly; faithful be
* To but one love, and not unjealously,
But never as a husband plight your troth;
Dabble in arts, but love them well; admit
Your faults, but scorn the ass's taunt and twit;
Like yourself, but seem not to; and, in sum,
Think yourself happy: so shall you become.

† MADRIGAL

Pleasant obsession, gift of poetry,
without you would my life most empty be:
no wealth have I, nor any seek from you.
Of you the gods have granted me small store:
    enough to please me, little more,
but not enough to make men jealous too.

Almanach des Muses, 1766

* The use of the word *objet* in the original to mean the female object of a man's affection was a commonplace in seventeenth- and eighteenth-century French literature and should not be considered a demeaning "objectification" of woman, especially from a woman herself. This poem from Guibert's *Poésies et œuvres diverses* was later reprinted in Laporte's *Histoire littéraire des femmes françoises.*

† A note in the source indicates that this poem served as a headpiece to the author's *Poésies et œuvres diverses.*

MADRIGAL

De ta fausse félicité,
ingrat, connois l'erreur extrême:
ah! si tu savois comme on aime,
vanterois-tu ta liberté?

MADRIGAL POUR METTRE SUR UNE ESTAMPE GRAVÉE, PAR M. DANZEL, D'APOLLON SERVI PAR LES MUSES

Sexe enchanteur, vous détournez les yeux,
quand par un burin précieux,
Danzel a fait servir Apollon par des belles:
craignez-vous pour vos droits? l'Amour veille sur eux;
les déesses servent les dieux:
mais les dieux servent les mortelles.

À MONSIEUR L***

Toujours, avec un ton égal:
on te voit critiquer ou rire:
ta bouche, Lisimon, fait-elle une satyre;
tes yeux disent un madrigal.

MADRIGAL

Though happy, rogue, you seem to be,
false is your joy; be sure thereof:
alas, if you knew how to love,
would you so vaunt your liberty?

Almanach des Muses, 1766

* MADRIGAL TO ACCOMPANY AN ENGRAVING BY
MONSIEUR DANZEL, OF APOLLO SERVED BY THE MUSES

Enchanting sex, you turn your gaze askew:
† does Danzel's mannered etching trouble you—
Apollo, by fair ladies wined and dined?
Do you fear for your rights? Love tends thereto:
goddesses serve the gods, 'tis true,
but gods serve mortal womankind.

Almanach des Muses, 1766

FOR MONSIEUR L***

Whether you quip or criticize,
dear Lisimon, you sound the same:
for, whilst your lips their satires may declaim,
madrigals come forth from your eyes.

Almanach des Muses, 1767

* Danzel was the family name of several eighteenth-century engravers and artists. Of
four brothers—Eustache (1735–1775), Jacques-Claude (1737–1801), Jérôme (1755–1810), and
Théophile (?–?)—either of the first two (and possibly the last, about whom little is known)
might, for reasons of chronology, be the one referred to. Though sources consulted fail to
indicate a specific engraving corresponding to the subject mentioned, Jacques-Claude's
frequent mythological inspiration would seem to make him the prime candidate.

† The *burin*, an engraving tool, can also refer, metonymically, to the engraving itself,
which I take it to mean here. A note after line 2 of the original, apparently by the edi-
tor of the *Almanach des Muses*, voices an aesthetic judgment—not an uncommon practice
in the pages of that annual collection—complaining of the phrase *un burin précieux*: "Cette
épithete [*sic*] n'est pas de bon goût" (This epithet is not in good taste), though without
specifying why.

Elisabeth Guibert 403

Pourquoi, Damon, à soixante ans,
vaut-il mieux que nos jeunes gens?
ma chanson vous l'expliquera,
    Alleluia.

Ils ont de l'amour, du dépit;
ils ont une tête, un esprit;
ils ont, que sai-je, & cætera.
    Alleluia.

Un tendre cœur vaut beaucoup mieux:
c'est le plus beau présent des cieux,
& c'est un cœur que Damon a.
    Alleluia.

À MONSIEUR DE ***

    Quoi! de l'amitié la plus tendre,
    vous me refusez le retour!
    ah! je n'y dois donc plus prétendre!
    vous ne m'offrez que de l'amour.
Un sentiment plus vif a pénétré votre âme:
    il passera, ce sentiment!
    je vois déja s'éteindre votre flâme.
Je voulois un ami: vous n'êtes qu'un amant.

    Vive jusqu'à l'étourderie,
Folle dans mes discours, mais sage en mes écrits,
    Ils sont presque toujours remplis
    Par des traits de Philosophie.
Sensible pour l'instant, mais facile à changer,
J'oublie, & quelquefois on peut me croire ingrate;
Je cherche à m'éclairer; je crois ce qui me flatte;

COUPLETS FOR MONSIEUR ***

Damon, at sixty... Why, in truth,
is he more dear than all our youth?
My song will tell you presently.
      Praise be!

They have love, they have spitefulness;
they have a head, a mind no less;
they have... Need I go on? Ah me...
      Praise be!

A tender heart is better, though;
the richest gift the heavens bestow:
like Damon's—tender-hearted, he!
      Praise be!

Almanach des Muses, 1767

FOR MONSIEUR DE ***

What? When I seek your friendship, why
do you deny me, cruelly?
You would not even have me try,
and love is all you offer me!
Your soul burned with a passion otherwise;
but it must pass, you will discover:
already it grows dimmer, dies.
I sought a friend; you would be but a lover.

Almanach des Muses, 1769

Pert, even unto thoughtlessness,
Daft in my talk, but in my writings wise;
Ever quick to philosophize;
Touched by one's favor, but, no less,
Fickle a bit, tending, perhaps, to let
Myself, at times, too soon a boon forget;
I try to be enlightened, yet can be
Convinced by simple flattery; I flee

Elisabeth Guibert 405

Je fuis les envieux, sans vouloir m'en vanger;
Mon esprit est solide, & mon cœur est léger.
Air gai, peau blanche, œil noir, & grandeur ordinaire;
Mes traits sont chifonnés; ma taille est réguliere.

À MONSIEUR ***

Judicieux Censeur, dont la plume légere
Sçait distinguer l'Auteur d'avec le plagiaire,
    Venge-moi d'un vol qu'on me fait;
    Je t'apprêtois quelques justes louanges,
    Lorsque, le cœur trop plein de mon sujet,
        Je laisse entrevoir mon secret
A celui dont je veux qu'aujourd'hui tu me vanges.
D'abord, sur mon dessein, il trace ton portrait;
Il peint de ton esprit l'enjouement, la justesse;
        Ah!... quand il t'écrira
    Les jolis vers que sa Muse t'adresse,
Pense qu'il m'a volé tout ce qu'il te dira.

À MONSIEUR ***

        Tu méprises les douces loix
    Que l'amitié sçut tracer dans ton ame;
        Pour te livrer à la perfide flamme,
Dont un cruel enfant t'aveugla mille fois;
Songe qu'un jour tes sens seront glacés par l'âge;
Cesse de carresser une trop douce erreur:
        L'amitié fait le vrai bonheur;
        L'amour n'en offre que l'image.

The envious, but no vengeful grudge I bear;
My mind is strong; my heart, light, debonair.
Air, gay; skin, white; eyes, black; size, ordinary;
* Homespun, my face; my shape, unexemplary.

FOR MONSIEUR ***

Wise Censor—you, who, with your gentle pen,
Can tell true authors from that race of men,
Base plagiarists—I beg you now indict
One who made free with what was mine: you see,
    As I was readying to write
My heartfelt praise of you—as well I might—
In my enthusiasm, carelessly,
    My thoughts, unfinished, came to light;
And he on whom I seek revenge this day
Stole them, to laud your taste, in form well-versed.
    Ah!... When his Muse indites them, pray
Realize that 'twas I who thought them first.

FOR MONSIEUR ***

    You scorn the rules of friendship, written
    Sweet in your soul, to yield your mind
To that false flame a cruel child, ill-inclined,
† Blinded you with, a thousand times, love-smitten.
But age will chill your senses, your affections:
Cease to clasp errant hope in your caress.
Friendship it is that brings true happiness:
    Love offers but its pale reflexions.

* The poet's description of her *traits* (features) as *chifonnés* (*sic*) gives pause. When used to describe a face the modern French *chiffonné* usually means "tired" or "drawn." It can, however, also have a less negative meaning, especially when applied to an individual feature. A *nez chiffonné* for example, would be an unusual but not unpleasant little nose. My translation assumes that the poet, while attempting to be objective, does not want to exaggerate her unattractiveness. My source for this self-portrait and for the three following tidbits of typical occasional verse is Laporte's *Histoire littéraire des femmes françoises*, 5: 572–73.

† It is with a touch of irony that the poet accuses Cupid—himself blind—of blinding his victim to the true nature of love and friendship.

MADRIGAL

Pincer les cordes d'une lyre,
Couronner les vœux d'un amant,
Ce sont deux sortes de délire;
Mais celui qu'Apollon inspire,
Est préférable au doux tourment
Que ressent un cœur qui soupire;
L'un, l'esprit a sçu le produire,
Et l'autre, le tempérament.

MADRIGAL

To pluck the lyre, or to submit
To suitor's urgings amorous:
Two follies, these; though one more fit—
Apollo's art: more worthy, it,
Than to lament, in querulous
Complaint, heart's torment exquisite.
One is the working of our wit;
The other, nature lays on us.

Marie-Amable de La Férandière (1736–1819)

The fable writer known as Madame de La Férandière, a native of Tours, ill de-
served the rather cavalier judgment of her verse that I had occasion to express
several years ago based on a reading of the scant body of work in the pages of
the *Almanach des Muses* available to me at the time.[1] Since then her collection,
Œuvres de Madame la Marquise de La Fer... of 1806, often referred to but hard
to find, has surfaced, and it has revealed to me both a skilled versifier, deft and
adept at her craft, and a thoroughly engaging poet, despite a generous dose of
late eighteenth-century cliché, difficult to avoid, and to be expected. Mea culpa,
madame!

Throughout the 168 fables that comprise the entire first volume of her *Œu-
vres*, one finds the same—and other—animal characters that had "peopled"
those of La Fontaine, the modern creator of the genre. And, as in his work, a
sprinkling of human beings as well. But, like most of his emulators, unable to
escape from his shadow yet eager to avoid the "anxiety of influence," she places
them in scenarios that are not simple repetitions of his. With a mischievous,
often tongue-in-cheek tone, she shuns the pitfalls of excessive saccharinity and
lets the joys of nature, virtue, and a down-to-earth moral sense shine, unforced,
through her neatly constructed "free verse"—in the rhymed pre-nineteenth-
century sense, of course—in much the same cordial manner as did the master
himself. The miscellaneous "poésies" of the second volume—incidental poems
with a variety of inspirations—delight no less with their wit, their gentility, and,
even when touching on well-worn subjects and sentiments, with a charm and a
grace that, close though they come at times, somehow manage not to cloy.

The fables of Marie-Amable Petitau, marquise de La Férandière (or "La-
férandière, or even "La Ferrandière"), began appearing in the *Almanach des
Muses* of 1780 and continued to be published in that anthology of *pièces fugi-
tives* through 1798, most often attributed, for whatever coy reasons, simply to
"Madame la marquise de La Fér***." (The "marquise" that she had acquired in
1756 through marriage to the marquis of that name, was noticeably, and perhaps
wisely, absent in the numbers printed during the height of the Revolution.) Her
literary career had begun in 1766, when a song she had composed for her ten-
year-old daughter was surreptitiously submitted to the *Mercure de France*. There
followed a variety of *poèmes de circonstance* in the *Journal des Dames* and con-
tributions to the *Almanach des Muse*, ending only with her death in 1819, three
years after the second edition of her *Œuvres* appeared. testimony to the high
regard in which her contemporaries held her.[2]

As indicated in the notes to the following translations, all but one of the eleven fables and ten *poésies fugitives* are found in the *Œuvres*, volumes one and two respectively.

NOTES

1. See Shapiro, *The Fabulists French* (1992), p. 116.

2. For some of the rare biographical data, see the entry on La Férandière in Fortunée Briquet's *Dictionnaire historique, littéraire et bibliographique*, pp. 187–88.

LE PAPILLON ET LA CHENILLE

A quoi, vil insecte, es-tu bon,
Disoit à la chenille, un très-beau papillon
Qui voltigeoit dans un parterre?
Oses-tu te fixer dans un riant jardin,
Y respirer le frais, y savourer le thim?
Je te trouve bien téméraire!
Es-tu donc faite, en bonne foi,
Pour approcher si près du lis et de la rose?
Cet honneur n'appartient qu'à moi...
Pourquoi t'enorgueillir de ta métamorphose,
Répliqua la chenille à l'esprit bien sensé?
Je te connois, et ris de ton humeur altière;
Tu fus ce que je suis, et tout le mois passé
Tu te traînois sur la poussière,
A mes côtés, auprès de ce rosier;
Si tu t'en souvenois, on pourroit l'oublier.
L'un de ces jours aussi tu me verras des ailes.
J'irai me reposer sur les fleurs les plus belles:
Mais, grâce à tes mépris, je songerai souvent,
Quand je pourrai voler sur les roses nouvelles,
Que je rampois auparavant.

LA POULE ET LE RENARD

Une poule égarée, en cherchant son poussin,
Aperçoit un renard guettant nouvelle proie;
Elle veut l'éviter, devinant son dessein;
Mais le fripon la suit, lui ferme le chemin,
Et se livre en secret à la plus vive joie:
Hélas! dit-il, feignant l'air de candeur,

THE BUTTERFLY AND THE CATERPILLAR

"You, caterpillar vile, what good are you?
       What purpose do you serve?" So said
A butterfly, beautiful creature, who
Went flitting roundabout a flower bed.
       "What? Do you dare to tarry here,
In this delightful garden, making free
With its cool shade, supping on thyme? I fear
       You go too far! How can you be,
In faith, so bold as to approach the rose,
The lily, when that honor, goodness knows,
       Is mine, my dear, and mine alone!"
       "Ah, but how can you take such pride
In your fine metamorphosis?" replied
The caterpillar, in the gravest tone.
       "I know you well and, frankly, must
Deride your high and mighty manner. Why,
You were, for one whole month, what now am I,
       Dragging your length along the dust
Beside me, by this very rosebush, no?
Were you more mindful of your past, one would
       Ignore it, in all likelihood.
       One of these days I too shall grow
A pair of wings for you to see; but when
I light on beauteous blooms, time and again,
       I shall, thanks to your scorn, recall,
       Flying amidst the rosebuds then,
That once upon a time I used to crawl."

"Fables," v

THE HEN AND THE FOX

       A hen there was who lost her way,
Trying to find her chick, when, lo! she spied
A fox, who meant to find some fresh, new prey.
       Guessing his foul intent, she tried
To step aside, avoid him... But the fox,
       Too clever, follows her and blocks

Marie-Amable de La Férandière 413

Que je vous plains, pauvre petite!
Oui, croyez-moi, sur mon honneur,
Pour la peur vous en seriez quitte,
Si depuis plusieurs jours je n'avois pas jeûné;
Mais par le ciel enfin repas m'est destiné,
Quand je vous rencontre à cette heure
Aussi loin de votre demeure,
Les dieux, et j'en frémis, vous mettent sous ma dent.
Ah! repart la poule à l'instant,
Langage d'hypocrite est un affreux tourment!
Puisque je ne peux fuir, puisqu'il faut que je meure,
Etrangle-moi sans compliment.

_____

LE LIS, LA ROSE ET LE TILLEUL

Deux fleurs, l'autre matin, disputoient de beauté.
Le lis de sa blancheur faisoit grand étalage;
Et la rose, avec vanité,
Disoit qu'à son éclat tout devoit rendre hommage:
A l'entendre, elle étoit le chef-d'œuvre des dieux.
Pour le lis, se croyant l'ornement de la terre,
Il ne trouvoit rien sous les cieux
Plus que lui capable de plaire.
Pendant ce débat important,
Près de ces fleurs, la violette
Emailloit du jardin le tapis verdoyant,
Ne disoit mot, et parfumoit l'herbette.
De leur éloge et de leur différent
Un vieux tilleul impatient
N'attendit pas le reste.
Je préfere, dit-il, la violette à vous;
Elle exhale en tous lieux des parfums aussi doux,
Et, qui plus est, elle est modeste.

Her flight; then, in his heart rejoicing, quite,
Exclaims, feigning pure innocence: "My poor,
Sweet thing! How I do pity you, for sure,
    To see your sad and sorry plight!
Had I not spent many a day without
    A bite to eat, there is no doubt
That fright is all that you would suffer, truly!
But heaven must sate my appetite; and when
The gods—alas!—present a straying hen
To satisfy my tooth... Well, forsooth, duly
Must I accept!" Replies the hen: "Oh? Then
Enough of your tongue's vile hypocrisy,
    Lest I become a woeful wreck!
Since die I must, and since I cannot flee,
Spare me your fancy talk! Just wring my neck!"

"Fables," x

THE LILY, THE ROSE, AND THE LINDEN TREE

Two flowers were arguing the other day
    As to which one the fairer was.
The lily bragged that it was he, because
None was so white; the rose, as vain, dared say
That all should bow to her, quick to declare
Herself the heavens' masterpiece; whereat
    The lily, giving tit for tat,
    Claims naught is there—not anywhere!—
    As fair as he beneath the sky.
While thus they trade their ayes and nays,
    A violet, blooming coy nearby,
Studding the verdant carpet, but too shy
To speak, over the grass her sweet scent lays.
An aging linden tree, hearing the praise
The pair heap on themselves, for honors vying,
    Finding their quarrel rather trying,
Scorning its outcome, says impatiently:
"I much prefer the violet to you two!
    Her fragrance is as fair; and she
Is far more modest, friends, than both of you!"

"Fables," xii

Marie-Amable de La Férandière 415

L'AIGLE ET LE PAON

Un aigle, auprès du paon, non sans quelque murmure,
De sa robe envioit l'éclatante parure.
Si vous devez briller aux yeux de l'univers,
    Dit le paon, c'est par le courage:
L'oiseau que la nature a fait le roi des airs,
    N'a pas besoin d'un beau plumage.

LA FEMME ET LE MIROIR

    Une femme étoit très jolie,
    Mais elle avoit une manie
    Qui déplaisoit, fatiguoit tous les yeux.
Les siens ne cessoient pas de chercher une glace:
Soit pour mieux ajuster ses pompons, ses cheveux,
Soit pour examiner son maintien et sa grace,
Ou bien en minaudant se regarder parler;
Enfin on la voyoit toujours se contempler.
On cesse d'admirer qui s'admire soi-même:
    Et puis cet amour propre extrême
    Blesse la vanité d'autrui;
Narcisse en se mirant n'aimoit, dit-on, que lui.
    Il méprisa les belles du bocage:
Et penché constament vers le cristal de l'eau
    Qui lui présentoit son image
Il fit sécher d'amour la pauvre nymphe Echo.
    Ah! notre Narcisse femelle
    N'eut pas le sort de son charmant modele:
Et trop tard se souvint des leçons, des avis,
    De ses parens et de ses vrais amis.
    Une cruelle maladie
En peu de jours lui ravit ses attraits,
    Mais elle ne perdit jamais,

THE EAGLE AND THE PEACOCK

An eagle, perching by a peacock, muttered
Jealously: "Ah! what splendid dress you wear!"
Whereat, "If you would shine," the peacock uttered,
   "It is through courage! I doubt whether
The bird whom nature made king of the air
   Needs must be very fair of feather!"

                        "Fables," xxxvii

THE WOMAN AND THE LOOKING-GLASS

   A pretty woman once there was,
But who could not control her eyes; and thus
All eyes that gazed on her found tedious
   The tiring looks she cast. The cause?
Ever they sought to find a looking-glass,
   Subjecting to minute inspection
   Every detail of her reflection,
As, with a little pout, she thought to pass
Judgment upon her mien, her gracious air;
   To primp and pose, adjust her hair,
Remaining there in constant contemplation.
But soon we cease admiring those who spend
Their time consumed in such self-admiration.
Besides, such vanity will, in the end,
Tend to give others umbrage and offend
Their vanity!... Narcissus, so they tell,
Kneeling above his crystal image, fell
   In love with it, and promptly spurned
Each woodland belle—especially the tender
Echo, poor nymph, she who with passion burned...
Ah! Our Narcissus of the female gender
Knew not her model's fate: too late she learned
The lessons that true friends and loved ones taught.
   A cruel disease its ravage wrought
Upon her loveliness: a few days took
   Their toll; and yet, grown ugly, still

Quoiqu'elle fût très enlaidie,
Son maudit penchant à se voir,
Et le trop fidèle miroir
Devint alors le tourment de sa vie.

L'ABEILLE ET LE LIMAÇON

Un limaçon disoit l'autre jour à l'abeille:
Dès le matin,
Sur ce jasmin,
Ou bien sur la rose vermeille,
Tu voltiges gaîment, puis tu viens t'y poser,
Et seule jusqu'au soir tu parois t'amuser.
Que ton sort est digne d'envie!
Hélas! malheureux limaçon,
Dans un jardin, dans la prairie,
Ou dans mon étroite maison,
L'hiver, l'été, bref, en chaque saison,
Partout je bâille et je m'ennuie.
Apprends-moi donc, dès aujourd'hui,
Comment tu fais pour éviter l'ennui:
Dis moi ton secret, je te prie.
— Oh! je vais te le confier;
A retenir il n'est pas difficile:
Je travaille, et toujours je sais me rendre utile,
Voilà le vrai secret de ne pas s'ennuyer.

LE BOURDON ET L'HIRONDELLE

Maudit soit le bourdon aussi vil qu'ennuyeux,
Disoit l'autre jour l'hirondelle;
Sans cesse il vient troubler les chants mélodieux
Du merle, du pinson, de ma sœur Philomèle.

She could not rid herself, for good or ill,
    Of that accursed desire to look
Upon herself... Too faithful now, alas,
What a tormentor was her looking-glass!

"Fables," xxxviii

_____

THE BEE AND THE SNAIL

A snail the other day addressed the bee:
        "When comes the dawn,
            You light upon
    The scarlet rose, or flittingly
Flutter about the jasmine, there to light
As well; and, though alone, you seem to me
    Most joyful, and contented quite.
    Much ought we envy such a state!
    Naught but a wretched snail am I,
    Alas! Mine is a woeful fate:
Whether in garden or in field I lie,
Or tight within my home, in every season—
    Winter, summer, the whole year through—
Little I do but yawn! What is the reason,
Friend, that you suffer not such boredom too?
    What is your secret? Tell me, pray!"
"Gladly! Nor is it hard to keep in mind:
    I work, and always seek to find
A way to be of use. A secret? Nay!
Labor it is that keeps boredom at bay."

"Fables," lix

_____

THE BUMBLEBEE AND THE SWALLOW

"Damned be the bumblebee, vile, bothersome,"
    Bemoaned the swallow recently.
    "It seems he always has to come
Droning his buzz amid the melody
*   Of blackbird, finch, and sister Philomele.

* "Philomele" is doubtless the nightingale (see, p. 501n).

Marie-Amable de La Férandière 419

A quoi cet insecte est-il bon?
Interrompre, étourdir, il n'a pas d'autre don.
Et toujours, près de nous, il vient faire sa ronde.
            L'ennuyeux bourdon l'entendit,
                    Et lui dit:
            J'ai bien des pareils dans le monde,
            Qui jamais n'ont fait que du bruit;
            Car notre espèce est très-féconde.
Nous recevons parfois incivil compliment;
            Mais nous nous en moquons, ma mie;
            Chacun de nous va répétant:
            Eh! que m'importe si j'ennuie!
            Moi, je m'amuse en bourdonnant.

JUPITER ET L'HOMME MARIÉ

Grand Jupiter, disoit tous les jours un époux,
De grâce! corrigez les défauts de ma femme!
            Mon encens brûlera pour vous:
Changez son caractère altier, vain et jaloux?
            Vous noterez que l'époux de la dame
            Etoit avare, et méchant, et joueur,
Fort superstitieux, libertin et grondeur,
Vif à l'excès; un rien allumoit sa colère.
Jupiter, las enfin de sa longue prière,
Lui dit: Chétif mortel, indigne de pitié!
Osez-vous m'invoquer pour les défauts des autres?
Je ne réprimerai ceux de votre moitié,
Qu'après que vous aurez corrigé tous les vôtres.

What is this insect good for? Well,
Not much! Only to interrupt and irk us:
No other talents, far as I can tell,
Only to fly and ply his blasted circus!"
The irksome bug, hearing himself decried,
                    Replied:
"Society has many a one like me,
          Whose only gift, I guarantee,
          Is to make noise, yet satisfied
To do no more, for we breed far and wide.
At times we are the butt of nasty twit
          And taunt, but we care not one whit;
We just keep saying: 'So? I bore you, coz?
Who cares? I'm happy, love, the more I buzz.'"

"Fables," LXXVI

JUPITER AND THE MARRIED MAN

"Great Jupiter!" a husband begs aloud,
          Day after day, and, zealous, prays:
          "Please! Cause my wife—vain, jealous, proud—
To change her character and mend her ways!
For you my incense shall be ever lit!"
Now, be it known, the lady's spouse was not
          Faultless: a nasty, greedy sot,
Quick, for no cause, to flare into a fit,
Given to gaming, superstitious—very!—
Ill-tempered, and much the voluptuary.
          Jupiter, tired at being thus
Constantly importuned, cries: "Cease the fuss!
Ought you be pitied? You, vile man who dares
          Invoke me with his endless prayers
To tend to others' faults that he endures?
Your wife's I will not mend till you mend yours!"

"Fables," LXXXIV

Marie-Amable de La Férandière 421

LE BŒUF ET LE COCHON

Le bœuf et le cochon alloient de compagnie
    Tristement à la boucherie,
L'un et l'autre bien gras. Les hommes ont grand soin
    De tous ceux dont ils ont besoin.
Le bœuf ne cessoit pas de gronder, de se plaindre,
Et disoit au cochon, ne pouvant se contraindre,
Vous étiez destiné de tout tems à la mort,
Vous n'étiez bon à rien, moi, j'ai rendu service
Et me faire mourir c'est horrible injustice,
    Je méritois un autre sort:
Les humains sont ingrats, ce fut toujours leur tort.
Son compagnon repart, le lâche! mets des bornes
    A ton chagrin, et ne t'en prends qu'à toi.
Si le ciel m'eût donné tes forces et tes cornes
L'homme n'auroit osé mettre la main sur moi
    Et quel intérêt peut on prendre,
    A celui qui se plaint au lieu de se défendre?

L'AGNEAU ET LE LOUP

    Messire loup enlevoit un agneau
    Et le portoit dans sa tanière,
On croit bien que c'étoit le plus fort du troupeau;
Se débattant de peur et presque de colère;
Enfin se dégageant de la dent meurtrière,
    L'agneau crioit: M'arracher à ma mère!
Contre nous appaisez votre injuste courroux!

THE BULL AND THE PIG

Sharing each other's company,
Off to the slaughterhouse together went,
Sadly, the bull, and, no less sad than he,
The pig, each most well-fed and corpulent.
(Man takes great care of what he needs!) The bull,
Lamenting in his accents sorrowful,
Could not resist telling the pig:
"You, friend, were raised for nothing but to die!
What are you good for? Not a fig!
Death was your lot since birth. But I,
I served Man! To kill me is scandalous!
I earned a better fate! But Man
Is an ungrateful wretch! 'Twas ever thus..."
Replied the pig: "Pish tush! I fear you can
Blame but yourself, so hush your whining.
If I had been bestowed, by heaven's designing,
A pair of horns and strength like yours, I vow
Never would Man have laid a hand on me!
Really! Do you expect much sympathy?
You could have saved your hide. Why whimper now?"

"Fables," cxxviii

THE LAMB AND THE WOLF

Sire Wolf kidnapped a lamb one day
And took it to his lair. They say
It was the hardiest of the flock, and it,
Flailing about in something of a fit
Of fear and rage, managed to find a way
Out of the deadly fangs, crying: "Permit
Me to observe... How unjust, you,
To snatch me from my mother! Ah, go to!

Marie-Amable de La Férandière 423

Qu'avons-nous fait pour vous déplaire?
Vous êtes l'animal le plus cruel de tous.
Tu ne connois donc pas celui qu'on appelle homme,
    Repart le loup en le flairant?
    Il fait la guerre à tout être vivant,
Et même à ses pareils; il fusille, il assomme,
    Et bien souvent sans la moindre raison.
        Je tuerai par fois un mouton,
Mais point de loup: tuer son frère est crime énorme:
Pour celui-là chez nous il n'est point de pardon.
Ton maître auroit déjà fini ta doléance,
Car du monde bientôt il te falloit sortir.
Je te mangerai cru, lui t'auroit fait rôtir,
Et voilà de ton sort toute la différence.

––––––––––

LE FINANCIER ET LES PAYSANS

Un financier voyant des paysans lui prendre
        quelques-uns des nombreux raisins
qui bordoient en festons les murs des ses jardins:
Scélérats, cria-t-il, je vous ferai tous pendre.
        Monsieur Mondor, lui répondit l'un d'eux,

What have we done? What do we do
To anger you? Surely there is no more
Bloodthirsty beast!" The wolf gives it a sniff
 And says: "Then I must ask you if
You know not one called Man? He wages war
 On all, even his own. The cause?
 Often, none. True, I sink my claws,
My jaws, into a sheep from time to time.
But kill another wolf? Oh no! The crime
Of fratricide is quite against our laws.
 We do not turn brother on brother!
Your fate is sealed: in one way or another,
 You're going to die, so why the fuss?
By now your master, doubtless, has forgot
Your loss. I'll eat you raw and on the spot;
 He would have roasted you. And thus,
That's all the difference betwixt him and us."

"Fables," cxiv

THE FINANCIER AND THE PEASANTS

A financier watches some peasants take
Some grapes that grow, thick, by his garden walls:
 "Wretches! You shall be hanged!" he calls,
 With angry cry. "For pity's sake,
† Monsieur Mondor," says one of them. "Ah, woe!

---

* I would not have committed this rather blatant repetition of a single rhyme over
three successive lines if the poet herself had not shown me the way in lines 4–6 of the origi-
nal, a phenomenon met with occasionally even in the works of La Fontaine, with whose
celebrated "Le loup et l'agneau" (see my version in *Fifty Fables of La Fontaine*, pp. 12–13)
this fable inevitably invites comparison. If La Férandière's wolf is no less vicious than his
ancestor's, his reasoning is, perhaps, a good deal more striking.

† The reader will appreciate the obvious symbolism of the name "Mondor," from *mont*
(mountain) and *d'or* (of gold). This fable, not found in the poet's 1806 *Œuvres*, was one
of many poems she published between 1780 and 1798 in the *Almanach des Muses*, where
it appeared in the volume for 1792. By that date, whether out of revolutionary conviction
or simply for self-protection, she had begun to sign herself "Madame de La Fer***" rather
than "Madame la marquise de La Fér***," and the fable itself strikes a suitably egalitar-
ian note. I reproduce the original with the idiosyncratic use of lower-case line beginnings
characteristic of the *Almanach des Muses*.

voilà vos fruits; nous allons vous les rendre.
Mais devenez plus juste envers les malheureux.
Nos pleurs, nos cris, enfin notre misère
    ce beau château vous a valu:
eh! devez-vous entrer en si grande colère,
quand nous voulons tâter de votre superflu,
vous qui nous avez pris souvent le nécessaire.

PORTRAIT DES MARIS

Un amant léger, frivole,
D'une jeune enfant raffole;
Doux regards, belle parole
Le font choisir pour époux:
Soumis quand l'hymen s'apprête,
Tendre le jour de la fête,
Le lendemain il tient tête;
Il faut déjà filer doux.

Sitôt que du mariage
Le lien sacré l'engage,
Plus de vœux, pas un hommage;
Plaisirs, talens, tout s'enfuit;
En vertu de l'hymenée,
Il vous gronde à la journée,
Bâille toute la soirée,
Et ronfle toute la nuit.

Sa contenance engourdie,
Quelque triste fantaisie,
Son humeur, sa jalousie,
Oui, c'est-là tout votre bien,
Et, pour avoir l'avantage
De rester dans l'esclavage,
Il faut garder au volage
Un cœur dont il ne fait rien.

Pray be not so unjust toward such as we!
Here! Take your fruit and let us go!
Our tears, our sobs, our life of misery
It was that got you such a fine château!
Oh! Must you rant, and rail, and shout,
When we make free with but a morsel, thus,
Of what, for you, is quite superfluous—
You, who take what *we* cannot do without?"

———————

PORTRAIT OF HUSBANDS

He, the lover frivolous,
Mad about the young belle; thus
Sweet words, glances amorous,
Make her choose him, marriage seeking.
Wedding nears: docile, monsieur
Bows low; let the *fête* occur,
Next day, he stands up to her:
Out already he goes sneaking.

Once the sacred marriage bond
Binds him ever and beyond,
Gone the vows, the tributes fond;
Pleasures, fled; and passion too:
Married now, our popinjay
Scolds and scolds the livelong day,
Yawns the evening hours away,
Snores and snores the whole night through.

Puffy-faced and plump, now he
Broods his fretful phantasy,
Grim and jealous as can be:
Such the dismal fate you choose—
Fate you pay for to the brim—
As, enslaved in life and limb,
You must save your heart for him;
One he deigns not even use.

Marie-Amable de La Férandière 427

POUR SOPHIE

Quand je vois cette aimable enfant
Caresser, adorer sa mère,
De cette fille, et tendre et chère,
Je voudrois être la maman.

Au récit de quelque malheur
Qui toujours attendrit Sophie,
Elle fait palpiter mon cœur,
Je voudrois être son amie.

Si je peins son minois charmant,
Et son maintien modeste et sage,
Je maudis mon sexe, mon âge,
Et voudrois être son amant.

L'AMITIÉ TRAHIE

Que je trouvois Thémire aimable!
Son air est séduisant, son esprit enchanteur;
Pour elle je sentois cette douce chaleur
De l'amitié tendre et durable;

Ses peines, ses plaisirs passoient jusqu'à mon cœur
Et de légèreté la croyant incapable,
Je répétois souvent: Je connois le bonheur.

Combien de fois sa voix délicieuse
M'assura d'un constant retour!
Combien de fois son amitié trompeuse
Me fit médire de l'amour!

De Thémire à présent j'éprouve l'inconstance...
Pour me venger de sa rigueur,
J'appelle en vain l'indifférence;
Elle ne peut, hélas! trouver place en mon cœur.

FOR SOPHIE

When I see that sweet child caress,
Adore her mother, lovingly,
So winsome and so dear is she,
Would I were her *maman,* ah yes!

To watch when some chagrin is told,
Some woe that saddens poor Sophie,
She makes my heart pound uncontrolled:
* Would I, at least, her friend might be.

When I portray her with my pen—
Pert face, coy manner, modest, tender—
Oh, how I curse my years, my gender:
Would that I were her lover then.

AFFECTION BETRAYED

†   Oh, how I loved Thémire! Her very
Air, so seductive, and her mind's allure,
Warmed in me feelings destined to endure,
    Not some mere fondness ordinary;
My heart shared in her pains, her pleasures, sure
That friendship was, for her, no temporary
Trifle, and found in it contentment pure.

How often did her sweet voice, promising
    Reward, foretell the fruits thereof!
How often did betrayed affection bring
    My tongue to curse the name of Love!

Dismayed, now must I bear her falsity.
    And to avenge, alas, the pain,
    I beg indifference visit me...
My heart can lodge it not: I call in vain.

---

* I follow the poet in her *abab* rhymes of the second quatrain, sandwiched, for no apparent reason, between the *abba* of the first and third.

† As early as the Middle Ages, it was not uncommon for women poets to affect the masculine voice in writing traditional love poetry. In this collection we have seen an example in Christine de Pizan's pithy *rondeau* LXVII (pp. 90–91 above). The cliché-ridden convention need not be assumed to have sexual overtones.

Pour chanter l'infidèle, au déclin de mon âge,
Des doux sons de mon luth je soutenois ma voix,
Et je comptois semer des roses quelquefois
Sur le chemin qui mène au funeste rivage.
    Plus de plaisirs, plus de douceurs!
    En me privant de sa tendresse,
    Elle a flétri le peu de fleurs
    Que je gardois pour ma vieillesse.

ÉPIGRAMME

Le beau Cléon nous disoit aujourd'hui:
Matin et soir je fais la même chose
    Et n'ai jamais connu l'ennui.
De ce bonheur nous savons bien la cause,
    C'est qu'il parle toujours de lui.

LE BON CHOIX DU RAT

    L'autre matin en me levant,
Je vois sur le parquet voler au gré du vent
    Nombre de feuilles imprimées
    Et la plupart très-écornées.
Qu'est-ce que ces papiers? des fables, dit Marton.
Ciel! un rat m'aura pris ma bonne édition
    De mon bien aimé la Fontaine.
    Et vite un piège, un chat en faction,
Que bientôt le gourmand subisse juste peine.
Quelle engeance bon dieu! que l'engeance des rats!
Je me baisse pour voir les débris du repas,
Disant, le maudit rat ne fera plus des siennes.
    Oui, ce sont des fables vraiment.
    Consolons-nous, oh! le mal n'est pas grand:
    Ce rat d'esprit n'a mangé que les miennes.

Grown old, yet have I spared my voice, my breath,
To praise this faithless one with lute and song,
And scatter roses, now and then, along
The path that leads us to the shores of death.
    But flown now are her winsome ways:
    Tenderness, pleasures, gone awry!
    She withered those few flowers that I
    Had saved for my last dying days.

———————

EPIGRAM

Cléon the fair has told us: "Yes, 'tis true,
    I do the same thing every day,
But never am I bored by what I do."
    And this, the reason, I daresay:
He talks about himself the whole day through.

———————

THE RAT'S WISE CHOICE

    One morning, as I rose from bed,
I saw, over the floor, here, there—wind-scattered—
    A pile of printed pages spread,
    Dog-eared and worn, and badly tattered.
"Marton, what are those papers, pray?" I cry.
    "Fables, I think," comes the reply.
"What? Can it be? A rat... Heavens! Perdition!
A rat has nibbled on that fine edition
    Of my belovèd La Fontaine!...
Be quick! A trap to catch the beast!... A cat,
To make the glutton pay his due!... Oh! That
Vile race! Him and his offspring too!" And, then,
Stooping to view the remnants of the feast,
    "No more," I shout, "that rat's audacious
Doings!... Fables, indeed!... Ah, but at least
We can take comfort; he was most sagacious!
    The damage is not very great:
Mine are the only ones the creature ate!"

STANCES À M. LE PREMIER PRÉSIDENT DORM*** LE PREMIER JOUR DE L'AN 1789

A cinquante ans je puis tout dire
Et sans manquer à mon devoir:
Pour qui souhaite de vous voir,
Oh! qu'il est ennuyeux d'écrire!

L'amour cache ce qu'il désire,
L'amitié peut tout révéler:
Et lorsqu'on brûle de parler,
Oh! qu'il est ennuyeux d'écrire!

Maintenant je pourrois sourire
Si vous m'étrenniez d'un baiser;
Et quand on songe à s'embrasser,
Oh! qu'il est ennuyeux d'écrire!

Mais tant que vos yeux pourront lire
Et ma main former quelques traits,
Je sentirai, non sans regrets,
Qu'il est encor bien doux d'écrire.

ÉPITAPHE DE M. LE PRÉSIDENT D'ORM*** MORT EN FÉVRIER 1789

Pleurez ce magistrat éclairé, vertueux,
Qui servit à la fois Dieu, les lois et son maître,
    Et qui n'a fait de malheureux
    Que le jour qu'il a cessé d'être.

STANZAS FOR CHIEF PRESIDING MAGISTRATE DORM***
ON NEW YEAR'S DAY 1789

At fifty years, admit I might,
That when one on your face would gaze—
One who her duty yet obeys—
Oh, what a woe it is to write!

Love hides its burning appetite,
Though friendship shows all that it will;
And when one yearns to speak her fill,
Oh, what a woe it is to write!

Now should I smile with pleasure, quite,
If you gave me a New Year's kiss;
And when one thinks of thoughts like this,
Oh, what a woe it is to write!

But while your eyes yet have their sight,
While yet my hand can push the quill,
Yes, I shall have regret, but still
Shall feel how sweet it is to write.

† EPITAPH FOR CHIEF PRESIDING MAGISTRATE D'ORM***
WHO DIED IN FEBRUARY 1789

Weep for this virtuous judge, wise, true and tried,
Who served God, and the law, with righteousness,
 Nor ever caused the least distress,
 Except, indeed, the day he died.

* The dedicatee was no doubt Louis-François de Paule Le Fèvre d'Ormesson (1718–1789), one of the scions of the d'Ormesson clan, a prominent family of magistrates and government officials of that name since the seventeenth century. The one in question, known for his intelligence and integrity, began his career as *avocat du roi* in 1739, and had, by the end of his life, risen to the position of *premier président,* chief of the eight presiding magistrates of the parliament under Louis XVI.

† See the preceding note. Despite the slight difference in the spelling of the gentleman's truncated name in the two originals ("d'Orm" and "Dorm")—a difference that does not occur in the first appearance of "Stances" in the *Alamanach des Muses* of 1789, and in spite of the date of his death being given as February, the two dedicatees would appear to be one and the same. The presiding magistrate referred to in the previous note died on January 29, 1789.

Marie-Amable de La Férandière 433

ÉPÎTRE À MA CHIENNE

Nous voilà vieilles toutes deux;
Consolons-nous, chère Zémire;
Mon œil s'éteint, et dans tes yeux,
Où brilloit l'amoureux délire,
On ne voit plus les mêmes feux.
Tu perds ta grâce, ta folie,
Mon esprit perd son enjouement;
Du jour tu dors une partie,
Et moi je rêve tristement.
Hélas! pour tous ceux qui vieillissent,
Tous les jours, à tous les momens,
Quelques plaisirs s'évanouissent.
Tu vois fuir bien loin les amans,
Et mes amis se refroidissent.
Mais laissons-là les inconstans;
Contr'eux, ni plainte, ni satire.
Ne les imitons pas, Zémire:
Chéris-moi comme en ton printems.
L'amitié fait couler la vie;
Elle embellit tous nos instans,
Et qui ne peut aimer s'ennuie,
Même à l'aurore de ses ans.
Tu ne peux parler; quel dommage!
Ton embarras me fait pitié:
De nos mots que n'as-tu l'usage!
Tout ce qui ressent l'amitié
Devroit avoir même langage.
Je serois heureuse avec toi,

* TO MY DOG FROM HER MISTRESS

See how we two are now grown old!
But let us not be unconsoled,
Zémire my pet; my eye is blear
And dim, and in your eyes, where shone
Love's ecstasies, one sees, my dear,
No more that flame: your grace is flown.
Your mischief's folly too is fled;
And I, no less dispirited,
Have lost the fire that once I knew.
By day, you seem to sleep and sleep,
Whilst I, as well, can little do
But dream in sadness, dark and deep.
Alas! When we are old, how few
The days that cast not, in some measure,
Shadows on yet another pleasure!
You see your lovers flee afar,
Shunning your presence; as for me,
My friends, once warm, grown colder are.
Ah well, amen! So let them be!
Against their fell inconstancy
Let us raise neither plaintive sigh
Nor bitter jibe; nor let us try,
Zémire, to emulate their ways:
Cherish me as in times gone by,
When spring adorned your greener days.
Friendship it is that drives us on,
Gracing with beauty all our hours,
Whilst boredom, dull and bleak, devours
Those who, though in the very dawn
Of youth, cannot express their love.
More do I prize your paw's caresses,
Fraught with the sweet intent thereof,
Than all the wheedling tendernesses
Of faithless friend's betraying hand!
Would that you had at your command

* I have seen fit to add a feminine pronoun to the title in order to reflect the feminine
gender of the French *chienne*, which the simple English "dog" would leave ambiguous, and
which "bitch" would disfigure.

Marie-Amable de La Férandière 435

Ma tendre et sincère Zémire,
Si tu t'exprimois comme moi.
Lorsque la confiance inspire,
On jase du soir au matin.
Etant du sexe féminin,
Il nous faudroit parfois médire.
Nous ririons des pauvres humains,
Foibles, petits, et toujours vains;
Je t'instruirois de nos usages,
Quelquefois fous, quelquefois sages,
De nos travers, de nos erreurs...
Enfin nous médirions, Zémire:
Ne faisant grâce qu'aux bons cœurs,
Combien de choses à nous dire!...
Mais quand j'y fais réflexion,
Si jamais tu pouvois m'entendre
Et répondre à notre jargon,
Serois-tu toujours aussi tendre?
Des humains tu prendrois le ton.
Devant toi je parle sans feindre,
De mes chagrins, de tous les maux
Que j'éprouve ou que je dois craindre;
Et je n'oserois plus me plaindre,
De peur de troubler ton repos.
Achève tes jours sans alarmes,
Sans songer que tu dois mourir;
Tu ne vois rien dans l'avenir,

The gift of speech! How well you would
Put it to use, if you but could!
Pity it is that you cannot.
For, all those bound in friendship should
Share the same tongue; and thus my lot
Would be much happier if you might,
In accents tender and sincere,
Speak as do I, O my Zémire.
Good, trusting friends will spend the night
Babbling till dawn; and since we two
Are of the gentle sex, no doubt
We should find much to carp about,
With sharp and twitting tongue! Yes, you
And I would laugh, and chaff, and flout
The human race, and make great sport
Of those too weak, too small, too short,
But not a whit less vain withal;
And gladly would I teach you all
Our manners—some, of prudent sort,
Others quite witless!—all our flaws
And faults as well... Yes, happily
Would we confound humanity,
And spare none but a few, because
Few are the good at heart... And yet,
Despite all we might say, my pet,
I wonder: if you knew, in fact,
This speech of ours, and could respond,
Would you be tender still, and fond,
As now you are? No, you would act
As human beings are wont to do,
I warrant; now I have no need
To feign before you when, indeed,
I speak of all the ills I rue
And all the woes I know, or fear
I might: but if your ear could hear
And comprehend, then dare should I
Lament no more, lest, by and by,
I trouble your tranquilllity.
No, best you end your days care-free,
Not knowing that, come time, you die,
Or worrying what tomorrows hold:

Le présent t'offre encor des charmes.
Oui, l'on envîroit tes plaisirs
S'il te restoit de ta jeunesse
Quelques aimables souvenirs,
Les seuls trésors de la vieillesse.

À UN JEUNE HOMME QUI POUR PRIX DE SES VERS ADRESSÉS À L'AUTEUR LUI DEMANDOIT UN BAISER

Quoi! pour prix de vos vers, vous voulez un baiser?
Y pensez-vous, Damis, un baiser!... à mon âge?...
Oui, pour votre intérêt j'ai dû le refuser.
     Quand les ans de notre visage
     Ont terni l'aimable fraîcheur,
Et que l'art se refuse à cacher leur ravage,
Un baiser, je le sais, n'est plus une faveur;
Qui le demande alors croit qu'il nous fait honneur,
     Et dire non, c'est être sage.

MON ÉPITAPHE

    Peu de biens et beaucoup de maux
    Hélas! avoient tissu ma vie;
     Ici j'ai trouvé du repos:
Tout passant malheureux va me porter envie.

Today still yields you charms untold...
Well might they envy you, all those
Who see that, though now long of tooth,
You keep sweet memories of your youth:
The only treasures age bestows.

FOR A YOUNG MAN WHO, IN RETURN FOR HIS POEM WRITTEN TO THE AUTHOR, ASKED HER FOR A KISS

What, Damis? For the poem you wrote, you would
Exact a kiss? Can you be serious?
A kiss?... At my age?... Ah, for your own good,
    Must I refuse. Yes, when years, thus,
    Wither the freshness of our face,
And art ill masks how time has ravaged us,
I know, a kiss is but a gentle grace:
    Who begs one honors us; but oh!
Wiser it is—alas!—to tell him "no."

MY EPITAPH

    Alas! Few riches, many woes
    Were weft in my life's tapestry;
    But here have I found my repose:
All who pass by, forlorn, will envy me.

Marie-Emilie Maryon de Montanclos (1736–1812)

Wearer of several different hats, Marie-Emilie de Montanclos's importance depends on the interests of those voicing their opinions. Observers concerned with revolutionary social issues and the role of woman, admire primarily her variety of journalistic writings. Those in theater emphasize the several plays and theatre commentary that she wrote. While those in letters point out that, although most of her poetry is traditional in form, she was in fact one of a number of eighteenth-century writers to experiment with what would come to be called the prose poem. (And that, almost a century before the genre, explored by Maurice de Guérin around 1835 and, more significantly, by Aloysius Bertrand with *Gaspard de la nuit* in 1842, was sanctified as an "official" genre with Baudelaire's *Petits poèmes en prose* in 1855.) Aestheticists will assert, rightly, that "prose" can be more "poetic" than much verse, and that line breaks, rhyme, and meter do not a poem make. At least, not necessarily.

Marie-Emilie Maryon, born in Aix-en-Provence, added the "de Montanclos" to her name with one marriage and "baronne de Prinzen" with another. Widowed by her first husband, she was legally separated from the second. As a low-key champion of women's rights, she became, in 1774, the editor of the *Journal des Dames* and used her pulpit to put forth that periodical's message on the importance of woman both in the arts and as mothers entrusted with the enlightened rearing of children. She used it also to preach against the frivolity of the court, exemplified in Versailles, and dedicated her message to Marie-Antoinette, hoping no doubt—rather too optimistically—for royal support for reasonable social reform. Her editorship was less than a resounding success, however, and the more vigorous utopian reformer Louis-Sébastien Mercier replaced her the following year.[1]

With her theatrical hat, Madame de Montanclos was director of the Théâtre Montansier at Versailles, and, between 1782 and 1804, she wrote several comedies, at least one of which, the one-act *Robert le bossu, ou Les trois sœurs*, in verse and prose, was performed in Paris in 1799. One other, *Le déjeuner interrompu*, appears to have been performed at the Comédie-Française in 1783; and still another was accepted at that theater but never performed. But it is for her poetry, published in *Œuvres diverses de Madame de Montanclos*, that she is included in this collection. The reader will notice, tucked in among the inevitable pastoral pieces and other fleeting trifles, several on the more striking subjects of excessive regal pomp, the masculine vigor of Catherine the Great, and a curious paean to a beautiful Jewess. Despite my commitment to presenting only complete poems,

I include also, as an example of an essential aspect of her work, an excerpt from one of her sensitively expressed poems in prose.

NOTE

1. For biographical details, see Nina Rattner Gelbart, *Feminine and Oppositional Journalism in Old Regime France*, pp. 170–206, as well as the brief entry in the *Bloomsbury Guide to Women's Literature*, pp. 827–28. The reader might also consult the unsympathetic account of Montanclos's career in the dyspeptic Alfred Marquiset's sarcasm-laced *Les Bas-bleus du premier Empire*, pp. 93–105. The latter's perspective is made clear from the outset by the epigraph to his volume, a bon mot by Alphonse Karr: "A woman who writes makes two mistakes: she increases the number of books and decreases the number of women."

STANCES SUR VERSAILLES

Palais des Rois, Temple de la Fortune,
Vous n'êtes point le séjour du bonheur;
Et votre aspect a produit sur mon cœur
Le triste effet d'une vue importune.

Je veux en vain fermer les yeux
Sur ce qui m'afflige ou me blesse:
Quand la fausseté me caresse,
Avec douleur je regarde les Cieux.

Par-tout ici je rencontre l'envie;
Et malgré ses déguisements,
Sous ses plumes & ses rubans,
On connoît encor la furie.

MADRIGAL FAIT DANS LE PARC DE VERSAILLES

Bientôt vous nous verrez, bocage frais & sombre,
Formé par la Nature, embelli par l'Amour,
Venir, Tircis & moi, pour jouir sous votre ombre,
Du spectacle riant qu'offre l'éclat du jour.
Mêlant toujours de la tendresse
Aux plus sages réflexions,
Nous éviterons la tristesse
Qui suit les méditations.
Ces superbes jardins, dignes de nos Monarques,
A notre esprit feront prendre l'essor:
Mais, par un doux regard, terminant nos remarques,
Nous nous dirons... tu me plais mieux encor.

STANZAS ON VERSAILLES

Kings' palace, Fortune's temple, you; and yet,
I fear that, here, resides no happiness:
I look on you and feel my heart beset
By sad and haunting visions of distress.

    In vain I try to close my eyes
    To what afflicts, beleaguers me:
    Embraced, caressed by falsity,
Sadly I turn my gaze unto the skies.

Envy abounds; no fine disguise can hide it,
    Try though it may, to failure doomed:
    Beribboned though it be, and plumed,
    One sees the madness deep inside it.

* ## MADRIGAL WRITTEN IN THE PARK AT VERSAILLES

O wood cool-shadowed, formed by Nature's art
And beautified by Love, soon will you see
Tircis and me come set ourselves apart
Beneath your shade, to welcome gleefully
    The smiling dawn: with tenderness
    And wise reflections mingled there,
    We shall cast off the sad duress
†   That follows oft on morning prayer.
Fine gardens worthy of our Monarchs, you
    Will make our souls take wing and soar;
But with a loving glance, at length, we two
Will tell each other: "Love, you please me more..."

---

  * The contempt expressed for Versailles in the preceding poem and the adulation expressed in this one are probably both hyperbolic: the former panders somewhat to the revolutionary spirit much in the artistic wind of the period and the latter to the tradition of sentimental pastoral cliché.

  † Given the time of day, I make a gentle interpretive leap here in supposing that the *méditations* referred to are of a religious nature.

Marie-Emilie Maryon de Montanclos 443

RÉPONSE DE L'AUTEUR À SON MARI, QUI LUI REPROCHOIT DE DORMIR LE JOUR

De mon sommeil que peut craindre l'Amour?
Il regne sur mes sens, & jamais sur mon ame.
Qu'il s'empare de moi, la nuit ou bien le jour,
    Il n'assoupira pas ma flamme.

IM-PROMPTU FAIT À CHAMPIGNI, APRÈS AVOIR VU MLLE MIKVÉ CALMER, JEUNE & BELLE JUIVE

Hier à mes regards s'offrit, d'un air modeste,
    Un rejeton des enfants d'Israël,
    Une beauté, que je trouvai céleste.
    Au même instant, je pense à Gabriel,
    Et je me dis: Si, du temps de Marie,
    Avoit paru l'adorable Mikvé,
L'Ange eût pu se tromper sur la Vierge choisie,
Et celle que je vois auroit eu son *avé.*

PLAINTES D'UNE ÉPOUSE TENDRE À SON MARI

    Non, je ne puis, mon cher Philinte,
    Cesser jamais de vous chérir.
    En vain vous évitez ma plainte:
    Je dois pour vous vivre & mourir.
    Semblable à la biche timide
Que le chasseur blessa d'un coup mortel,
    Par-tout où sa douleur la guide,
    Elle emporte le trait cruel.

THE AUTHOR'S REPLY TO HER HUSBAND, WHO REPROACHED HER FOR SLEEPING DURING THE DAY

Why must Love fear my sleeping, pray?
It reigns not on my soul but on my sense:
Whether it lay me low by night or day,
It will not quench my flame intense.

IMPROMPTU WRITTEN AT CHAMPIGNI, AFTER SEEING THE BEAUTIFUL YOUNG JEWESS MLLE MIKVÉ CALMER

Yesterday, to my eyes, most modestly
Appeared a damsel, child of Israel,
A truly heavenly beauty, she.
All at once, gazing on the belle,
I mused: "If Gabriel, in Mary's day,
Had seen Mikvé, the Angel might have erred,
And, by this Virgin's beauty led astray,
* Might, upon her, his *avé* have conferred."

LAMENT OF A LOVING WIFE TO HER HUSBAND

No, dear Philinte, I must remain
Ever in love. Forsake you? I
Cannot! You shun my plaints in vain:
For you I live, for you I die.
Just like the timid, wounded doe,
Who bears the hunter's dart, whithersoever
Her pain may lead, so too I go
Thither, in cruel distress; her woe will never

---

* "Cette pièce a paru dans plusieurs Journaux, au commencement de cette année, sous le nom de Madame de Bourdic. Mais elle appartient à Madame de Montanclos" (This piece appeared in several journals at the beginning of this year under the name of Madame de Bourdic, but it is by Madame de Montanclos), a footnote to the original tells us. Earlier, the poet's pride of authorship might have been outweighed by fear of accusations of a scandalous sacrilege.

A se guérir elle ne peut prétendre;
Tous ses maux, en fuyant, semblent se ranimer:
Mais toujours douce, & non moins tendre,
Elle gémit, & ne cesse d'aimer.

———————

IM-PROMPTU SUR UNE PÉNITENCE ORDONNÉE AU JEU

Vous me donnez pour pénitence
De faire un mauvais madrigal;
C'est plus aisé que l'on ne pense:
On réussit toujours au mal.

———————

LE DANGER DE LA RECONNOISSANCE

Quand un berger donne son chien,
Quel espoir pour une bergère!
Il ne faut plus qu'une faveur légere
Pour obtenir son cœur: c'est avoir tout pour rien.
Mais bientôt plus tendre que sage,
Lise donne à son tour un bijou précieux;
Et le berger, moins généreux,
N'offre plus qu'une humeur volage.

———————

SUR UN RENDEZ-VOUS

Demain, dans le palais de Flore,
Je dois rencontrer mon berger:
Amour! ouvre mes yeux à la naissante aurore,
Et ferme-les sur le danger.

———————

IM-PROMPTU SUR UN CHIEN QUI GRATTOIT À LA PORTE, APRÈS QUE LE MARI DE L'AUTEUR ÉTOIT ENTRÉ

Quand la fidélité suit de près la tendresse,
Laissez-les au logis pénétrer toutes deux;
Car en amour on n'est heureux
Que lorsque également notre cœur les caresse.

End, though she flee, but seems to grow the more:
Harsher the blow, deeper the wounds thereof.
　　Yet no less tender, she, therefor:
She moans her pain but cannot cease to love.

————————

IMPROMPTU ON A PENANCE IMPOSED AT GAMING

The penance you imposed on me—
To write a wretched madrigal—
Is easier than it seems to be:
To do ill is not hard at all.

————————

THE DANGER OF GRATITUDE

　　When shepherd lad his hound bestows,
A shepherdess's hopes rise ever higher!
She knows he will a modest boon require
　　If she would have his heart, and knows
He will be hers at little cost. But she,
Young Lise, less wise than tender, gives a jewel;
And, fickle lad—less generous, he, than cruel—
Offers her naught but his hypocrisy.

————————

ON A RENDEZVOUS

　　In Flora's palace, come the morn,
My shepherd shall I meet, by dawning sun.
Ah, Love! open my eyes to daylight born,
　　And close them to the risk I run.

————————

IMPROMPTU ON A DOG THAT KEPT SCRATCHING AT THE DOOR AFTER THE AUTHOR'S HUSBAND HAD COME IN

When faithfulness follows on tenderness—
Close on its heels—let both come through the door:
　　For love will but give joy the more
When our hearts both those qualities caress.

Marie-Emilie Maryon de Montanclos 447

À CATHERINE II, IMPÉRATRICE DE RUSSIE, APRÈS AVOIR REMPORTÉ UNE VICTOIRE SUR LES TURCS

Roi d'un peuple vainqueur, Reine d'un sexe aimable,
Que tu mérites bien le mirthe & le laurier!
Si ta valeur te rend un Héros redoutable,
Tes charmes font un voile à ton courage altier;
Et l'on ne sait en toi lequel est préférable
Des vertus d'une femme, ou du cœur d'un guerrier.

SUR LE RETOUR DE MON BIEN-AIMÉ

Enfin, tous mes maux vont finir;
De ce hameau Tircis approche:
Amour, je cesse le reproche,
Pour ne chanter que le plaisir.

Je vais me couronner de fleurs,
Pour charmer le Berger que j'aime.
Plaisir, viens essuyer toi-même
Toutes les traces de mes pleurs.

PREMIERS VERS FAITS APRÈS MON VEUVAGE: C'ÉTOIT LE DIXIÈME MOIS

Oubli de ma peine,
Desirs renaissants;
Charme qui m'entraîne,
Ranimez mes sens.
Ombre gémissante,
Objet de mes pleurs,
Mon ame constante
Chérit ses douleurs:
Et de ton amante
Si la main tremblante
Cueille quelques fleurs,

FOR CATHERINE II, EMPRESS OF RUSSIA, AFTER A VICTORY OVER THE TURKS

King of a conquering race, Queen gentle-sexed,
Myrtle and laurel set you well apart!
Hero, your foes shrink, fearful, sorely vexed,
Yet charms veil your proud mien with woman's art.
Which ought one prize in you the more, perplexed:
The woman's virtues, or the warrior's heart?

ON THE RETURN OF MY BELOVED

At last my woes are vanishing.
Tircis is drawing hitherto:
No more, Love, shall I harry you,
For naught but pleasure shall I sing.

I shall place garlands on my head
To charm my shepherd lad; I pray,
Pleasure, you come and wipe away
All traces of my tears, now fled.

FIRST VERSES WRITTEN AFTER BEING WIDOWED: TEN MONTHS AFTER

Grief be done, begone!
Let charm's consequences,
Reborn, lead me on,
And revive my senses!
O shade, moaning low,
As my tears flow free,
Doleful, my *esprit*
Holds woe dear... But oh!
If, hand-tremblingly,
Yet your lover, she
Now might choose to go

Marie-Emilie Maryon de Montanclos 449

Ces douces faveurs
Du Dieu du Permesse
Sont loin de l'ivresse
Qu'éprouvoient nos cœurs.

————————

CHANSON D'UNE BERGÈRE DE SAVOIE

(Extraits)

Réveille-moi, coq matinal, redouble ton chant bizarre. Je veux jouir du lever de l'aurore. Et je dirai alors à l'étoile qui brillera sous le firmament: "Je te salue, astre de nos bergers, je te salue; sois toujours le signal favorable qui m'annonce l'arrivée de Mirtil. Et je te consacrerai mes chansons du matin: elles me seront inspirées dans la plus belle heure de ma vie."

Fleurs qui venez d'éclore, oiseaux qui gazouillez d'un ton si doux, aubépine parfumée, verdure couverte de perles transparentes, et vous, nuages azurés, vous m'annoncez un nouveau bienfait du ciel: en vous voyant, je goûte le plaisir d'être et mon cœur s'agite dans mon sein comme le jeune ramier au retour de sa mère. . . .

Existence précieuse, il faut savoir, sans murmurer, vous rendre à l'Eternel; mais loin de nous, l'homme cruel qui cherche à précipiter votre fin: ses derniers regards porteront l'effroi dans le cœur innocent. . . .

J'entends les pipeaux rustiques; ils précèdent les moissonneurs. Aimable gaîté, compagne du berger vertueux, viens toujours l'aider dans ses travaux. Et toi, fidèle amitié, fais-le reposer dans tes bras et essuie son front brûlant avec des feuilles de roses.

Gather flowers... Although
    *   Phoebus' fair boon, this,
Gone that frenzied bliss
Our hearts used to know.

SONG OF A SHEPHERDESS FROM SAVOY

(Excerpts)

Cock of the morn, crow twice as loud your curious song, and waken me.
For I would revel in the dawning day. And I shall tell the star, hanging low
in the heavens: "Hail, you, our shepherds' star! Be ever the fair sign to me,
announcing that my Mirtil soon comes hither. And I shall sing to you alone
my morning songs. Their spirit will well up in me at this, my life's most
lovely hour."

O flowers newly bloomed, birds warbling on your soft, sweet notes. O
fragrant hawthorn, greenery spangled with transparent pearls. And you, O
azure clouds, who herald yet another boon of heaven: I look upon you and
delight in life. My heart pounds in my breast, as the young dove's when
nestward flies his mother. . . .

O precious life, we must learn how, with never a murmur of complaint,
to give you back to the Eternal. But away with the ruthless one who seeks
to cut you short. His final gazes will strike fear in the simple, guileless
heart. . . .

I hear the rustic flutes. They pipe the harvesters' return. Joyous delight,
you, mistress of the virtuous shepherd lad, attend him in his laboring. And
you, O faithful friendship, nestle him in your restful arms, and brush his
burning brow with leaves of roses.

    * The reference in the original is to the spring of Permessos, dedicated to Apollo and
the Muses. Though Phoebus and Apollo are not exactly synonymous, the former being the
latter's incarnation as god of the sun, I take the liberty of preferring one to the other for
metrical reasons.

Marie-Emilie Maryon de Montanclos 451

Fanny de Beauharnais (1737–1813)

When Marie-Anne-Françoise ("Fanny") Mouchard married the royal tax col-
lector comte Claude de Beauharnais in 1753, she became the aunt by marriage
of the future empress Joséphine. She was likewise to be the godmother to the
latter's daughter, the future queen Hortense, wife of Napoleon's brother Louis
Bonaparte, king of Holland (1806–1810). But her chief claims to fame among her
contemporaries were, not her imperial connections, but rather her beauty, her
social proclivities, and her devotion to letters; the latter, a love that some would
snidely affirm remained unrequited. Thanks to it, however, she composed sev-
eral less-than-successful plays, numerous poems twitting particular individuals
and the social mores of her salon coterie, and a quantity of prose tales, none of
whose picturesque narratives equaled the vagaries of her own erratic and erotic
existence. It was probably no exaggeration to say that "even though Fanny
would welcome any capable man into her bed, even into her eighth decade, she
maintained a special place in her heart for sixteen-year-old boys."[1]

Separated amicably from her husband after less than ten years of an unexcit-
ing union—the count, twenty years her senior, spent much time at sea—Fanny
entertained the Parisian intelligentsia in her weekly salons—her *vendredis*—
with no pretense at understanding their profound pronouncements. The poet
Claude-Joseph Dorat was one of her special admirers, and their liaison lasted
until his death in 1780, when he was replaced by others no less devoted. Her
salon was especially favored for the excellence of its cuisine. A celebrated gastro-
nome is said to have remarked that, much though she relished sex and would
take it where she found it, it truly came second to a "well-set table."

Fanny began her literary career in 1772 with a two-volume collection whose
title itself, *Mélanges de poésies fugitives et de prose sans conséquence*, expresses the
supposed triviality and capriciousness of much of her work. On the other hand,
that announced lack of *conséquence* was more likely than not a self-defensive
posture toward those who, unlike her faithful admirers, had little regard for her
talent. It is clear that, trivialize it though she might, she herself took her literary
endeavors very seriously, and devoted herself almost exclusively to them when
the pleasures of the flesh permitted. In 1782, she was named an associate of the
Académie française, though cynics would wonder if it was her beauty and so-
cial graces that were being rewarded, rather than a talent sincerely appreciated.
She was imprisoned briefly during the Terror, and it is even said that she was
tortured. Upon her release, it was to her life of letters that she immediately re-
turned.[2]

All the following examples of her verse, as deliciously piquant in its general as in its specific, personal mockery, are taken from her *Mélanges.*

NOTES

1. The quotation, which I hope is not apocryphal, is attributed to the brothers Goncourt, but I fail to find it anywhere in their voluminous writings. It was reported by Sanche de Gramont (a.k.a. Ted Morgan) to the culinary writer Daniel Rogov in personal correspondence, June 6, 1969.

2. For biographical details and varying amounts of critical appreciation, one has to depend largely on comments found in encyclopedias and literary dictionaries. See, e.g., Ranee Kaur's entry in the *Encyclopedia of Continental Women Writers,* p. 98, which cites also Maurice Pellisson, *Les hommes de lettres au XVIIIe siècle.* A study referred to in this and other sources, by the eminent scholar Daniel Mornet and supposedly entitled *La vie parisienne au XVIIIe siècle,* is actually a collection of eight essays by that title in which the fourth, by Mornet, "La vie mondaine des salons," devotes considerable discussion to Fanny. As for the snide comments in Alfred Marquiset's *Les Bas-bleus du premier Empire,* pp. 179–207—for whom "her poems scarcely reach the level of mediocrity" (p. 185)— they should be weighed in the spirit of the screed in which they were written.

AUX HOMMES

Fier d'une fausse liberté,
Sexe, qui vous croyez le maître,
Soyez, au moins, digne de l'être.
Justifiez votre fiérté,
Et puis, ce sera notre affaire,
Quand vous l'aurez bien mérité,
De vous surpasser pour vous plaire.
Pardonnez-moi cette candeur;
Qui peut vous paroître un outrage,
Mais qui convient à mon humeur.
Vive, indépendante & volage,
Ma plume obéît à mon cœur.
Disserter est votre partage:
Il est très-noble assurément;
Le nôtre, c'est l'amusement,
Qui, prouvant moins, vaut davantage.
A votre plus grave argument,
Nous répondons en nous jouant,
Avec un mot de persiflage.
Notre frivole Aréopage
Donne des loix à vos Héros,
Et nous cachons vos noirs bureaux,
Sous les pompons du badinage.
Vous vous battez bien mieux que nous;
Vous sçavez manier des armes:
Un grand sabre a pour vous des charmes;
Chez vous la force aide au courroux.
Oui, Messieurs, j'oserai le dire,
Depuis long-temps on sçait cela;
C'est d'elle que vient votre empire;
Le nôtre, il est vrai, n'est point là.
Le Ciel aussi nous dédommage.
Si la force manque à nos vœux,
Dans nos cœurs il met le courage;
Combien nos combats sont affreux!

TO MEN

Proud of a freedom desultory,
O sex who think you reign supreme,
Be, at least, worthy of your glory:
Deserve to be proud as you seem.
Then ours it will be to redeem
Our sex, and prove to you that we
Surpass you, if but for your pleasure.
Pardon me if too candidly
I speak, or past all proper measure;
My spirit, like my heart, beats free;
And ever must my pen concur...
Declaiming is what you prefer—
A noble enterprise!—We choose,
Rather, to say what will amuse,
Prove less, but be worth more, messieurs,
And, with a bit of persiflage,
However weighty your *message,*
Reply with banter, jibe, and jape.
* Our Areopagus decrees
Frivolous rules to twit and tease
Your heroes, and we gladly drape
Your lecterns, black, with fripperies...
True, you fight better than we might:
You ply your arms with passing skill—
A saber fills you with delight—
Strength serves your wrath and ever will.
Yes, messieurs, I admit your powers.
Long have we known that force it is
That gives to man that rule of his.
But power we have as well, though ours
Comes not from strength of body, nay...
But Heaven, ever magnanimous,
Requites us in a different way:
For it has granted unto us—
Though strength we lack, and fierce the fray—

* The tongue-in-cheek reference is to the Areopagus—named for a hill in Athens
dedicated to Ares—the highest tribunal in the Athenian state, noted for the wisdom of
its decisions.

Dans ces plaines, que Mars ravage,
Les vôtres sont moins douloureux;
Et l'ennemi qu'il vous faut craindre,
Ne sçachant, ni plaire, ni feindre,
Moins cher, est bien moins dangereux.
Vous faut-il dévorer des larmes,
Résister à votre vainqueur?
Sans honte, vous rendez les armes.
Mais, sous une feinte douceur,
Quand l'Amour blesse notre cœur;
Trop sinceres pour ne pas croire,
Pleurant la peine ou le bonheur,
Et la défaite & la victoire,
Et le triomphe de l'honneur,
Ou la perte de notre gloire,
Nous trouvons par-tout le malheur.
Sçavez-vous vaincre la Nature?
Connoissez-vous tous ces tourmens,
Vous, esclaves de vos penchans,
Vous, que l'impunité rassure?
J'ai tort, je vous condamne en vain;
Tous mes reproches sont des crimes:
N'avez-vous pas votre latin,
Qui vous rend des êtres sublimes?
Oui, Messieurs; le Sexe jaseur
Doit tout au Sexe raisonneur.
Trop heureuses, je suis sincere,
Que des demi-Dieux, tels que vous,
Daignent descendre jusqu'à nous,
Et s'humaniser, pour nous plaire.
Des Philosophes, des Penseurs,
Des Géomètres, des Docteurs,
Dont les discours sont admirables,
Et les écrits inexplicables,
S'occuper de jolis enfans!
En perdre par fois le bon sens!
Autour de nous jouer sans cesse!
S'abaisser à notre foiblesse!...
Tel est pourtant notre pouvoir.
Que la Nature forme un sage,
Si le sage vient à nous voir,

A heart endowed with virtue; thus,
On Mars' ferocious battlefield,
Ravaged by war, your combats are
Less perilous than ours, by far:
The foe whom you must fear can wield
Nor joy, nor ruse, nor tenderness:
Less dear than we, he threatens less.
When he, victorious, pummels you
To tears, do you, with derring-do,
Resist? Ah no! With much *noblesse*
You yield your arms, desist, and cease.
But we, when, with a sweetness feigned,
Love wounds our hearts, our tears increase:
Simple, sincere, we are constrained
Never to doubt; and weep shall we
Both our defeat and victory—
Our glory lost, our honor gained—
Finding in everything good cause...
And you? Can you best Nature's laws?
Know you these torments? You, in thrall
To instincts, passions, one and all,
Who deem yourselves exempt from pain?...
Ah, but I err: my criticisms,
Reproaches, cavils, are in vain.
Are you not filled with Latinisms,
Lodging sublimely in your brain?
Yes, messieurs, we, the prattling gender,
Owe all to you, the thinking sex,
Too grateful if, in all your splendor,
Demigods that you be—complex
Of reasoning (I speak sincerely!)—
You take a human form and deign
Descend to our banal domain,
And tarry here, to please us merely!
Imagine! Thinkers, *philosophes,*
Doctors, geometers—the lot!—
Orating; and, if not enough,
Writing (though who can say on what?),
All sharing in the company
Of pretty little *demoiselles*
(Though some quite lose their sense as well!),

Reconnoît-elle son ouvrage?
Enfin, tout adore nos fers;
Tout suit l'instinct qui nous dirige:
Par nos graces, par nos travers,
Si l'on veut, par notre vertige,
Nous enchaînons cet univers.
Nous lui prouvons, grace au prestige,
Qu'en vous ébauchant avant nous,
Le Ciel, de notre honneur jaloux,
Pour la fin garda son prodige,
Et que la main du Créateur
Commença vîte par la tige,
Pour donner ses soins à la fleur.

AUX PHILOSOPHES INSOUCIANS

Vous, que berce une vieille erreur,
Très-sots Disciples d'Epicure,
Connoissez la volupté pure:
Sçachez aimer, c'est le bonheur,
L'attrait, le vœu de la Nature:
Les sens trompent... je crois mon cœur.
Ici-bas, dites-vous sans cesse,
Il ne faut rien approfondir:
On y doit jouir, sans foiblesse;
Et la foiblesse est de sentir.
Excellente philosophie!
N'atteindre jamais qu'à la fleur!
Epicuriens, c'est, en honneur,
Brouter gaîment pendant sa vie.
Ces globes, qu'on enfle en soufflant,
Un vain prestige qui s'efface,

Stooping to our inanity!...
Yet, power immense is ours. Indeed,
Let Nature form a man as wise
As wise can be: then let his eyes
Light on us... Ah! Will she succeed
In recognizing her creation?
Everything follows where we lead,
Delighting in our domination.
Thanks to our loveliness, our flaws,
And even to our giddiness,
We rule the universe, because
We prove that Heaven prized you far less,
First forming you, then forming us,
Saving for last, in doing thus,
The best, with wondrous virtue graced:
For the Creator, with his power,
Fashioned the stem in careless haste,
* That he, with care, might form the flower.

FOR THE UNFEELING PHILOSOPHERS

O you, foolhardy, numb of skull,
Misguided Epicurean troops!
Still does that ancient error lull
And gull your souls! Denatured dupes!
You loll in sheer voluptuousness.
Learn, rather, how to love! Real love
It is that you know nothing of,
But that Nature, wise governess,
Urges—demands!—that you should know.
The senses—so my heart declares—
Guide ill. You say that, here below,
No need is there to plumb, to go
So deep. What matters it? None cares
What lies beneath! Enjoy!... Who dares
Have feelings is a weakling!... Oh!
What a superb philosophy!

* The reader will notice throughout this and several of the succeeding poems that I have taken as many liberties with my rhyme schemes as the poet takes with hers.

Ne satisfont que l'homme-enfant:
Pourvû qu'il joue, il est content;
Son œil s'arrête à la surface:
Le plaisir, voilà son lien;
Il y vole, & brûle ses aîles;
Le malheureux! c'est tout son bien...
Qu'ils sont pauvres, les infideles!
　　Mes froids amis, viendra le jour,
Où les tristes glaçons de l'âge,
Qui ne respectent que l'Amour,
Ne vous laisseront en partage,
Qu'un passé perdu sans retour.
"Que reste-t-il à ma vieillesse,"
Nous direz-vous languissament?
"J'ai dédaigné le sentiment:
Nul Etre à moi ne s'intéresse."
　　Les Dieux se vengent & font bien.
Ne vous dites pas leur image;
Je crois le diable Epicurien.
Le pauvre Satan n'aime rien;
Et c'est de cela qu'il enrage.

－－－－－－－

QUATRAIN

Beauté, fatal présent des Dieux,
Les peines sont votre partage.
Vous armez un Sexe envieux:
Fixez-vous un Sexe volage?

－－－－－－－

À LA FOLIE

Charme des Mortels & des Dieux,
Folie, aimable enchanteresse,
Tu sçais même embellir les jeux:
Le plaisir naît de ton ivresse.
Je me donne à toi pour toujours:
Je te préfere à la tendresse.
Répands la gaîté sur mes jours;

Touch but the surface, live your days
Savoring naught, a-browse, a-graze...
Like the child blowing playfully
His pretty bubbles, pleasure-bent,
Gazing upon their beauty, spent
In but a moment, then no more...
He burns his wings whilst seeking for
Mere joy, poor faithless malcontent!...
    My frigid friends, your ways presage
Days when, all ice-benumbed, old age,
With no respect for Love, will leave
You but your past, though ever flown.
"Why live I longer?" you will grieve,
Languishing in your woe, alone.
"Feeling I scorned—dull, wearisome!
Now none will mourn what I become."
    The Gods work vengeance: well they do;
Think not wrought in their image, you!
Satan it is, who—poor soul he!—
Of Epicurus treads the path.
Nothing he loves: and, probably,
Such is the reason for his wrath.

———————

QUATRAIN

O Beauty, fatal gift of Heaven!
Yours are the woes that grieve and vex:
You arm a sex to envy given;
Can you turn true a faithless sex?

———————

TO FOLLY

Charm of gods and of mortals, you—
Folly, lovable sorceress—
Beautify everything you do:
Joy is born of your drunkenness!
You I prefer to love's caress.
Fill full my days, and—*entre nous*—

Et j'aurai plus que la sagesse.
C'est en attendant ton retour,
Que les pauvres Amans sommeillent.
La raison seule endort l'Amour:
Ce sont tes grelots qui l'éveillent.

PORTRAIT DES FRANÇOIS

Tous vos goûts sont inconséquens:
Un rien change vos caracteres;
Un rien commande à vos penchans.
Vous prenez pour des feux ardents,
Les bluettes les plus légeres.
La nouveauté, son fol attrait,
Vous enflamment jusqu'au délire:
Un rien suffit pour vous séduire;
Et l'enfance est votre portrait.
Qui vous amuse, vous maîtrise:
Vous fait-on rire? on a tout fait,
Et vous n'aimez que par surprise.
Vous n'avez tous qu'un seul jargon,
Bien frivole, bien incommode.
Si la raison étoit de mode,
Vous auriez tous de la raison.

AUX SAUVAGES

Sauvages, soyez nos modèles!
Le sentiment guide vos pas;
A sa loi vous êtes fideles:
Que n'habité-je en vos climats!

More shall I be than wise! Ah yes...
You tarry, and poor lovers doze!
Cupid too! Slumbers overtake him...
Reason bores him to sleep; but those,
Your tinkling jester-bells, will wake him.

———————

* **PORTRAIT OF THE FRENCH**

With fickle tastes, all reason spurning,
A whit can change your whole *esprit;*
A whit, indeed, will set you yearning:
You take for passion-fire a-burning
The flightiest bit of coquetry.
The mad attraction of the new
Inflames you to ecstatic height;
A whit it is that well can woo
And win your hearts, won over quite;
As children one paints you aright!
Surprise alone can make you love;
And, might one be the master of
Your destinies? The secret is
To make you laugh: you will be his.
Yours, a strange gibberish cumbersome,
Frivolous tongue that reasons poorly;
Were reason, though, in fashion, surely
Well-reasoned would you all become.

———————

TO THE SAVAGES

Savages, be our models, pray;
Faithful to your life primitive,
Feeling it is that lights your way:
Why may I, in your climes, not live!

———————

* Though the plural *François—Francais* in modern spelling—can refer either to all the French or only to French men, hence my title, I would like to think that the countess is speaking specifically to, and about, the latter.

Fanny de Beauharnais 463

Chaque nœud s'y forme ou se brise,
Au gré des cœurs indépendans.
Parmi vous, il n'est point de Grands
Que l'on redoute, ou qu'on méprise.

Vous ne descendez pas au soin
De vous surpasser en richesse.
Chez vous, la seule qu'on connoisse,
C'est d'en ignorer le besoin.

Si vous ne donnez qu'une rose,
Elle vaut tous nos diamans.
Que fait la valeur de la chose?
Le cœur met un prix aux présens.

Vous vous aidez avec tendresse.
Nul secours n'est humiliant,
Et jamais la délicatesse
Ne rougit, même en acceptant.

Reconnoissante, & non séduite,
La beauté nomme son vainqueur.
Le penchant regle la conduite:
On n'y ment jamais à son cœur.

C'est, sous vos huttes, qu'on sçait vivre;
On végéte sous nos lambris.
La Nature vous sert de livre;
Son instinct vaut tous nos écrits.

———————

À M. LE MARÉCHAL DE ***

Vous valez César, à la guerre,
Et vous surpassez Annibal.
Vous sçavez vaincre, ainsi que plaire:
Je le sens bien; je le dis mal,
Et cela ne m'importe guere:
Apprend-on à rimer au bal?

Untrammeled urges, they, that stir
Your hearts to make or break your ties...
You have no noble *grands seigneurs*
To hold in fear or to despise.

To outstrip others overmuch
In wealth is not your goal: your one
Possession rich—second to none—
Is to ignore your need for such.

To match the gift of but one rose
Our diamonds all cannot suffice.
What value has what man bestows?
It is our heart that sets the price.

You aid each other tenderly;
And those whom thus you benefit,
Proud, prize your generosity,
Nor blush when they must bend to it.

Grateful, and not seduced, are they—
Your beauties—who their conquerors choose;
Never need they their hearts betray,
But follow what their taste pursues.

In huts, how rich the life you lead;
How poor, mid wainscots, ours, alas!
Nature is all the book you need:
Her instincts all our writ surpass.

———————

* FOR MONSIEUR LE MARÉCHAL DE ***

A Caesar, you, in war; and, true,
Greater than Hannibal's, your skill:
You conquer, yet are pleasing too.
I feel it well though speak it ill:
Who cares? When at the ball, we do
Not learn rhymes dancing the quadrille!

* The particular *maréchal* invoked, hero of battlefield and boudoir, would seem secure
in his anonymity. One reasonable guess, however, is Joachim Murat (1767–1815), *maréchal
de France,* who, as Napoleon's brother-in-law, was made king of Naples in 1808. He was
executed by firing squad after an unsuccessful attempt to reconquer his kingdom, lost in
1815. Murat was one of the host of imperial figures known to Fanny de Beauharnais.

Pardonnez mon insuffisance.
Chacun, en ce bon Univers,
A son défaut, par excellence.
Je suis novice en l'art des vers,
Tout comme vous pour la constance.

––––––––––

AU MARQUIS DE ***

Va, crois-moi, la mélancolie,
De l'esprit les calculs gênans,
L'importune Philosophie,
Ses systêmes impertinens,
Et sa raison si peu suivie,
Sont, n'en déplaise à nos Sçavans,
Des pavots semés sur la vie.
Si, pour la gloire qu'on envie,
On se livre à ces passe-tems,
Pour le bonheur, je m'en défie.
Nuls soins, nulle prétention,
Pour moi, voilà ce qui m'enchante.
Voi ta Nation si brillante:
Brille-t-elle par la raison?
Sous le moulinet de la mode,
On la voit tourner à tout vent:
Elle a le plaisir pour méthode,
Et pour instinct le sentiment,
Tant qu'il n'est pas trop incommode.
Es-tu François? voilà ton Code;
Et c'est ainsi qu'on est charmant.
Des travers, des métamorphoses,
Tel est le monde: prends son ton.
Le Printemps naît; cueillons des roses:
Qui voudra, songe à la moisson.

So, if I blunder, pardon me:
Each of us with some flaw must shine,
In this fine world, surpassingly.
Greenness in writing verse is mine,
Just as yours is inconstancy.

———————

FOR THE MARQUIS DE * **

Indeed! Dour, melancholic air,
Annoying counsels of the mind,
Philosophy (that guides one where
It will, be one or not inclined),
With systems to no end designed,
And reason, which most minds forbear
To follow... All these things specific—
Say what our sages may in their
Defense!—are but a soporific:
Poppies strewn wide... If one is there,
Whose glory or whose happiness
Demands one of these pastimes, such
An one I am not! I confess,
I am attracted far too much
By unpretentious things, not those
Rather groundless absurdities...
Your country—Reason's pride, they say!—
Goes whirling round with every breeze,
Changing its stance from day to day,
Following fashion's circumstance;
Pleasure is all that charms, enchants,
And instinct all that moves the senses—
So long as it cause no offenses!...
Well, French you are, and such your Code.
So goes society; and life,
With charming peccadilloes rife,
Invites you be *très à la mode.*
Come pluck the roses of the spring:
Await who will fall's harvesting!

AU COMTE D'H***

Oui, n'en déplaise à ma Patrie,
Vous avez ses aimables goûts:
Ses défauts, je vous en défie;
Et c'est encore tant-mieux pour vous.
Sur ces défauts-là, je vous prie,
Comte, gardez-nous le secret.
Taisez-vous, par galanterie,
Si ce n'est pas par intérêt.
Ne dites rien de nos caprices,
De nos Sages intéressans,
Qui, pour le progrès des talens,
Leur font de bonnes injustices,
Parlent, avec un très-grand sens,
De nos plumes & de nos vices,
Des Foyers, des Gouvernemens,
Du Conseil d'Etat, des Coulisses,
De Boston, & des vers courans,
De Bleds, de Finance & d'Actrices.
Vous avez vu, par-ci, par-là,
Oubliant jusqu'à leur coëffure,
Nos Raisonneurs en falbala,
Jaser sur la Littérature.
Que dites-vous de leur caquet?
O le plaisant Aréopage!
Ici, nous n'avons point de Sage,

May it my country not displease
If, Count, I say that you possess
All of her finest qualities;
As for her faults, I must confess
You show them not: so much the better;
Best you conceal them, to the letter,
Lest you reveal their pettiness.
Pray acquiesce to my request,
Whether it be through interest
Or gallantry that you do thus.
And so, say nothing of our age's
Whims and caprices, or our sages,
Who, with a wisdom generous,
On talent's progress bent, yet do
Many a nasty turn thereto;
Who talk—ah! with what sense!—to us
On everything: home, government,
The things we write, our lives ill spent,
Our vices, the affairs of state,
Tilling the soil, finance, the stage,
Actresses... How they prattle, prate,
Orate on verse now all the rage,
† On Boston, and all that... No doubt
Here and there you have seen them—these
Philosophes in their fripperies,
Hair all disheveled, and without
Even their wigs—eager to spout
Deep literary verities!
‡ O splendid Areopagus!
No sage have we who has not taught

---

* The dedicatee's anonymity is well preserved behind Fanny's asterisks. A perusal of her letters suggests one possible, albeit slim, candidate: the German, Franz Grafen von Hartig, who mentions her a number of times in his *Lettres sur la France, l'Angleterre et l'Allemagne*, of 1785. See Frederick King Turgeon, "Fanny de Beauharnais" (Ph.D. diss., Harvard University, 1929). This remains sheer conjecture, however.

† The reference to Boston makes special sense when one considers the publication date of this collection: 1776.

‡ See p. 455n.

Qui n'ait stylé son Perroquet.
Les jugemens sont un ramage
Qu'on répéte d'un air distrait;
Et, sur cet article, je gage
Que vous serez encor discret.
Sage & prudent, comme vous l'êtes,
Vous épargnerez nos Amans,
Fiers de leur amour à bluettes,
Et prodigues de faux sermens.
Vous ferez grace à nos Coquettes,
Qui, sçachant disputer au tems
Leurs prétentions indiscretes,
Hazardent leurs beaux sentimens,
D'après mille détails charmans
Qu'on leur arrange à leurs toilettes.
Motus encor sur nos Plaisans,
Nos historiques Ariettes,
Et nos Drames attendrissans,
Entrecoupés de Chansonnettes.
Autant en emporte le vent!
Chut encor!... mon Dieu! j'en ai honte.
Si vous étiez obéissant,
Il me semble, mon pauvre Comte,
Que vous vous tairiez trop souvent.
Tenez! je leve vos scrupules;
Dites tout ce qui vous viendra:
Trouvât-elle des gens crédules,
Votre critique nous plaira,
Même en frondant nos ridicules.

His parrot to discourse, discuss
Every opinion ever thought,
Cackled in a cacophonous
Display, and echoed with an air
Of debonair devil-may-care...
As for our lovers, I feel sure
That, prudent as you are, you will
Abjure from speaking all the ill
You might about their sham *amours,*
Profligate with their plighted troths,
Proud of their falsely proffered oaths...
You ought spare, too, our coy, demure
Ladies, longish of tooth, but both
Able to challenge time, secure
In their pretensions indiscreet,
And able, too, in manner meet,
To voice alluring sentiments
That match in style their costume; hence
Errant in all details, unfit...
As for our many a wag and wit,
Keep mum! And not a word concerning
Our ditty-airs historical,
Our *drames* with bourgeois passion burning,
* Our *vaudeville* tunes, to nonsense turning;
In matters such, rhetorical,
No oracle am I, but still,
Gone with the wind be they!... But nay!
Good God! How wrong I am! How ill
I serve you, Count! If you obey
And say naught of these things, what will
You have to say? It seems to me
That ever will you silent be!
I lift my strictures: speak your fill,
On anything that comes to mind.
Many believers might you find;
And your reproof will charm, delight us,
However much you might indict us.

* In these lines the poet alludes to both the sentimental *drame bourgeois,* popular mid-eighteenth-century forerunner of the melodrama, and—though not referring to it by name, as I have done—the genre of light comic theater characteristically interspersed with text set to tunes of the day.

REGRETS DU PREMIER ÂGE

Dans le monde, nos premiers ans
Sont dirigés par l'innocence.
Qu'elle est heureuse, notre enfance!
Toujours croire est sa jouissance,
Et tous ses rêves sont charmans.
Combien sa joie est vive & pure!
Il lui semble, du sein des jeux,
Que tous les cœurs sont vertueüx;
Qu'ils sont fermés à l'imposture.
Mortels, qui nous ouvrez les yeux,
Hélas! vous êtes bien coupables.
L'on perd tout, quand on vous voit mieux:
On perd ces prestiges aimables,
Par qui les Hommes sont des Dieux.
Ah! rendez-moi, s'il est possible,
L'opinion que j'eus de vous.
Sur la foi d'une erreur paisible,
J'aimois à vous estimer tous.
Je regrette un bandeau si doux:
La vérité m'est trop pénible.

AUX FEMMES

Mon sexe est injuste par fois;
Mais c'est un tort qu'un charme efface.
Ses travers même ont de la grace,
Et ses caprices sont ses loix.
Je voudrois le fléchir, sans doute.
Pour des titres, j'en ai plus d'un.
Mes traits n'ont rien que de commun.
Je me tais, & même j'écoute...
N'importe! il me faut renoncer
A l'espoir flatteur de lui plaire.
Auprès de lui, j'aurois beau faire:
Tout en moi paroît l'offenser;
Et mes Juges, dans leur colere,
M'ôtent jusqu'au droit de penser.

LONGINGS FOR THE EARLY YEARS

Here below, oh, how innocent
The first years that we live our life!
How happy, how enjoyment-rife,
Those childhood years so simply spent
With never a doubt, and confident,
In their unblemished naïveté,
That everything is as it seems.
How pure those years, how sweet their dreams!
How sure the virtue of their play,
Hearts closed to fraud's deceitful schemes...
Mortals, who open wide our eyes,
Ah me! How wrong, how cruel of you
To make us see life otherwise!
You let us look on you close to,
And let us see you through your guise:
No longer are you gods to us!
Oh! Give me back life's generous
Deceit; for sweet it was to wear
That blindfold that concealed you thus:
The truth is far too harsh to bear.

TO WOMEN

At times my sex is most unjust;
But women's charms efface their flaws
And lend them grace: whims are their laws,
Capriciously enforced. I must
Confess that I wish I could cause
Their nastiness to bend, of course.
Many a proper, fit resource
Have I therefor; to wit, my features—
Not in the least extraordinary—
My tongue—held still (for I am very
Willing to listen!...) But these creatures
Make me renounce the hope that I
May less displease them by and by.
Everything in me gives offense,
It seems; and, in their wrath intense,

Cependant j'exalte ces Dames;
J'encourage leurs défenseurs;
Je leur donne à toutes des ames;
Je chante leurs graces, leurs mœurs,
Et leurs combats, & leur victoire.
Je les compare aux belles fleurs,
Qui de nos jardins sont la gloire,
Elles rejettent mon encens,
Et, ce qu'on aura peine à croire,
Me traitent, dans leur humeur noire,
Presque aussi mal que leurs Amans.
Mes vers sont pillés, disent-elles.
Non, Chloé n'en est pas l'Auteur;
Elle fut d'une pesanteur!...
Le tems ne donne pas des aîles.
"Mon Dieu!" reprend avec aigreur,
A coup sûr, l'une des moins belles,
"Jadis, je la voyois, le soir;
Alors, elle écrivoit en prose,
Peut-être, hélas! sans le sçavoir,
Et hazardoit fort peu de chose."

Mesdames, à ne point mentir,
Je prise fort de tels suffrages:
Mais, craignez de m'enorgueillir,
En me disputant mes Ouvrages.
Ne me donnez point le plaisir
De me croire un objet d'envie.
Je triomphe, quand vous doutez;
Rendez-moi vîte vos bontés,
Et je reprends ma modestie.

These judges would, I fear, defy
My very right to think! But why?
Ever do I praise womanhood
And raise my voice on high for those
Champions who plead its case! I would
Even grant women souls, God knows!
I laud their grace, extol their mien,
Their manner; sing their struggles keen,
Their triumphs over feckless foes!
I call them flowers, the fairest seen,
In gardens blooming with their glory!...
My incense, rising laudatory,
Do they reject! Their humor, black,
Willingly lays me on the rack,
And, though hard to believe it be,
Almost as ill do they treat me
As they their lovers do: they say
*   I filch my verse... Ah no, Chloé
Is not the author... Heavier, she,
Duller of wit!... And wings are not,
Alas, of aging years begot!...
"My God!" one of the uglier cries,
"One night I caught her writing prose...
She knows the difference, I suppose!"

Mesdames, in truth I greatly prize
Your wise reflections; but I truly
Think you ought fear lest I, unduly,
Puff up with pride if, in your eyes,
My work is little worth. Beware
Lest too much pleasure you bestow,
Condemning me with envious air.
What triumph, mine, when you declare
My verse unworthy, ladies! So,
Quick! Once more with your praise make free,
That I once more may modest be.

* Not one of the poet's given names—Marie, Anne, Françoise ("Fanny")—"Chloé" was,
I suspect, one of those pet names not uncommonly assumed or imposed—in eighteenth-
century salon society, often, as here, with pastoral overtones.

Stéphanie-Félicité de Genlis (1746–1830)

Among the distinguishing characteristics of [Caroline-]Stéphanie-Félicité Du-crest (or Du Crest) de Saint-Aubin, comtesse Bruslart de Genlis and marquise de Sillery—besides her stunning abundance of names—was her musical ability. An accomplished artist on the harp and author of a pedagogical system for learning to play that instrument, she reigned over a salon that was as much devoted to chamber music as to letters, if not more so. But if she is known to eighteenth-century scholars today it is, without question, rather for her role as one of the more imposing and productive French women writers of the years straddling the Revolution.

Born in Champcéry, Burgundy, she was orphaned early in life and was taken under the wing of the royal tax collector Le Riche de La Poupelinière. In 1763, she married the comte Alexis Bruslart de Genlis and proceeded to devote her life, almost single-mindedly, to the education and edification of the young, both as governess to the children of Louis-Philippe-Joseph, duc de Chartres, later duc d'Orléans, and his duchess, Marie-Adélaïde (née de Bourbon-Penthièvre)— notable among them the future king Louis-Philippe—and to her voluminous literary production: theater, essays, memoirs, verse, and moral tales, all of didactic inspiration and intent. She was, in fact, the first woman in French history entrusted with the tutoring of princes, spending nineteen years in the royal household. This position of high moral responsibility did not prevent her, however, from having a notorious affair with the libertine Louis-Philippe-Joseph, whose ultraliberal views would later earn him the name "Philippe Egalité." Nor did it prevent her from being an active participant in the aristocratic political and social life of that troubled time; a time that saw both her husband and Philippe Egalité guillotined in 1793.

Madame de Genlis, who had emigrated in 1791, spent the following years in England, Switzerland, and Germany, continuing to mine the vein of her seemingly inexhaustible, if rather lackluster, inspiration. Allowed to return to France in 1802, she enjoyed the favor and largesse of Napoleon for a time, which permitted her to continue exploiting it further. She lived on long enough to see her former pupil Louis-Philippe ascend the throne of France in 1830, and when she died in Paris on the last day of that year, she was honored with a lavish state funeral.

Though the bulk—the word is well chosen—of her writing is of a didactic nature, and though she was little known for her verse, one of the more modest, though original, products of her decade of expatriation was her *Herbier moral, ou Recueil de fables nouvelles, et autres poésies fugitives.* The originality of the eighteen fables lies neither in their already-traditional form nor in their commonsense morality, but rather in the relative novelty of their characters. In the dedicatory *épître* to Lady Edward FitzGerald—reputed to be her daughter by Philippe Egalité—she writes that it had long been her ambition to compose fables, but that she had been discouraged from doing so by the imposing shadow of La Fontaine. And, echoing Rousseau, she found that the former's fables, with their frequent animal skullduggery, were not proper fare for the young. Her novel solution? To dramatize her fables with characters drawn from the vegetal kingdom, with their panoply of characteristics that give rise to a whole range of emblematic symbolism. Others had done so from time to time, but to Madame de Genlis belongs the credit, such as it is, of doing so almost to the exclusion of the sacrosanct *dramatis animalia*.[1]

The eight fables translated, as well as the four typically eighteenth-century *poésies fugitives* following them, are taken from the *Herbier moral*.

NOTE

1. For biographical and authoritative bibliographical details, see esp. Jean-Baptiste Harmand, *Madame de Genlis, sa vie intime et politique;* Alice M. Laborde, *L'œuvre de Madame de Genlis;* Violet Leverson Wyndham, *Madame de Genlis: A Biography;* and Gabriel de Broglie, *Madame de Genlis.* Marie Naudin's informative entry in *French Women Writers,* pp. 178–85, provides additional specialized titles, especially regarding the feminist import of her work.

LES FEUILLES

A sa branche attachée, une feuille naissante
      Exprimoit ainsi son chagrin:
Que j'envie en secret le glorieux destin
      De l'heureuse feuille volante,
   Qui dans les airs se frayant un chemin,
      Suivant le penchant qui la guide,
Tantôt jusques au cieux, sur l'aile des Zéphirs,
      Dirige sa course rapide;
   Tantôt cédant à de nouveaux desirs,
      Revient s'amuser sur la terre,
  Et caresser les fleurs de ce parterre,
   Ou voltiger à l'ombre des ormeaux,
Sur les flots argentés de ces limpides eaux!
    Du papillon rivale fortunée,
      Qu'elle est douce ta destinée,
Que je le sens, hélas! moi qui suis pour toujours
Au fond de ce bosquet sur cet arbre enchaînée!
     La branche entendit ce discours:
     Ton dépit, dit-elle, se fonde
     Sur l'ignorance et sur l'erreur;
     Cesse d'envier le bonheur
     De cette feuille vagabonde;
     Tu la crois libre, et cependant
     Elle obéit aveuglément.
     Son élan n'est qu'une secousse;
Quand tu la vois voler, c'est le vent qui la pousse,
Il ne la guide pas, il l'emporte, et toujours
De sa marche égarée il prescrit les détours.
Elle en est à la fois l'esclave et la victime;
Si parmi quelques fleurs il veut bien l'arrêter,
Plus souvent il se plaît à la précipiter,
    Et pour jamais, dans le fond d'un abîme.

THE LEAVES

A leaf, a-budding on its branch, expressed
    Its deep displeasure thus: "Ah me!
How jealous am I, and how sore distressed,
    To watch—albeit secretly—
The flying leaf that, glorious, leaves its tree,
Fluttering where it will: now to the sky
    On Zephyr's wing, hovering high
Above; now, on a whim, to earth once more
Returning for its pleasure, to caress,
Adore the blossoms in some patch, or soar
And swoop, in elm tree's shade, free, fetterless,
    Over the silver tide! How sweet
Your destiny, you, rival of the fleet
And fluttering butterfly, whilst I must spend
Forever in this wood, chained to this bough!"
    The branch gave ear and, in the end,
    Replied: "It seems, my friend, somehow
    You err: your judgment is askew,
    And you, I fear, much misconstrue.
    You think that leaf is free to fly
    Hither and yon? Well, let it try!
    For, though it wanders through the air,
    It flies not where it wants, but where
It must, blindly obedient in its flight,
    And subject to the gust's command!
Because it is the wind, with mighty hand,
That whisks it off, whips, buffets it—to right,
    To left, now up, now down—through all
The ins and outs of its erratic course:
    Victim and slave! And if, withal,
The wind will lessen now and then its force,
And let it share some flowers' company,
    More often will its fate be this:
To be cast, flung, for all eternity,
Down to the bottom of some dark abyss."

Ainsi que notre feuille, hélas! un jeune cœur,
Crédule et sans expérience,
Jouet des passions, cherchant l'indépendance,
Est entraîné par un espoir trompeur.
Sans doute le bonheur suprême
Réside dans la liberté;
Mais on ne peut jouir de ce bien si vanté,
Que par l'empire de soi-même.

LE PALMIER ET LE NOISETIER, DANS LE BOIS CONSACRÉ

Dans un bois aux dieux consacré,
Un palmier orgueilleux, richement décoré
Des attributs de Mars, de festons, de guirlandes,
Insultoit l'humble noisetier,
Qui ne portoit que de simples offrandes,
Des fleurs, une houlette, un fragile panier,
Dons ingénus offerts par l'innocence.
Contemple ma magnificence,
Disoit le superbe palmier,
Vois ces dépouilles éclatantes,
Que des rois les mains triomphantes
Ont déposé sur mes rameaux;
Ainsi paré des fruits de la victoire,
Je fixe les regards du peuple et des héros,
Et je suis devenu l'emblême de la gloire,
Mais écoutons!... Entends-tu les échos,
Qui du fond des antres sauvages,
Font retentir les bois d'un bruit harmonieux?
Le bruit s'augmente, et ces sons belliqueux
M'annoncent de nouveaux hommages.
A ces mots, un jeune guerrier,
Suivi d'une troupe nombreuse,
Se montre tout à coup, s'approche du palmier,
Et d'une main respectueuse,
Pose un énorme bouclier
Sur cet arbre si vain, dont la tige orgueilleuse
S'affaisse sous le poids; et bientôt se brisant,

The young heart, too, is like our leaf: without
    Experience, and credulous
Plaything of passions, it goes seeking thus
Its independence, thrown and blown about
    By a false hope. Yes, doubt it not,
Freedom brings happiness: much do we vaunt it;
But yours it will not be, though much you want it,
Unless you be the master of your lot.

II

THE PALM TREE AND THE HAZEL TREE
IN THE SACRED WOOD

In consecrated wood, the gods' domain,
A palm, richly festooned and decorated,
Bearing Mars' garlands, voiced haughty disdain
    As, loftily, he contemplated
A humble hazel tree who, rather, bore
Gifts offered on simplicity's behalf:
A fragile basket, flowers, a shepherd's staff—
    Innocent things, and nothing more.
"Gaze at my greatness!" said the palm with pride.
    "See how the hands of kings have plied
    My boughs with spoils of war! See how
I bear the fruits of glorious victory!
How simple folk and heroes honor me
    With awe!... But listen... Even now,
You hear? Those sounds off in the distance?... Clear,
Harmonious, martial sounds, that echo through
    The woods and reach our ear... You hear?
Louder and louder... Doubtless they bring new
Glories to heap upon me!" With these words,
Appear a soldier and his retinue,
All at once. There, the warrior ungirds
A monstrous shield, and, with utmost respect,
Places it on the palm. But, thus bedecked,
His slender trunk, for all his haughty air
Bows low beneath its weight; and, then and there,
Cracks with a crash and, groaning, falls to earth.

Eclate avec fracas, et tombe en gémissant.
L'arbre, éclairé trop tard par sa fin malheureuse,
Du noisetier modeste envia le destin;
Instruit par l'infortune, il reconnut enfin,
    Qu'une espérance ambitieuse,
Le desir des honneurs, et de vastes projets,
    Couronnés même du succès,
Ne produisent souvent qu'une chute honteuse.

L'OISEAU, LE PRUNIER ET L'AMANDIER

Un jeune oiseau, perché sur un prunier,
    Vit tout à coup un amandier.
Le bel arbre! dit-il, et quel charmant feuillage!
    Allons goûter ses fruits; je gage
    Qu'ils sont mûrs et délicieux.
A ces mots, fendant l'air d'un vol impétueux,
    L'oiseau bientôt, ainsi qu'il le desire,
Se trouve transporté sur l'arbre qu'il admire;
    Lors aux amandes s'attachant,
Il veut les entamer, mais inutilement:
Et de son bec en vain il épuise la force.
Ce fruit, dit-il, est dur, amer et dégoûtant.
Ne nous étonnons point de son raisonnement,
    Il ne jugeoit que sur l'écorce.

LE PAPYRUS

Devenu misanthrope, et sauvage et frondeur,
    Le papyrus, fort mécontent des hommes,
        Exhaloit ainsi son humeur:
"Quel maudit temps, grand Dieu, que le siècle où nous sommes!
    Et qui pourra nous rendre, hélas!
    Ces jours de bonheur et de gloire,

The palm, enlightened by his fate,
Comes to appreciate the hazel's worth
And envies him—but now, alas, too late!
Taught by misfortune, now must he confess
That vast ambitions, honors sought, and all
    Man's overweening eagerness,
    Even when not without success,
Most often lead to a most shameful fall.

VI

———————

THE BIRD, THE PLUM TREE, AND THE ALMOND TREE

A fledgling bird was perching in a tree—
    A plum it was—when suddenly
An almond tree he spied, exclaiming: "Oh!
How beautiful! What lovely leaves! Let's go
    And taste the fruit! I'll bet that it
Is ripe and succulent!" With that, he split
    The wind on eager wing, and now
Lights on a much admired and longed-for bough.
    Plucking the almonds, then, he tries
    To open them, but in no wise
Can he succeed; though he plies hard and well
His beak: in vain! Said he: "This fruit is tough!
    Vile! Sour!..." He reasoned well enough.
No surprise... He was judging by the shell.

VII

———————

THE PAPYRUS PLANT

    Grown mean, dyspeptic, dour and misanthropic,
    Venting his spleen against the human race,
        Papyrus Plant holds forth apace;
        And, ranting on his favorite topic,
*   Complains: "What times are these! Ye gods! Shame and disgrace!
        Gone are the days of heroes and their glory—

* I hope the reader finds my uncustomary use of the cumbersome 12-syllable line, here
and elsewhere in this version, appropriately bombastic.

Stéphanie-Félicité de Genlis 483

Dont le récit nous charme dans l'histoire!
Mais il n'est plus d'Agésilas!
De ces gens qui savoient discerner le mérite,
Et dont chaque discours et toute la conduite,
Et les goûts et l'opinion,
Excitoient l'admiration
Du sage ainsi que du vulgaire.
Aujourd'hui, sur toute la terre,
Le bon sens n'est plus de saison,
On a su le bannir; combien d'arts inutiles!
Combien d'inventions futiles!
L'esprit, les mœurs, tout est perdu,
On s'éloigne de la nature,
Et s'écarter d'une source si pure,
C'est renoncer à la vertu."
"Oui, je comprends," dit un arbuste,
"Le sujet de ce grand courroux:
On fait du beau papier, et tout vous semble injuste,
Depuis qu'on a cessé de recourir à vous."

LA FLEUR COMMUNE ET LE BEAU VASE

Dans un superbe vase, une triste immortelle
Se redressoit et s'épanouissoit,
En voyant les passans s'arrêter devant elle.
Mais elle s'enorgueillissoit
D'une erreur, et l'on n'admiroit
Que le porphyre et la forme si belle
Du vase qui la contenoit.
En la laissant dans le même parterre,
On la mit dans un pot de terre.
Elle perdit dans cet instant fatal,
Sa richesse, son piédestal,
Et la pauvre fleur, dégradée,
Depuis ce jour ne fut plus regardée.

Heroes in deed and word, masters of oratory—
    Moral exemplars gone before.
* The great Agesilaos and his like: no more!
    Today it's quite another story:
No more those souls whose mere thought moves the nation—
    Sages and proles—to admiration.
    Alas, today... Today, good sense
    Knows not the slightest recompense:
Futile and useless art, vain innovation,
    Have cast it out, driven it hence
With meaningless inventions. And the cost?
    Spirit, mind, morals... All is lost.
    Nature no longer sets the tone, and thus
    Is virtue vanished. Woe is us!"
Nodded a bush: "The interesting thing about you,
    My angry friend, is that no doubt you
    Look at the world with jaundiced eye.
    And, if I may, I'll tell you why:
Man makes fine paper now, and he can do without you!"

                                                                    VIII

———————

THE COMMON FLOWER AND THE BEAUTIFUL VASE

Placed in a splendid vase, an immortelle
Stood blooming—straight, erect—sad, but most proud
    To watch as an admiring crowd
Of passers-by stopped, gazed... The demoiselle,
    However, erred: her pride was not
Her own; for those fine glances that she got
Were for the vase's precious porphyry
    And comely shape. At length was she
    Placed in a vulgar earthen pot,
Still on the spot where she had been before.
Now, from that fatal moment, gone for good
Her wealth, the pedestal where she had stood:
Poor flower, undone, prized and admired no more.

    * In a footnote (p. 42), the author, citing the first-century Greek historian Diodorus
Siculus as her source, recalls that Agesilaos, king of Sparta, was said to have prized most
highly the gift of papyrus bestowed on him by an Egyptian pharaoh.

                                            Stéphanie-Félicité de Genlis 485

Combien de grands seigneurs, combien de parvenus
Verroient s'évanouir la foule qui, sans cesse,
        Et les environne et les presse,
S'ils perdoient les emplois dont ils sont revêtus!

LE VOYAGEUR, L'ORME ET LE MANCENILIER

        C'est l'ennui, la satiété,
        Qui font aimer la nouveauté.
Ce goût ne fut jamais donné par la Nature;
        Le Lapon dans sa hutte obscure,
        Le Sauvage au fond des forêts,
        Le sage dans sa solitude,
Craignent le changement et ne trouvent d'attraits
        Qu'à suivre la douce habitude.
Mais pour l'homme blasé, l'objet le plus nouveau
        Ne peut manquer d'avoir la préférence.
Il est neuf, inconnu, donc il est le plus beau.
        Ainsi raisonne l'inconstance,
Qui, lasse des vrais biens et cherchant à jouir,
Donne tout au hasard, et change sans choisir.
De ce goût dépravé, dont le pouvoir magique
        A gouverné plus d'un pays,
        Je vais citer un exemple tragique.
        Un voyageur (il étoit de Paris),
Sur le déclin du jour, surpris par un orage,
S'arrêta tout à coup au milieu d'un sentier,
        Et cherchant des yeux un ombrage,
Il vit auprès d'un orme un grand mancenilier;
        Comment ne lui pas rendre hommage?
        Pour lui cet arbre étoit nouveau!
        C'en fut assez pour dédaigner l'ormeau,
Qui cependant portoit un plus épais feuillage.
Sous le mancenilier l'imprudent voyageur,
D'un funeste repos savourant la douceur,

How many *grands seigneurs* are there,
And *nouveaux riches,* whose adulating mass,
Pressing about, would disappear, alas,
Were they to lose the dignities they wear!

X

<hr />

* THE TRAVELER, THE ELM, AND THE MANCHINEEL

Boredom it is, and dour ennui,
That make us turn to novelty.
But never was this taste imbued in us
By Nature, I would warrant. Thus
The Laplander in somber hut,
In forest deep the savage rude,
The wise man in his solitude,
Shun change and fear the unfamiliar; but
The worldly man, blasé to what he knows,
Avoids such things, preferring those
That he has never seen before;
For so he reasons, with fate's fickleness,
That what is tried and true gives pleasure less
Than what is new, which must, perforce, give more.
Let me relate a tragic case of this
Unseemly taste (whose magic is the cause
Whereby many a land is ruled amiss).
A traveler—a Parisian—one day was
Caught in a sudden storm at eventide,
Stopped in his tracks. Looking about, he tried
To find the shelter of some tree,
And there espied, beside an elm,
A stately manchineel. Never had he
Seen such a tree in all of Nature's realm!
Surely it was the one to which he should
Pay his respect—though, clearly, could
The elm protect him better with its many
Branches and leaves. So down he lay

* The manchineel, from the Spanish *manzanilla* (little apple), is a tropical tree of the
Western Hemisphere that exudes a poisonous rubbery sap, and whose bitter, apple-shaped
fruit is equally deadly. The Conquistadors early learned to avoid it.

Exempt d'effroi, de défiance,
S'abandonna sans résistance
Aux charmes d'un sommeil trompeur,
Qui fut le dernier de sa vie:
Une profonde léthargie
En peu d'instans mit un terme à son sort,
Dans les bras de Morphée il rencontra la mort.
L'ormeau n'auroit pas eu cette affreuse influence!
Mais il étoit privé de l'attrait si piquant
D'une nouvelle connoissance.

A nos anciens amis donnons la préférence,
C'est le plus doux parti, comme le plus prudent.

LE SÉNÉ ET LA TUBÉREUSE

Le Séné, d'humeur orgueilleuse,
Demandoit à la Tubéreuse,
Quels étoient ses emplois et son utilité.
—D'emplois, je n'en ai point.—Eh! quoi donc, la beauté
Seroit votre seul avantage?
—Hélas! oui. Mais modestement
Je sais me contenter d'un si mince apanage;
Il n'est pas glorieux, je le sais, cependant,
Se faire aimer et plaire innocemment,
N'est-ce donc rien? Il faut se rendre utile,
Reprit le Séné gravement;
Tout art, tout mérite est stérile,
Sans ce motif rare et touchant,
Qui fut toujours mon seul mobile.
Je me consacre à servir les humains,
Est-il de plus nobles destins!
De la plus cruelle souffrance
Que de fois j'arrêtai le cours!
Et j'offre du moins l'espérance,
Quand je ne puis donner d'autres secours.
Tout cela seroit admirable,

Under the manchineel, and without any
Fear, any qualm, prepared to drift away,
    With sweet abandon, willingly,
Into a sleep that was, alas, to be
His last. For deep the lethargy, the swoon
    That overcame him, and that soon
Ended his days in Morpheus's embrace.
The elm would not have been so deadly. Ah!
    But it had none of the *éclat*
Or the enticement of an unknown face.

Wiser it is, and how much sweeter too,
To give old friends the nod before the new.

XI

---

* THE SENNA AND THE TUBEROSE

    The senna, haughty, with his nose
Poised in the air, asked of the tuberose
What use she was, what useful tasks were hers.
    "Tasks? I have none." "What? Can it be
That beauty is your only quality?"
    "Alas, indeed! But..." she demurs,
"It is a worthy virtue—slight, but quite
Enough for me; not glorious, I know.
But is it not a virtue to bestow
Pleasure and, in all innocence, invite
Love and desire? Must one be useful too?"
"Ah," said the senna, in his darkest tone,
"Merit and art are worthless if they do
    No good at all! Myself, I own
Usefulness—virtue rare and dear—to be
My only reason to exist! I give
    My life so that the ill may live.
    Is there a nobler destiny?
How often have I cured the cruelest pain!
And when I cannot, one at least can gain

---

* As the author's footnote informs us (p. 60 of her text), senna is a medicinal plant. She
might have gone on to indicate that it is native to Africa and Asia, and that it was—and no
doubt still is in some parts of the world—used in infusions as a purgative.

Répliqua l'odorante fleur,
Si moins austère et plus aimable,
Vous aviez l'art, mon cher docteur,
En faisant tant de bien, de paroître agréable.

La Tubéreuse avoit raison:
Vous, auteurs, qui voulez instruire,
Profitez de cette leçon.
Songez bien que pour nous réduire
A préférer les routes du devoir,
Il faut ne laisser qu'entrevoir
Le dessein de nous y conduire.
Nous nous révoltons aisément
Contre un guide sévère, orgueilleux et pédant,
Pour nous bien éclairer, il faudroit nous séduire;
L'homme volage, indépendant,
Craint surtout l'ennui, fuit la gêne;
On ne peut le mener, encor moins l'asservir;
Il faut lui plaire, il veut bien qu'on l'entraîne
Par le doux attrait du plaisir.

———————

L'ENFANT, LE PÉDAGOGUE ET LA FIGUE

Dans une rue, un jeune enfant,
Suivi de près par son pédant,
S'arrête tout à coup, et tressaille de joie.
Une figue à ses pieds!... oh! quelle douce proie!
Une figue bien grosse et bien mûre, l'enfant
S'en saisit précipitamment;
Lors le Mentor, avec sagesse,
Lui tint ce discours éloquent:
Que faites-vous? quelle bassesse!
Quoi! ne vous souvenez-vous plus
Qu'une des plus belles vertus
Est la prudente tempérance,
Et que pour tout être qui pense,
La gourmandise est un vice honteux,
Aussi plat qu'il est odieux?
Quoi! pour vous corriger, vainement je travaille!...

A deal of hope from what I do." "Ah yes,"
Replied the fragrant flower, "and that, most surely,
Would be superb, if..." she went on, demurely,
"If, doctor, your art taught you to be less
Austere, and more well-versed in comeliness;
And if, with all the good you do, you were
        At least a good deal prettier!"

The tuberose was right in what she said.
        You, authors, who would but instruct,
Heed well the lesson. If you would conduct
Your readers in the righteous path, instead
Of showing clearly what you are intending,
        Let them but glimpse it: better thus,
        Because we find too onerous
The guide pedantic, haughty, and unbending.
The teacher must, at first, seduce; man yearns
To be unfettered, learning at his leisure.
        Boredom he fears; constraint he spurns:
To teach him, lead him in the path of pleasure.

                                                    XIV

————————

THE CHILD, THE PEDAGOGUE, AND THE FIG

        A young child, in the street one day,
        Walks with his tutor. On the way
He stops all of a sudden as he spies,
Agog with joy, a fig! Ah, what a prize!
Lying there at his feet, a big, ripe, fat,
        Delicious, juicy fig! At that,
        The child rushes to seize it, when
        His Mentor, wisest among men,
        Plies him with his fine rhetoric:
        "What's this? You little heretic!
        Have you so soon forgotten, then—
As any thinking person will agree!—
That man, of all the virtues that are his,
Loves moderation best; that gluttony,
As vile and odious as a vice can be,
One of the basest and the vilest is!

Après ce beau sermon, le pédant arracha
        A ce pauvre enfant sa trouvaille,
        Et tout assitôt la mangea.
Combien d'instituteurs pareils à celui-la!

    Ce trait falot nous fournit matière ample
    A réfléchir, comme Elien le dit.
    Un très-grand sens se trouve en ce récit;
        Que fait la leçon sans l'exemple?

VERS ENVOYÉS À GEORGETTE, POUR SON LIVRE DE SOUVENIRS

        A ton âge, ma jeune amie,
        Le plus important souvenir
        Qui puisse consoler la vie,
        Est déposé dans l'avenir.
        Ce n'est pas celui du plaisir,
        Des succès et de la richesse,
        Mais c'est celui de la sagesse;
        Il n'est de souvenirs heureux
        Que les souvenirs vertueux.
    O mon enfant, à peine à ton aurore,
Tu peux les préparer, en disposer encore,
    Ils sont à toi, ces souvenirs si doux,
        Ceux-là seuls dépendent de nous:
Puisses-tu les semer sur toute ta carrière,
        Et vers le déclin de tes ans,
        Dans la saison triste et dernière,
        Jouir des fruits de ton printemps!

What? All my teachings, preachings gone for naught?"
Then did he seize the poor child's prize; whereat
    He gulped it down, and that was that.
So much for what such pedagogues have taught!

* This waggish tale that Aelian once narrated
Gives ample food for thought: much sense indeed.
As for the fable, who would ever heed
Wise teaching were it not thus illustrated?

XV

LINES SENT TO GEORGETTE FOR HER MEMORY BOOK

Young friend, in this your tender age,
The most important memory
That might life's bitterness assuage
Lies in the future, yet to be.
Not one of wealth and high degree,
Success, or pleasure; rather, one
Of wisdom: for no other, none,
Will truly happy be unless
It be of good and virtuousness.
Dearest, your day has scarcely dawned; your sun
Barely appears: the power is yours, my child,
To form your memories, sweet, undefiled.
    Choose! For our choice alone decrees
That we are masters of our memories.
Scatter yours on life's pathway, where you may,
So that in your last days, remembering,
You taste the fruits you planted in the spring!

* The source of this apologue is found in the *Varia historia* (14.20) of the Roman rheto-
rician Aelian, i.e., Claudius Aelianus (ca. 170–ca. 235 C.E.), an admirer of Plato, Aristotle,
and Plutarch, who originally wrote his works, including *On the Nature of Animals,* in
Greek. The concluding lines of the English translation will give an idea of his spirit: "When
I read this story in the history of the Sybarites, I broke into laughter. And I recorded it in a
spirit of good will, in order not to begrudge anyone a good laugh" (*An English Translation
of Claudius Aelianus' "Varia Historia,"* ed. and trans. Diane Ostrom Johnson, [Lewiston,
N.Y.: Edwin Mellen Press, 1997], p. 215).

VERS À MADAME SUS. M***

En lui envoyant un petit tableau de mon ouvrage, composé de fleurs naturelles conservées et appliquées sous un cristal

Savoir conserver à jamais
Des fleurs la beauté fugitive,
Et leur éclat et leurs attraits,
C'est du Temps émousser les traits,
C'est briser sa faux destructive.
Je ne me flatte point d'avoir reçu des cieux
Ce rare et brillant avantage;
Ah! ce talent si précieux,
C'est vous qui l'eûtes en partage,
Et ce tabelau n'offre à vos yeux,
Que votre art et que votre image.

VERS SUR UN BOUQUET DE FLEURS PEINT AU MOIS DE JANVIER PAR MADEMOISELLE HELMINA DE KLENCKE

Une main de quinze ans nuança ces couleurs,
Elle eut la nature pour maître;
Et lorsqu'elle créa ces fleurs
(Malgré l'hiver et ses rigueurs),
C'est le printemps qui les fit naître.

ÉPITAPHE DE L'AUTEUR

Faite par elle-même, dans une longue et dangereuse maladie qu'elle eut en 1797

Je fus victime de l'envie
Et de l'affreuse calomnie;
Et cependant sans fiel, sans haine et sans courroux,
J'ai souffert l'injustice et terminé ma vie.
De mes travaux objets si doux,

LINES TO MADAME SUS. M***

Offered to her with a little tableau of my creation, composed of dried flowers preserved under crystal

To know how to preserve, unchanged,
The fleeting beauty of these flowers
In all their splendor, here arranged—
So may we halt Time's passing hours,
Destroy his scythe, blunt dull his powers.
I cannot claim that heaven bestowed on me
   That rare and precious gift; but it
   Granted the art, and generously,
   To you, its gracious favorite:
   Let this tableau an image be
   Of beauty, changeless, exquisite.

LINES ON A BOUQUET OF FLOWERS PAINTED IN JANUARY BY MADEMOISELLE HELMINA DE KLENCKE

When her hand, of but fifteen years, portrayed
   These flowers, with shades and colors rife,
   Nature itself tutored the maid;
But—in cruel winter's chill, dark shade—
Her springtime brought the blooms to life.

THE AUTHOR'S EPITAPH

Written by herself during a long and grave illness that she suffered in 1797

Victim was I of calumny,
   And vicious envy harried me;
Yet, in the end, with neither spite nor gall,
Calmly, I bore my unjust destiny.
   You, children, objects one and all

---

* A footnote in her volume (p. 86) explains that the author's anonymous dedicatee was a lady, then deceased, who even at the age of seventy-six had retained the freshness and beauty of youth.

Vous dont je dépeignis les jeux et l'innocence,
Vous dont j'ose espérer de la reconnoissance,
    Sur cette tombe, enfans, arrêtez-vous;
A vos cœurs ingénus elle doit être chère,
Jetez-y quelques fleurs, et gravez sur la pierre
        Ces mots: *Elle a su, sans effort,*
Aimer et pardonner, et se soumettre au sort.

Of my delight, whose simple innocence
Moved me to write; my only recompense:
    That, passing, you might stop withal
Upon this grave, which I hope you hold dear;
Strew a few flowers; and on my tomb carve here:
    Able was she, and tiring not,
To love, to pardon, and accept her lot.

Marie-Madeleine Joliveau de Segrais (1756–1830)

Although far less consequential a historical and social figure and far less var-
ied and prolific a writer than her contemporary Stéphanie de Genlis (see pp.
476–97), Joliveau de Segrais was, as a poet, much more productive and quite as
distinctive. The *femme de lettres* known affectionately to her intimates as "Adine"
Joliveau—née Marie-Madeleine-Nicole-Alexandrine Gehier—was drawn to the
verse fable not only because of her literary interest in general but also for very
practical reasons.

Born to a well-to-do family on November 10, 1756, in the Champagne town
of Bar-sur-Aube, she married early and had five children. Before long, however,
the ravages suffered by the schools during the Revolution posed a problem for
the latter's education, and she decided to undertake it herself, learning Latin,
Italian, and English in order to do so. Weaned, like so many of her compatriots
before and since, on the fables of La Fontaine, and with a natural gift for verse,
she soon began composing her own as well, as aids in her instruction.[1] Suppos-
edly it was only the encouragement of several other contemporary fabulists that
persuaded her to publish the six books of her *Fables nouvelles en vers, suivies de
quelques poèmes* in 1801, albeit reluctantly. A second edition followed, composed
of 175 fables divided into nine books (1807), and a third (1814), extensively re-
vised, in which a large number were omitted and new ones added. Many of her
fables were also published in the *Almanach des Muses* from 1803 to 1828 and in
other similar popular journals.

Besides the usual disparate *poésies fugitives*, Joliveau de Segrais also published
a supposedly "scabrous" four-canto poem, *Suzanne*, though with the "grace,
decency, and delicacy that only a woman could bring to it,"[2] followed by the
two-canto *Repentir*. But a variety of personal and familial misfortunes—the
premature deaths of her husband and four of her children—prevented a long-
announced fourth and definitive edition of her much-admired fables; an edi-
tion that was to include imitations of the then popular Russian fabulist Ivan
Krylov. At her death, in Paris, on December 27, 1830, she also left unfinished a
projected fifteen-canto poem on the English king Alfred the Great, which would
have been a happily coincidental link with her medieval artistic ancestor, Marie
de France.[3]

Joliveau de Segrais established a substantial reputation for the high moral
tone of her fables. But the reader should not be put off by what sounds like an
overpowering dose of virtue. While maternal concerns and undisguised didacti-
cism, clothed in the La Fontaine form, do dominate her inspiration, a number
of her fables—certainly the most distinctive—mute it in a charmingly epigram-

matic style that owes little or nothing concrete to her predecessor: brief scenes, whose tersely concluding dialogues clearly suggest their moral without explicitly stating it.

In addition to six fables, one of three "Quatrains moraux" (Moral quatrains), and one of three lengthier *contes*, all drawn from the 1814 edition of Joliveau's *Fables nouvelles*, included here in translation are four other fables of hers from the *Almanach des Muses:* "Le cochon, le coq et l'agneau" (1803), "Le lion et le sanglier" (1821), and "Le chien et le berger" and "L'horizon" (1824). As for the ne plus ultra of the epigrammatic fable, "L'aigle et le ver," it does not, curiously, figure in her final edition at all, though it is the most widely known and most frequently quoted example of her art.

NOTES

1. See H. Audiffret's entry in the revised *Biographie universelle, ancienne et moderne* ("Biographie Michaud"), 21: 113–14.

2. Ibid.

3. Enthusiasts of the anecdotal may also find their curiosity piqued by Audiffret's euphemistic account of her demise: "A stomach disorder, occasioned by former abuse of refreshing beverages, caused attacks of paralysis, the last of which ended her life."

LA FAUVETTE ET LA BANDE D'ÉTOURNEAUX

Sur le ton de l'allégorie
Une Fauvette un jour chantait.
Simple et sans nulle afféterie,
Sur les sots et les fous son humeur s'exerçait:
C'est rire de chacun, et pourtant de personne;
La volatile était si bonne
Que sa voix s'égayait sur ses propres défauts.
Son chant déplut à quelques Etourneaux:
—Entendez-vous la pédagogue,
Criaient les plus vains des oiseaux,
Qui nous siffle dans l'apologue?
Croit-elle, avec ses chiens, ses chats et ses oisons,
Nous cacher le dessein d'une amère satire?
De nous a-t-elle droit de rire?
Devons-nous souffrir ses chansons?
Grand débat sur ces questions.
Et pourquoi pas, dit-on, si la nature
Lui départit quelque filet de voix?
Instruire, ou se permettre une sage censure,
Est-ce un mal? C'est un bien, je crois.
Puis, le prend-elle en style académique?
A Philomèle elle céda toujours;

THE WARBLER AND THE FLOCK OF STARLINGS

In allegoric key, one day,
A certain warbler, debonair,
Was warbling forth a simple air
And gently venting her dismal dismay
  On dolts and fools; so numerous, these,
  That with her japes and railleries
She aimed at no one in particular,
So generous in her chirpings and her hummings
That she mocked, too, even her own shortcomings.
†　　Some starlings thought she went too far:
"Do you hear how this would-be teacher,"
The vainest of them cried, "makes sport
Of us? Say what she may, we come up short,
  No matter who or what the creature
  She blisters in her apologues!
Does she think that her goslings, cats, and dogs
Can hide her aim sarcastic? Who allowed her
Thus to berate us? Must we tolerate
  These songs of hers?" Long the debate...
"Why not," said one, "if nature has endowed her
With that thin voice? Is it a sin to teach,
And wisely criticize? Not so! Besides,
Is it in pedant fashion that she chides?
‡　No! Like the nightingale, she does not preach.

---

* This fable serves as the preface to the third edition of Joliveau de Segrais's *Fables nouvelles en vers*. Whether it was likewise included in any of the previous editions I cannot say, not having been able to consult any of them.

† The choice of starlings is significant in that *étourneau* is familiarly used in French to mean "scatter-brain."

‡ "Like the nightingale": in classical mythology, Philomela, after cleverly revealing to her sister Procne, wife of Tereus, king of Thrace, the latter's philanderings with her, was eventually changed by the compassionate gods into a nightingale to end the round of suffering that followed the irate Procne's baroque revenge. (She dismembered her son and served him up to his father for dinner.) To finish the transformation, Procne was turned into a swallow, and Tereus, into a hawk. Philomela's and Procne's metamorphoses are reversed by some authors.

Marie-Madeleine Joliveau de Segrais 501

Laissons la chanter les beaux jours,
Même pardonnons lui quelques traits de critique;
Ou, pour nous en venger, croyez-moi, chantons mieux:
C'est ainsi que devraient faire les envieux.
Dès-lors de la Fauvette on souffrit la musique.

———————

LES DEUX CHARRUES

Le soc d'une charrue, après un long repos,
S'était couvert de rouille. Il voit passer son frère
    Tout radieux, revenant des travaux.
—Forgé des mêmes bras, de semblable matière,
Lui dit-il, je suis terne, et toi, poli, brillant:
Où pris-tu cet éclat, mon frère?—En travaillant.

———————

LE CAVALIER AUX ÉCHECS

Deux enfans, aux échecs, jouaient une partie.
        Il leur manquait un cavalier.
Un pion superflu dans la cavalerie
Fut mis et prit un rang. Les anciens de crier:
—Tu marches notre égal: d'où sors-tu, je te prie?
        Et les enfans de répondre aux jaloux:
Qu'importe s'il nous sert, messieurs, autant que vous?

Let's let her sing her springtime; and, if she
Sees fit to carp a bit, well, let it be.
    Or, if you want revenge, let us
Each trill with fairer voice and greater skill,
As well befits the envious." And thus,
Thenceforth, they let our warbler sing her fill.

Préface

THE TWO PLOUGHSHARES

A ploughshare, long at rest, covered with rust,
    Watches his brother passing by,
Fresh from his labors, polished bright. Nonplussed,
    He asks: "How can it be that I
Am dull, and yet you shine? What is this quirk?
Both, the same metal, forged together... Why?
What gives you that fine lustre, brother?" "Work."

1.3

THE KNIGHT IN THE CHESS SET

Two children playing chess found that their set
Was lacking in a knight, and so they let
A pawn, no longer needed, take his place
    Among the knights, who, in disgrace,
Cry: "Who are you? You think you equal us?"
Reply the children to their jealous fuss:
"What does it matter whence, or how, or who?
He serves our needs, messieurs, as well as you!"

3.5

LA PAILLE ET L'AMBRE

La paille un jour disait: "quel charme ainsi m'attire?
Ne puis-je, ambre puissant, résister à ta loi?
—Tu le peux, mais il faut te tenir loin de moi."

L'ambre est la volupté qu'on craint et qu'on désire.

LE PORC ET LES ABEILLES

      Après dîner, seigneur pourceau
Dormait près d'une ruche: une petite abeille
De son faible aiguillon perce sa tendre peau:
      Lors en fureur l'adolescent s'éveille;
Il s'en prend à la troupe, attaque son palais,
      Et de son grouin le renverse.
Mais sur lui tout-à-coup l'essaim fond et s'exerce,
Le poursuit, et l'accable enfin de mille traits.
Qui cherche à se venger d'une légère offense
S'attire bien souvent plus de mal qu'il ne pense.

L'ASPIC

      Pour le seul plaisir de mal faire,
L'Aspic lançait son dard sur ce qu'il rencontrait;
      L'animal attaqué s'enflait,
Et la mort la plus prompte arrivait d'ordinaire;
Il s'exerça long-temps à cette cruauté.
Se roulant au soleil, par un ciel sans nuage,
Il aperçoit un jour son ombre de côté,

THE STRAW AND THE AMBER

Queried the straw: "What charm is this I yearn for,
O mighty amber? Have I no resistance?"
"You have, but only if you keep your distance!"
The amber is that bliss we fear yet burn for.

8.17

* THE PIG AND THE BEES

Proud piglet, after dinner, lay beside
    A beehive, sleeping, when a bee—
A small one—rather inoffensively
Pricked at the adolescent's tender skin.
    He wakes and, furious, lashes out
Against the lot, snout poking at the hive,
    Knocking it down. Swarm comes alive,
As pig, pursued, gets stung round and about.
He who, in rage, would settle a modest score,
Often gets more than what he bargained for.

9.7

THE ASP

    For nothing but the joy, in fact,
    Of doing ill, the asp would cast
His dart on all he met; the one attacked—
Poor beast—would swell, until death, fell and fast,
Would come dispatch it... Long, in truth, he plied,
†   His ruthless animalicide;
But then, beneath a cloudless sky, one day,
Coiling about under the sun, he caught

---

* This translation is a somewhat revised version of the one in Shapiro, *The Fabulists French*, p. 120.

† Before the professional flaw finders call attention to my outrageous overtranslation, let me acknowledge it, shamelessly, as one of those self-indulgent liberties that even scrupulously faithful translators will occasionally permit themselves to take.

Marie-Madeleine Joliveau de Segrais 505

Croit voir un Serpent plein de rage;
Il s'élance ainsi qu'un démon,
Trop aveuglé par sa furie,
Il mord sa queue, et perd la vie,
Par un effet de son mortel poison.

O calomniateur, songe à cette aventure,
Crains tôt ou tard l'effet de ta morsure.

—————

Il n'est plus aujourd'hui d'hypocrites en France,
Ceux qui jouaient ce rôle ont mis le masque bas;
Peut-on feindre en effet des vertus qu'on n'a pas,
Quand il serait honteux d'en avoir l'apparence?

—————

LE MÉDECIN COMPLAISANT

Soit ennui, tristesse ou vapeurs,
Julia, petite maîtresse,
Mourante, appelle des docteurs:
L'un d'eux vole, arrive, il s'empresse.
—Docteur, j'ai les nerfs agacés,
Des chaleurs! la fièvre peut-être.
Je suis, plus que vous ne pensez,
Malade... c'est... c'est un mal-être...
Au pouls, le docteur à l'instant
Décide qu'il faut un régime,
Mais calmant, mais adoucissant;
Et pardessus tout il supprime
Le café; c'est un vrai poison

Sight of his shadow next to him, and thought
  A vicious snake had crawled his way.
Demon-like, lashing out against his prey,
He bit his tail: his deadly venom filled him,
  And promptly killed him.

Muse on this tale, O cruel calumniator!
Your bite will do you in, sooner or later.

9.17

———————

In France, today, gone is the hypocrite;
Those who once played it have cast off their mask:
Can one feign virtue one has not, I ask,
When it were shame to have the look of it?

"Quatrains moraux"

*

———————

THE OBLIGING DOCTOR

Ill with the vapors, or ennui—
Or some such other malady—
Lying a-bed, young Julia, dying,
Summons her doctors; one comes flying.
"Doctor, my nerves are frayed! I fear
I have the fever! Doubtless I
Am sicker far than I appear!...
Sicker than you might think!... Oh, my!"
He takes her pulse and, then and there,
Declares that she must change her diet:
Naught but the simplest, mildest fare;
Foods that might calm her, keep her quiet...
And, above all, says he, she should
Forgo all coffee; for it is
An utter poison, one that could

* The indicated date of this quatrain, 1792, might explain its pithy revolutionary cynicism.

Dont une belle est la victime.
—M'ôter cette chère boisson!
Y pensez-vous? A votre guise,
Arrangez-vous pour me guérir;
Mais je l'avoue, avec franchise,
Sans mon café, plutôt mourir.
—Allons, allons, je lui fais grace:
Mourir, vous! ce serait pitié:
Prenez-en, mais peu; d'une tasse,
Je permets au plus... la moitié.
—Non, docteur, à mon ordinaire,
J'en veux prendre une jatte entière.
—Il faut donc qu'il soit bien léger,
Alors il ne vous nuira... guère.
—Allez vous encor m'affliger?
Je l'aime très-fort, au contraire.
—Mais... —Mais... —Sans doute qu'il est vieux?
—Très-vieux. —Et... du moka, je pense?
—Du plus parfait, docteur. —Tant mieux!
Continuez, plus de défense;
Avec vous votre médecin
En prendra chez vous dès demain.

—————

LE COCHON, LE COQ ET L'AGNEAU

Que dormir nuit et jour est un sort plein d'appas!
Disait, en soulevant une lourde paupière,
    Au jeune agneau, le cochon gras:
Vautré sur mon fumier, je ne m'informe guère
    Si le soleil tourne ou la terre.
    A notre agneau, le coq, de son côté,
    Recommandait, chantait la vigilance:

Destroy a lovely lady! His
Advice is not well met. "What? But...
Give up the precious drink I love?
Can you be serious?... Ah! Do what
You must to cure me, heavens above!
But I confess, I cannot do
Without that brew; and sooner might
I die than try!" "Now, now... For you,
I give it a reprieve! For quite
A pity were it, *entre nous,*
Were you to die! So, if you must,
Drink it, my dear; but mind you. just
A sip... A little... For example,
Half of a cup is more than ample."
"No, doctor! When I drink, I take
A whole large bowl!" "Then, for your sake,
Best it be weak; for then it will
Not harm you... Not too much, I mean."
"What? Must you mortify me still?
Weak?... Strong!" "But..." "But?..." "At least, not green,
I hope!" "No! Aged, as it should be."
"Aha... And mocha, I suppose?"
"The very tastiest bean that grows!"
"Oh? Then I lift the ban! Feel free...
Drink! And tomorrow, mademoiselle,
Your doctor will come drink as well."

"Contes"

THE HOG, THE COCK, AND THE LAMB

"Ah! What a joy it is, what sheer delight,
To doze the day away and sleep the night!"
Such were the thoughts a fatted hog suggested—
Raising a languid lid—to a young lamb.
  "Sprawled on my dungheap, here I am,
  Content, and quite uninterested
Whether it is the sun that turns, or earth..."
  Meanwhile, a cock, close by, was crowing
  Lustily to the lamb the worth
  Of wakefulness, ever bestowing

Elle entretient, disait-il, la santé
        Et la gaîté.
Sitôt que sur son char l'Aurore aux cieux s'élance,
De Morphée à l'instant secouant les pavots,
Je reprends mes plaisirs qu'assoupit le repos,
        Juges-en par mon alégresse.
L'agneau les écoutait, ouvrant ses deux gros yeux:
        De quel côté trouvait-il la sagesse?
Chacun lui conseillait ce qu'il aimait le mieux.

LE LION ET LE SANGLIER

Sous un ciel dévorant, altérés, hors d'haleine,
        Le lion et le sanglier
        Vers une petite fontaine
        Sont accourus; qui boira le premier?
Il faut voir; grand combat; puis suspension d'armes.
Comme ils se reposaient, s'offrent de noirs corbeaux,
Avides spectateurs, nourris aux champs d'alarmes,
        Et qui de l'un de nos héros
Guettaient la chute: à peine ils déguisaient leur joie.
—Réconcilions-nous, il vaut mieux vivre amis,
Se dirent nos guerriers, que de tomber en proie
        Aux corbeaux, nos vils ennemis.

LE CHIEN ET LE BERGER

        Un chien élevé par des loups,
Vint trouver un berger, et lui dit, d'un ton doux:
        "Sur tes troupeaux mon âme est attendrie,
Tes chiens sont trop peu forts, pas assez vigilans,
Pour triompher des loups, experts en fourberie;
A les apprécier j'ai passé mes beaux ans,
Comme eux, dans plus d'un art, j'acquis de l'exercice;
Eloigne tes mâtins, faibles et paresseux;
Me prendre à ton service, est un bien pour tous deux:

Good health—or so, at least, claimed he—
      And jollity!
"When Dawn drives forth her chariot through the skies,
And shakes Morpheus's poppies from our eyes,
When done my sweet repose, as you can see,
Joyful, I start anew..." Our lamb demurred,
      Intent on every word, wide-eyed;
But who was wiser? How should he decide?
Each one advised only what each preferred.

THE LION AND THE BOAR

Beneath a murderous sky, dying of thirst,
      Panting, a lion and a boar
      Approach a spring, and stand before
      Its waters. Which will be the first
To drink?... Oh, what a sight! Our pair at war!
That is, until, pausing to rest, they spy
A flock of crows, fed on life's battlefield,
      Eagerly watching from on high
To see which hero will be first to yield,
      To fall, to die... Their lustful glee
      Is scarce concealed. "Enough! Let's call
A truce," the two decide; "for, all in all,
      Better to live as friends than be
Food for the crow, our lowly enemy!"

THE HOUND AND THE SHEPHERD

    A hound raised up by wolves approached
A shepherd and, gently, discreetly, broached
    This thought: "My soul is sore distressed
To see your flock. Your dogs are feeble; they
Are far too weak to keep the wolves at bay,
Nor do they pay enough attention lest
Those masters of deceit attack. I spent
My salad years among them, and I know
The secret of their arts! Let your hounds go.
    Employ me, rather, and content

—Qui, moi! te prendre à mon service!
Chasser mes chiens! livrer mes moutons gras!
Un disciple des scélérats,
Ne peut être que leur complice."

L'HORIZON

Un précepteur, sur la géographie,
A son élève un jour donnait leçon;
Comme il se promenait dans la belle saison.
—O mon maître, je t'en supplie,
Satisfais sur un point ma curiosité.
Marchant toujours, toujours vers le même côté;
L'œil ne devrait plus voir ni cercle ni distance.
—Tu te trompes, mon fils, chaque pas qu'on avance,
On se trace à soi-même un nouvel horizon.
Ainsi l'ambitieux, dans ses désirs crédule,
Pense être au but, séduit par son illusion;
L'objet fuit, et, toujours, son horizon recule.

L'AIGLE ET LE VER

L'Aigle disait au Ver, sur un arbre attrapé:
"Pour t'élever si haut, qu'as-tu fait?" "J'ai rampé."

Shall we both be!" "What? Me, employ you?... Me,
Send off my dogs? Entrust my sheep to you?...
Ha! Those who learn from villains cannot do
Other than mimic their iniquity!"

THE HORIZON

A tutor taught his protégé
About geography one day,
Strolling along beneath the springtime skies.
"I beg you, master, for my sake,
Explain how this can be," the youngster cries:
"Though straight we walk, the distance swells in size.
Why? Why?" "You err, my child. Each step we take,
We trace ourselves a new horizon. Thus,
Likewise, do we—ambitious, credulous,
Lulled by illusion—ofttimes think that we
Have reached our goal, when, in reality,
Horizon-like, it merely flees from us."

THE EAGLE AND THE WORM

Eagle spied worm atop a tree and, calling,
* "How did you climb so high?" he asked. "By crawling."

---

* Reprinted from Shapiro, *The Fabulists French.* At the risk of writing a note longer
than the fable itself, I should point out that the verb *ramper* suggests the idea of groveling,
which "crawling" only hints at. Still, inadequacies aside, I can't resist concluding my selec-
tion of Mme Joliveau de Segrais's works with what is probably the shortest bona fide fable
in all the vast literature of that genre.

III

The Nineteenth & Twentieth Centuries

The Nineteenth and Twentieth Centuries

FROM VICTOIRE BABOIS TO ALBERTINE SARRAZIN

Introduction by Catherine Perry

"Hell is Others," Jean-Paul Sartre contended at the close of his 1944 play *Huis-clos.*[1] If this observation, which refers to the weight of outside influences on one's self-perception, is applied to French literature, perhaps at no time would it convey more appropriately the condition of women poets than during the nineteenth century and at least the first half of the twentieth. To be a woman with poetic ambitions meant facing a number of challenges, whose significance for literary history justifies the present anthology. In focusing exclusively on female poets, this anthology confirms the existence of a long-standing problem: readers and even students of French poetry will seldom encounter works by women in anthologies covering this period. To take a prominent example, in 2000, Gallimard published a two-volume anthology of French poetry in its prestigious Pléiade collection. The second volume, representing the eighteenth through the twentieth centuries, counts 1,174 pages of poems, with 768 pages assigned to the past two centuries.[2] For the entire period, only a handful of women poets are included, their works receiving a total of 16 pages: for the nineteenth century, Marceline Desbordes-Valmore; for the twentieth, Anna de Noailles, Marie Noël, Catherine Pozzi, Andrée Chedid, Barbara, Anne-Marie Albiach, Marie-Claire Bancquart, and Esther Tellerman. Among French anthologies published in the past fifty years, the major exception remains Jeanine Moulin's useful 1963 compilation, *Huit siècles de poésie feminine* (Eight Centuries of Feminine Poetry). In 1998, Christine Planté edited a more enlightening, critical anthology, which is nonetheless restricted to the study of nineteenth-century women poets, *Femmes poètes du XIXᵉ siècle.*[3] To date there has been only one comprehensive bilingual anthology of French women's poetry, edited by Domna C. Stanton in 1986, *The Defiant Muse: French Feminist Poems from the Middle Ages to the Present.* Valuable as it is for anglophone readers seeking information on a vaster corpus of works by French women poets than was previously available, Stanton's edition focuses on poetry written with a feminist agenda, excluding poetry of aesthetic significance by women who did not overtly rebel against patriarchal values or conventional notions of gender.[4]

Bearing these facts in mind, we might assume that the talent and intelligence of women poets were so inconsequential that very few among them deserve to be remembered, except within the parameters of historical, nonliterary studies. We might also infer that they were unable to carve out their poems in the "work of bronze" recommended by Théophile Gautier as the recipe for literary immortality in his 1857 Parnassian poem "L'art."[5] Or we might believe that "the genius of [the female] sex is no more durable than her beauty," as Jules Barbey d'Aurevilly asserted in 1862, and that women's verse was so entwined with their youthful, living being that old age and death ravished the vital flow from it as well.[6] It may be, however, that this slight representation of women in anthologies of French poetry is largely the result of cultural forces beyond their control. Brigitte Legars remarks how it was only in the early 1970s that one began to see "an irreversible transformation in the relationship of women to literature. Until then, common opinion considered women artists as exceptions. There was occasional interest in 'images of women' in the history of literary texts, but the practice of women writers was almost completely ignored."[7]

If anything, the care and toil that went into the composition of the poems in the present anthology should impress readers. Despite the efforts of women poets of the past few centuries to find a language that would suitably convey a vision of themselves as artists, with nearly unvarying single-mindedness, critics reduced their work to the articulation of a few themes perceived as belonging to a universal, timeless, and hence ultimately monotonous "feminine." According to these guardians of the French cultural establishment, the imagination of women poets was unable to extend beyond the private realms of family, religion, and lyrical sentimentality, the latter most often imbued with tearful suffering. As the poet and essayist Yves Bonnefoy reminds us, nineteenth-century women poets were "from the beginning judged as capable of imitative or minor works only," and they were "advised and even ordered to have very little ambition."[8] Given the social condition of women during this period, which was marked by a heightened codification of sexual differences, an overview of the French sociopolitical context and the critical reception of female poets become necessary first steps toward an understanding of their poetry in France from the early 1800s until the 1970s, when women acquired the strength and autonomy that enabled them to launch publishing houses of their own and thus, for the first time in history, to achieve greater control over the material and symbolic means of representing themselves.

Following the French Revolution of 1789, a number of women enthusiastically embraced its Enlightenment slogan "Liberté, égalité, fraternité" (Liberty, equality, fraternity), mistakenly believing that the political conversion from regal autocracy to popular democracy signaled a social revolution that would enable them to participate in the affairs of state as full citizens.[9] The zeal of the playwright Olympe de Gouges (1748–1793), who, on the basis of the 1789 "Declaration of the Rights of Man and of the Citizen," drafted a visionary declaration in 1791 arguing for the "natural" and "sacred" constitutional rights of women, earned her the guillotine.[10] When Napoleon Bonaparte rose to power, he established a definitive record of civil law in France, which culminated in the 1804 "Napoleonic Code." With this systematization of the law, inspired by Napoleon's statement that "[w]oman's role is not self-realization but to serve,"[11] even privileged women of the upper classes, who had enjoyed relative freedoms in the eighteenth century, saw themselves officially demoted to the status of minors, wholly dependent on their fathers before they fell under the rule of their husbands.[12] It was now the duty of men to watch over women, perceived as naturally lacking in judgment. The critic Joseph Nnadi remarks that the forty years following the first revolution marked a "black period" for feminism in France.[13] The subsequent revolutions of 1830 and 1848, as well as the Paris Commune in 1871, saw a resurgence of women's claim to be political agents and to enjoy equality under the law. During the Third Republic, the poet and activist Louise Michel was the most vocal in arguing for women's civil liberties. After each revolution, however, women were harshly restored to their "rightful" place as determined by the prevalent ideology. Michel herself was imprisoned and then exiled from France for her socialist and anarchistic positions. In 1848, when French legislators established universal vote for men, Delphine Gay de Girardin commented under her pseudonym Vicomte de Launay in the Parisian daily *La Presse:* "The most abject and idiotic man, if his imbecility has the honor of being masculine, matters more in [the legislators'] eyes than the most noble woman gifted with the best mind."[14] The nineteenth century also gave rise to scientific theories claiming to prove the biological inferiority of women, and hence their intellectual inferiority—steered by the uterus, women were simply unable to think. As evidence of continuing gender discrimination well into the twentieth century, although women in France had had access to public—hence systematic—education since 1850 in schools (where they learned "the classic virtues: chastity, modesty, composure, modest speech and frugality")[15] and since 1919 at universities, they were still barred from voting until 1944; and lest one think that France was more conservative than the other country represented in this anthology, Belgian women were granted the right to vote only in 1948. Until 1965, a Frenchwoman was still expected by law to request permission from her husband if she wanted to practice a profession, "because no one else is better informed of the extent of her intelligence," as the 1868 law stated it.[16] With little to say in the affairs of their country until the middle of the twentieth century, even the most talented and educated women found themselves legally inferior to the least educated among men. At the same time, however, the very principles that had brought about the first French Revolution, in shaking the foundations of Western civilization, initiated an irreversible social change that only the slow evolution of mind-sets would curb for more than a century.

As though answering a need to counter through symbolic means the emergent (perceived) threat of women in public space, this period of increasing literacy witnessed an unparalleled growth of texts and images that tended to enclose women in two conflicting categories, the goddess or the demon, with little room for depictions that would empower them in the world outside of male imagination. According to Bonnefoy, this predisposition has not abated in recent times: "In our society, men no longer exchange women as one would material goods, but they have nonetheless decided among themselves the values, ideas, perceptions, and projects that structure language; without even thinking of it, only they are free subjects for an act of speech in which woman is nothing but an object."[17] The first French Revolution hailed woman as "the divinity of the domestic sanctuary."[18] Romantic poetry in the hands of Alphonse de Lamartine and Victor Hugo (the latter particularly in writing about his drowned daughter Léopoldine) often portrayed ideal figures who, like Beatrice for Dante, died in the flower of youth and served as angelic guides investing the poet with the authority of a divinely inspired and visionary being. In his 1844 philosophical poem "La maison du berger" (The Shepherd's Home), Alfred de Vigny did not hesitate to instruct women about their nature and duties: "Eva, who are you? Do you know your own nature? / Do you know your purpose and your duty?" the poet asks, before revealing her to herself: God has designed woman, exalted though she may be, as the submissive companion of man, "reigning over his life while living under his law."[19] In 1854, raising the imagery of the virginal muse to a sublime level, the Catholic Church made the Immaculate Conception of Mary into an article of faith. Should a woman "fall from grace," she lost her distinction in a man's eyes. To Madame Sabatier, whom he had idealized in his poetry during a long Platonic courtship, even so innovative an artist as Charles Baudelaire wrote the morning after they had become lovers, "a few days ago, you were a divinity. . . . Now you are a woman."[20] In a complete reversal during the second half of the nineteenth century, women were often represented as femmes fatales, threatening men with their destructive sexuality, in imagery such as that of the biblical Salome, which met with lasting success in plays, operas, and paintings.[21] Given this situation, how could the majority of male critics and readers have an impartial view of women writers' intellectual and artistic abilities? Apart from one or two exceptions, such as Rachilde in the later nineteenth century, men ran the critical show; even Rachilde, who explained in a 1928 pamphlet why she was not a "feminist," refused to be identified with women by adopting a masculine persona in her writings, and she frequently unleashed acerbic critiques on women writers.[22] When becoming acquainted with female poets of this period in France, it is therefore crucial not to underestimate the social and cultural pressures that had a determining effect on their literary production. Examples of gendered prejudices toward them will serve to demonstrate this point.

To begin with, the very designation of poet is problematic in French when it comes to women practitioners of the art. The poet is customarily male: *le poëte* (a spelling that lasted throughout the 1800s), or *le poète* (the present-day spelling). Applied to women poets, the versatility of terms hints at the problematic situation of these artists: the masculine *le poète;* the rarer feminine *la poète* (a grammatical mistake, according to Barbey d'Aurevilly);[23] starting in the later nineteenth century, the aesthetically jarring *la poétesse;*[24] less commonly *la femme poète* (the woman poet); sometimes *la dame poète* (the lady poet); and, until the late 1940s, *la muse* (the muse), a term implying that the woman poet's role consists above all in inspiring male artists, and that she is thus poetry incarnate rather than its conscious vehicle.[25] Such is the reminder that the neoclassical poet Ecouchard Le Brun-Pindare inscribed in his 1795 "Ode aux belles qui veulent devenir poètes" (Ode to Beauties Who Would Become Poets): "Vous voulez ressembler aux Muses, / Inspirez, mais n'écrivez pas" (You wish to resemble the Muses, / Inspire, but do not write).[26] The private spaces of childlikeness, charm, sentiment, family, home, and biological reproduction, or "nature," were women's domain, unless they ventured into the outside world to become "courtesans," their only alternative according to the socialist-anarchist philosopher Pierre-Joseph Proudhon (1809–1865).[27] The fields of genius, reflection, politics, culture, and artistic (pro)creation belonged to men. As these terms reflect, women who overstepped their designated boundaries to enter the masculine world of poetry, especially when going against feminine modesty by publishing and selling their work, were abnormalities of sorts, no matter how much encouragement some might have found among relatives, friends, recognized (male) poets, or even the Académie française, which bestowed literary prizes on what it saw as the most deserving women when their poetry tended to affirm normative values. Examples of the reception of women's poetry in the nineteenth century suggest a growing unease among critics about this literary phenomenon, which seemed to imperil the fabric of a society based for the most part on gendered differences, particularly as women became bolder and more vocal in the pursuit of socioeconomic liberties.

Charles Baudelaire, the founder of modernist poetry as well as the precursor of late nineteenth-century symbolist and Decadent poetry, summarized prevalent opinions regarding women in his 1861 essay on Marceline Desbordes-Valmore, the most successful woman poet of the nineteenth century. This essay represents a significant departure from the romantics' "feminine" exaltation of the self and of the natural world toward the cultivation of a more ironic self, along with a rejection of nature. Though praising the poet for her qualities of heart and her spontaneous inspiration, Baudelaire excludes her work from the domain of authentic poetry: "If the clamor, if the natural sigh of an elite soul, if the heart's desperate ambition, if sudden, unthinking talents, if all that is gratuitous and comes from God suffices to make a great poet, then Marceline Valmore is and always will be a great poet."[28] As the reiterated conjunction "if" indicates, Baudelaire cannot conceive of Desbordes-Valmore as artistically creative. Despite the positive way in which he subsequently uses the word "nature" and its derivations in the essay, he locates them in terms that make nature antithetical to high art: "No poet was ever more natural; none was less artificial" (p. 146). "Nature" here is another term for inspiration that arises in unmediated fashion from the emotions, whereas "artifice" is the very definition of poetry as reflective construction. If at times Desbordes-Valmore's poetry contains "unmatched" beauty (p. 146), this is because it apparently depends on a sudden inspiration, without the participation of the intellect, whose task consists in selecting, and reflecting critically upon, the raw materials provided by inspiration. Ironic distance, which differentiates the author from the lyric voice, is a necessary premise in a modern definition of the poet. In contrast to female poets who, like Desbordes-Valmore, employ a "fervent and thoughtless style" (p. 147), those who challenge men on their own territory are altogether excluded from the realm of poetry. Such women produce "monstrous" works because, in trying to imitate intellect, with which they are not endowed, they are going against nature; that is, against female nature, hence against the nature of things. Desbordes-Valmore earns Baudelaire's approbation in great part because she modestly seems to remain in her "natural" place, whereas those other women he castigates can only be impious imitators, perpetrating breaches against male supremacy in the domain of art—"sacrilegious pastiches of the male mind" (p. 146). Thus, women who aspired to write poetry in the latter half of the nineteenth century found themselves caught in a bind: either they remained "natural" and were ultimately cast into irrelevance as poets, or they were perceived to imitate men, as did Louise Ackermann with her philosophical poems, and would be regarded as "blasphemers." It is no accident that Baudelaire used religious terminology in making his point—the gendered distribution of tasks among human beings reflects a hierarchical, immovable order of things, which should not be disturbed for fear of dire consequences, such as social chaos. Of course, this language is also designed to uphold male supremacy in the domain of poetry.

This Baudelairian approach to women's poetry continued throughout the nineteenth century and beyond. Barbey d'Aurevilly, for instance, derided women writers who aspired to learning, depicting them in his 1877 *Bas-bleus* (Bluestockings) as pretentious and pedantic in their attempts to imitate men. He conceded that poets such as Delphine Gay could be gifted with a vocation, but only insofar as they displayed typically feminine qualities: "poetry is so natural to woman, a being wholly made of sentiment, that a woman is not necessarily what one calls a *bluestocking*. . . just because she produces verse. . . . She is only a *lilac* stocking, which is to say that there is still some woman in her, a woman's grace, a light nuance!" Gay's attempts to write beyond these parameters met with ridicule, demonstrating for Barbey "the radical incapacity of any woman poet to sing anything beyond maternity and love."[29] By the turn of the twentieth century, women poets found reason for hope in new philosophies, such as that of Henri Bergson, which gave primacy to intuition over reason, or in the movement labeled "naturism," which advocated a sensory approach to reality as the primary means of knowledge and as the basis of all artistic endeavors. The cult of sensuality, as the philosopher Jean-Roger Charbonnel explained in a 1909 article on the rebirth of "paganism," was then part of an aesthetics grounded in the body, understood as "the original fount of all our joys and even . . . the initial condition of all aesthetics, harmoniously combining experienced sensations rather than lifeless ideas."[30] Poetry by women now daringly promoted the body and female desire. In the words of the critic Jean Larnac, "The romanticism of 1830 had liberated women's hearts, that of 1900 liberated their senses."[31] The number of published collections by women had expanded to such an extent and had met with such success during the Belle Epoque that several critics felt an urgent need to address what their colleague Jean Ernest-Charles disparagingly termed "the proliferation of poetesses."[32] Aware that they would reach an interested audience, critics seized the opportunity, once again, to return women to their place, while instructing readers about the moral danger of yielding to an attraction for bolder forms of lyricism. As Aimée Boutin puts it, "The standardization of the French poetic canon in the early twentieth century by literary scholars, historians and anthologists, such as Gustave Lanson, Henri Potez, and Ferdinand Brunetière, silenced the importance of women poets."[33] In a 1903 article entitled "Le romantisme féminin: Allégorie du sentiment désordonné" (Feminine Romanticism: An Allegory of Disorderly Sentiment),[34] the conservative critic, poet, and politician Charles Maurras cast four major contemporary women poets, Renée Vivien, Gérard d'Houville (Marie de Heredia), Lucie Delarue-Mardrus, and Anna de Noailles, as fundamentally anarchic and immoral. The epigraphs opening his article—"The insurrection of women" (Auguste Comte) and "Little souls, throbbing slaves to sensation" (Maurice Barrès)—give a foretaste of what is to come.[35] These women poets, in Maurras's view, perpetuate the worse traits of romanticism in their pursuit of sensation and emotion over reason (p. 207). Because they are foreigners to some degree, he points out that they are susceptible to "Germanic," "barbarian" influences (pp. 208, 210), the very constituents of romanticism as opposed to the values of classicism, which it is France's destiny to uphold (p. 221). With their literary education marked by male poets such as Hugo and Baudelaire, they do hardly more than imitate their "masters" (p. 225), a view that brings us back to Barbey d'Aurevilly's claim that the "destiny of a woman's brain is to imitate."[36] Finally, according to Maurras, because women poets "are heard" (p. 229), they endanger the "virtues of the feminine heart: resignation, gentleness, patience" (p. 232). Only d'Houville escapes Maurras's unmitigated blame on account of her respect for classical "measure," while Noailles, for instance, displays "a gluttonous little soul" (p. 196) in craving literary fame.

A few years later, in his influential 1909 study *La littérature féminine d'aujourd'hui* (Women's Literature Today), the critic Jules Bertaut judged women writers with like rigor, as unsuspecting emulators of Gustave Flaubert's fictional character Madame Bovary, whose yearning for freedom leads to self-destruction.

Lest readers be tempted to perceive women poets as original, he casts them as uniformly the same. Such conformity to a mold proves, in Bertaut's eyes—made sharper by evolutionary theories—the inferiority of women, "inasmuch as nature's law is to create beings all the more dissimilar as they occupy a higher rung on the organic ladder."[37] For Bertaut, "great poets were men . . . even the most romantic among them knew how to keep a sense of measure and still retained their lucidity in the most daring exaltations." Citing Noailles as an example, he writes that she, "on the other hand, is a woman. As such, she is a being lacking equilibrium, or at least who tends at every moment to lack equilibrium" (p. 144). Prompted by his study, other critics in 1909 subscribed wholeheartedly to Bertaut's argument.[38] With such information in mind, it will seem less odd that Alphonse Séché, who the previous year had compiled a two-volume anthology of French women's poetry, Les muses françaises (The French Muses), also wrote disparagingly about women's abilities for poetry. In his preface, Séché judges that this poetry reflects natural tendencies toward self-absorption, suffering, and principally love, the one goal that all women pursue, even when claiming social equality, as he cheerfully demonstrates: "This is the instinctive basis of their thought, the goal of . . . all their aspirations. . . . Why do they claim civil and political rights? In order to free themselves from the rule of man; why free themselves from man? In order to be his equal; why be his equal? In order to be free, and why be free: in order to love!"[39] Furthermore, according to Séché, a woman poet is unable to step outside herself, she "cannot differentiate much between the woman and the writer. This confusion harms her critical sense—which is already so reduced—and destroys in her the principle of impartiality, which is indispensable to the creator" (p. 12). Twenty years later, Jean Larnac, who embarked on the ambitious project to provide the first comprehensive history of women's writing in France, concurred. Although Larnac's stated goal is to evaluate the facts impartially rather than belabor commonplaces, his study reveals the persistence of this male-based criticism. Noting that "poetesses" were more numerous than women novelists owing to the "facility" of writing poetry—"it takes more time to compose a novel than to write a poem"[40]—just like Séché, he sees women as unable to step outside themselves (p. 241). And, when discussing Desbordes-Valmore, he observes that "no woman writer ever displayed less intelligence . . . did she even know what is meant by an assonance or an alliteration? No invention, no creative imagination; . . . only a complete guilelessness of the heart. . . . Love was the foundation of her life" (pp. 197–201). As for the poetry of contemporary women, it relies on "pure inspiration" and cannot bear the "least possible comparison with the chiseled, reasoned, meticulously pondered and assembled verse of a Paul Valéry" (p. 249).[41] As these examples show in criticism of women's poetry, one finds little discussion of the art of composition, of the writers' formal choices and talents for versification, or of the aesthetic value of their work; rather, the focus remains on themes, or what can be broadly construed as "content" over "form," because this poetry appears as the unmediated expression of an autobiographical self. As Bonnefoy remarks, however, the very notion of a spontaneous, unmediated poetry is an illusion.[42] Even the work of Louise Ackermann, the most philosophical, hence speculative, woman writer of the nineteenth century, is described by Larnac as a "philosophism [sic], . . . at bottom nothing but a sentiment, not a construction of the mind" (p. 203). Thus, poetry by women is defined either by an excess (of sentiment) or a lack (of mastery). Seemingly unable to renew itself, it cannot break away from the label "mediocre" that critics attach to it.

Notwithstanding exceptions, such as the poet Fernand Gregh's refusal in 1909 to distinguish between men and women poets—"There is no feminine poetry. There is poetry. Some men and some women excel in it, others do not"[43]—from most critical studies, a clear distinction emerges between that which is considered aesthetic and that which falls into a category deserving no other designation than "feminine poetry," a spontaneous, careless expression, unfit for literary survival. If this poetry drew the attention of critics, it is obviously because women form half the population and because their poetry appealed to contemporary readers, but also, it seems, because their apparent self-expression offered an opportunity to penetrate female psychology in order to demonstrate its limits and, in so doing, to participate in the preservation of the social status quo. Probably unaware that they were displaying among themselves the same derivative practices which they deplored in women writers, as well as the same inability to distinguish between the person and the poet, critics endeavored to control the reception of female poets by framing and shaping the canon. Largely on account of their efforts, literary history has excluded most talented women writers of the nineteenth and early twentieth centuries, an exclusion that dramatically impoverished French literature until recent years. Conversely, women writers must have failed to realize that they could produce an alternative literary history. Unless they had read Virginia Woolf in the 1920s, it was only in 1949, when Simone de Beauvoir published her carefully researched study, *Le deuxième sexe* (translated as *The Second Sex*), that women began to measure the full scope of their exclusion.

Bearing in mind the actual obstacles that women poets had to overcome, we may now imagine their ambivalence and misgivings when they ventured to publish. How many among them believed in the accuracy of this biological determinism and even reassuringly confirmed it to the very men who criticized their work? Ackermann, for instance, who ceased writing during her marriage out of deference for her husband, admitted to Barbey d'Aurevilly that "woman, compared to man, is an inferior being. She exists above all to carry out physical functions. Her main function is the reproduction of the species. . . . Woman has no more than a limited intelligence. Elevated concepts, abstract notions find no room in her narrow brain."[44] As Alison Finch has shown, women who aspired to literature even wondered "whether they should be writing at all."[45] Because many women took up the pen throughout nineteenth-century France, it is to be expected that a large number would have written in compliance with traditional patterns of gender, thus serving to confirm and perpetuate conventional views. In 1832, Laure Surville de Balzac, sister of the novelist Honoré de Balzac, shared with a friend her distaste for literature produced by women on account of what she perceived to be its poor quality: "Women's writings, raining down in buckets nowadays, make me ashamed of my womanhood. Their mediocrity is enough to disgust us with our sex, and more than ever I find the reputation of woman author undesirable, as it bestows a certificate of incompetence rather than of *eternity!*"[46] Even in the early twentieth century, women poets could reinforce prevailing stereotypes. Lucie Delarue-Mardrus, for instance, asserted that women were more "animal" than men, and she rejected equal rights for women, fearing a decrease in their power of seduction: "If women obtain the right to vote, equality, etc., they will exchange a kingdom for a district," she reportedly said in 1906.[47] Other poets, such as Renée Vivien and Natalie Clifford Barney at the turn of the twentieth century, claimed a "woman-centered" kind of writing, one that foreshadowed the late twentieth-century practice of *écriture féminine* (feminine writing)—which set them apart from men and could help them ignore the pontifications of critics; they were, according to Karla Jay, "committed to the full-scale redemption of the entire weight of Western literature and myth to serve their woman-centered philosophy."[48] Although it is true that for the first time since antiquity, women felt sufficiently confident to write about lesbian love, it may be judicious to consider, as Margaret Homans reminds us, that "[t]he call for a women's language that, on the model of a single-sex society, would be free of masculine fictions about women is . . . an anachronistic dream."[49] Indeed, Vivien did not obscure her debt to Baudelaire as well as to Decadent and symbolist poets; the verses "L'art délicat du vice occupe tes loisirs" (You spend your leisure hours in that discreet, / Delicate art of vice) and "Les deuils suivent tes pas en mornes défilés" (where / You tread, funereal footsteps follow there) (p. 871) are clearly reminiscent of Baudelaire's poems in *Les fleurs du mal* (*The Flowers of Evil*). It may be more accurate to say that, torn between "exaltation and anxiety," as Béatrice Slama characterizes their condition, women poets tended to use a "double discourse," because in order to write they either had to erase or to declare their difference.[50] Although we no longer view art as the direct expression of personal experience, a combination of factors within an individual's experience does lend a hand in fashioning art.[51] How could a woman poet, finding before her virtually little more than disempowering images of the female artist, discover a way of representing herself that diverged from them? In this perspective, Barbara Johnson correctly indicates that a poet like Desbordes-Valmore remained hesitant about the strength of her own poetic voice, often depicting herself "more as an object marked by love for death than as a desiring subject in her own right."[52] Approximately until the mid twentieth century, female poetry in France exhibits, ever so subtly at times, the ambivalences and contradictions of women who endeavored to become artists and to enter the public arena. Unsurprisingly, most successful women poets of the nineteenth and early twentieth centuries benefited from a privileged or liberal upbringing that gave them access to literature at a young age, providing them with the confidence and the necessary tools to develop a literary language.

The foregoing discussion raises the question on how we can profitably read French women poets from the early nineteenth century to the mid twentieth. It is important to note, of course, that their works display a greater diversity of tone, subject matter, technical skill, and formal experimentation than critics would have us believe; even as recently as 1997, the poet Louis Simpson, who compiled and translated a bilingual anthology of modern French poetry, declared that, except for Desbordes-Valmore, "the poetry women wrote in France in the nineteenth century and early decades of the twentieth is unadventurous in form and style. It is sentimental. In short, there is nothing modern about it" (although he immediately recognized that "[t]he women of France must have received very little encouragement to be poets").[53]

It was not only Desbordes-Valmore who unsettled poetic rhythms by inscribing heterometric lines in her poems; later poets, such as Renée Vivien, Cécile Périn, and Cécile Sauvage, applied the same freedom of rhythm to their verse, without altogether sacrificing classical forms. More prominently, the symbolist Marie Kryzinska (1864–1908) was the first French poet to break traditional patterns by writing in free verse as early as 1882;[54] if only for this reason, she should appear in the pantheon of modern French poets. Most often, however, because of their wish to be read and accepted, women poets of this period adopted recognizable forms, apart from the sonnet, which only a few, among whom Louise Colet, Louisa Siefert, and Cécile Périn, endeavored to compose. Formal ruptures, such as enjambments are unusual until the twentieth century, most women deferring to the rule of a complete meaning within each line. Even less frequent are poems that delineate an *ars poetica*, or a theory of poetry, comparable to Gautier's "L'art" (mentioned earlier) or Verlaine's 1874 "Art poétique" (Art of Poetry).[55] Ackermann's poem "Pour des sonnets" (Let those who favor sonnets), which consists in a brief reflection on the art of poetry and on her rejection of the sonnet in favor of "unfettered and unbound" verse (p. 695), is close to being an *ars poetica*. But for the most part, women demonstrated their poetic preferences through their practice.

According to Noailles, a poet's work provides sufficient material from which to derive insights into his or her poetic principles: "of course it is in the works of poets . . . that their preferences are affirmed and that one may find the laws they have accepted and the liberties they have chosen."[56] Rather than produce an *ars poetica*, women had a more urgent concern to establish their legitimacy as poets. Some did so by imitating proven models, the poetry of Lamartine, Hugo, Byron, or Thomas Moore, for instance. Others sought their origins in a nondualistic, mythical past, a gesture that evokes the romantic convention of visionary poet-prophets whose authority emanates from a transcendence of cultural limits. Noailles's 1907 poem "Commencement" (Beginning) harks back to time immemorial: "Je suis comme le temps, ma vie est faite avec / La matière du monde; / Je fus avant l'immense Egypte, avant les Grecs" (I resemble time, my life is made of the world's matter; I was before colossal Egypt, before the Greeks).[57] The following year, Marie Dauguet would also claim to have discovered her origins in a primeval past: "I know now, finally, who I am and whence / I come. Long did I live in rough-skinned tents, / Among my people, Indian shepherds" (p. 765). In romantic fashion, her speaker longs for an age when body, soul, and world were united: "Your soul was still one with the great design, / The universe; still joined with the divine" (p. 767). Also distinct from romanticism, and hence displaying its modernity, the work of both poets exemplifies an evolution among women toward a guilt-free affirmation of the female body and its sensuality; as Dauguet expressed it, "un dieu vit dans la chair" (a god [lives] in the flesh) (p. 769). In harmony with the speaker of Marie Nizet's "L'automne" (Autumn), these poets could have written, "Jouissons sans remords et mourons sans regret" ([Let us take pleasure] and guiltless let us die) (p. 732). As late as 1953, Cécile Périn would perpetuate the quest for an authentic source of inspiration in the depths of unrecorded time: "Cette source cachée en ton âme, . . . / O source, redis-moi d'anciennes ballades / Où je retrouverai l'écho mystérieux / Des profondeurs, le chant d'un invisible dieu" (That fount within your soul, deep hidden . . . / Fount! Sing me once more those / Lays of the deep, let me their echoes glean: / Mysterious singing of a god unseen) (p. 906). Even in 1960, the Belgian poet Liliane Wouters would similarly depict herself: "Je retourne au lieu solitaire / d'où le souffle un jour me tira . . . / Au pays d'avant la naissance / où je peux marcher sans mon corps" (I / am once more for that lone land bound / whence [one day a breath drew me forth] . . . / That land before birth where again / I'll go about without my flesh) (p. 1103).

Without referring specifically to the poets of this cultural period, Elisabeth Bronfen suggests another direction of study: "Because the historically real woman writer cannot articulate herself entirely devoid of cultural fictions of femininity, writing as a woman transpires into an act of *reading cultural texts critically*, so as to enact the implied contradiction."[58] In reading these poets, we can look for traces of ambivalence with respect to their dual and conflicting destiny, such as appear in Amable Tastu's chilling poem, "L'ange gardien" (The Guardian Angel).[59] The speaker, moving from childhood to her deathbed, constantly yearns for and affirms the intellectual and spiritual joys of a life dedicated to poetry, but alternating with her voice is that of her "guardian angel," the voice of religious and social conscience calling her back to woman's self-effacing duties within a domestic framework. By giving an independent voice to the angel and by omitting to evaluate his words, Tastu allows for a double reading. The nineteenth-century critic Charles-Augustin Sainte-Beuve interpreted the poem, which he considered Tastu's masterpiece, as praise of familial life, a "new type of domestic elegy" emanating from a "shy and modest muse."[60] It is possible, however, and more convincing, to read the very opposite; this poem would exemplify the condition of which Virginia Woolf so eloquently wrote in 1929: "who shall measure the heat and violence of the poet's heart when caught and tangled in a woman's body?"[61] With "L'ange gardien," Tastu left a testament for women engaged in the pursuit of art. If these poets intended to convey a message, they had practically no choice but to subvert convention. As Victoire Babois' poem "Remercîment des moutons" implies, contrary to the values of justice and fairness symbolized by the mythical "Astrée," in a world that did not readily welcome them, women poets needed to exercise caution and veil their message: "Tu sais qu'au temps d'Astrée et de ses douces lois, / Des plus faibles moutons on écoutait la voix; . . . / Ah! le faible toujours doit craindre de paraître. / Marchons sans bruit et taisons-nous: / Notre voix nous ferait connaître; / Qu'elle aille jusqu'à toi; mais n'en dis rien aux loups" (In Astrée's time, when earth was young and new, / Even the weakest sheep were listened to; . . . / Ah! But we talk too much! . . . / the weak must shun attention, fear it... / So let us go, but silently, / Else will our voice a traitor be. / May it reach you... But let the wolves not hear it!) (p. 543). Addressed to women, another poem by Babois, "A Mme B***, ma nièce," refers back to the eighteenth century and its Enlightenment philosophy—*lumière* (light) (p. 549)—in order to direct a message to men, who must learn to cultivate and esteem a woman's intellect; if she proves to be a friend worthy of respect, men will have to look beyond a woman's typically feminine traits to value her.

Even poets like Delphine Gay de Girardin, whose "Le bonheur d'être belle" (The Joy of Being Fair) (p. 627) seems at first glance to indulge in narcissism and would thus confirm prejudices about women, may reveal unsuspected depths. Gay wrote political poems as well, forcefully denouncing the government's repression of silk workers in Lyon following their 1834 uprising, for instance, in "Les Ouvriers de Lyon" (The Lyon Workers).[62] The same social solidarity with the oppressed appears in Desbordes-Valmore's poem "A Monsieur A. L."[63]

Female poets would also assist one another, the more experienced and affluent helping the less fortunate; several works recognize this "sorority" of poets or directly address other women, counting on their collaboration. Desbordes-Valmore, for instance, dedicated poems to Elisa Mercœur and Amable Tastu, among others. In a deceptively tearful poem, "Ecrire" (To Write) (p. 703), Marie Pape-Carpantier stresses her decision to write because, the speaker implies, her poetry may serve as consoling therapy for other women in the future.

Here we find poets blazing new trails for the traditional aspiration to immortality, which reaches its goal among women readers rather than in some all-male Academy. It is worth comparing this poem to Gay's "Envoi à M. Villemain," where the speaker hopes, in more traditional fashion, to "[e]ngrave [her] name beside [his] one day" (p. 637), or to Mercœur's "Un an de plus," where the speaker imagines her name reaching those who refused her love, in order to "[a]venge their cruel neglect" (p. 645). Intent on reviving their presence within the minds of future readers, d'Houville and Noailles inscribed seductively feminine speakers who would live on beyond the poet's death. This aspiration to poetic immortality frequently reveals itself to be problematic for women, however. The speaker in an untitled poem by Cécile Sauvage imagines the mark she will leave, but, because her footprint only appears for an instant, the poem betrays her apprehension that it might be judged unworthy of survival (p. 953). Around the same time, Amélie Murat's poem "Ne plus être" (To be no more) radically demystifies any belief in literary survival: "Et qu'il nous ment, l'espoir vaniteux que survive / Notre nom périssable à notre corps défunt" (That it is vain to hope our name might last / Beyond our mortal flesh's life and death) (p. 933). Years later, Lucienne Desnoues's memento mori, "Un crâne" (A Skull), will likewise present immortality as an illusion: of all the songs, poems, gods, and myths that "once dwelt" in this skull, "no trace" is left (p. 1081). With these poems, Murat and Desnoues resolutely situate themselves within the modern currents of poetry. Because artists are always engaged in the act of self-representation to some degree, a fruitful line of inquiry may consist in scrutinizing poetry that depicts the speaker's child as a metaphor for the survival of the poet's work. Louise Colet's sonnet "A ma fille" (For My Daughter) illustrates this tendency: "Tu t'élèves et je m'efface, / Tu brilles et je m'obscurcis, . . . / Ton destin, c'est mon destin même. / Vivre en toi, c'est vivre toujours!" (You grow and I decline; you glow / And I grow dim; . . . / my fate is yours to take. / Living in you, I live always!) (p. 699). In more recent versions of this theme, Desnoues's vigorous "La mise au monde" (The Delivery) (p. 1075) innovatively describes the poem as emerging from a midwife's labor, while Liliane Wouters's "Naissance du poème" (Birth of the Poem) is even more explicit in its account of the poem's birth (p. 1093); with Wouters, the poem is also shown as a "double" of the poet, an almost unrecognizable, "strange-voiced" being, reminiscent of the poet's *voix étrange* (strange voice) in Stéphane Mallarmé's sonnet "Le tombeau d'Edgar Poë" (The Tomb of Edgar Poe).[64]

The poems of Elisa Mercœur, in displaying epigraphs taken from her own poetry, imply how difficult it was for women poets to discover adequate models among their male predecessors and contemporaries. Other poems, which engage in a more or less explicit dialogue with these predecessors and contemporaries, suggest that the female poet may be positioning her work with respect to theirs. Poems directly addressed to Lamartine or Hugo, for instance, while praising these poets, provide insight into the woman poet's self-understanding. Rather than view them hastily as imitations, it is more productive to view them as attempts to rewrite poetry. Annoyed at the comparisons that critics made between her poetry and Lamartine's (in order to demonstrate her work's lack of modernity), in 1907, Noailles published a long, heavily intertextual poem, "Le Vallon de Lamartine" (Lamartine's Vale). At once homage and critique, this poem "corrects" Lamartine in significant ways in order to delineate the gap between his romantic aesthetics and Noailles's post-Nietzschean aesthetics.[65] Conversely, women poets may attempt to create a female line of transmission, more perceptibly through Sappho and the sixteenth-century Louise Labé, or more subtly through their ancestors, even when the latter left no written record of themselves. Such is the tenor of d'Houville's 1905 poem "Stances aux dames créoles" (Stanzas to Creole Women) and of Noailles's 1920 poem "Une Grecque aux yeux allongés" (A Greek Woman with Almond-shaped Eyes); not only do both acknowledge a poetic debt to their female ancestors but they attempt to revive those women by writing in their name.[66] Also noteworthy are poems such as "Demain" (Tomorrow) by Elisa Mercœur (p. 648), "Sans nom" (Nameless) by Marie Pape-Carpantier (p. 702), and "Je voudrais qu'on m'aime" (I Would Be Loved) (p. 754) by Marie Dauguet, in which the speaker appears as a masculine persona, signaling the author's desire to be recognized purely as a poet, beyond gender distinctions. Just as poetry is a unique language, so the writer is a person distinct from the social individual, as Marcel Proust articulated it: "a book is a product of a different *self* from the self we manifest in our habits, in our social life, in our vices."[67] D'Houville's "La prière" (Prayer) portrays the poet as an asexual being, or rather an energy, "pur élan / D'esprit insexué vers ce gouffre de grâce" (spirit free of lust, / Ready to bound in pure and sexless thrust / Up to the vast abyss of grace) (p. 830). Similarly, Louisa Paulin declared to a correspondent in 1941 that her true self was located only in her poetry: "It is in my poems that you must look for me . . . I have no other age, face, or form than those you will find in my poems."[68] As the title of Amélie Murat's posthumous collection indicates so clearly, *Poésie c'est délivrance,* "poetry is a deliverance" from the constraining realities of life. More significantly, it is life itself. Murat's earlier poem, "Chanson d'ennui" (Boredom Song) seems to foreshadow Proust's declaration, in the last volume of his work, that literature is the only life fully lived:[69] "Ah! Vivre un merveilleux poème / Dont les strophes soient des moments!" (Ah! But to live a poem, fine-wrought, / Whose stanzas are the stuff of life!) (p. 924). Reflecting a later twentieth-century emphasis on being as language, Wouters's poem "Ai-je demandé à naître? (Did I ask to be born?) shows the poet as a (masculine) being made up of words only: "Je refuse qu'on me nie / après m'avoir prononcé" (No! Don't you spirit life away / once you pronounced me into it) (p. 1109).

Another fruitful direction of inquiry in reading French women's poetry involves the use of irony, a rhetorical mode that is challenging to detect and that does not seem to appear much, in the period studied here, before the late nineteenth century. Irony may be applied to conventions, which women overturn without specifying their intention. A case in point is Nizet's poem "Le printemps" (Spring), which reverses gender expectations by feminizing the male beloved. The poem's first stanza presents a shy, almost fearful speaker, typical of an accepted perception of woman; the second stanza then surprisingly identifies the beloved with the feminine topos of nature, specifically equating his cheek with the "delicate" form and color of a peach. In more audaciously erotic poems such as "Les mains" (Hands), Nizet continues this process, depicting the form of the beloved's hands as feminine, "à la fois fine et grasse" (plump yet . . . fine of form) (p. 739), characteristics that a woman would not necessarily find attractive in a man. We may compare Nizet's images with those in a prose poem of her contemporary Marguerite Burnat-Provins (1872–1952), exalting the maleness of the beloved: "la force de tes bras, l'ardeur de tes reins puissants" (the strength of your arms, the ardor of your powerful loins).[70] It is also possible to detect an ironic practice in Dauguet's poems, "Tant d'ouate sanguinolente" (Cotton wool streaked with blood) (p. 744) and "Les purins noirs chamarrés d'or" (Spangled with gold, black liquid dung), which implicitly deride the preciosity of Decadent aesthetics by elevating mud and filth to the resplendent dignity of poetic objects: "Les purins noirs, chamarrés d'or, / Cernent de somptueux reflets / La ferme trapue" (Spangled with gold, black liquid dung / [spreads opulent reflections around the squat farm]) (p. 769). Though reminiscent of Baudelaire's poem "Une charogne" (Carrion) and the work of Decadent writers like Joris-Karl Huysmans (1848–1907), the violent contrast between the beautiful and the repulsive suggests not a rejection of nature in favor of the artificial, as with Baudelaire and Huysmans, but rather a recovery of nature, a willingness to accept and to integrate its multiple dimensions, including the lowly realities of peasant life, into the work of art. When the tropes of Decadent literature are thus overturned from their expected goals in order to enhance a new aesthetics, irony functions as a deeply serious device. Half a century later, in 1967, as though to acknowledge a literary debt to Dauguet, the Belgian Anne-Marie Kegels would adopt the same process of transfiguration in her brief poem "La Mare" (The Pond), this time turning mud into a royal pool: "L'eau pauvre, . . . / c'était la mare sans réponse . . . / Mais je ne sais par quelle grâce, / quel amour délivré du mal, / je voyais briller à sa place, / chaque soir, un étang royal" (Foul water, . . . / Such was the pond that answered not . . . / Nor do I know by what pure love, / what grace, I saw, casting its light / and gleaming bright in place thereof, / a royal pool, night after night) (p. 1033). Equally interesting are poems that openly quarrel with critics, such as Pape-Carpantier's "A une jeune Femme" (For a Young Woman), reprimanding those who deride women writers for their "great, sacred faith" in love (p. 707), precisely the kind of love that can redeem nature from its modernist detractors and, as in Kegels's poem "Ils ont dit" (They said) (p. 1039), reassess and welcome objects perceived as evil according to conventional values.

On account of the heterogeneity of their works, women poets of the past two centuries do not fall easily into set categories of the kind literary history tends to favor. Because, unlike male poets, they did not attempt to create "schools" or to write manifestoes—a common practice in male French poetry of the nineteenth and early twentieth centuries—women poets have been deemed unable to mark the literature of their times in any significant way. As Ernest-Charles put it in 1908, "It is undeniable that not one of the poetesses to whom overexcited people ascribe genius has exercised the least influence on today's literature or on the contemporary soul."[71] Such a view is highly contested among present-day critics. Adrianna Palyenko, for instance, states that nineteenth-century "women have indeed marked French literary history with their own poetic imagination."[72] According to Marcel Proust, poetry had even entered a new era at the turn of the twentieth century; his important 1907 essay on the poetry of Noailles compares the poet to the painter Gustave Moreau's rendition of the "Persian Poet," which Proust interprets as a woman, signaling for him a renewal of the genre.[73] It is therefore likely that the more women poets of the past two centuries are studied, the more their effect on other poets will become apparent. If it is at all possible to delineate general trends, one could tentatively say that toward the middle of the twentieth century, women's poetry, which had steadily grown in critical self-reflexiveness, began to align itself more closely with modernist aesthetics, often embracing the Mallarméan ideal of a poetry that reflects the artist's vision rather than her experience, that is deliberately composed of words, rather than sentiments, and that experiments with the magic of a "verbal alchemy." In becoming more "universal," it also freed itself from some of the characteristics that earned the critics' long-standing appraisal of this poetry as exclusively "feminine." Starting in the 1970s, the feminist recovery of women's literature prompted the revival of a more woman-centered poetry. We may now envision a shift in the focus of Sartre's infamous "Others." Women poets are emerging, not from hell, but from purgatory as scholars of both sexes work to reinstate these artists for the education and enjoyment of contemporary readers.

NOTES

1. Jean-Paul Sartre, *"Huis-clos": suivi de "Les mouches"* (Paris: Gallimard, 1947). All translations are my own, unless otherwise noted and except for quotations of poems translated by Norman Shapiro.

2. *Anthologie de la poésie française, XVIIIe siècle, XIXe siècle, XXe siècle*, ed. Martine Bercot, Michel Collot, and Catriona Seth, Bibliothèque de la Pléiade (Paris: Gallimard, 2000).

3. Christine Planté and her team of researchers counted seventy major women poets

for the nineteenth century, although they could only discuss nineteen in their anthology, *Femmes poètes du XIXe siècle* (Lyon: Presses universitaires de Lyon, 1998).

4. *The Defiant Muse: French Feminist Poems from the Middle Ages to the Present. A Bilingual Anthology*, ed. Domna C. Stanton (New York: Feminist Press, 1986). "People who don't enjoy reading poems of undiluted anger, bitterness, misery, frustration, defiance, written hollering, heart-burning depression, teeth-gnashing and snarling rage at men, may find (this volume) disturbing. . . . Long, droning, flatly-translated poems make up the first two-thirds of the French volume. . . . Because this is the most comprehensive anthology of feminist poetry to date, it will prove invaluable to women's studies programs. Only someone as ideologically intent as the editors will find it consistently engrossing," Diane Ackerman says of Stanton's anthology (*New York Times Book Review*, May 3, 1987, p. 38). Besides the literary value of its translations, the present anthology shows that poetry by female authors can be critical of accepted notions of women or the feminine in ways that may be more interesting than plain defiance.

5. "Les dieux eux-mêmes meurent, / Mais les vers souverains / Demeurent / Plus forts que les airains" (Even the gods die, / But sovereign verse / Endures / Stronger than bronzes) (Gautier, "L'art," vv. 49–52, in *Anthologie de la poésie française*, ed. Bercot et al., p. 597).

6. Jules Barbey d'Aurevilly, "Mme de Girardin: Œuvres complètes—Les poésies," *Le Pays*, March 29, 1862; online, *J. Barbey d'Aurevilly*, ed. David Cocksey, Université de Toulouse–Le Mirail, "Lettres, Langages et Arts," August 8, 2005, www.univ-tlse2.fr/lla/barbey/oc/oh3/oh3_17.htm (accessed May 20, 2007).

7. Brigitte Legars, "Le Féminisme des années 1970 dans l'édition et la littérature," *Encyclopædia Universalis*, electronic version 10 (Paris, 2005).

8. Yves Bonnefoy, "Marceline Desbordes-Valmore," preface to Marceline Desbordes-Valmore, *Poésies* (Paris: Gallimard, 1983), pp. 9–10.

9. See Germaine Brée, *Women Writers in France: Variations on a Theme* (New Brunswick, N.J.: Rutgers University Press, 1973), p. 40.

10. See Olympe de Gouges, *Ecrits politiques, 1788–1791*, ed. Olivier Blanc (Paris: Côté-femmes, 1993).

11. Napoleon, cited in Brée, *Women Writers in France*, p. 42.

12. For a discussion of these points, see *Histoire des femmes en Occident*, vol. 4, *Le XIXe siècle*, ed. Geneviève Fraisse and Michelle Perrot (Paris: Plon, 1991).

13. Joseph Nnadi, "Les femmes poètes françaises entre deux révolutions, 1789–1830," *LCMND e-Journal* 2003, 3 (September 5, 2005), http://umanitoba.ca/outreach/linguistic_circle/e_journal/v2003_3.html.

14. Delphine Gay de Girardin, cited in *Dictionnaire littéraire des femmes de langue française: De Marie de France à Marie Ndiaye*, ed. Christiane P. Makward and Madeleine Cottenet-Hage (Paris: Karthala, 1996), p. 279.

15. "Education and Gender Models in Europe," in *Women in the History of Europe*, ed. Pilar Ballarín, Margarita M. Birriel, et al. August 15, 2005, www.helsinki.fi/science/xantippa/wee/weetext/wee213.html (accessed May 19, 2007).

16. Cited in Nicole Arnaud-Duc, "Les contradictions du droit," in *Histoire des femmes en Occident*, vol. 4, *Le XIXe siècle*, p. 109.

17. Bonnefoy, "Marceline Desbordes-Valmore," p. 10.

18. Cited in Stéphane Michaud, "Idolâtries: Représentations artistiques et littéraires," in *Histoire des femmes en Occident*, vol. 4, *Le XIXe siècle*, p. 125.

19. Alfred de Vigny, "La maison du berger," *Les destinées*, in *Œuvres poétiques* (Paris: Garnier-Flammarion, 1978), p. 202.

20. Baudelaire, *Correspondance*, ed. Claude Pichois and Jean Ziegler (Paris: Gallimard, 1973), 1: 425 (August 31, 1857).

21. For more discussion on this topic, see Béatrice Slama, "Où vont les sexes? Figures romanesque et fantasmes 'fin de siècle,'" *Europe: Revue littéraire mensuelle* 69 (December 1991): 27–37. See also Bram Dijkstra, *Idols of Perversity: Fantasies of Feminine Evil in Fin-de-Siècle Culture* (New York: Oxford University Press, 1986).

22. Rachilde is the pseudonym of Marguerite Eymery (1860–1953), author of several "Decadent" novels, among which the scandalous 1884 *Monsieur Vénus*. After marrying Alfred Valette, co-founder in 1890 of the influential literary and critical journal *Le Mercure de France*, soon to become a publishing house, she contributed regular "chronicles" to it, in which she never shied from criticizing and ridiculing the work of other women writers, such as the poet Anna de Noailles, or from assisting those rare women writers of whom she approved, such as the novelist Colette. See *Pourquoi je ne suis pas féministe* (Why I Am Not a Feminist) (Paris: Editions de France, 1928).

23. "UNE poète" (a feminine poet), "a thing so rare that, in order to say it in the feminine, one must make a grammatical mistake!" (Barbey d'Aurevilly, "Mme de Girardin").

24. *Poétesse* can be read like "mistress" with respect to "master." See also Aimée Boutin, "Inventing the 'Poétesse': New Approaches to French Women Romantic Poets," *Romanticism on the Net, nos.* 29–30 (February–May 2003), "The Transatlantic Poetess," www.erudit.org/revue/ron/2003/v/n29/007725ar.html (accessed May 19, 2007).

25. In 1948, the critic Yves-Gérard Le Dantec compiled an anthology entitled *La Guirlande des muses françaises de Marceline Valmore à Marie Noël* (Paris: Emile-Paul).

26. Cited in *Femmes poètes du XIXe siècle: Une anthologie*, ed. Planté, xi. In a distich entitled "Sur une dame poète" (On a Lady Poet), Le Brun writes: "Chloé belle et Poète, a deux petits travers: / Elle fait son Visage, et ne fait pas ses Vers" (Chloe, beautiful and Poet, has two little flaws: / She makes up her Face and does not make her Verse) (in *Anthologie de la poésie française*, ed. Bercot et al., p. 177). Chloé in this distich serves as an allusion to the poet Fanny de Beauharnais, who responded with her own poem "Aux hommes" (To Men), reproduced in the present anthology.

27. Pierre-Joseph Proudhon cited in *The Red Virgin: Memoirs of Louise Michel* (1888), ed. and trans. Bullitt Lowry and Elizabeth Ellington Gunter (Tuscaloosa: University of Alabama Press, 1981), p. 142.

28. Baudelaire, "Marceline Desbordes-Valmore," p. 146. Page references to subsequent quotations are given in the body of this introduction.

29. Jules Barbey d'Aurevilly, *XIXe siècle: Les Œuvres et les hommes*, vol. 5: *Les Basbleus* (Paris: Palmé, 1878), Gallica http://gallica.bnf.fr/ark:/12148/bpt6k204451t (accessed August 13, 2007). In 1873, however, Barbey had praised the philosophical poetry of Louise Ackermann for its "magnificent blasphemies" ("Madame Ackermann," p. 158). He nonetheless removed from this poetry any force that it could have, characterizing it as "sterile," for it only "curses" rather than "seduces" (p. 163). Because this poetry is so "unfeminine," the poet, according to Barbey, "has consummated the suicide of her sex" (p. 166) and is no longer a woman but a "monster" (p. 165).

30. J[ean Ferval]-Roger Charbonnel, "La Renaissance du paganisme," *Akadémos* 1 (January 1909): 32.

31. Jean Larnac, *Histoire de la littérature féminine en France* (Paris: Editions Kra, 1929), p. 234.

32. Ernest-Charles, article in *La Grande Revue*, n.d., cited in Alphonse Séché, *Les Muses françaises: Anthologie des femmes-poètes (1200 à 1891)* (Paris: Louis-Michaud, 1908–9), 2: 359. In an article for *La Revue bleue* (October 3, 1903), however, Ernest-Charles professed his admiration for the poetry of Renée Vivien, whom he later befriended. In 1908, Jean de Bonnefon counted 738 women writers in France, a number that represents approximately 20 percent of all French writers at that time (*La corbeille des roses, ou, Les dames de lettres: Essais* [Paris: Bouville, 1909], cited in Larnac, *Histoire*, p. 223).

33. Boutin, "Inventing the 'Poétesse.'"

34. Charles Maurras, "Le Romantisme féminin: Allégorie du sentiment désordonné," *Minerva*, May 1, 1903, in id., *L'Avenir de l'intelligence* (1905; reprint, Paris: Flammarion, 1972), pp. 145–234. Page references to subsequent quotations are given in the body of this introduction.

35. The philosopher Auguste Comte (1798–1857) was the founder of positivism, or positive philosophy, in opposition to theological and metaphysical philosophy. Maurice Barrès (1862–1923) was a renowned novelist, essayist, and nationalist politician.

36. Barbey d'Aurevilly, "Mme de Girardin."

37. Jules Bertaut, *La littérature féminine d'aujourd'hui* (Paris: Librairie des Annales politiques et littéraires, 1909), pp. 16–17. Page references to subsequent quotations are given in the body of this introduction.

38. Pierre Lasserre, "La littérature féminine," *L'Action française: Organe du nationalisme intégral*, February 9, 1909; André du Fresnois, "Réflexions sur la littérature féminine," *Akademos* 10 (October 15, 1909): 503–13.

39. Séché, *Les muses françaises*, 1: 10–11. Page references to subsequent quotations are given in the body of this introduction.

40. Larnac, *Histoire*, p. 201. Page references to subsequent quotations are given in the body of this introduction.

41. The poet and essayist Paul Valéry (1871–1945) is well known for his rigorous work on language.

42. "Deprived of an intimate relationship with being through the interposition of words, those [poets] who rebel against language will imagine that women, not ensnared

as they are by the trap of language, benefit from the immediacy that they long for" (Bonnefoy, "Marceline Desbordes-Valmore," p. 11).

43. Fernand Gregh, cited in Séché, *Les muses françaises*, 2: 360.

44. Louise Ackermann, cited in Larnac, *Histoire*, p. 203. I have not been able to trace the original letter by Ackermann, which she must have drafted shortly after reading Barbey's 1873 article on her *Poésies philosophiques*, first published in 1871. According to Adrianna Paliyenko (personal e-mail), Ackermann was familiar with Schopenhauer's 1851 essay "On Women," which she paraphrases in her letter to Barbey (Arthur Schopenhauer, "On Women," in *Parerga and Paralipomena. Schopenhauer: Selections*, ed. De Witt H. Parker [New York: Charles Scribner's Sons, 1928], pp. 434–47).

45. Finch, *Women's Writing in Nineteenth-Century France*, p. 226.

46. Balzac, letter dated May 23, 1832. Cited in Christine Planté, *La petite sœur de Balzac: Essai sur la femme auteur* (Paris: Seuil, 1989), p. 10.

47. Delarue-Mardrus, cited in Hélène Plat, *Lucie Delarue-Mardrus: Une femme des années folles* (Paris: Grasset, 1994), p. 128. In the daily *Le Matin*, Delarue-Mardrus wrote an article entitled "A women poet declares that woman is nothing but a divine animal" (cited in Plat, p. 129).

48. Karla Jay, *The Amazon and the Page: Natalie Clifford Barney and Renée Vivien* (Bloomington: Indiana University Press, 1988), p. xiv.

49. Margaret Homans, *Women Writers and Poetic Identity: Dorothy Wordsworth, Emily Brontë, and Emily Dickinson* (Princeton, N.J.: Princeton University Press, 1980), p. 217.

50. Béatrice Slama, "De la 'littérature féminine' à 'l'écrire femme'": Différence et institution," *Littérature* 44 (December 1981): 56, 51.

51. See Linda Nochlin, "Why Have There Been no Great Women Artists?" in *Art and Sexual Politics: Women's Liberation, Women Artists, and Art History*, ed. Thomas B. Hess and Elizabeth C. Baker (New York: Macmillan [1971], 1973), 5.

52. Barbara Johnson, "The Lady in the Lake," in *A New History of French Literature*, ed. Denis Hollier (Cambridge, Mass.: Harvard University Press, 1989), p. 630.

53. *Modern Poets of France: A Bilingual Anthology*, ed. and trans. Louis Simpson (Brownsville, Ore.: Story Line Press, 1997), p. xx.

54. See Marie Krysinska's poem "Symphonie en gris," *Le Chat noir*, November 4, 1882, reprinted in *Femmes poètes*, ed. Planté, 157; also at http://poesie.webnet.fr/poemes/Pologne/krysinska/2.html (accessed May 20, 2007).

55. Verlaine, "Art poétique," in *Anthologie de la poésie française*, ed. Bercot et al., 743–44, also at www.poetes.com/verlaine/art.htm (accessed May 20, 2007).

56. Anna de Noailles, in *Le Figaro*, May 21, 1925.

57. Anna de Noailles, *Les éblouissements* (Paris, Calmann-Levy, 1907), p. 56.

58. Elisabeth Bronfen, *Over Her Dead Body: Death, Femininity and the Aesthetic* (New York: Routledge, 1992), p. 404; emphasis added.

59. Amable Tastu, "L'ange gardien," in *Femmes poètes*, ed. Planté, 65–68; also at www.biblisem.net/meditat/tastulag.htm (accessed June 7, 2007).

60. Charles-Augustin Sainte-Beuve, "Madame Tastu" (1835), in id., *Portraits contem-*

porains (Paris: Didier, 1855), 1: 381–96; also at http://gallica.bnf.fr/ark:/12148/bpt6k35426k (accessed May 20, 2007), p. 386.

61. Virginia Woolf, *A Room of One's Own* (1929; reprint, New York: Harcourt Brace Jovanovich, 1981), p. 48.

62. Delphine Gay de Girardin, "Les ouvriers de Lyon," in *Poésies complètes* (Paris: Librairie nouvelle, 1856), pp. 210–12. http://gallica.bnf.fr/ark:/12148/bpt6k202284t.

63. Marceline Desbordes-Valmore, "A Monsieur A. L.," in *Femmes poètes,* ed. Planté, pp. 48–50; also at www.poetes.com/aut_rom/d_monsieur.htm (accessed May 20, 2007).

64. Mallarmé, "Le tombeau d'Edgar Poë," in *Œuvres complètes,* Bibliothèque de La Pléiade (Paris: Gallimard, 1998), p. 38. In Wouters's poem "Instant qui dors" (Instant, who sleep), the lines "l'éternité qui te prend / tel qu'en toi-même te rend" (eternity that holds you, yet / would give you back yourself) clearly display their affiliation with Mallarmé's sonnet.

65. Noailles, "Le Vallon de Lamartine," in id., *Les éblouissements,* p. 219–24. For a fuller discussion of this poem, see Catherine Perry, *Persephone Unbound: Dionysian Aesthetics in the Works of Anna de Noailles* (Lewisburg, Pa.: Bucknell University Press, 2003), pp. 181–92.

66. Gérard d'Houville (Marie de Heredia), "Stances aux Dames créoles," in *Femmes poètes, ed.* Planté, pp. 196–97; also at www.florilege.free.fr/florilege/houville/stancesa .htm (accessed May 20, 2007). Anna de Noailles, "Une Grecque aux yeux allongés," in *Les forces éternelles* (Paris: Fayard, 1920), pp. 199–202.

67. Marcel Proust, *By Way of Sainte-Beuve,* trans. Sylvia Townsend Warner (London: Chatto & Windus, 1958), p. 76. See also *Contre Sainte-Beuve* (Paris: Gallimard, Folio, 1997), p. 127. This essay, written in 1909, was not published during Proust's lifetime.

68. Cited in Stephen Steele, "Le 'Cruel Silence' autour de Louisa Paulin, poète provenço-français," *Romance Notes* 37, 2 (Winter 1997): 194. This letter was first cited by Gui Sengès, *Una vida, una òbra, Loïsa Paulin* (Seccion de Tarn: L'Institut d'Estudis Occitans, 1994), n.p. given in Steele.

69. "La vraie vie, la vie enfin découverte et éclaircie, la seule vie par conséquent pleinement vécue, c'est la littérature." Marcel Proust, *A la recherche du temps perdu,* ed. Yves Tadié, Bibliothèque de la Pléiade, vol. 4, *Le Temps retrouvé* (Paris: Gallimard, 1989), p. 474.

70. Marguerite Burnat-Provins, *Le livre pour toi* (Paris: Editions Sansot, 1908), cited in Jeanine Moulin, *La poésie féminine: Epoque moderne* (Paris: Editions Seghers, 1963), p. 46.

71. Ernest-Charles, *La Grande Revue,* n.d., cited in Séché, *Les muses françaises,* p. 359.

72. Adrianna M. Paliyenko, "(Re)Placing Women in French Poetic History: The Romantic Legacy," *Symposium* 53, 4 (Winter 2000): 262.

73. Marcel Proust, "*Les éblouissements* par la comtesse de Noailles," *Le Figaro, Supplément littéraire,* June 15, 1907, reprinted in id., *Essais et articles,* ed. Pierre Clarac and Yves Sandre (1971; Paris: Gallimard, 1994), pp. 230–31. For further details on this subject, see Catherine Perry, "Flagorneur ou ébloui? Proust lecteur d'Anna de Noailles," *Bulletin Marcel Proust* 49 (1999): 37–53.

Victoire Babois (1760–1839)

If [Marguerite-]Victoire Babois spent her long literary life writing elegy after elegy, it is perhaps because, delicate in health and unlucky in love, both conjugal and maternal, her existence was not a very happy one. Daughter of a middle-class Versailles merchant family, she saw her marriage in 1780 end in separation eight years later, and, in 1792, she suffered the sudden death of her only child.

It was natural that this poet, many of whose very personal lyrics signal her as a forerunner of the romantics, should express her grief in sentiments that mark a break, from time to time, with the rather more artificial, traditional salon verse of her eighteenth-century predecessors. Commenting on her elegiac mode, the chronicler Alfred Marquiset, typically unsympathetic, would note that she "elegized" nonstop for some forty years, and he went on to remark sarcastically on her longevity: "Obviously, the elegy is a preservative."[1] Actually, many of the elegies one finds among Babois's works are *élégies* in name only—poems on a variety of subjects personal, anecdotal, topical, and often somewhat unexpected: vaccination, the theft of national art treasures, even the return of her pet dog... If nothing else, this inaccurate designation proves at least the desire to assume, in her poetry, a tragic stance before her readers.

A collection of *Elégies* in 1805 was followed by her *Elégies et poésies diverses* in 1810, and an expanded, two-volume edition in 1828, including a large number of letters—several to the neoclassical poet and Shakespeare translator Jean-François Ducis, and three dozen from him to her. It is from the last-named edition that the poems here translated are taken; works inspired by and dedicated to various friends and family members, pathetic in tone but with occasional glints of good humor, and always marked by an air of unforced and unfailing sincerity.[2]

NOTES

1. See Alfred Marquiset, *Les Bas-bleus du premier Empire*, pp. 161–76.

2. For biographical data, in addition to Marquisat's less-than-objective appreciation, see also Alexandrina E. M. Baale-Uittenbosch, *Les poétesses dolentes du romantisme*, pp. 72–73, 162–68, as well as a summary entry in the *Bloomsbury Guide to Women's Literature*, p. 310.

"Je hais l'amour," disait tout en colère
L'aimable Aglaure au jeune et beau Lisis,
Qu'elle avait vu, sous la coudrette assis,
Prendre en riant deux baisers à Glicère.
"Oui, je le hais," répétait la bergère.
"L'ingrat, hélas! lorsque dans ma candeur
Autant que moi je le croyais sincère,
Il ne voulait que déchirer mon cœur;
Mais à ce cœur il ne doit plus prétendre:
C'est un méchant, il faut l'abandonner."
"Non," dit Lisis d'un air soumis et tendre,
"C'est un enfant, il faut lui pardonner."

"Oh! I hate love!" proclaims the glowering, fair
Aglaure, as she espies the laughing Lisis,
Handsome young swain, stealing a pair of kisses—
† Sitting there, in the bower—from sweet Glicère.
"I hate love!" cries the shepherdess again;
"For, while I thought, in my simplicity,
That he, the blackguard, was sincere, like me,
He sought naught but to break my heart in twain!
Well, no more his, this heart, the foul offender!
Leave him I must! Be I no more beguiled!"
Lisis, all sighs, replies—so mild, so tender:
"You must forgive him... he is but a child."

---

* In his preface to the 1828 third edition of the poet's *Elégies et poesies diverses* (1: ix–x),
the publisher, A. Nepveu, acknowledges the curious labeling of this and several other po-
ems as *élégies*, with the defense that, having achieved her first notable success with her
Elégies maternelles, inspired by the death of her five-year-old daughter, she continued to
consider all those works marked by "deep and tender sentiments" under the same rubric.
It is hard, though, to see how the present rather traditional—if charming—little pastoral
ditty fits that description.

  † I allow myself the liberty of adding the adjective to the name "Glicère" for perhaps a
less than an obvious reason: namely, its Greek origin: *glykeros* (sweet).

Victoire Babois 541

REMERCÎMENT DES MOUTONS

A M. Voisin, médecin, qui venait de faire l'expérience
de l'inoculation du claveau

Tu sais qu'au temps d'Astrée et de ses douces lois,
Des plus faibles moutons on écoutait la voix;
Mais les loups dévorants, puis la peste et la guerre,
    Puis les méchants troublant la terre,
    Sur la crainte ont fondé leurs droits,
Et force fut, hélas! aux moutons de se taire.
    Peste, homme ou loup, c'est un pour nous.
    Toujours nous tombons sans défense;
    Car nous n'opposons à leurs coups
    Que la douceur et l'innocence.
Tristes, nus, dépouillés, nous bravons les hivers,
Heureux de n'avoir pu sous le joug le plus rude,
    Malgré l'exemple des pervers,
    Apprendre d'eux l'ingratitude.
    Mais hélas! si dans l'univers,
D'un art conservateur éprouvant la puissance,
A l'homme nous devons de la reconnaissance,
    C'est par toi, par toi seul encor,
Par toi, qui veux en vain nous rendre l'âge d'or.
Ah! d'un fléau, du moins, ta main savante et sûre
Suivit le cours affreux, trouva la source impure,
Et dans son poison même éteignit ses poisons:
On ne perd pas son temps en sauvant des moutons.

THE SHEEP GIVE THANKS

* *For Monsieur Voisin, doctor, who had just experimented with*
inoculation against the sheep-pox

† In Astrée's time, when earth was young and new,
Even the weakest sheep were listened to;
But soon fierce wolves appeared, and plagues, and war.
    Then evil man... And peace no more!
    Fear was the rule, and terror grew
Wherever he became the conqueror.
      We sheep, alas, are stilled! But man,
      Or plague, or wolves... What difference?
      Our sole defense, do what we can,
      Is tenderness and innocence.
Stripped bare, we brave the winters desperately,
Happy, indeed, that, though his yoke we bear,
    His dastardly perversity
    Has not taught us, in our despair,
    To share his thanklessness! For he,
In all the universe, no less it is,
Who, with that art and saving grace of his—
    Or, rather, *yours*... Yours, gentle sage!—
Would fain return us to life's golden age.
Yes, of one deadly scourge, at least, your hand,
Strong in the science at its sure command,
Retraced the course back to its poisonous,
Foul, and death-dealing source, and succored us

---

* The dedicatee, whose name crops up several times in the poet's works, was one Fran-
çois Voisin, a medical doctor whose experiments with vaccination against sheep-pox were
roughly contemporaneous with the discoveries of Edward Jenner. His findings were pub-
lished under the title *Rapport d'expériences sur la vaccination des bêtes à laine, et sur le claveau*
(Versailles, 1805). Voisin was also physician to the prominent tragic playwright Jean-François
Ducis, translator of Shakespeare into French and honorary "uncle" to Babois, with whom he
had a lengthy correspondence. See *Elégies et poésies diverses*, 3d ed., 2: 173–267.

† During the Golden Age, Astraea, daughter of Zeus and Themis, was responsible for
spreading sentiments of justice and equity to mankind, eventually being subsumed into
the constellation Virgo. Her name, in French, was given to the heroine of Honoré d'Urfé's
voluminous pastoral novel *Astrée* (1607–1627), which had a major influence on the gal-
lantry and preciosity of its own era and beyond. The poet's allusion here could well be to
either or both.

Quand les zéphirs viendront chasser l'âpre froidure
Tu nous verras plus gais, plus forts et plus nombreux
     Plus beaux, surtout moins malheureux,
Bondir dans les vallons sur la fraîche pâture.
Délivrés par tes soins d'un venin dangereux,
Au sein de la nature, à nos besoins propice,
     Nous laisserons couler les jours
     Qu'à nos destins, qu'à nos amours,
     Accorde l'humaine avarice,
Et nos riches toisons grossiront son trésor.
Mais nous nous oublions; moutons sont sans malice,
Et trop imprudemment moutons parlent encor.
Ah! le faible toujours doit craindre de paraître.
     Marchons sans bruit et taisons-nous:
     Notre voix nous ferait connaître;
Qu'elle aille jusqu'à toi; mais n'en dis rien aux loups.

À ***

Toi qui t'es proclamé notre libérateur,
Laisse tomber le masque et montre l'oppresseur.
Quand tu traînes l'Europe à tes lois asservie,
C'est pour sacrifier l'Europe à ta patrie.
Dans le piége à ton gré tu conduis l'univers:
Il dort; à son réveil il trouvera des fers.
D'Albion sur nos maux tu fondes la puissance;
Pour dominer le monde il lui fallait la France.
Oui, couvert de lauriers le Français est vaincu;
Sous tes coups un moment tu le vois abattu.
     Mais sa main, quoique désarmée,
Dispense encor la gloire et tient ta renommée.
S'il fut au champ d'honneur trahi par le destin;

By snuffing out the poison with the very
Poison itself: result extraordinary!
Nor is it wasted time to save our race:
When gentle zephyrs once again come chase
The bitter cold away, our flocks, grown merry,
Carefree, and bounteous, will go cavorting,
    Bounding with pleasure legendary
Over the valleys' fresh, cool grass, and sporting
A health restored. There, by your efforts freed,
We shall, in nature's tender bosom, pass
    Our days in peace, that man, alas,
    Accords our lives, our loves, to feed
    His avarice; and our rich fleece
Will fill his coffers, satisfy his greed...
Ah! But we talk too much! Best let us cease
Our chatter, lest, though free of malice, we
Be seen: the weak must shun attention, fear it...
    So let us go, but silently,
    Else will our voice a traitor be.
May it reach you... But let the wolves not hear it!

———————

* TO ***

You who proclaimed yourself our liberator,
Let fall the mask and show the devastator!
All Europe, subjugated to your laws,
Sacrificed to your country's selfish cause,
Cowers behind you: tight its bonds and strong
As you drag all the universe along
Into your trap. It sleeps, but let it wake,
And it will feel its chains! For Albion's sake
What woes you make us suffer in your thrall:
If she would rule the earth, then France must fall!
And so, though laurel-crowned, the Frenchman lay
Conquered, beneath your blows... But, come what may,
    His hand, though weaponless, bestows
Glory anew. For, as the whole world knows,
Though Fate, upon the field of honor, thus

———————

* One has to assume that the anonymous object of the poet's wrath is Wellington, Napoleon's bête noire, responsible for his and France's downfall at Waterloo.

Si, dépouillant nos murs, l'insigne perfidie
Sur le dieu des beaux-arts porte une main hardie;
A ses enfants chéris on le dérobe en vain,
Il nous laisse sa flamme et son trépied divin.
Notre Athènes moderne offre seule au génie
Cet encens, ces transports dont il aime à jouir.
Poètes et guerriers viennent, bravant l'envie,
Chercher dans ses arrêts l'arrêt de l'avenir,
Et d'avance goûter leur immortelle vie.
Elle saura peser une célébrité
          Qui, par la rapine avilie,
          Apporte au monde épouvanté
Les complots d'Albion et son joug détesté.
Dans ses foyers troublés malheur à qui t'appelle!
Ton secours est funeste et ta faveur cruelle.
L'Espagnol valeureux, que tu semblais chercher
Pour lui rendre à la fois ses droits et la lumière,
Quand il les a conquis, quand la raison l'éclaire,
Des champs de la victoire est conduit au bûcher;
Et ton cœur aujourd'hui l'abandonne à la rage
Du fanatique orgueil qui l'opprime et l'outrage.

Betrayed us; though, with treason scurrilous,
The god of arts, cast down, has vanquished lain;
* Though stripped and bare our walls... Ah, but in vain
Are his most favored children so despoiled:
Your blatant theft, your villainy stands foiled,
For, ever ours his pedestal divine,
His sacred flame! Our modern Athens, shrine
To genius, wafts that incense pure that he
Revels in, glorying, ecstatically.
Poets and warriors come, their one design—
Despite the rigors of vile jealousy—
To seek the judgment that posterity
Will tender, in the judgments that, today,
He offers of their worth, so that they may
Take pleasure in a taste, whilst yet they live,
Of the immortal life their fame will give.
The future will render its verdict, weigh
        Your name against the loathsome, base
        Ravage committed here, before
A world struck dumb with fear, the plots of your
Treacherous Albion, and the disgrace
Of her detested yoke! Woe stalks those who,
In their bale and confusion, call on you!
The aid you offer treads at treason's pace.
† Witness the doughty Spaniard, whom you seemed
To favor, so that soon might be redeemed
His honor and his reason... Yes, but when
He claimed them back and made them his again,
Enlightened, ah! who was it then that schemed
To lead him from the field of victory
Straight to the stake! Today your heart it is
That willingly abandons him to his
Fanatic pride and frenzied destiny...

* The reference is to the looting of French art works by the victorious British. It is
the subject of the first of Babois's "national elegies" included in her *Elégies et poésies di-
verses,* entitled "Sur l'enlèvement des tableaux et statues du muséum, et particulièrement
l'Apollon" (On the Removal of the Canvases and Statues from the Museum, and Especially
of the Apollo).

† The poet is alluding to the misfortunes of Spain during the Peninsular War (1808–
1814), originally encouraged by England to resist Napoleon but later victimized by Wel-
lington after he drove the French from Iberia.

Dans nos murs désolés tu voudrais à jamais
Noyer la liberté dans le sang des Français:
Et chez nous, sous nos yeux, consommant ton ouvrage,
Tu crois impunément jouir de tes forfaits!
Non, perfide étranger! nos muses gémissantes,
Loin du temple désert qui les vit triomphantes,
Rediront dans leurs chants ces tranquilles fureurs
Qui comptent les tourments, l'anxiété, les pleurs,
Les cris des nations sous tes pieds frémissantes.
Déja je les entends dans la postérité,
D'un langage divin déployant la puissance,
Au temps qui te poursuit demander leur vengeance,
    Et celle de l'humanité.
A leur voix, sur ton nom que d'horreur se rassemble!
Ah! cherche, mais en vain, cherche l'obscurité,
Connais aussi l'effroi. Vainqueur superbe, tremble
    Devant ton immortalité.

FROM "à mme b***, ma nièce"

O femmes! que d'attraits, de tendresse et de flamme,
    Que de trésors sont dans votre ame!
    Source d'amour et de bonheur,
    Vous trouvez tout dans votre cœur.
Suivez dans son essor le monde qui s'éclaire.
Aux partisans trompés des siècles ténébreux
    Vous ferez aimer la lumière,
    Quand de ce pouvoir salutaire,

Here, too, in our bare walls, you would spread round
The blood of France, shed deep, that liberty
Might sink within it, toppled, and be drowned.
You think that, here, before our eyes, you can,
Unpunished, ply your wicked felonies!
Ah no, perfidious stranger! Moaning, these
Wounded muses of ours, though broad the span
Betwixt them and the empty temple where
They reigned triumphant, yet will chant again,
With furious calm, their torment, their despair,
Their anguish, in the tearful cries of men,
Of nations quivering beneath your feet.
Now, at length, I can hear them groan, repeat
With all the strength at their command, the call,
In tongue divine—intent upon your fall—
    Seeking revenge for them, and for
All of humanity! They speak no more
Than the sounds of your name, and suddenly
Horror abounds! Proud, haughty conqueror,
Flee to the refuge of the darkness! Be
Ever afraid! Yea, tremble, quake before
    Your shameful immortality!

————————

* FROM "TO MY NIECE, MADAME B***"

O women! What vast stores of tenderness,
    Passion, and charms your souls possess!
    Your hearts are the rich sources of
    Treasures of happiness and love.
Follow the world, soaring in upward flight
Out of the darkness to enlightenment.
    Yours, the task to make love the light
    Those who have countless ages spent

* I depart here from my general principle of presenting only complete poems and avoid-
ing extracts. This, the second of five *épîtres* in the poet's collection, is actually a discrete
work of general interest sandwiched between two others of specific familial encomium.
As such, it stands quite well on its own; and the very feminine—if not at all "feminist"—
theme certainly makes it worthy of inclusion.

Que vous obtenez sur leurs vœux,
Vous ferez un usage heureux.
C'est en vain qu'on voudrait, dans notre belle France,
Anéantir votre influence:
Puisque des lois bannie elle agit sur les cœurs,
Puisqu'enfin elle est dans nos mœurs,
Qu'on ne peut, quoi qu'on fasse, éviter sa puissance,
Il faut la rendre utile, et personne n'y pense.
On vous admire, on suit vos pas,
On vous dit: "Vous avez des talents, des appas;
Plaire est votre destin; les belles sont parfaites."
Voilà ce qu'on vous dit; mais on ne vous dit pas
Que pour penser vous êtes faites.
Tout s'embellit pour vous aux rayons du printemps;
Il couvre de ses fleurs la vive étourderie;
Et des riens sont charmants quand la bouche est jolie.
Nul ne cherche querelle à des attraits naissants;
Mais elle brille, elle est éclose,
Bientôt va se flétrir la rose.
Les yeux s'ouvrent alors; le charme s'est enfui,
Et déja près de vous vient se glisser l'ennui.
Vous n'aviez qu'un moyen de plaire:
On enivra d'encens votre jeune saison,
Et vous voyez couler dans un triste abandon
Votre vieillesse solitaire.
Ah! dédaignez enfin ce funeste poison,
Et l'homme, que pour vous un zèle pur anime,
En parlant à votre raison,
Vous prouvera qu'il vous estime.
Vos pères, vos époux, vos frères sont Français.
N'est-ce que pour les bals, pour les modes anglaises,
Les concerts, les salons, que vous êtes Françaises?
Non; connaissez-vous mieux. Au fond de son palais,

In veneration of the night;
        Noble your purpose, if you might
Thus use your power for mankind's betterment.
        In our fair France one tries in vain
To quell your influence: it will remain
        Ingrained in how we feel and act.
Though banished from our laws, yet it, in fact,
Affects our hearts, and we can shun it not.
It should be put to use; yet, such your lot,
        That one thinks not a whit of it.
One finds you lovely, charming, exquisite,
Intelligent... But one will say to you:
"You have great talents, but, alas, unfit
        Are you except to please, and do
What your beauty's perfection tells you to..."
But not to think!... Sun's rays turn everything
Beautiful to your touch: and, should you err
In careless wise, then such the flowers of spring
That they disguise your lapse. For, all concur,
Trifles delight when lovely lips are they
That speak them, nor will anyone gainsay
        Charms fresh a-borning; whereas those
        There are that wither like the rose,
Blooming for but a moment... Then one's eyes
Gaze wide in awe: your charm bids its good-byes,
        Flies off, as dour and dull ennui
Slips thither in its place. You had, in truth,
One means of pleasing: man extolled your youth,
Burned incense to your beauty. Now you see
        The years flow by—forsaken, lonely—
Lying undone and long of tooth. If only
You scorned that deadly poison—beauty!—then
        Would you hear pure, well-meaning men
        Speak to your reason, and redeem
        Those others, with their true esteem.
Your fathers, husbands. brothers: Frenchmen all!
And you? Frenchwomen! For no purpose but
To haunt the salon and the concert hall?
The ball, decked out in English fashions? What?
        Is that your raison d'être? Nay! You
        Ought better know yourselves, I pray you!...

L'homme, dans la brillante Asie,
N'a qu'une vaine idole à ses lois asservie:
Il croit, sur vingt beautés promenant le desir,
Sans connaître l'amour connaître le plaisir.
    Il a, dans la molle Italie,
    Sous un ciel qui rit à ses vœux,
Pour troubler sa raison une trop vive amante;
Pour régir son ménage une femme indolente.
Chez nos voisins si fiers, dans ce moment joyeux
Qui réunit à table, avec la confiance,
L'esprit et la gaîté, les jeux et la décence,
L'homme existe pour boire, et seul il est heureux;
De ses grossiers plaisirs sa femme se sépare.
Enfin sensible et vrai, mais de parole avare,
    Le bon Germain fait en buvant,
    Sans qu'il y pense ou s'en souvienne,
    Une servante de la sienne,
    Dont il néglige trop souvent
    De cultiver l'intelligence.
    Mais l'homme a sa compagne en France;
    Elle est unie à tous ses vœux;
Il en peut recevoir un conseil généreux.
Voyez-la, dans les soins d'une active industrie,
Partager d'un époux les utiles travaux;
De moitié dans les biens, de moitié dans les maux,
    Son ame à ses devoirs s'allie,
    Et son époux sur ses enfants
La voit porter encor des regards vigilants.
O! de l'humanité moitié tendre et chérie,
Ce faible nourrisson, fruit des plus doux penchants,
Songez qu'il deviendra l'orgueil de la patrie,
    Et qu'il devra plus que le jour
    Aux soins touchants de votre amour,
    Si, dans l'âge de l'innocence,
Des vertus dans son cœur vous portez la semence.
Une tendresse aveugle est souvent un malheur.
Souvenez-vous toujours que sous votre influence
    Au berceau son destin commence;
Et que votre amour même éclaire votre cœur.
Dans vos leçons, dont rien n'égale la douceur,
A d'importants devoirs préparez son enfance;
De vos soins courageux gravez pour l'avenir

In Asia's distant glitter woman is
    Merely man's idol, nothing more—
A palace plaything—and he chooses his
Object of lust among a servile score,
For pleasure, and not love... In Italy's
    Lush climes, beneath her smiling sky,
    Man's lovers' passions bubble high;
But when it comes to household duties, these
Italian women languish lazily...
As for our haughty neighbors to the east,
When, in the sport and revels of the feast,
They give vent to their vulgar gayety,
Man's life is drink: his woman shuns the sot.
Our German, sensitive of soul, sits mum,
    Guzzles, and lets his spouse become
    His serving-wench, mean to or not;
    Respects her intellect but little;
    Nor fosters it one jot or tittle!
    Not so the French wife's state, however:
    She knows her mate's every design,
Offers him sound advice, and, idle never,
Shares in his labors; no mere concubine,
Hers, too, the good and ill that may befall.
    Her soul joins his endeavors all;
    And he looks on as, with benign
Vigilance, she cares for their young... You, O
Loving spouse, cherished by the human race,
    Think of the babe in your embrace,
Fruit of pure joy; weak now, but who will grow
One day to be his country's pride, and who
    Will owe more than his birth to you
And to your touching love, if you but sow
The seeds of virtue in his innocence.
Tenderness, with no purpose, blindly wrought,
May well bring woe: love that will influence
    His future, from the cradle taught,
Will light his life and light your heart no less.
Teach him with lessons fraught with gentleness,
    Virtue second to none; prepare
His childhood for the burdens he will bear
In life; let your courageous care impress
    Itself upon his mind, and there

Un immuable souvenir;
Et qu'un jour, citoyen, amant, époux ou père,
Il devienne meilleur en pensant à sa mère.
Mais trop souvent, hélas! une jeune beauté,
Négligeant son bonheur, dans un monde enchanté
Prodigue le temps qui s'envole,
Et des plus précieux instants,
Ses attraits, ses atours, quelques légers talents,
Occupent seuls le soin frivole.
Non que de ces talents heureux et séducteurs,
Qui règnent aussi sur les cœurs,
Dans quelques vers chagrins je prétende médire:
De la beauté qui passe ils prolongent l'empire;
Par eux du temps au moins l'emploi devient prescrit,
Et ce qui parle à l'ame éclaire aussi l'esprit.
Mais ce n'est pas d'eux seuls, ce n'est pas de ses charmes,
Que, malgré le pouvoir du temps,
La femme la plus belle obtient des vœux constants.
Non, ce n'est pas assez que, lui rendant les armes,
L'homme ébloui de sa beauté,
Ravi de ses talents, enfin d'elle enchanté,
Fasse parler l'amour et parvienne à lui plaire.
Quelques printemps, hélas! peut-être quelques jours,
Avec eux verront fuir cette flamme éphémère;
Mais la raison, l'esprit, embellissent le cours
D'une union tendre et prospère,
Et, plus touchante encor, l'ame attache toujours.
Avec elle plus pure, et plus vive, et plus belle,
L'existence se renouvelle,
L'esprit s'élève et s'ennoblit;
Elle-même ne peut épuiser sa richesse;
Ce qu'elle dit nous plaît sans cesse,
Et jamais elle n'a tout dit.
Heureuse la beauté belle de sa lumière!
A l'époux digne d'elle et que son cœur choisit,
Chaque jour la rendra plus chère;

Remain indelible, so that, one day—
Citizen, lover, father, mate—he may
Think of his mother and the better be...
Often, alas, the fair young belle, instead,
    Takes it into her pretty head
To trade her joy for vain frivolity,
Passing life's fleeting hours disdaining duty,
    Wasting her graces, talent-fed,
To dwell in the enchanted realm of beauty.
Think not that my intent it is to cast
Aspersions, in cantankerous verse, on these
    Seductive gifts, which, while they last,
    Rule hearts, prolonging properties
By beauty bred, in its dominion reigning.
    For, waning time, at least, will be
Well-spent, whatever time it has remaining;
And, what speaks to the soul lights equally
One's wit... Ah! But despite time's tyranny,
If beauteous woman's powers are such that still
    She wins man's constancy, it will
Not be her charms alone that earn it thus:
Bedazzled, the desiring, amorous
Monsieur can love, admire, and yearn his fill,
Yielding to her enchantment, arms surrendered.
Too soon, alas!—a few short springtimes, or
    Mere days—and, as they fly, no more
The passion that mere beauty had engendered!
Gone now that pleasing grace that shone before,
And, in its place, intelligence, wit, mind
    Are what embellish womankind:
Now, soul to soul, tenderly, the *rapport*
    Grows deeper, purer, lovelier,
    As, joining madame and monsieur,
Life springs anew, ennobling what it touches.
    She cleaves to him and he to her,
Reveling in her wealth of wit; for such is
The power it wields that never does it wane.
Happy is she with her fair intellect!
    Each day, yet greater the respect
That he, her wedded spouse—heart-chosen swain—
Will feel for her; and each day, yet more dear
Is she to him... At length, when it grows clear

Enfin elle saura, faisant mieux que lui plaire,
Lorsqu'à voir sur son front son âge qui s'écrit,
      Sagement elle se résigne,
Toucher encor son cœur, parler à son esprit;
Et de l'amitié sainte il la trouvera digne.
D'être belle dès-lors elle n'a plus besoin.
      Sans prendre un inutile soin
Contre le temps dont rien ne ralentit les ailes,
      Pour serrer de solides nœuds,
      Elle possède un charme heureux
      Auquel les graces sont fidèles.
Il n'est pas au pouvoir de ce mal redouté,
Qui trop souvent encore attaque la beauté,
      Ni du temps qui marche en silence,
      D'enlaidir jamais la bonté,
      La candeur et l'intelligence.

––––––––––

VERS À MADAME B***, JEUNE FEMME TRÈS AIMABLE, MAIS UN PEU SUJETTE À L'EXAGÈRATION

Quand vous exagérez même la vérité,
Mon aimable Zoé, vous vous éloignez d'elle.
Vous altérez, hélas! la grace naturelle,
      Et l'heureuse simplicité
      Qui vous rendent bien plus que belle.
Vous méprisez le faux, son ombre vous fait peur;
      Et, sans l'aveu de votre cœur,
      Dans le faux ce penchant vous plonge.
Ah! rougissez, Zoé, de placer le mensonge
      Sur les lèvres de la candeur.

That age begins to etch her brow,
No matter; for she will know how—
Wisely resigned—to touch his heart, to please
His wit, worthiest of the qualities
    Of friendship's sacred bonds; for, now,
No need has she of beauty. Fruitless, too,
The quest to stay time's wings; but she possesses
A charm that neither fades nor evanesces,
    And that, by grace endowed, ties true
The knots that bind them solidly together;
    So strong that one can wonder whether
Aught might yet sunder them: not the dread pox
    That preys on beauty's weak defense,
Whose thrall we suffer under, and that mocks
Our days; nor time, silently marching hence...
Nay! Naught mars goodness, wisdom, innocence.

———

* LINES FOR MADAME B***, A DELIGHTFUL YOUNG LADY,
BUT WHO TENDS SOMEWHAT TO EXAGGERATE

Sweet Zoé, when you tend—as tend you do!—
To use exaggeration even when
You speak the truth, you lie no less; and then
    You flaw the grace that makes of you
    A more than beauteous ingénue.
You loathe even the trace of false pretense;
    And, though your heart plead no defense,
    Your habit plunges you therein.
Ah, Zoé! Blush thus to lay falsehood's sin
    Upon the lips of innocence!

* More than one "Madame B***" figures in Babois's poems. Whether they were all different or one and the same, I cannot say; perhaps they were all relatives. The precise identity of this one escapes me, the vocative "Zoé" notwithstanding.

Victoire Babois 557

À MADAME B***

Aux charmes que sur toi nature a su répandre
Quand le sort ajouta les trésors de Plutus,
Sans doute par méprise il dotait les vertus;
Mais sa faveur volage il vient de la reprendre,
Et tu crois qu'il t'abaisse? Ah! respecte ton cœur,
Et sépare du moins la honte du malheur.
A son gré, j'en conviens, la Fortune humilie
L'insolent qui fut vain dans la prospérité;
Mais celui qu'on a vu riche avec modestie,
      Doit être pauvre avec fierté.

À MONSIEUR V***, EN LUI ENVOYANT MON PORTRAIT

Sur mes traits, je le sais, à peine si les graces
Vont laisser en fuyant quelques légères traces,
Que l'art le plus savant aurait peine à chercher;
      Et pour en offrir une image,
Le temps, que sans effroi je regarde marcher,
      M'avertit de me dépêcher.
Mais que m'importe ici sa fuite et son outrage?
L'aimable sentiment qui vous offre ce gage
De ce triste vieillard ne connaît point les coups.
Par lui son doux lien devient encor plus doux,
Et l'amitié toujours s'applaudit de son âge.

Perhaps it was mere accident that drove
Fate to add to your virtues, charms—endowed
† By nature!—Plutus's rich treasure-trove.
‡ Fickle, she takes her favor back! Unbowed
Pray be! Yours not the fault. Respect your heart:
Shame, in life's myriad woes, need play no part.
Fortune will humble those whose vanity
Let wealth and insolence dwell side by side;
§ But she who bore her riches modestly
    Should bear her poverty with pride.

** FOR MONSIEUR V***, IN SENDING HIM MY PORTRAIT

Youth's graces, in their flight—oh, well I know!—
Will leave precious few traces as they go,
That even cleverest skill would seek in vain;
    And thus, while some few have I still,
Old Time, whose ceaseless march I would disdain,
    Warns I make haste before they wane.
But what care I? Let Time fly, wound his fill!
The gentle love that offers you this token
Scorns his dour blows that fain would do me ill.
Friendship takes pleasure in Time's age: it will
Make sweeter still our tender bond, unbroken.

* Again, I can offer no proof of the specific identity of this charming, virtuous, once wealthy, and later impoverished "Madame B***."

† Plutus (or Plutos), in classical mythology—not to be confused with Pluto—was the god of wealth.

‡ Despite the masculine grammatical gender of *le sort* in French and the poet's referring to its personification with the masculine pronoun *il,* it seems more reasonable to refer to Fate as "she," and certainly more poetic.

§ By the same token, I take the liberty of particularizing the gender of Fate's victim to suit the case, rather than leave it a generic masculine (*celui*) as in the original.

** I suspect that the dedicatee of this poem, dated 1805, is the Doctor Voisin who figures frequently in the poet's works (see, e.g., "The Sheep Give Thanks," p. 543 above).

VERS FAITS SUR LE POÈTE LE BRUN,
QUELQUES JOURS APRÈS SA MORT

De son souffle immortel le dieu de l'harmonie
Sur le divin trépied vint animer ses chants,
Et toujours inspirés, ses lyriques accents
Ont porté jusqu'aux cieux l'audace du génie.
En nous peignant les champs et la paix des hameaux,
Il a de la nature égalé les tableaux.
Ses vers ont soupiré la touchante élégie.
Il perça de ses traits la sottise et l'envie.
Enfin sous les lois d'Atropos
Il repose, et laisse en repos
Les sots.

ON THE POET LE BRUN
A FEW DAYS AFTER HIS DEATH

The god of harmony, with breath undying,
On pedestal divine his song inspired:
Rising aloft, his genius, talent-lyred,
Sang boldly, with the very heavens vying.
Painting the fields, the peaceful hamlets, he
Equaled the skill of nature's artistry.
Soulful, his elegies touched deep our hearts;
His wit pierced folly, envy, with its darts.
†   Now Atropos grants him surcease:
He rests, and lets the dolts increase
    In peace.

* Ponce-Denis Ecouchard Le Brun (or Lebrun) (1729–1807), known for his odes, was dubbed the French Pindar. Babois added a footnote to this poem reading: "Le trait sans doute a porté souvent à faux, non seulement sur quelques hommes, mais surtout sur les femmes, envers lesquelles ce poète si galant fut toujours pour le moins injuste" (His barbed wit was, indeed, often ill-aimed, not only when directed at certain men, but especially at women, toward whom this poet, though most gallant, was always, to say the least, unjust). Perhaps, after penning this encomium to Le Brun, she was admonished for not acknowledging his frequent criticism of her own sex and preferred to add her rather tepid note rather than deleting it entirely. The following quatrain from his *Odes aux belles qui veulent écrire* (Odes to the Beauties Who Would Write) is characteristic of Le Brun's antipathy to women writers in particular: "Rassurez les Grâces confuses; / Ne trahissez point vos appas; / Voulez-vous ressembler aux Muses? / Inspirez, mais n'écrivez pas" (Distemper not the Graces fair: / Lest all your charms be misbegot, / if you the Muses' lot would share, / Inspire who write, but write you not).

† Regarding the Fate Atropos—to whose name the poet, curiously, gives an unconventional rhyme—see p. 179n above.

Victoire Babois 561

ÉPITAPHE À MLLE ***

(C'est sa mère qui parle)

Ma fille!... Je t'appelle, hélas! et tu n'es plus!
        Loin du climat qui te vit naître,
Comme une tendre fleur, tu n'as fait que paraître.
Je viens graver ici des regrets superflus.
Ici sont renfermés, sous cette froide pierre,
Tes graces, ta beauté, tes talents, tes vertus,
        Et le cœur de ta mère.

_____

VERS FAITS POUR RÉCLAMER UN CHIEN

Quand la jeunesse fuit loin d'un monde infidèle,
Il faut aimer pourtant, car aimer est un bien.
        En oubliant qu'elle fut belle,
Femme a vraiment besoin, j'en sais quelque nouvelle,
        D'un regard qui cherche le sien,
Et son chien seul encor n'a des yeux que pour elle.
        O vous qui m'enlevez le mien,
Lecteur, venez le rendre à son premier lien.
        Tandis qu'en vain ma voix l'appelle,
Par sa chaîne entraîné, craintif, obéissant,
        Il vous suit, mais en gémissant.
        Sur mes pas folâtrant sans cesse,
        Pour chaîne il avait sa tendresse.
De son bonheur aussi faites-vous un plaisir.
Vers celle qu'à vos pieds demande sa tristesse,
Dans son transport joyeux le voyant accourir,
        Jouissez de son alégresse.
        A peine il connaît votre loi:
C'est un jouet pour vous, c'est un ami pour moi.

EPITAPH FOR MADEMOISELLE ***

(Spoken by Her Mother)

My daughter!... Gone, alas!... Far from the land
    That saw you bloom, like a frail flower,
Here you came, and outspent your life's brief hour.
† Grim, the words—needed not!—carved by my hand:
Beneath this cold stone, lying tombed, there dwell
Your graces, beauty, talents, virtues... and
        Your mother's heart as well.

‡ LINES WRITTEN TO REQUEST THE RETURN OF A DOG

When youth far from this faithless world would fly,
Still must one love, for love all else outweighs.
    Woman, forgetting by and by
Her beauty fled, yet needs a tender eye—
    I know whereof I speak!—to gaze
Lovingly on her and her state belie.
    Such does her dog, whose silent praise
Is but for her! But tell me, why, oh why,
    Filched you mine from me? Sad my days,
Sad his as well... I call, in vain I cry:
Dragged by his leash, he follows you—ah, yes!—
    But fearful, whining nonetheless!
    My steps he dogged with playful glee,
    His only leash, his love for me!
Think of the pleasure that you, too, will share
When, begging at your feet, he joyously
Bounds once again before his mistress, where
    His heart says he should ever be.
    Your law scarce does he comprehend:
For you he is a toy... For me, a friend.

* The demoiselle in question remains a mystery.
  † It is hard to say if, as in many classical epitaphs, the poet intends here the fiction that the following lines were, in fact, the words graven on the stone.
  ‡ There exists a charming portrait of Victoire Babois done by her brother, the artist Paul-Nicolas Richer (1798–1864), showing her with a small Yorkshire terrier, more than likely the dog in question.

Rien ne songez qu'à vos moutons.
Si vous restait autres soucis en tête,
Très bien sauriez que ce n'est chose honnête
De laisser là femme qui n'est tant bête,
      Pour des moutons.

Si, douce comme vos moutons,
Comme eux encore étais simple et jeunette,
Ici seriez, beau diseur d'amourette;
Bien quitteriez, pour venir en cachette,
      Tous vos moutons.

Tandis qu'êtes à vos moutons,
Suis souffreteuse, hélas! en ma retraite:
Point n'est enfin ma guérison parfaite;
Bien la veux telle. Irez, quand l'aurez faite,
      A vos moutons.

Si me rendez, comme aux moutons,
Fraîche santé, sommeil que tant souhaite,
Lors vous promets que sur la tendre herbette
Irai chanter des airs sur ma musette
      Pour vos moutons.

EMMA

Emma d'un clair ruisseau regardait l'onde pure,
      Et n'y voyait pas ses attraits;
Près d'elle il murmurait sous un ombrage frais,
      Sans qu'elle entendît son murmure.
Une douce pâleur à ses touchants appas
      Semblait donner de nouveaux charmes:
Immobile et pensive, Emma ne pleurait pas,
      Elle laissait tomber ses larmes.

Nothing you think of but your sheep.
If other cares weighed upon your *esprit,*
Soon would you learn it is not meet—ah, me!—
To leave a lady—when no dumb beast she!—
      To mind your sheep.

If I, as tender as your sheep—
As simple, young, and sweet as they—should be,
Your tongue today would flow with flattery:
Here would you come to me, in secrecy,
      And leave your sheep.

But, whilst you care but for your sheep,
Alone, alas, I suffer! Hear my plea:
I seek my cure, but have no remedy;
Come, find one for me, then go presently
      Back to your sheep.

If you give me, as to your sheep,
Good health and sleep restored, I guarantee,
Over the young grass shall I frolic free,
* As my musette, droning its melody,
      Sings to your sheep.

EMMA

Emma stood gazing by the crystal spring;
    Saw not her charms therein reflected;
Heard not, in the cool shade, its murmuring,
    Deaf to its waters, deep dejected.
A gentle pallor rendered fairer still
    Her simple charms, as, silently—
Pensive and motionless—she stood. Then she
    Let fall her tears, that fell until—

* If we are to understand the original literally here, it presents the curious picture of the heroine singing and playing the bagpipe, or drone—her *musette*—at the same time. I adapt my translation somewhat to make less unusual artistic and physical demands.

Victoire Babois 565

Mais un soupir enfin vient soulager son cœur.
   "Oh! non," dit-elle avec douleur,
   "Non, non, Silvain n'est plus le même.
   En vain il me vante sa foi;
   En vain, s'il revient près de moi,
Touché de ma tristesse, il dit encor qu'il m'aime;
Il le dit, et des pleurs reviennent m'oppresser!
   Ah! dans ses yeux j'ai trop su lire:
   Il y pense pour me le dire;
   Il le disait sans y penser."

———————

SUR LA MORT DE TALMA

Vois l'asile où ton fils est venu nous attendre,
Divine Melpomène, et gémis sur sa cendre.
De tes pleurs à jamais, dans ses flots confondus,
   Grossis les ondes du Permesse;
Pleure, pleure son ame et la tragique ivresse
Qui ravissait nos cœurs et nos sens éperdus.
Dans sa tombe avec lui ta gloire va descendre.
Ton sceptre s'est brisé, tes accents sont perdus.
   Ah! renonce à te faire entendre:
      Talma n'est plus.

With sob and sigh to ease her woe,
Her heart's duress—she whispered: "No!
Silvain is not as he was then!
In vain he vaunts his faithfulness.
In vain, if—touched by my distress,
Returning—he protests his love again.
Say it he will, yet tears well in my eyes!...
    Alas! In his I saw my lot.
    Empty his words: mere sound, more lies...
He said it, yes, but meant it not!"

----

* ON THE DEATH OF TALMA

Here, the last refuge, where your son, laid low,
† Divine Melpomene, awaits us! O,
Weep for his ashes! Let your tears flow on
‡   And on, to swell Apollo's springs;
Mourn his soul, and his tragic rapturings
That wrenched our hearts, our minds, agog thereon.
Your glory joins him in the tomb: smashed, now,
Your scepter, stilled your voice, ever anon...
    How can it move, enthrall us? How?
        Talma is gone.

Victoire Babois 567

Marceline Desbordes-Valmore (1786–1859)

Admired both by her romantic contemporaries—Lamartine, Musset, Hugo, et al.—and her postromantic successors, Marceline Desbordes-Valmore was a poet of stature to her own and following generations. Verlaine appreciated the rhyming and rhythmic musicality of her verse no less than the frequent melancholy of her messages, and she was the only woman honored with inclusion among his *poètes maudits* (cursed poets). And even Baudelaire, a misogynist where women poets were concerned, was obliged to confer his grudging admiration upon her.[1] If she is not unanimously praised by today's promoters of a more militant feminism than her poetry displays, hers is nonetheless incontrovertibly a feminine voice, vigorous and intense even when discreetly and gently modulated. It is also a voice whose sensuousness and physical imagery, while never overpowering, lend themselves to contemporary poetic interpretations that should content even the most gender-conscious of today's readers.[2]

Born in the northern town of Douai on June 20, 1786, into a large working-class family, Marceline Desbordes was spirited off at the age of eleven by her mother, who had left her husband, impoverished by the Revolution, to take a lover. For several years, in what reads like a romantic adventure tale, mother and daughter eked out a modest livelihood as itinerant actresses, eventually leaving for Guadeloupe in 1799 in a desperate search for help from a wealthy relative. A slave rebellion and a yellow fever epidemic put an end to their hopes.

On the death of her mother in 1803, she returned alone to France at the age of sixteen, where the birth of two illegitimate and ill-fated children did not prevent her from continuing her acting and singing career, specializing—ironically—in ingénue roles and rising to modest prominence, thanks to the friendship of the composer Grétry, even at the Opéra-Comique. In 1817, while singing the role of Rosine in Rossini's *Barber of Seville* in Brussels, she married a fellow actor, Prosper Lanchantin, known as Valmore. Though her marriage, which produced four children, lasted all her life—despite mutual infidelities—her existence, constantly beset with monetary difficulties and sentimental entanglements, was far from idyllic. She gave up the theater in 1823, determined to live by her pen, and wrote, besides several volumes of poetry, a number of more financially productive children's tales and lyrics to musical romances. The death of her three adult daughters, her brother, and her only grandchild capped a pathetic life, which ended with her own solitary death in Paris.

Marceline Desbordes-Valmore's staggering misfortunes found artistic expression in her elegantly and passionately crafted poetry, romantic in inspiration and richly displaying a tone that no doubt owed much to her musical gifts.

From her first collection of elegies in 1819 through her posthumous *Poésies in-édites* of 1860, admiration for her talent continued to grow and to make of her, deservedly, one of France's most admirable and admired romantics, female or otherwise.[3]

The following varied selection of elegies, romances, apologues, and an array of touching lyrics, twenty in all, is reproduced from Marc Bertrand's most useful complete critical edition, which divides her poetic *œuvre* into the indicated sections corresponding to her originally published volumes.

NOTES

1. See Baudelaire's essay "Marceline Desbordes-Valmore" under the rubric "Réflexions sur quelques-uns de mes contemporains," in *Œuvres complètes*, 2: 145–49.

2. In this regard, see Michael Danahy's brief but excellent sketch of her life and penetrating discussion of her works, in *French Women Writers*, pp. 121–32.

3. Many studies are devoted to her life and art. Among them, see two early volumes by Lucien Descaves: *La vie douloureuse de Marceline Desbordes-Valmore* and *La vie amoureuse de Marceline Desbordes-Valmore*; and, more recently, Eliana Jasenas, *Marceline Desbordes-Valmore devant la critique*; Aimée Boutin's *Maternal Echoes: The Poetry of Marceline Desbordes-Valmore and Alphonse de Lamartine*; Francis Ambrière's minutely researched *Le siècle des Valmore: Marceline Desbordes-Valmore et les siens*; Barbara Johnson's gender-oriented *The Feminist Difference: Literature, Psychoanalysis, Race, and Gender*; Alison Finch, *Women's Writing in Nineteenth-Century France*, pp. 143–49; and the portions devoted to her in Wendy Greenberg, *Uncanonical Women: Feminine Voice in French Poetry (1830–1871)*, pp. 103–20, 131–51.

MÉDOR

Aimable chien, fidèle et bon Médor,
Tu restes seul à ta jeune maîtresse!
On m'abandonne... et toi, tu veux encor
    Me consoler par ta tendresse.

Cruel amant! sans regret tu me fuis!
Tu m'as laissée à ma douleur mortelle.
Ingrat! ton chien ne m'avait rien promis,
    Pourtant, il me reste fidèle.

Je le reçus pour gage de ta foi,
Le garderai pour sa reconnaissance.
Hélas! s'il est moins éloquent que toi,
    Il a du moins plus de constance!

SOUVENIR

Quand il pâlit un soir, et que sa voix tremblante
S'éteignit tout à coup dans un mot commencé;
Quand ses yeux, soulevant leur paupière brûlante,
Me blessèrent d'un mal dont je le crus blessé;
Quand ses traits plus touchants, éclairés d'une flamme
        Qui ne s'éteint jamais,
S'imprimèrent vivants dans le fond de mon âme;
        Il n'aimait pas, j'aimais!

MÉDOR

Good, faithful dog, Médor! All else is flown:
You, the last friend your mistress still possesses!
They all have left me... but you, you alone
    Console me with your tendernesses.

Cruel love! You fled from me, without regret!
You left me to my deathly, anguished lot.
Your dog promised me nothing, wretch! And yet
    Faithful is he whilst you are not.

You gave him to me, of your troth a token,
And I shall ever keep him, gratefully.
Though not, alas, like you, gallantly spoken,
    At least has he more constancy!

MEMORY

When he grew pale, one night, and suddenly
His quivering voice died in a word scarce spoken;
When, with his burning glance, he wounded me—
A glance I thought his own wounds must betoken;
When fire shone on his features, fire that never
    Seemed it could fade, or ever die—
Those features graven in my soul forever:
    It was not he that loved, but I!

Elégies

* Médor was long a traditional French name for a pet dog, especially of the more elegant breeds, coming from that of the Saracen knight Medoro in Ariosto's *Orlando furioso,* the chivalrous Moor known for his grace, beauty, and, especially appropriate here, his unflagging fidelity. This poem was originally published in the author's first collection, in 1819, but not subsequently, though a somewhat different version was eventually set to music. See *Les œuvres poétiques de Marceline Desbordes-Valmore,* ed. Marc Bertrand, 2: 771.

SOUVENIR

Son image, comme un songe,
Partout s'attache à mon sort;
Dans l'eau pure où je me plonge
Elle me poursuit encor:
Je me livre en vain, tremblante,
A sa mobile fraîcheur,
L'image toujours brûlante
Se sauve au fond de mon cœur.

Pour respirer de ses charmes
Si je regarde les cieux,
Entre le ciel et mes larmes,
Elle voltige à mes yeux,
Plus tendre que le perfide,
Dont le volage désir
Fuit comme le flot limpide
Que ma main n'a pu saisir.

LE PORTRAIT

Riant portrait, tourment de mon désir,
Muet Amour, si loin de ton modèle!
Ombre imparfaite du plaisir,
Tu seras pourtant plus fidèle.

De ta gaîté je me plains aujourd'hui;
Mais si jamais il cesse de m'entendre,
A toi je me plaindrai de lui,
Et tu me paraîtras plus tendre.

Si tu n'as pas, pour aller à mon cœur,
Son œil brûlant et son parler de flamme,
Par un accent doux et trompeur,
Tu n'égareras pas mon âme.

MEMORY

How his image, like a dream,
Ever haunts my destiny!
Though I plunge in crystal stream,
Yet does it chase after me.
Cool, the swirling waters; still,
All in vain: I burn, I smart,
Trembling; for his image will
Fly for refuge in my heart.

If, to breathe their charms, I raise
My sad glance to heavens on high,
There his image meets my gaze,
Hovering 'twixt tears and sky:
Gentler than the faithless beau—
He whose fleeting passion flees,
Fickle, like the limpid flow
That my fingers cannot seize.

Elégies

THE PORTRAIT

O smiling portrait, who so torture me!
Mute Love, shadow of pleasure; you, so far
    From him whose likeness you would be,
    Yet who more faithful surely are.

Today your good cheer I lament; but should
He ever cease, some day, my voice to hear,
    Lament to you I doubtless would,
    And you the gentler would appear.

If you, indeed, have not, to burn their way
Into my heart, his artful tongue and eyes,
    At least you will not lead astray
    My soul with sweet, deceitful lies.

Sans trouble, à toi, je livre mon secret.
S'il était là, je fuirais vite, vite.
　　Je suis seule... Ah! riant portrait,
　　Que n'es-tu celui que j'évite!

———————

LE BOUQUET

Non, tu n'auras pas mon bouquet.
Traite-moi de capricieuse,
De volage, d'ambitieuse,
D'esprit léger, vain ou coquet;
Non, tu n'auras pas mon bouquet.

Comme l'incarnat du plaisir,
On dit qu'il sied à ma figure.
Veux-tu de ma simple parure
Oter ce qui peut m'embellir,
Comme l'incarnat du plaisir?

Je veux le garder sur mon cœur;
Il est aussi pur que mon âme;
Un soupir, un souffle de flamme
En pourrait ternir la fraîcheur:
Je veux le garder sur mon cœur.

Non, non, point de bouquet pour toi:
L'éclat de la rose est trop tendre;
Demain tu pourrais me le rendre;
Demain... qu'en ferais-je? dis-moi.
Non, non, point de bouquet pour toi.

Gladly to you, O smiling portrait, I
Confess; but were he here, off would I run!
    I am alone... Ah, why oh why
    Are you not he, the one I shun!

Romances

———————

THE BOUQUET

No, you shall not have my bouquet.
Say that I am a fickle lass,
Capricious, vain, coquettish, crass,
Ambitious... Say what say you may:
No, you shall not have my bouquet.

Like pleasure's blush and tint of rose,
They tell me that it suits my face.
Would you deprive me of the grace
This simple ornament bestows,
Like pleasure's blush and tint of rose?

Clasp it I will in my caress.
Pure as my soul it is; and I
Fear lest a breath of flame, a sigh,
Wither and fade its loveliness.
Clasp it I will in my caress.

No, no bouquet of flowers for you.
Too tender is the rose, too bright;
Tomorrow, give them back you might:
What use, then, should I put them to?
No, no bouquet of flowers for you.

Romances

Marceline Desbordes-Valmore 575

LE SOUVENIR

O délire d'une heure auprès de lui passée,
　　　　Reste dans ma pensée!
Par toi tout le bonheur que m'offre l'avenir
　　　　Est dans mon souvenir.

Je ne m'expose plus à le voir, à l'entendre,
　　　　Je n'ose plus l'attendre;
Et si je puis encor supporter l'avenir,
　　　　C'est par le souvenir.

Le temps ne viendra pas pour guérir ma souffrance;
　　　　Je n'ai plus d'espérance:
Mais je ne voudrais pas, pour tout mon avenir,
　　　　Perdre le souvenir!

LE PREMIER AMOUR

Vous souvient-il de cette jeune amie,
Au regard tendre, au maintien sage et doux?
A peine, hélas! au printemps de sa vie,
Son cœur sentit qu'il était fait pour vous.

Point de serment, point de vaine promesse:
Si jeune encore, on ne les connaît pas;
Son âme pure aimait avec ivresse,
Et se livrait sans honte et sans combats.

Elle a perdu son idole chérie:
Bonheur si doux a duré moins qu'un jour!
Elle n'est plus au printemps de sa vie;
Elle est encore à son premier amour.

Ecstatic hour spent by his side! Pray, ever
    Abide with me; for never
Any joys will the future hold for me,
    Save in that memory.

To see, to hear him, be with him again,
    I dare not risk the pain;
If aught can ease the future's woe for me,
    It is that memory.

Time will not remedy, nor pacify
    My soul's despair; yet, I
Would not, though long the future be for me,
    Lose that one memory.

Romances

FIRST LOVE

Do you remember that young friend—so mild
Her glance, so sweet and gentle-mannered—who,
Scarce in the spring of life, alas! dear child,
Felt that her heart was meant for none but you?

No promises, no oaths, vain, meaningless:
So young, little one knows what such may be;
Her pure soul loved with passion's drunkenness,
And, shameless, gave itself ungrudgingly.

Now is her idol lost, deep her regret:
Less than a day's delight had she thereof!
Hers, now, no more the spring of life; and yet,
Hers ever and forever that first love.

Romances

* Desbordes-Valmore obviously had a liking for the title "Souvenir," with or without the article. Besides this one, she gave it to five other poems, two of which are translated in these pages (pp. 570–73).

LA SÉPARATION

Il le faut, je renonce à toi;
On le veut, je brise ta chaîne.
Je te rends tes serments, ta foi:
Sois heureux, quitte-moi sans peine,
Séparons-nous... attends, hélas!
Mon cœur encor ne se rend pas!

Toi qui fus mes seules amours,
Le charme unique de ma vie,
Une autre fera tes beaux jours,
Et je le verrai sans envie.
Séparons-nous... attends, hélas!
Mon cœur encor ne se rend pas.

Reprends-le ce portrait charmant
Où l'amour a caché ses armes;
On n'y verra plus ton serment,
Il est effacé par mes larmes!
Séparons-nous... attends, hélas!
Mon cœur encor ne se rend pas.

S'IL L'AVAIT SU

S'il avait su quelle âme il a blessée,
Larmes du cœur, s'il avait pu vous voir,
Ah! si ce cœur, trop plein de sa pensée,
De l'exprimer eût gardé le pouvoir,
Changer ainsi n'eût pas été possible;
Fier de nourrir l'espoir qu'il a déçu:
A tant d'amour il eût été sensible,
   S'il avait su.

S'il avait su tout ce qu'on peut attendre
D'une âme simple, ardente et sans détour,
Il eût voulu la mienne pour l'entendre,
Comme il l'inspire, il eût connu l'amour.

SEPARATION

I give you up; yes, must I now
Break loose your chain and set you free.
I give you back your faith, your vow:
Guiltless, begone, and happy be!
Let's go our ways... Ah me! Not yet!
My heart cannot so soon forget!

You, who were all the love I knew,
The only charm my life begot;
Now will another solace you,
And I shall watch, and envy not.
Let's go our ways... Ah me! Not yet!
My heart cannot so soon forget!

Take back this tender portrait, where
Love hid his darts; no more appears
Therein the vow you once would swear,
Washed pale, effaced by all my tears.
Let's go our ways... Ah me! Not yet!
My heart cannot so soon forget!

Romances

HAD HE BUT KNOWN

Had he but known the soul he wounded so;
Heart's tears, if he had seen you; if this heart
Of mine had still possessed the power to show
How full it was of him, had it that art,
Then could he not have changed: proud of the passion,
The hope—thwarted, alas!—his love had sown,
He would not spurn me in such faithless fashion,
        Had he but known.

Had he but known what gifts a soul benign,
Simple, and frank, can give—though one afire—
He might have chosen to commune with mine,
And would have seen the love he could inspire!

Mes yeux baissés recélaient cette flamme;
Dans leur pudeur n'a-t-il rien aperçu?
Un tel secret valait toute son âme,
        S'il l'avait su.

Si j'avais su, moi-même, à quel empire
On s'abandonne en regardant ses yeux,
Sans le chercher comme l'air qu'on respire,
J'aurais porté mes jours sous d'autres cieux.
Il est trop tard pour renouer ma vie,
Ma vie était un doux espoir déçu.
Diras-tu pas, toi qui me l'as ravie,
        Si j'avais su!

CHANT D'UNE JEUNE ESCLAVE

Imité de M. Moore

Il est un bosquet sombre où se cache la rose,
Et le doux rossignol y va souvent gémir;
Il est un fleuve pur dont le cristal l'arrose:
Ce fleuve, on l'a nommé le Calme Bendemir.

Dans ma rêveuse enfance, où mon cœur se replonge,
Lorsque je ressemblais au mobile roseau,
En glissant sous les fleurs comme au travers d'un songe,
J'écoutais l'eau fuyante et les chants de l'oiseau.

Je n'ai pas oublié cette musique tendre,
Qui remplissait les airs d'un murmure enchanté;
Dans ma chaîne souvent il m'a semblé l'entendre:
J'ai dit: le rossignol là-bas a-t-il chanté?

Penchent-elles encor leurs têtes couronnées,
Ces belles fleurs, dans l'eau que j'écoutais gémir?
Non, elles étaient fleurs; le temps les a fanées,
Et leur chute a troublé le Calme Bendemir.

But, downcast, my eyes hid the flame within.
What? Not one modest glimmer from them shone?
My silence lost the soul I yearned to win,
        Had he but known.

Had I but known the power his eyes could wield,
And their dominion over such as me,
I would have plied my course farther afield,
Beneath more distant skies, less fancy-free.
Too late is it to change my life one whit:
Naught was it but a sweet hope, hopeless grown.
Ah! Will you not say, you who ravaged it:
        "Had I but known!"

                                    Romances

---

* A YOUNG SLAVE'S SONG

Imitation of Moore

There is a darkling wood where hides a rose
And moans the nightingale, mournful to hear;
There is a crystal stream that through it flows:
A stream they called the Peaceful Bendemeer.

My heart goes coursing back to childhood, where,
A lissome reed, I dreamed my reverie,
Slipping betwixt the flowers, listening there
To songs of birds and waters flowing free.

Their murmured music lingering in my head
Would fill the air with its enchanted strain.
Enchained, I thought I heard it still, and said:
"Is that the nightingale moaning again?

"Do those fair blooms yet bow their brows, becrowned,
Over the waters, that I used to hear
Moan low? Ah, no! Time cast them, withered, round,
And they ruffled the Peaceful Bendemeer.

* The Bendemeer is also invoked by Desbordes-Valmore's contemporary Amable Tastu (see p. 613 below), who was even more devoted to Thomas Moore's poetry than Desbordes-Valmore.

Marceline Desbordes-Valmore 581

Mais lorsqu'elles brillaient dans l'éclat de leurs charmes,
Avant de s'effeuiller sur l'humide tombeau,
On puisa dans leur sein ces odorantes larmes,
Qui rappellent l'été dont le règne est si beau!

Ainsi le souvenir rend à mes rêveries
Les chants du rossignol que j'écoutais gémir;
Et ma chaîne s'étend jusqu'aux rives fleuries
Où je crois voir couler le Calme Bendemir.

CONTE IMITÉ DE L'ARABE

C'était jadis. Pour un peu d'or,
Un fou quitta ses amours, sa patrie.
(De nos jours cette soif ne paraît point tarie;
J'en connais qu'elle brûle encor.)
Courageux, il s'embarque; et, surpris par l'orage,
Demi-mort de frayeur, il échappe au naufrage.
La fatigue d'abord lui donna le sommeil,
Puis enfin l'appétit provoqua son réveil.

Au rivage, où jamais n'aborda l'Espérance,
Il cherche, mais en vain, quelque fruit savoureux;
Du sable, un rocher nu, s'offrent seuls à ses yeux;
Sur la vague en fureur il voit fuir l'existence.
L'âme en deuil, le cœur froid, le corps appesanti,
L'œil fixé sur les flots qui mugissent encore,
Sentant croître et crier la faim qui le dévore,
Dans un morne silence il reste anéanti.

"Their splendor shone, of brilliant charms possessed,
Before they fell to watery grave, stripped bare;
Plumbed were the fragrant tears deep in their breast,
That call to mind the summer's kingdom fair!

"Memory, thus, restores unto my dream
The nightingale's laments I used to hear;
Chained, yet I touch the flowering banks, and seem
To watch flow past the Peaceful Bendemeer."

Romances

---

* TALE FROM THE ARABIC

A fool, in days long past, forsook
His home, his loves, and undertook
To find a bit of gold. (That thirst, today,
Is far from quenched! I know more than a few
Who suffer from it!... Be that as it may...)
    Courageous, he embarks, sets to...
A sudden storm surprises him, but he
Escapes the wreck, wretched, half dead from fright.
At first he sleeps; but soon his appetite
Awakens him and will not let him be.

Over the shore, where never had Hope landed,
He sought a piece of fruit to please his taste:
Alas, in vain! Naught but a sandy waste,
A barren cliff, greeted his eyes. Thus stranded,
His body wracked, and sick at heart beside—
Soul sore—he sees his life borne off upon
The raging waves; he hears the angry tide
Before him, as his hunger, all hope gone,
Devours him, leaves him to his mute despair.

* The exact Arabic source is not indicated. The general subject, however—the value of
food over precious gems—is a common Aesopic and post-Aesopic topos, and no doubt
antedates Aesop as well. The poet was certainly familiar with La Fontaine's "Le coq et la
perle" (for a translation, see my *Fifty Fables of La Fontaine*, pp. 16–17). As in that celebrated
version, her hero's scorn is justified, whereas in most of the medieval settings, the hero is,
on the contrary, taken to task for not appreciating the intrinsic value of his find. For two
examples, see Marie de France, "The Cock and the Gem," in my *The Fabulists French*, p. 4,
and "The Cock the Gem," from *Isopet I,* in my *Fables from Old French*, pp. 50–51.

Marceline Desbordes-Valmore 583

La mer, qui par degrés se calme et se retire,
Laisse au pied du rocher les débris du vaisseau;
L'infortuné vers lui lentement les attire,
S'y couche, se résigne, et s'apprête un tombeau.
Tout à coup, il tressaille, il se lève, il s'élance;
Il croit voir un prodige, il se jette à genoux.
D'un secours imprévu bénir la Providence
Est de tous les besoins le plus grand, le plus doux!
        Puis, en tremblant, ses mains avides
Touchent un lin mouillé, rempli de grains humides;
Il presse, il interroge et la forme et le poids,
Y sent rouler des fruits... des noisettes... des noix...
"Des noix!" dit-il, "des noix! quel trésor plein de charmes!"
Il déchire la toile. O surprise! ô tourments!
    "Hélas!" dit-il, en versant quelques larmes,
        "Ce ne sont que des diamants!"

LES DEUX ABEILLES

A mon oncle

Au fond d'une vallée où s'éveillaient les fleurs,
On vit légèrement descendre deux abeilles;
Elles cherchaient des yeux ces fleurs, tendres merveilles,
Où l'aurore en passant avait laissé des pleurs.
        L'herbe brillait de perles arrosée;
        L'horizon bleu, les gouttes de rosée,
        Sur la colline une ardente clarté,
        Tout annonçait un jour brûlant d'été;
        Tout l'attestait; car un jardin rustique
Répandait à l'entour des deux errantes sœurs
        De frais parfums, d'attrayantes douceurs,
Et d'un souffle embaumé la langueur sympathique.

But gradually the sea retreats; and there,
Hard by the cliff, he sees the shipwreck, spread,
Shattered to pieces. Slowly, painfully,
He drags from here, from there, bits of debris,
Readies his tomb, resigned, soon to be dead...
But then, jumping for joy, his spirits soar!
A miracle!... Down on his knees he blesses
Fate for her help! Of all her tendernesses,
This is the one most sweet to thank her for!
    Trembling, his eager hands reach out,
Feel a wet satchel, filled with objects small
And round... He presses, hefts it... Fruits, no doubt,
Rolling about inside!... "And nuts!... And all
Manner of wondrous things to eat!" he cries...
He rips the sack... O torment! O surprise!
"No fruits!" he weeps. "No sweetmeats, nuts galore!..."
    Diamonds they were, and nothing more!

Poésies diverses

THE TWO BEES

* *For My Uncle*

Down in a valley's nethermost recess,
Two bees, a-flit among the waking flowers,
Were seeking tender blooms where dawn's first hours
Had wept her tears upon their tenderness.
    Pearls sparkled on the grass; the blue
    Horizon, and the beads of dew;
    The hillside's warm, clear light of morning,
Announced a torrid summer day a-borning.
A garden, lush with rustic blossoms, spread
Fragrant perfumes about the wandering pair;
Lured by its languid breath, its balm-filled air,
    The sisters, flying on ahead,

---

* The uncle that the poet refers to was her father's brother, Constant Desbordes, born in 1761, a Parisian painter of some repute. Despite his long-held disapproval of her youthful indiscretions, she was very much attached to him and deeply mourned his death in 1828, writing a touching letter to his departed spirit after learning of it. See *Œuvres poétiques*, ed. Bertrand, 1: 307–8.

Toutes deux ont franchi l'enclos vert du jardin:
"Voyez!" dit la plus vive; elle était frêle et blonde,
"Voyez, que de trésors! ce n'est rien que jasmin,
Lilas, rose, et je crois toutes les fleurs du monde."
Cette folle suivait son volage désir,
Aux suaves bouquets se suspendait à peine,
Prodiguant ses baisers jusqu'à manquer d'haleine,
Disant: "Demain le miel, aujourd'hui le plaisir!"

L'autre, plus posément, savourait les délices
Du banquet préparé pour les filles de l'air,
        Et, prévoyante aux besoins de l'hiver,
Pour la ruche épuisée en gardait les prémices.
Leurs ailes en tremblaient. Mais un globe fatal,
Suspendu dans les fleurs sous la méridienne,
Semble de l'ambroisie offrir le doux régal
        A la jeune épicurienne.
Sous ce cristal frappé de tous les feux du ciel,
        S'échauffe et fermente le miel;
Innocente liqueur pour l'homme préparée,
Mais qui donne la mort à la mouche dorée:
Sa force s'y consume, et sa raison s'y perd.
L'abîme transparent par malheur est ouvert:
L'imprudente n'y voit qu'un don de la fortune;
Sa sœur, qui l'en détourne, est presque une importune,
Et, malgré ses conseils, elle court s'y plonger:
Quand on veut le bonheur, en voit-on le danger!
"Par quel charme imposteur vous êtes asservie,"
Dit l'autre en soupirant; "vous me faites pitié:
Quittez ce doux breuvage, au nom de l'amitié,
        Peut-être, hélas! au nom de votre vie!
Vous ne m'écoutez pas. Je reviendrai ce soir;
O ma sœur! le travail est utile à notre âge.
Puissé-je ne pas voir bientôt, chère volage,
        Ce que je tremble de prévoir."

Elle retourne aux fleurs avec inquiétude.
Ce beau jour lui paraît plus lent qu'un autre jour;
Tout suc lui semble amer, et sa sollicitude
Implore, et croit du soir avancer le retour.

Crossed the green hedge about the garden. "See!"
Said one—the livelier of the two, frail, blond—
"A treasure! Jasmine, lilac, rose... Ah me!
All the world's flowers! From here, there, and beyond!"
About the blossoms hovering at her leisure,
Breathless, lavishing kisses by the score,
Said she: "Tomorrow, honey; but first, pleasure!"

The other daughter of the air, much more
Prudently savored the delicious store
    Of dainties spread before their eyes:
Musing upon the hive's meager supplies
Come winter's chill, she saves her booty... Now,
Still at their tasks, with flittering wings, they spy,
    Hanging amid the flowers somehow,
A fatal globe, beneath the noonday sky.
        Our gluttonous epicure,
Gazing upon the gleaming globe, is sure
It holds ambrosia; though, in point of fact,
Lashed by noon's fires, the brew she soon attacked
Was honey, for man's use, fermenting, heating:
    Harmless enough for human eating,
But death to any bee who enters in it,
Certain to lose her wits and waste her strength,
Struggling in vain!... The crystal nook, at length,
    Gave way, exposed the feast within it.
The foolish bee saw in the accident
A welcome stroke of fate; and she, next minute,
Despite her sister's urgings to relent,
Went to plunge in. (Where one sees happiness,
Can one perceive the risk he runs?) "Unless
    You care not for your life, or for
    The love betwixt us, I implore..."
So sighed the latter, "quit that sticky brew!
What false lure charms and masters you?... You scoff?
    Well, sister mine, I must be off;
For, at my age, I have much work to do.
When back I come, you silly thing, I pray
I not see what I fear, alas, I may."

Enfin à l'horizon le soleil va s'éteindre;
Elle vole à sa sœur, et, tout près de l'atteindre,
L'appelle en la grondant d'un ton craintif et doux:
"Allons, il se fait tard; me voici, venez-vous?"

"Il n'est plus temps, ma sœur, je suis trop accablée;
    Je ne puis plus me sauver de ce lieu.
Je vous regarde encor, mais ma vue est troublée;
Mon corps brûle et languit; venez me dire adieu,
Je ne puis me mouvoir. Un grand feu me dévore:
Mes ailes, je le sens, ne peuvent m'emporter;
Voyez comme je suis! mais soyez bonne encore;
Si mon crime (il est grand!) ne peut se racheter,
Ne me haïssez pas, je n'étais pas méchante.
La volupté trompeuse égarait ma raison;
Ce breuvage mortel dont l'ardeur nous enchante,
Que je l'aimais, ma sœur, et c'était un poison!
        Je me repens, et je succombe:
        Sous une fleur creusez ma tombe.
Adieu! Pourquoi le ciel créa-t-il le désir,
    S'il a caché la mort dans le plaisir?"

Elle ne parla plus. Ses ailes s'étendirent,
    Ses petits pieds doucement se raidirent;
Et sa sœur gémissante eut peine à s'envoler.
Ce tableau d'un long deuil accabla sa mémoire;
Elle fut toujours triste; et jamais, dit l'histoire,
Même au sein du travail ne put se consoler.

Anxiously, to her flowers she flies; and, spending
A day that seemed too long—aye, never-ending—
Finds all her nectar bitter; waits, broods, looks
For night's return, hanging on tenterhooks.

In time the sun begins to set, and so
Our bee comes back, with fear and trembling; gently
Chiding, she calls: "Come! It is time to go!"

Feebly, her sister answers: "Woe! Ah, woe
      Is me!" suffering evidently,
"I cannot leave this place! I burn! I die!
My sight is dim; too weak to move am I.
      Look! See my plight! My wings will never
Lift me from where I languish. But be not
      Harsh with me for my crime (however
Foolish it be!): I was a senseless sot!
Still, evil was it not that moved me; merely
Gluttony, sister dear, and I pay dearly!
That liquid's warm allure was deadly, very!
Repentant, I succumb... Farewell! Pray, bury
Beneath a bloom my poor remains... Ah, life!
Why did the gods invent desire, so rife
      With bliss, mere hiding-place for death!"

      So saying, she gasped her final breath;
Her wings gave one last flutter; and, thereat,
Her little feet grew stiff, and that was that.
      Transfixed, her sister sobs and sighs:
Ever that scene will loom before her eyes.
Her mourning knows no respite, no relief:
Even her toils, they say, ease not her grief.

JAMAIS ADIEU

Et vers le ciel se frayant un chemin
Ils sont partis en se donnant la main.
—Béranger

Ne t'en va pas, reste au rivage;
L'amour le veut, crois-en l'amour.
La mort sépare tout un jour:
Tu fais comme elle; ah! quel courage!

Vivre et mourir au même lieu;
Dire: au revoir; jamais adieu.

Quitter l'amour pour l'opulence!
Que faire seul avec de l'or?
Si tu reviens, vivrai-je encor?
Entendras-tu dans mon silence?

Vivre et mourir au même lieu;
Dire: au revoir; jamais adieu.

Leur diras-tu: Je suis fidèle?
Ils répondront: Cris superflus;
Elle repose, et n'entend plus.
Le ciel du moins eut pitié d'elle!

Vivre et mourir au même lieu;
Dire: au revoir; jamais adieu.

NOT THE LAST GOOD-BYE

They cleared a path to heaven's promised land,
Then took their leave, together, hand in hand.
*   *—Béranger*

Stay by the shore, stray not afar;
Believe love: love would bid you stay.
Death draws all things apart; you play
Death's game: alas, how brave you are!

One place to live and die; and sigh
† "Farewell": but not the last "Good-bye."

Trade love for wealth? Ah, what a choice!
What can gold to the lonely give?
If you return, will I yet live?
What will you hear when stilled my voice?

One place to live and die; and sigh
"Farewell": but not the last "Good-bye."

"Faithful am I!" you shall protest;
And they will say: "She hears you not.
Heaven, at least, pitied her lot;
And she takes her eternal rest."

One place to live and die; and sigh
"Farewell": but not the last "Good-bye."

Les Pleurs

---

* In *Mes mémoires* (Paris: Robert Laffont, 1989), chap. 179, Alexandre Dumas *père* discusses the background and political implications of the song from which these lines were taken, written around 1832 by popular revolutionary *chansonnier* Pierre-Jean de Béranger (1780–1857).

† Given the inadequacies of leavetaking vocabulary in English, my translation is a compromising attempt to deal with the poet's play on the difference between the two French ways of saying "good-bye": the temporary *au revoir*, "until we meet again," and the permanent *adieu*, commending one eternally "to God."

LA RONCE

I seek no sympathy.
Nor relief...
—*Byron*

Pour me plaindre ou m'aimer je ne cherche personne;
J'ai planté l'arbre amer dont la sève empoisonne.
Je savais, je devais savoir quel fruit affreux
Naît d'une ronce aride au piquant douloureux:
Je saigne. Je me tais. Je regarde sans larmes
Des yeux pour qui mes pleurs auraient de si doux charmes:
Dans le fond de mon cœur je renferme mon sort,
Et mon étonnement, et mes cris, et ma mort.
Oui! je veux bien mourir d'une flèche honteuse;
Mais sauvez-moi, mon Dieu! de la pitié menteuse.
Oh! la pitié qui ment, oh! les perfides bras,
Valent moins qu'une tombe à l'abri des ingrats.

À MES ENFANTS

Je ne reproche rien au passé: je l'oublie;
Je ne demande rien au douteux avenir:
Ma vie est dans vos yeux, et ma mélancolie
S'envole vers le ciel, quand vous allez venir!

THE BRAMBLE

> *I seek no sympathy,*
> *Nor relief...*
*   —Byron

No one seek I to love or pity me.
I knew—or should have known—what fruit that tree
I planted bore: that bush, that barren thorn,
Poisoned of sap, of prickly brambles born.
I bleed. Silent and tearless, I gaze on
Eyes that delight to see me woebegone,
Weeping. Ah no! No tears shall fill me eyes!
Deep, deep within my heart I hide my cries,
My woes, my death. Yes! Let a piercing dart
Kill me; but mercy, God! I want no part
Of pitying lies! I fear the tomb far less—
Safe from deceit—than false arms' faithlessness.

Bouquets et prières

† FOR MY CHILDREN

I blame the past for nothing, long forgot;
I ask naught of the future, dark and drear:
My life is in your eyes, and my sad lot
Goes flying heavenward when you draw near.

Bouquets et prières

* The epigraph cites, in truncated and inaccurate fashion, a passage from Byron's *Childe Harold's Pilgrimage* (4.10): "Meantime I seek no sympathies, nor need; / The thorns which I have reaped are of the tree / I planted,—they have torn me, and I bleed: / I should have known what fruit would spring from such a seed."

† This quatrain, probably dating from between 1827 and 1830, was evidently originally entitled *Retour* (Return) and addressed to only one child, given the use of the singular *tes* and *tu* where this version uses the plurals *vos* and *vous* (*Œuvres poétiques de Marceline Desbordes-Valmore*, ed. Bertrand, 2: 723n).

LE PAPILLON MALADE

Apologue

Las des fleurs, épuisé de ses longues amours,
     Un papillon, dans sa vieillesse,
(Il avait du printemps goûté les plus beaux jours)
Voyait d'un œil chagrin la tendre hardiesse
Des amants nouveau-nés, dont le rapide essor
Effleurait les boutons qu'humectait la rosée.

Soulevant un matin le débile ressort
     De son aile à demi-brisée:
"Tout a changé," dit-il, "tout se fane. Autrefois
L'univers n'avait point cet aspect qui m'afflige;
     Oui, la nature me néglige;
Aussi pour la chanter l'oiseau n'a plus de voix.
Les papillons passés avaient bien plus de charmes!
Toutes les fleurs tombaient sous nos brûlantes armes!
Touchés par le soleil, nos légers vêtements
     Semblaient brodés de diamants!
     Je ne vois plus rien sur la terre
     Qui ressemble à mon beau matin!
J'ai froid. Tout, jusqu'aux fleurs, prend une teinte austère,
Et je n'ai plus de goût aux restes du festin!
Ce gazon si charmant, ce duvet des prairies,
Où mon vol fatigué descendait vers le soir,
Où Chloé, qui n'est plus, vint chanter et s'asseoir,
N'offre plus qu'un vert pâle et des couleurs flétries!
L'air me soutient à peine à travers les brouillards
Qui voilent le soleil de mes longues journées;
Mes heures, sans amour, se changent en années:
     Hélas! que je plains les vieillards!

"Je voudrais, cependant, que mon expérience
     Servît à tous ces fils de l'air.
Sous des bouquets flétris j'ai puisé ma science,
J'ai défini la vie, enfants, c'est un éclair!
Frêles triomphateurs! vos ailes intrépides
S'arrêteront un jour avec étonnement:
Plus de larcins alors, plus de baisers avides;
Les roses subiront un affreux changement.

THE SICK BUTTERFLY

Apologue

Tired of his flowers, fatigued from loves long spent,
    An aging, time-worn butterfly—
Gone now spring's fairest days!—dour, malcontent,
Gazed on the loves of youth with jaundiced eye;
And lovers, brash but tender, newly born,
Who, flitting, grazed the blossom buds bedewed.

Lifting a much enfeebled wing one morn,
    He muttered in his lassitude:
"Alas for everything! How drab! How faded!
    What used to be so fair to see,
I can scarce even look on lest I be
Distressed at nature, grown so dull, so jaded!
The bird has lost his song; time was when we
Butterflies were a charming race: no flower
Was there but bowed before our glorious power!
    Sun-gilt, the airy garb we wore
    Seemed sewn with diamonds! Ah, no more!
Nothing is as it was in my sweet youth.
My limbs grow cold; the flowers, vile, uncouth;
Colorless, everything, in truth, becomes:
No taste, now, have the banquet's last few crumbs!
Those fields of downy grass—the favorite
Resting-place for my flight at end of day—
Where Chloe (gone too, now!) would come and sit,
    Singing her song... No more are they
    Fair, fresh, and green; now pale, bleak grays
Are all the hues I see; the air, turned thick,
Lies heavy on my wings, as, through the haze
That veils the sun, I trudge on, tired and sick...
    My hours seem years, loveless and cold.
Ah, how I pity those who must grow old!

"Still, I would like my brethren—sons of air—
To benefit from my experience:
Taught in the shade of withered blooms, I share
    My knowledge of life's paltry sense,
Finished in but a wink! My children, you,

"Je croyais comme vous qu'une flamme immortelle
Coulait dans les parfums créés pour me nourrir;
Qu'une fleur était toujours belle,
Et que rien ne devait mourir.
Mais le temps m'a parlé; sa sévère éloquence
A détendu mon vol et glacé mes penchants;
Le coteau me fatigue et je me traîne aux champs;
Enfin, je vois la mort où votre inconséquence
Poursuit la volupté. Je n'ai plus de désir,
Car on dit que l'amour est un bonheur coupable:
Hélas, d'y succomber je ne suis plus capable.
Et je suis tout honteux d'avoir eu du plaisir."

Près du sybarite invalide,
Un papillon naissait dans toute sa beauté:
Cette plainte l'étonne; il rêve, il est tenté
De rentrer dans sa chrysalide.
"Quoi! dit-il, ce ciel pur, ce soleil généreux,
Mon berceau transparent qu'il chauffe et qu'il colore,
Tous ces biens me rendront coupable et malheureux?
Mais un instinct si doux m'attire dans la vie!
Un souffle si puissant m'appelle autour des fleurs!
Là-bas, ces coteaux verts, ces brillantes couleurs
Font naître tant d'espoir, tant d'amour, tant d'envie!
Oh! tais-toi, pauvre sage, ou pauvre ingrat, tais-toi!
Tu nous défends les fleurs encor penché sur elles.
Dors, si tu n'aimes plus; mais les cieux sont à moi:
J'eclos pour m'envoler, et je risque mes ailes!"

Frail though you be, may think your glories last!
Yet will your vigorous wings fail one day too,
To your surprise; then will you stand aghast:
        Those fervent, stolen kisses? Flown!
Even the roses will have ugly grown.

"Like you, I thought that an immortal flame
Flowed in the scents wrought but to nourish me;
        That blooms shone fair eternally;
That nothing died. But then did time declaim
        The truth! Severe, his eloquent
Message cut short my flight, chilled my desire;
Hillock and meadow tire me; now my fire
Is quelled! I see death in that diffident
Folly where you pursue your blissful leisure.
Love is a guilty joy, or so they say!
No more, alas, can it lead me astray,
Ashamed that, yesterday, I knew its pleasure!"

        Close by our cripple sybaritic,
A butterfly a-borning, is about
To leave cocoon behind; but, almost out,
Fair to behold, he hears our moaning critic
And, musing on this life so much amiss,
Is tempted not to quit his chrysalis.
"What? That pure sky? That generous sun," says he,
"That warmed my crib to gold and sets me free,
Transformed? These gifts will sadden me, condemn
My life, you say?... But instinct draws me on!
The flowers beckon, lure me hither, yon,
With mighty breath, urge me to bide with them!
        Those gentle, brilliant-hued green slopes
        Raise my desires, my loves, my hopes!
Bah! Hush, poor thankless sage, a-fume, a-fret!
'Shun those vile flowers!' you tell me, though you yet
Hover about! Well, if no more you love,
Go sleep! Now mine to fly the skies above!
Life calls: I risk my wings with no regret!"

Poésies inédites, "Mélanges"

LES ROSES DE SAADI

J'ai voulu ce matin te rapporter des roses;
Mais j'en avais tant pris dans mes ceintures closes
Que les nœuds trop serrés n'ont pu les contenir.

Les nœuds ont éclaté. Les roses envolées
Dans le vent, à la mer s'en sont toutes allées.
Elles ont suivi l'eau pour ne plus revenir.

La vague en a paru rouge et comme enflammée.
Ce soir, ma robe encore en est toute embaumée...
Respires-en sur moi l'odorant souvenir.

LA COURONNE EFFEUILLÉE

J'irai, j'irai porter ma couronne effeuillée
Au jardin de mon père où revit toute fleur;
J'y répandrai longtemps mon âme agenouillée:
Mon père a des secrets pour vaincre la douleur.

J'irai, j'irai lui dire, au moins avec mes larmes:
"Regardez, j'ai souffert..." il me regardera,
Et sous mes jours changés, sous mes pâleurs sans charmes,
Parce qu'il est mon père il me reconnaîtra.

Il dira: "C'est donc vous, chère âme désolée!
La terre manque-t-elle à vos pas égarés?
Chère âme, je suis Dieu: ne soyez plus troublée;
Voici votre maison, voici mon cœur, entrez!"

O clémence! ô douceur! ô saint refuge! ô père!
Votre enfant qui pleurait vous l'avez entendu!
Je vous obtiens déjà puisque je vous espère
Et que vous possédez tout ce que j'ai perdu.

* THE ROSES OF SAADI

I brought you morning roses; but, too rash,
I took so many that my knotted sash
Was far too full to hold them carefully.

The knots gave way. The roses, flying on
The wind, flew to the sea... Each one, flown, gone...
Swept away, never to return to me.

The tide flamed red, flickering hither, yon.
Tonight their perfume still lingers upon
My gown... Come, breathe their fragrant memory.

THE CROWN OF DEAD LEAVES

Yes, yes, I shall my crown of dead leaves wear
Into His garden, where flowers bloom again.
There, on my knees, I shall my soul lay bare:
My father holds the keys to conquer pain.

Yes, yes, I shall, with but my tears, convince
Him of my woe: "Look! See?" And though I be
Much changed of mien, pallid of feature, since
He is my father, still will He know me.

And He will say: "So! It is you, poor soul!
What? Have your stumbling steps so errant been?
I am your God. Begone your bale, your dole;
Here is my heart, your home: pour soul, come in!"

O mercy! Refuge! Holy balm divine!
Father, you heard your child, weeping her prayer!
Long have I yearned for you; now are you mine,
And all that I have lost lies in your care.

* The reference is to the celebrated Persian poet Muslih ud-Din (ca. 1184–ca. 1291 C.E.), known as Saadi, author of *Gulistan,* or *The Rose Garden.*

Vous ne rejetez pas la fleur qui n'est plus belle,
Ce crime de la terre au ciel est pardonné.
Vous ne maudirez pas votre enfant infidèle,
Non d'avoir rien vendu, mais d'avoir tout donné.

———————

RENONCEMENT

Pardonnez-moi, Seigneur, mon visage attristé,
Vous qui l'aviez formé de sourire et de charmes;
Mais sous le front joyeux aviez mis les larmes,
Et de vos dons, Seigneur, ce don seul m'est resté.

C'est le moins envié, c'est le meilleur peut-être:
Je n'ai plus à mourir à mes liens de fleurs;
Ils vous sont tous rendus, cher auteur de mon être,
Et je n'ai plus à moi que le sel de mes pleurs.

Les fleurs sont pour l'enfant; le sel est pour la femme;
Faites-en l'innocence et trempez-y mes jours.
Seigneur! quand tout ce sel aura lavé mon âme,
Vous me rendrez un cœur pour vous aimer toujours!

Tous mes étonnements sont finis sur la terre,
Tous mes adieux sont faits, l'âme est prête à jaillir,
Pour atteindre à ses fruits protégés de mystère
Que la pudique mort a seule osé cueillir.

O Sauveur! soyez tendre au moins à d'autres mères,
Par amour pour la vôtre et par pitié pour nous!
Baptisez leurs enfants de nos larmes amères,
Et relevez les miens tombés à vos genoux!

You do not spurn the flower grown pale, and you
* Pardon, in heaven, our earthly crime of love.
You will not curse your child, unfaithful, who
† Sold not, but gave all that she had thereof.

Poésies inédites, "Foi"

RENUNCIATION

Lord, pardon this sad face of mine, bereft
Of smiles you wrought upon my joyous brow:
For tears you fashioned there as well; and now,
‡ Lord, of your gifts, that one alone is left.

Least coveted, and yet, perchance, the best:
Never my links to life shall see me dead.
My flowers have flown, sweet maker, to your breast;
Mine, now, naught but the salt tears I have shed.

For children, flowers; for woman, weeping; may
You wash me in their innocence, O Lord!
And when that salt has cleansed my soul, I pray
To love you ever, with a heart restored!

Life holds no more surprises now for me;
All my farewells are said; my soul prepares
To seize those fruits, shrouded in mystery,
That Death alone, discreet, plucks when she dares.

O Savior! Mercy! Pray more pity show
To others, for your mother's sake and mine.
Baptize their children with our tears of woe,
And raise mine, fallen at your feet divine!

Poésies inédites, "Foi"

* Following traditional interpretation of this line, I have taken the liberty of making explicit the "crime" implicit in the reference.

† It is generally assumed that the allusion here is to the Old Testament story of Esau, who was cursed by God for selling his right of primogeniture.

‡ I have retained the poet's rhyme scheme here, which for no apparent reason differs from that of her following quatrains.

Marceline Desbordes-Valmore 601

L'ESCLAVE

Pays des noirs! Berceau du pauvre Arsène,
Ton souvenir vient-il chercher mon cœur?
Vent de Guinée, est-ce la douce haleine
Qui me caresse et charme ma douleur?
M'apportes-tu les soupirs de ma mère,
Ou la chanson qui console mon père?...
    Jouez, dansez, beaux petits blancs;
    Pour être bons, restez enfants!

Nègre captif, couché sur le rivage,
Je te vois rire en rêvant à la mort;
Ton âme libre ira sur un nuage,
Où ta naissance avait fixé ton sort:
Dieu te rendra les baisers de ta mère
Et la chanson que t'apprenait ton père!...
    Jouez, dansez, beaux petits blancs;
    Pour être bons, restez enfants!

Pauvre et content jamais le noir paisible,
Pour vous troubler, n'a traversé les flots;
Et parmi vous, sous un maître inflexible,
Jamais d'un homme on n'entend les sanglots.
Pour vous ravir des baisers d'une mère,
Qu'avons-nous fait au dieu de votre père?...
    Jouez, dansez, beaux petits blancs;
    Pour être bons, restez enfants!

Land of the blacks! Cradle of poor Arsène,
Is it you that send me your memories?
You, Guinea's gentle breeze, that blows again
To ease my heart and calm my agonies?
Bring you the sighs my mother sighs for me?
The song that soothes my father's misery?
    You, sweet white tots! Play, dance... However,
    Would you be good? Stay young forever!

O black man lying captive by the shore,
I see you laugh; and, as you muse on death,
Your soul, cloud-borne, will go wafting once more
To where, by fate's decree, you first drew breath.
God-restored shall your mother's kisses be,
And the song taught you at your father's knee!
    You, sweet white tots! Play, dance... However,
    Would you be good? Stay young forever!

Never did peaceful black—poor but content—
To snatch you up, set sail over the waves;
Nor, in your land, does the intransigent
Master drone to the moan and sob of slaves!
To scorn and spurn your father's god, did we
Wrench you from mother's kisses, savagely?
    You, sweet white tots! Play, dance... However,
    Would you be good? Stay young forever!

* The original of this poem, with several minor variants, first appeared in the poet's novella "Sarah," printed in her collections *Les veillées des Antilles* (1821) and *Huit femmes* (1845).

Marceline Desbordes-Valmore 603

Amable Tastu (1798–1885)

Although scarcely remembered today, Amable Tastu was a poetic force to be reckoned with in her own time. One finds an obscure but probably typical testimony to her prestige in the dedication and adulatory verses thanking her for her counsel and encouragement by a francophone Louisiana poet, Charles Testut—by sheer coincidence almost homonymous, and even less known today than she—in his 1849 collection *Les échos*. Addressing her as a "muse bien chère à tous et, à moi, la plus chère" (muse dear to all, and dearest to myself), Testut recalls, rather grandiloquently, to be sure, her kindness to him as a debutant poet, with gratitude for "the balm of hope, with touching concern" that she lavished on his artistic self-doubt. It was this same generous spirit that expressed itself in the many works devoted to the young, which, as in the case of Marceline Desbordes-Valmore, formed a significant part of her prose (see p. 568 above). But it was also for practical reasons that she, like her *consœur,* turned to that literary vein.

[Sabine-Casimir-]Amable Voiart was born in 1798 in Metz (in whose museum her portrait hangs, along with those of other city notables, Verlaine among them). She lost her mother at seven and a dozen years later married Joseph Tastu, a printer originally from Perpignan and publisher of *Le Mercure de France*. After several youthful poetic successes, crowned by the venerable Académie des Jeux floraux de Toulouse, by recognition from the Académie française, and by a commission to compose a poem for the coronation of Charles X in 1824, she was quickly welcomed into Parisian salon circles—Madame Récamier's and others—and Charles Nodier's literary coterie, known as the Cénacle. She was befriended and admired by early romantics like Lamartine and Chateaubriand and praised even by the soon-to-be venerated Victor Hugo himself.

But the disinterested love of poetry for which she had shown a talent since childhood had to give way to more lucrative pursuits, because she was obliged to help support her family in the wake of her husband's financial ruin after the Revolution of 1830. A variety of popular children's stories, pedagogical treatises, translations—one, among them, of *Robinson Crusoe*, reprinted several times with great success—historical essays, travelogues, and literary history cast poetry into the background, though she continued to write as much as circumstances would allow, even throughout the virtual blindness of her latter years. Widowed in 1849, she spent those years with her only son, a diplomat frequently assigned to the Middle East, and died at Palaiseau, just outside Paris in 1885 after living through the upheavals of the Prussian siege and the Commune.[1]

Amable Tastu's poetic *œuvre* spans three collections in a dozen years, from

1826 through 1838, with her *Poésies complètes* published twenty years later. Tastu was strongly influenced by both medieval poetry and the English romantics, Shelley and Byron among them. She had been steeped in the bardic works of the pseudo-Celtic "Ossian" by her stepmother and was imbued with an obvious love of Irish and Scottish lore. The delicacy and music of her melancholy, no less motivated for being à la mode, indicate a poetic talent that would surely have delighted even more had life only not limited her productivity. It is not surprising that the musicality of her lyrics, with their frequent refrains, lent some of them to vocal settings (by Saint-Saëns and others). Nor is one surprised to find, on occasion, the gently muted complaints of a woman whose artistic freedom was compromised by the practical exigencies of living.

The first five of the poems here translated are taken from the 1826 collection *Poésies*; the last four, from *Poésies nouvelles* of 1838.

NOTE

1. Though Sainte-Beuve devoted several pages to her in his *Portraits contemporains*, pp. 158–76, there are far fewer studies of Amable Tastu's work than her lyrical talent might have led one to expect. Other than Earl Jeffrey Richards's brief biographical sketch in the *Encyclopedia of Continental Women Writers*, pp. 1224–25, especially valuable for its systematic bibliography of her work, see Alison Finch, *Women's Writing in Nineteenth-Century France*, pp. 48–49, 97–101, and passim; and, more recently, Afifa Marzouki's comprehensive study, *Amable Tastu, une poétesse à l'époque romantique*.

L'ÉCHO DE LA HARPE

Pauvre Harpe du barde, au lambris suspendue,
Tu dormais, dès long-temps poudreuse et détendue!
D'un souffle vagabond la brise de la nuit
Sur ta corde muette éveille un léger bruit:
Telle dort en mon sein cette harpe cachée,
Et que seule la Muse a quelquefois touchée.
Alors qu'un mot puissant, un songe, un souvenir,
Une pensée errante et douce à retenir,
L'effleurent en passant d'une aile fugitive,
Elle vibre soudain; et mon ame attentive,
Emue à cet accord qui se perd dans les cieux,
Garde du son divin l'écho mélodieux.

LAI DE LA MORT D'AMOUR

Merci, gentilles Jouvencelles,
M'avez reçu dans le châtel.
Soyez tendres autant que belles,
Saurez les chants du ménestrel;
Les retins de mon noble maître,
Car ai tout appris dans sa cour;
Vous conterai la Mort d'Amour,
Et vous verrai plorer peut-être!

Poor harp—a minstrel's once—from wainscot hung,
Long did you sleep, dust-covered and unstrung,
When lo! the night breeze, in its wanderings,
Wakened a murmur in your silent strings.
In my breast sleeps a harp that, quite as much,
Wakes, betimes, at the Muse's slightest touch.
Let but a dream, a thought sweet for the keeping—
A word, a memory—brush it, gently sleeping,
With grazing wing, and suddenly I hear
Chords from its quivering strings: my soul gives ear,
Holds fast the echoes of those notes that rise
Divine, soar... disappear beyond the skies.

† THE LAY OF THE DEATH OF LOVE

My thanks, ye comely *demoiselles,*
Who to your castle welcome me.
Well met and gentle be as well,
And you shall hear my minstrelsy.
My lays heard I from noble lord
And in his court learned all thereof;
So shall I sing *The Death of Love:*
Your tears, mayhap, be my reward.

---

* This poem's Celtic—bardic—inspiration, characteristic of much early French ro-
mantic poetry, is underscored by an introductory quotation from "The Coina, or Dirge" of
Thomas Moore: "My gentle Harp! once more I waken / The sweetness of thy slumbering
strain..." Moore would seem to have been one of the poet's favorites, judging by a number
of epigraphs and imitations in her work.

† As an epigraph to this lay in archaic style, the poet gives, in Old French, her final refrain,
which she indicates as being from the work of Thibaut, king of Navarre (1201–1253), usually
known as Thibaut de Champagne: "Cy gist amors qui bien amer faysait, / Le faulx amans
l'ont jeté hors de vie; / Amors vivant n'est rien que tromperie, / Por franc amors, priez Dieu,
s'il vos plaist." An exhaustive review of Thibaut's lyrics, in several editions—including one
contemporaneous with Amable Tastu (*Chansons de Thibaut IV, comte de Champagne et de
Brie* [Reims, 1851]—has failed to reveal anything resembling these lines, typical of the courtly
tradition though they are. Perhaps the poet was thinking of another of the love poets of me-
dieval France. Be that as it may, I am grateful to her for having encouraged my rereading (and
re-rereading) of Thibaut, which I doubt I would otherwise have done.

N'est plus amour qui bien aimer faisait;
Les faux amans l'ont jeté hors de vie;
Amour vivant n'est rien que tromperie;
Pour franc amour priez Dieu, s'il vous plaît!

Que franc amour avait de charmes!
Quel éclat brillait dans ses yeux!
De sa mort n'avais point d'alarmes,
Le croyais au nombre des dieux.
L'une de vous pourrait connaître
Que n'ai point flatté le portrait;
Ne veux pas trahir son secret,
Mais la verrai rougir peut-être.

N'est plus amour qui bien aimer faisait;
Les faux amans l'ont jeté hors de vie;
Amour vivant n'est rien que tromperie;
Pour franc amour priez Dieu, s'il vous plaît!

Las! bientôt, malgré sa jeunesse,
Il sentit la faulx du trépas;
Accablé d'ennuis, de tristesse,
Amour s'éteignait dans mes bras.
Voyais sa force disparaître,
Ses traits se faner et pâlir,
Un oubli le faisait mourir,
Un regard l'eût sauvé pent-être!

N'est plus amour qui bien aimer faisait;
Les faux amans l'ont jeté hors de vie;
Amour vivant n'est rien que tromperie;
Pour franc amour priez Dieu, s'il vous plaît!

Mis en bûcher lettre amoureuse,
Sermens félons, trompeurs aveux,
L'azur d'une écharpe menteuse,
Bouquets flétris et blonds cheveux;
L'astre du soir vint à paraître,
Y portai les restes d'amour.
Alors, pour le priver du jour,
Mes pleurs auraient suffi peut-être!

No more that love that wrought a lover true:
False lovers dealt a deathblow foul, complete.
Naught lives of love but ruse and fell deceit:
Pray God for loyal love, I beg of you!

What charms had loyal love! He shone
In splendor, gleaming, bright of eye.
How could I fear him dead and gone?
A very god he was, thought I.
One of you knows my words accord
With his true portrait; but I would
Not tell her secret: if I should,
A blush, mayhap, be my reward.

No more that love that wrought a lover true:
False lovers dealt a deathblow foul, complete.
Naught lives of love but ruse and fell deceit:
Pray God for loyal love, I beg of you!

The deathly scythe soon laid him low,
Alas, despite his youth, downcast
With many a dole and grievous woe,
And in my arms he gasped his last.
A glance might have his life restored;
But no: I watched him as his breath
Grew short, his features pale, as death
Bestowed his error's last reward.

No more that love that wrought a lover true:
False lovers dealt a deathblow foul, complete.
Naught lives of love but ruse and fell deceit:
Pray God for loyal love, I beg of you!

Onto the pyre, the billet-doux,
Oaths, faithless lies, *aye* turned to *nay*,
Perfidious scarf of azure hue,
Strands of blond hair; withered bouquet:
Off bear I love's remains adored
To where the evening star appears;
Enough, mayhap, my flood of tears
To send him to his last reward!

N'est plus amour qui bien aimer faisait;
Les faux amans l'ont jeté hors de vie;
Amour vivant n'est rien que tromperie;
Pour franc amour priez Dieu, s'il vous plaît!

Dans un bocage solitaire
S'élève la tombe d'amour;
On verra naïve bergère
Y rêver au déclin du jour.
Puisse un cœur inconstant et traître,
Dans ce lieu passer un moment!
Sur l'albâtre du monument
En soupirant lira peut-être:

"Ci-gît amour qui bien aimer faisait;
Les faux amans l'ont jeté hors de vie;
Amour vivant n'est rien que tromperie;
Pour franc amour priez Dieu, s'il vous plaît!"

LA GUIRLANDE

Je connais dans les bois, sur le front des montagnes,
La fleur qui sert d'asile aux songes incertains.
Cours, ô jeune beauté, dépouille les campagnes;
Que leurs dons parfumés s'assemblent sous tes mains.
Hâtons-nous de former la guirlande légère,
Qui doit rendre l'amour à tes vœux assidus;
Hâtons-nous, le temps fuit, la fleur est passagère,
Les songes et les fleurs demain ne seront plus!

Le songe de l'amour, vers la vierge timide,
S'élance chaque nuit de ce jasmin humide;
Le songe de l'espoir, plus fidèle au malheur,
Et dont le chant magique assoupit la douleur,
Naît de cet amandier qui dans les airs balance
De ses rameaux fleuris la pompeuse imprudence:
Hâtons-nous, profitons de ces rians tributs;
Les songes et les fleurs demain ne seront plus!

No more that love that wrought a lover true:
False lovers dealt a deathblow foul, complete.
Naught lives of love but ruse and fell deceit:
Pray God for loyal love, I beg of you!

A grove in woodland loneliness:
There will the grave of love be found.
Dusk finds a simple shepherdess,
Each night, to dream her dream, come round.
Ah! May some treasonous heart afford
A moment there, pause in the gloom,
And read the alabaster tomb,
Then sighs, mayhap, be love's reward:

"Here lies the love that wrought a lover true:
False lovers dealt a deathblow foul, complete.
Naught lives of love but ruse and fell conceit:
Pray God for loyal love, I beg of you!"

---

* THE GARLAND

On mountains' brow I know a woodland; there
Grow flowers where formless dreams take refuge: thence,
O my young beauty, run! Strip the land bare,
And let your fingers gather up their scents.
Make haste! Let us a dainty garland tress
That shall love's passion to your will restore.
Make haste! Time flees... Flowers blossom, evanesce...
Tomorrow, flowers and dreams will be no more!

Love's dream flies from this jasmine, pearled, by night,
And the coy virgin grasps it in its flight;
Hope's dream, more faithful to despair forlorn,
Whose magic song lulls woe and weal, is born
Out of this almond-tree that recklessly
Sways, wafts its flowered boughs' pomposity:
Make haste, and waste not these fond tributes; for
Tomorrow, flowers and dreams will be no more!

* A close imitation of Thomas Moore, this poem is preceded by the epigraph "I know where the winged visions dwell," from a lyric in Part X of his lengthy narrative poem "Lalla Rookh": "I know where the winged visions dwell / That around the night-bed play; / I know each herb and flow'ret's bell, / Where they hide their wings by day."

Cette fleur, où se cache une brillante image,
Teint des couleurs de l'or la dent du faon sauvage;
La noire mandragore, en inspirant l'horreur,
Poursuit le meurtrier d'un fantôme vengeur.
Garde-toi d'approcher cette plante ennemie
Qui jette la terreur dans nos sens éperdus;
Tressons, tressons ces fleurs, hâtons-nous, jeune amie,
Les songes et les fleurs demain ne seront plus!

Voici le cannellier, à l'écorce odorante;
Le songe du cœur pur qui l'habite le jour,
Oppose au noir soupçon la douceur caressante:
Ah! ce songe puissant ramènera l'amour.
Hâtons-nous, hâtons-nous, achevons la guirlande,
Les instans différés sont des instans perdus;
Cours au front d'un amant déposer ton offrande,
Les songes et les fleurs demain ne seront plus!

L'ODALISQUE

Imitation de Thomas Moore

Aux bords du Bendemir est un berceau de roses
Que jusqu'au dernier jour on me verra chérir;
Le chant du rossignol, dans ses fleurs demi-closes,
        Charme les flots du Bendemir.

J'aimais à m'y bercer d'un songe fantastique;
M'enivrant de parfums, de repos, d'avenir,
J'écoutais tour à tour l'oiseau mélancolique
        Et les ondes du Bendemir.

This flower, of brilliant image, hidden, tints
The wild and free fawn's tooth with golden glints...
* But flee the mandrake, black, fear-redolent,
That stalks the killer of a phantom bent
On vengeance! Draw not close, young friend. Abhor
That plant that casts our wits in disarray!
Make haste! Tress these... Fit to be tressed are they:
Tomorrow, flowers and dreams will be no more!

The cinammon-tree's buds, its fragrant bark...
The pure heart's dream that, by day, dwells within,
Parries with sweet caress the fearsome dark;
Dream that will raise up love that once had been.
Make haste! Let us complete the garland now!
Moments postponed are moments lost; ignore
Time not: gird round, enwreathed, a lover's brow:
Tomorrow, flowers and dreams will be no more!

———————

THE ODALISQUE

Imitation of Thomas Moore

† The Bendemeer flows by a rosebush bower
That, till my dying day, I shall hold dear;
The nightingale charms, midst the buds a-flower,
   The billows of the Bendemeer.

Cradled, I mused my fancies by the stream:
By turns I listened to the bird's song, drear—
Glutting on sweet repose, scents, future's dream—
   And the waves of the Bendemeer.

* Numerous superstitions, mostly unpleasant, have surrounded the mandrake root
since ancient times. Though it is associated with female fertility in the Old Testament
(Gen. 30:14–16), it was also associated with death and long believed to have been engen-
dered by the sperm of a criminal hanged for murder. Shakespeare refers to its supposedly
stupefying properties in *Antony and Cleopatra:* "Give me to drink mandragora . . . / That I
might sleep out this great gap of time / My Antony is away" (1.5).

   † Like the preceding poem, this too is a close imitation of a lyric from Moore's "Lalla
Rookh" inserted in Part I ("There's a bower of roses by Bendemeer's stream, / And the
nightingale sings round it all the day long"); the river Kur, or Kyrus, in southern Iran, was
mistakenly called the Bendemeer by Moore and other foreigners.

Maintenant, loin des lieux où fleurit mon aurore,
Je dis: Voit-on encor la rose s'embellir,
Et le chantre des nuits soupire-t-il encore
        Sur les rives du Bendemir?

Non, le printemps n'est plus, la rose s'est flétrie;
Le triste rossignol de douleur va mourir,
Et je ne verrai plus couler dans ma patrie
        Les flots d'azur du Bendemir.

Mais il nous reste au moins, quand la rose est passée,
Un parfum précieux que l'art sait obtenir,
Pareil au souvenir qui rend à ma pensée
        Les bords rians du Bendemir.

RÊVERIE

Alors que sur les monts l'ombre s'est abaissée,
Des jours qui ne sont plus s'éveille la pensée,
Le temps fuit plus rapide, il entraîne sans bruit
Le cortége léger des heures de la nuit.
Un songe consolant rend au cœur solitaire
Tous les biens qui jadis l'attachaient à la terre,
Ses premiers sentimens et ses premiers amis,
Et les jours de bonheur qui lui furent promis.
Calme d'un âge heureux, pure et sainte ignorance,
Amitié si puissante, et toi, belle espérance,
Doux trésors qui jamais ne me seront rendus,
Ah! peut-on vivre encore et vous avoir perdus!

Now, far from where blossomed my early dawn,
I ask: "Blooms yet the rose of yesteryear?
And does night's warbler still sigh on and on
    By the shores of the Bendemeer?"

No, spring is gone, the rose is withered; and
Doleful, the nightingale will disappear.
No more shall I see flow in my fair land
    The azure of the Bendemeer.

But, though the rose is fled, it leaves behind
A fragrance wrought of art; sweet souvenir,
Memory calling evermore to mind
    The gay banks of the Bendemeer.

----

*   REVERIE

When evening on the hills its shade has cast,
Memories waken of those days long past;
Time, in its silent course and gentle flight,
Whisks, one by one, the swift hours of the night.
Dreaming, the lonely heart relives, consoled,
Joys that this life delighted in of old:
Its earliest passions, friendship's first caresses,
And days on days of promised happinesses.
Calm of a carefree age—chaste, naïve, pure;
Fast friend; and you, O my hoped-for *amour:*
Sweet treasures, lost forever, pleasure-rife...
Ah! Can one lose you all and still live life?

* The poet, in her obvious admiration for the English romantics, introduces her poem
with lines from Byron's *Childe Harold's Pilgrimage*: "'Tis night! . . . / The soul forgets her
schemes of hope and pride, / And flies unconscious o'er each backward year."

LA FLEUR DU VOLCAN

Ce n'est pas la nature qui est triste, c'est la vie.
—Jules Lefèvre

Humble et chétive fleur, par le sort condamnée,
Sur le flanc d'un volcan pourquoi donc es-tu née?
Qu'as-tu fait à ce sort, dont l'injuste dédain
Te refusa l'enclos d'un rustique jardin?
Au gré de sa faveur, ta grace solitaire
Eût fait même l'orgueil d'un somptueux parterre,
Sous les yeux satisfaits d'opulens possesseurs,
Qui te proclameraient belle parmi tes sœurs!
Hélas! telle n'est point la part qui t'est restée!
Sur un sol frémissant, sans relâche agitée,
Tu fleuris sans repos, tu souffres sans témoins;
Ceux qui t'auraient pu voir sont émus d'autres soins;
Qu'importe qu'à leurs pieds un doux parfum s'exhale
Dans l'ombre et le secret de ta corolle pâle,
Qui, long-temps exposée à tous les vents du ciel,
Garde encore à l'abeille une goutte de miel?
Quand une ville, un peuple, un empire s'efface,
Qui songerait à toi, qui chercherait ta trace,
Pauvre fleur oubliée au sein des rocs déserts,
Où tu subis long-temps l'inclémence des airs?...

THE VOLCANO'S FLOWER

Nature is not what is sad; it is life.
*   —Jules Lefèvre*

Poor, lowly flower, condemned by fate's cruel prank
Thus to be born on the volcano's flank!
Why? What ill have you done to fate, that she
Refused you the rustic tranquillity
Of garden penned? Had her favor so willed,
Your solitary grace might have fulfilled
The pride of some lush, sumptuous flower bed,
To please the gazes of well-pursed, well-fed
Lords of the manse, who would claim you to be
Fairest among your sisters!... Destiny,
Alas, did not decree that such a share
Be yours. And so, quaking, you blossom where
Earth shakes you endlessly, and where no one
Is there to see your suffering, never done.
Other concerns have they who might have been
Moved by your sight; but what they have not seen,
Not smelled, they know naught of: your sweet perfume
Wafted unsavored in the shadowed gloom;
Your pale corolla's secret, fragrant yet
Of honey, that the bee can scarce forget
Despite the winds of heaven unleashed! But then,
When cities fall, when races die, and when
Whole empires disappear, who will give but
A thought to you, poor flower, or wonder what,
Lost in the rockbound wastes, you have become,
After your long and gale-tossed martyrdom?...

---

* Jules-Alexandre Lefèvre-Deumier (1797–1857), a medical doctor and minor poet, was a member of the Paris literary group called the Cénacle, important in the early days of the romantic movement. Besides a number of Byron-inspired works, he also wrote several prose poems and works of literary history and criticism. I have not been able to trace the present quotation—likely from one of his prose writings, given its length, unorthodox for a work of verse at the time.

Amable Tastu 617

LA BARQUE

Frale barca
Mi trovo in alto mar senza governo.
—Pétrarque

Mon œil rêveur suit la barque lointaine
Qui vient à moi, faible jouet des flots;
J'aime à la voir déposer sur l'arène
D'adroits pêcheurs, de joyeux matelots.
Mais à ma voix, nulle voix qui réponde!
La barque est vide, et je n'ose approcher.
    Nacelle vagabonde,
    A la merci de l'onde,
Pourquoi voguer sans rame et sans nocher?

La mer paisible et le ciel sans nuage
Sont embellis des feux du jour naissant;
Mais dans la nuit grondait un noir orage;
L'air était sombre et le flot menaçant!...
Quand l'espérance, en promesses fécondes,
Ouvrit l'anneau qui t'enchaîne au rocher,
    Nacelle vagabonde,
    A la merci de l'onde,
Pourquoi voguer sans rame et sans nocher?

Oui, ton retour cache un triste mystère!
D'un poids secret il oppresse mon cœur.
Sur cette plage, errante et solitaire,
J'ai vu pleurer la femme du pêcheur!
Es-tu l'objet de sa douleur profonde?
Ses longs regards allaient-ils te chercher?
    Nacelle vagabonde,
    A la merci de l'onde,
Pourquoi voguer sans rame et sans nocher?

THE BARQUE

> *Frail barque,*
> *Here am I, on the high seas, rudderless.*
> *   —Petrarch

Musing, I spy a barque, far from the land,
Approaching, plaything of the tides; anon,
How I will love to watch the joyous band
Of sailors, fisherfolk, step forth upon
The sandy shore... But no voice answers me!
Empty the skiff: draw near I dare not, for,
  Barque adrift, aimlessly
  Afloat, how can it be
That you sail with no oarsman and no oar?

Calm now the sea and beautiful the sky,
Cloudless, aflame with dawn's first fires. But night,
Growling, had churned the black waves, and let fly
A howling tempest with its fearsome might!...
When fertile hope, heavy with progeny,
Unloosed the chain that moors you to the shore,
  Barque adrift, aimlessly
  Afloat, how can it be
That you sail with no oarsman and no oar?

Yes, back you came from some sad fate unknown!
How heavy on my heart your secrets press:
I saw, wandering along the strand, alone,
A fisherman's wife, weeping her distress!
Are you the object of her woe? Did she
Peer her gaze deep into the night, heartsore?
  Barque adrift, aimlessly
  Afloat, how can it be
That you sail with no oarsman and no oar?

---

* The quotation is from the first tercet of Petrarch's sonnet CXXXIII: "S'amor non è, che dunque è quel ch'io sento?" (If not love, this, what is it that I feel?).

Amable Tastu 619

LA JEUNE FILLE

De Gil Vicente

Qu'elle est gracieuse et belle!
Est-il rien d'aussi beau qu'elle?

Me diras-tu, matelot,
Sur ta galère fidèle,
Si la galère, ou le flot,
Ou l'étoile est aussi belle?

Me diras-tu, chevalier,
Toi dont l'épée étincelle,
Si l'épée, ou le coursier,
Ou la guerre est aussi belle?

THE DAMSEL

*   *After Gil Vicente*

Damsel, beauteous as can be!
Is there aught as fair as she?

Seaman sailing in your skiff—
Trusty barque that plies the sea—
Tell me if the barque, or if
Waves, or stars, are fair as she!

Knight, you with your sword, perforce—
Sparkling, gleaming brilliantly—
Tell me, is your sword, your horse,
War itself as fair as she?

---

* This poem is a very close imitation of "La Doncella" by the medieval Portuguese-born dramatist Gil Vicente (ca. 1470–1536), thus making my version—as with the poems of Thomas Moore—a translation of a translation. The poet cites the original in its entirety (not without a few lines of debatable prosodic accuracy):

> ¡Muy graciosa es la Doncella!
> ¡Como es hermosa y bella!
>
> ¿Digas tu, el Marinero,
> Que en las naves vivias,
> Si la nave o la vela
> O la estrella es tan bella?
>
> ¿Digas tu, el Caballero,
> Que las armas vestias,
> Si el caballo, o las armas,
> O la guerra es tan bella?
>
> ¿Digas tu, el Pastorcito,
> Que el ganadico guardas,
> Si el ganado, o las valles,
> O la tierra es tan bella?
>
> ¡Muy graciosa es la Doncella!
> ¡Como es hermosa y bella!

Vicente's original speaks of *velas* (sails), not our poet's *flot* (waves). But since I am translating the French, I preserve her liberty, one she obviously took for the sake of rhyme.

Me diras-tu, pastoureau,
En paissant l'agneau qui bèle,
Si la montagne, ou l'agneau,
Ou la plaine est aussi belle?

Qu'elle est gracieuse et belle!
Est-il rien d'aussi beau qu'elle?

PLAINTE

O monde! ô vie! ô temps! fantômes, ombres vaines,
Qui lassez, à la fin, mes pas irrésolus,
Quand reviendront ces jours où vos mains étaient pleines,
Vos regards caressans, vos promesses certaines?
   Jamais, ô jamais plus!

L'éclat du jour s'éteint aux pleurs où je me noie;
Les charmes de la nuit passent inaperçus;
Nuit, jour, printemps, hiver, est-il rien que je voie?
Mon cœur peut battre encor de peine, mais de joie
   Jamais, ô jamais plus!

Shepherd lad, who watch will keep
As your bleating sheep graze free,
Tell me, are the hills, the sheep,
Or the plain as fair as she?

Damsel, beauteous as can be!
Is there aught as fair as she?

———————

[*] LAMENT

O world! Life! Time! Vain shadows, phantoms, who
Weary my aimless steps, whithersoever...
When will those days return, dear days when you
Gave with full hands, sweet looks, promises true?
        Nevermore! No... No, never!

Daylight dies in the tears that drown my woe.
The charms of night fly past, ignored forever:
Night, day, spring, winter... Do I know them so?
My heart beats yet with grief. But joy? Ah, no!
        Nevermore! No... No, never!

* A brief borrowing from Shelley's "A Lament"—the last line of both its five-line stanzas ("No more, oh never more!")—serves to introduce this imitation, typically faithful to the original, in both content and form.

Amable Tastu 623

Delphine Gay de Girardin (1804–1855)

Delphine Gay was born with many advantages that seemed to single her out for prominence. Not the least of them was an ambitious mother. Sophie Gay was herself a salon stalwart and talented *femme de lettres* of distinguished family background, and she was determined to see to it that her daughter, an exceptional beauty (according to the then prevailing canons), would not prove wanting in either the social or literary spheres of the Empire and the Restauration.

On the contrary, Delphine, born in Aix-la-Chapelle, with roots supposedly plunging deep into the time of Charlemagne, early displayed an exuberance of wit and spirit that endeared her to others. Added to that was a seemingly natural talent for self-expression—in verse, especially—that bubbled charmingly, albeit with a dose of de rigueur melancholy, in her frequent recitations before her mother's salon friends-in-letters. One of the young admirers of the eighteen-year-old Delphine was the poet Alfred de Vigny, dashingly uniformed and seven years her senior. Their idyll was brief, however, community of talent notwithstanding, and the budding romance was soon ended, though Vigny was to dedicate his *Poèmes antiques et modernes* to her years later (see p. 627n, 629n below).

One cannot say how much the admiration that greeted young Delphine's first poetic endeavors—her *Essais poétiques* and *Nouveaux essais poétiques,* published in 1824 and 1825—was sincere and how much was the natural result of social pandering to her influential mother. It is clear, however, that, letting that youthful success go to her head, she penned a pompous encomium for the coronation of Charles X in 1824. "La vision," invoking the shades of Joan of Arc and her mission to Charles IX, was roundly ridiculed, especially when compared to a similarly inspired work of Amable Tastu (see p. 604 above). In an effort to prop up her sagging self-esteem, a family friend, Abel Villemain, suggested that she employ her literary and charitable talents in the cause of Greek independence (see p. 637 below). Her success, both poetic and eleemosynary, was considerable; and it was probably for both reasons that, on a trip with her mother to Italy—in part, at least, to help her forget Vigny—she was fêted by the Roman literati with honors no less imposing than a previous commendation from the Académie française had been.

When, in 1831, Delphine married Emile de Girardin, *député* and director of *La presse,* virtual founder of the modern daily, most of her poetic production already lay behind her. Receiving the elite of Parisian letters—Balzac, Gautier, Musset, and many others—in her own salon, which was even more distinguished than her mother's, she eventually saw her career take a different direction, turning to the theater with a number of plays, serious and comic. One of the latter, *L'école des journalistes* (1840) reflected the role that she had assumed as commentator on the social and political scene in a column written for her husband's paper under the pseudonym Vicomte Charles de Launay—a position for which one imagines she did not have to compete—and which eventually produced a popular collection of ephemera under the title *Lettres parisiennes* in 1843. It may or may not be significant that another of her comedies, *Une femme qui déteste son mari* (A Woman Who Loathes Her Husband) did not appear until after her death in 1855.[1]

Six volumes of Delphine Gay de Girardin's complete works appeared posthumously in 1860–1861. Her *Poésies complètes* had appeared in 1842 and the collection was reprinted in 1876. The small group of poems translated in the following pages are reproduced from the section titled "Poésies" in the latter and are among her best known.

NOTE

1. The most detailed biography of Delphine Gay de Girardin (and her mother) is probably still Henri Malo, *Une muse et sa mère*. See also Eugène de Mirecourt's more venerable *Madame de Girardin (Delphine Gay)*. For a less straightforwardly biographical study, with more emphasis on her works in their historical context, see François de Bondy, *Une femme d'esprit en 1830. Madame de Girardin,* as well as the pages devoted to her by Joanna Richardson in *Genius in the Drawing-Room,* ed. Peter Quennell, pp. 71–83, and a variety of other studies, over the years. Most recently, she is one of the authors treated in Whitney Walton's *Eve's Proud Descendants: Four Women Writers and Republican Politics in Nineteenth-Century France.* A concise summary in English of her life and work is provided in Dorothy Kelly's entry in *French Women Writers,* pp. 188–95.

LE BONHEUR D'ÊTRE BELLE

Dédié à Madame Récamier

Quel bonheur d'être belle, alors qu'on est aimée!
Autrefois de mes yeux je n'étais pas charmée;
Je les croyais sans feu, sans douceur, sans regard;
Je me trouvais jolie un moment par hasard.
Maintenant ma beauté me paraît admirable.
Je m'aime de lui plaire, et je me crois aimable...
Il le dit si souvent! Je l'aime, et quand je voi
Ses yeux, avec plaisir, se reposer sur moi,
Au sentiment d'orgueil je ne suis point rebelle,
Je bénis mes parents de m'avoir fait si belle!
Et je rends grâce à Dieu, dont l'insigne bonté
Me fit le cœur aimant pour sentir ma beauté.
Mais... pourquoi dans mon cœur ces subites alarmes?...
Si notre amour tous deux nous trompait sur mes charmes;
Si j'étais laide enfin? Non... il s'y connaît mieux!
D'ailleurs pour m'admirer je ne veux que ses yeux!
Ainsi de mon bonheur jouissons sans mélange;
Oui, je veux lui paraître aussi belle qu'un ange.
Apprêtons mes bijoux, ma guirlande de fleurs,
Mes gazes, mes rubans, et, parmi ces couleurs,
Choisissons avec art celle dont la nuance
Doit avec plus de goût, avec plus d'élégance,
Rehausser de mon front l'éclatante blancheur,

THE JOY OF BEING FAIR

*   *Dedicated to Madame Récamier*

What joy to be so fair! For love it is
That has transformed me, now that I am his!
Before, my eyes held little charm for me:
I deemed them lifeless, dull; no radiancy
Flashed in their drab and vacant glance. But when
I found I pleased him, quite by chance, ah! then
At once my beauty seemed to shine; and now,
How happy am I to have changed somehow...
So much does he declare his love! And I
Love him no less; and when, at times, I spy
His gaze happily lighting on my face,
I do not try to spurn or to erase
The pride within me. Rather do I bless
My lineage for my wondrous loveliness!
And I thank God, whose goodness exemplary
Gave me, to sense it, not an ordinary
Heart, but one full of love... Ah, but... What fear
Is this I feel? What troubling thoughts appear,
Haunting me suddenly? What if, instead,
We are both, simply, by our love misled?
What if... Ah! What if I am ugly?... Oh!
He knows better than that! It is not so!
I want no eyes but his with which to see
My charms, and peer on them admiringly!
No! Let my joy be unalloyed... Yes, let
Me be fair as an angel for him, set
Amidst my jewels, my blooms of many hues,
My veils, my bows; and, artful, let me choose
The one whose shade, with taste and elegance,

---

* Madame Récamier, born Jeanne-Françoise Bernard (1777–1849), was a famous beauty, immortalized in a celebrated portrait by the painter David. Her salon at L'Abbaye-aux-Bois was a meeting place for the elegant social, literary, and artistic luminaries of Paris during the Restauration, one of the most faithful of whom was Chateaubriand. As a longtime acquaintance of her mother's, Récamier frequently crossed paths with the young Delphine at both her own salon and others of the period. Its dedication notwithstanding, the poem is not about Madame Récamier; rather, it is an outpouring of Delphine's elation at the beginning of her romance with Alfred de Vigny. See Malo, *Une muse et sa mère*, pp. 234–35.

Sans pourtant de mon teint balancer la fraîcheur.
Mais je ne trouve plus la fleur qu'il m'a donnée:
La voici: hâtons-nous, l'heure est déjà sonnée,
Bientôt il va venir! bientôt il va me voir!
Comme, en me regardant, il sera beau ce soir!
Le voilà! je l'entends, c'est sa voix amoureuse!
Quel bonheur d'être belle! Oh! que je suis heureuse!

LE MALHEUR D'ÊTRE LAIDE

En vain sur mon malheur Alfred veut me tromper,
Aux torts qu'il se reproche il ne peut échapper;
En vain il se promet de me rester fidèle;
Sa tristesse me dit que je ne suis plus belle.
Hélas! son inconstance est peinte en ses regrets.
Depuis qu'un mal affreux a dévasté mes traits,
Dans mes yeux autrefois embellis par mes larmes,
La douleur elle-même a perdu tous ses charmes.
L'orgueil de mon amour est détruit pour jamais,
Et je crains les regards de celui que j'aimais!
Pourquoi ses tendres soins m'ont-ils rendu la vie:
Dans la tombe du moins la beauté m'eût survie;
La mort ne m'aurait point enlevé son amour,
J'aurais charmé ses yeux jusqu'à mon dernier jour,
Et, rendant à ma cendre un douloureux hommage,
Son cœur serait resté fidèle à mon image!

Maintenant il s'épuise en serments superflus
Pour exprimer encor l'amour qu'il ne sent plus.
Sans espoir de bonheur, sans trouble, sans ivresse,
C'est dans ses souvenirs qu'il cherche sa tendresse,

Will the white splendor of my brow enhance,
Yet not match my fresh tint... Where is that flower
He gave me?... Here it is!... Be quick!... The hour
Has struck... He will arrive! And he will be
Handsome tonight, as his eyes gaze on me!...
I hear him! Oh, that loving voice!... Ah yes,
What joy to be so fair! What happiness!

————————

THE WOE OF BEING UGLY

*   In vain does Alfred seek to ease my woe.
He cannot flee his wrongs repented; though
He promises that ever will he be
A faithful lover, when he looks on me
His sadness says I am no longer fair.
Inconstancy, alas, is written there
In his regrets, and all his look belies
The loving words he speaks. My face, my eyes
That tears once beautified, have been laid waste,
Undone, by frightful malady debased;
And even grief has lost its charms. The pride
I felt in love lies ravaged, mortified;
I shudder lest he look upon me! Why,
Why did his tender care not let me die?
At least I should have perished lovely yet,
And still beloved, for he would not forget
How I once looked, though in the grave I dwell;
Bidding my ashes one last, sad farewell,
His heart would linger faithfully forever
On that fair image, and forsake it never.

Now he consumes himself in useless oath
And pledge, to prove that he still plies a troth
Undying, though he could not love me less,
In truth! No hope of joy, no heart's distress,

* The allusion is certainly to Alfred de Vigny. The biographical similarities end there, however, since Delphine was far from being ugly; nor would she sacrifice her lover to a beautiful sister, as suggested at the end of the poem, but lost him, rather, to an English-woman whose supposed wealth had seduced Vigny's socially pretentious mother. See Malo, *Une muse et sa mère*, p. 237.

Et, triste lorsqu'il veut m'admirer aujourd'hui,
Ses yeux sur mon portrait se fixent malgré lui.
Pour être plus sincère, en sa pitié touchante,
Il dit que je suis bonne, et que ma voix l'enchante.
Quand, des soins d'une amie implorant la douceur,
Je repose mon front sur le sein de ma sœur,
Il sourit tendrement, il nous regarde ensemble,
Et dit, pour me flatter, que ma sœur me ressemble.
Mais celle qui garda ses attraits séduisants,
Et celle qui, mourante à la fleur de ses ans,
A vu s'évanouir une beauté trop chère,
Ne se ressemblent plus qu'aux regards d'une mère.

En vain la mienne aussi cherche à me rassurer,
Et des mêmes atours veut encor me parer;
Sa ruse ne saurait tromper celui que j'aime,
Et pour lui seul, hélas! je ne suis plus la même!
Ah! puisque son bonheur n'est plus en mon pouvoir,
Qu'une autre l'accomplisse!... et je saurai le voir!
Qu'il lui porte ces fleurs, ces voiles d'hyménée,
Cette blanche couronne à mon front destinée,
Oui... de ma jeune sœur qu'il devienne l'époux,
Qu'elle rende la joie à ses regards si doux,
Et qu'Alfred, dégagé de sa foi généreuse,
Oublie en l'admirant que je suis malheureuse!

No bliss... Nothing but tender recollection.
And when he would look on me with affection,
Sadly, despite himself, his gaze falls on
This ugly image of me, woebegone!
Then, to seem all the more sincere, he would
Have me believe that I am kind and good;
And, with a touching pity, tells me how
He finds my voice enchanting. And when, now
And then, yearning for friend's caress, I rest
My weary head upon my sister's breast,
He looks at me, and, with a gentle smile,
Hoping to flatter me and to beguile
My woe, he tells me that she looks like me.
But oh! Only a mother, lovingly,
Could see the slightest likeness now between
That one—still fresh, and of enticing mien—
And me, the other, dying, who—sad truth!—
Saw beauty vanish in the bloom of youth.

In vain mine reassures me, and would try,
With the same finery, to prettify
My wretchedness; but she cannot deceive
Him whom I love with all her make-believe:
He knows that I am not the one I was!
Not in his eyes, I fear!... And so, because
The power is mine no more, alas, to bring
Him joy, let someone else be everything
To him that I am not! At least I still
Shall see his face!... Yes, let him come and fill
Her arms with flowers; let him place on her brow
The white wreath and the veils that suit her now,
Though meant for me!... Ah yes... Let my Alfred—
This noble, kind, and generous one—now wed
My sister! Let his love for her restore
Sweet joy to his admiring gaze once more;
And, from his promise set forever free,
Let him forget how deep my misery!

LE LOUP ET LE LOUVETEAU

Fable

Un soir, il m'en souvient, j'errais sous la feuillée;
J'écoutais d'un troupeau le bêlement lointain,
    Et de l'orage du matin
L'herbe fleurie était encor mouillée.
Dans la forêt j'entendis tout à coup
Une lugubre voix; c'était celle d'un loup.
A son élève il parlait de la sorte;
    Car ce vieux loup était sage, prudent,
        Et même un peu pédant:
"—Mon fils," lui disait-il, "avant tout il importe
D'examiner ici les rapports différents
Qui peuvent exister entre la nourriture,
Les costumes, les mœurs et la magistrature
Des moutons dévorés et des loups dévorants;
Déjà nous connaissons, grâce à l'arithmétique.
        Le nombre des agneaux,
        Des brebis, des chevreaux
Que nous avons croqués par ordre alphabetique;
        Maintenant il nous faut songer
        A démêler avec adresse
        La politique du berger.
        Ainsi donc, partez, le temps presse;
        Vous savez mes desseins secrets.
Allez, et secondez nos communs intérêts."

Fable

One evening, I remember, as I strolled
Under a leafy arbor, listening
   To bleating from a distant fold—
   With drops of moisture glistening
Still, from the morning storm, over the grass—
   Off in the woods it came to pass
   That, all at once, I chanced to hear
   A voice, somber and dour: it was
   An old wolf who spoke so, because
Prudent and wise—pedantic, too, I fear—
He lectured a young cub, his pupil; thus,
"My son," said he, "we must be curious
And study in detail all the relations
That may exist, in all their permutations,
   Betwixt the lambs devoured, and us,
The wolves devouring, as pertains to such
As costumes, customs, laws, and nourishment.
   We know already the extent—
In alphabetic order, forasmuch,
And thanks to calculations arithmetic!—
To which we have consumed lambs, kids, and ewes.
Now must we, in wise no less energetic,
   Study the shepherd too, and muse
Upon his manners and his means. So go!
   Time passes, and no doubt you know
My secret plans. Go!" the old wolf requests,
   "And serve our common interests."

* The poet informs us in a note that her fable is adapted from one in a collection by "M. le comte Orloff." A prose version that she also provides (translated from the Russian) indicates that she has taken a number of artistic liberties. Of the many Orloffs (or Orlovs) that run through Russian literary and political history, the one in question was Alexander Anfimovich Orlov (1791–1840), an artistically rather undistinguished ideologue of the bourgeoisie and virulent anti-aristocrat, whose favorite genre was the "moral-satirical novel," usualy written in a stilted, archaic style, but who also composed a variety of verse satires and fairy tales in a more simple, "folksy" language.

Alors le jeune loup obéit à son maître,
Il part. L'instant d'après je le vis reparaître:
"—Venez," s'écriait-il, "venez, ils dorment tous.
Jamais vous ne verrez une plus belle proie:
C'est un festin royal que le ciel nous envoie."
"—Bon," dit l'autre, "et les chiens, ami, qu'en pensez-vous?"
"—Les chiens? ils sont chétifs et de peu d'apparence;
Ils ne m'ont point senti, je leur crois mauvais nez.
Le parc n'est pas très-haut, nous sauterons, venez."
     "—Et le pasteur?"—"Oh! quelle différence!
     Chacun prétend qu'au milieu des dangers
Il conduit ses moutons en maréchal de France:
        C'est le Turenne des bergers."
     "—S'il est ainsi, changeons de batterie,
Et pour un coup plus sûr réservons nos moyens;
Croyez qu'un bon berger a toujours de bons chiens.
Je sais sur la montagne une autre bergerie,
        Dont les chiens gros et gras
        Font beaucoup d'embarras;
     Mais je crains peu leur humeur difficile.
        Sans doute ils n'ont point de talent,
        Car ici leur maître indolent
        Passe pour être un imbécile"

De connaître les grands si vous êtes jaloux,
Mettez, mon jeune ami, cela sur vos registres:
Dans le gouvernement des hommes et des loups,
Un sot roi n'a jamais que de mauvais ministres.

The young wolf listens and, quick to obey
      His master, leaves, but stays away
Only an instant; for, a moment later,
I see him reappear. "Come quick, I say!"
      He cries out to his educator.
"Never will you see such a prey as this!
They sleep, each blessèd one! What joy, what bliss!
Heaven sends us the most regal of feasts!"
      "Aha!" replies the other, "But
What of his hounds?" "His hounds? Poor, paltry beasts!
      They could not even smell me, what!
Come! We can leap the sheepfold wall with ease."
"What of the shepherd?" "Everyone agrees—
Not that it matters!—that he is a very
Model of France's genius military:
*   They call him sheepdom's Maréchal Turenne!"
"Aha!" the wolf responded, "Think again!
Better we use our tactics customary
Against a more submissive prey; for, when
Clever the shepherd, so his hounds as well.
I know a sheepfold on the mountainside
      Whose hounds leave others terrified,
So big and fat are they! But, truth to tell,
Their lazy master is a mindless twit,
And I fear not their talent! Not one whit!"

If you yearn to frequent the great, best, then,
You add this fact into your reckonings;
My young friend, as with wolves, so too with men:
A stupid king has worthless underlings.

---

* Maréchal de France Henri de la Tour d'Auvergne, vicomte de Turenne (1611–1675),
was one of Louis XIV's most successful military commanders and distinguished himself
especially during the latter years of the Thirty Years' War.

ENVOI À M. VILLEMAIN, QUI M'AVAIT CHARGÉE DE QUÊTER POUR LES GRECS

Vous le voulez: qui peut résister à sa voix
    Lorsque l'éloquence commande?
Pour ceux que votre esprit eût charmés autrefois,
Pour ces Grecs malheureux voilà mon humble offrande.
La Fortune en fuyant m'a ravi ses trésors,
    Et ma richesse est dans ma Lyre;
Je n'ai, pour seconder vos généreux efforts,
Que les bienfaits de ceux qui daigneront me lire.
Puisse ma faible voix, unie à vos accents,
Rendre à ce beau pays tout le bonheur du nôtre!
    Puissent un jour les Grecs reconnaissants,
Sur le marbre sacré de leurs murs renaissants,
    Graver mon nom auprès du vôtre!

L'ANGE DE POÉSIE

Volez, ange de poésie;
Déployez vos ailes de feu;
Au guerrier qui m'avait choisie
Allez porter un doux aveu.
Allez, et secondez vous-même
L'ardeur dont il est enflammé:
Ne lui dites pas que je l'aime,
Mais faites qu'il se sente aimé.

MESSAGE TO MONSIEUR VILLEMAIN,
WHO HAD ASKED ME TO RAISE MONEY FOR THE GREEKS

Such is your wish! And who would not give ear
　　To your most eloquent command?
For those your wit might have charmed yesteryear—
For those Greeks, in that fair, unhappy land—
　　This is my humble offering.
Fortune has fled me, borne off all her treasures;
My only wealth is in the Song I sing.
To match your efforts, your heroic measures,
Naught have I but the boon of those who may
　　Deign read my verse. And so I pray
My feeble voice, joined to your bold discourse,
Give the Greeks back their joy, like ours, perforce!
Grateful, on marble walls reborn, may they
Engrave my name beside your own one day!

THE ANGEL OF POETRY

　Take flight, angel of poetry:
　Spread wide your wings of fire; unto
† The warrior who had chosen me,
　Carry my heart's avowal, you
　Whose help I now implore. Go fill
　With flame that ardent soul of his:
　Tell him not of my love; but, still,
　Let him feel how much loved he is.

* The poem is addressed to the educator and literary historian Abel-François Villemain
(1790–1870), a regular at the salons of Sophie Gay and others, and eventually a member
of the Académie française. It is dated August 25, 1825, during the bloody defense of Meso-
longhi in Greece. Regarding Villemain's request to the poet to help raise money for the
Greek struggle for independence from the Turks and her success in doing so, see Malo,
Une muse et sa mère, pp. 217–20.
　† The *guerrier* (warrior) is clearly Alfred de Vigny, a dashing lieutenant in the Garde
royale when he and Delphine met. See Malo, *Une muse et sa mère,* pp. 234–35.

Près de lui, pour vous faire entendre,
Imitez ma timide voix;
Apprenez-lui qu'une âme tendre
Préside à ses nobles exploits:
L'amour fait chérir la victoire,
Et l'amour le rendra vainqueur,
S'il sait que le bruit de sa gloire
Retentit dans un autre cœur.

Portez-lui les sons de ma harpe,
Mes vœux et mon premier serment,
Et que l'azur de votre écharpe
Lui rappelle mon vêtement.
Chantez-lui les vers qu'il m'inspire;
Peignez mon trouble, mon effroi,
La tristesse de mon sourire,
Et tout ce qu'il aimait en moi.

Que son oreille soit charmée
Des accords qui nous ravissaient;
Que votre aile soit parfumée
Des roses qui m'embellissaient.
Caché sous un brillant nuage,
Allez protéger son sommeil;
Offrez-lui ma fidèle image,
Pour qu'il me nomme à son réveil.

Fly to his side and imitate
My timid voice; pray let him hear
How tenderly my soul would wait
On such a noble cavalier.
It is for love that one succeeds!
And love it is that will impart
His triumph, if he knows his deeds
Ring, valorous, in another's heart.

Bear him my lyre's sweet melodies,
And the first troth I swore; and all
My hopes for him; and, if it please,
May your pure azure sash recall
The clothes I wear. Sing him each line
His love inspires; and, even more,
My woes, fears, this sad smile of mine,
And all the things he loved me for.

May the chords that enraptured us
Delight his ear; may your wings' grace
Waft him those fragrant, glorious
Roses that rendered fair my face.
Hidden beneath a cloud of light,
Protect him there, his slumber taking;
Show him my image, that he might
Call out my name upon his waking.

Elisa Mercœur (1809–1835)

Truly a poet to the tips of her fingers, Elisa Mercœur possessed a talent that was, unhappily, to be short-lived, snuffed out in her twenty-seventh year by that "preferred" disease of the romantics, consumption. Like Delphine Gay de Girardin (see pp. 624–39), she had an enthusiastic and doting mother to sing her praises. Unfortunately, they would have to be sung more post- than prehumously. It was the mother who assembled the young woman's poems and who, after repeatedly soliciting subventions from this personage and that, published them at her own expense with a sketch of her daughter's life.

Elisa Mercœur was born on January 24, 1809, in Nantes—where a plaque in her likeness adorns the entry to the Jardin des Plantes—and died on January 7, 1835, in Paris, where she and her unwed mother had moved when she was twenty. As a child, she had been obliged to give private lessons to support them. Once in the capital, however, the young poet's talent attracted early attention.

Honored by the Académie de Lyon in 1826, despite her youth, and awarded a pension by the Ministère des Beaux-Arts the following year, Mercœur frequented the salons of Paris, notably that of Sophie Gay. She was preceded by the modest fame of a volume of poems published in 1827 with a dedication to Chateaubriand, which was celebrated by the romantic icon Lamartine himself. A five-act verse drama, *Boabdil*, less successful, was refused at the Théâtre-Français, and it was no doubt in hope of monetary gain that she wrote a short novel, *La comtesse de Villequieu*.

Mercœur's romantic angst and well-founded melancholy were more than a simple expression of the fashionable *mal de siècle*. Her brooding resignation and nostalgia for better times fill the seven lyrics translated here, and reveal the sensitive yet forceful artist that she might, indeed, have become.[1]

NOTE

1. Elisa Mercœur's mother's biographical introduction to her *Œuvres complètes* remains the most authoritative source of details on her life, if hardly impartial. See also Wendy Greenberg, *Uncanonical Women: Feminine Voice in French Poetry (1830–1871)*, pp. 43–68. Marilynn J. Smith has provided a summary of her life and work in the *Encyclopedia of Continental Women Writers*, 2: 802.

LE JEUNE MENDIANT

A ce monde bruyant qui paraît vous sourire,
Dérobez un regard pour le jeter sur moi.

. . . .

Ne fermez pas votre âme à la voix qui supplie:
Pour le pauvre le ciel a réclamé des soins.
—Elisa Mercœur

Je souffre, le besoin me contraint à le dire;
Le malheur me retient sous sa méchante loi.
A ce monde bruyant, qui paraît vous sourire,
Dérobez un regard pour le jeter sur moi.

L'eau pure du Léman vient baigner ma patrie;
Là, comme vous, jadis j'eus aussi mon bonheur.
Je suis pauvre à présent, je pleure, je mendie:
Près du beau lac Léman n'est resté que mon cœur.

Je serais sans désir, si vous viviez encore,
Bons parens, que vers lui rappela le Seigneur!
Mais je suis repoussé par la main que j'implore,
Et je n'obtiens jamais un mot consolateur.

Du pain, hélas! voilà ce qu'il faut à ma vie,
Je ne sais point créer d'inutiles besoins;
Ne fermez pas votre âme à la voix qui supplie:
Pour le pauvre le Ciel a réclamé des soins.

Vous n'osez m'approcher!... L'habit de la misère
De celui qu'il recouvre est-il le déshonneur?
Quand votre œil dédaigneux (ou du moins je l'espère)
S'attache au vêtement, Dieu regarde le cœur.

Il lit au fond du mien ce qu'il a de souffrance,
Ah! puisse-t-il au vôtre inspirer la pitié;
Donnez! bien peu suffit à ma frêle existence;
Donnez! j'ai faim! j'attends!... aurai-je en vain prié?

THE YOUNG BEGGAR

Cast on your gleeful revels one glance less,
And let it, filched, come fall on me instead.

.   .   .   .

Pray, close your soul not to my eager pleas:
"Succor the pauper," heaven's voice has said.

*   *—Elisa Mercœur*

I suffer, and must needs my pain confess;
Bane is the force that rules my destiny.
Cast on your gleeful revels one glance less,
And let it, filched, come fall instead on me.

† Leman's pure waters bathe my native land;
There I knew joy, like you; but now no more.
Poor am I, weeping, begging, cap in hand:
My heart alone bides by the lake's fair shore.

Naught would I want if you, O parents dear,
Lived still, you whom the Lord called to His side.
Rebuffed, rebuked am I as I draw near:
Even kind words are to my woe denied.

I seek no futile, vain frivolities:
Alas! I need but a mere crust of bread.
Pray, close your soul not to my eager pleas:
"Succor the pauper," heaven's voice has said.

You dare approach me not... Why? Is the worn
And tattered cloak I wear a shame, a sin?
When your eye—so I hope!—brings down its scorn
Upon my garb, God sees the heart within.

In mine He reads my suffering... Give! Oh, give!...
May He fill yours with pity for my pain!
A pittance must my frail life have to live:
Give... What say you?... Ah! Have I prayed in vain?

---

* Most of Mercœur's poems are introduced by an epigraph, probably chosen by her mother, often drawn from the poem itself, or another by her. This poem, dated February 1826, is echoed in Victor Hugo's similar poetic appeal "Pour les pauvres" (For the Poor), originally entitled "Qui donne au pauvre prête à Dieu" (Who Gives to the Poor Lends to God), first published in February 1830, during an especially harsh winter.

† Lac Léman is the French name for Lake Geneva.

LA FEUILLE FLÉTRIE

Un printemps, un été, furent toute ta vie...
—Elisa Mercœur

Pourquoi tomber déjà, feuille jaune et flétrie?
J'aimais ton doux aspect dans ce triste vallon.
Un printemps, un été, furent toute ta vie;
Et tu vas sommeiller sur le pâle gazon.

Pauvre feuille! il n'est plus le temps où ta verdure
Ombrageait le rameau dépouillé maintenant.
Si fraîche au mois de mai! faut-il que la froidure
Te laisse à peine encore un incertain moment!

L'hiver, saison des nuits, s'avance et décolore
Ce qui servait d'asile aux habitans des cieux;
Tu meurs, un vent du soir vient t'embrasser encore,
Mais ses baisers glacés pour toi sont des adieux.

UN AN DE PLUS

Triste rose, au désert j'exhale mon odeur!
—Elisa Mercœur

Quoi! tout un an de plus écoulé sans bonheur!
L'hiver est mon printemps, la nuit est mon aurore;
Aucun rayon d'espoir sur moi ne brille encore:
Triste rose, au désert j'exhale mon odeur!
Ceux que j'aurais aimés ne m'ont point accueillie,
Leur main jamais vers moi ne se tendit, hélas!
Et l'oubli, de son voile enveloppant ma vie,
Semble dire à leur cœur: ne le soulevez pas.
Ah! puissent mes succès, réveillant leur mémoire,
Pour ma vengeance, un jour, leur apporter mon nom.
Et puissé-je, oubliant ce funeste abandon,
Leur dire: un an de plus écoulé pour la gloire!

THE WITHERED LEAF

One spring, one summer: your life, all too brief...
—Elisa Mercœur

Why fall already, yellow, withered leaf?
I loved your sweet look in this dismal vale.
One spring, one summer: your life, all too brief;
Now must you slumber on a ground grown pale.

Poor leaf! Gone is the time your green would fill
The branch with shade—now bare, so lush before—
So fresh and cool in May! What? Must the chill
Grant you now not even one moment more!

Winter, season of darkness, dulls the hue
Of this refuge for dwellers of the sky:
You die... A night wind comes, caresses you,
But, cold, its every kiss is a good-bye.

December 1826

YET ANOTHER YEAR

Sad rose, I waft the desert with my scent!
—Elisa Mercœur

What? Yet another year unhappy spent!
The winter is my spring, the night my dawn;
And still no ray of hope on me has shone:
Sad rose, I waft the desert with my scent!
Those whom I would have loved have turned aside;
No hand, alas, have they held out to me!
Disregard to their hearts seems to have cried:
"Lift not my veil about her: let it be."
Ah! May their memories waken to the story
Of my success, one day, and may my fame
Avenge their cruel neglect, as I proclaim
To them: "Another year spent for my glory!"

January 1827

L'AMOUR

C'est toi qui sur l'homme prononces:
Couronné de fleurs ou de ronces,
Il est esclave de ta loi.
—Elisa Mercœur

Riant ou pénible mensonge,
De la raison fatal sommeil;
L'amour n'est bien souvent qu'un songe,
Dont la vieillesse est le réveil.

LE CLAIR DE LUNE

Elégie

Viens avec ta lueur verser l'oubli du jour,
Toi, qui sembles jaillir du flambeau de l'amour...
—Elisa Mercœur

A toi que vient chercher l'œil de la rêverie,
Doux et charmant soleil de la mélancolie,
Salut. Tel qu'une vierge au sourire enchanté,
Qui s'embellit encor de sa timidité,
Quand tu montres aux cieux ton rayon solitaire
J'aime à le voir au loin prolongé sur la terre!
Viens avec ta lueur verser l'oubli du jour,
Toi, qui sembles jaillir du flambeau de l'amour;
Ecarte de ton front ce passager nuage;
Viens, la brise s'endort sur l'humide feuillage.
Vois ces astres jetés dans un ciel calme et pur,
Immortels diamans, ils nuancent l'azur.
Dans un champ de saphirs, quand t'avançant timide,

LOVE

Ever you hold man in your thrall;
And, crowned with thorns or flowers, withal,
A slave unto your law is he.
*   *—Elisa Mercœur*

Falsehood that drear or joyous seems,
And reason's deathly slumbering:
Love, oftentimes, is naught but dreams,
Whence old age is the wakening.

January 1827

MOONLIGHT

Elegy

> *Come, pour forgetfulness*
> *Of day around us, you whom one might guess*
> *Sprung from the torch of love...*
> *—Elisa Mercœur*

To you, object of reverie's musing glance,
† You—melancholic orb that charms, enchants—
Greetings! You, like a virgin, spellbound, smiling,
Fairer still for her coy, shy stance beguiling,
When you cast your lone light about the sky
I love to watch it spread before my eye,
Over the land. Come, pour forgetfulness
Of day around us, you, whom one might guess
Sprung from the torch of love; wipe from your brow
That passing cloud: the breeze is slumbering now
In trees' moist greenery, The stars festoon
The azure pure, like deathless diamonds strewn,
Sprinkling the calm with their variety.
And when, in sapphire field, you timidly

---

* The epigraph, almost as long as the poem itself, is found in the last stanza of the ten-stanza ode "L'illusion," in the poet's *Œuvres complètes*, 1: 145, whose composition post-dated "Amour" by several months.

† Rather than retain the original's curious *soleil* (sun) as metaphorical for the moon, I have opted to avoid possible—even probable—confusion by using a more neutral noun.

De ta molle clarté que le silence guide,
Des nuits le dôme obscur s'éclaire et s'embellit,
Tu parais effacer l'étoile qui pâlit.
Au paisible rayon que cherche ma paupière,
On dirait qu'un secret d'amour et de mystère
Le plongeant transporté dans un trouble rêveur,
Comme apportant l'espoir se relève à mon cœur.
Loin de moi le sommeil et sa vaine magie;
Ta céleste lueur enchante l'insomnie:
Blanche reine du soir, que de brûlans soupirs
Doivent monter vers toi sur l'aile des zéphyrs!
Long-temps, vierge du ciel, que la nuit se prolonge;
T'admirer est plus doux que se bercer d'un songe!
Combien j'aime à te voir briller au bleu séjour,
Que tu plais à mes yeux, et que je crains le jour!
Charme de mon regard, tu pâlis: ah! demeure!
Ou fuis plus lentement, et reviens avant l'heure.

DEMAIN

Ah! laissons un bandeau pour parure au destin...
—Elisa Mercœur

Chaque flot, tour à tour, soit qu'il sommeille ou gronde,
Emporte mon esquif où le conduit le sort;
Et, passager sans nom sur l'océan du monde,
Je m'éloigne incertain de l'écueil ou du port.

J'ai vu s'enfuir le but de qui pensait l'atteindre;
J'ai vu ce qu'au sourire il succède de pleurs;
Combien de purs flambeaux un souffle peut éteindre:
Ce qu'un baiser du vent peut moissonner de fleurs.

Stride on your soft beams, by the silence led,
As over night's dark dome there starts to spread
A glowing dawn, it seems that you erase
The very stars, now growing pale apace.
As my lids seek the gentle ray, one might
Almost say that some secret recondite,
Some hidden love, plunging my heart down deep
Into a muddled dream, makes it yet leap
With hope... Away with sleep's vain sorcery!
You, evening's virgin queen! Your heavenly
White charms my sleeplessness. How many the burning
Sighs, borne aloft on zephyrs' wings, rise, yearning!
I pray you, let night long—nay, endless—seem:
Sweeter to gaze on you than by mere dream
Be lulled and cradled! Ah! How I delight
To see you shine in the deep blue of night...
But look! Daylight, I fear, is on the rise!
You wax pale even as you please my eyes!
Stay!... Go not!... Or, at least, less quickly flee,
And then, before day's end, come back to me.

February 1827

TOMORROW

> *...best bind*
> *A scarf about Fate's eyes...*
> —Elisa Mercœur

Bearing my barque off to its destiny,
Each swell, in quiet sleep or groaning roll,
Sweeps on; and, nameless traveler on life's sea,
* Unsure, I leave behind the port, the shoal.

I saw the goal flee from my eager grasp;
I saw how smiles give way to tears, and, oh!
How pure flames can be snuffed out in a gasp:
How many the blooms the wind's kiss reaps, lays low.

* The masculine forms *passager* and *incertain* might strike one as rather odd, but it is not unusual for some female poets to speak with a generically masculine voice.

Et j'ai dit: S'il s'éloigne, oublions le nuage:
Qu'importe le matin notre destin du soir;
De la tombe au berceau charmons le court passage;
Un moment de bonheur vaut un siècle d'espoir.

Pour chanter, pour aimer, pourquoi toujours attendre?
Jamais a-t-on vécu deux fois un même jour?
Et le flot du passé jamais sut-il nous rendre
Un seul de nos momens emportés sans retour?

Un songe d'avenir trouble la jouissance;
Ah! laissons un bandeau pour parure au destin:
Que le malheureux seul existe d'espérance,
S'endorme sur sa chaîne, et se dise: A demain.

RÊVERIE

Une heure vaut un siècle alors qu'elle est passée...
—Elisa Mercœur

Qu'importe qu'en un jour on dépense une vie,
Si l'on doit en aimant épuiser tout son cœur,
Et doucement penché sur la coupe remplie,
Si l'on doit y goûter le nectar du bonheur.

Est-il besoin toujours qu'on achève l'année?
Le souffle d'aujourd'hui flétrit la fleur d'hier;
Je ne veux pas de rose inodore et fanée;
C'est assez d'un printemps, je ne veux pas d'hiver.

Une heure vaut un siècle alors qu'elle est passée;
Mais l'ombre n'est jamais une sœur du matin.
Je veux me reposer avant d'être lassée;
Je ne veux qu'essayer quelques pas du chemin.

And I said: "Let it go! Let us forget
The clouds: at dawn, who cares what night may bring?
From birth to death: brief joy! But better yet
* Than a whole hundred years of dallying."

Why wait to live, to sing? Has mankind ever
Been twice born in a single day's sojourning?
Can the past, flowing on, flowing forever,
Give back one moment, gone, never returning?

Dreams of the future cloud our joy: best bind
A scarf about Fate's eyes; then, in his sorrow,
Let the lone wretch live hopeful, unresigned,
And, as he slumbers, chained, mutter: "Tomorrow..."

September 1827

———————

REVERIE

One hour is as a century, once past...
—Elisa Mercœur

What matters that in one day a whole life
Be spent, if one drains all one's draught—no less—
Of love, head bowed over the goblet, rife,
And tastes the nectar born of happiness!

Must the year ever reach its term, consumed?
Yesterday's flower fades in today's chill breath;
I want no rose, withered and unperfumed:
Suffice one spring, I want no winter death.

One hour is as a century, once past,
But shadow is no kin to breaking day.
I want to rest while yet my powers last,
And venture but few steps along the way.

January 1828

* Because of the lack of quotation marks, it is not clear where this quotation actually ends. I have made one of several possible guesses.

Louise Colet (1810–1876)

Louise Colet is one of those figures that every student of French literature has
heard of but none of whose works any but a specialist can name. They may well
have read at least part of her now one-sided correspondence with Flaubert dur-
ing their famous liaison. (The revealing letters from him to her, that is—post-
humously "laundered" by his niece—since hers to him were destroyed.) And
they may also know that she was a beauty, recalling perhaps the lush abandon
with which Théodore de Banville would glorify her "little turned-up nose—the
kind that change the laws of an empire—her pretty arched lips, her pink chin,
and that great mass of bright golden ringlets falling in profusion on a bosom
whose luxuriant white splendor sang, shouted in all its glory, the glories of a
Rubens."[1] They might also remember some of her other amours—the philos-
opher Victor Cousin, the poets Vigny and Musset—and even her scandalous
(but harmless) revenge wrought on the journalist Alphonse Karr with a kitchen
knife, in 1840, for his insinuations about the paternity of the child she was ex-
pecting. In short, a most colorful and memorable character in French letters.
But a poet? Indeed...

When Louise Révoil, born in 1810 in Aix-en-Provence, came to Paris as the
wife of the musician Hippolyte Colet of the Conservatoire—some said to escape
from the provinces—she was already the author of *Les fleurs du midi*, an 1836
collection composed "in the desert of Provence," as she says in her preface, that
quickly attracted the attention of the popular poet and *chansonnier* Béranger.
In the years to follow, her talent (perhaps abetted by her beauty) won for her
repeated honors from the Académie française, though wagging tongues won-
dered how much of her success was owing to the patronage of the academician
Cousin, who had, in the meantime, become her lover, and who would eventu-
ally claim to be the father of her daughter Henriette.

Colet would continue her poetic and other literary endeavors before and
during her liaison with Flaubert, whom she met in 1846 while posing for the
sculptor James Pradin, and who, some assume, retouched her work. The rather
inconsequential Hippolyte had died in 1851, and when she and Flaubert finally
broke up in 1854, she moved from part-time friend to full-time mistress of Mus-
set, later to write the novel *Lui, roman contemporain* (1860), one of several ro-
mans à clef about their relationship, chronicling his affairs with her and George
Sand, and earning for her the latter's unalloyed loathing. Specialists consider
the novel her most important work, revealing as it does, in addition to titillating
gossip, a picture of the tribulations of the woman writer of the time. Colet's final
years were not nearly as tumultuous as the nostalgic glory days of her youth.

Marred by bitterness and ill health, they were given over to literary hackwork to support herself and her daughter. She died at the age of sixty-six, mourned by Flaubert, who, despite her other entanglements, had probably been the only true love of her life.[2]

Her earlier poems are less socially or literarily relevant than her later prose, but she displays far more truly poetic sentiment and tone in them than in the rather stilted academic competition pieces honored by the Académie française. The first six lyrics translated in these pages are taken from her *Poésies complètes,* reproducing texts from *Fleurs du midi* and other early collections. The remaining seven, more clearly autobiographical, are from *Ce qu'on rêve en aimant,* of 1854.

NOTES

1. Théodore de Banville, *Camées parisiens,* 2d ser., pp. 79–80.

2. For several recent studies, see Janet Beizer, *Ventriloquized Bodies: Narratives of Hysteria in Nineteenth-Century France,* pp. 99–166; Francine DuPlessix Gray, *Rage and Fire: A Life of Louise Colet, Pioneer Feminist, Literary Star, Flaubert's Muse;* Fraser Kennedy, *Ornament and Silence: Essays on Women's Lives,* pp. 99–113; Julian Barnes, *Something to Declare: Essays on France,* pp. 173–92; and the more chatty *L'indomptable Louise Colet,* by Serge Grand and a Colet descendant, Micheline Bood, who had inherited many of her papers.

LASSITUDE

Il est de ces longs jours d'indicible malaise
Où l'on voudrait dormir du lourd sommeil des morts;
De ces heures d'angoisse où l'existence pèse
      Sur l'âme et sur le corps:

Alors on cherche en vain une douce pensée,
Une image riante, un souvenir fécond;
L'âme lutte un instant, puis retombe affaissée
      Sous son ennui profond.

Alors tout ce qui charme et tout ce que l'on aime
Pour nos yeux dessillés n'a qu'un éclat trompeur;
Et le bonheur rêvé, s'il vient, ne peut pas même
      Vaincre notre torpeur.

SONNET

Avoir toujours gardé la candeur pour symbole,
Croire à tout sentiment noble et pur, et souffrir;
Mendier un espoir comme un pauvre une obole,
Le recevoir parfois, et long-temps s'en nourrir!

Puis, lorsqu'on y croyait, dans ce monde frivole
Ne pas trouver un cœur qui se laisse attendrir!
Sans fixer le bonheur voir le temps qui s'envole;
Voir la vie épuisée, et n'oser pas mourir!

Car mourir sans goûter une joie ineffable,
Sans que la vérité réalise la fable
De mes rêves d'amour, de mes vœux superflus,

Non! je ne le puis pas! non, mon cœur s'y refuse;
Pourtant ne croyez pas, hélas! que je m'abuse:
Je désire toujours... mais je n'espère plus!

LASSITUDE

Long, those unspeakably dull, sickly days,
When one would sleep death's heavy sleep; when dole
And anguish toll the hours, and all life weighs
    On body and on soul.

One seeks in vain to raise a tender thought,
A happy scene, a fruitful memory;
The soul struggles a moment, then swoons, caught
    Deep in its dour ennui.

And all we love, charm's every loveliness,
Shines false before our eyes, now clearly viewed;
And even joy, long-dreamt, is powerless
    To thwart our lassitude.

September 1833
Fleurs du midi

SONNET

To be the image of pure candor, be
Upright of mind; yet, suffering, to try
To beg a *sou* of hope, and, niggardly,
For my sole sustenance, long put it by!

To trust... But, midst the world's frivolity,
Find not one tender heart! To watch time fly,
Leaving no trace of happiness; to see
That life is empty, bare, yet dare not die!

For, to die with no taste of joy supreme,
Not to have lived, in truth, my fable-dream
Of love, my fruitless, vain desires galore:

Ah, no! My heart cannot allow it! Still,
Think not that I, deluded, lose my will!
No, I yearn yet, alas... but hope no more.

1834
Fleurs du midi

LA DEMOISELLE

Dans un jour de printemps, est-il rien de joli
Comme la demoiselle, aux quatre ailes de gaze,
Aux antennes de soie, au corps svelte et poli,
Tour à tour émeraude, ou saphir ou topaze?

Elle vole dans l'air quand le jour a pâli;
Elle enlève un parfum à la fleur qu'elle rase;
Et le regard charmé la contemple en extase
Sur les flots azurés traçant un léger pli.

Comme toi, fleur qui vis et jamais ne te fanes,
Oh! que n'ai-je reçu des ailes diaphanes!
Je ne planerais pas sur ce globe terni!

Aux régions de l'âme, où nul mortel ne passe,
J'irais, cherchant toujours dans les cieux, dans l'espace,
Le monde que je rêve, éternel, infini!

L'INDIENNE

Souvent, au bord du Gange, à l'heure où le soleil
Jette un réseau de feu sur le fleuve vermeil,
Dans le kiosque embaumé qui se baigne à la rive
Sous ses voiles flottants la bayadère arrive;
Une esclave la suit en portant des parfums.

THE DRAGONFLY

On a spring day, what sight more charms the eyes
Than glints of sapphire, emerald, topaze, spread
Gleaming on gossamer-winged dragonfly's
Lithe form, antennae spun of silken thread?

It flits about the air as daylight dies;
Lifts perfumes from a flower, with skimming tread;
And, as we gaze on it, bliss-surfeited,
* Traces a weightless seam on azure skies.

O, flower that never wilts or withers, would
I too had wings diaphanous! Then could
I fly from this dull globe, abandon it!

Off would I go, where never mortal went,
Seeking amid the spacious firmament
My world of dreams, eternal, infinite!

May 1834
Fleurs du midi

THE HINDU MAIDEN

Often, by Ganges' shore, at daylight's ebb,
Just as the sun spreads wide its fiery web
Over the crimson tide, appearing there,
† The nautch girl, veils floating upon the air,
Enters the scent-filled kiosk where, a-swirl,
Waves lap at water's edge; another girl—
Her slave—bearing perfumes, follows close on
Her heels. The Hindu dancer, thereupon,

---

* The poet frequently takes liberties with the rhyme scheme of her sonnet quatrains. The scheme here—*abab abba*—is one of several that she uses, and I follow it in my version.

† Readers are no doubt more familiar with India's sinuous dance the "nautch" in its variation known as the "coo(t)ch," especially in its carnivalesque incarnation, the "hootchy-kootchy." The French *bayadère*, from the Portuguese *bailadeira*, though today referring to any theatrical dancer, was originally applied specifically to so-called nautch girls.

Louise Colet 657

Alors, se délivrant des voiles importuns,
L'Indienne se plonge en un bain de porphyre,
Et du store entr'ouvert, où glisse le zéphire,
Elle voit fuir les flots en longs rubans d'argent,
Laisse errer son regard sur leur prisme changeant,
Suit un nuage d'or dans les cieux, ou contemple,
En rêvant à Brama, la coupole du temple.
Son esclave à genoux agite l'éventail,
Répand sur son sein nu l'essence du sérail,
Ou berce mollement son extase rêveuse
Aux accents de sa voix pure et voluptueuse.
Et quand le soir, chassant la chaleur du midi,
Fait courir un air frais sur le fleuve attiédi,
Abandonnant le bain d'où l'aloès émane,
L'Indienne s'assied sur la molle ottomane,
Et l'esclave attentive, abaissant le rideau,
Etanche sur ses bras les blanches perles d'eau,
Noue autour de son sein la tunique de gaze,
Suspend à son oreille une étoile en topaze,
Voile sous ses cheveux sa fraîche nudité,
Et la sirène émue attend la volupté.

SONNET

Le malheur m'a jeté son souffle desséchant:
De mes doux sentiments la source s'est tarie,
Et mon âme abattue, avant l'heure flétrie,
En perdant tout espoir perd tout penser touchant.

Mes yeux n'ont plus de pleurs, ma voix n'a plus de chant,
Mon cœur désenchanté n'a plus de rêverie;
Pour tout ce que j'aimais avec idolâtrie
Il ne me reste plus d'amour ni de penchant.

Casts off her irksome veils and, presently,
Settling into a tub of porphyry,
Peers through the zephyr-parted drapes onto
The silvered ribbon-waves, fleeing from view;
Lets wander on their rainbow hues her eyes;
Watches a gilded cloud traverse the skies
Above; or, musing upon Brahma, gazes
About the temple dome; and, as she lazes,
Languid, her slave, kneeling, fans her and strews
The harem's fragrance on her breast, or coos
In accents soft and sensuous, as she
Cradles her dream, coddles her ecstasy.
When evening, banishing the midday heat,
Blows the warm river cool, she takes a seat—
Stepping forth from her bath, amid the scent
Of aloes wafting heavy, redolent—
On the soft ottoman; the slave, thereat,
Blind lowered, stems the gentle pitter-pat
Of droplets, pearling white, along her arms,
Draping in gossamer her bosom's charms;
Hangs from her ear a topaze star... And thus
The siren, in her pose voluptuous,
Tresses veiling her nakedness—cool, fresh—
Aroused, awaits the blisses of the flesh.

1835
Penserosa, xxv

SONNET

The breath of woe blows barren my distress:
Dried up now are my soul's sweet-flowing streams—
My soul, too soon laid low; nothing redeems
Its withered hope, nor can its thought redress.

Tears flee my eyes; songs flee my throat no less;
My disenchanted heart dreams no more dreams;
Of all I worshiped and adored, it seems
Nothing remains: no love, no eagerness.

Louise Colet 659

Une aride douleur ronge et brûle mon âme,
Il n'est rien que j'envie et rien que je réclame;
Mon avenir est mort, le vide est dans mon cœur.

J'offre un corps sans pensée à l'œil qui me contemple;
Tel sans divinité reste quelque vieux temple,
Telle après le banquet la coupe est sans liqueur.

LE TRAVAIL

Travail! fidèle ami qui sur ma pauvreté
Répands ton noble orgueil et ta sérénité,
Tu relèves mon cœur; durant mes longues veilles,
C'est toi qui me soutiens, c'est toi qui me conseilles;
Tu soumets à ton joug mes désirs renaissants,
Et mes rêves vaincus n'assiègent plus mes sens.

Les folles passions et la gloire futile,
Qu'est-ce, après tout, mon Dieu?... Mais une vie utile,
Qui dans l'obscurité se résigne au labeur,
Peut donner le repos à défaut du bonheur.

LE BAISER DU POËTE

Quand je reçois avec recueillement,
Comme on reçoit le baiser d'un amant,
Le pur baiser qui clôt votre visite,
Si sur mon front une rougeur subite
Monte soudain, si mon cœur bat plus vite,
Si du bonheur j'ai le tressaillement,
C'est que je sens une clarté divine
Par ce baiser passer dans ma poitrine,

An arid anguish burns, gnaws at my soul:
Naught do I yearn for, vanished now my goal;
Empty my heart; my future, long deceased.

I offer to the eye a being bereft
Of thought; like some old temple ruin, left
Godless; a goblet drained after the feast.

1834
Penserosa, xxxiv

_____

WORK

Work! Faithful friend, who, ever by my side,
Bedeck my poverty with noble pride
And calm serene; through my long wakeful nights
You lift my heart, sustain me; by your lights
I live my life: you quell my passion-fires,
Bridle my dreams, rein in my vain desires.

Mad yearnings, and a futile glory! What
Matter they in the end, my God? Ah, but
A life of useful works, in darkness done,
Can grant you peace, though pleasure have you none.

October 1843
Mezza vita, xxv

_____

* THE POET'S KISS

When, lost in thought, my brow receives a pure
Kiss, like the kiss a lover gives, as your
Parting farewell, if suddenly there glows
Upon my brow, thus kissed, the tint of rose;
If my heartbeat faster and faster grows;
If I shudder with happiness; for sure,
The reason is, I feel a spark divine
Pass through that kiss into this bosom mine;

* Although, to my knowledge, it corresponds to no particular form, I have maintained
the poet's capriciously unorthodox rhyme scheme.

Louise Colet 661

C'est que je crois, poëte créateur,
Que votre esprit, que la muse domine,
Répand en moi son souffle inspirateur.
Oui, par un Dieu mon âme est possédée,
Et dans mon sein il fait germer l'idée.
La fleur, dit-on, est ainsi fécondée
Par le baiser des vents de l'équateur.

——————

ORGUEIL

Va! cherche encor de femme en femme;
Je crains peu l'infidélité:
Tu ne trouveras pas mon âme,
Si tu trouves plus de beauté!

Je crains peu ces pâles jeunesses,
Ces fleurs que fanent vos amours.
Ces couronnes de vos ivresses,
Où le parfum manque toujours.

Vos forces succombent frappées
Par ces esclaves sans orgueil;
Faibles têtes inoccupées,
Cœurs bornés qu'on lit d'un coup d'œil.

Leur main, quand leur bras vous enlace,
Dans la vôtre n'a pas frémi,
Et leur lèvre reste de glace
En murmurant le nom d'ami!

Elles vous rendent infidèles
Durant la nuit, dans le festin;
Mais, mornes, vous rougissez d'elles
Aux blanches lueurs du matin.

Leur regard vous semble la vie:
Leur parole, le sentiment;
Mais, après la chair assouvie,
Sans maîtresse reste l'amant;

Feel that your poet's spirit, exquisite,
Bending unto the muse's own design,
Infuses me, spreads its breath, infinite.
Yes, then is my soul by some god possessed,
Warming to thought the seed within my breast.
So the Equator's hot breeze-kisses, pressed
Against the bud unbloomed, breathe life in it.

August 1846

————————

PRIDE

Faithless! From woman to woman go!
Search here, search there: I pay no mind.
You will not find my soul's like, though
You may, indeed, more beauty find!

I fear not those fair lasses, young
Pale flowers that fade and wilt your love—
Wreaths for your wild excess, unstrung—
But lacking the sweet scents thereof.

Those slaves to lust, who have no pride—
Vain hearts one plumbs in but a trice,
Weak heads with nothing much inside—
Will bring you down with vile device.

When locked in your embrace, your hand
In theirs, they quiver not, and mutter,
Murmur through lips of ice: how bland
The words "my love" those lips would utter!

For them are you unfaithful, when
Your festive revels fill the night,
Only to gaze on them again
And, mournful, blush at dawn's first light.

Their glance is life; their word, its sense—
Or so you think!—but you discover
That soon the flesh is sated: whence,
Their ardor flown, alone the lover.

Sans idéal reste l'artiste,
Sans appui, le cœur désolé;
Vers elles, celui qui va triste,
Ne s'en revient pas consolé!

De votre mère, absente ou morte,
De votre ami, de votre honneur,
Des choses qui font l'âme forte,
De l'art et de Dieu... du bonheur,

Ne leur parlez pas: leur sourire
Accueille tout mot sérieux,
Leur main avide vous retire
De chaque sentier glorieux.

Elles enchaînent la pensée
Aux lourds cordages de la chair,
Et la font tomber affaissée,
Comme la voile où manque l'air.

Va! cherche encor de femme en femme,
Je crains peu l'infidélité:
Tu ne trouveras pas mon âme,
Si tu trouves plus de beauté!

––––––––––

SONNET

Laissons au Nord brumeux les moroses pensées,
Les ronces qui toujours aux fleurs vont se mêler.
Nous, enfants du grand fleuve aux ondes cadencées,
Comme son vif courant laissons nos cœurs aller.

Pur miroir du soleil, beau Rhône au doux parler,
Ecloses sur tes bords, deux âmes enlacées
N'ont point le pâle amour de froides fiancées;
Gais rayons, on les voit sourire et scintiller.

In them the artist, sick at heart,
Finds no ideal when dull and cold
His soul: to them he brings his art,
And, helpless, comes back unconsoled.

Of your dear mother, absent, dead;
Your friend, your honor even less;
Of things wherewith strong souls are fed;
Of art, of God... of happiness;

No. Of such things speak to them never:
They sneer at solemn repertory;
And with an avid hand they ever
Steer you away from paths of glory.

Like the sail, windless, they enmesh
Your thought in earthy passion, tying
It round with riggings of the flesh,
Drag it down, sagging, useless lying.

Faithless! From woman to woman, go!
Search here, search there: I pay no mind.
You will not find my soul's like, though
You may, indeed, more beauty find!

1847

SONNET

Let the drear North keep, in its fog-bound waste,
Its thoughts morose: brambles midst blossoms sown.
We, children of the river grandeur-graced,
Let our hearts course, pound to its waves alone.

Sun's crystal mirror, O sweet-murmuring Rhône!
Two souls, bloomed by your shores, shimmer, enlaced,
Spurn the cold love of lovers pallid-faced;
Glimmering rays of joy, and smiles full-blown.

Transports, amour, folie, ivresses débordantes,
Comme la mer au flux, à vos vagues ardentes
Un cœur chaud du Midi se gonfle impétueux:

Il plane, il chante, il rit au monde qu'il embrasse;
Mais profond est ce cœur qui bout à la surface,
Autant que l'est ton lit, fleuve majestueux.

LE LION CAPTIF

> Conseil d'ami, conseil à vous,
> Conseil d'un jour et pour la vie.
> —Alfred de Musset

Lion du Sahara, dans ta cage enfermé,
Le désert passe-t-il sous ta fauve paupière?
Ta lionne à tes flancs, revois-tu l'antre aimé?
Revois-tu le soleil qui dora ta crinière?

A ton rugissement en écho transformé,
Sens-tu trembler encor quelque tribu guerrière?
Libre et reconquérant ta grandeur prisonnière,
Roi! berces-tu l'ennui dont tu meurs consumé?

Et vous, poëte, aux fers que vous a mis la vie
Arrachez-vous parfois, palpitante et ravie,
Votre âme qui revient aux premiers horizons:

A l'amour qui l'inspire, à l'art qui la couronne!
Oh! rendez à vos jours ce passé qui rayonne,
Sortez de l'esclavage où meurent les lions!

Love, folly, drunk excesses, fancy free:
In your tide's fervor, like the swelling sea,
A southern heart, untamed, in passion bred,

Soars and sings, mocks the world clutched to its breast.
Yet deep, this heart, though froth foams on its crest:
As deep, majestic stream, as is your bed.

1850

THE CAPTIVE LION

> *Friendly advice, advice to you,*
> *One day's advice, and evermore.*
>
> *   *—Alfred de Musset*

Sahara's lion, caged! Can you still be
Dreaming, fierce beast, your desert days of old?
Lioness by your flanks, do you still see
That mistress-sun, who turned your mane to gold?

Your roar an echo now, nostalgically
Sense you some quaking tribe of warriors bold?
King! Do you languish, pent in prison-hold,
For grandeur past, consumed in your ennui?

And you, O poet, shackled by life's chains!
Snatch free your fervent soul, trembling its pains,
Back to those first horizons that you cherish:

Let your days gleam anew with crowning art,
And, ah! let love once more inspire your heart!
Cast off that bondage where proud lions perish!

1852

* The citation, whose source escapes me, bears witness both to Colet's passion for Musset (with whom she began her liaison in 1852, the year when this poem was written), and to the eminent romantic poet's need for encouragement at a physically and emotionally difficult time of his life, despite his recent election to the Académie française.

Louise Colet 667

SOIR D'ÉTÉ

Oui, je me souviendrai de ce couchant d'été
Sur les flots de la Seine, en face de cette île
Où des hauts peupliers l'ombre fraîche et mobile
Frissonnait, rideau vert au bord du ciel jeté.

Au-dessus, dans l'azur de l'éther velouté,
Des vagues de rubis se roulaient à la file,
Et nous étions assis sur la rive tranquille,
De ce déclin du jour admirant la beauté.

À MA FILLE

Tu t'élèves et je m'efface,
Tu brilles et je m'obscurcis,
Tu fleuris, ma jeunesse passe;
L'amour nous regarde indécis.

Prends pour toi le charme et la grâce,
Laisse-moi langueurs et soucis;
Sois heureuse, enfant, prends ma place,
Mes regrets seront adoucis.

Prends tout ce qui fait qu'on nous aime:
Ton destin, c'est mon destin même.
Vivre en toi, c'est vivre toujours!

Succède à ta mère ravie;
Pour les ajouter à ta vie,
O mon sang! prends mes derniers jours.

VISITE À UN ABSENT

Il fait froid, ton foyer s'allume,
Tu t'habilles, tu vas sortir;
Tu pars, et j'accours me blottir
Dans ton fauteuil. Je prends ta plume.

SUMMER EVENING

I shall remember, on Seine's billowing
Waters, that summer sunset, evermore;
That poplar-shaded isle, spread out before,
Draping the sky's edge—green, cool, shimmering.

In down-soft azure, over everything,
Ruby waves, rolling, rolling by the score...
And we sat watching, on the peaceful shore,
Delighting in day's last fair glimmering.

FOR MY DAUGHTER

You grow and I decline; you glow
And I grow dim; you bloom: I see
My youth pass by, and older grow;
Love looks, unsure, at you, at me.

Take all the charm and grace, but oh,
Leave me the languor, the ennui;
Be happy, take my place. For, so
Will my regrets the sweeter be.

Take from me all those things that make
Men love: my fate is yours to take.
Living in you, I live always!

Your mother, blissful, bids you add
To your life all she might have had:
O blood mine! Take my life's last days.

1852

AT THE HOME OF HIM WHO LEFT

It's cold. You light the fire, and then
You dress... You go. You leave me there,
Alone. I hurry to your chair,
Nestle deep, and I take your pen.

Louise Colet 669

Je n'écrirai pas un volume...
Mais un seul mot pour t'avertir
Que mon cœur n'a plus d'amertume
Si le tien s'ouvre au repentir.

Mais ce mot, pourras-tu le lire?
Ma main, en tremblant, l'a tracé,
Et mes pleurs l'ont presque effacé.

Oh! ce mot, pourquoi le récrire?
A ton âme comme à tes yeux
Une larme parlera mieux.

I will not write a volume! Men
Need but one word: no grudge I bear,
Nor shall my heart be bitter when
I hear your heart its fault foreswear.

But that word... Will you understand
What I would write with trembling hand?
My tears all but wash out each letter!

Ah! Why write it again? One tear
Will, to your eyes, your soul, appear
More eloquent, and speak still better.

Louise Ackermann (1813–1890)

Born in Paris on November 30, 1813, Louise-Victorine Choquart was thoroughly educated by a father steeped in Enlightenment rationalism, and was widowed after two years of apparently happy, if admittedly passionless, marriage to an Alsatian philologist and poet, Paul Ackermann. Upon her death in Nice, on August 2, 1890, she left a slim but congenial—and, at times, even most introspective—body of verse, as well as a volume of memoirs.

While only on the fringes of the romantic movement in France, chronologically speaking, she nonetheless inherited much of the emotional baggage of her immediate forebears, especially in the melancholy poems written after her husband's death. Not only did she mourn the injustices of life and personal suffering, and display the typical romantic angst at the passage of time, but, despite her own intellect-dominated perspective, she even bemoaned the would-be substitution of science for faith. Her *contes,* in easy-going verse, are pleasantly cynical commentaries on social mores, treating such properly romantic themes as the unappreciated artist who, like her bee, is crushed before her potential treasure can be enjoyed by society.

Louise Ackermann's collections present a certain amount of bibliographical confusion owing to considerable overlap of materials. A modest volume of verse tales—*Contes en vers,* cited by several sources—appears to date from 1855. It was followed by two longer and more easily accessible collections: *Contes et poésies* (1863) and *Poésies* (1874). The former reproduces the earlier *contes* and adds several new ones, as well as a group of eleven "Pensées diverses" in verse of various lengths, and sixteen "Poésies." The latter reproduces these "Poésies" (under the youthful rubric of "Premières poésies") and adds a group of eighteen poems on more or less philosophical themes ("Poésies philosophiques") some of which, to compound the confusion, had also appeared in the 1863 collection.

Happily, the artistry of Louise Ackermann's verse, imbued with a Vignyesque pessimism and a stolid acceptance of the rigors of existence and the absurdity of the human condition—making of her what one observer calls an existentialist before the fact[1]—transcends such details, which I explain (or try to) for those concerned with scholarly precision. Included in these translations is a chronologically and thematically diverse group of her poems, found (as indicated in the notes) in one or both of her 1863 and 1874 collections.[2]

NOTES
1. See the headnote introducing a selection of her poems in Jeanine Moulin, *La poésie féminine,* 1: 286.

2. Biographical data—scant at best—come principally from the preface to her memoirs, *Pensées d'une solitaire* (1883); from Moulin (where several other bio-bibliographical sources are suggested); and from *Nineteenth-Century French Poets,* ed. Robert Beum, *Dictionary of Literary Biography,* 217: 299. See also sections on Ackermann in Wendy Greenberg, *Uncanonical Women etc.,* pp. 110–13, 120–29, 151–59, and in Alison Finch, *Women's Writing in Nineteenth-Century France,* pp. 12–13, 166–67, 178–80, 198–99, and passim.

ADIEUX À LA POÉSIE

Mes pleurs sont à moi, nul au monde
Ne les a comptés ni reçus;
Pas un œil étranger qui sonde
Les désespoirs que j'ai conçus.

L'être qui souffre est un mystère
Parmi ses frères ici-bas;
Il faut qu'il aille solitaire
S'asseoir aux portes du trépas.

J'irai seule et brisant ma lyre,
Souffrant mes maux sans les chanter;
Car je sentirais à les dire
Plus de douleur qu'à les porter.

LE DÉPART

Il est donc vrai? Je garde en quittant la patrie,
O profonde douleur! un cœur indifférent.
Pas de regard aimé, pas d'image chérie,
Dont mon œil au départ se détache en pleurant.

Ainsi partent tous ceux que le désespoir sombre
Dans quelque monde à part pousse à se renfermer,
Qui, voyant l'homme faible et les jours remplis d'ombre,
Ne se sont pas senti le courage d'aimer.

Pourtant, Dieu m'est témoin, j'aurais voulu sur terre
Rassembler tout mon cœur autour d'un grand amour,
Joindre à quelque destin mon destin solitaire,
Me donner sans regret, sans crainte, sans retour.

FAREWELL TO POETRY

No one has yet, nor will one ever,
Count all my tears: they are my own;
No stranger's eye need try, endeavor
To plumb the sorrows I have known.

The sufferer is a mystery,
Alone among his earthly brothers;
And never, at death's gates, shall he
Sit in the company of others.

Breaking my lyre, off will I go
In pain, alone, yet not declare it;
For suffer will I more my woe,
Singing it, than if I but bear it.

† LEAVE-TAKING

What? Can it be? I quit my native France—
How deep the grief!—yet passionless my heart.
No image loved, no gentle, loving glance
To fill my eyes with tears as I depart.

Thus leave all those whom dismal hopelessness
Moves to seek refuge from the pain thereof;
Who, seeing how weak is man, how lusterless
His days, have not felt brave enough to love.

Yet, as God is my witness, how I should
Have drawn about my heart a great love, let
My lone fate share another's; how I would
Have given myself with no fear, no regret!

* Written in 1835, when the poet was in her early twenties, this conventionally romantic "farewell"—which, given its early date in the poet's career, seems somewhat premature—serves, curiously, as the prefatory poem in the section "Premières poésies" of her volume *Poésies* (1874).

† How much of the poet's lament at a loveless leave-taking one can attribute to sincerity, and how much to a fashionable romantic posturing, is difficult to say. What is clear, however, is that the poem was occasioned by her departure from France to Berlin in 1838, at age twenty-five, to study German. It was there that she was to meet her future husband (see p. 672).

Aussi ne croyez pas qu'avec indifférence
Je contemple s'éteindre, au plus beau de mes jours,
Des bonheurs d'ici-bas la riante espérance:
Bien que le cœur soit mort, on en souffre toujours.

———————

LA LYRE D'ORPHÉE

Quand Orphée autrefois, frappé par les Bacchantes,
Près de l'Hèbre tomba, sur les vagues sanglantes
On vit longtemps encor sa lyre surnager.
Le fleuve au loin chantait sous le fardeau léger.
Le gai zéphir s'émut; ses ailes amoureuses
Baisaient les cordes d'or, et les vagues heureuses,
Comme pour l'arrêter, d'un effort doux et vain,
S'empressaient à l'entour de l'instrument divin.
Les récifs, les îlots, le sable à son passage
S'est revêtu de fleurs, et cet âpre rivage
Voit soudain, pour toujours délivré des autans,
Au toucher de la lyre accourir le Printemps.

Ah! que nous sommes loin de ces temps de merveilles!
Les ondes, les rochers, les vents n'ont plus d'oreilles,
Les cœurs mêmes, les cœurs refusent de s'ouvrir,
Et la lyre en passant ne fait plus rien fleurir.

And so, think not that I, indifferently,
Watch, in my salad days, the withering
Of laughing hopes for joy in store for me:
Though dead the heart, long lasts the suffering.

September 13, 1838

———————

ORPHEUS'S LYRE

When Orpheus, by the Hebrus' shore attacked,
* Fell to the Bacchants, and his body, hacked,
Bloodied the waves, long did his lyre thereon
Go floating; and the river, thereupon,
Would sing beneath the tender weight it bore.
The zephyr blew, impassioned; and the more
It blew, the more its love-inspired wings
Gaily caressed and kissed its golden strings.
Happy, the waves—in vain—had one intent:
To gather round the heavenly instrument
And keep it for their own. And, as it passed,
Sands, islets, reefs flowered and bloomed; the blast
Now spared the savage bank its bellowing:
Touched by the lyre, it welcomed endless Spring.

How far from us such wondrous times! For, here,
Rocks, billows, breezes now turn a deaf ear;
Hearts—even hearts, alas!—close tight: and, lo!
The lyre may pass, but nothing more will grow.

* The Hebrus, or Evros (also known today as the Maritsa, among other names), is the river in Thrace, emptying into the Aegean, into which the priestesses of Bacchus—also known as the Maenads—threw the head and lyre of the dismembered Orpheus after his ill-fated return from the underworld in search of Eurydice.

Louise Ackermann 677

HÉBÉ

Les yeux baissés, rougissante et candide,
Vers leur banquet quand Hébé s'avançait,
Les Dieux charmés tendaient leur coupe vide,
Et de nectar l'enfant la remplissait.
Nous tous aussi, quand passe la Jeunesse,
Nous lui tendons notre coupe à l'envi.
Quel est le vin qu'y verse la déesse?
Nous l'ignorons; il enivre et ravit.
Ayant souri dans sa grâce immortelle,
Hébé s'éloigne; on la rappelle en vain.
Longtemps encor sur la route éternelle,
Notre œil en pleurs suit l'échanson divin.

L'ABEILLE

Quand l'abeille, au printemps, confiante et charmée,
Sort de la ruche et prend son vol au sein des airs,
Tout l'invite et lui rit sur sa route embaumée.
L'églantier berce au vent ses boutons entr'ouverts;
La clochette des prés incline avec tendresse
Sous le regard du jour son front pâle et léger.
L'abeille cède émue au désir qui la presse;
Elle aperçoit un lis et descend s'y plonger.
Une fleur est pour elle une mer de délices.
Dans son enchantement, du fond de cent calices
Elle sort trébuchant sous une poudre d'or.
Son fardeau l'alourdit, mais elle vole encor.
Une rose est là-bas qui s'ouvre et la convie;

* **HEBE**

When, blushing, eyes downcast, Hebe drew near
The banquet where, enthralled, the gods would sup,
As each held out his empty glass, the dear
Young maid, once more, with nectar filled it up.
We too, with goblets drained—to our chagrin—
Seeing Youth pass, hold them out greedily
What wine does heaven's cupbearer pour therein?
We know not, but how drunk, enraptured, we!
Smiling her grace's sweet, immortal smile,
Hebe draws off and, slowly, disappears.
We call her back: in vain; and, all the while,
Our gaze pursues the goddess with our tears.

THE BEE

When, in the spring—charmed, confident—the bee,
Quitting the hive, takes to the scented air,
All nature smiles on her invitingly.
The dog-rose wafts the breezes with its fair,
Scarce-opening buds; the bellflower gently nods
Its frail and pallid brow before dawn's gaze.
Then it is that the bee, as passion prods
Her on, gives way to lust; and, as she lays
Her eyes upon a lily, she will sweep
† Low in her eager flight and plunge in, deep:
A flower, for her, is a sea of delight.
From bloom to bloom she flies, enchanted quite,
But stumbling, tottering, dragging her store

---

* In Greek mythology, Hebe (rhyming in English with "Phoebe"), daughter of Zeus and Hera, and eventually the wife of Herakles, was cupbearer of the gods, goddess of youth—the *échanson* of line 12—whose province it was to make the aged grow young and beautiful again. Eventually she was replaced in that function by Ganymede.

† After establishing a rhyme scheme of *abab cdcd*, the poet lapses into a series of rhymed couplets, later resuming her scheme and subsequently altering it with even further liberties, which do not seem to serve any aesthetic purpose other than to lend a minor freedom typical of traditional animal fables, of which this might be considered a de facto if not a de nomine example, complete with moral. My version respects her form in its broad lines.

Sur ce sein parfumé tandis qu'elle s'oublie,
Le soleil s'est voilé. Poussé par l'aquilon,
Un orage prochain menace le vallon.
Le tonnerre a grondé. Mais dans sa quête ardente
L'abeille n'entend rien, ne voit rien, l'imprudente!
Sur les buissons en fleur l'eau fond de toute part;
Pour regagner la ruche il est déjà trop tard.
La rose si fragile, et que l'ouragan brise,
Referme pour toujours son calice odorant;
La rose est une tombe, et l'abeille surprise
Dans un dernier parfum s'enivre en expirant.

Qui dira les destins dont sa mort est l'image?
Ah! combien parmi nous d'artistes inconnus,
Partis dans leur espoir par un jour sans nuage,
Des champs qu'ils parcouraient ne sont pas revenus!
Une ivresse sacrée aveuglait leur courage;
Au gré de leurs désirs, sans craindre les autans,
Ils butinaient au loin sur la foi du printemps.
Quel retour glorieux l'avenir leur apprête!
A ces mille trésors épars sur leur chemin
L'amour divin de l'art les guide et les arrête:
Tout est fleur aujourd'hui, tout sera miel demain.
Ils revenaient déjà vers la ruche immortelle;
Un vent du ciel soufflait, prêt à les soulever.
Au milieu des parfums la Mort brise leur aile;
Chargés comme l'abeille, ils périssent comme elle
Sur le butin doré qu'ils n'ont pas pu sauver.

UN AUTRE CŒUR

Serait-ce un autre cœur que la Nature donne
A ceux qu'elle préfère et destine à vieillir,
Un cœur calme et glacé que toute ivresse étonne,
Qui ne saurait aimer et ne veut pas souffrir?

Ah! qu'il ressemble peu, dans son repos tranquille,
A ce cœur d'autrefois qui s'agitait si fort!
Cœur enivré d'amour, impatient, mobile,
Au-devant des douleurs courant avec transport.

Of golden dust, much heavier than before,
Yet flitting still, until she spies a rose,
Open, beckoning to her. As she goes
Wooing, oblivious, on the fragrant breast,
Dark grows the sun. But, eager in her quest,
Although the northwind plots a tempest wild
Against the valley, lo! the bee, beguiled,
Hears not the thunder and sees even less!
Down pours the torrent, but too far the hive!
Too late! And as the rose's powerlessness
Yields to the storm, the bee, now trapped alive,
Within the rose-tomb's calyx lying pent,
Dies in the drunken bliss of one last scent.

Who will see in her death our destiny?
How many the unknown artists who, hope burning
High in their breasts, sky cloudless utterly,
Fly to the fields, never to be returning!
With sacred passion, but too drunk to see
Where spirit leads, putting their faith in spring,
Without a qualm, off they go foraging.
Ah! What a glorious fate awaits them here!
Art's divine love guides them along the way
Unto the myriad treasures that appear
Spread vast before them. What is flower today
Tomorrow will be honey!... But as they
Would turn back to their deathless hive, wind-tossed,
Wings clipped by Death, no longer can they fly:
And, weighed down, like the bee, like her they die,
Midst fragrant golden booty, lying lost.

A DIFFERENT HEART

Does favoring Nature give a different heart
To those destined, unloving, to grow old;
Those who are loath to suffer, set apart,
And who live life emotionless and cold?

How unlike, in its calm tranquillity,
That pulsing, pounding heart of long ago:
Heart drunk on love, impetuous and free,
That, passionate, embraced even its woe.

Il ne reste plus rien de cet ancien nous-mêmes;
Sans pitié ni remords le Temps nous l'a soustrait.
L'astre des jours éteints, cachant ses rayons blêmes,
Dans l'ombre qui l'attend se plonge et disparaît.

A l'horizon changeant montent d'autres étoiles.
Cependant, cher Passé, quelquefois un instant
La main du Souvenir écarte tes longs voiles,
Et nous pleurons encore en te reconnaissant.

À LA COMÈTE DE 1861

Bel astre voyageur, hôte qui nous arrives
Des profondeurs du ciel et qu'on n'attendait pas,
Où vas-tu? Quel dessein pousse vers nous tes pas?
Toi qui vogues au large en cette mer sans rives,
Sur ta route, aussi loin que ton regard atteint,
N'as-tu vu comme ici que douleurs et misères?
Dans ces mondes épars, dis, avons-nous des frères?
T'ont-ils chargé pour nous de leur salut lointain?

Ah! quand tu reviendras, peut-être de la terre
L'homme aura disparu. Du fond de ce séjour
Si son œil ne doit pas contempler ton retour,
Si ce globe épuisé s'est éteint solitaire,
Dans l'espace infini poursuivant ton chemin,
Du moins jette au passage, astre errant et rapide
Un regard de pitié sur le théâtre vide
De tant de maux soufferts et du labeur humain.

Of the self that we were, naught we remain:
Time filched it from us, pitiless, austere.
Yesteryear's dead suns hide their drear rays, wane,
Dip in the waiting dark, and disappear.

As the horizon changes, new stars rise.
And yet, dear Past, there are brief moments when
Memory's hand unveils you to our eyes,
And we weep, recognizing you again.

---

[*] ## TO THE COMET OF 1861

Fair, wandering star, guest unexpectedly
Come from the depths of heaven to visit us,
Where do you go? What plan impels you thus?
You, who go sailing on that shoreless sea,
Have you, far as your gaze can reach through space,
Seen naught but pain and woe, as we know here?
Do we have brethren on some far-flung sphere?
Do you bring us their distant saving grace?

Alas! When back you come, mankind, perchance,
Shall be no more. If, thus, from this domain
No mortal eye may look on you again,
And this lone globe be but a dead expanse,
Then, as through endless realms you come and go,
At least, O wandering star, as you pass by,
Cast on our empty stage a pitying eye
For all the human toils we suffered so.

* The so-called "Great Comet of 1861" was discovered by an Australian, John Tebbutt, in May of that year, and was visible in the Northern Hemisphere from the end of June to mid-August. In the United States, it is of historical interest in that superstition saw in it a foreshadowing of the Civil War and the assassination of Abraham Lincoln.

LE POSITIVISME

Il s'ouvre par delà toute science humaine
Un vide dont la Foi fut prompte à s'emparer.
De cet abîme obscur elle a fait son domaine;
En s'y précipitant elle a cru l'éclairer.
Eh bien, nous t'expulsons de tes divins royaumes,
Dominatrice ardente, et l'instant est venu:
Tu ne vas plus savoir où loger tes fantômes;
        Nous fermons l'Inconnu.

Mais ton triomphateur expîra ta défaite.
L'homme déjà se trouble et, vainqueur éperdu,
Il se sent ruiné par sa propre conquête;
En te dépossédant nous avons tout perdu.
Nous restons sans espoir, sans recours, sans asile,
Tandis qu'obstinément le Désir qu'on exile
Revient errer autour du gouffre défendu.

LE PERROQUET

Conte

Un perroquet vivait chez un jeune ménage,
        Couple aimable autant qu'amoureux;
        La lune de miel sur eux
        Répandait ses douceurs d'usage.
Mille amours s'ébattaient entre nos gens épris.
Le perroquet, témoin de plus d'une caresse,
        En pleurait souvent de tendresse.
Qu'un regret s'y mêlât, je n'en serais surpris:
Tout seul dans sa prison depuis son plus jeune âge
Du bonheur d'être aimé l'oiseau sentait le prix;
Je le sentirais bien, moi qui ne suis en cage.

There is, beyond Man's ken, an emptiness—
Dark abyss past all human knowing—one
That Faith was quick to capture and possess,
Thinking the darkness by her light outdone.
Well, now we cast you from your heavenly fief,
You, once victorious in your quest therefor.
No place now for your ghosts, your vain belief:
    Closed, the Hereafter's door!

But he who won will pay for your defeat.
Already Man, the haughty conqueror,
Suffers his conquest, feels a loss complete:
Casting you out, oh! what a woe we bore!
Hopeless, comfortless, we; and, now returning,
Banished Desire, deep in its exile yearning,
Haunts the forbidden chasm all the more.

THE PARROT

A Tale

A couple had a parrot; young, these two,
    And much in love they were,
No less beloved than loving: he loved her,
She, him. And what all honeymoons will do,
    Theirs did, shining upon the pair
    Its fair delights, a thousandfold.
    The parrot watched as they would hold
Each other in embrace, and, *solitaire,*
    Much touched, would often weep, and rue
His lot: since early life, imprisoned there,
    Little of love he knew he knew!
(Feelings that even I, uncaged, can share.)

---

* One can assume, clearly, that this pleasantly sarcastic defense of faith against the anti-religious attacks of the materialistic positivism of Auguste Comte (1798–1857) must have been written during or after the promulgation of that philosopher's very influential *Cours de philosophie positive* (1830–1842).

Voici qu'un beau matin auprès d'un vieux parent
Riche, Dieu sait! mais pour l'heure mourant,
Appelé fut l'époux; il se mit en voyage.
Il ne fallait rien moins qu'un leurre d'héritage
      Pour séparer nos deux amants.
La dame désolée et pleurant à cœur fendre,
D'un millier de baisers, d'un millier de serments
Chargea notre partant. Ces marques d'amour tendre
Sont bagage léger; il en prit tant et plus.

D'abord, pour consoler sa dolente maîtresse,
L'oiseau fit de son mieux, mais, efforts superflus!
"Quel babil odieux! il trouble ma tristesse.
Quand donc pourrai-je en paix soupirer un moment?"
Le perroquet se tut, admirant en lui-même
L'effet de la douleur sur un cœur trop aimant.

Pendant les premiers mois, de l'un à l'autre amant
Missives de trotter. Or, parmi les je t'aime,
Les jamais, les toujours, entre deux au revoir,
Le jeune époux mêlait un mot de ses affaires.
Notre parent susdit avait fait son devoir:
Il était mort. Restaient encor les inventaires,
Les scellés, les procès, ce n'est jamais fini.
Qu'y faire? on attendit, et, qui mieux est peut-être,
On essuya ses pleurs. "Pour ne point reparaître,
L'éclat de nos beaux yeux serait déjà terni?
C'est fort mal entendu de s'enlaidir soi-même.
Quoi! nous irions gâter ce qui fait qu'on nous aime,
Nos charmes?... Non, l'amour ne nous en saurait gré."
Contre tant de soupirs à peine rassuré,
Sans qu'à deux fois pourtant besoin fût de le dire,
Sur sa bouche charmante il revint un sourire,
Puis deux, puis trois; ils ne se comptaient plus.

Now then, one lovely morning our young lad
Learned that an agèd relative he had—
Agèd and rich!—lay dying, whitherto
He must repair. No sooner had they bade
    Him come, than he rode thither. True,
Only the love of wealth could draw apart
Our lovers: she, sobbing, with aching heart,
Broken in two, laid on him many a kiss,
Many an oath! But baggage such as this
Weighs naught, and he left, taking all he could.

At first, trying to soothe the belle, the bird
Did what he thought might cheer her: nothing would.
"What hateful chatter!... Oh! Must it be heard
Day in, day out?" she cried. "Let him be still,
And let me pout in peace and sigh my fill!"
The parrot ceased his talk, surprised at such
Proof of how sad the heart that loves too much.

The first few months, the missives come and go,
Trotting their tender way. Midst all the "Oh,
I love you so!", and all the "Leave me never!",
And all the "Ah! My love is yours forever!",
Our husband, 'twixt two "Till we meet again!",
Slipped in a word about his task. Indeed,
The old gent did his duty... died. Amen.
But there was many a thing that yet would need
Much care: take stock of his estate, and all
Manner of endless legal folderol.
What could she do but wait; and, waiting, dry
Her tears. "Who knows if, long concealed, my eye
Might duller grow, or have already done!
It is not right that such a charming one
As I spoil what my lover loves me for!...
Love itself would think ill." And, more and more
Confident now, there shone a little smile—
Timid at first—on her fair lips, erstwhile
Given to dismal sigh and moan; then two,
Then three... Then on and on, smiles without number.

La beauté renaissant ainsi que sa compagne,
La grâce, les amours se mirent en campagne.
D'anciens adorateurs, autrefois bien voulus,
Du temps qu'on était fille, au logis de la belle
Revinrent tout d'un vol et sur le pied d'amis.
D'un cœur à l'amitié l'accès est bien permis,
Mais trop souvent l'amour se faufile avec elle.
Croyez qu'il n'y manqua. Bientôt la citadelle,
On le prétend du moins, se rendit à merci,
Après un court combat. L'époux de tout ceci
Paya les frais. Déjà la dîme est prélevée
Sur les biens de l'absent et sans son agrément:
   Sa femme ainsi patiemment
   Put attendre son arrivée.

Notre consolateur à qui n'échappait rien,
Vit donc la brèche ouverte à l'honneur de son maître.
   Il en gémit en perroquet de bien.
   "Quoi!" disait-il, "deux cœurs que j'ai vus naître.
   Grandir, se chercher, s'entr'aimer!
Le plus charmant ferait à l'autre cette injure!
Non, foi de perroquet! De sa mésaventure
Je veux à son retour mon bon maître informer."
Ce retour ne tarda. Vers sa moitié chérie
Notre époux revola plus tendre et plus aimant.
   Que fleurette et cajolerie
Eussent passé chez lui sous forme d'un amant,
Il ne s'en aperçut; ce n'est chose vraiment
Qui laisse de soi trace, et même en laissât-elle,
Par un objet aimé qui n'est vite aveuglé!
Comment ne l'être point? Tout des mieux régalé,
Accueilli, caressé fut l'époux par la belle.
N'était-ce qu'un semblant? Grâce au remords, l'amour
Avait-il tourné bride, et par un beau retour

Arising from their long and deathly slumber,
Beauty, and grace—her kin—are born anew,
Paving the way for those who used to woo
To pay their court again. Fine suitors, whom
She fancied well when she was in the bloom
Of youth, came flocking back; all quick to tell—
Assure—Madame that it was only... well...
As friends, no more. For should the heart not stand
Open to friendship? Ah! But often, love,
Crawling and creeping by the side thereof,
Slithers in too. And so it did. Unmanned,
The citadel, they tell us, after but
A brief defense, laid down its arms; and what
Was lost was paid for at Monsieur's expense,
Without his knowledge or consent. And, thence,
    While absent overlong was he,
    Madame awaited patiently.

Our chattering consoler watched, missed naught,
    Saw all the many breaches wrought
    In Monsieur's trust; and since he was
An honorable bird, "What? What?" he caws,
"This love that I saw born, that I watched grow?
These hearts that yearned for, sought each other? Why,
    How can a charming creature so
    Betray her mate! No! By and by,
When he returns, then—parrot's honor!—I
Will tell him all, good master that he is!"
Return he does. To that dear spouse of his
He fairly flies. Warmer now his caresses,
Stronger, indeed, his love... That others had
    Proffered their flirting tendernesses—
To say the least!—was something that our lad
Saw nothing of, for such like leave no trace.
And, even if they did, does not the face
Of one beloved blind us to everything?
The belle, with many a welcoming embrace
Regaled him, glad—or so it seemed—to fling
Her arms about him. Real or counterfeit,

Réparait-il une erreur passagère?
Il se peut; toutefois je n'en jurerais pas,
Car, s'il faut tout vous dire, on ne rencontre guère
De cœurs qui s'égarant reviennent sur leurs pas.

Aussitôt cependant que l'oiseau dont la langue
Etait sur les charbons, trouva jour à parler,
"Propos de perroquet! Je m'en irais troubler?
Quelque sot!" L'indiscret, bien qu'étouffant de rage,
 Ne se tint pas ce jour-là pour battu;
Il revint à la charge. "Oiseau, te tairas-tu?"
L'autre ne se taisait; vingt fois et davantage
Il répéta son dire. "Oh! l'animal têtu!
Le maudit babillard!" Cependant le pauvre homme
Devenait tout rêveur. Du jour au lendemain
Il perdit l'appétit. La joie avec le somme
 Avait pris le même chemin.
Il n'ose point encor s'avouer qu'il soupçonne
A son honneur aucune atteinte pour cela.
Son épouse, c'était la sagesse en personne,
Et l'amour. Cependant qu'une mouche bourdonne
Aux environs, notre homme est sur le qui-va-là.
Une ombre, un soufle, un mot, tout tire à conséquence
Lorsqu'on est à ce point.

 L'oiseau, voyant l'effet
Que produit son discours, redouble d'éloquence;
Il cite ses témoins, il précise le fait,
Il parla, mais perdit sa peine et sa harangue.
Il jure ses grands dieux, il proteste, il s'entête.
"On vous trompa," dit-il, "j'en mets ma patte au feu."
La patte? ce n'est guère, il jouait plus gros jeu
Et perdit davantage: il y laissa la tête.
—Comment! la tête?—Hélas! on lui tordit le cou.
 Notre mari crut pour le coup
Recouvrer le repos par ce trait exemplaire.
Crut-il bien? Je ne sais. L'oiseau, dans cette affaire,
Fut malgré sa vertu le plus sot de beaucoup.

Her feelings? Did remorse, perhaps,
Redeem her from her momentary lapse?
Possibly, but I would not swear to it:
Errant hearts seldom change the path they take.

Our feathered prattler's tongue begins to ache,
Burning to give report of what his eyes
Beheld; but better had he held it: "Lies!"
His master shouts. "Mere parrot-talk! You dare
Trouble my mind with doubts, you stupid bird?"
Choking with rage, the tattler, undeterred—
No skittish battler!—charged again; and, there
      And then, despite commands to shut
His beak, he rattled out his accusation
A score of times, and even more. "Damnation!"
Chided Monsieur. "What blasted babble!" But
Despite himself, poor thing, night after night,
Day after day, gone were his appetite,
      His sleep, and all the joy it brought;
Gone his tranquillity. For, though he thought
His wife could not have smutched his honor, yet,
Though love and virtue in the flesh, she set
His mind to wondering: let the merest fly,
Flitting about, go humming, buzzing by,
And he pricks up suspicious ears. A word,
A breath, a shadow... Everything presents
A danger in such circumstance.

                              The bird,
Seeing the product of his eloquence,
Doubles his rhetoric: still more intense,
He names names, cites the times, the places, bares
Every detail. "By all the gods," he swears,
Insists, protests, "Madame has been a cheat,
And Monsieur, indiscreetly cuckolded!
See? Cross my heart..." (For parrots, no mean feat!)
"And hope to die!" With that, he lost his head...
His head? Quite! Monsieur wrings his neck. The latter
      Thinks that, now freed from his foul chatter,
He will regain his peace. Did he? Who knows?
I only know that, virtuous in the matter,
The parrot fared the worst. And so it goes.

Si par cas d'aventure, ô belles! je me trouve,
Sans le vouloir, témoin de quelque méchant tour,
Comptez sur mon silence, encor que je n'approuve
De pareils manquements aux devoirs de l'amour.
Des amants, des époux inquiéter les flammes,
C'est périlleux; j'honore après tout leur erreur.
Dieu la permet toujours; sans sa grâce, mesdames,
Qui pourrait vous aimer en sûreté de cœur?

———————

Partant pour Troie, à ce que dit Homère,
De son honneur un grand roi soucieux
Laissait auprès de sa moitié légère,
Pour tout gardien, un chantre aimé des Dieux.
Tant que la voix chanta, la jeune reine
Demeura sourde aux vœux du séducteur;
Une puissance aimable et souveraine
Veillait sur elle aux abords de son cœur.

Se pourrait-il que nos accents, mesdames,
Eussent perdu ce pouvoir chaste et doux?
Je n'en crois rien; à l'entour de vos âmes
Qu'un chant résonne, et je réponds de vous.
L'essaim furtif des mauvaises pensées
Vers vous en vain accourt de toute part;
Contre l'attrait des amours insensées
La lyre encore est un divin rempart.

———————

On dit qu'Adam sur la pelouse en fleur
Trouva la femme au sortir d'un long somme;
Mais sur un point ce récit fait erreur:
Pour la créer ce que Dieu prit à l'homme
Ce n'était point sa côte, mais son cœur.

If I, despite myself, should be, perchance,
Witness to such skulduggery, O beauties!
Count on my silence, though I look askance
On such defections from one's spousely duties.
Husbands' or lovers' passions? Let them be!
God leaves them to their blindness though he sees
Your ways, Mesdames: without his charity,
What man could love you with a heart at ease?

———————

As off he went to Troy, so Homer tells,
A king, to mind his honor, left to guard
His spouse—one of your none-too-solemn belles—
A lyrist: much loved of the Gods, this bard.
As long as he would sing, no libertine
Could reach the young queen's ear; his tender art,
A power as sovereign as had ever been,
* Lovingly kept its watch upon her heart.

Can it be that our notes have lost, mesdames,
The sweet and gentle power of chastity?
No. Let song spread about your souls its balm,
And chaste will you remain, I guarantee.
Furtively, swarms of evil thoughts conspire
To charge, assail you, from every direction:
Against the lure of mindless loves, the lyre
Is yet a sure and heavenly protection.

———————

They say that Adam, waking, found God's art
Made flesh, beside him, on the grass; they err,
However, on a single point: the part
The good Lord took from him to fashion her
Was not his rib, alas! It was his heart.

* To the best of my knowledge, there is no classical tradition of a worried king assigning
a bard whose singing might keep his queen faithful, but the scenario would seem to recall
the first two books of the *Odyssey*, in which Phemios sings for the pleasure of Penelope's
suitors and her own mixed pleasure and sorrow.
    This poem and the several following are from among eleven brief works of varying
lengths grouped under the title "Pensées diverses," and dated at Nice, May 1861.

Pour des sonnets en fasse qui les aime;
Chacun son goût, mais ce n'est pas le mien.
Un bon, dit-on, vaut seul un long poëme;
Heureux qui peut en amener à bien.
Mon vers, hélas! a l'humeur vagabonde;
Ne lui parlez d'entraves seulement.
Un peu de rime, encor Dieu sait comment!
S'il peut souffrir, c'est tout le bout du monde.
Ruisseau furtif, je le laisse courir
Parmi les prés, le livrant à sa pente;
Il saute, il fuit, il gazouille, il serpente,
Chemin faisant il voit ses bords fleurir.
Qu'un voyageur parfois s'y désaltère,
Et d'un merci le salue en partant,
Ou ses attraits qu'une jeune bergère
Vienne y mirer, c'est un ruisseau content.

L'amour, hélas! c'est la rose sauvage
Sur l'églantier s'entr'ouvrant au zéphyr;
Si la beauté la met à son corsage,
Près de son cœur, c'est pour l'y voir mourir.

C'est en vain que les ans et la raison morose
Vous diront qu'à l'amour il faudrait renoncer;
Les ans ni la raison ne font rien à la chose,
Et le cœur est toujours prêt à recommencer.

———————

Let those who favor sonnets write them: one
Follows one's taste, and sonnets are not mine.
A good one, so they say, concisely done,
* Can rival works of lengthier design;
Good luck to those who do them well! My verse
Goes wandering off, unfettered and unbound.
A touch of rhyme—God knows how it is found!—
A whit of suffering for its pains, or worse...
I set it free, a bubbling brooklet, flowing
Where it will—babbling, snaking furtively,
Leaping through field and meadow, glad to see
Its banks, along the way, flowering, growing...
And if a traveler slakes his thirst a bit,
Offers his thanks; or if, kneeling beside,
A shepherd-lass admires herself in it,
Happy the brooklet then, and satisfied.

———————

Love is the dog rose growing wild and free,
Spreading its petals to the zephyr's breath;
If beauty clasps it to her breast, ah me!
It is for naught but there to watch its death.

———————

In vain, age and dour reason say you ought
Abandon love wth a "farewell, amen!"
Reason and age will ever count for naught:
Never the heart is loath to try again.

* As if to prove her point, the author proceeds to write here a sixteen-line poem—two
lines longer than a sonnet—and one that, even with the requisite number of lines, would
not appear intended to fit any of the usual sonnet forms.

On fait un reproche à ma lyre
D'avoir rendu des sons joyeux.
Le poëte ne doit pas rire;
Son art est toujours sérieux.
Les pleurs, voilà son vrai domaine;
Le sourire de l'âme humaine
Echappe à cet enfant des Dieux.

A mêler donc pour plus de charme
Tous les tons il faut renoncer.
Pourtant, voisine d'une larme,
Ma gaieté raillait sans blesser.
Oui, mon rire et les pleurs sont frères,
Et mes rimes les plus légères
Laissent un bout du cœur passer.

My lyre, they chide, is much too gay,
And too much given to sounds of mirth.
Poets' art must be grave, they say,
And one who laughs is little worth.
Rather are tears the poet's lot;
Laughter, alas, behooves him not,
This child to whom the Gods gave birth.

And so I must renounce the charm
That mingled notes bring to our ears.
Gayly I chaffed, but did no harm,
Nor ever strayed too far from tears:
Yes, my sobs and my laughs are kin;
And, though carefree my rhymes, therein
Part of my heart, albeit, appears.

May 1861

Marie Pape-Carpantier (1815–1878)

Like a nun of centuries past, devoted to her calling but happily finding time for a poetic avocation as well, the woman born Marie Carpantier did not let her vocation as a reformer silence her poetic inspiration. Almost, that is, but not entirely. That inspiration, somewhat reminiscent of Lamartine's blend of classical rhetoric and romantic passion, produced only a single volume, to my knowledge; one well enough considered at the time to earn a preface by the then-prestigious Amable Tastu (see pp. 604–23).

But the several dozen lyrics of *Préludes* (1841) display a sincerity, harmoniously expressed, romantic clichés notwithstanding, that lets us appreciate that collection's existence while regretting the lack of successors. "Preludes" to what? She does not say, but her well-crafted rhetoric allows us to guess: to human love and fulfillment, to spiritual awakening, and to woman's martyrdom and inevitable demise. An enigmatic and anonymous dedication (just conceivably to Tastu) offers her volume—"the first and only wealth I possess in this world"—to "her, who delivered my soul from its painful cares," and who eased "my beloved mother's final days."

Marie Carpentier was born at La Flèche, near Le Mans, on September 10, 1815. The death of her father, one of Napoleon's officers, killed toward the end of the Hundred Days, resulted in a childhood marred by poverty and interrupted education. (Clearly not interrupted, however, before she had had the opportunity to familiarize herself with the poetry of her forebears and contemporaries.) It was no doubt her personal misfortunes that determined her long career as a reformer of the so-called *salles d'asile* (asylum classes) for the children of the poor and her transformation of them into the institution of lay *écoles maternelles* (nursery schools), providing the early education that working mothers were unable to give their young.

Her later years, in the turmoil of 1848, were troubled by accusations of irreligion—Protestantism, in a word—by a variety of enemies who saw her advocacy of practical lay schooling as a threat to the social fabric. But the support of influential individuals—the popular Béranger, the philosopher Victor Cousin, and Marceline Desbordes-Valmore's daughter Ondine, among them—helped maintain her in her mission. She married her long-time friend Léon Pape in 1849, spending the rest of her productive life as a force in the laicisation of the French educational system. When she died on July 31, 1878, she was recognized as one of the most important educators of her time.[1]

The four poems translated here, all written in the 1830s, are taken from

Préludes, a collection that stands as a solitary promise of a lyrical talent left unfulfilled.

NOTE

1. Several studies chronicle Marie Pape-Carpantier's career and pedagogical writings: Fanny Dupin de Saint-André, *Madame Pape-Carpantier;* Emile and Richard Loubens, *Madame Pape-Carpentier: Sa vie et ses ouvrages;* Emile Gossot, *Madame Marie Pape-Carpentier: Sa vie et son œuvre;* and Colette Cosnier's recent and thorough *Marie Pape-Carpantier.* They do not, however, have much to say about her poetic aspirations.

Oh! que j'aime le soir d'une forêt ombreuse!
Sa majesté sauvage et sa clarté douteuse,
Quand un pâle rayon timide et vaporeux
Blanchit ces noirs sapins dont les fronts sourcilleux,
S'élançant vers le ciel pour en montrer la route,
S'étonnent du zéphir qui caresse leur voûte!
Semblable au vol d'une âme, un bruissement plaintif
S'élève harmonieux, et vague et fugitif;
L'oreille en s'inclinant veut saisir ce murmure,
Mais le cœur seul comprend la voix de la nature,
Qui, dans ces sombres nuits, d'un ton mystérieux
Se révèle aux mortels et soupire avec eux.
Ou bien, quand tout-à-coup, déchirant le silence,
Un hurlement affreux de la terre s'élance,
Et qu'un fils de Borée, accourant en fureur,
Remplissant les forêts d'épouvante et d'horreur,
Déracine en passant les plus antiques chênes,
Souffle au loin leurs débris dont il couvre les plaines,
Ebranle l'univers et menace les cieux...
Ses clameurs sont pour moi des sons mélodieux!
D'une sainte frayeur tout mon être palpite,
Et cède en frémissant au trouble qui m'agite!

BREEZE AND STORM

Oh, how I love the evening's forest shade:
Its savage grandeur—low-lit, dimly-grayed—
When one pale, timid ray, like a light cloud
Whitens the firs' black tips that, solemn-browed,
Rise to the sky, showing the way, while much
Surprised are they at zephyr's gentle touch!
Like a soul's flight, a plaintive swish, a-flutter,
Skyward flies in a vague, harmonious mutter
That the ear wishes it could seize, bowed low
To comprehend its message... Ah, but no!
It is the heart and heart alone that can
Learn what the voice of nature says to Man;
That voice that chants, in solemn tone, on these
Dark nights; that voice that utters mysteries,
And sighs in tune with mortals' moaned laments.
Or else, that frightful groan; that fierce, intense
Roar that goes rising, suddenly, from the earth,
Rending the silence as the North gives birth
To its more fearsome offspring, casting round
About the woods, the most horrendous sound;
Whose breath uproots the age-old oaks; goes strewing
Shattered boughs, scattered limbs, bent on subduing
*   The universe and all the heavenly sphere...
What joy I feel! What blessèd, quivering fear
Before that blaring tempest melody,
A-shiver with the woe tormenting me!

1834

* One is inevitably reminded, in these final lines, of the climactic scene in La Fontaine's celebrated fable "Le chêne et le roseau" ("The Oak and the Reed"). For an English translation, see my edition of *Fifty Fables of La Fontaine*, pp. 17–18.

SANS NOM

Souvent, la nuit, loin du bruit et du monde,
Seul, égaré dans l'épaisseur des bois,
Aux sourds éclats de la foudre qui gronde,
En souriant j'aime à mêler ma voix.
Et quand, des pics noircis qui pendent sur ma tête,
L'éclair étincelant a fait pâlir le faîte;
Quand, des vastes forêts la sombre majesté
Resplendit tout-à-coup d'une vive clarté;
Qu'un roulement, profond, majestueux, terrible,
Ebranlant jusqu'au pied le roc inaccessible,
Semble, du haut des cieux, une éclatante voix,
Qui, comme au Sinaï, vient proclamer ses lois;
Exalté par ce bruit que mon cœur sait comprendre,
Je crois qu'un Dieu s'annonce, et, brûlant de l'entendre,
Je vole avec l'éclair au sommet du rocher;
Car de ce Dieu puissant je voudrais m'approcher.
Tremblant d'un saint effroi, je contemple la nue,
Qui dans ses sombres flancs se dérobe à ma vue.
Et, prêt à l'adorer, mon esprit confondu
Attend qu'il se découvre à mon œil éperdu!

ÉCRIRE

Répandre avec amour les secrets de son âme
Sur la page où pourront se fixer d'autres yeux;
Y verser ses douleurs, ses souvenirs, ses vœux,
S'y dévoiler enfin, est un besoin de femme.

NAMELESS

Lost in the woodland depths, alone,
Often, at night, far from the world's ado,
Amid the thunder's muffled moan,
* Smiling, I love to join my voice thereto.
And when the lightning bolt above my head
Brightens the blackened peaks rising outspread;
When the vast forest's dusky majesty
Flashes a sudden burst; then, fearsomely,
A deep and stately groan grumbles a low
Roar at the foot of the remote plateau,
Rumbling, splitting the very firmament
Like The Law's voice on Sinai, heaven-sent;
Then, in a tongue that my heart comprehends,
It is as if some god almighty sends
Word of His presence; and, ecstatic, I
Give ear, yearning to hear His voice and fly,
Borne on the lightning, to the topmost peak,
† Trembling with holy dread to meet and speak
With God Himself... I gaze upon the cloud,
Whose flanks conceal Him, like a somber shroud;
And, worshipful, I wait, until He might
Bare Himself to my soul-enraptured sight.

1836

TO WRITE

To spread with love, for others' eyes to read
Upon the page, her soul's deep secrets; there
To pour her memories, wishes, woes, and bare
Herself to all: such is a woman's need.

* Not unusually, the poet affects a male persona, as revealed in the masculine gender of her self-referential French adjectives, in the opening lines and later in the poem.

† Given the sense of the concluding lines, I suspect that the original *se*, referring grammatically to *la nue*, ought to read *le*, referring to *ce Dieu*, and have taken the liberty of translating it as such.

Nous savons, essuyant des pleurs inaperçus,
Aux profanes regards cacher notre souffrance.
Et pourtant nous cédons à la triste espérance
De révéler nos maux quand nous ne serons plus.

Avides de bonheur, de bonheur dépouillées,
Lasses d'un cœur désert comme d'un lourd fardeau.
Nous voudrions aimer... aimer semble si beau!
Mais donner son amour à des âmes souillées?

Non non! mieux vaut souffrir! mieux vaut, dans le secret,
Arroser de ses pleurs sa route solitaire;
Renverser son idole et la briser à terre,
Qu'accepter un amour que Dieu réprouverait!

Et pourtant, ô Jésus! au fond de quelques âmes
Brûlent des feux sacrés dignes de ton autel...
Faudra-t-il donc couvrir d'un silence éternel
Ces transports délirants, ces extases de flammes?...

Non! j'écrirai! Peut-être, à mon tombeau désert
Le soir viendra pleurer, quelque femme isolée
Qui dira, par mes vers tristement consolée:
"Tout ce qu'on peut souffrir, son âme l'a souffert!"

À UNE JEUNE FEMME

J'ai compris ta souffrance, ô triste jeune femme!
De ton front altéré quand j'ai vu la pâleur;
Quand j'ai vu ton regard, mélancolique flamme,
Se tourner vers le ciel confident de ton âme,
   Va, j'ai lu dans ton cœur!

J'ai lu qu'un froid hymen a défloré ta vie;
Qu'un lugubre avenir, veuf de joie et d'amours,
Couvre comme un linceul ta jeunesse flétrie;
Et qu'hélas! tu subis, de dégoûts poursuivie,
   D'interminables jours.

Brushing our unseen tears—heart suffering, sore—
We hide our grief from eyes profane, and yet
Yield to the hope that one will not forget
Our pain, revealed when we are here no more.

Yearning for joy but joy-bereft, laid low
Beneath the weight of barren heart, we would
Happily love... Love seems so fair, so good!
But, give one's heart to souls impure?... Ah, no!

No!... Better, far, to suffer! Better, hidden,
To let drear life with bitter tears abound;
To smash one's idol, crashing to the ground,
Than to accept a love by God forbidden!

Still, Jesus mine! in some souls there must be
Sacred fires fit to burn before your shrine.
Must we, to endless silence, then, resign
Ourselves, and quell those flames of ecstasy?

No! Write I shall! Perhaps, one night, will come
Some woman to my grave—abandoned, cold—
To sob, alone, by my sad verse consoled:
"Hers was each suffering soul's dour martyrdom!"

1838

FOR A YOUNG WOMAN

O sad young woman! On your brow—pale, yearning—
I gazed and saw how anguish played its part!
I saw the flame of melancholy burning
Deep in your trusting eyes, heavenward turning.
          Ah, how I read your heart!

I read a wedlock fading your life's bloom;
A future, widowed of the bliss of love;
Your withered youth, spread with a pall of gloom,
Shrouding, alas, as in a mournful tomb,
          The endless days thereof.

Se peut-il que ces biens si communs dans le monde,
Ces maux qui font au moins sentir la vie en soi;
Ivresse, désespoir, amour, haine profonde,
Délices ou tourments, dont le sort nous inonde,
      Ne soient jamais à toi!

Quoi! jamais sur tes jours d'astre qui les éclaire!
Quoi! toujours dans ton cœur la fatigue et l'ennui!...
Jamais, jamais d'enfant qui t'appelle sa mère!...
Et savoir qu'il faudra demain, la vie entière,
      Souffrir comme aujourd'hui!...

Ne pleure pas; tes pleurs éveilleraient le blâme:
Le monde?... ah! comprend-il tous les maux qu'il nous fait?
Cache-lui, cache à tous les douleurs de ton âme;
Chante et ris, si tu peux, mais surtout, pauvre femme,
      Garde bien ton secret!

Car si, leur découvrant le trait qui te déchire,
Tu leur disais: "Eh bien! ce mal que je ressens,
C'est le besoin d'amour, d'ineffable délire!... "
Ils se diraient entre eux avec un froid sourire:
      "Elle a lu des romans... "

Honte et mépris sur vous, blasphémateurs impies
Du culte grand et saint qu'on professe à genoux!
Par l'égoïsme ardent vos âmes sont flétries;
Vous reniez l'amour, les nobles sympathies...
      Honte à jamais sur vous!

Can it be that life's vast variety—
Passion, love, hate, despair (not joys alone,
But woes and torments too, that endlessly
Prove that we live and feel!)... Ah! Can it be
      That they be never known?

What? Not to let a star, no light whatever,
Brighten your days, heart empty, languishing!...
Never a child to call you "mother"!... Never!...
And know that your tomorrows bring forever
      Today's same suffering!...

Weep not: your tears would but stir blame withal.
The world?... Can it know how it treats us ill?
Let none perceive your soul's distress, its gall;
Sing, laugh, poor thing... Try, try... But, most of all,
      Hush! Keep your secret still!

For, if you should confess to them the cause
Of your distress, and say: "It is the need
For love's wild passion that thus rips and gnaws
At me," they would but smile with cold guffaws:
      "What novels must she read!"

Shame on you, vile blasphemers, virtueless,
Of that great, sacred faith you kneel before!
Your souls burn, withered by your selfishness;
Love's noble tenderness you scorn... Ah yes,
      Shame on you evermore!

Louise Michel (1830–1905)

Readers who may feel that true art and "engagement" do not mix will find the poetry of Louise Michel a rude revelation. No champion of "art for art's sake," she proved with the inflammatory energy of her anarchistic pen that committed, "propagandistic" literature—in this case, poetry—can cause artistic chords to vibrate no less forcefully than the apolitical tributes to love, death, nature, God, and the lyrical variations on same that many poets have felt to be the only worthy province of their art and craft. To be sure, many a masterpiece of Hugo and others could give the lie to such a notion. But poetic purists often persist in the feeling that anything as utilitarian as the expression of a social ideal or political idea is an affront to Apollonian purity. In modern times they can, rightly, smirk at such abominations as Soviet odes to reforestation or Communist Chinese paeans to the fulfillment of factory quotas. But in the hands of a real poet, if one can put aside the absurdity of their premise, even such exaggerations might well be rhetorically powerful.

Louise Michel was such a poet. Whether singing her solidarity with the American black or the Russian moujik, the fire of her verse, intoned in the cause of anarchy, never loses its rhetorical power, its rigorous fidelity to the canons of French prosody, and its passionately personal voice inherited from the romantics.

She was born on May 29, 1830, in Vroncourt, close to Domrémy, birthplace of another firebrand, Joan of Arc. Daughter of an unwed servant girl and a small landowner, she was raised largely by her paternal grandfather, an eighteenth-century rationalist and survivor of the Revolution. Trained as a schoolmistress, with a marked gift for poetry, she lost her local teaching post because of her vigorous criticism of the Second Empire and, in 1856, went to teach in Paris, taking her anti-government sentiments and her literary talents with her. She spent the following years participating in republican groups, fighting for the budding cause of women's rights, and, at the same time, writing several protest novels and a body of verse. Encouraged by her lover, Théophile Ferré, she became more and more militant in her socialistic stance, (wo)manning the barricades in the siege of Paris during the Franco-Prussian War and the disruptions of the Commune in 1871. Condemned as one of the Commune leaders, she was exiled to New Caledonia, where a French penal colony for political dissidents had been established in 1853.

During her years there, she continued writing—poetry, theatre, novels, essays—and fighting for the cause of the indigenous Kanakas. When a general amnesty returned her to Paris in 1881, participation in more socialist and anarchistic unrest landed her in prison on several other occasions. Eventually released, but always flirting with incarceration, she exiled herself on and off to England, whose political freedom was more congenial to her political activities. These continued unabated until, returning ill from Algeria, she died in Marseille on January 9, 1905, mourned by thousands as a martyr to her deeply held convictions.

In addition to her own *Mémoires* (1886), there is, to put it mildly, no dearth of biographical studies of Louise Michel and her work, political as well as literary.[1] Her poetry is most easily accessible in the collection titled *A travers la vie et la mort*, edited by Daniel Armogathe, which is chronologically divided into the principal periods of her tempestuous life, appropriately titled, and in which the nine poems here translated, spanning the years 1850 to 1896, are found.

NOTE

1. For several recent studies see Edith Thomas, *Louise Michel*, trans. Penelope Williams; Xavière Gauthier, *La vierge rouge* (The Red Virgin) (the name by which she was affectionately known); Paule Lejeune, *Louise Michel l'indomptable;* Christine Ribeyreix's politically oriented *Louise Michel, quand l'aurore se lèvera;* Alison Finch, *Women's Writing in Nineteenth-Century France*, pp. 187–89, 199–205, 221–22; and Wendy Greenberg, *Uncanonical Women*, pp. 161–69.

Vent du soir, que fais-tu de l'humble marguerite?
Mer, que fais-tu des flots? Ciel, du nuage ardent?
O mon rêve est bien grand et je suis bien petite,
Destin, qu'en feras-tu de mon rêve géant?

Lumière, que fais-tu de l'ombre taciturne,
Et toi qui de si loin l'appelle près de toi,
O flamme, que fais-tu du papillon nocturne?
Songe mystérieux, que feras-tu de moi?

SERMENT

Les noirs devant le gibet de John Brown

Frères, il est donc vrai, la guerre est déclarée.
Venez... Qui d'entre nous, pour la cause sacrée,
    Ne donnerait cent fois son sang?
Quand l'arène est grondante on brûle d'y descendre,
Les restes des martyrs sont plus froment que cendre,
    Qui d'entre vous ne prendrait rang?

Venez, frères, venez; la torture est délices,
Le gibet même est beau; la flamme des supplices
    Est l'immense foyer d'amour,
L'éclair du glaive reste en sillon de lumière,
Et quand le juste meurt, sa parole dernière,
    Dans l'air, retentit nuit et jour.

*   What do you with the daisy, winds of night?
    And you, sea, with the waves? You, sky agleam,
    With clouds of fire? So small am I, so slight—
    What will you do, Fate, with my giant dream?

    What do you do, light, with mute shadows lit?
    And you, O flame, who beckon distantly
    To the night moth? What do you do with it?
    Mysterious dream, what will you do with me?

"Album de jeunesse, 1850–1860"

OATH

†   *The Blacks Before John Brown's Gallows*

‡   "Yes, brothers, war has been declared. Come... Come...
    Who would refuse to bleed his martyrdom
         For sacred cause so glorious?
    When the arena roars, we burn to try
    Our arms, to let our ashes fructify
         The land. Will you not stand with us?

    "Come, brothers... Torture is delight; the stake's
    Flames are love's vast expanse: our torment makes
         Even the hangman's noose seem fair.
    The blade's gleam furrows in a flash of light;
    And when the just man dies, then day and night
         His last words echo on the air.

   * This untitled, undated poem, marked only "Vroncourt," is undoubtedly one of Michel's earliest.

   † Typical of her socially and politically engaged verse, the poet here draws her inspiration from the ill-fated pre–Civil War slave insurrection at Harper's Ferry in Virginia on October 16, 1859, instigated by the white abolitionist John Brown, for which he was subsequently hanged.

   ‡ Though the original omits quotation marks, I take the liberty of inserting them in the hortatory stanzas, resulting in the poet's own voice of the climactic final three lines.

Venez, vous les grands cœurs, vous les âmes ardentes
Il faut des bras géants pour ces luttes géantes,
      Des fronts que rien ne fait pâlir.
Il faut, quand le chemin est sillonné d'abîmes,
Les traverser au vol; venez, esprits sublimes,
      Venez, vous qui savez mourir.

Venez et jurons tous, jurons-le par nos pères,
Jurons par nos martyrs, nos frères et nos mères,
      De combattre jusqu'au dernier!
Ah! si nous mourons tous, sacrifice suprême,
Sur l'immense tombeau viendra le peuple même.
      Maudit celui qui sait plier!

Frères, jurons donc tous! L'horreur nous environne;
Du vieux parti, bercé par le vent monotone,
      Tombe le dernier fort.
Mais à nous les déserts, les solitudes mornes,
L'inconnu, l'infini dont nul ne sait les bornes,
      Les secrets que garde la mort.

Jurons aussi par toi, qui dans les catacombes,
O mage, dans les cieux, dans les flots, dans les tombes,
      Entends sonner l'éternité!

Et le peuple, prenant la nuit, au gibet sombre,
Le linceul de l'esclave et l'agitant dans l'ombre,
      En fait surgir la Liberté.

DANS LES MERS POLAIRES

La neige tombe, le flot roule!
L'air est glacé, le ciel est noir,
Le vaisseau craque sous la houle,
Et le matin se mêle au soir.

"Come, you of noble hearts, souls passion-wrought...
With giants' arms must giant frays be fought,
    And brows that pallid fear defy.
When fraught the path with long and deep abyss,
We must fly high above the precipice:
    Come, pure souls, who know how to die.

"Come, let us all swear by our fathers, mothers;
Let us swear on our martyrs' heads, our brothers,
    To fight unto the bitter end!
If—sacrifice supreme!—we meet our doom,
Each one, the people will flock to our tomb.
    Cursèd be who his knee would bend!

"Brothers, come swear! Horror abounds about us:
Fallen, our last fort, to those who would flout us,
*   Rocked by the wind's relentless breath.
But ours the deserts' lonely wilderness,
The endless, the unknown, the limitless,
    And secrets held by naught but death.

"And by you, let us swear, who, in the seas,
The skies, the tombs, working your mysteries,
    Hear the eternal infinite!"

The people, that night, by the gallows, take
The slave's shroud, in the dark, and shake
    Till Freedom surges forth from it.

May 2, 1861
"La légende républicaine, 1861–1870"

---

† IN THE POLAR SEAS

The snow falls thick, the sea rolls on!
Frigid the air and black the skies...
The ship creaks in the waves, and dawn
Turns into dusk before your eyes.

* The original six-syllable line, instead of the eight syllables of her established pattern,
is probably an oversight, and I do not reflect it in my translation.
    † This is one of a number of works inspired by the poet's South Sea exile as a result of
her revolutionary activities.

Formant une ronde pesante,
Les marins dansent en chantant;
Comme un orgue à la voix tonnante,
Dans les voiles souffle le vent.

De peur que le froid ne les gagne,
Ils disent au pôle glacé
Un an des landes de Bretagne,
Un vieux bardit du temps passé.

Et le bruit du vent dans les voiles,
Cet air si naïf et si vieux;
La neige, le ciel sans étoiles,
De larmes emplissent les yeux.

Cet air, est-il un chant magique,
Pour attendrir ainsi le cœur?
Non, c'est un souffle d'Armorique
Tout rempli de genêts en fleur.

Et c'est le vent des mers polaires
Tonnant dans les trompes d'airain,
Les nouveaux bardits populaires
De la légende de demain.

———————

OCÉANIDE

Avec les vagues, sous la houle,
Les temps présents, les temps passés
Se mêlent et viennent en foule,
Montant au cœur à flots pressés,

Et tout ce qui vit sur la terre,
Et tout ce qui dort sous les eaux,
Lève le voile du mystère
Et parle avec la voix des flots.

The sailors, in a weighty ring,
Sing and dance as the wind blows round,
Organ-like, howling, bellowing:
Deep in the sails, its mighty sound.

To hold the deadening chill at bay,
They tell the icy Pole how cold
The Breton moors can be: a lay
Sung by the bards, long years untold...

And the sails moaning loud and low;
That simple, time-old lay; the blear,
Starless sky; and the blowing snow...
All fill the eye with many a tear.

Is it a magic litany,
Mystic chant, this? Heart-rending air?
No, only a breath of Brittany
Lush with the broom-flowers looming there;

And with the wind of Polar seas
As well, blaring their trumpets' brass:
The people's bardic legends, these
* Lays of tomorrow's ruling class.

"Le livre du bagne, 1873–1880"

OCEAN NYMPH

With rolling waves, in ocean deeps,
The present and the past as well,
Mingling in surging bounds and leaps,
Pound at my heart in mounting swell,

And all that sleeps beneath the sea,
And all that on the land abides,
Lifting the veil of mystery,
Speaks with the voices of the tides.

"Le livre du bagne, 1873–1880"

* My translation here may seem a little far-fetched. But I think that readers familiar with the poet's social and political leanings will agree that her adjective *populaire* in the next-to-last line of the original is used in its original French meaning, "of the people," and that the utopian vision of her conclusion justifies my apparent liberty.

LE CYCLONE

Les cyclones hurlent dans l'ombre;
La nuit emplit la terre et l'eau;
L'écueil est noir, la mer est sombre;
Plus de fanal sur le vaisseau.
La tempête sonne ses trompes,
Dans cet abîme où rien ne luit.
Navire, faut-il tant de pompes
Pour t'engloutir dans cette nuit.

La mort ici c'est l'épousée,
Sous le voile humide des flots;
Sa pâle tête est couronnée
Des magnifiques fleurs des eaux.
Sonnez, ô flots, l'appel de guerre;
Tonnez, tonnez, clairons des vents;
Passez, terribles sur la terre,
En Marseillaises d'ouragans.

Est-ce le continent qui sombre
Ou le navire qui périt?
Qui sait ce que recouvre l'ombre
Et ce que le navire engloutit:
Les tempêtes frappent leurs ailes;
Les mâts tombent avec fracas;
Les luttes terribles sont belles
Noirs éléments dans vos combats.

THE CYCLONE

Out of the shadows, swell and roar
The gales; the sea, dark, fore and aft;
Black are the waves, the reef, the shore;
No beacon on the foundering craft.
The tempest-trumpets blast, blare free;
In the abyss, no gleam of light.
* Boat, do you need such obsequy
To be sucked deep within this night?

See, here, the bride: Death, ocean-crowned,
Entwined beneath her tide-tossed veil.
Splendid, the water-flowers wreathe round
About her head, so wan, so pale.
Shout loud the war-cry, mighty sea!
Blow loud, you wind-borne menaces;
Sweep loud the land: fierce clarions be;
Thunder your cyclones' "Marseillaise."

Is it the continent that hovers,
Or but one boat astride the pit?
Who knows what ills the darkness covers,
† What the boat will drag down with it...
The storm winds beat their wings; masts crack
And crumble: deafening is the rattle.
How beautiful is strife, how black,
All nature in your glorious battle!

"Le livre du bagne, 1873–1880"

---

* I feel certain that the *pompes* referred to here, profusion of water notwithstanding, are not pumps but *pompes funèbres* (funeral rites). Unfortunately (or, perhaps, fortunately), the ambiguity cannot be carried over into English.

† Either the poet or her modern editor has inadvertently added a ninth syllable to the expected eight of this line in the original, which I reproduce as published.

Les cœurs sont chauds comme la braise
Dans vos froides plaines du Nord,
Et sous notre ciel de fournaise,
Les cœurs sont froids comme la mort.
Le sang tombe en gouttes vermeilles
Aux rouges verveines pareilles,
Sur vos froides plaines du Nord.

Quand le vent des steppes balance,
Braves, vos pâles ossements
Aux bras hideux de la potence,
Les ténèbres, les loups hurlants
Disent ton hymne menaçante,
O liberté! dans la tourmente
Où sont vos pâles ossements.

Le vent mugit et souffle en foudre...
Enfin serait-ce le réveil?...
Le clairon sonne, on sent la poudre;
L'Egalité brille au soleil
Ainsi qu'un phare, elle illumine,
Dans le ciel rouge, elle domine;
Enfin, serait-ce le réveil?...

FOR RUSSIAN FRIENDS

Your hearts are hot as embers' breath,
There, in your Northland, frigid, bare;
And hearts are barren, cold as death,
Here, in the furnace of our air.
† Like vervain flowers of crimson red
Your blood's vermilion drops are shed
Over your Northland, frigid, bare.

Brave souls, when, from the steppes, the gale
Whips at your white bones, rattling, swaying—
From hideous gibbet-arms—bleached pale,
The shadows, the wolves howling, baying,
Ring out the hymn that freedom sings,
Menacing, with its blusterings
About your white bones, rattling, swaying.

Growls the wind, huffs, puffs, thundering louder...
Is it the wakening? Can it be?...
The clarion sounds, we smell the powder:
See? In the sun, Equality
Shines like a beacon, casts its beam
‡ In the red sky, superb, supreme.
Is it the wakening? Can it be?...

"Germinal, 1881–1901: La légende future"

* On the poet's admiration for and sympathy with the Russian peasants of her time, "nos camarades de lutte" (our comrades in the struggle), and the influence of prominent anarchists on her thinking, see *A travers la vie et la mort*, p. 243n.

† I intentionally suppress the apostrophe "O liberté!" since the direct address both to the "brave souls" and to personified Freedom would cause a confusion, one not present in the original thanks to the distinction between the plural (*vos*) and the singular (*ton*) possessive forms in French.

‡ While the redness of the sky might be seen as no more than the color of daybreak, it suggests as well the image of blood and suffering. In addition, though the Red Army of the Bolsheviks was several years down the road, the color red had for some time already been taken as a symbol of revolution.

Louise Michel 719

LA NOCE DE MISÈRE

Chanson du nord

La fille du moujik apprête sa couronne
    (Une couronne à quatre fleurs).
Elle fait son bouquet au matin qui frissonne.
    Et le bouquet a quatre fleurs,
    Quatre fleurs aux faibles couleurs.

Celles de la couronne ont pour noms la Misère,
    La Maladie et le Chagrin,
Et la Fatalité; ses autres, peine amère,
    La Travail, la Douleur, la Faim.
    Elle tient son bouquet en main.

Mais la Fatalité s'irradie en aurore,
    Le froid l'a prise sur le seuil;
Il la glace pendant que la chanson sonore
    En riant la donne au cercueil.
    La vie eût été plus grand deuil.

La fille du moujik avec sa robe blanche
    Et la couronne aux quatre fleurs
Dort en paix dans la fosse où le tilleul se penche,
    Le tilleul aux rameaux rêveurs
    Qui sur elle s'effeuille en pleurs.

Song of the North

The moujik's daughter braids her diadem—
With flowers four, one shivering dawn—
And plaits a nosegay with four more of them;
Four flowers of colors weak and wan,
Four withered flowers, blooms woebegone.

The diadem's four flowers are each named so:
Grief, Sickness, Doom, and Poverty;
The other four of them bear the names Woe,
Hunger, Travail, and Misery.
She clasps her nosegay eagerly.

But Doom goes spreading like the rays of dawn;
The cold has snatched her at the door,
† Chills her deep—as the wedding song brawls on—
Laughs her into the coffin; for
Life would have grieved her all the more.

The moujik's daughter, with her wedding gown,
And flowers four of her diadem,
Sleeps, tombed in peace; the linden tree bends down
Its dreaming boughs and, bowing them,
Weeps her a leafless requiem.

"Germinal, 1881–1901: La légende future"

---

* In his note to this poem, the manuscript of which is apparently lost, Daniel Armogathe indicates that it had remained unpublished until it appeared in the *Revue anarchiste* 12 (November–December 1930). See *A travers la vie et la mort*, p. 243.

† I take the liberty here, given the context, of assuming the *chanson* in question to be specifically a wedding song.

Jeune fille douce et rieuse
Fraîche comme un matin d'été
Gentille abeille travailleuse
Tu fus la grâce et la bonté

Les tiens te pleureront sans cesse
Ayant perdu tout leur bonheur
Ta sœur te garde sa tendresse
Malgré la mort glaçant son cœur

Et l'impression m'est restée
A moi qui te vis un instant
D'une rose pâle penchée
Dans une urne de marbre blanc

À SARAH BERNHARDT

Les chants auprès de vous ce matin ont fait trêve
Et je veux à mon tour offrir un souvenir
Des vers pleins du brouillard de Londres et du rêve
Puissent-ils près de vous en fleurs s'épanouir

FOR JULIA VAUVELLE, DEAD AT THE AGE OF NINETEEN

Fresh as a summer morning, you,
† Demoiselle of the laughing face...
Busy bee, never idle, who
Naught were but goodness, sweetness, grace...

Your dear ones will not cease to mourn,
For all their happiness is fled;
Your sister weeps, yearning, forlorn,
Heart chilled by death, uncomforted.

And though but once, briefly, we met,
Never will I forget the sight
Of a rose, gently bowing, set,
Pale, in an urn of marble, white.

August 16, 1893
"Germinal, 1881–1901: La légende future"

‡ **FOR SARAH BERNHARDT**

The odes of the adoring throng agog
Subside this morning and I rhyme for you
A souvenir of dream and London's fog
§ To flower about you as fair blossoms do

* Clearly, the ill-fated young subject of this bit of occasional verse was related to Charlotte Vauvelle, the London anarchist whom Michel had met in 1890, who became her constant companion until the poet's death and the executrix of her will.
† The original does not suffer from the poet's rather uncustomary total lack of punctuation, but my translation would, and I have seen fit to supply it.
‡ Armogathe explains this poem, in part at least, by Louise Michel's hopes that the celebrated first lady of the French stage would perform her drama *Prométhée*, hopes that were never fulfilled. See *A travers la vie et la mort*, p. 244.
§ As opposed to the previous poem, the total lack of punctuation in this curious encomium seems too integral a part of its structure for me to presume to "rectify" it in my translation.

A travers les courants les forces inconnues
L'éternité d'après l'éternité d'avant
Et les mondes voguant dans l'infini des mers
A travers les progrès l'un sur l'autre montant

Qu'ils aillent écoulant la lointaine harmonie
Les accords et les chants dans les airs emportés
Puisque vous êtes l'art sublime et le génie
Et fleurissent pour vous en rameaux étoilés

Que les parfums les sons les étoiles ardentes
Se mêlent vous disant quelque chant de demain
Et que flottent dans l'air les ailes flamboyantes
De l'idée éternelle éclairant le chemin

Forces unknown currents mysterious
Eternities of what was and will be
Worlds floating in the infinite lift us
* Through the clouds higher and higher endlessly

May they spread far and wide upon the breeze
The art sublime the genius that you are
And in your melodies your harmonies
Bloom laurels for you touched by many a star

May the hot-passioned stars the sounds the scents
Blend for you sing you a tomorrow-song
May pure thought's wings eternal glow intense
Waft on the air and light your way along

December 9–10, 1896
"Germinal, 1881–1901: La légende future"

* Before the outraged reader leaps on my seeming lapse and insists that *mers* in line 7 of the French means "seas," not "clouds," I hasten to note that I believe the original here is a misreading. I have not seen the manuscript of the poem in the Internationaal Instituut voor Sociale Geschiedenis in Amsterdam, but I cannot believe that the poet did not intend the rhyming word *nues*, rather than the clearly unrhyming *mers*. The two words could easily be confused in a handwritten manuscript. My assumption is bolstered by the need, according to the demands of French versification, for a "feminine" rhyme—i.e., one ending in a mute *e*: *nues* would fit the requirement whereas *mers* does not.

Marie Nizet (1859–1922)

Born in Brussels on June 19, 1859, and one of Belgium's finest poets, female or male, Marie Nizet came by her wordsmithing talents naturally. Her father, François-Joseph Nizet, an erudite scholar in several fields and assistant curator of the Bibliothèque royale, was also a published poet; and her brother Henri Nizet, a journalist and writer, was a poet as well. It is obvious, too, that she was endowed with a rich imagination when one considers that her early poems, "Moscou" and "Bucarest," published at eighteen, extolled the beauties of a Russia and a Romania that she had, in fact, never visited. Not unlike Marceline Desbordes-Valmore, who was touched by the plight of the Greeks eager to throw off the Turkish yoke (see pp. 568–602 above), Marie Nizet, influenced by her liberal lay education at the prestigious Institut Gatti for girls in Brussels, and, no doubt, by some of her father's students, was an eager champion of the cause of Romanian independence from Russia. In 1877 or 1879—sources differ—the same imagination produced an early novel, *Le Capitaine Vampire*, one of the many vampire tales based on Transylvanian folklore—indeed, one of the first, preceding Bram Stoker's celebrated *Dracula* by some eighteen years.

Unhappily married—hence the marriage name Mercier by which she is sometimes known—Marie Nizet bore a child and soon ended her marriage in divorce. It was not until after her death, at Boisfort, Belgium, at age 63, that her love affair with a Scandinavian sailor lost at sea—one Cecil-Axel Veneglia, mourned and immortalized as "Axel"—came to light in a posthumous collection of passionate, nostalgic, and eventually resigned laments addressed to him by his despairing "Missie."

Lacking precise biographical details, one cannot even say how much of the affair depicted in *Pour Axel* (1923), of which nine poems are here translated, was historically true and how much was a fictionalized fantasy no more solidly based than her descriptions of the Romanian landscape. No matter. The poetic result is the same: a stirring document, written from the soul, from the first of its forty poems to the tender resignation of the last, dated the year of her death, in 1922.[1]

NOTE

1. Frequently anthologized, Marie Nizet and her work have, curiously, been only sporadically studied. In addition to Edith Joyce Benkov's entry in the *Encyclopedia of Continental Women Writers*, 2: 919, see the special supplement no. 23 to the *Journal littéraire* of July 2002 devoted to Belgian authors, as well as Renée Linkhorn and Judy Cochran's recent volume, *Belgian Women Poets*, pp. 1–9.

A Venise, un verrier, maître d'art, fit un jour
Ce verre de cristal ambré, veiné de rouge,
Et pailleté d'or fin, qui paraît, tour à tour,
Une fleur qui s'incline, une flamme qui bouge.

Le pied trop frêle porte un calice profond,
Comme un lys jaune sur sa tige trop chargée.
La lumière à travers court, s'irise et se fond;
Et l'eau que l'on y verse en vin semble changée.

A Sèvres, l'autre siècle, un homme a façonné
La tasse que voici d'une pâte si tendre
Que l'ongle y laisse un trait, et d'un ton bleu fané
Que le Temps, sans égard, couvre d'un peu de cendre.

Une ronde d'Amours soutient comme un miroir
Le médaillon où rit une dame poudrée
Et sur les bords, cernés d'un filet or et noir,
Une grecque circule, à moitié dédorée.

Ces deux objets, dit-on, sont sans prix. Toutefois,
Le verre de Venise et la tasse de Sèvres
N'ont pour moi de valeur que parce qu'autrefois
Il les a consacrés au contact de ses lèvres.

VIEILLE LÉGENDE

Le Dieu cruel, le Dieu terrible, impérissable,
Prit quelques gouttes d'eau, prit quelques grains de sable,
Les mêla d'un peu de lumière et de chaleur,
En fit la Terre, y mit l'homme pour son malheur,
Puis il précipita le tout au fond du gouffre,
Ayant dit: Tourne à l'une, à l'autre ayant dit: Souffre!
Et créant à la fois la Vie et la Douleur.

THE GOBLET AND THE CUP

In Venice, once, a master blower blew
This gold-flecked amber goblet, veined with red,
Whose crystal seems, to glances turned thereto,
Like dancing flame, or flower's tilting head,

With calyx deep, poised on a stem too slim—
A yellow lily's stem—too frail to bear
* Its weight. Light shines through, opal, then melts, dim;
And water glimmers with a wine-like air.

In Sèvres, someone, many years long past,
Fashioned this cup of fine, delicate clay,
Easily marred, in tenderest blue shade cast,
That Time, unwitting, gently turns to gray.

A ring of Cupids, circling, gaily hold
A medal where a powdered belle is found
Laughing; the rim, in fading black and gold,
Decorates, Grecian-style, the border round.

Venetian goblet, Sèvres cup: they say
These things are priceless. But, if they are such
For me, it is because I know, today,
That, then, his lips hallowed them with their touch.

VI

ANCIENT LEGEND

Eternal God—cruel, fearsome—in His hand
Took a few drops of water, grains of sand,
Mixed in a little light and heat, and so
Made Earth, placed Man thereon, alas, when, lo!
He said: "Turn, Earth, and suffer, Man!" then cast
Everything into the abyss: at last
He had created Life, and, with it, Woe.

* I have to believe that *se fend* (cracks) in the original is a misprint for *se fond* (melts),
for obvious reasons of rhyme as well as, perhaps, less obvious reasons of sense, and I have
altered it accordingly.

Marie Nizet 729

Et la Terra tourna. L'Homme eut la Conscience,
La Raison. Il mordit à l'amère Science.
Il apprit à pleurer; il put haïr aussi.
Le Cœur rongé de Doute, il connut le Souci,
La morne Envie et la Colère qui flamboie.
Il naissait dans les maux; il engendrait sans joie...
Il mourait... Cinq mille ans, dit-on, ce fut ainsi.

Or, Satan qui traînait son ennui solitaire
A travers l'Infini, rencontra cette Terre.
Il la trouva mal faite et le dit sans détour.
Il voulut y changer quelque chose à son tour
Et, plein d'orgueil, autant que de pitié profonde,
Il souffla, de sa bouche en flammes, sur le monde
Et fit la Volupté, le Plaisir et l'Amour.

LE PRINTEMPS

La terre est refleurie; elle est verte, elle est blanche.
Mon cœur enamouré vers votre cœur se penche,
Mais si timidement que je n'ose approcher...
Tant je crains de troubler le charme de cette heure
Pour qu'il s'effraye et qu'il s'envole et que je pleure
De n'avoir pas compris qu'il n'y fallait toucher.

Et je songe au pêcher fleuri qui vous ressemble
Car votre joue, ô mon amour, est tout ensemble
Ronde comme son fruit, rose comme sa fleur.
Je ne veux même pas l'effleurer d'une lèvre
Tant j'ai peur de ternir, sous mon baiser de fièvre,
Sa fraîcheur délicate et sa tendre couleur.

Earth turned. Man got Awareness, Reasoning,
Conscience. He bit into that bitter thing
Called Knowledge, learned to weep, to hate; and, yea,
Doubt gnawed his Heart: he knew Distress, Dismay.
Bleak Envy, blazing Anger filled his Earth:
Born would he be in ills; joyless, give birth...
And die... So passed five thousand years, they say.

Now, Satan, loping through the Infinite,
Lonely and bored, came upon Earth, found it
Very ill-made, cried: "What a cock-up, this!"
Thus, to repair what was, he felt, amiss—
Prideful, but moved by a deep pity too—
Over the land his flaming breath he blew,
And so made Pleasure, Love, and lustful Bliss.

VII

SPRING

Earth blossoms once again in whites and greens;
And so in love my heart, that it yearns, leans
To yours, but shyly, timidly... For such
My fear that I disturb the charm, not keep
This hour, frighten it off, that I would weep
Not to have understood I ought not touch.

And I think of the blooming peach-tree, so
Like you, my love; you, with your cheek aglow,
Pink as its flowers, full as its fruit; and I,
Fearing my passion, let my lips—so hot
The fever of my kiss—touch, graze it not,
Lest, delicate, its hue fade, wither, die.

IX

Marie Nizet 731

L'ÉTÉ

Nous rôdons par les blés roussis que midi brûle.
Une fièvre amoureuse en nos veines circule.
Nous nous sommes couchés aux pentes des talus,
Sous le ciel bleu, moins bleu que le bleu de nos âmes,
Sous un soleil moins fort, moins ardent que la flamme
Qui consume nos sens... Et nous n'en pouvons plus.

Puis nous avons cherché les étangs et les saules.
J'ai posé mes deux mains, ainsi, sur vos épaules,
Afin de m'absorber mieux en votre beauté...
Et d'elle j'ai joui plus que je ne puis le dire
Et de vous je me suis grisée, et j'ai vu rire,
Dans vos yeux clairs, le rire immense de l'Eté.

L'AUTOMNE

Voici venir l'automne, âpre et voluptueuse.
Conseillère perverse en robe somptueuse.
Nos cœurs désordonnés l'attendent tout exprès...
Et c'est elle qui veut que je mette ma bouche
Contre la vôtre et que j'y morde et que je touche
Votre corps de mon corps, plus près, encor plus près...

Car ses derniers rayons seront aussi les nôtres.
Défuntes ces amours, nous n'en aurons plus d'autres:
L'hiver nous guette ainsi qu'il prendra la forêt.
Hâtons-nous: Entassons les baisers, les caresses.
Crispons nos nerfs, brûlons notre sang en ivresses.
Jouissons sans remords et mourons sans regret.

SUMMER

We amble through the gold-red, noon-burnt wheat
As, in our feverish veins, pounds passion's heat.
Beneath the sky we take our rest upon
The highroad's sloping banks: blue, the sky, yes,
But our souls, bluer; hot, the sun, but less
Than flames that char our sense... How to go on?

So we sought willows, pools revivifying.
I placed my hands upon your shoulders, trying
To seep into your beauty, one with it.
More did it pleasure me than you surmise;
And, drunk on you, I saw in your bright eyes
Summer laughing its laugh, vast, infinite.

                                                                    X

AUTUMN

Now comes the autumn, harsh, voluptuous
Mentor perverse, in robe luxurious.
Our hearts, unstrung, await her, sore beset...
She it is who would have me stroke, caress
Your lips with mine, bite them; would have me press
My flesh to your flesh, closer, closer yet...

In her last rays we see our destiny:
Once dead these loves, no other loves have we.
Forest-foe winter stalks us: by and by
We, too, fall... Quick! Let us pile kiss on kiss,
Nerves tingling, blood aflame in drunken bliss,
Nothing held back; and, guiltless, let us die.

                                                                    XI

L'HIVER

Dans la tiède langueur de la chambre bien close
Le sommeil doucement vous a gagné. Je n'ose
Bouger car vous dormez au creux de mes genoux.
Et je reste à rêver devant votre visage
Si beau, si jeune encor, si peu touché par l'âge
Qu'on dirait que le temps s'est arrêté pour vous.

Mais malgré le front lisse et la moustache blonde,
Je sais qu'il marque aussi pour vous chaque seconde
Et que vous souffrirez quand ce jour aura lui
Où la jeunesse meurt dans la beauté flétrie.
Et je pleure en baisant d'une lèvre attendrie
Vos cheveux d'or hier et d'argent aujourd'hui.

PLUS HAUT

Ami, quand nous avons escaladé les cieux,
Que notre amour a fait de nous presque des dieux
Quand nous avons franchi les limites sublimes,
Que nous ne pouvons pas descendre encor des cimes
Et que nous palpitons au plus haut des sommets
Que nos sens révulsés puissent joindre jamais...
Ne sens-tu pas qu'il est encore d'autres sphères,
Et d'autres régions et d'autres atmosphères?...
Si haut que nous soyons, nous contemplons d'en bas
Cet Eden interdit où nous n'atteindrons pas...

Et vois-tu pas alors, par une grâce insigne,
La radieuse Mort qui de loin nous fait signe?

WINTER

Here, in our chamber's warm, close, languorous air,
Sleep overcame you gently, and I dare
Not budge: there, nestling by my knees you lie;
And I, dreamily, gaze upon your face,
So fair, young, so untouched by age's pace
That one might think time stopped, or passed you by.

And yet, despite the blond mustache, smooth brow,
I know that every second marks you now;
That, when your beauty wilts and fades away,
Suffer you will as well... And so I shed
Tears as, sad-lipped, I kiss that lovely head:
Yesterday's golden hair, silver today.

                                                    XII

STILL HIGHER

Friend, when we've scaled the heights; when, finally,
Our love has made us almost gods; when we
Have risen past that utmost farthest end
Sublime, and from the peaks cannot descend,
Quivering on the topmost point that each
One of our senses, glancing high, can reach,
Do you not sense many a vast domain
Lying still higher?... Ah, but we gaze in vain:
Though high we rise, always are we below
That Eden, barred, that we shall never know...

Then, don't you see, grace-bestowed, glorious
Death, in the distance, radiant, beckoning us?

                                                    XIII

LA BOUCHE

Ni sa pensée, en vol vers moi par tant de lieues,
Ni le rayon qui court sur son front de lumière,
Ni sa beauté de jeune dieu qui la première
Me tenta, ni ses yeux—ces deux caresses bleues;

Ni son cou ni ses bras, ni rien de ce qu'on touche,
Ni rien de ce qu'on voit de lui ne vaut sa bouche
Où l'on meurt de plaisir et qui s'acharne à mordre,

Sa bouche de fraîcheur, de délices, de flamme,
Fleur de volupté, de luxure et de désordre,
Qui vous vide le cœur et vous boit jusqu'à l'âme...

LE PÉTALE

Sous le portrait de mon amant
Une rose meurt dans un verre.
Elle agonise exquisément
Avant de s'effeuiller à terre.

Un large pétale bombé,
Ainsi qu'une chose très lasse,
Se détache, glisse, est tombé...
Pieusement je le ramasse.

A son doux contact satiné,
Mes doigts s'émeuvent de tendresse.
D'un lent mouvement obstiné
Ce n'est pas lui que je caresse...

Mon baiser pervers s'est posé
Et mes lèvres se pâment d'aise
Sur le beau pétale rosé...
Et ce n'est pas lui que je baise.

THE MOUTH

Neither his thoughts, winging from distant skies,
Nor his brow, shining fair, lit glowingly,
Nor his young body, god-like, tempting me,
Nor that two-fold caress—his two blue eyes;

Neither his arms, his neck, nor anything
One sees of him, can match the rapturing
Wrought by his mouth, fierce with its biting kiss,

That mouth—fresh, hot as flame, a joy apart,
A flower of lust, of disarray, of bliss—
That drinks deep of your soul, drains dry your heart...

XVI

THE PETAL

Beneath a portrait of my love
A rose stands in a goblet, dying,
In the exquisite pain thereof:
Soon on the ground will it be lying.

Like some tired creature, lazy, lolling
About, a petal staunch sees fit
To come undone, slips, glides, goes falling...
Piously I go gather it.

And, as I touch that satin-fine
Softness, moved by its gentleness,
With slow strokes of these fingers mine,
It's not the flower that I caress...

A kiss, long and perverse, I pose;
And, though my lips would swoon with bliss,
Pressed to the petal of the rose...
It's not the petal that I kiss.

XVIII

Marie Nizet 737

LES MAINS

Chères mains que la Mort pour jamais a croisées,
Si pleines autrefois de tout ce qui fut doux;
Mains de belle vaillance, aujourd'hui reposées,
    Comme je me souviens de vous!

Mains de blancheur, mains de tendresse, mains de grâce,
Mains de triomphe avec des gestes caressants,
Dans votre forme pure à la fois fine et grasse
    Je vous subis et je vous sens.

J'ai conservé sur moi votre empreinte invisible:
—Le souvenir demeure où vous avez passé—
Et je garde de vous le désir impossible
    Et le regret inapaisé.

Et je veux retenir de l'illusion brève
D'un songe où m'apparaît votre dessin charnel
Votre toucher d'amour avec des doigts de rêve,
    O chères mains mortes d'Axel...

OFFRANDE

Devant le grand mystère où vous êtes perdu,
Dans le néant ou vers quelque aurore nouvelle,
Comme un oiseau qui cogne à la vitre, éperdu,
Mon amour obstiné se heurte et bat de l'aile.

Si je ne peux lever le voile descendu,
Si rien de votre essence à moi ne se révèle,
Je peux du moins forcer, sur le seuil défendu,
Ma pensée à rester adorante et fidèle...

HANDS

Dear hands that Death forever on your chest
Has crossed; so full, before, of everything
Tender and mild: hands valiant, now at rest,
    I think of you, remembering!

Hands pale and graceful, hands victorious;
Hands that caressed, hands plump yet staunchly set,
So fine of form, so pure, so sensuous;
    I yield to you and feel you yet.

I keep your touch unseen upon me still—
The memory lingers where once you had been—
And my desires that nothing can fulfill,
    And my unsoothed, uncalmed chagrin.

And I would hold that brief illusion of
A dream wherein your fleshly form yet stands
Before me, your dream-fingers stroking love,
    O you, Axel's dear, lifeless hands...

                                XXXII

OFFERING

Before the nothingness, great mystery
Where you lie lost, or some new, unknown dawn,
My love goes flailing, flapping stubbornly,
Like a bird, frantic, to the window drawn.

But if the veil must never lifted be,
Your essence never more be looked upon,
Still, at this gate closed on eternity,
Live is my love, true, ever and anon...

Je veux qu'elle se plaigne en rythmes assouplis,
En mots agenouillés et rares, tout remplis
Du regret de votre être où le mien se recueille...

Et je jette, parmi l'amas désordonné
De roses et d'œillets que je vous ai donné,
Mon âme qui se fane et mon cœur que j'effeuille...

———————

ADIEU

Je ne veux pas ainsi vous quitter, mon ami.
Tant de jours passeront avant que je revienne...
Et je ne trouve pas, dans mon cœur endormi,
Les paroles qu'il faut et l'adieu qui convienne.

Je cherche vainement. Et je reste à genoux
Devant ce marbre en deuil où je m'attarde à lire
Les quelques mots de bronze où l'on parle de vous...
Dites-moi, mon amour, ce que je dois vous dire...

Mais tout auréolé, voici que je le vois,
Votre cher nom, et je comprends que je dois mettre,
Comme sur votre bouche adorée, autrefois,
Un baiser, un baiser fervent sur chaque lettre...

Would that in supple rhythms, eloquent
With rare and suppliant words, it might lament
Its longing for your being, where mine reposes...

And so I throw this withered soul of mine,
My heart stripped bare of petals, to entwine
There, midst my scattered heaps of pinks, of roses...

XXXV

———————

FAREWELL

My love, I would not leave you so. It will
Be long before I come again to you...
And in my heavy heart, slumbering, still,
I find no words to bid you my adieu.

Vainly I seek them. And I kneel above
You here, pause at this mourning marble, read
The few bronzed words that speak of you... My love,
Tell me what words to say, what words you need...

But now your dear name, halo-graced, I see;
And, as upon your lips that once I craved—
Adored—so must I place, passionately,
A kiss upon each letter, here engraved...

XXXVIII

Marie Nizet 741

Marie Dauguet (1860–1942)

"Love of nature" is one of those clichés that trip easily off the tongue in describing poets from Virgil onward, and even before: most lyric poets, in some degree or other, all stylistic differences and particularities being equal. In the case of Marie Dauguet, prolific but far-too-little-known poet of the French *terroir,* it describes neither mere respect for the beauties of sunsets and seascapes, romantic awe before a volcano's power or the simple grandeur of the budding branch, nor the mere cerebral recognition of the boons conferred by Mother Earth. For her, it is a sensuous, almost voluptuous identification. More than simply "loving" nature, she subsumes herself in it, in a kind of mystical, pantheistic union with every one of its parts, from the smallest of her pet cats to the vastest of the surrounding landscapes.

The poems of *Les pastorales* (1908) are typical in this regard. With a sonorous lexicon rich in the language of the senses, and one that mirrors in its lush profusion the natural world it describes, she seems to revel synesthetically in the music and the passion that her poetry produces, and that invites the reader to do so too. All poems, I am convinced—indeed, all works of literature, ideally—are written to be heard; in the mind's ear, at least, if not actually spoken aloud. And some beg to be recited even more than others. Marie Dauguet's are eminently such. To let her poetry lie languishing in silence on the printed page—as it has largely done, no doubt, for many years of obscurity—is to subject it to a fate that it does not deserve.

Marie Dauguet, née Julie-Marie Aubert, was born in the village of La Chaudeau, in Haute-Saône, on April 2, 1860, and died quietly in a clinic in Ville d'Avray on September 10, 1942, after living the country life that she much preferred to the chaotic existence of the city.

In 1880, having moved with her family to the Vosges, she married Henri Dauguet, gave birth to a daughter, and produced four collections of poems—*La naissance du poète* (1897), *A travers le voile* (1902), *Par l'amour* (1904), and *Paroles du vent* (1904). Her devotion to hearth and home notwithstanding, she did travel with her husband to Italy (though, to be sure, not until after some twenty-five years of marriage). The trip resulted in the volume *Clartés* (1907), a journal of prose reflections and poems celebrating the joys of the sunlit Italian landscape and its no-less-sunny human fauna. A few years before, *Par l'amour* had been honored by the Académie française, and *Paroles du vent* had attracted the attention of the editors of the *Mercure de France* and the dean of French critics, Emile Faguet. The latter's ecstatic review—one of many that the same journal would devote to her—spread her name through the literary salons of the capital, where the reluctant celebrity would spend yearly "command performances" with the likes of the poets Henri de Régnier and Gabriele d'Annunzio, Rémy and Jean de Gourmont of the *Mercure*, the novelist Rachilde, and a distinguished coterie of literati (and literatae). Many would come to share the opinion of André Fontainas that Dauguet was "among the most remarkable women poets of our time... sensitive to nature and concerned with philosophical questions."[1] But one feels that she begrudged the moments spent away from home, away from her husband, and even from her animals, to the latter of which, we are told—and perhaps to the former as well—she would often recite her poems.

Dauguet's happy life was not immune to misfortune, however. Her daughter's husband perished at sea during World War I, and her own husband died in 1924, the year of her most philosophical collection, *Ce n'est rien, c'est la vie*. She continued writing, producing, during the last few years of her life, two more volumes of verse and a novel, though with little recognition.[2]

Since much of Marie Dauguet's poetry is difficult to come by, the selection of translations in the following pages represents, unfortunately, only three of her volumes: *Par l'amour, Clartés,* and *Les pastorales.*

NOTES

1. See André Fontainas, *Tableau de la poésie française d'aujourd'hui,* p. 154.

2. For early appreciations of Dauguet's work, in addition to Fontainas's *Tableau,* see Adolphe Van Bever, *Les poètes du terroir,* 2: 160–64; Jean de Gourmont, *Muses d'aujourd'hui,* pp. 85–107; and, later, Jean Héritier, *Essai de critique contemporaine. Première série,* pp. 298–301. A concise summary of her career is found in Edith Joyce Benkov's entry in the *Encyclopedia of Continental Women Writers,* pp. 290–91.

LA FOLIE DES PARFUMS

Que je les goûte et que j'en meure,
Tel un philtre aphrodisiaque,
Les parfums déments qui m'effleurent
Embrumant les nuiteux cloaques.

Que j'en comprenne le mystère
De cet étourdissant breuvage,
Effluve de Pan solitaire
Dansant par les tourbeux pacages.

O voluptés exténuantes,
Odeurs, qui sont des mains tenaces,
Des souches que l'hiver crevasse,
Des champignons aux chairs gluantes.

Comme un Dieu qui m'enlacerait,
Que votre errance me possède,
Plus mythique qu'un chant d'aède
M'enseignant le divin secret.

_____

Tant d'ouate sanguinolente,
Parmi les marais s'entassant,
Toutes ces odeurs si ferventes
Qu'exhale l'étang croupissant...

Il monte des mauves bourbiers
Où pourrit l'herbe par torchées,
Des parfums comme extasiés
Vers quelles déités cachées?

———————

How I would savor, unto death,
Those wild scents misting round night-black
Cesspools that graze me with their breath:
Potions, strong, aphrodisiac.

How I would pierce, as best I can,
That brew that leaves me drunk, agog:
Smells that a lone, abandoned Pan,
Dancing, exudes about the bog.

Brute bliss that leaves me powerless,
Like hands that will not loose their hold,
Tree-stumps that crack with winter's cold,
† Toadstools oozing their tackiness...

Like god that would his being entwine
About me, let your waftings, free,
More mythic than bard's elegy,
Teach me the secret, deep, divine.

Par l'amour, "Odorant automne, mélodieux automne"

———————

Cotton wool streaked with blood, piled high
Among the marshes; fervid scents
Seep from the wallowing swamp and fly
Off, by its fevered breath blown hence...

Toward what gods, hidden, do they rise
From mallowed mire, these rare perfumes
Whipped up to ecstasy, as dies
The moss that rot decays, consumes?

---

* Given the very physical, even voluptuous, implications of the poet's vocabulary, I interpret her title to imply something of the *folie* suggested in the rather coarse phrase *en folie,* as in *une chienne en folie* (a bitch in heat). Some may take issue.

† Here and in many of her succeeding poems, the poet often changes her rhyme scheme in mid-opus, and I usually respect her practice.

Marie Dauguet 745

Des parfums d'un tel idéal
Evocateurs et d'une ivresse
Si pénétrante qu'ils font mal:
Poignard aigu qui vous transperce,

Ou langoureux baiser qui mord.
Quel secret profond balbutie
Par delà l'amour et la mort
La vase où baignent les orties?

———————

Quelle douceur d'allumer un feu de bruyère
A la nuitée et d'y accrocher sa marmite,
De souper en rêvant au seuil de sa chaumière
Quand la lune fleurit comme une clématite,

Et de tendre à une biche familière
Se faufilant silencieuse au ras des branches,
Le reste de son pain et de la voir, légère,
Danser en s'ébrouant par les clairières blanches!

———————

LA GERBE

Je ressemble au bouleau humide sous la pluie,
Au frêne desséché que drape au bord de l'eau
Le salissant brouillard de ses voiles de suie;
Mon âme a la couleur verte d'un vieux tombeau.

Perfumes that call to mind the pure
Ideal, and of such heady brew
That, dagger-like, they torture your
Poor flesh, pierce it, and run you through;

Or like a languid, biting kiss...
Nettles bathed in the muck thereof
Give ear: what stammered secret, this,
Beyond the pale of death and love?

Par l'amour, "Odorant automne, mélodieux automne"

———————

How sweet to light a briar fire at night;
To hang a pot, sup, muse, and sup the more,
Dreaming of how the moon, clematis-white,
Blossoms, shining above your cottage door;

To offer to a doe, tame, and who might—
Silent, sly—graze the branches, your last crust;
Watch her go bounding, weightless, through the light,
* Over the clearings, snorting in the dust!

Par l'amour, "Par les bois"

———————

THE SHEAF

Like a birch sodden in the rain am I,
An ash-tree, by the shore, veiled in a dress
Of sooty fog, standing withered and dry;
My soul, an old grave, weed-strewn, spiritless.

* I have tried to resolve a curious ambiguity presented by the French verb *s'ébrouer*. Applied to birds, it means to flutter the wings rapidly, usually in the dust; to smaller animals, like dogs, simply to shake the body, as if to shake the dust off. It becomes more complicated when the word is applied to large animals, in which case it refers not to a motion but to a sound, a whinnying kind of snort. I doubt that the poet is inviting us to imagine the doe simultaneously bounding off and shaking itself too, and assume that the latter, more usual, meaning was intended. Still, to give at least a suggestion of the former, I include an allusion to the dust, not literally found in the original.

Marie Dauguet 747

Je suis le naufragé cramponné au radeau
Que la vague, linceul, de ses longs pans essuie;
Mon cœur que le labeur trop lourd de vivre ennuie,
Comme un galérien courbé sous un fardeau,

Succombe et se révolte en la fadeur des choses.
Et me voici, fantôme assis sur un tombeau,
Groupant entre mes doigts, dernier bouquet de roses,

La gerbe de mes désirs morts.—O noirs corbeaux,
Parmi le ciel flétri promenant vos ténèbres,
Autour de ma pensée, errez, troupes funèbres!

———————

LE SILENCE

Je n'écouterai plus la chanson des ramiers,
Le bleu roucoulement lentement qui palpite
De leurs couples errants parmi les alisiers;
Je n'écouterai plus la feuille qui crépite,

Eclate hors du bourgeon et s'ouvre en la clarté
D'une aurore d'Avril. Ce que je vois se fane
Et le silence étend sa morne aridité
Dans mon bois intérieur que la bise décharne.

Le paysage est dur, fait de bronze et d'acier
Où le soleil répand des lueurs funéraires
Près des étangs mangés de rougeâtres ulcères.

Le jour souillé vacille aux bords où je m'assieds,
Et tombe ivre d'erreur, de doute et de blasphème:
Tout meurt immensément au dedans de moi-même.

I am the shipwrecked traveler in distress,
Clutching his flotsam raft, foam-swathed, as by
A shroud; my heart—that life's woes sorely try,
Like a slave-oarsman, bowed in his duress,

Bent low—would yet resist the fell, the fey.
And on this grave I sit: my ghostliness
Holds in its grasp this one last rose bouquet,

Sheaf of dead dreams... O black crows! Come, possess
The heavens' dull-blighted realm with your drear shade:
* Come fly about my thoughts, in death arrayed!

Par l'amour, "Le sens de la vie"

_____

SILENCE

I'll listen no more to the ringdoves' coo,
That slow, blue-pulsing warble that they utter
Among the berry bushes, two by two.
I'll listen no more to the crackling sputter

Of budding leaf that comes bursting anew
On the bright April dawn. All I see there
Withers, as silence lays its drought all through
The woods within me, that the wind strips bare.

The sun casts a funereal glow about
The landscape's bronze and steel, and overspreads
Its ponds, consumed in pinkish ulcer-reds.

Here by their banks I sit, as, drunk on doubt
† And sin, foul day wavers, falls, darkening:
And in me all is one vast perishing.

Par l'amour, "Le sens de la vie"

* In this sonnet, I have followed the very free and unorthodox rhyme scheme of the original: *abab baab cbc bdd.*

† It seems that the original here, although syntactically ambiguous, is referring not to the poet but to the day, transformed from dawn to dusk in the space of two quatrains. I try to suggest something of the same ambiguity.

Marie Dauguet 749

LE REÎTRE

Je rêve parfois d'une existence brutale:
Le donjon sur un roc inaccessible, au loin
L'humanité courbée et vague, et surtout point
De frein. Comme un fleuve ma volonté s'étale.

Je ne suis vraiment sous la couronne comtale
Qu'un reître violent, dépourvu de tous soins
Autres que le pillage et l'orgie, et j'ai moins
D'âme que mon épervier. Nulle décrétale

Ne contraignit jamais mon désir et je vais
Triomphant, au trot lourd de mon cheval de guerre
Ecrasant sans le voir tout ce qui grouille à terre:

Prêtres, soudards, vilains. Je vais le cœur en paix
Et trempant, pour le teindre aux couleurs de la gloire,
Parmi le sang versé mon étendard de moire.

LA DIVINE FOLIE

Au comte M. de Vasselot

Je veux être celui qui sur sa chevelure
Attache un brin d'ortie avec la grappe mûre,
Qui danse titubant, bestial et divin
Et porte la nature entière dans son sein;
Celui qui sent frémir et couler dans ses moëlles
L'âme errante du vent, des mers et des étoiles,

THE RUFFIAN

I dream at times of a life wild, inflamed:
A dungeon on some cliff, remote, set high;
Far off, vague masses, bowed and bent, that I
Harass without relief. Free, unashamed,

My will flows like a stream. Ruffian untamed,
I ride in some count's retinue, but my
Only wish is to sack and pillage, ply
Debauch. As for my soul—a "soul" misnamed!—

My hawk has more! Never has a decree
Reined in my will; and proudly forth I go,
To my steed's heavy trot—as his *sabots*

Crush everything: priests, soldiers, knaves—carefree,
Dipping my shimmering banner in the flood
Of glory-tinting, beautifying blood.

Par l'amour, "Simplicité"

MADNESS DIVINE

†   *For Count Monsieur de Vasselot*

I want to be the one who, in his hair
Hanging a bunch of grapes, ripe, dangling there
Upon a bramble, dances—staggering—
Bestial, divine; with every living thing,
All nature, in his breast; and who feels deep,
Quivering in his bones, the flowing sweep
Of winds' and stars' and oceans' errant soul;
Who fastens to his belt, all in one whole

---

   * The *reîtres* (from the German *Reiter,* horseman) were cavalry mercenaries hired by France from the fifteenth to the seventeenth centuries, whose name, owing to their generally bad manners and less-than-elegant behavior, eventually lost the military connotation that it has in this Baudelairean sonnet.

   † There are several counts and non-counts, with a variety of hyphenated names, to whom this dedication might refer. I suspect that the most likely is the sculptor Marquet de Vasselot, curator of the Musée de Cluny in the late 1890s.

Marie Dauguet 751

Accroche à sa ceinture en un même bouquet
La ronce, le chardon, la ciguë et l'œillet;
Qui, ne distinguant plus son regard de l'aurore,
Sent parmi les couchants sa chair qui s'évapore.

Je veux être celui qui rit dans le soleil
Et savoure le jour ainsi qu'un fruit vermeil;
Le berger ou l'outlaw dormant sur la javelle
Comme un enfant bercé aux genoux de Cybèle.
Je marcherai rêveur, épris de l'inconnu,
Aux sentiers ignorés, froissant de mon pied nu
L'herbe, le laurier rose et l'ingrate bruyère.
Debout sur les sommets, libre dans la lumière,
Mendiant triomphant, je tendrai vers l'éclair
Le geste avide de mes bras à travers l'air.

Je serai le glaneur idéal qui recueille
La rosée au matin, le rayon, le reflet
Du fleuve et s'en nourrit; le gueux dans la forêt
Elevant son palais frissonnant sous les feuilles.
Possesseur des trésors qu'on dédaigne, j'irai
Boire aux lèvres du vent quelque nectar sacré;
Frôler à l'eau qui fuit par les mousses humides
Le torse transparent des pâles néréides;
Et jouissant des odeurs, des sons, voluptueux,
Avec les sens aigus d'un sauvage et d'un dieu,
Je glisserai subtil à l'herbe où le vent joue
Et je serai le bond du dix-cors qui s'ébroue.

Etoiles qui brillez au bord du ciel serein,
Tendresse de la nuit qui monte et qui m'étreint,
Mystérieux baisers, soupirs sur le rivage
Du flot diamanté où se mire un nuage,

And same bouquet, carnation, nettle, thorn,
Hemlock; who cannot tell the dawning morn
From his own glance; and who, when day is done,
Feels his flesh and the sunset melt as one.

I want to be the one who savors day
Like a lush crimson fruit, and laughs away
The sunlight hours; shepherd lad or scofflaw
Vagabond, sleeping on their sheaves of straw
* Like a child wrapped in Mother Cybele's
Earthy embrace, rocked, cradled on her knees.
In love with the unknown, I will walk toward
The heights, free in the light, on unexplored
Paths; and, unshod, I will trample beneath
My feet, grass, oleander, meager heath,
My arm outstretched, triumphant beggar-wise,
In eager gesture, upturned to the skies.

† I shall the perfect gleaner be: collect
River's reflection, sun's rays, morning dew
To feed upon; the woodland idler, who,
Beneath the foliage, trembling, would erect
His palace-home. With treasures scorned, I will
Go off and, from the wind's lips, drink my fill
Of sacred nectar; run my fingertips
‡ Over pale nereids, as water drips
Gently over their form transparent, from
The humid beds of moss; and, venturesome,
In the voluptuous bliss of sound and scent,
With sharpened sense, godlike or violent,
I shall fuse with the wind-played grassy ground,
One with the ten-point stag's bellowing bound.

O evening stars, who shine low in the skies;
O tender night, who hug me as you rise
In darkness; kisses full of mystery;
Sighs spread along the water's banks, in whose

---

   * The allusion is to Cybele, the Earth Mother of early Asia Minor religions, evenually
assimilated under a variety of names into Greek and Roman mythology.
   † Although it does not seem to have any particular effect, I have respected the poet's
sudden change of rhyme scheme in the first four lines of the third section.
   ‡ The sea-divinity Nereus's fifty sea-nymph daughters of classical mythology eventu-
ally gave their name to any general sea sprite, as here.

Marie Dauguet 753

Fantômes devinés de blanches déités,
Accordez à mes vœux votre complicité,
Accordez à mon cœur la grâce qu'il implore,
La divine folie! Et toi, morne ellébore,
Que ton rameau flétri se dessèche infécond
Qui guérit de l'ivresse et nous rend la raison.

Je voudrais qu'on m'aime avec de belles paroles
Palpitantes comme au ciel bleu des banderolles,
Avec des mots qui soient d'un métal précieux:
Des carillons d'argent dans un beffroi pieux;

D'un mystique métal rendant le son d'une âme
Où beaucoup d'infini se trouve emprisonné,
D'un métal fulgurant, la pointe d'une lame
Qui lentement pénètre en mon cœur forcené.

Très-pâle théorie emmy des bouleaux frêles,
Je voudrais écouter des mots comme envolés,
Musique d'ailes d'ange où l'inconnu révèle
Les lointains paradis dont je suis exilé.

LE TAMBOURIN

Dans l'odeur des marais, les nixes
Grelottantes claquent des dents
Et dansent sous la lune fixe
Au son d'un tambourin strident.

Diamond-strewn waves a passing cloud looks, views
Itself; and you, god-ghosts, white, vaguely seen,
Grant me the help of heavenly go-between:
Grant to my heart the grace it begs you for:
* Madness divine! And you, dour hellebore,
May your branch wither, you whose regimen
Cures folly, and makes our minds whole again.

Par l'amour, "Rayons"

I would be loved with many a pretty word,
Like banners in the blue sky, wind-bestirred,
Quivering, and with words of metal rare:
Silver bells calling out to pious prayer;

Of mystic metal, pealing a soul's sound
Where a great infinite imprisoned lies;
Lustrous, bright metal, to a point sharp-ground.
Slowly piercing my mad heart, dagger-wise.

Words would I hear in pale procession flown
Among the fragile birches, tree to tree:
Angel-wings' music, singing the unknown,
Lost paradises that have banished me.

Par l'amour, "Rayons"

THE TAMBOURINE

Teeth chattering, trembling, nymph and sprite—
In swamp-stench, caught betwixt, between—
Beneath the moon's unwavering light
Dance to the twanging tambourine.

* The hellebore, with its dried roots' long-supposed curative powers against mental illness, would clearly make the plant a dour and unwelcome spoilsport to the persona of the poem.

Marie Dauguet 755

C'est l'heure où la Bête à sept têtes,
Rêvant à la fille du roi,
Aux murs du donjon qu'elle guette
Heurte ses lugubres abois;

L'heure où dans sa noire chaumière
Presqu'effondrée au bord de l'eau,
Quelque incertaine filandière
Tourne un invisible fuseau;

L'heure des chansons ambiguës,
Baisers cyniques, serments faux,
Où la mort d'une pierre aiguë
Sournoisement rebat sa faux.

———————

LA CHANSON DE LA LUNE

Au lac de claire améthyste
Se mire la lune blonde
Et sa lumière m'inonde,
Fausse, à travers tes yeux tristes.

Mais trop d'incertaines dunes
Sous les pêchers qu'on émonde,
Pleines de fosses profondes,
Roses dans du clair de lune,

En la vague violette,
De la couleur qu'ont les prunes,
Des vergers où dort la lune
Vraiment trop d'effroi qui guette!

*   The seven-headed Beast, this hour,
    Dreams of the princess, waiting, spying,
    Flinging against her dungeon-tower
    Bayings and barks, glum, mortifying;

    The hour when, in her darkened hut,
    Drenched at the water's edge, there lingers
    Some spinning wench capricious, but
    Unseen the spindle in her fingers;

    The hour of songs that lie, beguile,
    Cynical kisses, pledges blithe,
    When death, with pointed stone the while,
†   Slyly goes hammering sharp his scythe.

                                    Par l'amour, "Frissons"

_____

MOON SONG

False, the moon sees herself reflected
In the dark amethystine pond,
Showering me with moonlight, blonde,
Mirrored there in your eyes, dejected.

Too many dunes, too ill-defined,
With pits so deep, so silver-mooned—
Beneath the peachtrees newly pruned,
‡   Pink in the soft beams intertwined;

Fright lies in wait, quietly keeping
Watch in the purple water, whose
Color matches the plums' dark hues
In orchards where the moon is sleeping.

---

    * "Then the angel carried me away in the Spirit into a desert. There I saw a woman sitting on a scarlet beast that was covered with blasphemous names and had seven heads" (Revelation 17:3ff.).
    † As elsewhere, I opt for the masculinization of death—the Grim Reaper—despite the feminine gender of the French *la mort.*
    ‡ The impressionistic mood of this piece is rendered all the more imprecise by some of the poet's punctuation, which I have seen fit to alter here and elsewhere.

Marie Dauguet 757

Eparse à travers cette onde
Que brise et meurtrit la rame,
Aux étangs bleus de mon âme
Se mire la lune ronde.

C'est ta tendresse ambiguë
Qui sourit au ras des vagues:
Fleurs des pêchers qu'on élague,
Rameaux des pourpres ciguës.

Je cueillerai ces fleurs tristes,
Hélas! sans créance aucune,
Au songe du clair de lune
Sur les étangs d'améthyste.

———————

LE NAIN

Sur l'escalier de marbre où le couchant se joue
Des groupes enlacés s'attardent en l'odeur
Des jets d'eau frémissants et des jasmins en fleur;
Les belles vont rêvant, l'éventail à la joue;

Et le nain blottissant dans l'ombre sa laideur,
Sa guitare aux genoux, lui, triste, qu'on bafoue
Pour son échine en dôme et sa flasque bajoue,
Brûlant, meurtri, hagard, apaise son ardeur

En caressant du doigt, en pressant sur sa lèvre,
Chair douce et accueillante au désir qui l'enfièvre,
Une rose en bouton: épaules, seins nacrés...

O tendresse et pitié qui s'émanent des choses,
Loin des rires cruels, des dédains acérés,
Sous les baisers du nain s'est ouverte la rose!

Billowing on the watery space,
Bruised by the oar—a fractured whole;
And in the blue pools of my soul
The round moon gazes on her face.

A tenderly ambiguous mood:
Bright smile over the lake, dark-rimmed;
Blossoms from peach-boughs, timely trimmed,
And hemlock branches, purple-hued.

And I shall pick those blooms dejected,
Without the slightest faith, alas,
That moonlight makes dreams come to pass
On amethystine pond reflected.

Par l'amour, "Chansons"

———————

THE DWARF

At day's end, in the joyous setting sun,
Amid the fountain-rustling, jasmined air,
Couples, enlaced, loll on the marble stair;
Fans poised on cheeks, miladies muse, each one.

The dwarf, bejowled and humpbacked, does not dare
Stray from the shade, ugly, second to none.
Sitting with his guitar—jeered, bruised, undone—
He calms his fervor with a passing fair

Flower—enticing, soft of flesh; and pressing
His lips against it, lovingly caressing
The rosebud—shoulders, pearl-hued breasts... Oh, wonder!

Ah, what compassion some things will disclose!
Far from their cruel and scornful taunts, there, under
The kisses of the dwarf, blossoms the rose!

Par l'amour, "Les baisers"

MÉLUSINE

Le vent sifflait au loin les meutes de la mort
Et la tour frissonnait parmi les ronces sèches
D'où fuyaient des corbeaux dispersant leur essor,
C'est alors qu'apparut, s'avançant vers la brèche,

Un spectre que l'amour jusqu'en la tombe allèche,
Mélusine: serpent, femme, vampire, un corps
Fragile et que cinglaient épars en lourdes mèches
Des cheveux déroulés croulant d'un flot retors.

Dans la nuit qu'une lune écarlate illumine,
La voici qui se noue au fantôme évoqué
D'un chevalier hautain sous l'armure et casqué,

Colle sa bouche au dur métal qui l'embéguine
Et, glapissant ainsi qu'un loup sur un charnier,
Froisse sa lèvre blême à l'impassible acier.

SALOMÉ

Parmi les cèdres bleus dont l'épaisseur l'encastre,
Dans un parfum d'encens, de cinname et de rose,
Le lourd palais d'Hérode aux somptueux pilastres,
Aux escaliers d'onyx, en silence repose.

Seul un chacal gémit, précurseur de désastres,
Flairant l'odeur du sang au bas des portes closes;
Et l'écoutant, perdue en quelqu'étrange hypnose,
Dans la salle déserte où pleut un frisson d'astre,

The wind, far off, whistled the deathly hounds;
The brambled tower shuddered a flight of crows,
Strewn here and there. And then, reaching the grounds'
Divide, a spectral figure! One of those

Whom love lures even from the tomb's repose:
Frail Mélusine... Thick, tousled hair surrounds
Her—woman, vampire, snake!—heavy, abounds
Cascading in great twirling, twisting flows.

And, in the darkness, she entwines—advancing
Beneath a moon glowing a scarlet red—
About a haughty ghost knight, helmeted,

Her mouth pressed to his armor, hard, entrancing;
Like wolf atop a corpse heap, with a squeal,
Bruising her pale lip on the callous steel.

Par l'amour, "Les baisers"

SALOME

Mid cedars' thickset blue serenity,
Heavy with incense, cinammon, and rose,
Lush, Herod's onyx-staircased, sumptuously
Pilastered palace, silent, seems to doze.

A jackal bays disaster, doom, as he
Sniffs blood, seeping beneath closed porticoes;
And, listening, lost in strange hypnotic pose—
† Empty, the hall, save for a quivery

* The reference is to the fairy heroine of a famous medieval French legend, condemned, for an offense against her father, to become a serpent from the waist down once a week. When she married the unsuspecting Raymond, count of Lusignan, she made him swear never to look upon her on the fateful day. He, however, consumed with curiosity, broke his vow. Melusina was obliged to leave him and was destined to wander about till doomsday, in spectral form.

† Whether intentionally or inadvertently, the poet alters her rhyme scheme between the two quatrains and, not wanting to second-guess her, I duplicate her liberty.

Marie Dauguet 761

Salomé enraidie et droite sur sa couche,
Rappelant son désir criminel, croit voir Jean,
Fantôme torturé, d'une étreinte d'amant

L'enlacer et défaille en sentant qui la touche
Et se colle à sa lèvre ardente, la mordant,
La bouche douloureuse où se glacent les dents.

———————

L'air est d'un bleu trop vif de préraphaélite,
Limpidement qui coule et tout rebrodé d'or,
En noirâtres massifs des buis taillés limitent
L'allée, et deux grands lys ouvrent leur pur trésor;

De frêles rosiers blancs rehaussent le décor,
Où du silence errant si doucement palpite,
Leur floraison de marbre au gré du vent s'effrite,
Sous les murs de feuillage étouffant leur essor.

Et là-bas, tout au fond du sombre corridor,
Que forment les buis noirs au somptueux parfum,
C'est Rome en la lumière éclatante qui dort,

Morte sous le ciel bleu près du Tibre défunt,
Dont le cours arrêté visqueusement étreint
Sa berge abandonnée au pied de l'Aventin.

———————

Je veux t'appartenir et que ton poids m'accable,
Mer, puisque nous entoure un rivage désert;
Prends-moi, je suis à toi, voici mes bras ouverts
Et mon corps étendu sur ta couche de sable

Sprinkling of starlight—upright, stiff, upon
Her sofa, Salome recalls her sin,
Her lust; swoons, feels an anguished ghost within

Her love-embrace; feels her hot kiss on John
The Baptist's tortured face, pressed like a vise,
And bites his lips, his teeth now turned to ice.

Par l'amour, "Les baisers"

---

*   The air, a limpid blue—Pre-Raphaelite,
Too sharp!—flows in a tapestry of gold;
Boxwood trees line the lane, thick, gray as night,
And lilies twain their treasure pure unfold.

Rosebushes, white, enhance the scene: behold
How frail! Stray silence trembles gently where
Their buds, white-marbled, in the gusting air,
Trapped by the leaf-walls, fall, still, lifeless, cold...

There, mid the boxwoods' scent, sumptuous and bold,
Beyond their shadowed path, Rome sleeps the sleep
Of death, in light, bright as in days of old,

Beneath the blue sky, by the Tiber, deep
And dead as well, whose viscous waves entwine
†   The bank, deserted, by the Aventine.

Clartés: Notes et pochades, "Rome"

I would belong to you completely, sea;
Beneath your weight, on this unpeopled shore,
My open arms reach out: would I were your
Creature entire, my body feverishly

* In this sonnet, Dauguet, never one to shrink from innovative rhyme schemes, uses a most unusual one, which I think I can say was original with her—*abab bccb bdb dee*—especially unorthodox in that it repeats one of the quatrain rhymes in the first of the tercets.

† The Aventine is one of the seven hills of Rome, and the site from which the poet contemplates the city is, as she tells us in the lush prose passage into which this poem is inserted, the garden of the Grand Masters of the Order of Malta.

Marie Dauguet 763

A tes baisers trop lourds intensément offert.
Pour ta langueur perverse et ta folle tristesse
Pour ta brutalité subtilement qui blesse,
Il me semble t'aimer mieux qu'un être de chair,

Quand sous le firmament pâlement violet,
Près des pins d'azur noir à l'écorce vermeille,
A ton âme j'unis mon âme si pareille,

Abîme gémissant que nul don ne comblait,
Et dont je trouve en toi l'image et la réplique,
O ma beauté suprême et si mélancolique.

———————

J'ai découvert enfin qui je suis, d'où je viens.
J'ai vécu très longtemps mêlée à tous les miens
Sous la tente rugueuse ouverte à la nature,
Où rien ne vous limite, où rien ne vous emmure,
Des pasteurs aryens. Leur main la dépliait
Quand s'endormait au fond du couchant violet
Et sur l'Himalaya, dont les longs bras s'écartent,
Le soleil grandiose; à l'heure où les troupeaux,
Par le steppe égarés, vers le bercail repartent,
Précédés par leurs pâtres aux dissonants pipeaux.
Je regarde mon sang tout au fond de mes veines,
Qui fleurissent ma peau comme de bleues verveines,
Et je songe: ils sont là poursuivant leur chemin.
Je regarde mes mains et rien ne les suspecte
En mon esprit. Je dis: mes mains je vous respecte,
Vous avez la douceur des brebis et du lin.

Dans ma chair, dans mon cœur immense, d'autres êtres
Par milliers sont morts. Mais ces lointains ancêtres
Se survivent, malgré tant de soleils éteints,
Indéniablement à travers mes instincts

Couched on your sand, heavy your kisses... For
Your frenzy, your sad, languid testiness,
And for the subtle wounds you deal, no less
Than human form I love you—even more;

And, in the pallid violet of the sky,
By the pines, crimson-barked, of deepest blue,
I join my soul to yours, its image true:

Howling abyss no gifts can fill; there I
Seem to see our two kindred souls combine,
O peerless beauty, melancholic, mine!

*   *Clartés: Notes et pochades,* "Città Vecchia"

———————

I know now, finally, who I am and whence
I come. Long did I live in rough-skinned tents,
† Among my people, Indian shepherds, where,
Unfettered in the Himalayan air
Unwalled, they would unfold them once the sun,
Grandiose in its splendor, had begun
Its purple sleep, deep in the mountainous
Embrace, and as the straying flocks, spread thus
Over the steppes, went following once again
The shepherds' twanging pipes, back to their pen.
I watch my blood as it flows blue within
My veins, like vervain blossoms on my skin,
And I muse, gazing at my hands: "They keep
Wending their endless way..." And, in my mind
I say: "Hands—mine and theirs—nothing I find
Displeasing in you, soft as flax, as sheep.
And I respect you, as you are and were..."

In my flesh, in my vast heart, others stir,
Dead by the thousands. Forebears mine, long gone,
From myriad sunsets past, still carry on,
Live in my tastes, my instincts' deepmost spaces.

* The name of the port of Rome is usually written as a single word, Civitavecchia.
† My translation of the original *aryens* (Aryans) attempts to avoid confusion with the word's later, much deformed, usage.

Marie Dauguet 765

Les plus profonds, parmi mes goûts les plus sincères.
L'impériale race en moi se régénère.
Vraiment n'étiez-vous pas les princes de la terre,
Vous qui ne disiez pas en élevant les bras:
"Nous sommes des bannis, qui nous recueillera?"
Le divin, dont toujours notre désir s'affame,
Ne se séparait pas encore de votre âme,
Ni rien de l'univers; tout restait confondu
Dans un rayonnement jusqu'au ciel répandu;
Dieu formait avec vous un lumineux mélange;
C'est en vous regardant que l'on inventa l'ange.
Vous trouviez pour la bête aimante des mots doux;
Quand la rose s'ouvrait, vous tombiez à genoux.
Vous causiez avec l'eau, dont la voix sourde flue,
Et vous disiez au vent joyeux: Je te salue!
Quand l'aurore, fontaine de clarté, noyait
L'espace, vous mettiez sa blancheur sur vos lèvres
Pour les purifier, tandis que s'écriait
Dans l'enclos le troupeau des béliers et des chèvres
Impatient d'être délâché par les champs;
Et si vous rapportiez, les faucilles aux flancs,
Entre vos bras heureux, l'énorme et lourde gerbe
D'orge ou de blé teintés d'un feu pur et vermeil,
Vous croyiez, contre vous, d'un grand geste superbe,
Presser, tout palpitant, le cœur chaud du soleil.

Le soir, au seuil bleuâtre et tranquille des tentes,
Dont sur la solitude on relève les pentes,
Vous parliez longuement, paisibles et hautains,
Et d'égal à égal, aux astres vos voisins,
Poursuivant leur regard parmi l'espace sombre,
Et vous en décriviez les circuits et le nombre.
La lune s'asseyait songeuse près de vous
Ou, lente, se couchait au creux de vos genoux.

Risen in me again, the royal race's
Blood... Were you not the princes of the earth?
You, who had never a cause to doubt your worth,
Nor raised your arms in laments dolorous:
"Exiles are we! Who will deliver us?"
Your soul was still one with the great design,
The universe; still joined with the divine
That we all hunger for; and everything
Rose to the heavens in one emblazoning:
You were God's models for the angels; and
You it was, too, that His almighty hand
Wrought in His shining image. Nature was,
For you, in all her parts, a happy cause
Of love. You whispered gently to the beast;
Knelt to the rose when her petals released
Their grasp and let her bloom; chatted with fleeting
Brooklet and hush-voiced stream; even gave greeting
Willingly to the joyous wind! When dawn,
Great fount of light, drowned space, you daubed upon
Your lips its purifying white, as all
The while, the goats and rams, with caterwaul
And bleat, would call, impatient to be gone
Already to the pastures. Then, when your
Harvests were done, with sickles by your side,
Homeward you trod again; and if you bore
Armfuls of wheat, of barley—sunset-dyed
Sheaves of pure fire—you thought that you had pressed,
Proudly, the sun's heart, pounding, to your breast.

Evenings, before the tranquil blue-black tents,
Whose slopes rose on the solitude immense,
You would have conversations without end—
Haughty but peaceable, as friend to friend—
With all your neighboring stars; and you would trace
Their paths as they gazed over somber space.
Dreaming, the moon would sit by you, or set
Slowly within your lap. The dogs would let

Les chiens tendres baignaient leur regard dans le vôtre;
S'il pleuvait, vous goûtiez le parfum de l'épeautre
Comme un baiser profond dont s'ébranlent les sens,
Comme un geste d'amour aux attraits tout puissants.

Ah! que je vous admire et combien je vous aime,
Magnifiques bergers, qui d'un pas entêté,
Sans doute accomplissant une tâche suprême,
Vers son destin futur meniez l'humanité
Et gardiez d'un foyer céleste la lumière
Aux lampes de vos cœurs. Combien je vous vénère
Pour vous être aperçu qu'un dieu vit dans la chair,
Dans l'élément, le cèdre et le brin de fougère,
Comme aux subtils remous du raisonnant éther;
Qu'à l'extase lucide, amoureux, il se livre
Et pour m'avoir transmis ce cœur fervemment ivre.

———————

Les purins noirs, chamarrés d'or,
Cernent de somptueux reflets
La ferme trapue et qui dort
Sous ses lourds tilleuls violets.

La porte entrouverte, l'étable
Ardente pesamment parfume
L'air du soir. Un lis adorable,
Un grand lis élancé consume

Son cœur, au bord de la croisée,
Près du fumier évaporant
Sa buée... La vitre irisée
Chatoie, teintée d'un bleu mourant.

Their tenderness's glance bathe in your eyes;
And, when it rained, the cow-grass scents would rise,
Sweet to the taste, in a sense-quavering kiss,
One huge embrace of all-consuming bliss.

Ah, glorious shepherds! How I love, admire
You for your mission, your unswerving will
To keep your hearts' lamps burning with the fire
And light of a celestial hearth, while still
Leading Man to his future, ever higher.
I worship you for having understood
That a god, living in the flesh, yet could
Live in the fern sprig, in the cedar bough,
The rustling, murmuring winds; for knowing how,
Loving, He yields to splendrous ecstasy;
And for bequeathing rapture's heart to me.

Les pastorales, Prologue

———————

Spangled with gold, black liquid dung
Rings the squat, little farm, stiff-necked
Rich-speckled, as it sleeps among
Its weighty lindens, violet-flecked.

The stable, door ajar, secretes
Its heavy, hot perfume upon
The evening air. A lily eats
Its heart out—long, slim-stemmed—as on

The window-pane, close by, the mist
Clears in the vapors of manure...
Mottled, the glass seems rainbow-kissed
And tinged with blue, lifeless, obscure.

* For the agriculturally untutored—like myself—I should explain that *épeautre,* known in English as "spelt" or "German wheat," is a grain of inferior quality cultivated since prehistoric times and found nowadays in a few parts of Europe and Asia, where it is generally used as animal fodder.

† I am uncertain whether the poet's original *raisonnait* (reasoned) might not be a misprint for the more logical homonym *résonnait* (resounded), and I confess that my translation skirts the issue by trying to suggest both possibilities.

Marie Dauguet 769

L'anis, le souci, les troènes
Embaument l'âme de la nuit
Et la lune baigne incertaine
Ses pieds frileux à l'eau du puits.

————————

RÉVEIL

Partout s'entremêlent, brouillés,
Des rayons troubles et mouillés
A l'ombre mal évanouie.

L'aurore se réveille en larmes;
On entend s'égoutter les charmes
Au bord des routes éblouies.

Au-dessus des orges violettes
Et rosées, un chant d'alouette
Eclate rapide et vivace;

Et, venant des lointains perdus,
Un son de cloche répandu
Moire, en larges ondes, l'espace.

————————

Les si naïfs parfums fanés et radotants
Qu'exhalent les seuils gris du village en automne,
S'entournant et si doux, voguant parmi le temps,
Tournoiements, dans le vent, de biniou monotone.

Les si naïfs parfums, sourds bruissements de vielle,
Des cuisines noircies au lit à baldaquin
Où quelque mère-grand, en fruste casaquin,
File près du foyer. Les parfums de vieux poêles

Anis, privet, and marigold
Scent the night's soul; coy demoiselle
Moon—timidly, shy of the cold—
Bathes her feet softly in the well.

Les pastorales, "Les champs"

———————

AWAKENING

Everywhere, in the mist, dark rays
And moist mix in the dimming haze
Of shadows, fading, but not quite...

The dawn awakes in tears; and one
Hears, by the road's edge bathed in sun,
* The yoke elms trickling in the light.

Above the barley's violet
And pink, pipes a lark's *chansonnette,*
Bursting in bright and sprightly sound;

And, from the distance, rolling in
Broad waves, a bell's peal, opaline,
Shimmering in the air, spreads round.

Les pastorales, "Les champs"

———————

The oh-so-simple scents—drab, jabbering—
That autumns, from gray village thresholds, waft
In gentle twirls, sailing on weather's wing;
Bagpipe notes, wind-blown, droning fore and aft.

The oh-so-simple scents, low fiddle twangs,
Smoke-blackened stoves, niches with baldaquin
Beds, where some *grand'maman,* in blouse worn thin,
Spins by the fire. Old hearthside scents, where hangs,

* The *charme* of the original, not to be confused with its homonym, is the European hornbeam, a small hardwood tree in the birch family; "yoke elm" is a somewhat more poetic-sounding synonym.

Marie Dauguet 771

Où pend aux murs le crucifix, où l'ombre ourdie
Parfois est traversée d'un jet de soleil rouge
Qui perce l'épaisseur de la vitre verdie
Et sur le dos du chat poussiéreusement bouge.

Against the walls, the crucifix, and where
A jet of sunlight through the glaucous pane,
Piercing the shadows' weft, now and again,
Plays on the cat's back, in the dusty air.

Les pastorales, "Les champs"

Rosemonde Gérard (1866–1953)

It is not unusual that a single line should be all that the world recalls of a talented author, or even that almost no one remembers who it was that wrote it. How many even literate French readers know, for example, that it was the much-forgotten poet-playwright Edmond d'Haraucourt who wrote the now proverbial "Partir, c'est mourir un peu" (To leave is to die a little)? The same is true, unfortunately, of the pithy claim to fame of another poet-playwright, Rosemonde Gérard, a quotation translated the world over and cited popularly as a supremely simple definition of love: "je t'aime davantage, / Aujourd'hui plus qu'hier, et bien moins que demain" (I love you more today than yesterday, and much less than tomorrow).

Rosemonde (née Rose-Etiennette) Gérard deserves certainly to be remembered for more than that quotation, lovely though it is. Born in 1866—some sources say 1871 and even 1872—of an eminent family, she was the granddaughter of one of Napoleon's generals, who later served under Louis-Philippe and was a senator under Napoleon III. An orphan, raised in a convent, she began writing poetry as a child. It was to great critical and popular acclaim that she produced her major collection, *Les pipeaux,* published in 1892 and frequently reprinted. The rustic charm of these "Shepherd's Pipes" captivated the critics. The praise of Alfred Marchand is typical: "It has been a long time since I have read poems whose sentiments are as remarkably fresh and natural as those that Mlle Rosemonde Gérard offers us."[1] Reminiscent at times of Verlaine, the airy delicacy of subject and graceful nostalgia of her verse play neatly against its perfect (but not inflexible) formality. Not one to scorn the traditional dictates and constraints of structured French prosody, she handled them with graceful skill and, at times, even playfulness. She was no avant-garde experimenter, no free-versifier like many of her more famous contemporaries.

And understandably so. As the wife of the dramatist Edmond Rostand, of *Cyrano de Bergerac* fame, it would be surprising if she had not shared his elegantly formal aesthetic. She had been, in fact, the soon-to-be-famous dramatist's muse when, in 1887, he dedicated to her his first major work, a collection of postromantic poems, *Les musardises,* whose pastoral "dawdlings" may well have inspired her own opus. She was married to him the same year and was the mother of two other celebrated Rostands: the writer Maurice and the biologist-academician Jean. Perhaps influenced by her husband's success, she also turned to the theater, writing several verse plays—imaginative *féeries* (extravaganzas) typical of her rich, imaginative style—at least one of which, *Un bon petit diable,* written in collaboration with her son Maurice, was produced in English by the famous Broadway impresario David Belasco in January 1913, including in the cast such later luminaries as Mary Pickford and Lillian Gish. Many of her poems were also set to music by the prominent composers Emmanuel Chabrier and Cécile Chaminade.

Rosemonde Gérard outlived by many years her celebrated husband, who died in 1918 in the famous influenza epidemic. She continued to write, bringing out several more collections of verse—among them *Rien que des chansons* (1929), with his posthumous collaboration, and a historical account, *La vie amoureuse de Madame de Genlis* (1926). She also compiled an anthology of French women poets, *Les muses françaises* (1948), from which her typically light-hearted self-portrait deserves to be quoted: "Elle ne sait que peu de choses, / On pourrait dire presque rien, / Rien... quelques noms de quelques roses, / Et pas un seul mot de latin" (Nothing, in fact, is what she knows— / Well, a few things, but almost none: / A few names of this or that rose. / And Latin? Not a word, not one). She died five years later after a long, distinguished, and well-respected life.[2]

The selection of twenty-three of her poems in translation may help slightly to acquaint the reader with her work. They are taken from two of the three sections into which the collection *Les pipeaux* is divided, "Rustica" and "Ritournelles."

NOTES

1. See Alfred Marchand, *Poètes et penseurs*, pp. 271–75.

2. Except for very sporadic details gleaned from a number of disparate sources, there is a surprising lack of studies devoted to Rosemonde Gérard's life and works. Among the few, see Henriette Charasson's appreciation in *Vingt-cinq ans de littérature*, ed. Eugène de Montfort, 2: 67, and André Fontainas, *Tableau de la poésie française d'aujourd'hui*, p. 22.

SOIRÉE

Le ciel est couleur d'émeraude;
La terre est couleur d'horizon;
Dans l'air du soir, un parfum rôde,
Une odeur fraîche de gazon.

La grenouille verte clabaude;
L'étang se ride d'un frisson...
Le ciel est couleur d'émeraude;
La terre est couleur d'horizon.

Oubliant sa grâce faraude,
La fleur penche vers le buisson;
Et, déjà la lune minaude
De son joli visage rond,
Dans le ciel d'un vert d'émeraude.

───────────

LE VILLAGE ANCIEN

Village ancien, que fais-tu de tes pommes?...
L'arbre s'écroule aux pentes du gazon;
Le cidre d'or mousse aux lèvres des hommes;
Et le parfum dépasse la saison.

Village ancien, que fais-tu de tes âmes?...
Le soir soupire au seuil de la maison;
Le fil d'argent se mêle aux doigts des femmes;
Et la dentelle a brodé l'horizon.

Village ancien, que fais-tu de tes heures?...
Tes souvenirs dorment sur tes demeures;
Le temps, qui vole à côté d'un ramier,

N'oublia rien dans ta brise sylvestre;
Et le parfum du paradis terrestre
Se trouve encor près de chaque pommier!

EVENING

The sky is hued an emerald green;
The earth sports the horizon's hue.
The evening wafts perfume—cool, clean—
The scent of fresh grass, sprung anew.

The green frog blurts, betwixt, between:
The marsh wrinkles its face, chilled through...
The sky is hued an emerald green;
The earth sports the horizon's hue.

Forgetting her sham-graceful mien,
The flower bends toward the bush, askew:
And now the moon begins to preen—
Prettily round-faced ingénue—
In the sky, hued an emerald green.

"Rustica"

THE OLD VILLAGE

Old village, what becomes of all your apples?
The tree has crumbled on the grassy hill;
Cider froths, gold, on men's lips, where it dapples,
As, past its time, the sweet smell lingers still.

Old village, what becomes of your souls, dead?
Evening, before the threshold, sighs its fill:
The women's fingers tat with silvered thread,
And the horizon wears a lace-like frill.

Old village, what becomes of your hours, gone?
Asleep, your memories haunt your hearths, live on.
With ringdove by its side, time, flying free,

Could never, in your woodland breeze, forget;
And earthly paradise's fragrance, yet
Hovering, wafts about each apple tree.

"Rustica"

PROMENADE À L'OMBRE

On s'aventure à travers champs... on se promène...
On découvre une fleur... on aperçoit un nid...
On rencontre un bourdon... le ciel sent la verveine...
Et la voix du silence a dominé le bruit.

Quel est cet écureuil? Quelle est cette fontaine?
Quels sont ces peupliers inconnus? et voici
Que, dans l'immensité déserte de la plaine,
On a perdu la route et trouvé l'infini.

Ah! qu'on aille plus loin dans la forêt profonde!
Qu'on aille au bord du soir, qu'on aille au bout du monde,
Cueillir l'immortel fruit de l'arbre surhumain!

Qu'on aille au cœur caché de la nature fraîche!
—Mais voici le poteau qui parle avec sa flèche...
On a perdu le rêve et trouvé le chemin.

LES PETITS OISEAUX

Que dites-vous, petits Oiseaux du cimetière,
Vous qui chantez autant que les autres oiseaux?
Vous chantez! et pourtant vous devriez vous taire,
Ici, où les maisons ne sont que des tombeaux;

Ici, où les rameaux qui tremblent sur la pierre
Sont des âmes peut-être autant que des rameaux.
Que dites-vous, petits Oiseaux du cimetière,
Vous qui chantez autant que les autres oiseaux?

STROLL IN THE SHADOWS

We saunter through the fields... Stroll aimlessly...
* Here a flower, there a nest, all shadowed round...
The sky smells of verbena... Look! A bee...
And silence's loud voice drowns out each sound.

What squirrel is that?... And there, a fountain... See?
Poplars, unknown till now, rise from the ground...
Yes, we have, in this vast immensity,
Lost our way, but infinity we've found.

Could we but plumb the forest depths, go right
To earth's edge, to the very end of night,
Where grows the tree eternal, pluck its fruit!

Could we reach nature's unspoiled hideaway!...
Ah, no!... The signpost arrow chides: "Nay nay!..."
We lose our dream and find once more the route.

"Rustica"

THE LITTLE BIRDS

† What are you saying, you dear graveyard Bird,
You who sing quite as much as others do?
You sing? Yet mute should be your voice, unheard!
Here abides death: these tombs are home thereto.

Here, where the trembling vines the gravestones gird,
Dwell souls as numerous as the vines. Ah, you...
What are you saying, you dear graveyard Bird,
You who sing quite as much as others do?

---

* To justify my minor addition to the original here I would point out that, without it or something like it, the reader does not know until line 10, title notwithstanding, that the poet is painting an evening scene.

† I have taken the liberty—admittedly for facility of rhyme—of singularizing as a prototype the poet's plural, *Oiseaux*, with, I hope, no detriment to her intent.

Rosemonde Gérard 779

Mais, puisque vous chantez ici des chants si beaux,
Qui sait si ce n'est pas, ici, que vit la terre?
Et qui sait si, là-bas, ce n'est pas, au contraire,
Nos vivantes maisons qui sont les vrais tombeaux...
Qu'en dites-vous, petits Oiseaux du cimetière?

————————

LE DERNIER PAPILLON

Quand ne chante plus le grillon
Et qu'on est avant dans l'automne,
Quelque matin gris l'on s'étonne
De voir un dernier papillon.

Plus d'or, d'azur, de vermillon;
Son coloris est monotone;
La cendre dont il se festonne
Se mêle au sable du sillon.

D'où vient-il?... et par quelle porte?...
Est-ce, parmi la feuille morte,
Le seul des papillons vivants?

Ou, parmi la neige vivante,
La petite ombre transparente
D'un papillon mort au printemps?

————————

LE CRAPAUD

Perdrix dont le cœur se tracasse
En longeant le pré de colza,
Aronde dont le chant se casse
Sitôt que le vol se posa,

Lézard dont le rayon traverse,
Vert, le mur des abricotiers,
Colimaçon des jours d'averse,
Rose, au bord de tous les sentiers;

And yet, so sweet your song, could it be true
That life lives here, though in the tomb interred,
And that, out there, we may, alas, have erred;
That life is death, and our homes tombs thereto...?
What do you say to that, dear graveyard Bird?

"Rustica"

———————

THE LAST BUTTERFLY

When cricket sings its last good-bye
And autumn plods its mournful way,
Our eyes, one drab morn, chance to stray,
Surprised, on one last butterfly.

Dull now, its colors are well-nigh
Undone: blues, reds, golds... Its display—
Dim, drearisome—is all of gray,
Like furrow sands that ashen lie.

Whence does it come?... Through what door flying?...
Is it, amid fall's leaves, all dying,
The last live butterfly a-wing?

Or, ghost amid the snow's chill storm,
Is it only a spectral form:
A butterfly, dead since the spring?

"Rustica"

———————

THE TOAD

Partridge—you of the worrying heart's
Concern, grazing the colza leaves;
Swallow—you of the song that starts
To break as you light on the sheaves;

Lizard—you of the darting ray,
Green, through the apricot trees sprawling;
And snail—you of the rainy day,
Pink, along every roadside crawling;

Nous connaissons votre manière
De vivre, enfantine et légère,
Mais vous, Crapaud, toujours si vieux,

Est-ce vrai qu'une année entière
Vous demeurez dans une pierre
Avec du soleil dans les yeux?

———————

LA CHANSON DU MONDE

Ancienne légende

Jupiter, un jour que le temps était parfait,
Dit aux humains: "Le vieux monde est votre héritage:
Je veux vous le donner. Faites-en le partage."
Et, fraternellement, le partage fut fait.

Le laboureur aux mains calleuses prit la terre;
Le chasseur prit les bois, la plaine et le ravin;
Le pêcheur prit les mers, le lac et la rivière;
Le buveur prit la treille et les grappes de vin;
L'usurier prit l'argent et l'or dans ses mains viles:
Le roi barricada les routes et les villes;
Et le peintre prit l'arc-en-ciel; et les amants
Prirent tous les oiseaux et les fleurs du printemps.

Chacun vivait heureux: l'un fou, et l'autre sage,
Quand le poète vint prendre part au partage.
"Hélas," fit Jupiter en fronçant le sourcil,
"Hélas, j'ai tout donné, par là et par ici;
Je n'ai plus rien pour toi: pas même un paysage!
Mais où donc étais-tu?—J'étais dans un nuage... "

Et, comme le rêveur aux regards vagabonds
S'en allait, n'ayant eu qu'une larme pour geste...
Jupiter s'écria: "A propos, il me reste
Encor mon ciel! Veux-tu que nous le partagions?"

We know your lives and, *entre nous,*
Find them banal, and childish too;
But you, O Toad, ever so old,

Is it true that, the whole year through,
You live beneath a rock, and do
Nothing but eye the sun, we're told?

"Rustica"

THE SONG OF THE WORLD

Ancient Legend

Back when time knew no imperfections—none!—
Jupiter said to Man: "It's my decision
To give you this old world. Make a division..."
In fashion brotherly his will was done.

The rough-palmed ploughman said: "I take the land."
The hunter said: "Wood, plain, and dell are mine."
The fisherman took sea, lake, river; and
The drunkard took the trellis and the vine.
The usurer's vile hand seized silver, gold;
The king held cities in his stranglehold;
The painter took the rainbow; lovers got
The flowers of spring and the birds for their lot.

Some daft, some wise, each lived his laissez-faire,
Content, when there appeared, seeking his share,
The poet... Frowning, with a "Welladay!"
Jupiter sighed: "I gave it all away!
There's nothing left for you! Alas, no more
Have I to give!... But, where were you before?"
"I was up in a cloud," the dreamer said...

And, as he turned to leave, raising his head,
With far-off glance, he shed a tear. And there it
Remained, to mark his sadness... "Wait, good sir!
One thing is still my own," cried Jupiter.
"The sky... And, if you would, friend, we can share it!"

"Ritournelles"

Rosemonde Gérard 783

LA CHANSON DU NUAGE

Fait de brouillard et de lumière
Entre le matin et le soir,
Lorsqu'il se penche sur la terre
Le nuage n'est qu'un miroir.

Il voudrait bien, lorsqu'il se penche,
Être peuplé infiniment
De fleur rose, de verte branche,
D'un mot, d'un cœur, d'un sentiment;

Il voudrait qu'une onde l'enivre
D'un ruisseau bleu comme un saphir,
Il voudrait, ce nuage, vivre
D'un projet ou d'un souvenir;

Il voudrait, charmante souffrance
Dont il embellirait le jour,
Voir passer sur sa transparence
L'ombre fatale de l'amour!

Mais hélas, brouillard et lumière
Entre le matin et le soir,
Lorsqu'il se penche sur la terre
Le nuage n'est qu'un miroir:

Et, dès qu'un divin paysage
Monte à son cœur aérien,
Voici qu'il passe, le nuage...
Et c'est un autre qui revient!

RONDES

I

Les premiers refrains de la vie,
Qu'on chantait d'une voix d'enfant,
Ont une musique infinie
Qui reste dans un cœur battant,

SONG OF THE CLOUD

Fashioned of mist and daylight-crowned,
After the dawning and before
The dusk, with head bowed toward the ground,
The cloud's a mirror, nothing more.

With head bowed, it would like to be—
Bough-green and blossom-pink of hue—
Peopled with an infinity
Of word, of heart, of point of view;

It would like to grow drunk upon
The sapphire blue of brooklet streaming;
To live on memory, done and gone,
Or on some hoped-for project, dreaming;

It would like—torment of delight,
Gracing the day—to watch as passed
Over its brow, transparent, bright,
Love's deathly, deadly shadow cast!

Ah! But, of mist and daylight-crowned,
After the dawning and before
The dusk, with head bowed toward the ground,
The cloud's a mirror, nothing more.

And, as some divine landscape spanned
Goes rising to its heart on high,
See how the cloud goes passing, and...
Another one comes floating by!

"Ritournelles"

ROUNDS

I
The first of our life's *chansonnettes*,
A simple tune, a child's refrain,
Is an air infinite that yet
Beats in our hearts, long to remain.

Un peu plus tard, on les oublie;
Beaucoup plus tard, on les reprend,
Les premiers refrains de la vie
Qu'on chantait d'une voix d'enfant.

O source de mélancolie
Qui fais de nos pleurs un torrent,
Daigne parfois, je t'en supplie,
Nous redonner, rien qu'un instant,
Les premiers refrains de la vie!

II
Toutes nous avons, de nos lèvres,
Juré de n'aller plus au bois.
Les bois sont pleins de vertes fièvres,
De dangereux airs de hautbois.

Et, la plus gardeuse de chèvres
Comme la plus fille de rois,
Toutes nous avons, de nos lèvres,
Juré de n'aller plus au bois.

Cœurs de fillettes, cœurs de lièvres
Aussi tremblants au bord des bois...
Nous n'avons qu'à nouer nos doigts.
Les mots reviennent dans la voix...
Et la voix revient sur les lèvres!

III
Les chansons veulent qu'on les chante
Quand il fait beau, quand il fait noir.
Elles viennent, troupe émouvante,
Et cherchent à nous émouvoir.

Penchant vers nous, comme un miroir
Leur allegro ou leur andante...
Les chansons veulent qu'on les chante
Quand il fait beau, quand il fait noir.

L'étoile, qui n'est pas méchante,
Voudrait nous remplacer l'espoir;
Les fleurs, étoiles de la plante,
Voudraient qu'on les respire un soir...
Les chansons veulent qu'on les chante!

A little later, we forget;
Much later, we recall again
The first of our life's *chansonnettes,*
A simple tune, a child's refrain.

O doleful source of sad regret,
Who make our tears fall thick as rain;
I pray you, but one moment, let
Us hear once more—would you but deign!—
The first of our life's *chansonnettes.*

II
We women never, willingly,
Will venture to the woods, we swear;
The woods, where hectic greenery
Snares us with oboe's treacherous air.

And, whether goatherd lass we be
Or regal princess, debonair,
We women never, willingly,
Will venture to the woods, we swear.

Timid, our girlish hearts; and we
Quiver and quake, like forest hare...
We need but join our hands, declare
Once again not to venture there...
And we, again, swear willingly!

III
Songs must be sung: they wish it so,
Whether by day or night's dim light.
Inspiring troupe, they come and, lo!
Attempt to move us as they might.

Mirror-like, they cast on us, bright,
Their lento or prestissimo...
Songs must be sung: they wish it so,
Whether by day or night's dim light.

The stars would, with their courteous glow,
Help turn our hopes once more aright;
And flowers, whose petals star-like grow,
Would have us breathe their scents by night...
Songs must be sung: they wish it so!

IV

On chante. Et tout est emporté
Sitôt qu'on a fini la ronde;
Dans la forêt, folle ou profonde,
Un laurier est vite coupé.

Un oiseau, dans l'arbre arrêté,
S'écrie après une seconde:
"On chante, et tout est emporté
Sitôt qu'on a fini la ronde."

Ah! chevelure brune ou blonde!
Rubans volant au ciel d'été!
Petits pieds sonnant sur le monde!
L'oiseau disait la vérité:
On chante... et tout est emporté!

––––––––––

VIEILLES CHOSES

I

Il est un tas de vieilles choses,
Qui nous parlent des temps passés,
Au fond des vieux bahuts moroses:
Vieux bijoux, éventails froissés

Jadis par des doigts fins et roses,
Par des doigts aujourd'hui glacés...
Il est un tas de vieilles choses,
Qui nous parlent des temps passés.

Fauteuils branlants aux pieds cassés,
Coussins nuancés de vieux roses,
Ecrans aux sujets effacés...
Plus vivantes qu'on ne suppose,
Il est un tas de vieilles choses.

II

Dans le vieux salon délabré,
Pend le pastel d'une marquise;
Si charmant qu'on madrigalise
Devant son cadre dédoré.

IV
They sing. And off flies everything,
No sooner do they end their round:
In the wood—daft or deep, profound—
A laurel falls with just one swing.

Perched in a tree, a twittering
Bird, in a trice, chirps, sound by sound:
"They sing... And off flies everything,
No sooner do they end their round."

Ah! Ribbons fly, hair comes unbound—
Brown, blond—aloft on sky-bound wing!
Little feet, pattering on the ground...
Yes, the bird told the truth: they sing...
They sing... And off flies everything!

"Ritournelles"

OLD THINGS

I
Those oh-so-many time-worn things
That speak to us of life grown old
In gloomy, time-worn chests: old rings,
Gems, fans that hands—today grown cold—

Once crumpled with the flutterings
Of fine pink fingers' tender hold...
Those oh-so-many time-worn things
That speak to us of life grown old.

Chairs, broken, tottering uncontrolled,
Old cushions' rose embroiderings,
Screens with their faded stories told...
Time... Strange how, back to life, it brings
Those oh-so-many time-worn things.

II
Here, in the shabby old salon,
Hangs a marquise's miniature,
Extolled by poet-troubadour
Before its frame, gold leaf now gone.

Tout rose et doublement poudré
De poudre et de poussière grise,
Dans le vieux salon délabré,
Pend le pastel d'une marquise.

Sous le sourire évaporé,
La bouche est tellement exquise
Qu'un moineau qui serait entré
La prendrait pour une cerise
Dans le vieux salon délabré.

III
C'est un vieux gilet de marquis,
Brodé d'une façon galante;
Un gilet rose, au ton exquis;
Sur son étoffe chatoyante,

Le jabot dut faire jadis
Sa cascatelle éblouissante;
C'est un vieux gilet de marquis,
Brodé d'une façon galante;

Et fleurant la poudre de riz.
Au fond du gousset, on a pris
Deux billets tendres d'une amante
Et trois tabatières de prix...
C'est un vieux gilet de marquis.

IV
La chaise à porteurs d'un bleu tendre
A petits bouquets pompadour,
Seule en son coin, paraît attendre
Quelque dame en galant atour.

Balancée, elle a dû se rendre
A plus d'un rendez-vous d'amour,
La chaise à porteurs d'un bleu tendre
A petits bouquets pompadour.

With a gray dust spread thick upon
Her pink and powdered *fin amour,*
Here, in the shabby old salon,
Hangs a marquise's miniature.

Beneath her vaporous smile, grown wan,
Her pursed lips—exquisite, demure—
Would make a sparrow, lit thereon,
Think them a cherry, such their lure,
Here, in the shabby old salon.

III
This antique vest of some marquis,
Embroidered waistcoat richly made:
Pink of hue, gallant filigree,
Fabric of shimmering brocade...

Its ruffled front undoubtedly
Once dazzled in its frilled cascade,
This antique vest of some marquis,
Embroidered waistcoat richly made,

Perfumed with powder's fragrancy.
And in the pocket, deep, would be
Billets-doux from some escapade
D'amour, and fine snuffboxes three...
This antique vest of some marquis.

IV
Sedan chair, with its pale blue air
* And little pompadour bouquets,
Waits in the lonely corner where
Fine *dame* might live her yesterdays.

† A-bob, a-sway, it plied its share
Of love-tryst rendezvous, this *chaise:*
Sedan chair, with its pale blue air
And little pompadour bouquets.

* Less familiar to anglophone readers than the hairstyle made famous by the Marquise
de Pompadour (1721–1764), celebrated mistress of Louis XV, the reference here is to the
characteristic fabric of the period, decorated with intricate little floral designs.

† Another reading is possible here, based on the popular meaning of the verb *balancer,*
"to throw out," suggesting that, though now discarded, the *chaise* did, indeed, once have
a more noble use.

Il ne faudra jamais la vendre;
Car on dit qu'au bal de la cour
Jadis on vit la Pompadour,
Avec un gros bouquet descendre
De la chaise à porteurs bleu tendre.

V

Le clavecin à la voix grêle
Se tait dans le boudoir vert d'eau.
Adieu, l'air du berger fidèle;
Adieu, le menuet nouveau;

Adieu, la grande ritournelle
Du cœur de Glück ou de Rameau...
Le clavecin à la voix grêle
Se tait dans le boudoir vert d'eau.

Mais, quand la nuit tombe au château,
Il fait danser incognito
Les tanagras de Praxitèle
Et les bergères de Watteau,
Le clavecin à la voix grêle.

VI

L'éventail de nacre irisée,
Qui s'est échappé d'une main,
Conserve une branche brisée
Mais garde une odeur de jasmin.

D'une brise inutilisée
Il n'a pu refaire un destin,
L'éventail de nacre irisée
Qui s'est échappé d'une main.

Fut-il, auprès d'une croisée,
Le tendre appel d'un cœur lointain?
Ou le paravent clandestin
D'une lèvre à l'autre posée,
L'éventail de nacre irisée?...

Sell it? Ah no! One must forebear;
For, at one of Court's lush soirées,
La Pompadour dazzled men's gaze,
Bouquet'd, they say, alighting there
From that sedan, with pale blue air.

V

This harpsichord, with twang and wheeze,
Stands mute in sea-green boudoir yet.
Farewell, fair shepherds' melodies!
Farewell, new unplayed minuet!

Farewell Rameau, Glück, whom its keys
Once sang in heartfelt *chansonnettes*...
This harpsichord, with twang and wheeze,
Stands mute in sea-green boudoir yet.

But, come the night, it wakes to let
Masked dancers fill the château: those
* Tanagras of Praxiteles,
Watteau's shepherd maids and soubrettes,
This harpsichord, with twang and wheeze.

VI

This pearled fan, shimmering with a frill,
That a hand once let fall, so free,
Has a cracked rib, and yet it will
Waft jasmine's scent unendingly.

Its breeze, unused, has had its fill
Of its unfinished destiny,
This pearled fan, shimmering with a frill,
That a hand once let fall, so free.

Was it, beside some window sill,
The distant call of heart's ennui?
Or a screen, in coy secrecy,
Betwixt two mouths, poised silent, still,
This pearled fan, shimmering with a frill?...

---

* Less familiar to readers than the Greek sculptor Praxiteles (ca. 370–340 B.C.E.)—
accent on the *i*, fortunately for the rhyme—this esoteric allusion refers to the terracotta
figurines first found in tombs in the Beoetian town of Tanagra, and an especially popular
inspiration for nineteenth-century Parisian artists.

VII

Voyez, c'est une boîte à mouche,
Avec son vrai petit tiroir.
D'une dame assez peu farouche
Elle ornait jadis le boudoir.

Mouche pour le coin de la bouche;
Mouche pour le coin de l'œil noir;
Voyez, c'est une boîte à mouche,
Avec son vrai petit tiroir.

Tout y est resté: le miroir,
Le carmin, la poudre à retouche...
Et l'on trouve, dès qu'on y touche,
De la beauté pour plus d'un soir
Dans la petite boîte à mouche.

VIII

Tremblant toujours sous du cristal,
C'est une petite tortue.
Microscopique, elle est venue
Du Japon qui sent le santal.

Oh! comme il doit lui faire mal,
L'éternel frisson qui la tue!
Tremblant toujours sous du cristal,
C'est une petite tortue.

Hélas, cette angoisse éperdue,
Où donc l'avais-je déjà vue?
Dans un rêve? dans une rue?
Ou dans un cœur sentimental
Tremblant sous des yeux de cristal?...

IX

Le fond de la tapisserie
Est d'un rose fleur-de-pêcher.
Un papillon d'allégorie
Sur un front semble se pencher;

See? Just a wee cosmetic-case—
Small drawer and all!—that, once upon
A time, shone with her dainty grace
In *dame*'s boudoir... Her face? Thereon,

The dots, therein, she used to place
* By her dark eye, sweet lips: "bon ton"!
See? Just a wee cosmetic case—
Small drawer and all!—that, once upon

A time, she used... Then she was gone;
But, in it yet, her beauty's trace,
Still there: rice powder for the face,
Rouge, mirror... Grace to linger on
And on, in that cosmetic-case...

VIII
Trembling in closure crystalline,
A tiny turtle, nothing more...
Minute, it came to live therein
† From Japan's sandal-scented shore.

Oh how it shudders! What chagrin,
What grievous torments, woes galore
For tiny turtle, nothing more,
Trembling in closure crystalline!

Where have I seen that look before?
That anguish? In some nightmare? Or
Eye of some passerby, heartsore?
Or sentimental heart, done in,
Trembling beneath gaze crystalline?...

IX
The background of the tapestry
Is of a pink, peach-blossom shade.
A butterfly, symbolically,
Hovers in tender accolade

* I hope the reader will not cringe at this anglicized pronunciation of "bon ton." While my linguistic instincts and good judgment give more than a slight shudder at it, the authorization of several respectable dictionaries has won out over my own perhaps overly fusty qualms.

† I trust that the reader will not be tempted to interpret the "sandal" in "sandal-scented" as referring to anything other than sandalwood.

Ce front, c'est celui de Psyché,
Papillon d'une autre prairie...
Le fond de la tapisserie
Est d'un rose fleur-de-pêcher.

Et les yeux, remplis de féerie,
Ne savent plus où s'attacher:
Quel ciel est le plus rapproché...
Le petit front blanc de Psyché?
Ou le fond de tapisserie?

X
Mais il est, sur une gravure,
Un indéfinissable ciel:
Plein de ramiers et de ramure
Et d'un roman presque irréel.

Certes on voit, dans la nature,
Des heures d'azur et de miel;
Mais il est, sur une gravure,
Un indéfinissable ciel.

Dans un océan de verdure,
Deux amants, au pied d'un autel,
Se donnent, d'un regard qui dure,
Un baiser qui semble éternel...
Mais il est sur une gravure!

————————

RÉCRÉATION

Ma poupée aux yeux de faïence
Dormait dans l'herbe aux yeux de fleur.
Le jardin n'était qu'une danse
De soleil rose et de bonheur.

*   By Psyche's brow... Butterfly, she,
As well, from distant meadow strayed...
The background of the tapestry
Is of a pink, peach-blossom shade.

Before such faerydom displayed,
Our gaze knows not where best to be:
Closer, which heaven? Which phantasy?
Psyche's pale brow? Or, there arrayed,
The background of the tapestry?

x
But it's an etching that we see,
This vaguely pictured sky outspanned:
With doves aloft from tree to tree—
Like some romance's wonderland.

Surely in nature there can be
Azure-sweet hours at love's command.
But it's an etching that we see,
This vaguely pictured sky outspanned.

There, in a sea of greenery,
Two lovers by an altar stand,
With tender gaze unending, and
Seeming to kiss eternally...
But it's an etching that we see!

"Ritournelles"

PLAYTIME

My doll, with her glazed porcelain eyes,
† Lies in the garden's flower-eyes, sleeping.
Dancing, the grasses bow and rise,
Swaying with joy, in pink sun steeping.

* The poet's allusion is not to any of the mythological Psyche's various adventures and
misadventures with Venus, Pluto, and—especially—Cupid, but rather to the meaning of
her name, Greek for both "soul" and "butterfly": a double meaning that allegorizes death,
entombment, and resurrection in the form of the butterfly emerging from its chrysalis.
† I have opted for a change of tense, from past to present, both to intensify the poet's
vision and, incidentally, for exigencies of rhyme.

Rosemonde Gérard 797

Le printemps réglait sa cadence
Au métronome de mon cœur.
Ma poupée aux yeux de faïence
Dormait dans l'herbe aux yeux de fleur.

Et, sur une vieille crédence,
Un sablier, d'un air moqueur,
Disait: "Qu'est-ce que l'existence?
Des yeux en fleur... des yeux en pleur...
Puis... de pauvres yeux de faïence!"

Year beats its rhythm in springtime wise,
To my heart's metronome, time keeping.
My doll, with her glazed porcelain eyes,
Lies in the garden's flower-eyes, sleeping.

And, on an old credenza, cries
An hourglass, sand-filled, leering, heaping
Scorn: "What is life—this pack of 'whys'!—
But eyes a-bloom and eyes a-weeping...
And... Ah, yes, poor glazed porcelain eyes!"

"Ritournelles"

Lucie Delarue-Mardrus (1874–1945)

Multi-talented writer, musician, painter, sculptor. Self-assertive woman, flamboyant in her rejection of middle-class mores. Sexually independent to the point of ambivalence, and unconvinced of the inevitability of the female role of motherhood. All these qualities, describing Lucie Delarue-Mardrus, should, one would think, make her an ideal Belle Epoque standard-bearer in the cause of today's feminism. And yet she is not unconditionally embraced and claimed as an ancestor by all her twentieth- and twenty-first-century *consœurs*. Despite her several lesbian affairs and her willingness to make of them openly the stuff of some of her novels, she not only pooh-poohed female suffrage, but, even more unforgivable, also never rejected the traditional values of feminine physical seductiveness and masculine chivalry that, historically at least, had differentiated the sexes. For her it was proper that woman should make the most of her pulchritude, her social grace, in a word, her "femininity." If she was to compete with man, creature of base and corrupt reason, it should not be on his own grounds but rather on hers, as a creature of passion and instinct. A nonconformist of the first order, yet attached to political and social values of the past, she was quite the contradiction.

Delarue-Mardrus's values are reflected especially in her essays and, to varying degrees, in her forty-odd novels (many of which appeared in serial form), as well as in her short stories and occasional plays. Less directly, perhaps, in her poetry, more oblique by the very nature of the genre. Ironically, although she hoped to be considered primarily as a poet, and although she produced several respectable collections of verse, they were not always appreciated by the male-dominated critical establishment, despite the unrealistically lavish praise of some, like the poet Renée Vivien (see pp. 868–85 below), her lesbian colleague, for whom she was the poet of the age. An exaggerated opinion, to be sure. But we can still be grateful that the young Lucie had ignored the contrarily inspired advice of poet François Coppée that she give up poetry and take up needlework and housework instead.[1] Perhaps, of all her contemporaries, the one whose middle-of-the-road judgment should be taken the most seriously is the literary historian André Fontainas, who, while acknowledging her "fervent heart" added that "the use to which she puts her talent is sometimes rather disconcerting."[2]

Lucie Delarue was born on November 3, 1874, in Honfleur, Normandy, the youngest of a wealthy lawyer's six daughters. When she married Joseph-Charles Mardrus at twenty-six, that eccentric translator of *The Arabian Nights* dismissed her avowed lesbian tendencies despite several schoolgirl attachments that she had already formed. After spending seven years in the Near East with her husband, where she is said to have learned fluent Arabic, she returned to Paris, where, at his urging, she entertained prominent musicians and writers of the day and frequented various literary salons à la mode. Among the most à la mode was that of Aurélie de Faucanberge—known to her contemporaries as Madame Aurel—which hosted such figures as Cocteau, Apollinaire, and Delarue-Mardrus's rival Anna de Noailles (see pp. 834–57 below). Divorcing in 1913, she would nourish an unrequited passion for the American expatriate poet Natalie Clifford Barney (see pp. 858–67 below), chronicled in her posthumous collection of poems *Nos secrètes amours* (1957) and novelized in *L'ange et les pervers* (1930). Her longer-lasting affair with the Jewish opera singer Germaine de Castro (née Victoria Gómez), whom she met at the age of fifty-eight, created considerable anti-Semitic difficulties for her during the Occupation. She continued to write until her death in 1945, just before the end of World War II.[3]

The eighteen poems that follow, from three of her nine collections (the early *Ferveur* and *Figure de proue*, and the mid-career *Les sept douleurs d'octobre*), give a modest sampling of Lucie Delarue-Mardrus's varied and colorful, if sometimes overly oratorical, and at times even droll, inspiration.

NOTES

1. Cited in Pauline Newman-Gordon's entry in *French Women Writers*, p. 108. In addition to presenting a concise biography and bibliography, this essay deals in detail primarily with Delarue-Mardrus's novels.

2. André Fontainas, *Tableau de la poésie française d'aujourd'hui*, p. 22.

3. For a variety of biographical information and aesthetic appreciation, among many studies and articles, see Miriam Harry, *Mon amie, Lucie Delarue-Mardrus;* and, more recently, Hélène Plat, *Lucie Delarue-Mardrus: Une femme de lettres des années folles*, and a study of specialized interest, Agnès Cardinal, Dorothy Goldman, and Judith Hattaway, *Women's Writing on the First World War*. The poet's own *Mes mémoires* offers biographical details of her early life.

CHUTES

Je regarde en rêvant les marronniers rameux:
Les bourgeons ont crevé, les feuilles sont sorties...
O! les arbres en or aux chutes amorties
Dans la calamité de l'automne orageux!

Il semble que jamais ne reviendra Novembre,
Et pourtant, marronniers! quand vos bras fleuriront,
Le vent chaud jettera vos fleurs jusqu'à ma chambre
Et ce sera déjà comme une allusion...

ŒILLETS

L'odeur des œillets épicés
Transporte notre âme attentive,
En une vaine tentative,
Vers les étés de nos passés...

Avec ce flot de souvenance,
Œillets, œillets, ah! rendez-nous
Ces jardins verts de notre enfance
Restés dans votre poivre doux!

Du bout de ses tuyaux gris,
Dans le ciel fume Paris;

Le jardin se ramifie
Sur cette lithographie;

Tout le long d'un rameau sec
Les moineaux se font le bec;

FALLINGS

Musing, I watch the chestnut trees, lush-limbed:
The buds have burst, the leaves have sprung... O trees
Of gold, of fallings gently, softly dimmed
In stormy autumn's harsh calamities!

November, so it seems, will nevermore
Return! But, chestnut trees, when your boughs bloom,
Warm winds will blow your flowers to my room,
And that will be another metaphor...

Ferveur, "Poèmes terrestres"

CARNATIONS

The spice scent of carnations casts
Our souls in backward flight, in vain
Attempting—yearning—once again
To reach the summers of our pasts...

With that flood of remembrance, please,
Carnations, ah! carnations! let
Us live your peppered memories
Of childhood gardens, greening yet!

Ferveur, "L'âme des choses"

From her gray pipes, rising high,
Paris smokes against the sky;

Garden boughs spread fore and aft
On this image lithographed;

On a dry branch sparrows sitting
In a row, are pecking, twitting;

Et quelque bateau qui passe
Sur la Seine lourde et lasse

Vient mêler de temps en temps
Son sanglot au mauvais temps.

———————

L'ombre de Verlaine est au jardin d'automne
Qui s'est assise au long des bancs vermoulus
A recevoir longtemps la pluie monotone,
Comme un mendiant triste qui n'en peut plus
Et qui regarde sans parler, bouche bée,
Devant soi, mourir une feuille tombée...

———————

Ton cœur intact plus frais qu'un fruit encore à l'arbre
S'est offert pour tenter la morsure de marbre
De mes cruelles dents prêtes à saccager.

Mais j'ai reçu le don, et, tremblant de songer
Que sa beauté mourrait du péché de ma bouche,
J'ai respecté ce fruit qu'il ne faut pas qu'on touche.

———————

ALLUSION

Petite ombre, dieu lare ou démon familier,
Sans bruit, la chatte rôde autour du mobilier,
S'assied avec sa queue au côté, ronde et sage,
Et, fixement, allume au centre du tapis

And along the weary Seine
Some boat passing now and then

Sobs a sob, mixing together
Its low moan with the foul weather.

Ferveur, "Fumées"

———————

An autumn garden, where shades of Verlaine
Haunt the worm-eaten benches, there to be
* Buffeted by the rain, again, again,
Like a poor beggar in his misery,
Gaping in silence as, before his eye,
† He sees a fallen leaf, watches it die...

Ferveur, "Fumées"

———————

Your heart offered itself intact to me,
Fresher than fruit still clinging to the tree,
Bade my cruel marble teeth to wrench a bite.

I took the gift, but, trembling lest I might,
Sinful, lay waste its beauty unprotected,
Rightly, I left the fruit untouched, respected.

Ferveur, "Déclarations"

———————

ALLUSION

Dark household god or demon imp, the cat
Roams, noiseless, in and out, then, sitting pat,
Humped in a rounded mass—tail by her side,
Curled—debonair and well-behaved; and, there,

———————

* There is probably meant to be an echo here of Verlaine's famous lines "Il pleure dans mon cœur / Comme il pleut sur la ville," from his *Romances sans paroles* (1874), for my translation of which, see *One Hundred and One Poems of Paul Verlaine,* pp. 78–79.

† Delarue-Mardrus intentionally casts the original in eleven-syllable verse in tribute to Verlaine's frequent use of the odd-syllable (*impair*) line. I have not followed suit, however, since the subtlety, clear enough to a well-tuned French ear, would be lost in English, and would sound more like a mistake than an intent.

Deux lunes dans la nuit noire de son pelage.
Mais, dans sa patte, cinq durs ongles sont tapis
Que pourrait dégainer son humeur décevante,
Et je sais la souris de son dernier repas
Si lentement cruel! et qu'elle représente
Certain intime fond dont on ne parle pas.

———————

Genève, teints proprets et prunelles contentes
Pleines de calvinisme et de neutralité,
Ville sans passions, tranquille probité,
Sur quoi tombent de haut tes cloches protestantes.

Genève, montre en règle! Au rythme langoureux
Des orchestres, ton lac berce son flot fameux;
Et, le Mont Blanc montrant son gros dos sans vertèbre,
La satisfaction de tes Dimanches bleus
Danse pompeusement dans un jet d'eau célèbre.

———————

MÉMOIRE

Nous montâmes souvent, les nuits, sur nos terrasses
Au plus chaud des printemps royalement fanés
D'Orient, pour sentir, enfants passionnés,
Les étoiles pleuvoir doucement sur nos faces.

Et, comme les champs gris trépidaient de grillons,
Nous étions étonnés de sentir jusqu'aux moelles
L'espace clignoter et vibrer les sillons,
Et qu'il y eût autant de grillons que d'étoiles...

Stares to light two bright black-furred moons, astride
The rug... But her deceptive mood might bare
That paw's five rugged claws! I know, just now,
Her meal of mouse was cruel and slow... A token
Of something intimate that, anyhow,
Most surely must remain down deep, unspoken.

Ferveurs, "Heures intimes"

Geneva, tidy colors, and the people's
Neutrality-gazed, Calvinistic eyes,
Passionless city, from whose tranquil skies
Trusty bells peel from your Protestant steeples,

Geneva, watch well-set! Orchestras play
Their languorous rhythms and your lake's waves sway,
As Mont Blanc's boneless back lies arching, lo!
Smug in your sky-blue Sunday holiday,
* You dance, proud, in the spray of your *Jet d'eau.*

Ferveur, "Regards"

MEMORY

Often, at night, we climbed the terrassed spaces
In Orient's torrid-wilted springs, to sense—
Passionate children, we!—the stars commence
To rain down tenderly upon our faces.

Gray fields quivered with crickets, and we were
Awed to feel, in our bones, that, equally,
Skies winked and furrows buzzed, and to infer
That crickets matched the stars' infinity.

La figure de proue, "Premier Islam"

* The allusion is to the man-made waterspout in Lake Geneva, the city's celebrated
tourist trademark.

Lucie Delarue-Mardrus 807

SECONDE

Une longue forêt de reflets est dans l'eau;
L'altitude du ciel qui s'y est renversée
Est un abîme bleu sans fond.
Je me tiens sur ce bord, seule avec ma pensée;
Ce n'est rien que mon cœur, ce n'est rien qu'un peu d'eau,
Mais la vie éternelle en moi s'est renversée
Ainsi que la forêt et le ciel dans cette eau,
Et je me sens, avec des reflets jusqu'au fond,
Plus profonde, magique et menteuse que l'eau...

BERCEMENT

Les barques dorment dans ton port au bruit du large,
      Comme des oiseaux dans leur nid.
Elles dorment ayant leurs mâts dans l'infini,
Autour d'elles leur ville et la mer grise en marge.

Autour de toi ta ville et la mer grise en marge,
Tu dors aussi devant le natal infini.
      Comme un oiseau chaud dans son nid,
Tu dors parmi le bruit des barques qu'on décharge.

SECOND

Long forest of reflections in the water;
In it, the height of sky, turned upside down,
† Is an abyss, blue, endless, deep.
My thought and I stand by this bank, alone;
Only my heart, only a little water,
But life eternal has turned upside down
For me, like sky and forest in this water,
And I feel, joined to these reflections deep,
Deeper, more magic, falser than the water....

‡   *La figure de proue,* "En Kroumirie"

CRADLING

Boats sleep in port, lulled by the murmuring sea,
    Like birds reposing in their nest.
They sleep with masts turned toward infinity,
About them, the gray sea, their town at rest.

About you, the gray sea, your town at rest,
You sleep amid birth's never-ending spring.
    Like a bird warming in its nest,
You sleep amid the boats' unburdening.

* I have followed the author here in her curious rhyme-scheme—or non-rhyme-scheme.

† I follow her too in her unexpected short line, not uncommon in her verse, though unmarked by the usual indent.

‡ "Kroumirie" is the French name for the mountainous and heavily wooded area on both sides of the border between Algeria and Tunisia, originally inhabited by the K(h)roumir brigands. This poem and two dozen others in the collection were inspired by the author's travels in that region.

Les barques, toi, tous les oiseaux sont dans leur nid.
A dormir, la tête sous l'aile...
Dors! Ton âme-mouette est bien ici chez elle,
Dans son port, et devant le natal infini.
Dors! Ton âme-mouette est bien ici chez elle,
A dormir la tête sous l'aile.

RONDEL ÉQUESTRE

Galoper dans les boutons d'or
Sur un cheval de bonne race,
Voici qui tout à coup efface
Ces rêves couleur de la mort.

Comme j'étais dolente, lasse!
A présent, non! J'aime si fort
Galoper dans les boutons d'or
Sur un cheval de bonne race!

Dans mes cheveux de jeune lord
Le vent de mai passe et repasse.
En selle, je suis à ma place.
Oh! puissé-je longtemps encor,
Derrière une invisible chasse,

Galoper dans les boutons d'or!

SOUPIR

Le malaise secret de l'arbre qui bourgeonne
Doit ressembler à ceux que nous sentons en nous.
Le printemps vient. L'air est trop doux.
Il faudrait roucouler comme fait la pigeonne.

Boats, birds, you: everything sleeps in its nest,
    Head nestled, tucked beneath its wing...
Sleep! Here your seagull-soul will find its rest,
Its port, amid birth's never-ending spring.
Sleep! Here your seagull-soul will find its rest,
*   Head nestled, tucked beneath its wing.

La Figure de proue, "Au port"

———————

RONDEAU ON HORSEBACK

Galloping through the buds of gold
On a fine horse of pedigree
Wipes quickly from my memory
Those dreams, death-colored, drab and cold.

How doleful, sad I used to be!
But now, no more! What joy untold,
Galloping through the buds of gold
On a fine horse of pedigree!

My hair, like some young lord's! Behold
How the May wind plays and makes free!
The saddle is the place for me...
Ah! To ride on, like huntress bold,
Chasing a pack no eye can see,

Galloping through the buds of gold!

Les sept douleurs d'octobre, "Mai, joli mai!"

———————

SIGH

The budding tree's secret malaise must be
Much like our own. Spring comes. The air is just
    A bit too mild. We feel we must
Coo like a pigeon when contented she.

* Without copying exactly the author's unorthodox and quite informal rhyme-scheme, with its word repetitions and homonyms, I have tried to produce something of the same effect.

Lucie Delarue-Mardrus 811

Mais, quand on n'a plus rien qui roucoule en son cœur,
Le printemps qui s'annonce a-t-il sa raison d'être?
    Il faut nous consoler, peut-être:
Bonheur d'autrui, ton nom est toujours le Bonheur.

––––––––––

L'HUMILIATION

Puante à plein nez, cette race
Que les chiens suivent à la trace,

Fléau qui détruit, incessant,
Monstre qui marche dans le sang,

Faux gorille, ample pourriture,
Teigne et lèpre de la nature,

Cette race pleine d'horreur,
J'en suis cependant, ô douleur!

––––––––––

LASSITUDE

O rêves de mes jours, ô travail de mes nuits,
Occulte pouvoir qui me mène,
Quelquefois, je sens que je suis
Une étonnante force humaine.

Ainsi qu'un austère devoir
Je pousse plus avant mon intime science.
Seule avec mon travail, je suis la conscience
D'autrui, qui ne sait pas sentir, entendre et voir.

Mais je fléchis parfois sous le poids de cette âme,
    Mes mains repoussent l'inconnu,
Et je voudrais alors n'être rien qu'une femme
Qui vit sa vie, et meurt quand le temps est venu.

But when our heart coos no more tenderness,
What reason is there for spring's transformation?
    Perhaps this is our consolation:
You, Joy, are Joy for others nonetheless.

Les sept douleurs d'octobre, "Mai, joli mai!"

HUMILIATION

So vile, this foully stinking race,
That only dogs will give it chase;

Scourge that destroys, monster forever
Marching in blood, whithersoever;

Failed ape, vast store of rot incessant,
Nature's scurf, leprous spawn putrescent;

This loathsome race! Yes, I admit—
O woe!—that I am part of it!

Les sept douleurs d'octobre, "De la vie à la mort"

LASSITUDE

O days' dreams and nights' labor, mystery
Of obscure power that leads me on,
At times I feel myself to be
Some natural phenomenon.

I ply my skill as though I fear
It were a duty, harsh, within me; and
I play the lonely conscience, work in hand,
Of those who neither feel, nor see, nor hear.

But now and then I bow to my soul's weight,
*   My hands spurn the unknown, and I
Would be the woman who accepts her fate:
Merely to live, and, when time comes, to die.

Les sept douleurs d'octobre, "L'Angoisse"

* I preserve the author's disposition of lines, curious though it is, since her previous
short lines (2, 3, 4, and 5) are not indented, as one might expect them to be.

Lucie Delarue-Mardrus 813

MON CHIEN

Mon berger jaune et noir, tranché comme un drapeau,
    Environne ma bicyclette,
    Et sa vigilance inquiète
    Garde un invisible troupeau.

Je vais. Il court devant et s'en revient bien vite,
    Car je suis pour lui ses moutons.
    Et, chaque fois que nous sortons,
    Son humeur joyeuse, m'invite.

"Viens! Viens!... La vie est bonne et tentant le chemin.
    Mon cœur bat! Comme je m'amuse!
    Je t'aime! Fidèle et sans ruse,
    Toute ma vie est dans ta main!"

Il repart au galop jusqu'au bout de sa zone;
    Et moi je me sens le cœur gai,
    Malgré mon rêve fatigué,
    Rien qu'à voir son derrière jaune.

KIKI

Mon chat si beau qui me méprise,
Ne m'accordant que de le voir,
Porte des fleurs de velours noir
Parmi sa douce couleur grise.

Les dessins persans du tapis
Sont moins compliqués que ses taches
Quand il s'étend, les pattes lâches,
Avec des regards assoupis.

* My shepherd—black, gold—like striped flag, goes leaping
    About my bicycle; and there,
    With vigilant and restless air,
    On flock unseen his watch is keeping.

I pedal... Off he runs, thither and yon,
    Comes dashing back... For him, no doubt,
    I am his sheep. When we go out,
    In joyous mood he prods me on.

"Come! Life is good! My heart pounds... The road stands
    Beckoning... Ah! The joys thereof!
    Faithful am I, and true my love...
    My very life lies in your hands."

Once again off he flies, though disinclined
    To cross his bounds. And I, despite
    Worn dreams, am heart-cheered at the sight—
†   Delightful—of his gold behind.

Les sept douleurs d'octobre, "Bonheurs"

KIKI

My lovely cat, scornful, remote,
Whom my affections importune,
Wears blossoms of black velvet, strewn
Over his soft gray-shaded coat.

My Persian rug's complex design
Is less so than his spots when he,
Paws spread, stretches out languidly
With looks of lassitude benign.

---

* I chose not to insult the reader's intelligence by translating *berger* as "sheep dog," assuming it would not be thought that the rump-revealing "shepherd" referred to was human rather than animal.

† The last line, as anti-climactic in French as it is in English, is a pleasant example of Delarue-Mardrus's occasional drollery.

Lucie Delarue-Mardrus 815

O merveille de son pelage
Conçu par un pinceau chinois!
O féroce et câlin minois
Rayé d'un si fin tatouage!

Frère nain des tigres royaux,
Beauté familière et féline,
Voici ses prunelles, joyaux,
Son nez, cachet de cornaline.

Petit sphinx qui rêve au néant,
Je le contemple et je l'envie
Quand ses yeux couleur d'océan
Regardent plus loin que la vie,

Car je sais qu'à ces instants-là
Ce chat, fantastique chimère,
Ne songe pas à l'au-delà,
Mais, égoïstement, digère.

———————

COUP D'ŒIL

Il sort de l'estuaire un grand nuage fou.
    Le vent le pousse on ne sait où.
    Il semble plus grand que la ville.

Son ombre gigantesque au loin dessine une île
    Sur l'eau mourant dans les pâleurs
    Parmi le couchant en couleurs.

Cette création soudaine de l'espace
    Qui paraît un moment et passe
    Enchante si bien mon esprit

Que tandis qu'à pas lents je vais, ma bouche rit
    A cause de la belle image
    Que font l'eau, l'ombre et le nuage.

How splendid-furred, this wondrous beast,
Art of a Chinese brush! Those kitty
Features—conniving, fierce, but pretty—
Striped by some fine tattoo artiste!

Tiger-prince kin in miniature,
Homey his feline grace! Ah yes,
His pupils, jewels; his nose, a pure
Gem of carnelian loveliness!

Little sphinx deep in reveries,
I envy him to see him so,
When his eyes, color of the seas,
Seem lost past life; because I know

That surely he, at times like this—
Chimera-cat, as he lies resting—
Muses not on the vast abyss,
But, self-absorbed, is just digesting.

Les sept douleurs d'octobre, "Bonheurs"

————————

GLIMPSE

A great wild cloud comes from the bay, blown where
    The wind's whim wishes, and bids fair
    To look still bigger than the town.

It joins the sun's hues, dying, sinking down,
    Over the graying waters, while
    It casts a giant shadow-isle.

This nonce-created figure forms, moves on,
    Lasts for a moment, and is gone,
    Charming so much my mind and soul

That I break into laughter as I stroll,
    Thanks to the lovely image made,
    Briefly, by water, cloud, and shade.

Les sept douleurs d'octobre, "Bonheurs"

* The carnelian (or cornelian), rather as abstruse in English as its French equivalent, is a reddish variety of chalcedony.

Lucie Delarue-Mardrus 817

Six modernes dans la forêt
Vont, sur leurs douze jambes roses,
S'asseoir en différentes poses.

Six Princes Charmants, on dirait,
Devisant sous les hêtres-fées,
Car, en robes d'un ton de fleur,
Cheveux courts, têtes bien coiffées,
Elles ont la tendre couleur
Qu'on voit dans les belles histoires.

Il tombe, au soleil, des nuits noires
Sous les troncs argentés et droits
Laissant la Seine, en bleu, paraître.

Et, quand le couchant, mis en croix,
Jette du sang sur chaque hêtre,
Les six Princes Charmants, peureux,
S'en vont en fraîche ribambelle,
Retournant, prudents, deux à deux,
Vers le klakson qui les appelle.

OUTING

Six modish personalities—
Twelve-legs—go to the forest, sit,
Pink-fleshed, in poses favorite.

One would say six Prince Charmings, these,
Tattling under the fairy-beeches;
For, in the bloom-hues of their dress,
With hair cropped close, chic-hatted, each's
Colors boast that soft tenderness
One finds in pretty storybooks.

Sun turns to shadow as their nook's
Silver shafts let the eventide
Reveal the Seine, a darkening blue.

And, when the sunset, crucified,
Bleeds on each tree, then, two by two,
Grown circumspect, our six Prince Charmings,
Flurrying off again—nor hem
Nor haw—resume their arm-in-armings
* Back to the auto summoning them.

Les sept douleurs d'octobre, "Bonheurs"

* The gender of these caricatures is, perhaps intentionally, ambiguous. Is the poet poking fun at effete, effeminately dressed, effeminately acting males? Or, with her typical self-mockery, is she twitting her mannish, "Prince Charming" sisters-under-the-skin? A case can be made for either interpretation, I think.

Lucie Delarue-Mardrus 819

Gérard d'Houville (pseud.) (1875–1963)

Daughter of one poet, wife of another, and mistress to several more, Gérard d'Houville was—and, by those who know her work, is—considered one of the most gifted of the bevy of women writers that her age produced. No less appreciated today than during her life, this "Muse de la Belle Epoque" was posthumously honored most recently with a fourteen-week exposition at the Bibliothèque de l'Arsenal in Paris (February 13 to May 23, 2004). Her early novels had attracted a good deal of attention and even notoriety—not a little blue-nosed concern, in fact, thanks to their subjects of less than scrupulous morality. Her first, *L'inconstante* (1903), was only one in a lengthy series of works marked by plots of an almost savage energy and a style that, although often brutal, was always elegantly rendered. One of them, *Jeune fille* (1919), won for her the prize for literature and poetry of the Académie française.

Born in 1875, this daughter of the expatriate Cuban poet José-María de Heredia, a disciple of the Parnassian school of French verse, was the wife of the poet Henri de Régnier, and it was first under the name "Marie de Régnier" that she published. With the success of her first novels, her fear of accusations of literary nepotism no doubt prompted her to choose a pseudonym. She found a fashionably masculine one by slightly altering the name of a distant aristocratic Norman ancestor, Girard d'Ouville, and it was as Gérard d'Houville that she soon achieved celebrity. Not only as a controversial novelist, but, from time to time, as a poet as well, brought up "on the lap of a father who chased after his rhymes through the thousand tasks of daily life, spending six months, if need be, to perfect a magnificent sonnet."[1]

As early as 1910, the critic Jean de Gourmont singled her out among the many women poets of the day with the opinion that "no woman handles the French language, in the act of writing, with a greater suppleness." Going so far as to compare her aesthetic to Mallarmé's, he praised the artistry with which she "suggests, rather than describes"—like her symbolist colleagues—and appreciated the aristocratic dignity of her verse, a relief from the "shameless and at times vulgar shrieks of other poetesses" (whom he tactfully declined to name).[2] Other observers—Charles Maurras, not the least prominent among them, and not the most sympathetic to women poets—would point out, in her later work, the classical affinities of her inspiration as well as the picturesque echoes of her Antillean heritage.[3] Others would also suggest the influence of Mallarmé on her strong yet supple versification.

Many of Gérard d'Houville's (or Marie de Régnier's) poems were originally published semi-anonymously—three discreet asterisks replacing her name—in the *Revue des Deux Mondes*. Two collections (*Clowns* and *Vingt poèmes*) appeared in 1925, with a comprehensive volume, *Les poésies de Gérard d'Houville*, in 1931, and, fifteen years later, the little-known *Enfantines et amoureuses*. Six years before her death in 1963, she received the Grand Prix des Poètes français, though, typically modest, she refused the accompanying decoration. Her poetic production, however, was less extensive and less studied than her novels, which would seem to have been a more colorful reflection of her own amorous involvements with two lovers: the *décadent* novelist Pierre Louÿs (whom some sources claim to have been her brother-in-law) and, from 1914 to 1921, the flamboyant Italian author Gabriele d'Annunzio. And that, despite vague suggestions of lesbianism, encouraged by her artistic association with openly lesbian colleagues. Perhaps it was her own passionate adventures that prompted her to pen *La vie amoureuse de l'impératrice Joséphine* (1927) and *La vie amoureuse de la Belle Hélène* (1928).[4]

Of the eighty-nine flawlessly crafted lyrics in *Les poésies*, evidence of the Parnassian ideal inherited from her father, the ten I present in translation offer a necessarily limited view of Gérard d'Houville's majestic and much too neglected *œuvre*.

NOTES

1. See Paul Flat, *Nos femmes de lettres,* p. 105.

2. Cited in Jean de Gourmont, *Muses d'aujourd'hui,* pp. 51–53.

3. See the section devoted to her work in Maurras's *L'avenir de l'intelligence* (1904), reprinted in *Romantisme et révolution,* pp. 148–57.

4. For a few of the early biographical details readily available, see Flat, *Nos femmes de lettres,* pp. 102–39, which devotes most of its comments, however, to one of her early novels, *Esclave*. For more interpretive detail, as regards her poetry, see also Catherine Perry, "Celles par qui le scandale arrive: Ethique de l'innocence chez Gérard d'Houville et Anna de Noailles," in *Le mal dans l'imaginaire littéraire français,* ed. Metka Zupancic and Myriam Watthée-Delmotte, pp. 275–89.

CENDRE

Tu t'arrêtes devant la tombe parfumée
Où tout ce qui fut moi gît sous une herbe en fleur,
Et, lisant ces seuls mots, ô jeune voyageur:
"Nulle femme ne fut plus longuement aimée,"
L'âpre et vivant désir gonfle et remplit ton cœur
Du rêve de ma chair, hélas! inanimée.

Mon cher miroir, qui meurt de n'avoir reflété
Que l'ombre où j'ai voulu près de moi le suspendre,
Mon miroir revivrait, si tu pouvais le tendre
Au jour pur, et rirait de toute sa clarté;
Mais tu n'y verrais pas ma grâce triste et tendre;
Jamais tu ne sauras ce que fut ma beauté.

La cendre de mon corps que consume la terre
En d'ardentes saisons me refleurit au jour;
Cueille une de ces fleurs au prix de ton détour,
Et passe... car, berçant mon sommeil solitaire,
J'entends, dans le refrain que murmure l'Amour,
Le regret éternel de ma forme éphémère.

PETITE MORTE

Sur ton sein ténébreux, enfant triste endormie,
O Terre! je repose, et serre entre mes bras
La poupée aux yeux peints qui fut ma seule amie
Et qui sait mes secrets, qu'elle ne dira pas.

Si petite, j'étais si pensive et si sage
Que je tins peu de place, et je fis peu de bruit;
Je négligeais la joie et les jeux de mon âge
Et songeais à la mort lorsque venait la nuit.

Je n'étais pas encor femme quand je suis morte;
C'est pourquoi mon tombeau, étroit comme mon lit,
N'enferme ni parfums, ni fards d'aucune sorte,
Ni mon premier miroir d'acier pâle et poli.

ASHES

You pause before the fragrant grave where lies
All that was me, beneath the flowering grass;
And, seeing these words, young traveler, as you pass:
"No woman was loved longer," your dreams rise—
Living dreams for my lifeless flesh, alas!—
Swell, fill your heart, aching in lustful wise.

My mirror, dying—now dull, reflectionless,
Save for the shades it hangs in, next to me—
My mirror would spring to life and laugh to see
You hold it to the day's pure light. Ah, yes...
But no, my wistful grace unseen must be,
And never will you know my loveliness.

My body's ashes, to the earth returning,
Bloom me anew in burning heat of day;
Take a flower for your pains, then go your way...
Lulled, in eternal, lonely sleep sojourning,
I hear Love sigh its unrequited lay:
Fleeting my form, but endless is the yearning.

DEAD DEMOISELLE

O Earth! Here, in your shadowed breast, so lonely
And sad, I lie at rest, young demoiselle,
Clutching my doll with painted eyes, my only
Friend, who knows all my secrets, but won't tell.

I didn't take much room or make much noise—
So small and quiet, so well-behaved was I;
I had no use for childhood toys and joys,
And thought of death whenever night came by.

I wasn't yet a woman when I died;
That's why I don't keep in my bedlike tomb's
Scant space, my mirror, long kept by my side—
Pale polished steel—or powders, or perfumes.

J'ai voulu, loin de l'ombre et des funèbres marbres,
Suspendre ce miroir dans les bois que j'aimais;
Il s'y balance ainsi qu'un fruit clair dans les arbres
Bien haut, pour que nuls doigts ne l'y cueillent jamais.

Et qu'il puisse, parmi les bouleaux et les saules,
Voir l'astre féminin s'arrondir lentement,
Puisque entre mes cheveux flottant sur mes épaules
Mon miroir n'a pas vu croître mon sein charmant.

———————

LE POTIER

Aujourd'hui je suis triste. Ecoute, ô cher potier,
Je t'apporte le don de mon corps tout entier,
Si tu veux avec art, dans ta durable argile,
Peut-être, éterniser une forme fragile.
Dans une terre rose et semblable à ma chair,
Modèle le contour de mon bien le plus cher:
Mes petits seins égaux aux deux pointes aiguës.
Qu'il reste au moins cela des grâces ingénues
Que j'offre à ton désir, si de chaque côté
De l'amphore funèbre où toute ma beauté
Doit dormir, poudre éparse et cendre inerte et grise,
Au lieu de l'anse, creuse à la main qui l'a prise,
Tu renfles la rondeur de ce double contour
Presque enfantin et prêt à peine pour l'amour.
...Et celui qui, pensif, sous le sol séculaire,
Trouvera quelque jour mon urne funéraire,
Saura que je fus femme, et femme tendrement,
Amoureuse et malicieuse par moment,
Et se demandera devant la terre sombre
Pourquoi tant de clarté dut naître pour tant d'ombre.

Far from death's gloomy graveyard stones, I chose
To hang that mirror in the woods I love;
It sways, high, like a bright fruit, safe from those
Hands that would pluck it from the boughs above.

Midst birch and willow, let it watch as she—
The woman-moon—slowly grows rounder; for,
Through my long locks it never got to see
My bosom swelling, lovely, more and more.

THE POTTER

How sad I am today! Friend potter, I
Give you my being entire, if, by and by,
You should desire, with all your skill and art,
In your clay, firm and changeless, to impart
A lasting life to fragile form. I pray
That, in an earth pink as my flesh, you may
Model the shape of what I prize the most:
My small breasts—small, but well-matched, and that boast
Two pointed tips... Let that remain, at least—
Last of the simple graces that, deceased,
I offer to your lust—if, on each side
Of death's amphora, wherein, rarefied
Into a gray and lifeless powder, ashen,
My beauty must repose, your craft might fashion,
Rather than handles concave to the hand,
Two shapes, round, swelling, almost childlike, and
Not ready quite for love... And he, perchance
A century hence, who finds my urn, will glance
Pensively on it, and will realize
That I a woman was, and, woman-wise,
Tenderly loved, although now and again
A trifle impishly; and, musing then
Upon the somber earth, will wonder why
Such light was born only in dark to die.

LE VERGER DE L'AURORE

L'espoir qui plane encore au fond du ciel vernal,
De son vol immortel frôle les fronts moroses
Et fait tinter l'or clair du rire matinal
Dans l'éblouissement des rayons et des roses;
Des arbres printaniers ne vois-tu pas neiger
En l'herbe haute les pétales blancs et roses?
Sens-tu dans tes cheveux frémir le vent léger
Imprégné de l'ivresse unanime des choses,
Et l'heure resplendir dans l'auroral verger?

Le hautbois chante au loin un chant irrésistible
Et tendre, qu'il alterne ou confond tour à tour
Avec les sons vibrant sous l'archet invisible,
Voluptueux et long, des violes d'amour;
Dans l'air harmonieux passent en vols de rêve
Les ramiers roucoulants dont voici le retour.
Savoure la douceur de l'instant qui s'achève,
L'allégresse infinie et l'extase du jour;
L'heure délicieuse est l'heure qu'on sait brève.

Les lumineux parfums, les odorants rayons
Montent vers le ciel rose où vibre leur lumière
Dans un palpitement d'ailes de papillons.
Sois la divine sœur de la rose trémière!
Fais rire aux gais échos tes rires puérils,
Et loin de la tristesse à ton cœur coutumière
Laisse, oublieuse enfin de ses futurs périls,
S'ouvrir comme une fleur ton âme printanière,
Et refleurir en toi tous les anciens avrils.

LE VENT PLUS TRISTE

Le vent plus triste encor de défleurir les tombes,
A dispersé le vol des candides colombes
Dont l'essor tournoyant n'argente plus l'azur.
Comme la nuit fut longue! et que l'air fut obscur
Sans le palpitement des invisibles ailes!
Comme mon jeune cœur se sentit seul sans elles!
Ah! sur les grands rosiers du jardin matinal,

DAWN'S ORCHARD

Hope, hovering still in vernal skies, soars after
Our somber brows, grazed in its deathless flight,
Its golden bells pealing their morning laughter
In dazzling flash of roses and of light;
Can you not see the springtime trees strew on
The reeds their snowflake petals, pink and white?
Do you not feel the fluttering breeze upon
Your hair, drunk with life's oneness, and the bright
Hour, in its splendor, of this orchard-dawn?

Distant, the oboe's soft, resistless song
Blends with the notes drawn by an unseen bow
From viola d'amores' low sighs—long,
Voluptuous—in quivering tremolo.
Borne on the air's pure harmonies, upcast,
Dream-flights of ringdoves, cooing, come and go.
Savor this instant, precious, all but past,
Infinite joy, morning's ecstatic glow:
Sweetest, the hour we know must end too fast.

Light's lush perfumes and fragrant-scented rays
Rise to the pink skies, trembling, flickering
On wings of butterflies, flecking the haze.
Sister to heavenly hollyhock, let ring
Gay echoes of your childlike laughter through
The air, heedless of perils time will bring;
To your heart's melancholy bid adieu:
Opening, like a flower, your soul's fair spring,
Let bloom your bygone Aprils' days anew.

THE CHEERLESS WIND

The cheerless wind, sad to have cast astray,
Scattered, the graveyard flowers, has borne away
As well the pure white doves, whose wheeling flight
Silvers the blue no more. How long the night!
And I, young and alone! How dour the air
Without their unseen wings, fluttering there,
Aloft! Ah! shall I see again, at dawn,

Reverrai-je posé leur blanc vol virginal?
De mon âme d'enfant les trop mornes pensées
Seront-elles par l'aube à jamais effacées,
Et d'avoir effleuré les fleurs d'un heureux jour
Le vent sera-t-il pur tel qu'un parfum d'amour?
Doux oiseaux de jadis, reviendrez-vous encore?...
Mais je vois dans le ciel empourpré par l'aurore,
Au lieu du cher retour de mes légers espoirs,
Planer, assombrissant les fleurs, des cygnes noirs.

_____

REFUS

Va, pars! Je ne veux rien du bonheur vil des hommes.
Qu'ai-je besoin d'avoir un enclos plein de pommes,
Sous des mains pleines d'or, un cœur plein de souci,
D'inutiles désirs et de colère aussi,
Un front barré d'orgueil, un esprit lourd d'envie?
Pourquoi? N'ai-je donc pas à moi toute la vie
Et le soleil et l'ombre avec la terre et l'eau?
Mon corps n'est-il pas jeune et mon visage beau?
N'ai-je pas tout l'amour et toute la jeunesse?
Pourquoi me parles-tu de gloire et de richesse?
Les heures en collier orneront ma beauté,
Ainsi que les saisons, de leur diversité,
Changent à l'infini la parure du monde.
Pars seul. Ecoute en toi l'ambition qui gronde.
Travaille, lutte et crie, et crois-toi libre et fort,
Sans regarder la vie et sans croire à la mort.
Cours, vers l'espoir humain des chances incertaines!
...Moi, je verrai le soir assombrir les fontaines
Avec des yeux emplis de sagesse et d'amour;
J'accueillerai la nuit sans regretter le jour,
Etant sûre d'avoir toujours toutes les choses
Dans ma tombe allongée, où fleuriront les roses.

The virgin whiteness of their flight perch on
The roses in the garden? Will the drear
Thoughts of my childhood soul fade, disappear,
Ever erased by breaking day; and will
The wind that stripped fair daylight's petals fill
The air above with fragrance, pure as love's
Redolent scent? And you, yesterday's doves?
Sweet birds, will you return?... Ah! In the sky,
Crimsoned, I see soaring toward me, not my
Gentle and air-borne hopes, come winging back,
But, shading dark the flowers, great swans of black.

———————

REFUSAL

Leave me alone! Men's wretched happiness
Is not for me! Do I need to possess
An orchard full of fruit, hands full of gold,
A heart full of distress, desires untold
Of little worth, anger as well, a brow
Furrowed with pride, an envious soul? Come now!
Why? Have I not my life ahead of me,
With earth and water, sun and shadow? See?
Have I not love, youth, beauty? Must you chatter
On about wealth and glory? Do they matter?
Just as the changing seasons decorate
The world's variety, the hours—ornate
Necklace—will set my loveliness aglow.
So leave! Heed your growling ambition! Go,
Alone! Slave, struggle, howl, as though you were
The mighty master of your fate, monsieur,
Without a glance at life, without a thought
Of death! Run toward man's hopes of fortune, fraught
With their uncertainties!... Meanwhile, my eyes
Will watch, brimming with love and worldly-wise,
As evening shades the fountains; I shall call
On night, with no regrets for day at all,
Sure to be put to rest with everything
Laid in my grave, and roses blossoming.

LES LIS

Un pétale est tombé comme l'aile d'un ange...
C'est qu'un bouquet de lis s'effeuille en l'ombre étrange
Où tout semble rempli d'un deuil qu'on ne sait pas.
Que dois-tu donc pleurer, en silence, tout bas,
Dis, ou de quelle horreur pressens-tu le prélude?
Le savez-vous, lis blancs et verts, lis des Bermudes,
Lis royaux, qui venez de si loin pour la voir
Rêver sinistrement aux approches du soir?
Un long pétale blanc, comme une larme nue
Coule encor. Le parfum s'exalte et s'exténue;
Quelque chose de pur, ici défaille et meurt...
Est-ce ton âme, ô femme? est-ce ton rêve, ô fleur?

LA PRIÈRE

Pareille aux formes que l'on voit sur les verrières,
Les mains étroitement rejointes, la Prière,
Longue et haute, plongeur inverse, pur élan
D'esprit insexué vers ce gouffre de grâce,
L'élément violet de son nouvel espace
Où déjà sa ferveur la soutient en tremblant,
Hésite, monte, souffre, en l'ombre d'améthyste;
Elle s'égare et pleure, inconsolable et triste,
Car l'ange encore humain ne connaît pas son ciel...
Quand, perdu dans l'espoir des choses étoilées,
Soudain, s'ouvrent en lui des puissances ailées,
Qui divisent son être, et le font immortel.

THE LILIES

A petal fell, light as an angel's wing...
Lilies there were, windblown, unraveling
In shadow, strange, filled with some unknown mourning.
What do you weep for? Why those tears a-borning
In silent sobs? What horror unforeseen
Can you foretell? You, lilies white, and green,
Bermuda lilies, royal lilies? You
Who come so far to keep this rendezvous,
To watch her dreaming dolefully, as night
Slowly descends?... A petal, long and white,
Flutters still, dripping like a naked tear.
Its heady scent soars, flags, and fades; and here,
Now, something pure grows weak, dies, it would seem...
Woman, is it your soul? Flower, your dream?

PRAYER

Hands joined, held high, long, palm to palm, like those
Figures one sees outlined in stained-glass pose...
Diver poised skyward, spirit free of lust,
Ready to bound in pure and sexless thrust
Up to the vast abyss of grace: sky's blue
Element, heavenly space, crimsoned anew,
Where fervor nourishes it, quivering... Prayer,
Pained, hesitates; then, rising, rends the air,
Into the purpled shade. Losing its way,
It weeps in bitter, unconsoled dismay;
For, human still, the angel casts his eye
Over his strangely unfamiliar sky...
When, lost in star-graced hope, his staunch wings splay—
Outspread—his being, divided now, and he
Stands forth in sudden immortality.

Gérard d'Houville 831

LE PUITS

Je voudrais me pencher sur le vieux puits, qui songe
Là-bas, au coin du clos où saignent les mûriers,
Et revoir, dans sa nuit où la fougère plonge,
Mes rêves d'autrefois, de moi-même oubliés.

Je voudrais me pencher sur la margelle rousse,
Désaltérer mon âme à mon passé dormant,
Et, parmi les reflets des plantes et des mousses,
Tout au fond du miroir, rire à mes yeux d'enfant.

Je voudrais, je voudrais... ô bonheur! ô détresse!
Boire le philtre vert du vieux puits enchanté,
Et grâce à lui revivre un jour de ma jeunesse,
Tout un jour d'innocence et de limpidité.

ÉPITAPHE

Je veux dormir au fond des bois, pour que le vent
Fasse parfois frémir le feuillage mouvant
Et l'agite dans l'air comme une chevelure
Au-dessus de ma tombe, et selon l'heure obscure
Ou claire, l'ombre des feuilles avec le jour
Y tracera, légère et noire, et tour à tour,
En mots mystérieux, arabesque suprême,
Une épitaphe aussi changeante que moi-même.

I would look down the old well dreaming there,
Beside the blood-red mulberries, and peer
Into its fern-reflecting blackness; stare
At my forgotten dreams of yesteryear.

I would look down over its rim, rust-red,
And quench my thirsting soul where my past lies,
Deep in the mirror's moss and weeds outspread,
Laughing with joy to see with my child-eyes.

I would, I would—O happiness! O woe!—
Drink of the charmed old well's green potion, whence
I might relive one day of childhood! Oh,
One day of purity, of innocence.

EPITAPH

I want to sleep deep in the forest, where
The wind will shake the leaves, like locks of hair,
Trembling, stirring the air above my tomb,
And where, in bright day or in twilight gloom,
Leaf-shadows, with a wisp of light, will trace,
Weightless and black, here, there, like a fine lace
Of obscure words—arabesque filigree—
An epitaph in constant change, like me.

Anna de Noailles (1876–1933)

A poet of undeniable stature, whose reputation has lasted beyond the popu-
larity of her actual works, the comtesse Anna de Noailles was respected, fêted,
and beloved by fin-de-siècle France's literary and lay population alike, count-
ing among her admirers such figures as Proust, Cocteau, Colette, Sarah Bern-
hardt... Even her lifelong friend, the writer-statesman Maurice Barrès, whose
anti-Dreyfus views in the *affaire* that divided France ran counter to her own en-
lightened sentiments. Her official honors included the Grand Prix de Littérature
of the Académie française in 1921, election to the Royal Belgian Academy the
following year—the first woman to be so honored—and the most prestigious
Légion d'honneur in 1930, of which she was, likewise, the first of her sex to be
promoted to the rank of commander.

Seemingly unconcerned with the tenets of this or that poetic school, she
tuned the traditional elements of French prosody to her personal lyrical use,
refusing however to be straitjacketed by their limitations. Without abandoning
its meters and rhymes, she was not against taking liberties with both when the
flow of her inspiration demanded; an inspiration often lush and musical, often
visual, now synesthetically sensual and even erotic, as much at home in evok-
ing the eternal as in rhapsodizing briefly on the Parnassian plasticity of her cat.
Even when, in her later poems, her subjects were the heaviest—preoccupied
as she was with thoughts of death and the nothingness that she was convinced
must ensue—still, her poetic touch remained light and dextrous. Some saw in
this delicacy of style a characteristic trait of the female poet. But Noailles's tech-
nique and talent transcended her gender. When an article in the London *Times,*
in 1913, called her "the greatest poet that the twentieth century has produced in
France—perhaps in Europe,"[1] and when the poet Léon-Paul Fargue supposedly
referred to her as "our last inspired poet," neither saw fit to modify the word
"poet" with the word "woman."

An exotically connected princess by birth, Anna-Elizabeth Bassaraba de
Brancovan was born in Paris on November 15, 1876, to a Romanian father—the
prince Grégoire Bibesco de Brancovan, whose death in 1885 would affect her
deeply—and a mother from an old Greek family, daughter of Musurus Pasha,
one-time Turkish ambassador to London. Surrounded by artists of every stripe
in her mother's salon, she was an avid reader of poetry and writer of her own
from early childhood. Her last volume, posthumously published in 1934 as *Der-
niers vers,* contains nine of her *poèmes d'enfance* (childhood poems), neatly clos-
ing the poetic circle of her life, and about which she had herself confided in her
memoirs, *Le livre de ma vie:* "Even then I knew what I was to become."[2]

In 1897, the princess married Comte Mathieu de Noailles, producing, first, a son, three years later, and then her first collection of poetry, *Le cœur innombrable* (1901). The son would be one of two children, but the volume, received with great admiration and recognized by the Académie française, was followed over the years by over a dozen more, interrupted only by World War I. The success of her poetry, and of three rather racy novels as well, continued despite the dissonant voices of a few dyspeptic critics (Henri Clouard and Charles Maurras especially), as did her active involvement in the salon society of the day. It was only failing health—tangible reason, as it were, for her poetry's increasing preoccupation with suffering and death—that put an end to both. She died on April 30, 1933, and was accorded a state funeral celebrated at the church of La Madeleine, for more than ten thousand devoted mourners.[3]

My twenty-four translations represent eight of Anna de Noailles's many impressive collections.

NOTES

1. Quoted in Tama Lea Engelking's detailed entry on the poet in *French Women Writers*, p. 335.

2. Cited, from her memoirs, in the preface to the 1934 republication of *Derniers vers et poèmes d'enfance*, p. 13. *Derniers vers* had been published by itself the preceding year, and *Poèmes d'enfance* had originally appeared in 1927.

3. As one would expect, there is no lack of factual and critical study of Noailles's work. For bio-bibliographical detail, the most concise source is Engelking's essay, cited in n. 1 above. See also the poet's *Le livre de ma vie* (1932) for details up to her adolescence. A listing of her principal poetry collections can be found in Jeanine Moulin, *La poésie féminine*, 2: 107, and even before her death, Jean Larnac had compiled a compendious volume of critical works: *La comtesse de Noailles: Ssa vie, son œuvre*. Among later studies one can consult the following: Edmée de La Rochefoucauld, *Anna de Noailles* (a 1976 reprint, honoring the centenary of her birth, of a 1956 publication); Louis de Perche, *Anna de Noailles*; the largely archival volume by Claude Mignot-Ogliastri: *Anna de Noailles: Une amie de la princesse Edmond de Polignac*; Elisabeth Higonnet-Dugua's voluminous biography, *Anna de Noailles, cœur innombrable*; and three recent studies by Catherine Perry: "Celles par qui le scandale arrive..." pp. 275–89, (see p. 821n4); *Persephone Unbound: Dionysian Aesthetics in the Works of Anna de Noailles*; and her study in *Dictionary of Literary Biography*, vol. 258: *Modern French Poets*, pp. 297–310, not to mention a profusion of specialized articles in numerous French and international publications.

Il fera longtemps clair ce soir, les jours allongent,
La rumeur du jour vif se disperse et s'enfuit,
Et les arbres, surpris de ne pas voir la nuit,
Demeurent éveillés dans le soir blanc, et songent...

Les marronniers, sur l'air plein d'or et de lourdeur,
Répandent leurs parfums et semblent les étendre;
On n'ose pas marcher ni remuer l'air tendre
De peur de déranger le sommeil des odeurs.

De lointains roulements arrivent de la ville...
La poussière, qu'un peu de brise soulevait,
Quittant l'arbre mouvant et las qu'elle revêt,
Redescend doucement sur les chemins tranquilles.

Nous avons tous les jours l'habitude de voir
Cette route si simple et si souvent suivie,
Et pourtant quelque chose est changé dans la vie,
Nous n'aurons plus jamais notre âme de ce soir...

CHANSON DU TEMPS OPPORTUN

Le Temps, de ses pipeaux, tire de clairs accords:
Bondissez au soleil, les âmes et les corps;

Par les chemins poudreux et la verdure épaisse
Epuisez les plaisirs, c'est la seule sagesse;

Prenez-vous, quittez-vous, cherchez-vous tour à tour,
Il n'est rien de réel que le rêve et l'amour.

Sur la terre indigente où tant d'ombre s'éploie
Ayez souci d'un peu de justice et de joie;

Retenez, du savoir, ce qu'il faut au bonheur;
On est assez profond pour le jour où l'on meurt.

Vivez; ayez l'amour, la colère et l'envie,
Pauvres êtres vivants, il n'est rien que la vie!

The days grow long: this evening's light will gleam
Into the shade; day's murmur flitters, flees...
Wakeful, beneath a pallid sky, the trees
Wonder what has become of night, and dream...

The chestnuts strew their scents, heavy and deep,
Over the evening's golden breath; we dare
Not take a step, nor stir the tender air,
Lest we arouse the perfumes from their sleep.

The echoes rumble from the far-off town;
A weary tree shakes loose its cloak of dust,
That rises, wafted on a gentle gust,
Over the tranquil paths, and settles down.

Daily we saw this road laid out before
Our eyes, traveled its calm simplicity;
But life, tonight, is changed somehow, and we
Have lost this evening's soul forevermore...

Le cœur innombrable

SONG OF THE PROPER TIME

Time pipes its chords: and you, bodies and souls,
Leap, in the sun, your lusty caprioles!

On dusty path, in verdure lush and dense,
Wring delights dry: life has no other sense;

Take lovers, leave them, look for more thereof:
Nothing in life is real but dreams and love.

In poor earth's shadows, spread in ample measure,
Seek out a bit of justice and of pleasure.

Learn only joy's demands; for, by and by,
Wise enough will we be the day we die.

Live! Keep your love, your wrath, your eagerness,
Poor humans: life is all that you possess!

Le cœur innombrable

Anna de Noailles 837

LA QUERELLE

Va-t'en, je ne veux plus regarder ton regard,
Voir tes yeux plus lointains et plus doux que la nue,
Ta joue où les rayons du jour d'or sont épars,
Ta bouche qui sourit et qui ment, ta main nue...

Va-t'en, éloigne-toi de mon désir ce soir,
Tout de toi me ravit, m'irrite et me tourmente.
Loin de tes bras, trompeurs et chers, je vais m'asseoir
Dans la plaine assoupie où se bercent les menthes.

Et là, oubliant tout du mal que tu me fais,
J'entendrai, les yeux clos, l'esprit las, le cœur sage,
Sous les hêtres d'argent pleins d'ombre et de reflets,
La respiration paisible du feuillage...

LA POURSUITE

Les cœurs voudraient bien se connaître,
Mais l'Amour danse entre les êtres,
Il va de l'une à l'autre attente
Et, comme le vent fait aux plantes,
Il mêle les douces essences;
Mais les âmes qui se distancent
Sont plus rapides dans leur course
Que l'air, le parfum et la source
Et cherchent en vain à se prendre.
L'amour n'est ni joyeux ni tendre...

Vous que jamais rien ne délie,
O ma pauvre âme dans mon corps,
Pourrez-vous, ma mélancolie,
Ayant bu le vin et la lie,
Connaître la bonne folie
De l'éternel repos des morts?

THE QUARREL

Go! I no longer want to see that glance
You glance at me, softer than cloud-mist, and
More distant; or your cheek, where sun's rays dance
Their gold; your mouth, false, smiling; or your hand...

Go! Flee my evening passion, let me be,
You who are all my bliss, ennui, and woe.
Far from your dear, deceiving arms, let me
Doze where the mint goes swaying, to and fro.

Forgetting all your hurtfulness, content
In silvered beeches' glinting shades, eyes closing,
I shall give ear, heart wise but spirit spent,
To the calm breathing of their leaves reposing...

L'ombre des jours

THE CHASE

Hearts yearn to know each other, yet
Love does its little minuet
Amongst them, now between, betwixt,
Full of its lush aromas, mixed,
As when the wind goes blowing on
The plants; but souls are quickly gone,
Fleeing, more rapid in their going
Than air, perfume, or river flowing:
Each would, in vain, its mate possess.
Love knows nor joy nor tenderness...

L'ombre des jours

O melancholic soul of mine!
Poor soul, ever a part of me,
Will you, once you have drunk the wine
Down to the dregs, seize the design
Of endless rest, folly benign:
Death, life's eternal destiny?

Anna de Noailles 839

—Vous si vivace et si profonde,
Ame de rêve et de transport,
Qui, pareille à la terre ronde
Portez tous les désirs du monde,
Buveuse de l'air et de l'onde,
Pourrez-vous entrer dans ce port?

Dans le port de calme sagesse,
De ténèbres et de sommeil,
Où ni l'amour ni la détresse
N'étirent la tiède paresse,
Et ne font,—mon âme faunesse,—
Siffler les flèches du soleil!...

———

JOUR D'ÉTÉ

Le matin lumineux semble une chaude neige,
Et luit comme un dessin qu'une vitre protège.
Nulle ombre ne ternit ce calme long, égal;
L'azur a l'éclat net et dur d'un minéral;
La verdure est d'un vert trop doux, plus doux encore...
A chaque arbre s'enroule une liquide aurore;
Un geai semble emporté vers la claire hauteur
Par la force et l'élan d'un battement de cœur!
Les fleurs, sur la pelouse où des agneaux vont paître,
Ont le rouge et le bleu d'une fête champêtre;
L'ombrage se déverse et fait de noirs étangs
Où l'insecte et l'oiseau se reposent, contents.
Douce diversité des feuilles et des lignes!
Sous les ormes luisants où s'agrafent les vignes
On croit voir s'élancer, au son du tympanon,
Les nymphes et les beaux garçons d'Anacréon!...
—O tendre flamboiement, l'immense gratitude
Pour tant de paix, de joie heureuse, d'altitude,

—You, sage so spry, so debonair,
O soul of bliss, of reverie,
Who all the weighty passions bear
Of earthly sphere; do you bid fair,
You, who glut, gorge on sea and air,
To enter that port willingly?

That port of wisdom's restfulness,
Of shades and sleep's oblivion,
Where neither love nor life's duress
Tug at the calm—mild, motionless—
Or—O my soul, my satyress!—
Cast whistling darts down from the sun!...

L'ombre des jours

SUMMER DAY

The morning glistens, like a warm snowshine,
And glitters like some glass-encased design.
No shadow dulls this long, smooth calm; a sheen
Glows on the azure, like a metal, clean
And hard; the foliage lies soft, too soft...
A liquid dawn surrounds each tree; aloft,
A jay seems swept up toward the sunlit height,
Borne on a heartbeat! In the meadows, bright,
Where sheep will graze, the blossoms, blue and red,
Look like a village fair; shadow-pools spread
Patches of darkness here and there, in which
Insect and bird, contented, find a niche,
To rest. Under the elms, where vines entwine—
Gentle diversity of leaf and line!—
* Dreaming, one sees Anacreon's nymphs, beaus,
Reveling in the timbrel's tremolos!...
—O blaze of tenderness, my limitless
Thanks for this peace, these heights of happiness

* In referring to the Greek lyric poet Anacreon (ca. 570–480 B.C.E.), the author most likely has in mind the love poems and drinking songs long incorrectly attributed to him, and to the imitations they inspired, since his own authenticated compositions are fragmentary and few in number.

S'agite dans mon cœur comme un flot triomphant,
Comme des rameaux clairs portés par des enfants!
Les coteaux, dans le ciel léger, s'évanouissent
A force de chaleur, de vapeurs, de délices.
Une exaltation soulève l'Univers,
Les cieux, tranchants et vifs, pénètrent les bois verts,
Le mol pétunia, l'œillet, les chèvrefeuilles
Donnent leur goût divin aux brises qu'ils recueillent.
Luxurieuse ardeur du languissant été!
Les monts d'argent sont des soupirs de volupté;
Tout mon cœur vaporeux d'entre mes bras s'envole,
Je ris, je tends les mains, je baise l'herbe molle,
Et là-bas, dans l'azur, un train s'est enfoncé
Avec son cri de joie et ses sanglots pressés,
Tandis que, détaché d'une invisible fronde,
Un doux oiseau jaillit jusqu'au sommet du monde!...

———————

Avoir tout accueilli et cesser de connaître!
J'avais le poids du temps, la chaleur de l'été,
Quoi donc? Je fus la vie, et je vais cesser d'être
       Pendant toute l'éternité!

J'ai voulu vivre afin d'épuiser mon courage,
Afin d'avoir pitié, afin d'aimer toujours,
Afin de secourir les humains d'âge en âge,
Puisque l'ambition n'est qu'un plus long amour...

—Un bondissant désir comme un torrent me gagne.
Ah! que je hante encor le sommet des montagnes,
Que je livre mes bras aux vents de l'Occident;
Le vert genévrier de ses senteurs me grise,
Un frein couvert d'écume éclate entre mes dents,
Se pourrait-il vraiment que l'univers détruise
       Ce qu'il a fait de plus ardent!

Stirring my heart in floods of triumph, streaming,
Like boughs, fronds wafting in young hands, light, gleaming!
So much the heat, the haze, such the delight,
That hillocks in the sheer sky fade from sight.
The Universe wells up in ecstasy,
The heavens' sharp edge cuts through the greenery;
Pinks, woodbines, frail petunias, breeze-embraced,
Offer their gift divine of scent and taste.
Languorous, torrid, sumptuous summer day!
Distant, the hills and hummocks, silver-gray,
Are sighs of bliss; my heart melts, mistlike, flees
My grasp, goes soaring, and I laugh, and seize
The soft grass in my hands and kiss it, as
A train, whistling its cry of triumph, has
Gone lunging in the azure, off somewhere,
Gasping its breathy sobs, while, in the air,
A bird, loosed by a sling unseen, is hurled
Heavenward, to the summit of the world!...

Les éblouissements

———————

To have accepted all life's gifts, then, by
And by, be done! I felt time's weight on me,
And summer's heat. Ah! I was life, yet I
      Must die, for all eternity!

I should have lived to use up all my share
Of pluck, affection, pity, ceasing never
To serve mankind from age to age; for, where
There is ambition, there is love forever...

Bounding, a flood of passion stirs, excites
My soul! Oh, that I might still haunt the heights,
The mountaintops, reach out my arms, caress
The West Wind's breath! The juniper's fresh scent
Dizzies me, panting, frothing, bridleless...
What? Can the universe be so intent
      To waste its ardentmost success!

Les vivants et les morts

Anna de Noailles 843

Les vivants se sont tus, mais les morts m'ont parlé,
Leur silence infini m'enseigne le durable.
Loin du cœur des humains, vaniteux et troublé,
J'ai bâti ma maison pensive sur leur sable.

—Votre sommeil, ô morts déçus et sérieux,
Me jette, les yeux clos, un long regard farouche;
Le vent de la parole emplit encor ma bouche,
L'univers fugitif s'insère dans mes yeux.

Morts austères, légers, vous ne sauriez prétendre
A toujours occuper, par vos muets soupirs,
La race des vivants, qui cherche à se défendre
Contre le temps, qu'on voit déjà se rétrécir;

Mais mon cœur, chaque soir, vient contempler vos cendres,
Je ressemble au passé et vous à l'avenir.
On ne possède bien que ce qu'on peut attendre:
Je suis morte déjà, puisque je dois mourir...

Je ne veux pas savoir s'il fait clair, s'il fait triste,
Si le printemps, exact, va reverdir encor,
Si l'orgueilleux soleil jette son cerceau d'or
Sur les chemins légers de la bleuâtre piste,
Ni si le vif matin a son joyeux ressort,
Et le soir ses couleurs de lin et d'améthyste,
Je sais que pour les morts plus aucun temps n'existe:
        Je suis jalouse pour les morts.

MATIN D'ÉTÉ

La chaud velours de l'air offre à la rêverie
Un divan duveteux où mon esprit s'ébat,
La verte crudité de la jeune prairie
Est pour l'œil ébloui un exaltant repas.

Mute are the living, but the dead have spoken.
Their ageless silence teaches me what stands
Unchanged. Far from the human heart—vain, broken—
I've built my pensive dwelling on their sands.

—Your sleep, O Dead, eyes closed in grim, grave wise,
Casts upon me a long and savage glance;
Words' breath yet fills my mouth; the vast expanse
Of fleeting universe invades my eyes.

Dour, fickle Dead! You cannot hope to bend
Time's will, with voiceless sighs, to occupy
Those living yet, who, watching time, defend
Against it, ever shrinking, passing by.

Still, nightly comes my heart here to attend
Your ashes: you, like time to come, and I,
Time past. Ours? What we wait for till the end:
I am already dead, since I must die...

Les vivants et les morts

I do not care if days are sad or bright;
If spring, on schedule, spreads its greening; or
If the sun, haughty, rings—behind, before—
The bluish pathways in its golden light;
Nor if crisp morning crackles gaily; nor
If evening glows, purple and linen-white...
The dead care little for the day, the night:
    I envy those who are no more.

Les vivants et les morts

SUMMER MORNING

The air's warm velvet lays out, for my dreaming,
A downy couch for revels of the mind;
The meadow's fresh and untamed green shines, gleaming,
A heady banquet for the eye, sun-blind.

L'ombrage et le soleil quadrillent la pelouse
Où le brûlant matin se repose, encagé;
Il semble qu'en volant une guêpe recouse
Le merveilleux éther par ses jeux dérangé.
Mon immobile rêve a l'ampleur d'un voyage;
J'entends le bruit mouvant et lointain de l'été,
Murmure énigmatique où tout est volupté.
Le ciel, aride et pur, est comme un bleu dallage,
Mon cœur calme bénit les dieux aériens,
Et je croise les mains, n'ayant besoin de rien
Que de penser à toi dans un clair paysage...

———

Pour oublier la morne houle
Humaine, affairée et frivole,
Ecoutons respirer la foule
Des belles choses sans paroles.

Calme du soir, fraîche candeur!
—Que j'aime ces abords des bois
Où gît, invisible et sans poids,
La masse immense des odeurs...

———

CONSOLATION

Réjouis-toi d'avoir tant souffert, car enfin
Toute fureur ayant son déclin, la détresse
Connaît aussi la lente et paisible paresse
Qui trouve son repos, et n'a ni soif ni faim.

Il n'est pas que la joie et l'espoir qui faiblissent,
La fringante douleur pâlit aussi. Comment
Ne pas goûter du moins, après tant de supplices,
L'absence de l'atroce et neuf étonnement?

Shadow and light, aligned, map out the lawn
Where lies the sweltering morning, caged; a flitting
Wasp seems to keep restitching—hither, yon—
The glowing ether that its play keeps splitting.
My dream is a vast voyage, motionless;
The summer's distant rustlings strike my ear:
Blissful, the puzzling rumblings that I hear;
Barren, the sky, like azure tiles; I bless
The gods of air with peaceful heart; and I,
Folding my hands, need nothing more than my
Thoughts of you in a landscape's limpidness...

Les forces éternelles

———————

To help forget the dreary tide
Of trifling human putterings,
Let's listen to the soft breath, sighed
By hosts of lovely wordless things.

Cool, evening's calm spreads artlessly!
—Oh, how I love these woods, where lies,
Weightless, transparent to the eyes,
The fragrances' immensity...

Les forces éternelles

———————

CONSOLATION

Be glad that you have suffered greatly, for
No turmoil is there but subsides; distress
Slowly sinks into gentle listlessness
That finds repose, and hungers, thirsts, no more.

Not only joy and hope grow weak; one's pain,
Stinging, will pale no less. For how can one,
After great torment, not know peace again?
Once the first shock is past the worst is done.

Car le pauvre être humain, instruit par la souffrance,
A l'espoir comme au deuil oppose un calme esprit,
L'infortune et la mort n'ont plus rien qui l'offense,
Et c'est vaincre le sort que n'être pas surpris.

———————

Mon esprit anxieux, qui n'est jamais distrait,
Vous palpe, ombre où plus rien de l'être ne subsiste,
Eternité d'avant, éternité d'après,
Double vertige autour de la vie! Et j'existe!
Et mes yeux exercés aux célestes secrets
S'enchâssent dans la nuit comme un astre. Est-il vrai
Que l'on meurt, ayant tout aimé! Que je mourrai
Sans qu'un dieu fraternel à ce moment m'assiste?
O ma vie, accident somptueux, vain et triste...

———————

TRANQUILLITÉ

Après le jour luisant d'entrain
Voici la nuit, dévote et fine,
Il semble que le ciel s'incline
Par le poids des astres sereins.
Le souffle saccadé d'un train
Transmet à la calme colline
Sa palpitation d'airain.
Dans l'ombre, les bruits qui scintillent,
—Bruits de pas, de voix, de volets—
Semblent polis comme des billes,
Comme les grains d'un chapelet.
—O Nuit, compatissant mystère!
Se peut-il, quand l'air est si doux
Et semble penser avec nous,
Qu'il y ait des morts dans la terre!
—Je n'ai besoin de rien ce soir
Grâce à ta tendresse amoureuse,
Une âme n'est vraiment heureuse
Que sans projets et sans espoirs.

Poor humankind, schooled in the ways of woe,
Can bear both hope and grief with calm complete;
Death, dole have no more anguish to bestow;
Not to be shocked: such is fate's best defeat.

————————

Anxious, my mind, alert, will ever try
To probe you, all-consuming shade-domain,
Eternities before and after! I
Exist between your dizzinesses twain!
Starlike, embedded in the evening sky,
My eyes see all the secrets wrought on high.
What? Die despite our loves? What? I must die
Without some brother-god to ease my pain?
O life of mine, lush accident, sad, vain...

Les forces éternelles

————————

TRANQUILLITY

Gone, now, day's dazzling energy,
And falls the night, so gentle, so
Devout. The sky seems to bow low
Beneath the stars' serenity.
A huffing train puffs fitfully
Its brassy-breathed fortissimo
Over the calm hill, pounding free.
Sounds flashing in the dark, galore
—Shutters, steps, voices—sparks of light,
Seem like so many marbles, or
Rosary beads, smooth, polished bright.
—Night! Pact mysterious! Can it
Be—when, in tune with us, the air
Hangs soft—that there are corpses there,
In earth! Ah! I need not one whit
This night, so sweet your tenderness.
A soul is happy only when
It has no hopes, no dreams; for then,
Finished, its yearning. We profess

Anna de Noailles 849

Nous parlons sans cesse de l'âme,
Pourtant, après ce long plaisir,
Tout nous est paresse et loisir,
Plus rien en nos cœurs ne réclame;
Nous pourrions vivre ou bien mourir
Contents ainsi, calmes, à l'aise.
—O mon cher compagnon, serait-ce
Qu'on ne souffre que de désir?

———————

L'être ne recherche que soi
A travers le multiple choix
De l'amour et de ses orages.
O Désir, somptueux voyage
Vers notre fascinante image
Qui nous exalte ou nous déçoit!
—C'est à soi-même qu'on veut plaire
Sur le cœur brûlant qui nous plaît,
Où, dans l'ivresse et la colère,
Ne sachant si l'on aime ou hait,
Par la volupté l'on espère
Mourir, et ne mourir jamais!

———————

Ni l'éblouissement du regard qui reçoit
L'aurore, l'horizon et les coteaux sur soi;
Ni les vergers avec leurs tentures de pêches,
Ni le ciel pur par qui la chaleur semble fraîche,
Ni le subit bonheur d'un noir oiseau, cloué
D'extase, semble-t-il, sur l'azur large et tendre,
Ne valent la douceur de ce que peut entendre
Daphnis se reposant sur le cœur de Chloé...

To plumb the soul with talk; and yet,
After life's pleasures and life's fire,
At length, no more do we require,
Nothing more need our hearts beget,
Either to covet or aspire:
Then might we live, die, peaceably.
—O dear companion, can it be
We suffer only from desire?

Les forces éternelles

———————

Each being seeks but itself, throughout
The many choices that spread out
Before it: love tempestuous...
Desire! Passionate, sumptuous
Voyage to our image of us,
That fascinates, or makes us doubt
Our worth!... It is ourselves that we
Would please as we lie, drunk, upon
His burning breast, where, blissfully—
In love? hate? anger?—we go on,
Yearning at once to die, yet be
Alive forever and anon!

Les forces éternelles

———————

Neither the dazzling dawn beyond the high
And distant hills, falling upon the eye;
Nor orchards hung with peaches; nor the fair,
Pure sky that seems to cool the torrid air;
Nor, soaring on the azure's tenderest
Expanse, a black bird's sudden ecstasy,
Can match the sweet bliss Daphnis knows when he
Reposes, calm, upon his Chloe's breast...

Les forces éternelles

Anna de Noailles 851

Comprends que je déraisonne,
Que mon cœur, avec effroi,
Dans tout l'espace tâtonne
Sans se plaire en nul endroit...

Je n'ai besoin que de toi
Qui n'as besoin de personne!

———————

Sans doute ma vie est plus morne,
Et plus stable aussi qu'autrefois.
Ce n'est plus l'espace sans borne
Que je poursuis; j'assiste à toi.

Mais tandis que mes pas s'arrêtent
Auprès de ton cœur grave et sûr,
Des dieux offensés me regrettent
A quelque banquet de l'azur!

———————

Vivre, permanente surprise!
L'amour de soi, quoi que l'on dise!
L'effort d'être, toujours plus haut,
Le premier parmi les égaux,
La vanité pour le visage,
Pour la main, le sein, le genou,
Tout le tendre humain paysage!
L'orgueil que nous avons de nous,
Secrètement. L'honneur physique,
Cette intérieure musique
Par quoi nous nous guidons, et puis
Le sol creux, les cordes, le puits
Où lourdement va disparaître
Le corps ivre d'éternité.

—Et l'injure de cesser d'être,
Pire que n'avoir pas été!

Listen how I rave, undone,
How my fearful heart, askew,
Looks for pleasure, finding none,
Though it grope the whole world through...

You alone I need; and you
Have no need of anyone!

Poème de l'amour

_____

My life seems duller, I confess,
Than once it was, more staid withal.
I seek no boundless, limitless
Expanse of space; you are my all.

And yet, though I stray not from this
Grave heart of yours, so solid, stable,
Banqueting gods, offended, miss
My presence at their azure table!

Poème de l'amour

_____

Life, permanent surprise! Self-love,
Say what you will! To rise above,
Strive to rise higher, ever higher,
First among equals, vain desire
To best the human landscape: breast,
And face, and knee, and hand—whatever!
All of them, each the tenderest!
The vanity we feel, but never
Dare to express. Our body's pride,
Honor, a music deep inside,
Guiding our steps, driving us on,
And then, the empty sod, anon,
The cords, the body lowered in,
Soon gone, drunk on eternity.

—And, worse than having never been,
The curse of ceasing now to be.

L'honneur de souffrir

Anna de Noailles 853

J'ai dormi, j'ai pendant quelques instants rejoint
La vide immensité où ne se trouvent point
Ni ton sort, arrêté, ni le mien, continu.
—J'ai reposé sous l'arc interminable et nu
Où tout être s'ignore avant, après la vie.
En quittant ce néant, je porte au cœur l'envie
De retourner sans fin vers ce suave site
Dont j'eus en m'éveillant le contact et le goût.

—Les ténèbres! l'oubli! Plus rien, ni moi, ni vous!
Lieu d'avant la naissance, unique réussite!

CHATTE PERSANE

La chambre, où l'été monotone
Confine les ors de sa gloire.
Une brise tiède frissonne
Et creuse d'argentines moires
Sur la chatte aux yeux de démone
Qui, sournoise et longue, vient boire
Dans le vase des anémones...

SAGESSE

Vis sans peur, sans remords et sans contrainte. Crains
De dépasser les jours consacrés aux caresses,
Puisque tout n'aboutit qu'au lit où l'on étreint,
    Qu'à la tombe où l'on cesse!

I slept, and for a moment joined that vast
Void, where neither my present nor your past
Abide; where every creature that draws breath
Is mystery—before life, after death:
—Beneath its timeless vaulting arch I lay;
My heart yearned, as I quit that void, to stay
Endlessly in its gentle nothingness
That still I savored, sensed, when sleep was done.

—You? Me? No, nothing! Shades! Oblivion!
That space before our birth, life's one success!

L'honneur de souffrir

PERSIAN CAT

Bedchamber... Boring summer's frieze
Of glorious gold... And, by and by,
Quivering warm, a silvered breeze
Shimmers the cat—she of the eye
Demonic!—lithe, who, if you please,
Laps from the long vase—ah, so sly!—
The one filled with anemones...

Derniers vers

WISDOM

Live fearless, guiltless, free. Fear only lest
You spend more days embracing than one ought:
All ends in bed—caressing and caressed—
    And in the grave, where all is naught!

Derniers vers

EXIGENCE

L'être recherche le plaisir,
Toute sa force le réclame,
Nous conférons le beau nom d'âme
A la puissance du désir.

Il faudrait que toujours nous tente
Quelque appel ou bien quelque attente,
Et, repoussant le morne effort
Qu'exige la vie humble et creuse,
L'homme se ruerait vers la mort,
S'il la savait voluptueuse.

CONSCIENCE

Quand le sort semble pur et franc
Et que la jeunesse s'efforce,
Comme la sève sous l'écorce,
A dominer le corps souffrant,
Périr paraît inique et lâche;
On s'acharne à la dure tâche,
Comme un travailleur dans le rang.

J'ai craint d'avoir tort en mourant.

DEMANDS

The human creature has one goal,
Pleasure: he yearns for it, unending;
Beautiful is that name, "the soul,"
We give to our desires unbending.

Something must always be, that should
Call to us, tempt us; and man would
Reject the effort, still the breath
Of this drear, hollow life of his,
And would go chasing even death
Could he but know what bliss it is.

Derniers vers

CONSCIENCE

When life is pure and hope is high,
And youth strives hard, like sap within
The bark, to conquer pain's chagrin,
Subdue the body, then, to lie
Undone and dead seems a disgrace;
Workmanlike, one assumes one's place,
Attacks the task, and asks not why.

I feared that I was wrong to die.

Derniers vers

'Natalie Clifford 'Barney (1876–1972)

If the name "Natalie Clifford Barney" sounds distinctly un-French, it is for good reason. This prima ballerina of countless pas de deux in the intellectual and artistic lesbian society of fin-de siècle Paris, and well beyond, was born on October 31, 1876 (or 1877, according to many sources), in Dayton, Ohio. And if that society can be said to have had a spiritual leader—indeed, a high priestess—certainly it was she. Lover to many and friend to many more, of both sexes, she touched the lives—amorous and artistic—of a great swath of the Tout Paris of several generations, thanks to her own exceptionally long life and the vigor with which she lived it almost to her death, on February 2, 1972.

Nor is one surprised to find, among her distinguished and distinctive coterie, such other un-French names as those of Gertrude Stein, F. Scott (and Zelda) Fitzgerald, Sylvia Beach, Ernest Hemingway, Truman Capote... And of musicians—she herself was a violinist—like Virgil Thomson, George Antheil, Wanda Landowska... Even the infamous Mata Hari, who is said to have often ridden naked through her garden on a horse with beturquoised trappings... (No less excellent a horsewoman than Barney herself, dubbed "L'Amazone," but who usually rode in less ostentatious fashion.) The list is long. So too the list of her variously tenured lovers: the courtesan Liane de Pougy, Dolly Wilde (Oscar's niece), the painter Romaine Brooks, whose liaison with her lasted over fifty years, and especially the poet Renée Vivien (see pp. 868–85). Not to mention the amorous extras or the unsuccessful would-be lovers like Lucie Delarue-Mardrus (see pp. 800–819).

Barney's interest in the arts apparently came from her mother, a portraitist and a student of Whistler's, and her fortune—an inheritance of two-and-a-half million dollars, it is said—from her tycoon father, who, scandalized by the life she had already begun to lead in Paris, conveniently died before he was able to force her into a conventional marriage. A permanent expatriate by 1909, she began her famous Turkish-decor salon on the rue Jacob, which survived, through wars and riots, for the next sixty-plus years, and where exotic delicacies (and ever-present cucumber sandwiches) vied with the panoply of artistic delights for the attention and admiration of her devoted guests.

During her own time, it was especially Barney's lifestyle and the eccentricities that she seemed to cultivate that people found worthy of note. Those who wrote and gossiped about her or included her, not-so-veiled, in their fictions, were not always aware that she was a most prolific writer, both in her native English and in her excellent French, which she had learned early during her parents' many stays in Paris. In today's climate of social freedom, her life is no less a subject of study; but, since her death, her writing—long almost ignored—is also attracting its share of artistic and scholarly consideration, taking its place as a precursor of the women's movement. Of the many works she wrote in her long life—essays, a novel, an occasional play, Wildean aphorisms like *Pensées d'une Amazone* (1920) and *Nouvelles pensées de l'Amazone* (1939), and, of course, poems—only a dozen were published in her lifetime. Several have been, and are being, republished today, as interest in her grows.[1]

As an aspiring poet, Barney brought out a pair of collections: her first, *Quelques portraits-sonnets de femmes* (1900), love poems to a variety of lovers and others; and the second, twenty years later, *Poems & poèmes: Autres alliances,* half of them in English and half in French (with an ampersand cleverly avoiding the choice of either an "and" or an *et*). It is from the latter collection, poems that alternate between openly lesbian and quite asexual inspiration—respectful of traditional prosody but not stiflingly so—that I have translated the seven following examples of her rich sensuality.

NOTE

1. Barney is the subject of a legion of individual studies and is also included, to varying degrees, in even more numerous general works on the period by a variety of writers. Among the sources in which she is discussed over the years, the following are especially worthy of attention: Jean Chalon, *Portrait d'une séductrice,* translated by Carol Barko as *Portrait of a Seductress: The World of Natalie Barney;* George Wickes, *The Amazon of Letters: The Life and Loves of Natalie Barney;* Shari Benstock, *Women of the Left Bank,* passim, and esp. pp. 268–307; Karla Jay, *The Amazon and the Page: Natalie Clifford Barney and Renée Vivien;* Andrea Weiss, *Paris Was a Woman,* pp. 100–113; and Suzanne Rodriguez, *Wild Heart, a Life: Natalie Clifford Barney's Journey from Victorian America to Belle Epoque Paris.* In addition, Charlene Ball provides an excellent overview in the *Encyclopedia of Continental Women Writers,* pp. 82–84.

FEMME

Femme à la souple charpente,
Au poitrail courbe, arqué pour
Les gémissements d'amour,
Mon désir suivra tes pentes—
Tes veines, branchages nains—
Où la courbe rejoint l'angle;
Jambes fermant le triangle
Du cher coffret féminin.

—O femme, source et brûlure—

Je renverse dans ma main
Ta tête—sommet humain,
Cascade ta chevelure!

SUFFISANCE

Quand ton regard mi-clos, luisant entre tes cils,
Peut évoquer l'amour sans forme et sans visage,
Tu ne rêves donc plus aux amants de passage?
—Quelle joie égalant ton dégoût t'offrent-ils?—
Ils rôdent tels des loups à l'affût d'une proie,
Désirant mal ton corps que leur désir salit;
Mais, loin d'eux, ton désir, seul maître de ton lit,
Reste le créateur nocturne de ta joie.
Et lorsque le désir te tient éperdûment
Livrée, et qu'il te rend plus ardente et plus souple,
Lorsque ton être double, à la fois ton amant
Et ta maîtresse, sait te prendre, mieux qu'un couple
Tu t'exaltes, ton geste est plus harmonieux.
N'aimant que Toi, tu plains la femme qui s'encombre
Du danger des amours faciles; toi, les yeux
Pleins d'orgueil, tu ne sers qu'à ta beauté, dans l'ombre.

WOMAN

Woman, supply built, lithe-fashioned,
* You of lissome bosom, of
Breasts meant for the moans of love,
I shall trace each mound, hot-passioned—
Every tiniest vein!—to where
Lines, curves, join in gentle wise:
Boxed within your loins, your thighs,
That triangle, female-fair!

—Woman! Scald, and soothing spring—

In my hands your head hangs down—
From what heights!—and from your crown
Fall your tresses, billowing.

COMPLACENCY

When, eyes half-closed, your lashes let flash through
That look of formless, faceless love, ah! then
Dream you no more of transient lover-men?
—How can they please rather than sicken you?—
A-prowl, like wolves stalking their prey, they blight,
Befoul your body with their ill-spent lust;
But your desire, your bed's sole master, must
Spurn them, and spawn joys that befit your night.
And, when desire holds you in fevered thrall,
Renders you lithe, supple of flesh; when she
Who is your double—mistress, lover, all!—
Shows that she knows your pleasure, harmony
Sings in your movements: two become as one.
Yet you, Self-loving, pity her, your booty,
Caught in the toils of easy loves, undone...
Proud-eyed, you serve only your darkling beauty.

* The French *poitrail*, usually referring to the upper body of a horse, unlike the human *poitrine*, has no poetically appropriate equivalent in English. Since the animal image, not continued in succeeding lines, seems accidental—dictated by the need for two syllables to fit the seven-syllable line, whereas *poitrine* would count here as three—I have not tried to incorporate it in my rendering. Then again, perhaps the poet's—the "Amazone's"— affection for horses had something to do with her choice.

Natalie Clifford Barney 861

Effluve d'un vieux livre,
Humide odeur du temps—
Console bien de vivre
—De vivre trop longtemps—
Dans ces pages respire
Le passé des élans,
Des voyages à lire
Par ce vieux nouvel an!

_____

DIFFÉRENCES

Vous vivez du temps qu'il fait,
De projets et de voyages;
De tel ennui, de tel fait,
D'un besoin d'air, de visages
Nouveaux, de rien et de tout.

Je ne vis que de vous...

De vous... et sans voir les pages
Des livres, de tout distrait,
Ma barque est un lit défait,
Vos traits sont mes paysages,
L'air qu'il me faut sont vos doux

Parfums: je vis de vous!

An old book's musty scent,
Exhaled—time's humid breath—
Consoles for life long spent—
Too long—waiting for death.
Over its pages spread,
Breathe yearnings, gone their way,
Adventures to be read
This agèd New Year's day!

DIFFERENCES

You live on the weather; on
Little projects, problems, or
This trip, that trip, hither, yon;
On a need for air and for
Faces new, or nothing known.

Myself, I live on you alone...

You... Books left unread—anon!—
* And my boat: the bed with your
Crumpled sheets; my distant shore:
Your face, and the look thereon;
And the air I need: your own

† Sweet scents... I live on you alone!

---

* The masculine *distrait* is rather curious here, given the poet's gender and the prob-
able female voice in which she is no doubt speaking. My translation attempts to skirt the
problem.
   † My rendering, capricious in structure and rhyme, is less so than the original.

NUIT BACHIQUE

Ivre de boire à flots la belle nuit bachique,
Je n'avais plus besoin que vous vous soyez Vous:
—Je n'avais plus besoin de la bonne musique!

Je mâchais des débris d'étoiles—tels des fous
Se reposant enfin d'être de trop eux-mêmes
—Des dieux impersonnels courtisent mes genoux.

Les ombres prenaient corps. Je leur disais "je t'aime"
—Disant à tout: "je t'aime" est-ce à toi seule, à Toi
Nuit dont je partageais les vastes diadèmes!

J'étais libre un instant, universel et roi
—Libre des sentiments qui font notre esclavage,
Mais me voici repris par tout le désarroi...

Par le doute et le trouble et le double engrenage!
Je ne suis plus que moi! Les choses d'alentour
Ne sont plus qu'à leur place... Et sûr d'un seul visage
J'ai quitté tout amour pour retrouver l'Amour!

SONNET D'AUTREFOIS

(Genre anthologie!)

Sans plus tâcher de plaire ou même d'émouvoir,
Laisse-moi m'approcher de toi, plus virginale
Que la neige; apprends-moi ta paix impartiale,
Anéantis en moi la force et le vouloir.

Je veux cacher mes yeux, plus tristes que le soir,
A tes yeux, oublier jusqu'au petit ovale
De ta face, et, mon front dans le frais intervalle
De tes seins, sangloter des larmes sans espoir.

BACCHIC NIGHT

Drunk on a glut of Bacchic night's excess,
No more I needed that you be your You:
—No more I needed music's loveliness!

I chewed on scraps of stars, as madmen do,
Content with their identities no more.
—Gods of a sort caress my knees (but who?).

The shades took shape. "I love you," so I swore.
—But is "I love you," said to everything,
* Meant but for you, Night, whose vast crowns I wore!

† One instant I was free, a cosmic king
—Free of those feelings that enslave us so.
Now, lo! Again, floundering, wavering...

Caught up in doubt, ground down by double woe!
Myself, alone! Things roundabout, above,
Below: in place... Sure of one face, I know
That loves galore I spurned, searching for Love.

SONNET OF YESTERYEAR

(Anthology-style!)

With no more wish to please or move you, I
Would lie with you, more virginal than snow
Untouched: teach me your passive calm; for, oh!
Might you but quell my lust, leave it to die.

I would conceal my glance, sadder than sky
Of night; my thoughts would let your image go—
Petite, round face—as, hopeless, sobbing low,
My brow between your breasts, I weep and sigh.

---

* I avoid following the poet's capitalization of *Toi* here, since doing so would cause a confusion with the capitalized "You" of line 2, modern English being unable to distinguish conveniently between the French formal and informal pronouns.

† As in the previous poem, the use of the masculine form *universel* (and, in subsequent lines, *repris* and *sûr*) leads one to wonder if the poet is intentionally letting her sexuality intrude on her grammar. Likewise the use of the masculine *roi*, in line 10, and, perhaps, *fous*, in line 4, though the latter can be explained as a general, rather than a personal, reference.

Natalie Clifford Barney 865

Mes pleurs sont un poison très lent que je veux boire,
Au lieu de mendier à quelque amour banal
L'ingrate guérison, l'aveuglement final.

Près de toi mon désir se consume, illusoire.
O mes regrets! combien j'éprouve encor ce mal
De rêver au bonheur auquel on ne peut croire.

———————

MÉDUSES

Dans la forêt de mort, sans saisons, sans feuillages,
—Où la sève des pins, de leurs troncs mutilés,
Coule en lente agonie—il est un exilé
De la vie, attendant de vains appareillages.

Il regarde la vague apporter sur la plage
Les masques transparents, aux traits annihilés,
Des méduses.—Semblable aux ruines de Philae,
A ces visages d'eau s'oppose son visage.

Masques faits et défaits du mouvement des flots,
La mer toujours les roule à même ses sanglots,
Des soleils de minuit jusqu'à l'aube des lunes.

Les immolés ont tous la face de Jésus,
Qui, des sables passifs, rejetés par le flux,
Comptent le temps sans fin au sablier des dunes.

Rather than ask a cure, in beggar-wise,
From love banal—that final blindness!—those
Poison tears shall I drink: slow my demise.

Lying beside you, how my woe belies
My lust consumed! Alas! It grows and grows:
* That pain of dreaming joy the heart denies.

———————

† MEDUSAS

In death's seasonless, leafless wood, stripped bare—
As pine stumps seep with tortured sap the while—
A being, cut off from life, a drear exile,
Waits for boats bound, in vain, for anywhere.

He sees waves spread clear-masked medusas there—
Featureless, with no grimace, frown, or smile;
‡ Like one awed by the ruins along the Nile,
Staring, his face returns their watery stare.

Masks formed, deformed by each new wave: the sea
Sobs them along, billowing endlessly,
From midnight suns to daybreaks' fading moons.

Victims, they bear a Christlike look, as they,
Tide-tossed from passive sands and cast away,
Count time's grains in the hourglass of the dunes.

* Despite the close similarity of the rhyme-sounds in the quatrains (-*oir* and -*ale*) and those in the tercets (-*oire* and -*al*), virtually identical to the non-French ear, the mute *e*, by its presence or absence, renders them inexact. I have tried to approximate this very unusual effect with the rhymes between my quatrains and tercets, related but not identical.

† The "medusas" in question are, of course, not mythological creatures but jellyfish. The latter word, however—distinctly unpoetic—dictated choice of the less-common English term for the common French *méduse*.

‡ The specific reference, which I have generalized, is to the island of Philae, in the upper Nile, sacred to Osiris and Isis, and site of the ruins of a temple to the latter.

Renée Vivien (pseud.) (1877–1909)

Destined to live a much briefer life than her co-expatriate sometime lover Natalie Clifford Barney (see pp. 858–67), Renée Vivien—*née* Pauline Mary Tarn—was nevertheless a more productive poet and one of greater aesthetic substance. It is safe to say that she was one of the most genuinely gifted of her generation of lesbian writers. A tormented soul, whose dark-toned, almost Baudelairean angst colors the lush sensuality of her Sapphic inspiration, she was to produce some fourteen verse collections, including two volumes of prose poems, continuously revising her works, to the point of actually withdrawing some of them from sale, before alcohol, laudanum, and anorexia—some say consumption—ended her life at the age of thirty-two. At times rather daring in her versification, she could move from the regularity of traditional eight-syllable quatrains to *impair* verse whose eleven-syllable—or, even more unusual, thirteen-syllable—lines impart a sense of uneasiness and irresolution that seem to reflect her state of mind and heart. Though a morbid pessimism and fascination with death infuse virtually all her verse, it is so elegantly expressed that one reads it with pleasure, even if only for its harmonious sonorities, all the more remarkable in that French, which she had learned as a child, was not her native language. Like Natalie Clifford Barney, but even more convincingly, she expressed it with sensitivity, passion, and an often better-than-native sense of nuance.

Sources differ as to the place of Pauline Mary Tarn's birth—London or Long Island!—but it is generally accepted that she was born in the former, Paddington to be specific, of a Scottish father and a Hawaiian-American mother. Educated in Paris and Switzerland, she lost her father when she was nine and was brought back to England by her mother, who unsuccessfully attempted to cheat her out of her inheritance by having her declared insane. A ward of the court, she remained in England until she turned twenty-one, at which time she returned to Paris, where her childhood amour Violette Shillito introduced her to Natalie Clifford Barney, with whom she promptly began an openly avowed lesbian relationship.[1] Seeing it as a symbolic rebirth, she adopted the pseudonym "René Vivien"—no doubt evoking the French *rené* (reborn) and the root of the verb *vivre* (to live)—using it for her first few collections and subsequently feminizing the first name to "Renée."

From 1901 until the year of her death, she actively pursued her double career of writer and lover. The former produced more collections of poetry, an unpublished play about Sappho, and several volumes of stories. The latter saw her continuing her on-and-off relationship with Barney, which was definitely over by 1902 (despite the pair's poetic pilgrimage to Mytilene, Sappho's Lesbos), a passionate exchange of love letters with one Kérimé Turkhan-Pasha in a harem in Constantinople,[2] and her liaison with the protective baronne Hélène de Zuylen de Nyevelt (née de Rothschild), with whom she also collaborated on a number of works under the pseudonym "Paule Riversdale." By 1906, even that latter heated affair had withered away, as did Vivien herself a few years later. In her waning years, betwixt transient loves and in declining health, she had become something of a recluse, seldom leaving her morbid and exotic apartment, where it is said she kept a coffin as a writing desk. A final liaison with the poet Madeleine Rouveirollis (known variously as Cécile or Camille Arnot) resulted in her brief conversion to Catholicism shortly before her death on November 18, 1909.[3]

The poetry of this fascinating woman is not easily classifiable. Nor need it be. Neither quite Parnassian nor quite symbolist, yet at times both, she is, as Hubert Juin has observed "an exceptional example of French Pre-Raphaelitism."[4] One thinks of her, all things being equal, as a sort of French-language Dante Gabriel Rossetti; a muse too early stilled, of that fin-de-siècle, anti-bourgeois aesthetic that proudly and rather aggressively gave itself the French name of *décadence*.

The fourteen poems translated here, taken from several collections, can be found in *Poèmes de Renée Vivien* (1923).

NOTES

1. See, among other sources, Karla Jay, *The Amazon and the Page: Natalie Clifford Barney and Renée Vivien.*

2. Her one-sided correspondence has been published by Jean Leproux, *Lettres de Renée Vivien à Kérimé.*

3. Like Natalie Clifford Barney, Renée Vivien is discussed in greater or lesser detail in general works on the period, among them Jeannette H. Foster's *Sex Variant Women in Literature*, pp. 150–73. For studies devoted primarily to her, see Charles Brun's and André Germain's works, each entitled *Renée Vivien;* and Yves Le Dantec, *Renée Vivien, femme damnée, femme sauvée.* Henk Vynckier's entry in the *Encyclopedia of Continental Women Writers*, pp. 1308–9, is concise and informative, as are Jeanine Moulin's comments in *La poésie féminine*, 2: 120–22. Marie Perrin, who has also detailed the Sapphic inspiration of her poetry (see *Présence de l'antiquité grecque et romaine au XXe siècle*, ed. Rémy Poignault), has recently produced a psychologically oriented study, *Renée Vivien: Le corps exsangue: De l'anorexie mentale à la création littéraire.* For a most useful bibliography, see Paul Lorenz, *Sapho 1900, Renée Vivien*, pp. 185–87.

4. Vivien, *Cendres et poussières*, ed. Hubert Juin, preface, p. 16.

CHANSON

Le vol de la chauve-souris,
Tortueux, angoissé, bizarre,
Aux battements d'ailes meurtris,
Revient et s'éloigne et s'égare.

N'as-tu pas senti qu'un moment,
Ivre de ses souffrances vaines,
Mon âme allait éperdument
Vers tes chères lèvres lointaines?

LUCIDITÉ

L'art délicat du vice occupe tes loisirs,
Et tu sais réveiller la chaleur des désirs
Auxquels ton corps perfide et souple se dérobe.
L'odeur du lit se mêle aux parfums de ta robe.
Ton charme blond ressemble à la fadeur du miel.
Tu n'aimes que le faux et l'artificiel,
La musique des mots et des murmures mièvres.
Ton baiser se détourne et glisse sur les lèvres.
Tes yeux sont des hivers pâlement étoilés.
Les deuils suivent tes pas en mornes défilés.
Ton geste est un reflet, ta parole est une ombre.
Ton corps s'est amolli sous des baisers sans nombre,
Et ton âme est flétrie et ton corps est usé.
Languissant et lascif, ton frôlement rusé
Ignore la beauté loyale de l'étreinte.

SONG

The bat, in twisting zigzaggings,
Flying its anguished path, bizarre,
Fluttering on bruised, battered wings,
Comes, goes, returns, flits off afar...

Did you not feel this soul in me,
Drunk on its fruitless pains; and how
It flew, one moment, desperately,
Toward your dear lips, so distant now?

*

Etudes et préludes

LUCIDITY

You spend your leisure hours in that discreet,
Delicate art of vice; and, though you heat
Fires of desire, yet your perfidious
And supple flesh steals off, abandons us.
Your gown, steeped in your couch's heady scent,
Wafts the perfume of love, rich, redolent.
Pale, honey-haired, you love only what springs
From artifice: meaningless murmurings
And words' mere music. And well you resist—
Head turned aside—to let your lips be kissed.
Your eyes are winters, pallid-starred; and where
You tread, funereal footsteps follow there.
Your gesture is an empty echo; what
Your tongue is moved to say is nothing but
A shadow. And your body, worn and jaded—
So much embraced—betrays a soul, dull, faded.
Languid, your hands' lascivious caress
Knows not the beauty of true tenderness.
You lie as others love, and one can sense,

* Many of the poet's lyrics bear the title "Chanson." This one originally appeared only in the first edition of the collection *Etudes et préludes* (Paris: Lemerre, 1901), and is reproduced from the volume *Poèmes de Renée Vivien* (Paris: Lemerre, 1923). The latter volume reproduces also a three-quatrain *chanson,* from the second edition of *Etudes et préludes* (1903), in which the second quatrain is almost exactly the same as in the present poem.

Tu mens comme l'on aime, et, sous ta douceur feinte,
On sent le rampement du reptile attentif.
Au fond de l'ombre, telle une mer sans récif,
Les tombeaux sont encor moins impurs que ta couche...
O Femme! je le sais, mais j'ai soif de ta bouche!

SOMMEIL

O Sommeil, ô Mort tiède, ô musique muette!
Ton visage s'incline, éternellement las,
Et le songe fleurit, à l'ombre de tes pas,
Ainsi qu'une nocturne et sombre violette.

Les parfums établis et les astres décrus
Revivent dans tes mains aux pâles transparences,
Evocateur d'espoirs et vainqueur de souffrances
Qui nous rends la beauté des êtres disparus.

CHANSON

Il se fait tard... Tu vas dormir,
Les paupières déjà mi-closes.
Au fond de l'ombre, on sent frémir
L'agonie ardente des roses.

Car la déesse du Sommeil,
De ses mains lentes, fait éclore
Des fleurs qui craignent le soleil
Et qui meurent avant l'aurore.

Beneath your sweetly innocent pretense,
A snake a-crawl, waiting to strike. Deep, deep
The dark, like reefless sea, wherein you sleep—
Bed fouler than the tomb!... I know all this,
O Woman! yet I thirst to taste your kiss!

Etudes et préludes

SLEEP

O Sleep, O tepid Death, mute melody!
Your face, forever weary, nods to us
And, like night-blooming violets, tenebrous
* Dreams blossom in your shadows, gloomily.

In your translucent hands there live once more
Fragrances past and stars long on the wane,
You who revive our hopes, conquer our pain,
Bring back the beauty of those gone before.

Cendres et poussières

SONG

It's late... You are about to sleep,
Eyelids half-closing, languidly.
I feel the roses, shadowed deep,
Quiver their amorous agony.

The Slumber goddess has begun,
Slowly, with gentle hands, to spawn
Flowers that wither in the sun,
And that must die before the dawn.

Cendres et poussières

* In his preface to the 1977 edition of *Cendres et poussières*, p. 19, Hubert Juin suggests that the poet's frequent allusion to the violet is a tribute to her first lesbian lover, Violette Shillito, who died in 1901, several months before the publication of *Cendres et poussières*. Although the dedication reads "A mon Amie H. L. C. B."—perhaps a veiled reference to Clifford Barney?—Juin contends that it was Shillito, *l'amie aux violettes,* who inspired the collection.

VELLÉITÉ

Dénoue enfin tes bras fiévreux, ô ma Maîtresse!
Délivre-moi du joug de ton baiser amer,
Et, loin de ton parfum dont l'impudeur m'oppresse
Laisse-moi respirer les souffles de la mer.

Loin des langueurs du lit, de l'ombre de l'alcôve,
J'aspirerai le sel du vent et l'âcreté
Des algues, et j'irai vers la profondeur fauve,
Pâle de solitude, ivre de chasteté!

ÉPITAPHE

Doucement tu passas du sommeil à la mort,
De la nuit à la tombe et du rêve au silence,
Comme s'évanouit le sanglot d'un accord
Dans l'air d'un soir d'été qui meurt de somnolence.
Au fond du Crépuscule où sombrent les couleurs,
Où le monde pâlit sous les cendres du rêve,
Tu sembles écouter le reflux de la sève
Et l'avril musical qui fait chanter les fleurs.
Le velours de la terre aux caresses muettes
T'enserre, et sur ton front pleurent les violettes.

LE TOUCHER

Les arbres ont gardé du soleil dans leurs branches.
Voilé comme une femme, évoquant l'autrefois,
Le crépuscule passe en pleurant... Et mes doigts
Suivent en frémissant la ligne de tes hanches.

INCLINATION

O Mistress mine, loosen your feverish arms!
And, from your bitter kiss's yoke set free,
Far from your scent's shameless, oppressive charms,
Let me breathe deep the breezes of the sea.

Far from the shadowed nook, the languorous bed,
I'll breathe the pungent sea-plants' salt, wind-blown,
And to the wild depths let myself be led,
Drunken on chastity, pale and alone!

Cendres et poussières

EPITAPH

Gently, you passed from sleep to death, from night
To tomb, from dream to silence, like a sighing
Chord in a summer evening's waning light,
Somnolent in the air, vanishing, dying...
Deep in the Twilight colors, darkening,
Where fades the world, beneath dream's ashes burning,
You seem to listen to the sap's returning,
And April's voice, that sets the flowers to sing.
Earth wraps you in her mute velvet caress,
† And on your brow weeps violets' tenderness.

Cendres et poussières

TOUCH

The trees hold the sun's glintings as it dips
Down low. Veiled, like a woman, twilight lingers,
Weeps for the Once Upon a Time... My fingers,
Quivering, trace the contour of your hips.

* It is probably significant that "Velléité," the word chosen by the poet for her title, implies only a passing desire; one that, even as she composed her poem, she knew would be short-lived.

† Again, probably a reference to Violette Shillito (see above).

Mes doigts ingénieux s'attardent aux frissons
De ta chair sous la robe aux douceurs de pétale...
L'art du toucher, complexe et curieux, égale
Le rêve des parfums, le miracle des sons.

Je suis avec lenteur le contour de tes hanches,
Tes épaules, ton col, tes seins inapaisés.
Mon désir délicat se refuse aux baisers:
Il effleure et se pâme en des voluptés blanches.

———————

CHANSON

Du ciel poli comme un miroir
Pleuvent les langueurs enflammées,
Et nous suivons, au cœur du soir,
L'irréel essor des fumées.

J'adore tes gestes meurtris
Et tes prunelles embrumées...
Tu regrettes... Dans tes yeux gris
Passent et meurent des fumées...

———————

AIGUES-MARINES

Des gouttes d'eau—de l'eau de mer—
Mêlent leur lumière fluide,
Glauque et pareille aux flots d'hiver,
A tes longs doigts d'Océanide.

Comment décrire le secret
De leurs pâleurs froides et fines?
Ton regard vert semble un reflet
Des cruelles aigues-marines.

Your shivering flesh, in petal-smoothness gowned,
Yields to my fingertips' soft, artful strokes...
Strange and complex, the art of touch evokes
The dream of scent, the miracle of sound.

Slowly, my hands, with delicate caress,
Follow your shoulders' curve, your neck's, your hips',
Your anxious breasts'... My lust, shunning your lips,
Grazingly, swoons in pale voluptuousness.

*   *Evocations*

SONG

From the sky, mirror-polished, light
Rains down its languorous flames, and we
Gaze, in the heart of falling night,
As wisps of smoke rise hazily.

I love your gestures, passion-bruised,
Your glances that dim mist evoke...
You languish... In your eyes, infused
With gray, rise, die the wisps of smoke.

Evocations

AQUAMARINES

Seawater droplets blend, combine
The pallor of their liquid light—
Like winter waves'—with your long, fine
Fingers of fabled Ocean-sprite.

How to describe their lithe and cold
Pale mystery? Your glances' greens
And grays reflect the secrets told
Darkly by harsh aquamarines.

* I follow the supposedly definitive version of the French original, as found in the second edition of *Evocations*, which differs only slightly from that found in the first edition of two years earlier.

Ton corps a l'imprécis contour
Des flots souples aux remous vagues,
Et tes attitudes d'amour
Se déroulent, comme les vagues...

———————

CHANSON

L'ombre vient, les paupières closes.
O ma Maîtresse, j'ai mêlé
Des iris noirs aux roses roses
Dans le crépuscule troublé.

Savourons l'intime détresse,
La langueur que verse le soir...
Pour toi je mêle, ô ma Maîtresse,
La rose rose à l'iris noir.

Tes yeux ont des lueurs mystiques
Comme la lune sur les flots...
Que nous importent les musiques
Où ne vibrent point les sanglots?

L'ardeur de vivre m'abandonne
Vers la nuit... mais je garde encor
Le reflet du soleil d'automne
Sur tes cheveux de pourpre et d'or.

Your body's contour dimly flows
Like supple tide, hither and yon;
And, in love's poses, vaguely goes
Rolling on, wavelike... On and on...

*   *Evocations*

_____

SONG

The shadows fall, the eyelids close...
O Mistress mine, I have combined,
In the dusk's dimming haze entwined,
The iris black and rose-pink rose.

Let's sip a draught of languorousness
From twilight's sweet "Alas!... Alack!..."
For you, O Mistress mine, I tress
The rose-pink rose and iris black.

Mysterious glimmers, like the moon's
Glints on the waves, glow in your eyes...
What matters now the music, tunes
Untouched by quivering sobs or sighs?

Life's burning passion-fire has done
With me. Night falls... And yet, I hold
Still dear, the trace of autumn sun
About your hair, purple and gold.

†   *Evocations*

* I follow the poet's definitive version in the 1905 edition of *Evocations*.
† Here I have translated from the version of the poem in the first edition of *Evocations*, with its added final quatrain, rather than the three-quatrain, rearranged version of the second.

Renée Vivien 879

Je serai toujours vierge

Je demeurerai vierge comme la neige
Sereine, qui dort là-bas d'un blanc sommeil,
Qui dort pâlement, et que l'hiver protège
    Du brutal soleil.

Et j'ignorerai la souillure et l'empreinte
Comme l'eau de fleuve et l'haleine du nord.
Je fuirai l'horreur sanglante de l'étreinte,
    Du baiser qui mord.

Je demeurerai vierge comme la lune
Qui se réfléchit dans le miroir du flot,
Et que le désir de la mer importune
    De son long sanglot.

DANSES SACRÉES

De leurs tendres pieds les femmes de la Crète
Ont pressé la fleur de l'herbe du printemps...
Je les vis livrer à la brise inquiète
    Leurs cheveux flottants.

*   *Ever shall I be a virgin*

Virgin shall I be forever, as the snows,
Tranquil and serene, sleeping their sleep of white,
Pallid, shielded by the winter's chill repose
      From the sun's cruel light.

Free of foot-tracks' vile corruption shall I be,
Like clear rivers, like the North's gusts of pure bliss.
Blood-stained horror of caresses will I flee,
      And the biting kiss.

Virgin shall I be forever, as the moon,
Shining on the mirror-waters from on high;
Moon that ocean's waves lust after, importune,
†   With their long-drawn sigh.

Sapho

SACRED DANCES

The Cretan women's tender feet would press
The spring's new-budding grass with their caresses...
I saw them heap the breeze's eagerness
      With flowing tresses.

   * Vivien's tersely eloquent epigraph is a quotation from a Sapphic lyric in which Artemis, goddess of the chase, affirms: "By your head, I shall always be a virgin untamed, hunting on peaks of solitary mountains" (*Sweetbitter Love: Poems of Sappho*, trans. Willis Barnstone [Boston: Shambhala, 2006], p. 23).

   † The reader will notice—perhaps after unsuccessfully attempting to scan these lines in conventional fashion—that I have tried to duplicate the effect of the poet's Sapphic-inspired quatrains: three eleven-syllable lines followed by a five-syllable line.

Renée Vivien 881

Leurs robes avaient l'ondoiement des marées.
Elles ont mêlé leurs chants de clairs appels
En rythmant le rire et les danses sacrées
      Autour des autels.

———————

CHANSON POUR ELLE

L'orgueil endolori s'obstine
A travestir ton cœur lassé,
Ténébreux comme la morphine
Et le mystère du passé.

Tu récites les beaux mensonges
Comme on récite les beaux vers.
L'ombre répand de mauvais songes
Sur tes yeux d'archange pervers.

Tes joyaux sont des orchidées
Qui se fanent sous tes regards
Et les miroitantes idées
Plus hypocrites que les fards.

Tes prunelles inextinguibles
Bravent la flamme et le soleil...
Et les Présences Invisibles
Rôdent autour de ton sommeil.

Their gowns, like waves, would flow and ebb. And they
Circled the altar with the gleeful chants
And sacred dances, rhythmic roundelay,
        Of celebrants.

*

Sapho

SONG FOR HER

Your wounded pride, obstinately,
Disguises your dour heart, downcast
In morphine-shadowed mystery,
Dark as the secrets of the past.

You speak your lies—beautiful lies—
As some speak verse of beauty rare.
Shade spreads with fearsome dreams your eyes—
Archangel's eyes, perversely fair.

Your gems are orchids that, before
Your gaze, like shimmering thoughts, begin
To fade—thoughts hypocritic, more
False than the rouge that tints your skin.

Unquenchable, your glances vie
With sun and flame... And, without number,
Those of the Life Unseen, draw nigh
To prowl about you as you slumber.

La Vénus des aveugles

* This poem, from the collection *Sapho* (1903), also appears in the first edition of *Evocations* (1903), but in a substantially different version, though maintaining its Sapphic structure:

> De leurs pieds fleuris les femmes de la Crète
> Pressent le duvet de l'herbe du printemps:
> Je les vois livrer à la brise inquiète
>   Leurs cheveux flottants.
>
> Leur robe a les plis ondoyants des marées...
> Je les entends rire avec de clairs appels,
> En rythmant les chants et les danses sacrées
>   Autour des autels.

I suspect that, since the poem does not appear in the second edition of *Evocations* (1905), the present version is the definitive one.

Renée Vivien 883

J'erre au fond d'un savant et cruel labyrinthe...
Je n'ai pour mon salut qu'un douloureux orgueil.
Voici que vient la Nuit aux cheveux d'hyacinthe,
Et je m'égare au fond du cruel labyrinthe,
O Maitresse qui fus ma ruine et mon deuil.

Mon amour hypocrite et ma haine cynique
Sont deux spectres qui vont, ivres de désespoir;
Leurs lèvres ont ce pli que le rictus complique:
Mon amour hypocrite et ma haine cynique
Sont deux spectres damnés qui rôdent dans le soir.

J'erre au fond d'un savant et cruel labyrinthe,
Et mes pieds, las d'errer, s'éloignent de ton seuil.
Sur mon front brûle encor la fièvre mal éteinte...
Dans l'ambiguïté grise du Labyrinthe,
J'emporte mon remords, ma ruine et mon deuil...

THE MAZE

I wander in a cruel and artful maze...
Only my pride redeems my doleful course.
Hyacinth-haired, Night falls, and in her haze
I lose my way within the deep, cruel maze,
O Mistress! you, my doom's, my ruin's source.

My hypocritic love, my brazen hate,
Are two ghosts, prowling drunk on their despair;
Curled lips their death-mask traits accentuate:
My hypocritic love, my brazen hate,
Are two cursed ghosts haunting the evening air.

I wander in a cruel and artful maze;
Undone, I quit your door, footsore perforce,
My feverish brow with passion yet ablaze...
There, through the gray-blurred Labyrinthine maze,
I bear my doom, my mourning, my remorse...

La Vénus des aveugles

Cécile Périn (1877–1959)

For a poet with her extensive bibliography, the rather scant available biography of Cécile Périn is indeed a surprise. Few sources, few concrete facts... One is tempted to assume that she either led a rather uneventful life or jealously guarded her privacy. But certainly her twenty-odd collections, produced between 1906 and her death in 1959, offer posterity a more valuable legacy than the reams of biographical detail and engaging historical chitchat with which many less productive poets provide readers and scholars.

From *Vivre*, first of those collections, published in her native Reims, to the last, published—like most of the rest—in Paris, three years before her death, she gave her native, instinctive poetic talent free rein, apparently untouched by the theories and techniques of the literary movements of the moment, producing a seemingly spontaneous, uncomplicated, and (mercifully) not overly sophisticated body of verse that can be read with all the more pleasure in that it seldom invites the reader into complex or subtle byways of interpretive ingenuity. In short, whether singing the joys of motherhood and family, the delights or mysteries of the natural landscape, or firsthand folkloric evocations of Provence or Brittany, Cécile Périn seems to take a simple joy in the transparency of her subjects. No less straightforward, too, are her patriotic poems in *Les captives* inspired by the horrors of World War I, which affected her deeply. As Jeanine Moulin observes, these sincere elegies "avoid that jingoistic bombast into which the finest poets let themselves fall."[1]

Born Cécile Martin in 1877, she began writing poetry as a lycée student and sharing her creative enthusiasm with music, painting, and sculpture. In 1898, she married Georges Périn, a native of Metz, who, himself an accomplished poet, encouraged her to develop her obvious talent.[2] United by their common interest, both husband and wife frequented many of the leading poets and other literati of the day, most prominent among them Apollinaire, Gustave Kahn, Georges Duhamel, and Jules Romains. Both were regular contributors to the influential journal *La Plume*. After her husband's death in 1922, Cécile Périn married a childhood friend, the ethnographer and painter Daniel Réal. Several of her collections bear witness to their extensive travels. Réal died in 1931 and Périn herself twenty-eight years later, as the result of an auto accident, still writing poetry, it is said, on the very morning of her death. Her final collection, *Images*, had been published just a few weeks before.

The following twenty-five free forms, sonnets, and assorted melodious scenes and sketches of striking imagery represent seven of Périn's collections: *Les captives* (1919), *La féerie provençale* (1930), *Dicté par une ombre* (1934), *Mélodies*

(1943), *Bretagne* (1951), *D'une chambre ouverte sur le ciel* (1953), and *Paroles à l'enfant* (1954), and offer a substantial cross-section of her verse, gracefully undemanding but no less rewarding for all that.

NOTES

1. See *La poésie féminine*, 2: 141–42, which also presents a bibliography of her collections. For such discussion of her life and works as is readily available, see also Elie Moroy's *La littérature féminine définie par les femmes écrivains*. I am especially indebted to the poet's granddaughter, Madame Lise Jamati, for providing a number of basic details.

2. For a recent study devoted to her husband, see Catherine Boschian-Campaner, *Georges Périn, poète messin*.

Beaucoup ne verront plus palpiter la lumière,
Ni l'éclat délicat des matins de printemps.
Un doux soleil entr'ouvre en vain les primevères;
Je pense aux jeunes morts qui n'avaient pas vingt ans.

Le destin les coucha dans l'ombre, à peine en vie.
Et les vieillards et les femmes regarderont,
La flamme vacillant dans ces mains engourdies,
S'éteindre les divins flambeaux;—et survivront.

Mais ils ne pourront plus connaître cette ivresse
Qui les envahissait, jadis, au temps joyeux.
Pour un rayon posé sur les pousses qui naissent,
Pour un jeune arbre en fleur, pour un pan de ciel bleu.

Ils n'auront plus jamais l'exaltation douce
De ceux que la beauté seule autrefois rythmait.
Leur cœur se souviendra de l'horrible secousse
Quand l'oubli s'étendra sur les jardins de Mai.

MIDI

Nul bruit dans le village et nul éclat de voix.
Les contrevents sont clos et la rue est déserte.
Le soleil ruisselant semble écraser les toits
Et pèse lourdement sur la campagne inerte.

Midi, cloche d'argent, heurte aux portes fermées.
Et rien ne lui répond; pas un chant, pas un rire...
Mais tu montes dans l'air, fumée, humble fumée,
Et par toi les maisons immobiles respirent.

Many will never see light throb again,
Or spring's soft mornings sparkle—nevermore!
Sun will coax open primrose buds in vain
For those young dead, whose years scarce reached a score...

Fate plunged their youth into obscurity.
Women, old men, will cast their gaze upon
Their quivering flames in hands benumbed, and see
Their divine torches die—yet they live on.

No more they feel life's passions, dead and done,
That sweet-time joy that filled them, through and through.
At new-sprung seedlings fingered by the sun,
Or a young tree in flower, a patch of blue...

Never will they that calm ecstasy know
That pulsed to beauty's rhythms limitless.
But their hearts will recall the deathly blow
When May lies blooming in forgetfulness.

Les captives

* NOON

Quiet the village: no sounds, voices, none.
Closed are the shutters, empty is the street.
The roofs seem crushed by the cascading sun,
The land lies heavy in a calm complete.

Noon, silver-belled, raps at the doors, tight-shut...
Silence. No song, no laughter in reply...
But you, smoke, prove these houses live; you, but
A humble wisp of breath reaching the sky.

La féerie provençale, "Provence"

* The original title is somewhat ambiguous since, in this encomium on the French southland, it could refer either to the time of day, noon, or to the whole geographical area of "Le Midi." The context makes the former seem more logical.

Cécile Périn 889

PETITE PLUIE

Petite pluie, ô douce pluie!
Est-ce un souffle dans le feuillage,
Une source dans la prairie
Ou l'haleine d'un nuage?

Entre les plombs de son vitrail
L'ombre cerne une aile azurée...
Mais le vent pousse le vantail
Sur les visions éthérées.

Et voici qu'on entend soudain
Courir par la plaine assombrie
Tes menus pieds par le chemin,
Petite pluie, ô douce pluie...

LE MOULIN

Pensif, découronné, le vieux moulin demeure,
Ronde tour échancrée au faîte du coteau,
Inutile ruine où s'écoulent les heures
Sans qu'un grain soit moulu dans un effort nouveau.

Ta tâche est faite. Ecroule-toi, vieux centenaire.
Une brèche déjà ronge tes flancs épais,
Et voici que s'accroche à tes pierres le lierre
Qui jadis à tes pieds sournoisement rampait.

Que n'es-tu mort, moulin, lorsque tu n'eus plus d'ailes,
Lorsque de tout élan tu fus dépossédé!
Mais tu chois, pierre à pierre, et dans le vent chancelles,
Toi dont l'âme jadis fut le vent déployé!

SOFT RAIN

Soft rain, O gentle little rain!
Is it the puff of greenery,
A brooklet rising in the plain,
Or a cloud sighing? Can it be?

* See? In her stained-glass traceries,
A wing, azured in shadow-rings...
Wind blows the casement shut on these
Ethereal imaginings.

Then, all at once, upon the ground—
Over the meadow's darkening lane—
One hears your dainty feet run round,
Soft rain, O gentle little rain...

La féerie provençale, "Provence"

THE MILL

Pensive, uncrowned, the old mill stands, round tower
Nestled atop a gentle-sloping hill;
Useless, this ruin, as each passing hour
Sees no grain ground, no new life springing still.

Your task is done. Crumble, you battered, bruised
Hundred-year-old! Cracks gnaw your thick flanks. See?
Your stones bear now the ivy vines that used
To crawl about your feet, once, furtively.

Why did you not die, mill bereft of wings,
When first you stood, still and undone, unwhole!
Now, stone by stone, in the wind's buffetings,
You fall, you whom the wind once gave a soul!

La féerie provençale, "Vers la sérénité"

* The original, with its possessive adjective *son* (his/her/its) implies a possessor of the *vitrail* in question, though one that the context leaves vague. I have opted for "her," assuming—admittedly on interpretive faith alone—that the poet is, in fact, referring to herself.

Cécile Périn 891

TRANSMISSION

Tu n'entends plus chanter ces voix sur la colline
Ni rire les enfants au pied des arbres-fées
Dont le fluide étain qu'un souffle dissémine
Encadre de l'azur les scintillants trophées.

Tu ne vois plus danser sur la vague divine
Les lumières, blondeurs par le soleil coiffées,
Et pourtant ton esprit m'obsède, et je devine
Dans le moindre frisson ses forces étouffées.

Tu poses sur mon front ta main surnaturelle;
Tu veux que je t'écoute encor, et que je mêle
Ton soupir à mon souffle en la nuit inspirée

Où ces rires, ces chants qui déjà se dispersent,
Ces clartés dont je fus tout le jour entourée,
De mon âme en ton âme, ondes d'or, se déversent.

LA SOURCE

La source emprisonnée aux griffes de l'hiver,
Muette, sur l'abîme en glaçons suspendue,
Semble morte. Qui donc l'a jamais entendue
Bruire, ivre d'espace, aux jardins frais de l'air?

Elle était cependant un sistre d'argent clair
Et palpitait, laissant sur sa corde tendue
Glisser les doigts légers d'un sylphe, âme ténue,
Ou, ruisselante, elle vibrait comme un éclair.

MESSAGE

You hear no more those hillside voices sing,
Nor children laughing by the fairy-trees,
Their glistening trophies, in a shimmering
Of tin-blue tide, blown on the azure breeze.

You see no more, over the billowing
Divine, these sun-capped glints go dancing, these
Blonde flecks of light; yet, with each shuddering,
I sense your spirit's muted energies.

You place your hand ethereal on my brow;
You would I heed you still, and that, somehow,
I blend my sigh, your breath, here in this night

Inspired, where waves of gold, already soaring
Off to the past—my daylight laughter—might,
Singing, from my soul into yours go pouring.

Dicté par une ombre

THE BROOK

This brook, imprisoned, mute, in winter's drear
And frigid grasp, seems dead, over the vast
Chasm hung still. It murmured, in the past,
Drunk on the blooms of space, but who gave ear?

* And yet, it was a silver cittern, clear,
Trembling; and on its strings, held taut, stretched fast,
A light-souled sylph's deft fingers softly cast
An air, or throbbed her sparkling music here.

* The context would indicate that the poet intended to refer here to the *cistre,* a medieval long-necked lute, known in English under various names—"cither," "cittern," "gittern," and so on—rather than to the homonymous *sistre* (sistrum), an ancient Egyptian rattle.

Cécile Périn 893

Nul ne se souvient plus des grâces de sa course...
Mais je me pencherai sur l'invisible source.
Avec un stylet d'or, au plus profond des bois,

Je briserai la glace et, sur le lit de mousse,
Je ferai rejaillir, fluide, cette voix
Qui naguère enchanta le silence, si douce!

―――――――

NOVEMBRE

Novembre refleurit à nos rosiers de Mai.
La mer berce en rêvant ses épaules soyeuses;
Et l'air a ce parfum d'oranger que j'aimai
Naguère, en le jardin des minutes heureuses.

Les pétales de fleurs qu'un vent souple semait
Semblent encor joncher l'allée. Et les pleureuses
S'étonnent d'écouter un glas dans l'air quiet
Et de porter un voile noir, mystérieuses.

Comme un ciel de printemps ce ciel d'automne est pur.
Au pied des longs cyprès qui transpercent l'azur
Le Jour des Morts s'éploie ainsi qu'un jour de fête.

Mais sur les chemins clairs que nous avons suivis
Vibre, deuil de cristal, un sanglot de poète...
Solitaire, tu dors... Solitaire, je vis.

―――――――

CAUCHEMAR

Que le sommeil me soit doux comme une colombe!
A peine un battement d'aile autour de mon front;
Invisible plumage où, mols, se berceront
Des rêves dont la trame au mystère retombe.

Mais dans la nuit d'émail et de velours succombe
Sous la griffe d'acier sanglante d'un faucon
La colombe. Et, brisant le funèbre flacon
De morphine, un vampire émerge de la tombe.

None now recalls its sweet meandering...
But I shall lean over this unseen spring,
Deep in the wood, and, with a golden prong,

Shall pierce the ice, make leap to life again
Over the mossy bed, that liquid song
That, gentle, charmed these silences back then.

Dicté par une ombre

NOVEMBER

November blooms on rose trees of our May.
The sea shrugs silken billows, dreamily;
Orange scents I so loved waft free, the way
They did, then, in our garden ecstasy.

Blown on a supple breeze, petals that lay
About, seem yet strewn on the lane. Look! See
Our willows, weeping, listening with dismay
To death's calm knell, veiled in black mystery!

Pure as a sky of spring, this autumn sky.
The azure-piercing cypresses rise high:
All Souls' Day spreads, like feast-day, at their feet.

But on the bright paths we once trod upon,
Poet's grief, sobbing, throbs a crystal beat...
Alone, you sleep... And I, alone, go on.

Dicté par une ombre

NIGHTMARE

Would that my sleep might gentle, dovelike be!
Scarcely a wing grazing my brow; unseen
Plumage, to cradle, soft—betwixt, between—
Dreams woven in the weft of mystery.

Instead, velvet, enameled night will see
That dove beneath a bloodied-red, steel-keen
Claw of a hawk; and, drinking his morphine,
A vampire, risen from his tomb, set free.

Cécile Périn 895

Mon sang lourd coule ainsi qu'un fleuve empoisonné;
La hyène et le chacal en l'ombre ont ricané.
—Il rive à mes poignets une chaîne d'esclave;

Vibrante, je me lève à l'appel de sa voix,
Et, dans la moite horreur de l'alcôve, je vois
Luire le vert phosphore au fond de son œil cave.

———————

GRELOTS

Nostalgique, la nuit en grelottant s'effeuille
Mais laisse encor traîner son souffle sous la nue.
Dans un miroir sans tain ne s'est pas reconnue
L'aurore que nul cri léger d'oiseau n'accueille,

Mais un long friselis de gouttes que recueille
Sous les taillis la nymphe invisible et menue
Qui sur les rocs déjà gonfle sa gorge nue,
S'étire, et seule, il semble, en pleurant ne s'endeuille.

Au linceul de l'azur la lumière fanée
N'est plus au fond du ciel qu'une étrange araignée
Qui tisse incessamment des fils gris et les noue.

Jour morne, sans espoir. Et l'âme qui s'ennuie,
Comme la nymphe en la fontaine, pleure et joue
Au cachot de cristal musical de la pluie.

———————

ORGUEIL

Au sommet de la tour d'onyx et de porphyre
Notre âme s'est drapée en un royal manteau,
Opposant à la joie impure son veto
Et daignant la douleur et ses pourpres élire.

Heavy as poisoned stream, my blood. Midst jackal's
Barking, and midst hyena's jeering cackles,
He chains my wrists: I lie, slave acquiescent.

Shivering, I rise to his strident cry,
And, in the alcove's sultry horror, I
See shine his hollow orbs, green, luminescent.

Dicté par une ombre

———————

* PITAPAT

Nostalgic night, shivering, peters out,
Trailing her breath beneath the clouds. Dawn breaks:
But, dim and dull her glass, no notice takes,
Nor chirp the birds morn's welcome roundabout;

Droplets, rather, that pitapat without
Design, sipped by woodsprite unseen, who slakes
Her thirst, yawns, proud of breast: though tearful, wakes
To joy, alone untouched by fear or doubt.

On azure's winding-sheet, spreads, by and by,
The faded light, deep on the mournful sky:
Weird spider, weaving endless threads of gray.

Day: hopeless, dark... The soul, spent and in pain,
Will, like some river nymph, now weep, now play,
Pent in the cell of music's crystal rain.

Dicté par une ombre

———————

PRIDE

Atop the tower—onyx and porphyry—
We draped our souls in regal mantles; chose,
Rather than joy impure and sullied, woe's
Raiments of purple, royal panoply.

———

* The literal "little bells" of the title has obviously given way to its metaphorical meaning expressed in the poem.

Cécile Périn 897

Nul souffle désormais aux cordes de la lyre.
La voici suspendue ainsi qu'un ex-voto
Aux murs de la chapelle obscure du château.
Silence! Solitude! Inaccessible empire!

Mais offensés les Dieux ont encerclé la tour,
Franchi le pont-levis, et, de leur glaive lourd,
Ils fustigent la porte. Un cri jaillit. Ecoute!

Où les armures d'or, les carquois précieux,
Et nos pauvres orgueils blessés dans la déroute
Qui meurent en fuyant sous l'étreinte des Dieux?

———————

SOIR

Nous irons vers la mer dans le soir ténébreux,
Bercés par les soupirs de musiques câlines
Et guidés par l'éclat des lueurs opalines
D'invisibles bateaux dont s'allument les feux.

Frémira dans la nuit notre cœur douloureux.
L'espoir fera tinter ses subtiles clarines.
Nous humerons l'odeur des saumures marines
Au bord de la calanque où fuit le flot peureux.

Sur le sable mouillé par la frange d'écume
Nous errerons, pensifs, dans un voile de brume,
De nos chastes secrets n'ayant rien échangé.

Mais, souffle insidieux épandu dans l'espace,
Nous rejoindra, glissant d'une proche terrasse,
Voluptueuse, l'âme en fleur d'un oranger.

———————

MÉLODIE

Le fragile éclat,
L'odeur d'une rose
Qu'un souffle apporta;
Un vol qui se pose
Sur l'acacia;

No lyre's breath now, strings mute. No melody.
Sacrifice-like, it hung from the château's
Dim chapel walls, in somber, dark repose.
Silent! Alone! Realm unassailed and free!

But soon the Gods were circling round the tower...
Storming the drawbridge... With bare broadswords' power,
Smashing the gate... A cry... Oh, woe betide!

Where, now, our precious quivers? What? No trace?
Where, our gold armor-mail? Where, our poor pride
That, wounded, died while fleeing the Gods' embrace?

Dicté par une ombre

EVENING

Off in the evening darkness shall we go,
Rocked by the wheedling song of lulling sighs,
And led on by the light, dazzling our eyes,
Of boats unseen, lit with an opal glow.

In black night will our hearts tremble their woe;
Delicate notes, tinkling with hope, will rise.
We shall breathe deep the scent of brine, that flies
Over the inlet's timid, fleeting flow.

On sandy shore, moist with a froth of lace,
Pensive, veiled in the mist, we'll stray apace,
Our secrets, chaste, kept hidden deep in us.

There shall we be, together, joined as one,
By that sly breath from terraced grove outspun:
Orange tree's soul, in bloom voluptuous.

Dicté par une ombre

MELODY

How fragile-lived these:
Perfume of a rose
Blown light on the breeze,
Bird striking a pose
On acacia trees;

Cécile Périn 899

Un chant qui soupire
Au fond du jardin
Et semble traduire,
Cœur qui se souvient,
L'ancien délire;

Un amour qui meurt,
Mais qui se délie
Sans drame, sans pleur,
Chaste mélodie
Ou souffle de fleur...

———

LIED

Sur l'herbe de la clairière
Aux aigrettes de cristal
Vibre le chœur musical
Des tristesses éphémères.

Hors des voûtes des tilleuls
Leurs formes pensives glissent.
Mais le clair de lune tisse
A ces ombres des linceuls.

Elles flottent, dispersées.
Et de leur souffle subtil
Demain que restera-t-il?
—Quelques gouttes de rosée...

———

ESSAIM

Dans les cerisiers,
Neigeuse merveille
Prête à s'effeuiller,
Vibrent les abeilles.

In grove's greenery
A song, sighed withal,
That brings back to me—
Heart quick to recall—
The old ecstasy;

A love's final hour—
Calm-dying amour—
No scene, no tear-shower,
Tune simple and pure,
Or breath of a flower...

Mélodies

SONG

In the clearing, on the grass
Crystal-tufted, trills the choir:
Music that day's woes inspire,
But that, in a day, will pass.

From the linden grove, arch-boughed,
Pensive figures come, a-slither,
But the moonlight, wending thither,
Weaves each shadow-form a shroud.

Off they float, fading from view.
And tomorrow what will be
Left of their breath's frailty?
—A few drops of morning dew...

Mélodies

SWARM

Leaves about to fall
From the cherry trees'
Wondrous snow, and all
Around buzz the bees.

Cécile Périn 901

Tu cherches en vain
A capter, furtive,
Jeunesse, l'essaim
Divin qui s'esquive.

Tout va s'évadant
Des nids et des branches,
Abeille, aile, chant
Et molles fleurs blanches.

––––––––––

DIMANCHE

Dimanche... Sur le quai passent les jeunes filles
Et l'on entend siffler et rire les garçons
Dans la salle de danse où déjà s'éparpillent
Au son d'un aigre biniou les airs bretons.

Quelques vieilles, en coiffe blanche et robe noire,
Assises à l'abri d'un bateau renversé,
Ressassent lentement leur monotone histoire
Ou parlent à mi-voix des marins trépassés.

Mais les vieux, pipe aux dents, remâchant l'amertume
D'être sans force alors que leurs yeux restent clairs,
Sur la digue où s'écrase en paquets mous l'écume
Regardent inlassablement s'enfler la mer.

––––––––––

SUR LA PLACE DU VILLAGE

Le plus humble village a dressé vers le ciel
Sur la place, au milieu de ses maisons serrées,
Ou devant l'horizon, symbole essentiel,
      Le granit d'une croix sacrée.

"Souffre...," dit cette croix aux bras écartelés.
Et le Seigneur, le front penché, murmure: "Espère."
Ainsi jaillit d'un phare au fond des soirs voilés
      Le rayon dont la mer s'éclaire.

Vain, Youth, your design:
Slyly though you may
Stalk the swarm divine,
Still, it slips away.

Fleeing nest and bough,
Everything takes flight—
Bee, bird, song... and now
Blossoms, soft and white.

Mélodies

———————

SUNDAY

Sunday... Along the quay the girls pass by;
One hears the lads laughing and whistling there,
Inside the dance-hall, where a bagpipe's wry,
Sour notes go sprinkling many a Breton air.

Old women—white coif, black dress, neckerchief—
Slowly retell their stories, on and on,
Sitting beside a beached, overturned skiff,
Or whisper tales of sailors, dead and gone.

Old men suck on their pipes, drone their distress
At flesh grown weak, though clear their glance, sharp-eyed,
As, on the dyke splashed with foam's gentleness,
They watch the waves, untiring, swell the tide.

Bretagne

———————

ON THE VILLAGE SQUARE

Even the humblest village raises high
Amongst its houses on the square—pressed taut,
Each to the next, or stark against the sky—
     A sacred cross of granite wrought.

Unerring symbol, this! With arms spread wide,
"Suffer!" it says. But, head bent, "Hope!" sighs He,
Our Lord... Thus does a lighthouse light the tide
     Despite veiled night's obscurity.

Cécile Périn 903

Et le pêcheur s'en va sur les flots en priant;
Et la femme s'en va vers la lande infertile.
Mais sur les marches du calvaire un jeune enfant
    S'assied, et rit aux vents hostiles.

———

PAYSAGE

Un ciel délicat
Couleur de bruine;
Dans l'ombre l'éclat
D'une eau cristalline;

Des hêtres autour
D'une humble chapelle
Qui niche le jour
Dans son clocher frêle;

Silence où l'oiseau
Jase, où le feuillage
Bruit comme l'eau...
—Le doux paysage!

———

HOULE

L'espace est alourdi de stagnantes nuées;
A peine un flot ronge la grève, et vibre, et gronde.
Les furieuses déesses exténuées
Reposent un instant dans leurs grottes profondes.

Mais le vent s'engouffrant aux cavernes du ciel
Ebranle tout à coup les nuages qui croulent
Et, jetant aux échos son redoutable appel,
Fait courir sur la mer l'effroi des grandes houles.

Off goes the fisher, praying, on the brine;
Off goes the woman to the barrens bare...
But, a lad, on the steps before the shrine,
　　Sits and guffaws at winds' gruff air.

Bretagne

LANDSCAPE

A fragile sky, mist-grayed
And delicate; and in
A flash, there, in the shade,
Rivulet crystalline;

Frail, humble spire that reaches
Up in the nestling light,
And round the chapel, beeches
Standing in their full height;

Silence: only the bird,
Chirping, the rustling hiss
Of leaves, like water, heard...
—O gentle landscape, this!

Bretagne

SWELL

Heavy, space lies beneath a stagnant shroud;
Scarcely the tide moans, quivers, gnaws the shore.
The fury-goddesses—tired, bent, and bowed—
Take their rest on the grottoed ocean floor.

But then the surging wind, swooping within
The caverns of the sky, crumbles and fells
The clouds, raises the echoes with its din,
And spreads over the sea its dreaded swells.

Bretagne

L'OISEAU POSÉ

Comme un oiseau posé sur le sommet d'un mât,
Va, replie un instant tes ailes frémissantes,
Désir ivre de ciel et qui toujours aimas
Parcourir dans l'espace une invisible sente.

Tu ne touches pas terre ici; mais cependant
Tu contemples de loin le port aux maisons grises;
Immobile, tu suis le lent balancement
Qu'imposent au bateau le flot, la moindre brise.

Et déjà tu sens naître en toi l'immense essor
Qui t'emportera loin des barques et des voiles,
Vers la roche sauvage où tu niches encor,
N'ayant pu t'évader jamais jusqu'aux étoiles.

SOURCE

Cette source cachée en ton âme, entends-la
Si pure, frissonner comme une aube. Là-bas
L'air souple t'apportait le parfum des lavandes,
L'odeur du buis, du thym, des fraises, de la menthe...
Source! Jaillissement d'onde au creux des rochers,
Rire de l'ombre, éclat des verdures rayé
Par le verre filé, fluide des cascades,
O source, redis-moi d'anciennes ballades
Où je retrouverai l'écho mystérieux
Des profondeurs, le chant d'un invisible dieu.

Like a bird perched atop a mast, O my
Desire, fold back your wings, you who would trace
With quivering joy your unseen path, and fly,
Drunk on the ecstasy of sky and space.

Lighting not on the land, you fix your gaze
Upon the grayish houses standing there
In port, motionless on your mast, that sways
With each wave, each breeze wafted on the air.

And even now you feel surge in your breast,
That flight from sail, boats, sweeping you afar,
Off to that rugged cliff, where you still nest,
With never a hope to reach your distant star.

Bretagne

FOUNT

That fount within your soul, deep hidden... Hear
How pure it murmurs, like a dawn, how clear.
The supple breeze brought you the fragrant scent
Of boxwood, thyme, mint, strawberry, redolent
Lavender... Trickles spurting to cascades
From rocks' recess... O fount of laughing shades
And bursts of green, striped with the twists and flows
Of liquid glass... Fount! Sing me once more those
Lays of the deep, let me their echoes glean:
Mysterious singing of a god unseen.

D'une chambre ouverte sur le ciel

Cécile Périn 907

COUCHANT

Contre le ciel d'un bleu de lin
Les blonds transparents et les cuivres,
Le roux, le chrome, le carmin
D'orgiaques rayons s'enivrent.

Entrelacs de soleil, d'azur,
Vibre, flamboie, Esprit que guette
La mort et son cortège impur.
Dans cette fantastique fête

Où l'or spiritualisé
Aux veines de l'ombre circule,
Sois l'arbre jailli du brasier
Où s'effondre le crépuscule.

CRÉPUSCULE

A André Germain

Vois, les flambeaux du jour sur les monts se concertent
Pour jeter sous les pas de la nuit leurs trophées.
Mais dans le lit profond d'une combe déserte
Tu t'enivres de clair-obscur aux ombres vertes,
De mousse, de fontaine et de torche étouffée.

SUNSET

Against the sky of flaxen blue,
Transparent gold and copper spreads
* Rays—ruby, chrome, and *acajou*—
Drunk on a glut of yellows, reds.

Azure and sun entwined, sky spanned,
Trembling, aflame... Soul's orgiastic
Flight against death and its foul band!
Here, in this revelry fantastic,

Where spirit-gold, pure liquid fire,
Flows in the shadow's veins, you must
Be the tree sprung safe from the pyre,
Where twilight crumbles into dust.

D'une chambre ouverte sur le ciel

TWILIGHT

† *For André Germain*

See how day's hilltop torches now conspire
To fling beneath the footfalls of the night
Their trophies! Yet, still drunk on your desire,
In barren vale's green-shadowed darkling light,
You gorge on fount, on moss, on muted fire.

* If justification is needed for my use of the French *acajou* (mahogany), found in the *OED* and various other dictionaries, though rarely met with in English, I would point out that it not only has the advantage of offering a convenient rhyme, but also that it has a distinctly poetic ring.

† André Germain was the author of literary appreciations of Aragon, Gide, and Proust (see especially his *De Proust à Dada* [1924]). It is possible that Périn admired his anti–World War I sentiments, which she appears to have shared, at least on occasion.

Cécile Périn 909

Gorgé d'azur, tu guettes l'impalpable cendre
Qui neigera d'un ciel aux langueurs d'élégie
A l'heure où le rayon clignotant va descendre
De la première étoile à l'orient surgie
Ainsi qu'un regard d'ange évadé d'une orgie.

———————

Près de toi qui souris et t'éveilles, j'ai peur
De tout ce que je sais, de tout ce que j'ignore,
De tout ce qui se jette entre nous deux. J'ai peur...
Un crépuscule rose évoque en vain l'aurore.

Ah! pouvoir appuyer mon amour doucement
Sans l'opprimer ni le meurtrir sur ton cœur tendre!
Mais je suis une femme et tu n'es qu'un enfant.
Hélas! Comment s'aimer assez pour se comprendre?

———————

Ouvre ta porte à ceux que le sort exila.
Que sera ton foyer si l'amour ne l'éclaire?
Ouvre ton cœur à ceux qui souffrent. De ton bras
Soutiens cet inconnu qui chancelle: ton frère.

Ne capitonne pas les murs de ta maison
Pour que n'y siffle pas le vent né dans la plaine.
Et lorsque sous ton toit des gerbes brilleront
Songe aux champs dévastés de la détresse humaine.

Glutting on azure, you await the snow
Of phantom ash that, from the languorous skies,
Will fall with elegiac pace, as, lo!
The first star blinking in the east will rise
* Like fleeting orgy-glance from angel-eyes.

D'une chambre ouverte sur le ciel

———————

Close to you—waking, smiling—I'm afraid
Of all I know and don't know: vast terrain
Of all that comes between us, I'm afraid...
My twilight, pink, calls to your dawn, in vain.

Would I could gently press my love, and do
Your heart no hurt! Ah, but my little friend,
Woman am I, and a mere child are you.
How can we love enough to comprehend?

Paroles à l'enfant, "La plus belle aventure"

———————

Open your door to fate's outcast cohort.
How dark your home without love for another!
Open your heart to those in pain. Support
That poor, tottering nameless soul: your brother.

Don't pad your walls to shield them from that cold
Wind that comes whistling from the plain. Ah, no!
And when, beneath your roof, sheaves flash their gold,
Think of the fields laid waste in human woe.

Paroles à l'enfant, "La plus belle aventure"

* Although the poet's change in rhyme scheme between the two stanzas (*ababa/ababb*) has no obvious formal aesthetic justification, I follow it in my version.

Cécile Périn 911

LUXEMBOURG D'ANTAN

Un petit air vieillot tourne dans ma mémoire.
La girafe, le cerf et les chevaux de bois
S'ébranlent. Et déjà, le bras tendu, victoire!
Enfilant des anneaux, l'enfant rit d'être adroit.

Les fleurs des marronniers roses sur les allées
Glissent. Le vent d'avril joue avec les pigeons;
Et toute la douceur du printemps s'est mêlée
Au petit air vieillot qui grince, tourne en rond.

Un visage ravi de fillette s'anime,
Tacheté d'or par les caprices palpitants
De l'ombre, du soleil, du vent parmi les cimes...
—O petit air vieillot, nostalgique et touchant!

A little bygone air runs round my head.
Giraffe, deer, wooden horses, child astride,
Arm outstretched, turning, turning, fingers spread,
Grasping the ring, laughing, beaming with pride...

The April breeze plays with the pigeons. There,
Falling, pink chestnut blossoms strew the ground,
And all of spring's sweet breath blends with that air—
A creaking little bygone air, round... round...

A young girl's face sparkles to life, aglow,
Flecked gold by the caprice of shade, of sun,
Of wind, pulsating among the hilltops... O
Sweet little bygone air, longed-for, long done!

Paroles à l'enfant, "Aubes et aurores"

---

* It should need no explanation that the reference is to the Jardin du Luxembourg in Paris, long a favorite haunt for the young and not-so-young alike.

Cécile Périn 913

Amélie Murat (1882–1940)

Considered by some the foremost modern woman poet of her native Auvergne, Amélie Murat was able to play her lyrics on many different strings. Serious and even somber, she could sing the traditional wonders of nature in Lamartine-type tones, now giving voice to the winds, the trees, now apostrophizing the animals as a loving disciple of Saint Francis or lamenting the power of death by rhapsodizing on deathless portraits whose models are no less dead for all their specious immortality. She could dedicate her works, as she herself said, "to her sisters, those women who have suffered for love and yet who have not cursed it."[1] Doleful, she could mourn the loss of her sister Jeanne, two years her senior, or the living death of her own soul, as a lonely, love-starved spinster, able to gaze on her long-awaited lover, real or fantasized, only "in dreams' dark bluish depths" and certain to be denied the joys of motherhood. Yet she could also, and no less deftly, poetize in mock-majestic verse the banalities of everyday life: her neighbor lady's cock, "fluffed up like a plate of whipped-up eggs"; the nightingale's "mini-throat / Burning with passion in its every note"; the household-spirit cat, with its "silver-tinkling bell / Dancing its jig across the stairs, pell-mell." And she could do so with a delicious, almost tongue-in-cheek banter, without losing her graceful and seemingly intuitive stylistic elegance.

Amélie Murat was born on December 19, 1882, in Chamalières, a small town in Puy-de-Dôme. Grief would seem to have singled her out early in life. Orphaned by age six—her mother died when she was two and her father four years later—she and her sister were given a properly religious convent-school education by their grandmothers. When both ladies died in 1903, the two teenagers were left virtually without family. An avid reader, Amélie—multicultural before it was fashionable—was particularly attracted by the poetry of the Belgian Georges Rodenbach, the Italian Gabriele d'Annunzio, and the Indian Rabindranath Tagore. Living in Paris by the time she was twenty, she had already begun to write poetry herself and to frequent its literary circles, finding favor, despite her youth, among such eminences as the poet Henri de Régnier and, especially, the historian-academician Pierre de Nolhac. Her first volume, *D'un cœur fervent*, appeared in 1908, followed in 1912 by *Le livre de poésie*. Both collections, not without the expected, de rigueur touches of melancholy, are inspired by a variety of subjects—nature foremost among them—and, at any rate, are not yet filled with the deep pessimism that her personal misfortunes, physical and emotional, as well as the disillusionment of war, would later engender. Her sister's death in 1926 was to be the most severe of these blows.

She continued to write, however, producing three well-received novels and several more poetry collections; and—modest consolation for her solitude and sadness—she saw her work awarded a number of literary prizes and honors, not the least of which was the Légion d'honneur, in 1932. In the last volume published during her lifetime, *Vivre encore* (1937), she makes an effort to escape from the personal doldrums that characterize such collections as *Passion* (1929) and *Le rosaire de Jeanne* (1933)—the latter devoted entirely to the memory of her sister—and, without a whole-hearted return to faith, at least to accept the value of the simple phenomenon of living. When she died on March 8, 1940, in Montferrand, possibly from the lingering aftermath of the influenza epidemic of 1918, she left unfinished, in addition to two novels, an even more optimistic collection with the revealing title *Poésie c'est délivrance*. As a lasting tribute—probably longer lasting than the street named after her in her hometown, and which, in French fashion, would doubtless be frequently rebaptized—an award, the Prix Amélie Murat, was established in her honor three years after her death.

Several of the poems translated here are from four of the sections of the early *Le livre de poésie*, and are followed by two from *Passion*, an almost light-hearted group from *Le chant de la vie* (1935), and an appropriately concluding quatrain from *Vivre encore*.[2]

NOTES

1. Quoted in André Fontainas, *Tableau de la poésie française d'aujourd'hui*, p. 28.

2. Besides Edith Joyce Benkov's concise entry in the *Encyclopedia of Continental Women Writers*, pp. 888–89, see Jeanine Moulin's brief note in *La poésie féminine*, 2: 163–64, and occasional journal articles. For more extensive bio- and bibliographical details, however, see Paule Bouvelot-Ulrich, *Le lyrisme d'Amélie Murat*, as well as the brief comments in Fernand Delzangles, *Biographies et morceaux choisis d'écrivains d'Auvergne*, pp. 281–82.

ARBRES D'AUTOMNE

L'Automne, aventureux bûcheron qui voyage,
A marqué pour un coup prochain notre feuillage.
Déjà son vent brutal, incisif et tranchant
Comme un outil d'acier qu'il affûte en marchant,
Sur l'abondant taillis de nos branches, prélève
Quelques feuilles encor souples d'un peu de sève,
Dont on voit voltiger les fragiles copeaux...
—Et pourtant, nous n'avons jamais été plus beaux!

Oui, le vert printanier du bourgeon qui s'éveille,
Le vigoureux essor des rameaux, la merveille
De fleurir en bouquets, en grappes, en chatons,
Tous les reflets, tous les parfums que nous portons
En notre immense ombrage où l'Eté se repose,
Ont longtemps préparé la brève apothéose
Dont s'éblouit, ce soir d'octobre, la forêt!
Chacun de nous, selon sa nuance, apparaît
Dans le groupe infini qui se dore et rougeoie;
Nous allumons en l'air un triste feu de joie,
Un bûcher pathétique, où la Belle Saison
Meurt, et voile en ses yeux l'éclat de l'horizon.
Le peuplier rapide élance sa fusée,
Le platane secoue une torche embrasée,
Le hêtre épanouit un globe incandescent;
Et comme une fumée inverse, qui descend,
Notre ombre sinueuse et molle, tiède et rousse,
S'allonge, flotte, ondule et tourne sur la mousse...

Ainsi, nous composons le fastueux décor
Où, quand la chasse éloigne et sa meute et son cor,
Le poète dont l'âme à la nôtre se lie
Goûte l'enthousiasme et la mélancolie;
Où les amants fiévreux exaltent leur désir
D'effeuiller les rameaux délicats du plaisir;

AUTUMN TREES

Autumn, brash woodsman, ever coming, going,
Has marked our foliage, soon to feel his blowing
Winds' biting, cruel attack, that, in his wrath—
Honed to a blade-sharp edge along his path,
Like knife of steel—already levies its
Toll on our tangled limbs, as scraps and bits
Of leaves, still supple with their sap, take flight...
—Yet never has our beauty shone so bright!

Ah yes, the spring-born green of bud in bloom,
Our branches' hearty surge, bouquets that loom
In wondrous clusters, cat-tails, all our glints,
All our perfume, all the reflections, tints,
That form our vast shade where fair Summer lies
At rest: all this it is that glorifies,
At last, our being in one brief blaze, to leave
The woods bedazzled this October eve!
Each of us, in this maze of manifold
Hue and nuance, this endless red and gold,
Ignites a bonfire in the air; pathetic
Pyre, where the Summer, with one last frenetic
Breath, faces the horizon, veils its eyes
Against the brilliance of its glare, and dies.
The poplar sends its rocket reaching high,
The plantain torch shakes flames against the sky,
The beech tree's globe blooms a translucent glow;
And, like a smoke-cloud—sinuous, soft, bowed low,
Head down—our shadow's warm and ruddy mass
Undulates, floats, twists, overspreads the grass...

And so we shape this sumptuous splendor, where—
As the hounds take their distance, and the blare
Of hunting-horn grows dim—the poet, whose
Very soul and our own mingle and fuse,
Knows melancholy's moan and passion's fire;
Where zealous lovers glory in their desire
To pluck the leaves from pleasure's tender boughs;
Where the wan, pallid youth fervently vows,

Amélie Murat 917

Où l'adolescent mince et pâle, aux mains brûlantes,
Vient s'unir à la mort fraternelle des plantes,
Et peut-être, implorer le consolant secret
De finir sans laideur, sans effroi, sans regret!...

———————

VOIX DU VENT

Je suis le vagabond éternel, qui chemine
Nuit et jour, dans la libre immensité de l'air...
Vos yeux n'atteignent pas le mur de la colline:
Moi, je parcours le monde et traverse la mer.
Tour à tour caressant ou vif, brise ou tempête,
J'effleure ou violente, et je chante ou gémis;
Je traîne le nuage ainsi qu'une conquête,
Et les arbres, géants peureux, me sont soumis.
Nul ne peut diriger ma fougue ou ma paresse,
Et nul ne peut prédire ou fixer mon vouloir;
Mon caprice est la loi qu'à plaisir je transgresse:
Je ne sais pas moi-même où je serai ce soir!
        J'aime à lutter, dans l'eau marine, avec la houle,
Et j'en sors imprégné d'embrun et de sel fin;
Au sein de la forêt profonde, je me roule,
Jouant parmi les troncs feuillus, comme un sylvain;
Dans la plaine déserte et nue, ivre d'espace,
Comme un fier étalon je m'élance au galop;
Quand sur la route sèche en hennissant je passe,
La poussière tournoie au choc de mon sabot!
Je sème un goût de large, un frisson d'aventure...
Je dis ce que j'ai vu par delà l'horizon;
Amant passionné de la tendre Nature,
Je dérobe un bouquet des fleurs de la saison.
Il n'est pas de farouche asile, de retraite
Où ne vienne rôder mon souffle curieux:
La source qu'un rocher gardait froide et secrète,
Se trouble de sentir mon baiser sur ses yeux...
Parfois, ma fantaisie est agréable et douce:
Je promène mes mains au fifre des roseaux,

With feverish hands, to be, in death, still more
Our brother; and, perhaps, to beg us for
That all-consoling secret we possess,
To die without regret, fear, ugliness!...

Le livre de poésie, "Des arbres et du vent"

VOICES OF THE WIND

I am the wanderer, the vagabond
Eternal; night and day, I ply the free,
Vast realms of air... Your eyes pass not beyond
That hill, but I travel the world, the sea.
Now sharp, now gentle, storm or breeze, I blow
Tempestuous or calm, I groan or croon;
I drag the clouds along, like beaten foe
Enchained; the trees, great timid giants, swoon
Before me. None can tame my passion or
Spur on my laziness. Where will I fly?
My whim is law, which I myself ignore:
Where shall I dwell tonight? Who knows? Not I!
      I love to struggle with the ocean, swelling,
Heavy with froth, shrouded in mist and salt;
Deep in the forest, I writhe, waning, welling,
Like faun at play beneath an arbored vault;
And on the barren plain, drunk with expanse,
I gallop free, like stallion proud; and when,
Whinnying, I go dashing by, a-prance,
A-trot, over the dry dirt road... Ah, then
The dust whirls, swirls about my hooves! I spread
A shudder of adventure, sow a taste
For open seas, tell where my path has led
And what my eyes have seen, the journeys traced...
Tender Dame Nature's earnest lover, I
Steal flower bouquets; no untamed spot has she,
No niche, where my breath fails to satisfy
The proddings of my curiosity.
The hidden spring, cooled in a rock's retreat,
Trembles to feel my kiss pressed to its eyes...
At times my fantasy is soft and sweet:
My hands go probing where they will, as rise

Amélie Murat 919

Puis j'invite la feuille à danser sur la mousse,
Et je berce la branche où dorment les oiseaux.
Je poursuis les enfants dans leurs rondes agiles,
Et fais sur leurs cous blancs voler leurs longs cheveux;
J'emporte, destructeur des ivresses fragiles,
Les roses, les serments d'amour ou les aveux.
Je dévide à mon gré les soyeuses fumées
Comme des rubans bleus enroulés sur mes doigts;
Je m'engouffre et me rue au fond des cheminées;
Je meus la girouette alerte en haut des toits.
Et visitant ainsi les demeures humaines,
Je recueille l'écho des douleurs que je sens,
Et parais, certains soirs, pleurer mes propres peines,
Tant votre désespoir entre dans mes accents!...

———————

LES ÉPHÉMÈRES

A Fernand Gregh

Nous n'avons ni pays, ni cité, ni maison.
Un rayon de soleil marque notre horizon,
Et le soir d'un beau jour d'été, notre saison.

De tout l'élan fougueux de nos petites ailes,
Nous projetons dans l'air nacré nos rondes frêles,
Que la lumière change en rondes d'étincelles.

Ne nous immole pas d'un jeu dur de ta main,
Toi qui nous suis des yeux, toi, l'Ephémère humain...
Fais grâce aux condamnés qui seront morts demain!

Nous n'avons que ce bref et divin crépuscule
Pour bercer sans repos notre vol minuscule,
Sous le grand ciel paisible où la clarté recule...

And fall the fluted notes the reeds are playing.
I bid the leaf dance with me on the moss,
And lull to sleep birds on the branches, swaying.
I chase the children in their games, and toss
Their locks about their young white necks. My breath
Destroys the roses' fragile drunkenness—
Vows of eternal love!—whisked to their death.
My hands unwind wisps of blue smoke, caress
Its silken ribbons, twirled about... Down in
Your chimneys I go wafting, plunging deep;
And on your roofs, with twist and turn, I spin
Your flighty weathercocks... Thus do I keep
Watch on your human dwellings, where I gather
The echo of your woes, until, with sighs
And sobs, I seem to weep my own grief, rather,
So much does your despair invade my cries!...

Le livre de poésie, "Des arbres et du vent"

——————

THE MAYFLIES

*   *For Fernand Gregh*

We have no country, city, home... A ray
Of sun is our horizon, and the gray
Dusk is our death, eve of fair summer's day.

Frail dots, we dart the air's pearl shimmerings
With all the fervor of our tiny wings,
Turned, by the light, to sparkling glimmerings.

Stay your harsh hand! Don't call death down upon
Our heads, you, human Mayfly gazing on
Poor creatures doomed, soon to be dead and gone.

We have this moment only—dusk's dim light
Divine!—for our minute, unceasing flight
Beneath the vast, calm sky, fading to night.

* The prolific poet Fernand Gregh (1873–1960), member of the Académie française, author of several dramatic works, and biographer of Victor Hugo, is best known for his elegiac inspiration and a humanistic love of nature that characterizes much of his elegant and formally rather traditional verse. It was probably this concern for the natural world that endeared him to our poet.

Amélie Murat 921

Nous n'avons que ce peu de temps, ce peu de jour
Dont la fuite abolit le rêve d'un retour,
Pour posséder le monde, et la vie, et l'amour!

C'est pourquoi notre essaim silencieux se grise,
—Poussière d'or avant d'être poussière grise,
De rayons, de parfums, de rythme, d'air, de brise!

Ne nous repousse pas d'un geste de tes doigts,
O rêveur vaniteux et naïf, qui nous dois
La sécurité fausse où tu dors sous tes toits:

Puisque c'est en voyant si faible et mesurée
Notre vie en essor dans une heure azurée,
Que tu connais l'orgueil de croire à ta durée!

FRÈRES ENNEMIS

J'ai pour les animaux, captifs ou vagabonds,
Faibles ou forts, charmants ou laids, méchants ou bons,
Le cœur tout fraternel de Saint François d'Assise...
Et sous un ciel baigné de lumière et de brise,
Pareil au ciel d'Ombrie, où le Poverello
Lorsqu'il marchait, pieds nus, exhortant sa sœur l'Eau,
Discernait un reflet de l'angélique fête,
Je les voudrais voir vivre en une paix parfaite.
C'est pourquoi je m'afflige, ô mon frère le Chien,
De convenir que vous, doux, franc, presque chrétien,
Aveuglé par l'éclair d'une haine de race,
Ne pouvez rencontrer sans lui donner la chasse
Notre frère le Chat, compagnon de logis.
Et vous, le Chat, malgré vos instincts assagis
Par la sécurité d'une honnête existence,
Vous, gorgé de bien-être, accablé de pitance,
Mais trouvant à la proie un farouche intérêt,
Je sais que vous guettez la Mésange, tout prêt
A déchirer d'un coup de dent, d'un coup de griffe,
Son joli corps tremblant que la peur ébouriffe...

We have this moment, and this one alone,
This wisp of day—dream done, forever flown—
To make the world, and life, and love our own.

And so our swarm, in silent riocochets—
Gold specks of dust, soon to be flecked to grays—
Gluts, drunk, on day's scents, rhythm, wind, and rays!

Don't wave us off, dreamer vain and naive,
Who, thanks to us, under your roofs, believe
You sleep secure! For, when your eyes perceive

Our fragile life that all too soon is past—
One azured hour of flight, over so fast—
Proud, you suppose that yours will last and last!

Le livre de poésie, "Nos amis"

HOSTILE BROTHERS

For all the beasts—those who live footloose, free,
Roaming the wild, or in captivity—
Lovely or ugly, good or bad, the meek
And mild, the fierce untamed, the strong, the weak:
For all of them my heart brims with the love
That Francis of Assisi taught men of;
And I, beneath a breeze-blown, sun-bathed sky,
Like Umbria's, when, "The Pauper," he would ply
His barefoot way... That sky whence he would seem
To glimpse, glistening in his sister-stream,
Reflections of the angels' feast... Ah yes,
I too would have them live in happiness
And harmony, at peace with one another.
Thus do I grieve to see, O Dog, my brother,
That you, although a creature stalwart, kind—
Almost a Christian!—let race hatred blind,
With hellish flash, your noble eye, such that
You cannot come upon our brother, Cat,
Household companion, but that you give chase.
And you, O Cat, who will (ah, the disgrace!)—
Despite your calm, bourgeois existence, sated,
Well-fed, glutting on comfort, satiated—
Nevertheless turn fierce, lurking, dissembling,

Amélie Murat 923

Mais quoi! vous-même, avec vos mines de douceur,
O vous, Mésange bleue, ô vous, petite sœur,
N'êtes point à couvert d'un semblable reproche:
Car votre bec, aigu comme un éclat de roche,
Forant le sol, le tronc, la feuille en maint endroit,
Détruit l'insecte obscur,—et qui pourtant a droit
A son moment d'amour, de soleil et de vie!

N'est-ce donc pas assez que la haine et l'envie
Chez vos maîtres chagrins et durs portent leurs maux?
Faut-il encor que vous, les simples animaux,
Vous combattiez sans cesse à l'exemple des hommes?...

Ah! Seigneur, dans l'extrême indigence où nous sommes,
Faites tomber du van large et doré du ciel
La manne au frais parfum de froment et de miel,
Qui nous rassasiant chaque jour, nous délivre
De la nécessité rigoureuse de vivre...
Et que nous, vos enfants, avec ces compagnons
Qu'en notre pauvre orgueil humain nous dédaignons,
Pratiquant le conseil légué par vos apôtres,
Nous nous aimions enfin, Seigneur, les uns les autres!...

———————

CHANSON D'ENNUI

C'est toujours le décor tranquille
Du haut clocher, des toits penchants;
La route qui mène à la ville,
Le chemin qui finit aux champs.

Quand donc la fuite, où l'on s'isole
Dans l'Inconnu grave ou riant?
Quand donc l'Italie et Fiesole,
Constantinople et l'Orient?

C'est toujours l'étroite existence:
Travail, promenade ou repos;
La solitude du silence,
Et la fatigue des propos.

Waiting to bite and claw to shreds the trembling
Fright-ruffled Titmouse!... Ah, but are not you,
Little blue Tit, our sister, guilty too?
For, here and there and everywhere—around,
About—you peck and poke beneath the ground,
Under the leaves, within the trees, and seek
That hidden insect with your shardlike beek,
Who has no less a right than anyone
To live and love his moment in the sun.

Is it not quite enough that jealous hate
Infects your masters? Must you emulate
Their evils, simple beasts, with war unending?

Lord! In our moral poverty unbending,
Open your vast and golden bin: pour free
Your honeyed manna, grain-perfumed, that we
Might gorge on it until, feasting our fill,
We stand delivered of life's every ill...
That we, your children, Lord, may feel no more
Our prideful scorn for these, our friends, whom your
Disciples taught us we should love, and thus
Deserve the love that they, in turn, give us.

Le Livre de poésie, "Nos amis"

BOREDOM SONG

The same scene—calm, serene, homespun—
Tall steeple, sloping rooftops, and
Two roads: one to the town, and one
Out to the fields and meadowland.

Ah! When, the flight into the gay
Or grave Unknown, cast free, released?
When Italy? When Fiesole?
Constantinople? Oh, when the East?

Each day, hemmed in, like those before:
To work, perhaps to stroll, to rest;
The solitude of silence, or
Tired, worn-out thoughts once more expressed.

Amélie Murat 925

Quand donc l'enthousiasme extrême
Des actes et des sentiments?
Ah! vivre un merveilleux poème
Dont les strophes soient des moments!

Vous rêviez d'être, ô cœur crédule,
La harpe qu'un souffle conduit:
—Et vous êtes l'humble pendule
Qui bat dans l'ombre, à petit bruit...

BRUMES

Les crépuscules gris d'octobre et de novembre
Estompent le contour du fuyant horizon,
Où l'on discerne encor le toit d'une maison,
Un rang de peupliers que la bise démembre,
Et ce coteau, qui n'est peut-être qu'un brouillard...
Sur la route allongée au couchant, molle et lisse,
Le pas d'habituels passants s'étouffe et glisse;
Chacun, courbé, frileux, a l'air d'être un vieillard.
Déjà la nuit hâtive au jour faible se mêle;
Pourtant le ciel varie à peine de couleur,
Et la brume conserve un peu de sa pâleur
Dans le rapide afflux de l'ombre fraternelle.
Les vitres des logis scrutent de leurs fanaux
Cette mer de silence où pas un flot ne bouge,
Et leur rayonnement attentif, jaune ou rouge,
Semble au loin propager de funèbres signaux.
Ah! que de lassitude et de mélancolie
Dans cette mort d'un jour qui se meurt de langueur!
—Mais je n'évoque point votre chaude splendeur,
O pays du soleil: lumineuse Italie,
Egypte où le grand sphinx royal sculpte ses traits,
Orient où le soir est blond comme un grain d'ambre...
Les crépuscules gris d'octobre et de novembre
S'enveloppent pour moi de trop tendres attraits.
Mon cœur, frère dolent du dolent paysage,
Voit sévir son automne et son brouillard aussi:

When, all those deeds, those feelings, fraught
With ardor, zeal, and passion-rife?
Ah! But to live a poem, fine-wrought,
Whose stanzas are the stuff of life!

O callow heart! You thought, for sure,
To be the lyre inspired to song:
Naught are you but the clock obscure,
Ticking its humble hours along...

Le livre de poésie, "Nostalgies"

MISTS

October's and November's twilights, gray,
Dull the horizon's distant silhouette:
A rooftop, dimly seen; and poplars, set
In single file, wind-wracked, in disarray;
That hillock—or is it perhaps a cloud?...
And the road, soft, smooth, to the sunset spreading,
Where passers-by, each slowly, mutely treading,
Pick their steps, like an old man, chilled, head bowed,
Back bent... Already eager night has blended
Into the weakening day: barely the skies
Change color, as, still pale, the mists arise,
Hang in the dark's congenial swell, suspended.
Lamps in the windows of the houses shine
Questioning glances on this still, hushed sea;
Burning their reds and golds, they seem to be
Signals cast far and wide, some deathly sign.
Ah! The ennui, the melancholy of
This day, gasping its last in languidness!
And yet, I sing no praise of you, nor bless
Your splendorous heat, you whom the sun above
Graces with light, O Italy! Or you,
O Egypt, of the royal-sculptured sphinx!
Or you, O East, where daytime gently sinks
Into the evening's golden-ambered hue...
October's and November's twilights, gray,
Have for me charms to wrap themselves within.
My heart, the doleful landscape's doleful twin,
Watches his autumn and his mists, as they

Amélie Murat 927

L'horizon de son rêve en est tout obscurci;
Et loin de s'affranchir de l'ombre, fol ou sage,
Mon cœur se livre avec un impuissant remords
A ses charmes profonds comme des maléfices.
Et vous m'apparaissez, ô froides tentatrices
Que poursuit mon ardent désir: villes du Nord,
Villes de Flandre avec vos canaux blancs de cygnes,
Vos légers carillons tombant des beffrois lourds,
Et villes d'Angleterre où s'enfièvre le cours
De la vie âpre, au clair des globes rectilignes.
Dans ma mémoire et sur mes lèvres vous chantez,
Vers fluides de Rodenbach et de Verlaine,
O musique subtile à l'égal d'une haleine,
Dont mes songes et mes souvenirs sont hantés!
Et tandis que le feu palpite dans la chambre,
Je savoure et recueille en moi, jusqu'à la nuit,
Le mal délicieux et le fervent ennui
Des crépuscules gris d'octobre et de novembre.

_____

PORTRAITS

J'ai bien souvent scruté le regard des portraits
Qui dédaignent, contraints à l'exil du musée,
La foule, d'un détail ou d'un nom amusée,
—Morts attentifs frôlés par les vivants distraits...

Tous: les rois somptueux, les bruns infants d'Espagne,
Et les princes anglais des tableaux de Van Dyck,
L'heureux fumeur flamand, le bourgeois, le syndic,
Les donateurs qu'un ange ailé d'or accompagne;

Threaten to form: his dream's horizon is
Darkened by them as well; but, mad or wise,
He yields to their cursed charms, and weakly tries
To make amends... And, like those lures of his,
You, O chill temptresses, loom frigidly—
Cities of northern climes that I lust for:
Flemish towns, with white-swanned canals, and your
Stone belfries' light-voiced chimes; and dear to me,
Also, those English towns where life's duress
Streams in its fervent course, lighted by those
* Square globes on streetlamps, set in proper rows;
While in my mind, and on my lips no less,
You, O smooth-flowing verses of Verlaine,
Of Rodenbach, pour out your northern heart
In music fragile as a breath, whose art
Fills, haunts my thoughts, my dreams, again, again!...
And, while my hearth-fire flames, crackles away,
I gather up and savor, till the sky
Grows dark, the sweet malaise wrought in me by
October's and November's twilights, gray.

Le Livre de poésie, "Nostalgies"

PORTRAITS

Often have I gazed at that scornful stare
That portraits, in museum-exile, cast,
Glaring, upon the living, who brush past,
Amused by some detail, some name seen there.

Princes—dark Spaniards, English—rich-garbed kings,
That happy Flemish smoker of Van Dyck,
Syndics, contented burghers and the like,
And patrons grazed by angels' gilded wings;

* If the allusion to the *globes rectilignes* illuminating English cities is somewhat obtuse—
I think I have understood it correctly—the reference to the "northern" inspiration of the
symbolist poets Paul Verlaine (1844–1896) and Georges Rodenbach (1855–1898) should be
clear enough; the former, for the poems of his "Paysages belges" in the collection *Romances
sans paroles,* largely the fruit of his wanderings with Arthur Rimbaud, and the latter, for the
many poems inspired by his Belgian homeland.

Amélie Murat 929

Les dames en atours du temps passé, haussant,
Plein de charme étranger ou de grâce française,
Leur visage poudré sur la guimpe ou la fraise,
Et les nymphes qui sont des princesses du sang;

La vierge que posa quelque beauté célèbre,
L'innocente accordée en fichu de linon,
Les figures dont nul n'a deviné le nom,
Et dont l'image, acquise à l'oubli, s'enténèbre:

Ils ont agi, parlé, senti, vécu, ces morts!
Ils furent comme nous des hommes et des femmes;
L'angoisse et l'espérance ont possédé leurs âmes,
Le sommeil, le plaisir, l'effort, soumis leurs corps.

Leurs lèvres au baiser d'amour se sont écloses;
Leurs paumes où la vie affluait en chaleur,
Ont tenu l'éventail, ou l'épée, ou la fleur,
Et leurs yeux ont connu les êtres et les choses.

Du ciel dont s'imprégnait leur regard lumineux
Quand naquit l'effigie au geste de l'artiste,
Le reflet dilué dans la couleur persiste,
Et l'histoire d'un siècle obscur s'éclaire en eux.

A travers le brouillard du temps, ils semblent suivre
Un songe, un souvenir subtil qui leur fut cher,
Et malgré la froideur inerte de leur chair,
Au fond de leur passé, continuer à vivre...

———————

Ne plus être. Ne plus assister à la fête
Des matins de cristal et des couchants de feu,
Des automnes où l'or dans de l'or se reflète,
Des printemps où le bleu se baigne dans du bleu.
Ne plus goûter la saine et primitive joie
De mouvoir au soleil un corps souple et dispos,
Choisir un but, gravir un mont, suivre une voie,
Alterner le plaisir, la tâche et le repos.
Quand le conseil du froid ou de l'ombre nous livre
Au tiède et lumineux abri de la maison,
Ne plus veiller la flamme ou feuilleter le livre,

Fine regal ladies robed in antique wise,
Heads fraught with foreign charm or Gallic graces,
Ruffled and wimpled, powdered white their faces,
And royal princesses in nymphlike guise;

The virgin, posed by beauteous paragon;
The innocent betrothed, fine kerchief tied
About her head; figures unknown, who hide
Their features, shadowed, in oblivion:

And yet, these dead once lived, felt, spoke! Nor ever
Less were they than ourselves, women and men.
Woes, hopes possessed their souls: oft and again
Their bodies knew sleep, joy, and hard endeavor.

Their lips once bloomed to love's kiss and caress;
Their hands, warm with the heat of life, once held
The fan, the sword, the flower; their gaze once dwelled
On things and beings, and all their world's largesse.

Dark story of a century shines through
Their forms, born of the artist's brush, inspired
By their luminous glances, heaven-fired:
Lasting reflections, though age-dimmed their hue.

Across the mist of time they seem to give
Eye to a fragile dream, memory still fresh
And dear; and, though lifeless and cold their flesh,
Appear, deep in their past, yet still to live....

Le livre de poésie, "Nostalgies"

To be no more. No more to join the bright
Crystalline feast of morning and the blaze
Of sunset; autumns, when golds cast their light
On gold; springtimes, when blues bathe in the day's
Pure blue... No more to taste the joy, the sheer
Bliss of a body moving in the sun,
Supple and strong and fit; to persevere,
To reach a goal, to climb a hill, to run,
To stroll; to know, by turns, work, pleasure, rest...
And when the cold and darkness dismally
Urge us to seek our refuge, and suggest

Amélie Murat 931

Ou laisser à son rêve obéir sa raison...
Ne plus joindre ses doigts sur son cœur de poète
Qui sait diviniser tout sentiment humain,
Et qui, l'œuvre du jour lui semblant imparfaite,
Se confie et s'exalte en l'œuvre de demain.
Ne plus être. Prévoir qu'aussitôt notre place
Sera prise et comblée, et que des pas nouveaux
De nos pas éloignés disperseront la trace,
Que d'autres cueilleront le fruit de nos travaux;
Que l'arbre lent planté par notre main tardive
N'étendra pas sur nous son ombre ou son parfum,
Et qu'il nous ment, l'espoir vaniteux que survive
Notre nom périssable à notre corps défunt.
Ne plus être... Et songer que nulle force au monde,
Ni ce grand flot d'amour vital et créateur
Que la nuit haute verse à la terre profonde
Où la rosée a l'air d'une douce moiteur,
Ni les larmes, les cris, la plainte ou la prière
De l'être dont le moindre appel fut notre aimant,
Rien ne pourra briser le sceau, lever la pierre,
Et rompre ce terrible et morne enchantement!
Ah! comme il est heureux que la Vie infidèle,
Chaque jour, nous portant l'angoisse de souffrir,
Epuise ce désir fou que nous avons d'elle,
Et lasse notre effroi révolté de mourir:
Peut-être, à l'heure où vient le terme inévitable,
Que, vaincu par l'épreuve et meurtri par l'effort,
Comme un enfant chagrin que la fatigue accable,
On se couche, et le front sur ses bras, qu'on s'endort?

The comfort of the hearth, ah! not to be
Able to watch the fire, no more to skim
A book, or let the mind go wandering where
The dream will take it, bending to its whim!...
No more to sit with a poetic air,
Hands clasped upon our breast, like one who will
Render divine each human sentiment,
And who, if work performed today turns ill,
Yet revels in tomorrow's, confident...
To be no more. To see that soon our place
Will be taken and filled; that other feet
Will leave new tracks as, blithely, they efface
Our own, more and more distant in retreat;
That others, too, will pluck the fruits that our
Labors produce; that the slow-growing tree,
Late planted by our hands, will never flower
Or spread its fragrant shade for us to see;
That it is vain to hope our name might last
Beyond our mortal flesh's life and death.
To be no more... To think that, in this vast
Expanse, this world of ours, neither the breath
Of life, born of the floods of love that night
Pours down on earth, moist in the dew-soft air,
Nor any other power at all—despite
The tearful cries, laments, even the prayer
Of him whose merest call I never could
Resist... No, nothing is there that can break
This dark and frightful spell, no force that would
Shatter the deadly seal, or undertake
To raise the stone! How fortunate that each
Day of perfidious Life, heaping on us
Ever more woe, more suffering, helps us reach
The end with less wild will to live, and thus
Calms our rebellious fear of dying! Yes,
Perhaps, bruised, spent by toil and moil, we keep
That rendezvous like child—glum, spiritless—
Who lies, cradling his head, and falls asleep?

Le livre de poésie, "Vers la mort, et au-delà"

Amélie Murat 933

POUR L'ATTENTE

Quand je vous reverrai, vous que je ne vois plus
Qu'à travers le bleuâtre enfoncement du rêve...
—Et si la nuit me tend, sa sœur l'aube m'enlève
Le fil dont me guider en ces lacis rompus:

Je chercherai vos yeux, ma source et ma clairière,
Et ce tout petit point tremblant de leur clarté
Dont le rayonnement est pour moi dilaté
Jusqu'à couvrir le monde et dorer la lumière.

J'approcherai du temple clos de votre front
Mes poignets réunis et mes paumes tressées,
Pour sentir la chaleur de vos mille pensées
Fluer en mes dix doigts qui s'en imprègneront.

Je ne verrai plus rien que votre seul visage...
Jusqu'à l'heure où cessant de le trop regarder,
Je fermerai les yeux pour le mieux posséder
En ma pupille où s'est empreinte son image.

Je n'entendrai plus rien, dans la chaude langueur
Où les mots sont couchés à l'ombre du silence,
Rien que le petit bruit... le petit bruit immense
Que fait mon cœur battant... battant sur votre cœur!

POUR L'AMOUR OPINIÂTRE

Reprendre jour par jour un cœur qui s'est dépris,
Mais dont l'indifférence exhausse encor le prix;
Enrober de silence, et de ruse, et d'adresse,
Le brusque et bondissant retour de la tendresse
Qui veut forcer la porte en criant: Je suis là!
Se parer pour la lutte ainsi que Dalila,
Mais l'amour, non la mort, sera notre victoire;
Ne point se désister devant l'échec, mais croire
Qu'on obtiendra demain ce qui manque aujourd'hui.
N'avoir pas plus d'orgueil que le pauvre éconduit

FOR THE WAITING

When I see you once more, you whom I gaze
On but in dreams' dark bluish depths... (Ah! When
Night gives, and dawn, her sister, takes again
That thread that guides me through their well-worn maze!...)

I shall seek out your eyes—my fount, my bright,
Flickering little spot of clarity,
Whose radiance spreads about, and that, for me,
Covers the whole world with its golden light.

I shall place at the altar of your brow
My hands—wrists joined and fingers intertwined—
To feel the warmth that, flowing from your mind,
Will steep them in its thousand thoughts somehow.

I shall look at your face, no other—none!—
Until that moment when, gazing no more,
I close my eyes to hold it dearer; for
They keep its features graven, every one.

I shall hear nothing in the languorous heat
Where words lie, in the shadow-silence cast...
Only the little sound—little, but vast—
Of my heart beating to your own heart's beat!

Passion, "Avec l'amour"

FOR LOVE UNYIELDING

To bring to love again, day after day,
A heart that cast love out, and yet to play
Cold and indifferent, so that it might be
Prized all the more; to disguise artfully,
With silence and with ruse, the rash return
Of passion, rushing headlong, that would yearn
To burst in, crying: "Here I am!"; to dress
And primp, Delilah-like—for combat, yes:
But love, not death, will be the victor's spoils;
To be not she, disheartened, who recoils
Before defeat, but hopes to realize

Amélie Murat 935

Qui vers le même riche, ouvre, à la même place,
La même main toujours frustrée... et jamais lasse!
Mais réprimant la plainte ou le geste chagrin,
Sourire... et si l'on voit que l'autre élude ou craint
La grande passion téméraire et sauvage,
Ne dévoiler qu'un tout petit amour bien sage.

Sentir qu'à ce jeu grave où l'espoir est tendu,
On regagne... on reprend ce qu'on avait perdu;
Que cette main, distraite hier, cherche la nôtre,
Et ne convoitera la chaleur d'aucune autre;
Lire enfin notre grâce au clair de ce regard...
Mais lorsque, ô mon amour, tremblez qu'il soit trop tard!
Lorsque s'achèvera l'épuisante conquête,
La mort qui s'embusquait dans nos pas, louve en quête
D'un bonheur à broyer tout vif, viendra manger
Cet agneau pantelant sur le cou du berger!
Et ces soins, ces combats, cette attente, ce zèle,
Ce frémissant espoir que sa ferveur décèle,
Ce don définitif du cœur qui nous revient
Trop tard, ô mon amour!—ne serviront de rien!

PETIT BESTIAIRE

Amour des êtres

Quelque moine bouddhiste en moi revit peut-être,
Qui, gardant le respect et l'amour de tout être,
Evite en son chemin d'écraser la fourmi,
Sauve du jardinier le bourdon endormi
Dans la rose, permet à l'obscure araignée
De parfiler sa toile, au plafond, rencognée,

The fruits, tomorrow, that today denies;
To be not prideful, any more than that
Poor soul who begs the wealthy plutocrat,
Each day, yet, empty-handed, begs again;
To smile a smile without reproach... And when
She sees that he avoids, in timid fashion,
The slightest aspect of a savage passion,
To show the merest, gentlest trace of love.

Hopeful, to play this solemn game, whereof
The aim is to restore what is no more—
Might yesterday's daydreaming hand reach for
Our own, and not, with covetous desire,
Seek out another's, warming to her fire!
To see our grace illumined in his glances...
But when, my love—tremble, lest circumstances
Conspire: too late, too late!—when our campaign
Wears itself out, then death, long having lain,
Coy, in our footsteps, she-wolf out in quest
Of some still-living joy to gnash, will wrest
This lamb, torn from the shepherd's breast, and fall
To feasting on its shivering flesh! And all
Those fervent cares, that struggling, quivering
Hope that her zeal discloses... Everything...
And that heart, too, at last bestowed, long sought—
Too late, my love! Too late!—will go for naught!

Passion, "Avec l'amour"

———————

LITTLE BESTIARY

Love of Creatures

Perhaps there lives some Buddhist monk in me,
Who loves, respects all life so much that he
Steps carefully aside when, on his path,
He spies an ant; saves from the gardener's wrath
The bee asleep inside the rose; permits
The sombre spider, curling up in its
Dark corner of the ceiling, hanging high,
To ravel out its threads (but frees the fly!);

(Mais délivre pourtant la mouche), et voudrait voir,
Si, d'abolir la Faim, il avait le pouvoir,
L'aigle aider l'alouette... et l'agneau qui se trouve
Perdu dans la forêt, téter la mère louve.

Visite du pigeon

Ce bruit d'une eau qu'on fouette ou d'un satin qu'on froisse,
Disjoint, mais d'un réveil sans heurt et sans angoisse,
Le repos méridien de ce long jour brûlant.
Salut! c'est toi, voisin d'en face, pigeon blanc,
Qui t'introduis chez moi, patte oblique, aile haute.
Colombe de la Bible, Esprit de Pentecôte,
Ramier de La Fontaine, es-tu le messager
Que je dois, d'un symbole ou d'un pli, décharger?
Non, ton vol est vacant. Posé sur la fenêtre,
Tu sembles, de ton œil latéral, reconnaître
Le gîte et l'habitant... comme si tu pensais
Qu'un grenier de poète offrant facile accès,
Ce voisinage aérien rend fort licite
Ta brusque, familière et charmante visite.

Le coq de la voisine

C'est un coq blanc, gonflé comme un plat d'œufs battus,
Quand, juché noblement sur un tas de fétus,
Il semble, du soleil, s'affirmer l'oiseau-lige.
Un coq loyal, qui sait comment l'honneur l'oblige,
Cherche, d'un bec soigneux, pour ses poules, des vers,
Trousse équitablement des plumages divers
Et boute le chien hors de la cour, son domaine.
Mais une vanité candide, presque humaine,

And who, could he quell Hunger, would delight
To see the eagle aid the lark's frail flight...
And see the lamb, lost in the forest, pressed,
Suckling, against the she-wolf's ample breast.

Visit of the Pigeon

That sound of water whisked or satin crumpled
Severs, like an awakening—calm, unrumpled—
The noontime pause in this long, torrid day.
Greetings! You, neighbor from across the way,
White pigeon—high your wings, outspread your feet—
Who visit me. Are you the Paraclete,
The Holy Spirit, or are you that dove
* That La Fontaine so fondly tells us of?
Are you the faithful messenger come winging
Hither, some billet doux or symbol bringing?
No, you bring nothing in your flight. Perched by
The window, as you cast your sidewise eye
Here, there, you seem to recognize the space,
And me as well... as if you thought this place,
This poet's loft, easy of access for
An airborne neighbor living just next door—
No closer to the ground than yours, now is it?—
Permits your brash, but charming, friendly visit.

The Neighbor Lady's Cock

White cock, fluffed like a plate of whipped-up eggs,
Perched nobly on a pile of straw, he begs
Inform us (so it seems) that loyally
His Fowlship serves the sun in fealty.
As honor dictates, and with cautious bill,
He digs for worms to feed his hens, and will
Tumble the lot, of every feather, fairly—
No favorites!—and chase the dog out, squarely,
From his farmyard domain. But often he
Is moved by almost human vanity—

---

* While the eminent fabulist La Fontaine populates his fables about a dozen times with
pigeons and *colombes* (doves), in point of fact, he never actually does include the *ramier*
(ringdove) among his fauna, as the poet categorically declares.

Le pousse, lorsqu'on dit, l'admirant: "Qu'il est beau!"
A redresser du col son glorieux jabot
—La crête en majuscule et la queue en paraphe—
Tout comme s'il posait devant le photographe.

Chant du rossignol

Rossignol, je t'en prie, éloigne ta chanson!
Qu'un merle négligeable, un infime pinson,
Viennent, si c'est leur goût, filer jusqu'à ma porte
Un couplet gentiment anodin, il n'importe.
Mais toi, toi dont le chant, dressé comme un pistil,
Recueille l'amoureux pollen des nuits, faut-il
Que du faubourg banal, on t'entende... on t'écoute?
Il est des cœurs en peine où ton doux lied s'égoutte
Comme, sur une plaie irritable, un mordant.
On croyait apaisés ou vaincus, cependant,
Cet amour, ce chagrin... et ta voix les réveille.
Emporte au fond du bois la néfaste merveille
D'un tout petit gosier brûlant de passion:
Rossignol, ta musique est de perdition!

Chat sauvage

Velu, souple, onduleux ainsi qu'une chenille,
Quand tu viens, de façon résolue et gentille,
M'aborder d'un seul bond au travers du chemin,
Que veux-tu, petit chat? qu'attends-tu de ma main?
Sors-tu de la forêt... ou bien de la cuisine?
(Le bourg est proche, mais la campagne est voisine.)
Tes ancêtres les grands félins t'ont, je le crois,
Légué l'instinct premier de l'affût dans le bois,
Cependant qu'une mère aimable et domestique
T'inspira de plus près—ton manège l'indique—
Quelque désir second d'un geste d'amitié.
Le cœur d'un petit chat peut être, par moitié,
Sauvage et confiant, irréductible et tendre.
Tu sais ma paume vide... et qu'il n'en faut attendre,
Fût-ce à l'heure des chauds fumets, aucun régal.

When he hears: "Oh, how beautiful!"—to puff
His chest with pride, ruffle his splendid ruff—
Paraph-tailed, crest all caps!—as if he were
Striking a pose for the photographer.

Song of the Nightingale

Nightingale, pray be still, off with your song!
Let some poor finch, mere blackbird, come along,
If sing they will, and spin before my door
A harmless couplet! I don't care! But your
Song, yours!—that stands out, pistil-like, full of
The nighttime gatherings of pollen-love...
What? Must this banal borough have to hear
Your song? Many's the suffering heart, I fear,
Whose woe lies calmed—or so it seems! But when
Your warblings drip their sweet drops once again
Onto the smarting wound... Ah, then the bitten
Heart wakes to its chagrin, all the more smitten.
Go, take your ill-starred wonder—mini-throat,
Burning with passion in its every note—
Into the woods, to voice your exultation:
Your music, nightingale, sings our damnation!

Wild Cat

Soft as a caterpillar is your fur,
Supple, and smooth, and lithe, as you bestir
Yourself to cross my path, my little cat,
With one determined bound. Is it a pat
You're after, pet? What promise is there in
This hand of mine? Tell me, where have you been?
The woods? The kitchen?... (Both are quite close by.)
Your feline instinct has taught you to lie
In wait, like your great cousins, but a mother—
Tamed to more pleasant ways—inspired another
Wish (as your tactic proves)! to wit, a gentle,
Loving, and friendly touch, quasi-parental.
A cat's heart can be both wild, unsubdued,
And tender, mild. You know I have no food
Here in my palm, no feast, even when through
The air waft warm, delicious scents. Yet you
Come, on a sudden whim, lest I ignore

Tu viens pourtant, d'un vif coup de tête amical,
Me rappeler ta prompte et légère présence.
Car si ton appétit trouve sa suffisance
Dans la jungle facile où tu tends tes appâts,
Il y manque, à ton gré, au plus fameux repas
—Et voilà quelle faim sur mon sentier t'amène—
Le souverain dessert de la caresse humaine.

Génie du foyer

La maison dort... mais le chat veille. Entre deux sommes
Réintégrant le monde et les aîtres des hommes,
J'entends le fin grelot d'argent de son collier
Mener la farandole à travers l'escalier.
La maison dort. Le chat, fidèle agent-vigile,
Monte un guet rigoureux, ouvre une ronde agile,
Fait détaler, devant ses retours querelleurs,
Les souris... et peut-être, écarte les voleurs?
Ou mieux, ce chat, plus qu'un exact fonctionnaire,
Est le dieu familier, non point imaginaire,
Mais réel, mais vivant, du nocturne logis.
Et ses yeux incisifs, des ténèbres surgis,
Savent pourfendre, ainsi que d'adroits petits glaives,
Les fantômes chagrins qui menaçaient nos rêves.

Maintenant l'étape est brève
Qui conduit au Pays noir.
Séché, le rosier du rêve
Qu'arrosait le jeune espoir.

Your lissome loveliness's presence; for,
If, in the yielding jungle, where you spread
Your snares, your appetite is better fed,
Your meals, even as fine as fine can be,
Lack the one thing you sought to find with me—
Hungering for a bit of tenderness—
That fine dessert: a human being's caress.

Household Spirit

The house sleeps... but the cat's awake. Between
Two naps, returning to the human scene,
I hear his collar's silver-tinkling bell
Dancing its jig across the stairs, pell-mell.
The house sleeps. But the cat, night watchman, keeps
His faithful, earnest vigil, round-eyed; peeps
And peers about with darting glance, and sends
Packing the mice before his growls; defends
The house—perhaps?—from thieving robbers... Or,
Not a mere functionary but, much more,
This cat is the nighttime divinity—
Real, living, not imagined—of the home.
His eyes, like blades, piercing the darkling gloam,
Run through, with agile little dagger-gleams,
The phantoms, dour, that would destroy our dreams.

Le chant de la vie

———————

Brief the stay and short the way
Toward the Black Land. Withered, dead,
Now, the rosebush, dream-bouquet,
Watered by youth's hope, long fled.

*   *Vivre encore,* "Reliquat des doutes"

* This quatrain introduces the second section of the volume *Vivre encore,* each of whose
seven groupings contains a brief liminary piece, from one to six lines in length.

Cécile Sauvage (1883–1927)

Daughter of a schoolteacher father with peasant roots and a mother of Walloon ancestry, Cécile-[Anne-Marie-Antoinette] Sauvage was born at La Roche-sur-Yon, southwest of Paris, on July 20, 1883, and moved at the age of five with her family to the Basses-Alpes town of Digne, where her father was appointed to teach history. It is said that it was to him that she owed her early love of poetry, memorizing almost all the fables of La Fontaine by the time she was sixteen—no mean feat—and steeping herself, at his urging, in the French classics, as well as in translations of Shakespeare and Dante.

A poem, "Les trois muses," written when she was twenty, seems to have been doubly responsible for the course that the rest of her life was to follow. On the one hand, it was brought by her doting father to the attention of his idol, Frédéric Mistral—the patriarch of modern Provençal poetry, riding the crest of a wave that was leading to the Nobel Prize for literature in 1904—who, perhaps sincerely, perhaps pro forma, encouraged her to keep writing. And she did. On the other hand, it was the hyphen that would link her to Pierre Messiaen, schoolmaster-translator of Shakespeare and Emily Dickinson, and editor of a review in Saint-Etienne in which her opus was published, and who became her husband shortly thereafter. As it happened, the musical world would also benefit from this concatenation of results all stemming from the same small cause: the first of her two sons, Olivier Messiaen, born in Avignon in 1908, became one of the major avant-garde composers of the twentieth century, admired especially for his extravagant and monumental ten-movement symphony, *Turangalîla* (1948).

It was also for this son that Cécile Sauvage, having already produced a brief, rather traditional, nature-steeped collection *Tandis que la terre tourne*, composed *L'âme en bourgeon,* inspired by and dedicated to him while he was still in the womb. Whatever posthumous celebrity she has continued to enjoy—less, unfortunately, than she desired or deserves—has come from these paeans to mother- and childhood, sensitive and often profound lyrics on the miracle of maternity. The collections that followed were more and more dissonantly tinged with an introspective melancholy, attributed by some contemporaries to disillusionment over her lack of literary acclaim. Others saw it as an indication that, as a lapsed Catholic, like her husband, she yearned to be able to accept her former faith. (Ironically, Olivier, to the bafflement of his agnostic parents, was—and remained—particularly devout, as his vast body of religious compositions would attest.) The delicate, at times almost Verlainean, poems in

Mélancolie and *Fumées* bear progressive witness to the poet's ever more mournful state of soul. The birth of her second son in 1912, the same year as the publication of her last collection, the Keats-and-Shelleyesque *Le vallon,* would seem to have deepened rather than lightened her depression, though she continued sporadically to write. A lyrical drama, *Aimer après la mort,* and short poems interspersed with prose for a collection to be entitled *Primevère,* were left unfinished at her death in 1927. The following year, a bevy of distinguished contemporaries—Anna de Noailles (see pp. 834–57), the novelist Georges Bernanos, the poet Tristan Derème, and a dozen more—eulogized her in glowing terms, though a bit too late, unfortunately, to lift her spirits.[1] Lucie Delarue-Mardrus (see pp. 800–819) sounded a particularly emphatic (and not uncontroversial) note: "At a time when womanhood is howling so much for equality of the sexes, it is good to keep in mind the lines of this simple young woman who, thanks to her being a poet, responded in advance to all of its errant ways."[2]

As indicated in the notes to the following selection, I have chosen for translation poems from five of her published collections and the unfinished *Primevère.*

NOTES

1. The tribute appeared in a special number of the Saint-Etienne journal *Les Amitiés* in September 1928.

2. Quoted in Jean Tenant's introduction to the comprehensive volume of the poet's work, *Œuvres de Cécile Sauvage,* p. xv. This introduction provides the fullest available— though perhaps not wholly objective—biographical sketch of the poet and an appreciation of her *œuvre.* The reader can also consult, in addition to the number of *Les Amitiés,* Jean de Gourmont's *Les muses d'aujourd'hui,* pp. 189–204, and Henri Pourrat's *La veillée de novembre.*

Sors de ta chrysalide, ô mon âme, voici
L'Automne. Un long baiser du soleil a roussi
Les étangs; les lointains sont vermeils de feuillage,
Le flexible arc-en-ciel a retenu l'orage
Sur sa voûte où se fond la clarté d'un vitrail;
La brume des terrains rôde autour du bétail
Et parfois le soleil que le brouillard efface
Est rond comme la lune aux marges de l'espace.
Mon âme, sors de l'ombre épaisse de ta chair:
C'est le temps dans les prés où le silence est clair,
Où le vent, suspendant son aile de froidure,
Berce dans les rameaux un rêve d'aventure
Et fait choir en jouant avec ses doigts bourrus
La feuille jaune autour des peupliers pointus.
La libellule vole avec un cri d'automne
Dans ses réseaux cassants; la brebis monotone
A l'enrouement fêlé des branches dans la voix;
La lumière en faisceaux bruine sur les bois.
Mon âme en robe d'or faite de feuilles mortes
Se donne au tourbillon que la rafale apporte
Et chavire au soleil sur la pointe du pied
Plus vive qu'en avril le sauvage églantier;
Cependant que de loin elle voit sur la porte,
Ecoutant jusqu'au seuil rouler des feuilles mortes,
Mon pauvre corps courbé dans son châle d'hiver.
Et mon âme se sent étrangère à ma chair.
Pourtant, docilement, lorsque les vitres closes
Refléteront au soir la fleur des lampes roses,

O soul of mine, burst from your chrysalis,
Autumn is come. The sun, with long-drawn kiss,
Gilds red the ponds; far off, a crimson glow
Colors the leaves; the rainbow, bending low,
Drives back the storm atop its arch, where blend
Clear stained-glass hues; the ground-mists form, suspend
Their droplets round the flock, now and then rise
Skyward, before the sun, that, to our eyes—
Befogged flat disk—presents a full-moon face,
Enshrouded, on the very edge of space.
My soul, burst from your flesh's shadows deep:
Now is the moment when the meadows keep
Their silence pure and still, and when the breeze,
Holding its chill wing back, rocks reveries
To sleep—adventure-dreams—entwining there
Among the boughs and, sweeping through the air,
With chubby fingers, golden leaves that fall,
A-heap, about the poplars, pointed, tall.
The dragonfly, in brittle zigzaggings
Flitting here, there, the cry of autumn sings;
The lamb's hoarse voice cackles and cracks, repeats
The sound of crackling branches in its bleats;
The sunbeams drizzle on the woods in sheaves…
My soul, in golden robe, woven of leaves
Now dead, yields to the whirlwind swirling round,
Gust-blown, goes falling to the sun-lit ground
On tiptoes, yet brisker than spring's wild rose.
And, all the while, she sees in distant pose
My body, bent, listening at the door,
Wrapped in a winter shawl as, more and more,
The dead leaves pile; and my poor soul feels quite
The stranger to my flesh. But when, by night,
The windows, closed, reflect the pink lamps' flower,
Pale in the docile darkness of the hour,

* There seems to be a curious incongruity between the title of this poem, suggesting the
end of autumn, and its text, evoking its arrival, but I translate it as given.

Cécile Sauvage 947

Elle regagnera le masque familier,
Et, servante modeste avec un tablier,
Elle trottinera dans les chambres amères
En retenant des mains le sanglot des chimères.

———————

Si la lune rose venait
En robe de petite fille
Danser sur le foin nouveau-né
Devant la source qui frétille,
Elle aurait tes deux mollets ronds
Et tes yeux argentés d'eau brune,
Mon fils, poupée en court jupon,
Au visage de clair de lune.

———————

J'entends tout bas pleurer les roses,
Les branches vertes, l'eau d'argent;
Mon pauvre cœur tant indigent
Est plus sûr de ses jours moroses
Que le lac ne l'est de son eau
Calme où nagent des feuilles rondes
Et que l'amour du jeune oiseau
Ne l'est des ramures profondes.

Then will she wear again her mask long-worn,
And, servant pertly-aproned, modest-born,
Will patter through the bitter chambers, trying
To hold back her chimeras, sobbing, sighing.

*   *Tandis que la terre tourne*

————————

If the moon, tinted pink, perchance—
Dressed like a little girl—drew nigh
The quivering spring to do her dance
Over the new-born hay hard by,
She would have your plump calves, your brown,
Deep water-silvered eyes, son mine—
My doll, in dainty baby-gown—
And your face, where the moonbeams shine.

†   *L'âme en bourgeon*

————————

I hear the roses weeping low,
The silvery water, boughs of green;
More sure is my heart of its woe—
Poor heart!—than is the pond serene
Of its smooth face, leaves floating free;
More sure than is the young bird's love
Sure of the woodland greenery,
And branches twining thick above.

* I include this poem as an example of the poet's somewhat traditional youthful manner—not without its stylistic inconsistencies—quite different from that of her later years. It is one of the dozen poems dated 1905–1908 in this, her first collection, published in 1910 and dedicated to her parents.
    † The twenty-odd poems of *L'âme en bourgeon*, dating from 1908 and chronologically the second of her collections, were inspired by the birth of the poet's first son, Olivier Messiaen, and were dedicated to him.

Langueur pure, douce harmonie
Des pelouses et des sentiers,
Les crapauds chantent dans ma vie
Avec leurs violons mouillés.

☾

Les mélancoliques crapauds
Avec leurs violons sous l'eau
Font une musique à la lune.

O crapauds, vos violons verts
Faits d'eau morte et de cristal clair
Sont cachées sous la mare brune.

La lune est au milieu de vous
Dans l'eau et son visage doux
Pleure la pâle destinée
D'une musique insoupçonnée.

☾

La lune blanche au rire éteint
Glisse dans l'air où rien ne pèse;
On entend le frisson lointain
D'un long murmure qui s'apaise.

L'heure est si pure qu'on dirait
Que la montagne est transparente
Et que les arbres dilués
Sont les reflets d'une eau dormante.

☽

The languor, the harmonious air
Of greenswards, pathways, and the song
* The toads sing in my life, as their
Violins moistly hum along...

☽

Sad, the toads bow their fiddle strings
Beneath the water: offerings
Of music to the moon beyond.

O toads! Yours, each green violin,
Stillwater-wrought, and crystalline,
Down in the brown depths of the pond.

The moon's light, in the waters traced,
Plays there amongst you: gentle-faced,
It mourns the pale fate—weeping, grieved—
Of a dim music, scarce perceived.

☽

The white moon, her smile pallid grown,
Glides on the air with lightsome glimmer;
One hears the distant trembling moan
Of a long murmur, dimmer, dimmer...

So pure the hour, one might suppose
The hills transparent; on inspection
Even the trees, in weightless pose,
Seem but the sleeping pool's reflection.

* Rather than second-guess the poet, I translate her *crapauds* as "toads," though, given the aquatic context here and in the following lines, frogs (*grenouilles*) would be more expected, the toad—especially the variety found in France—being basically a land animal. Perhaps there is a subtle—far-fetched?—intent here, since the toad does come to the water to spawn.

❨

Après moi celui qui viendra
Sur la route grise et poudreuse
Verra l'empreinte de mon pas
Dont l'argile un instant se creuse,
Mais ne se demandera pas
Quelle peine appuya ce pas
Sur la route silencieuse.

———————

Dans l'herbe trottine un chien,
Une brindille remue,
Un oiseau fuit et plus rien
Ne bouge sur l'avenue.

———————

Je ne veux qu'un rêve
A demi-flottant,
Que mon âme brève
Passe en voletant,
Que la brume fine
L'enveloppe aussi;
Qu'elle s'achemine
Sans autre souci
Que celui d'errer
Avec une brise,
Sur l'arbre léger,
Sur la terre grise.

𝇋

And he who comes here after me,
Over the clay path gray with dust,
Will see my footprint pressed, but he,
I warrant, will not wonder just
What woe it was that someone must
Have labored under, painfully,
Over the path's tranquillity...

Mélancolie

*

———————

In the grass dog toddles by;
Twig goes crackling on the ground;
Bird goes flitting, flying high;
Path grows still now. Not a sound...

Fumées

†

———————

In midair suspended,
But one dream wish I:
One my soul, ascended,
Might dream, fluttering by;
That might swaddled be
By the mist-pearled air,
And that might roam free
With no other care
But to ride a breeze—
Here, there—wander round
In gossamer trees,
On the clay-gray ground.

Fumées

* This coherent grouping of five consecutive vignettes is taken from the hundred-odd
that form the introspective collection *Mélancolie*, dated 1909.

† The twenty-nine poems of *Fumées*, most of which are brief vignettes characteristic of
the poet's style, date from 1910. A number of them, like the present quatrain, are written in
odd-syllable (*impair*) lines, whose lapidary quality I try to approximate.

Cécile Sauvage 953

Des baisers sont échangés;
La bergère et le berger
Se promettent à la brune
D'unir la même infortune;
Et tous deux à pas plus longs
S'éloignent dans le vallon
Enveloppés par la lune.

Ils vont. De tranquilles fleurs
Sous les ombres sans couleur
Frôlent leur marche légère
Et peut-être dans ces cœurs
Font naître avec leur odeur
La tristesse du mystère.

Depuis que je suis aimée,
Quand je vais sous la ramée,
Mes pieds caressent la mousse;
Ma chevelure est plus douce
Sur mon front. Les fleurs se taisent
Et poussent sur mon passage.
Le vent baise mon corsage,
Mon voile me baise.

Here a kiss and there a kiss...
Shepherd lad and shepherd miss
Swear, with twilight tendernesses,
Ever to share life's distresses;
And they saunter, strolling on,
From the valley, thither, yon,
Midst the moon's gentle caresses.

Far they wander. Flowers serene—
Darkling shadows, scarcely seen—
Graze them lightly as they go
Sprightly passing; whose scents might
Give birth in their hearts this night
To dim mysteries of woe.

*   *Le vallon*

Ever since love has come to me
I stroll the bowers fancy-free;
My feet fondle the moss; my hair
Gentles my brow with sweet loving air.
The flowers, in silent genesis,
Spring as I pass. The winds embrace
My breast, and my veil, on my face,
Places a kiss.

†   *Primevère*

* The forty typically bucolic poems of *Le vallon*, the poet's last complete collection, bearing the date 1911, were, curiously, dedicated to her second son, Alain Messiaen, not born until the following year. See *Œuvres de Cécile Sauvage*, pp. xiv, 177.

† Begun around 1913, *Primevère*, a collection of verse somewhat freer than its predecessors, and of a number of prose poems as well, was left unfinished at the time of the poet's death. Though written years after the fact, it was inspired by the remembrance of her engagement and marriage, and was to bear a dedication to her "cher Pierrot."

Cécile Sauvage 955

Louisa Paulin (1888–1944)

A little-known poet in latter-day Occitan, Louisa Paulin presents a link with her literary ancestor Na Castelloza (see p. 63–69 above) and other female representatives of medieval troubadour art. Unlike her distant predecessors, however, who wrote only in what one generally calls by the umbrella-term "Provençal," she was no less proficient in French; and, though she claimed to prefer the former for poetry, she wrote no less in the latter. Reading the frequently light-hearted and almost nonsense-type verse that shared her inspiration with more serious works, one would hardly suspect that she had led anything but a most congenial and even carefree life. The facts, sadly, prove quite the opposite. Jeanine Moulin sums up the rigors of her life in a single sentence: "The love of people and poetry were the only wealth of this woman, who knew two short-lived pregnancies, divorced, suffered a lengthy illness, and finally lost her sight."[1] She might have added that Paulin died quietly on April 23, 1944. Behind those unadorned details lies the story of a simple schoolmistress cum poet, whose capricious imagination endeared her to her pupils over an eighteen-year career, and who, in her personal misfortunes as well as in her several collections of verse—which she published grudgingly, it seems—maintained a stoic resignation, unwilling to burden her friends and readers with her woes. As she herself confided: "I should like to write only poems of light, only songs of joy."[2]

Louisa Paulin was born on December 2, 1888, in Réalmont, near the historic medieval town of Albi, to which she returned in 1930, after spending most of her teaching career in the Limousin town of Tulle. Ill health forced her premature retirement in 1932. The dozen years that followed found her back in her birthplace, receiving accolades for her verse and folkloric prose, which she contributed to a variety of local journals and anthologies in both French and Occitan. Numerous manuscripts were left unpublished at her death.[3]

The translations in the following pages, including four from Occitan, present a selection of Paulin's characteristically varied verse—now playful, now somber—dating from before the onset of her debilitating disease and eventual blindness. The first poem, from her youth, was published posthumously in *Rythmes et cadences,* and appears, along with the others, in French and in Occitan, in the comprehensive collection *Poèmes* (1969), edited, with great affection, by the prominent Albi historian, politician, and Occitan apologist Louis-Charles Bellet. The volume is divided, somewhat arbitrarily, into several sections, and the reader interested in prior publication of much of her work should consult the editor's remarks preceding each of these.

NOTES

1. *La poésie féminine,* 2: 233.

2. Quoted in Louis-Charles Bellet's introduction to *Poèmes,* p. xiii.

3. Bellet's introduction to *Poèmes* (pp. vii–xv) and its bibliography (pp. 319–27) give the most useful, if necessarily incomplete, account of her life and work. See also Théodore Briant, Georges Bouquet, and Pierre Menanteau's *Florilège poétique* of 1955, a collection of her poems in French and Occitan, as well as several other anthologies cited in the same bibliography.

CHANT POUR LE VENT DU SUD

O brise du Sud, viens boire la neige,
nous sommes repus de gel et de vent,
un doux pissenlit a tiré de terre
un petit soleil tout en or vibrant.

O brise du Sud, viens boire la neige,
nous sommes repus de froid et de pluie,
une pâquerette a tiré de terre
un petit soleil frangé de sang vif.

O brise du Sud, qu'Amour te protège,
nous avons tous faim et soif d'être heureux;
chaque œil de bourgeon épie, tout peureux,
ton souffle d'azur qui boira la neige.

LE CHANT DU COQ

Chaque matin le coq demande:
Heu! eu eu eu!
Fait-on mon feu?
Chaque matin le coq demande:
Ha! a a a!
Qui me cuira?
Chaque matin le coq demande:
Ho! o o o!
Est-ce bientôt?

Hé! grand nigaud!
C'est pour Noël,
Pour fêter la terre et le ciel.
C'est Mélanie qui va te cuire,
Découpé en friands morceaux
Dans un joli vin de coteau,
Tout doucement tu vas bruire
Embaumé d'oignons et de thym
Et tu seras un coq au vin.

SONG FOR THE SOUTH WIND

O breeze blown from the South, come drink the snow,
we have had quite our fill of frost and cold;
a dandelion pulls up from the ground
a tiny sun all quivering with gold.

O breeze blown from the South, come drink the snow,
we have had quite our fill of rain and gale;
a gentle daisy pulls up from the ground
a tiny sun fringed with a blood-red veil.

O breeze blown from the South, Love keep you! Oh,
how we all hunger, thirst for happiness:
timid, each bud keeps watching, nonetheless,
to spy your azured breath come drink the snow.

Rythmes et cadences

THE SONG OF THE COCK

Each dawn the cock crows, querying:
"Ho ho!... Rrrit rrrit!...
Is my fire lit?"
Each dawn the cock crows, querying:
"Ho ho!... Rrroo rrroo!...
Who'll cook me? Who?"
Each dawn the cock crows, querying:
"Ho ho!... Rrroon rrroon!...
Will it be soon?"

Ha! You buffoon!
Christmas is when
We'll feast on you, and not till then,
Praise heaven and earth! We'll cut you up
In tasty chunks to simmer, panned
With fragrant thyme and onions, and
Steeped in nice wine—a heaping cup—
Mélanie's favorite recipe:
A coq au vin is what you'll be.

Louisa Paulin 959

Chaque matin le coq demande:
Heu! eu eu eu!
Fait-on mon feu?
Chaque matin le coq demande:
Ha! a a a!
Qui me cuira?
Chaque matin le coq demande:
Ho! o o o!
Est-ce bientôt?

Hé! grand nigaud!
Pour la moisson.
Et c'est la vieille Louison
Qui va gonfler ta maigre panse
D'une farce—quelle bombance!—
Dorée d'œufs frais, parfumée d'ail,
Hâchée bien fin—ah! quel travail—
Et dans l'arome des poireaux
Tu seras une poule au pot.

Chaque matin le coq demande:
Heu! eu eu eu!
Fait-on mon feu?
Chaque matin le coq demande:
Ha! a a a!
Qui me cuira?
Et l'écho, fatigué, lui mande:
Ho! o o o!
Tais-toi, nigaud!

CHANT DE NEIGE

L'Ange de la géométrie, mon cœur,
Ce matin d'hiver veut nous prendre au piège.

L'Ange étincelant nous ouvre, mon cœur,
Le blanc paradis des cristaux de neige.

Each dawn the cock crows, querying:
"Ho ho!... Rrrit rrrit!...
Is my fire lit?"
Each dawn the cock crows, querying:
"Ho ho!.... Rrroo rrroo!...
Who'll cook me? Who?"
Each dawn the cock crows, querying:
"Ho ho!... Rrroon rrroon!...
Will it be soon?"

Ha! You buffoon!
When harvest's done,
That's when we'll glut on you, each one!
Your skinny belly's going to be
Crammed full of goodies, goldenly
Basted with fresh eggs: leeks divine
And pungent garlic, minced up fine—
Old Lise's stuffing, just for you:
And there you'll be, a chicken stew.

Each dawn the cock crows, querying:
"Ho ho!... Rrrit rrrit!...
Is my fire lit?"
Each dawn the cock crows, querying:
"Ho ho!... Rrroo rrroo!...
Who'll cook me? Who?"
Answers the echo, wearying:
"Ho ho!... Rrroon rrroon!...
Be still, buffoon!"

Poèmes, "Choix de poèmes"

SNOW SONG

The Angel of geometry, my heart,
this winter morning, wants to do us in.

The glistening Angel offers us, my heart,
the paradise of white flakes, crystalline.

Et nous sommes là, fascinés, mon cœur,
Par sa merveilleuse et pure science.

Et nous sommes là, prisonniers, mon cœur,
De son ineffable et cruel silence.

DANS LA NUIT

Depuis que l'on t'a pris le ciel de ton enfance
Avec ses grands nuages glorieux
Où se glissaient les doigts de Dieu
En purs rayons décelant sa présence,
De Dieu le père avec sa barbe emmêlée comme un nid
Où se glissait innocent et contrit
Le vol divin de tes mains en prière;

Avec ses arcs-en-ciel précis et vaporeux
Que les anges victorieux
Déroulaient en ouvrant leurs ailes de lumière;
Depuis que la voûte des cieux
Ne s'appuie plus sur nos bonnes collines
Et que les étoiles ne sont plus ces fleurs divines
A la mesure de tes yeux,
Tu as perdu le chemin d'espérance
Qui te livrait les jardins de la nuit
Et tu pleures, dans l'ombre, un royaume détruit.

LA PAUVRE MORTE

Quand le Prince viendra, adieu! je serai morte
—Beau jeune homme étourdi s'est trompé de saison—
Tu viendras quand sur moi on fermera la porte,
La porte de la vie et de l'humble maison.

And here we stand, utterly stunned, my heart,
by its pure science and its wondrousness.

And, prisoners, here we stand entrapped, my heart,
by its sheer silence, awesome, merciless.

Poèmes, "Choix de poèmes"

_____

IN NIGHT'S DARKNESS

Since they've borne off your sky of childhood's days
With its great clouds a-glorying
That God's sly hands were fingering
To prove his presence in the sun's pure rays—
Of God the Father, with His nestlike beard unkempt,
To which your hands, in prayer, would rise, attempt
Contritely innocent, to finger too;

With its rainbows, clean-cut yet raveling,
Work of the angels triumphing
With outspread wings of light spanning the blue;
Since the skies' vault no more lies balancing,
Pressing upon our lovely hills; and since
The stars no more are heavenly flowers whose glints
Echoed your eyes, your gaze...
Ah! You have lost the path of hope once dreamt
That gifted you night's garden, and you cry,
* Mourn in the dark a kingdom gone awry.

Poèmes, "La chanson des regrets"

_____

THE POOR DEAD MAIDEN

When the Prince comes, farewell! Dead shall I be—
Dunderhead beau, you wait too long: time's past!
You'll come, and they'll have shut the door on me,
The door of life, my hovel's door, shut fast.

* I have tried to maintain something of the original's freely rhyming and freely metered
lines, with their curious echoes over unconventional distances.

Louisa Paulin 963

Je tissais pour tes pieds un doux tapis de laine,
Je tissais pour tes yeux un doux tapis de fleurs.
Mais le soir est venu qui a noyé la plaine,
Mais la nuit est venue qui a noyé mon cœur.

Tu n'es pas le soleil, je ne suis pas la rose;
Tous deux suavement accordent leur plaisir:
Tu resteras muet devant ma porte close
Et je n'aurai pas su le nom de mon désir.

LES DEUX CHANSONS

Tandis que s'enivraient les merles
dans les branches des cerisiers
je rêvais d'un collier de perles
et toi tu rêvais de baisers.

Et tandis que chantaient les merles
dans les branches des cerisiers
je parlais d'un collier de perles
et toi tu taisais les baisers.

Et tandis que sifflaient les merles
les deux colliers se sont brisés,
je regardais rouler mes perles
et tu voyais fuir tes baisers.

LA DÉLAISSÉE

Ramier, ramier sauvage
dis-moi, où est ton nid
pour que je m'y repose
auprès de tes petits.

Ramier, ramier sauvage
dis-moi, où est ton nid
pour y porter ma peine
et mon amour aussi

A carpet soft, of wool, I wove your feet,
A carpet soft, of flowers, I wove your eyes.
Dusk came and drowned the plain, covered complete,
Night came and drowned my heart: dark, dead it lies.

You're not the sun, I'm not the rose; each one
Bestows its pleasure, gentle and benign:
You'll stand mute at my closed door; and, undone,
I'll not have known what longing had been mine.

Poèmes, "La chanson des regrets"

———————

THE TWO SONGS

As blackbirds glutted, high among
the cherry boughs, in drunken stance,
I dreamed of a pearl collar, strung,
and kisses loomed before your glance.

As blackbirds sang their song among
the cherry boughs, in drunken stance,
I spoke of a pearl collar, strung,
and kisses dimmed before your glance.

And as the blackbirds chirped among
the boughs, the collars broke, askance.
I saw my pearls come all unstrung,
and all your kisses fled your glance.

Poèmes, "La chanson des regrets"

———————

FORSAKEN, SHE

Ringdove, O ringdove wild,
Tell me, where is your nest?
There, with your little ones,
I would go take my rest.

Ringdove, O ringdove wild,
Tell me, where is your nest?
There would I leave my pain,
And the love I possessed.

Ramier, ramier sauvage
dis-moi, où est ton nid
pour cacher la blessure
qu'a faite mon ami.

Ramier, ramier sauvage
par où s'en va ma vie
Ramier, ramier sauvage
depuis qu'il est parti.

————————

CHANSON POUR RIRE

Le Rat, la Rate sont partis
    —Quel beau voyage!—
Le Rat, la Rate sont partis
    Pour voir Paris.

Ils sont partis en avion
    —Quel beau voyage!—
Ils sont partis en avion
    avec Raton.

En arrivant se sont assis
    —Quel beau voyage!—
En arrivant se sont assis
    Pour voir Paris.

Sur Notre-Dame de Paris
    —Quel beau voyage!—
sur Notre-Dame de Paris,
    quel beau pays!

Ils ont mangé la Tour Eiffel
    —Quel beau voyage!—
Ils ont mangé la Tour Eiffel
    au caramel.

Ringdove, O ringdove wild,
Tell me, where is your nest?
There would I hide the hurt
My beau wrought in my breast.

Ringdove, O ringdove wild,
Where now my life, my quest?—
Ringdove, O ringdove wild—
* Now that he's left my nest.

Poèmes, "La chanson des regrets"

NONSENSE SONG

The Rats went traveling—He and She—
    What a nice trip!
The Rats went traveling—He and She—
    To see Paree.

They went by plane—just fancy that!—
    What a nice trip!
They went by plane—just fancy that!—
    With young son Rat.

When they arrived they settled down—
    What a nice trip!
When they arrived they settled down
    In Paris-town.

On Notre-Dame they found a space—
    What a nice trip!
On Notre-Dame they found a space—
    What a nice place!

They ate the Eiffel Tower, much savored—
    What a nice trip!
They ate the Eiffel Tower, much savored,
    Caramel-flavored.

* I hope that my liberties are in keeping with the simplicity of both the scenario and the rhymes (and non-rhymes) throughout.

Louisa Paulin 967

Ils reviendront tous par "sans fil"
—Quel beau voyage!—
Ils reviendront tous par "sans fil"
Ainsi soit-il!

———————

POUR L'ENFANÇON

Jean-Jean notre bon marchand
ne vend que des ânes blancs.

En a vendu un, lundi,
pour un pied de céleri.

En a vendu deux mardi
pour deux bottes de radis.

Et puis trois le mercredi
pour trois petits canaris.

Et puis quatre le jeudi
pour quatre grosses souris.

Et puis cinq le vendredi
pour cinq puces dans son lit.

Et puis six le samedi
pour sa place au Paradis.

Dimanche n'a rien vendu
Il les avait tous perdus.

They'll all come back via radio—
    What a nice trip!
They'll all come back via radio...
*   Amen! Just so!

Poèmes, "L'escalier de verre"

———————

FOR THE TOT

Jean, nice merchant, sells the masses,
and sells nothing but white asses.

Monday he sold one, did he,
for a head of celery.

Tuesday he sold two, he says,
for two bunch of radishes.

Wednesday he sold three—it varies—
† for a trio of canaries.

And on Thursday four he sold
for four fat mice, so we're told.

And on Friday, five, it's said,
for five fine fleas for his bed.

And Saturday, six—the price
for his place in Paradise.

Sunday was the one day when he
lost them all, so sold not any.

Poèmes, "L'escalier de verre"

---

* I have not reproduced the poet's capricious avoidance of capitals beginning certain lines, probably a decision, for no apparent reason, on the part of her latter-day editor.

† I realize that my version makes sacrifices to rhyme here and in much of this ditty but plead obviously extenuating circumstances.

Louisa Paulin 969

Ah! qui fait pleurer mon enfant?
Voici la fête de Saint-Jean
Nous allons danser tout à l'heure
Il ne faut pas que l'enfant pleure.

Oh! qui fait pleurer mon enfant?
Voici la fête de Saint-Jean
Nous mettrons une robe bleue
Non, non, ne dites pas qu'il pleut.

Oh! qui fait pleurer mon enfant?
Voici la fête de Saint-Jean
Nous achèterons un sifflet
Non, non, mon enfant n'est pas laid.

Oh! qui fait pleurer mon enfant?
Voici la fête de Saint-Jean
Nous sifflerons dans les nuages
Voyez comme l'enfant est sage.

Voyez comme il s'est endormi
Le blanc petit agneau chéri
Jésus, que nous sommes contents
Voici la fête de Saint-Jean.

SOSC

Soscarem, dins la nèit, a de sorgas perdudas,
borrons d'aiga e musicalas flors de lutz
que jamai, jamai plus,
vos vestiran d'amor, ò pauras tèrras nudas!

VILLAGE LULLABY

Who makes my baby cry? Who? Ha?
Tonight's Midsummer Eve! Hurrah!
We'll all be dancing by and by
It's wrong to make my baby cry.

Who makes my baby cry? Who? Ha?
Tonight's Midsummer Eve! Hurrah!
We'll wear a dress blue as the skies
Don't say it's going to rain! Lies, lies!

Who makes my baby cry? Who? Ha?
Tonight's Midsummer Eve! Hurrah!
We'll buy a pennywhistle. Oh!
Don't say my baby's ugly! No!

Who makes my baby cry? Who? Ha?
Tonight's Midsummer Eve! Hurrah!
We'll whistle at the clouds. See? See
What a good baby he can be?

Look! Now, at last, he's slumbering,
Little white lamb, sweet little thing
God above! We're so happy! Ah!
Tonight's Midsummer Eve! Hurrah!

Poèmes, "L'escalier de verre"

---

* DREAM

At night we shall dream of lost freshets, springing,
blossoms of water, flowers of singing light
that nevermore—no, never!—might
clothe you in love, bare lands, poor naked things!

* The collection *Poèmes* contains a number of Louisa Paulin's poetic and prose works in Occitan, one of the Provençal dialects of southern France, "French" by reason of geography if not of language. The present poem was originally published in the volume *Sorgas* (Freshets), in the section entitled "Aigueta" (Brooklet). Clearly, my version avoids a precise reproduction of the poet's whimsical rhymes and repetitions, without sacrificing—I hope—the elements of sound and rhythm characteristic of Occitan poetry since the days of the medieval troubadours.

Louisa Paulin 971

Miracle del silenci, de l'aiga, de la lutz,
ò belòias perdudas!
Qun vent vos a begudas,
ò vos, sorgas perdudas
que podètz plus florir?
Soscarem, dins la nèit, a de sorgas perdudas
e pausarai mon front sus tas bèlas mans nudas...
Mas lagremas, tant-pauc, las veirás pas florir.

COMA L'ÒRT

Coma l'òrt ont florís una darrièra ròsa
—l'òrt tot poirit de plèja, ablasigat de vent—
s'espanta d'aquela flor maienca,
la meu ama t'agaita, ò paure amor tardiu,
e tremòla en t'aparant
de sas doas alas esquissadas.

MALANCONIA

M'aimarás totjorn! Pòd èstre...
Te remembras, al campèstre,
La ròsa que florissiá
Dins lo randal, ufanosa,
Sens saber—la tant urosa!—
Que l'autan la passiriá?

M'aimarás totjorn! Pòd èstre...
Mas l'autan bufa al campèstre.
Nòstra ròsa pòd sofrir!
Ròsa d'amor malurosa,
Ela qu'es pas ufanosa
E que sab que deu morir!

Miraculous, the water, silence, light—
O beauties lost, poor things!—
drunk by a wind come winging...
And you, lost freshets, springing
no more... Nevermore blooming?
At night we shall dream of lost freshets, springing,
and I shall lay my brow in your hands, fair—
so fair, poor things, but now so bare—
and there you will not see my tears spring, blooming...

Sorgas

JUST AS THE GARDEN

Just as the garden with one last rose blooming—
rain-sodden garden blasted by the wind—
looks on with wonder at that Maytime flower,
so my soul looks on you, poor late-hour love,
and, trembling, tries to keep you whole
beneath its worn-out wings, torn all asunder.

Sorgas, "Per un ser d'auton"
[On an autumn evening]

MELANCHOLY

You'll always love me!... So it goes...
Do you recall that country rose
That we saw blooming fair that day
Under the hedge, disdainfully,
With no idea—oh! happy she!—
That autumn would bear her away?

You'll always love me!... So it goes...
But autumn blows on country rose,
And this rose—ours—in torment lies!
Rose of our love—unhappy she!—
And blooming not disdainfully
Because she knows in time she dies!

Poèmes, "Cançons per mon amic"
[Songs for my friend]

LO BÈL MATIN

Aquel matin de Junh s'es pausat sus mon còr
com un vòl de colombs sus la vièlha gleiseta,
frenisent d'alas blancas e de rocols d'amor,
de sospirs tremolants d'aigueta.
Aquel matin de Junh camina al bòrd del cèl,
al bòrd del azur siaud ont navega la glèisa:
belèu, mos bèls espèrs, vèrs aquela aiga vièrja,
vos poiretz enaurar com un ramat d'ausèls.

That June morn lighted on my heart like doves
lighting on the old chapel with their wings
of white, and with their trembling sighs, their love's
cooings and brooklike murmurings.
That June morn wends its way along the sky,
along the calm blue, where the church sails free:
perhaps, fair hopes, in that stream's purity
you will rise up, like birds, and fly on high.

Sorgas, "Prima" [Spring]

Lise Deharme (1898?–1980)

Lise Deharme, née Anne-Marie Hirtz, was born on May 5, 1907. Or 1902. Or
1898. It depends on whom one believes—an example of the uncertainty sur-
rounding much of her biography. All three dates have been given by credible
authorities: respectively, the poet-anthologist Jeanine Moulin, the eminent
scholar Henri Peyre, and, more recently, professor Marie-Claire Barnet, prob-
ably the most credible, who has devoted much critical attention to this once-
admired but little-remembered "muse of the surrealists," whose movement the
latter would, typically, both champion and parody.[1] Even the date of her de-
mise, which no amount of coyness could alter—1980, according to the no doubt
reliable Barnet—is occasionally found as 1990, and bears witness, at least, to
the near-oblivion that attends her today. As the latter observes, anyone seeking
documentation on Lise Deharme is faced with "a flagrant lack of biographical
and bibliographical references," and her work "seems buried in total silence."[2]
When an authority of the stature of an Henri Peyre devotes a scant half-dozen
lines to her, we have to be grateful to Barnet for shedding more light on her
career than can be culled from miscellaneous references and snippets scattered
here and there.[3] Even from her own engaging diary, which, informative though
it is, covers less than a decade of her life and does so in disjointed and anecdotal
fashion.

Of Deharme's early years, little can be easily deduced, though comments in
Les années perdues make clear a Germanic background, which would seem to be
confirmed by her original name.[4] By 1940 she was the mother of two children,
who were with her in her two wartime country retreats of Montfort and So-
ligny, and who are frequently mentioned in her journal. (We know from other
sources that she had been the wife of Paul Deharme, pioneer of the French radio
drama, who died in May of 1933.) It was for these two—Hyacinthe, the elder,
and Tristan, the younger—that friend Robert Desnos had written, in 1936, two
collections of fanciful children's poems, *Le parterre d'Hyacinthe* and *Le ménage
de Tristan,* whose flora and fauna, surrealism-born, bespeak that movement's
relationship with the dream creatures of a child's imaginings, qualities that
many of Deharme's own poems, published three years before, display as well.

Desnos was, indeed, only one of a veritable catalogue of literary and artistic
figures—surrealists and others—whom Deharme counted among her acquain-
tances: dinner and theater companions, intellectual partners both before and
during the Occupation, and frequenters of her salon gatherings of the 1950s.
Eluard, Aragon, Dali, Man Ray, Barrault, Cocteau, Auric, Picasso (and his long-
time paramour Dora Maar, to whom she had introduced him in 1936 in Saint-

Tropez)... And André Breton himself, who was, they say, madly in love with her (which did not, however, prevent his wartime self-imposed "exile" to America). The entries in her journal read at times like an artistic register of Parisian life, even during the rigors of the Occupation.

It is as a prolific author of novels and stories that Deharme is remembered by those who remember her at all, works that Barnet discusses extensively and in interpretive detail, calling attention to their often contradictory complexities—sexual and psychological—in what Marcel Schneider characterizes as a "fairyland universe" whose frivolity is actually "a solitary retreat where one can flee from Man in favor of plants, animals, and objects that speak to the imagination."[5]

Deharme's verse exhibits much of the same quality, childlike in its surrealistic, often playful ambiguities. Of four early collections published between 1922 and 1937, *Cahier de curieuse personne* (1933) is the most widely known. Its poems obey its whimsical epigraph, "Write whatever comes into your window," with "window" replacing "head," and calling to mind, in visual terms, a Daliesque or Magritte-type figure with an open window in place of a brow. Two others— *Le pot de mousse* and *L'amant blessé*—date from 1952 and 1966 respectively. Another, *Farouche à quatre feuilles* (1954), taking its title from a type of four-leaf clover and composed in collaboration with André Breton, Julien Gracq, and Jean Tardieu, grew out of a series of radio broadcasts that Deharme hosted in the 1950s. The eighteen examples presented here in translation are from the *Cahier*, with two other texts from her entry in *Les années perdues* dated December 14, 1942.

NOTES

1. See Moulin, *Huit siècles de poésie féminine*, p. 402; Peyre, *French Novelists of Today*, p. 410; and Barnet, *La femme cent sexes ou les genres communicants*, p. 293. Deharme's *Les années perdues (1939–1949)*, her diary of the war and postwar years, with an unexplained lacuna from 1946 to 1947—provides the month and day. And her reference, in an entry during the year 1939, to "those of us who will have reached forty in five or ten years" makes any of the three dates plausible, at least if one assumes a little age-ist coquettishness on her part.

2. Barnet, *La femme cent sexes*, p. 22.

3. Marie-Claire Barnet's article on Deharme's transient review of 1933, "To Lise Deharme's Lighthouse: *Le Phare de Neuilly*, a Forgotten Surrealist Review," *French Studies*, July 2003, pp. 323–34, also provides significant information.

4. The French given names of those to whom she refers would suggest, possibly, a childhood in Alsace.

5. Schneider, *Histoire de la littérature fantastique en France*, p. 379.

LA CAGE VIDE

J'ai raté
le livre de ma vie
une nuit
qu'on avait oublié
de mettre un crayon taillé
à côté de mon lit.

UNE CHAUMIÈRE ET TON CŒUR

Une petite maison
grande comme un mouchoir
où j'irai vous dire bonsoir
mon amour
et bonjour
chaque jour.
Nous serons heureux
comme ceux
qui sortent de prison.

Un revolver
un chemin de fer
sont des bijoux
dont je suis fou.

THE EMPTY CAGE

I never got
to write
my book of life that night
when they forgot
to put a sharpened pencil right
beside my cot.

Cahier de curieuse personne

* A LOVE NEST

A house no bigger
than a handkerchief
where I will go if
I would tell you good night
my heart's delight
and where I would say
good morning each day.
How happy we'll be
like prisoners set free.

Cahier de curieuse personne

Two jewels: a gun,
a train... each one
of the above
† I madly love.

Cahier de curieuse personne

---

* The title, literally, "A Cottage and Your Heart," pokes obvious fun at a common bourgeois cliché.

† The use of the masculine *fou* merely underscores the capriciousness of this trifle. I apologize to the shades of the poet for yielding to the exigencies of English punctuation where her original has none.

Lise Deharme 979

LE PEINTRE

Je peins cette dame toute noire
même les idées.
Pourquoi?
C'est le soir
et je n'ai pas dîné.

LE PÊCHEUR AU SOLEIL

La ligne d'or
danse sur l'eau
de chaque rayon
sort un oiseau.

Pêcheur qui dort
abasourdi
croit que le lac
est plein de nids.

Dans la tour où rien ne luit
où le désespoir et l'ennui
me traquent dans le noir
il faudrait voir
malgré le soir
malgré la nuit
si je puis me passer de lui.

Mon amour
qui êtes parti
pour la nuit
pour la vie
ou pour toujours.

THE PAINTER

I'll paint this lady by and by
all black even her mind.
But why?
It's night and I
have not yet dined.

*

                                  Cahier de curieuse personne

THE FISHERMAN IN THE SUN

Fishing-line gleams
bobbing gold string
and from each ray
a bird takes wing.

Fisherman dreams
and awe-possessed
thinks that the lake
is one big nest.

                                  Cahier de curieuse personne

In the tower's blackness where
my ennui and my despair
darkly stalk and shadow me
I must see
if I might
despite the night
do without him utterly.

Lover you left
for one night
but I might be
eternally
lover-bereft.

                                  Cahier de curieuse personne

    * The reader may notice that I try to be more punctilious with my rhymes than the poet is with hers.

                                    Lise Deharme 981

VŒUX SECRETS

Des chansons sortaient de la bouche des égouts.
—Aragon

Etre une belle fille
blonde et populaire
qui mette de la joie dans l'air
et lorsqu'elle sourit
donne de l'appêtit
aux ouvriers
de Saint-Denis.

Aux quatre coins du bois
je crie
hou-hou, où es-tu?
qui es-tu?
en pleurant
et le vent me répond
le vent
rien que le vent...

SECRET DESIRES

*   *Songs used to issue from the sewers' mouths.*
    —Aragon

To be a beguiling
young thing blonde and fair
who spreads joy in the air, never stops
and when she's smiling
deliciously
† workmen from Saint-Denis
lick their chops.

Cahier de curieuse personne

To the four corners of the wood
I cry hou-hou
where are you?
who are you?
tears in my eyes
and the wind replies
the wind
just the wind...

Cahier de curieuse personne

* The line is from Aragon's "La transfiguration de Paris," from the collection *La grande gaieté* (1931).

† The Saint-Denis quarter of Paris is generally regarded as a blue-collar and rather activist neighborhood.

Lise Deharme 983

MIRA

Le hanneton cogne lourdement
au carreau—c'est le printemps
et le miroir d'argent
pendu   qui se balance   jette
des pigeons blancs
dans le cabinet de toilette.

CURIEUSE

Tes cheveux sont des araignées
noires et griffues
ton front un désert de sable blond
ton nez une vague de son
tes dents ont faim
ta bouche est fine
ton menton
une colline aiguë
mais tes yeux sont deux cratères
de lave et de gouffres ouverts
semés d'étincelles et de feu
Tes yeux sont deux mondes perdus

MIRA

The clumsy maybug goes banging
into the window-pane—it's spring
and the silver mirror hanging
swinging   swaying   starts to fling
white pigeons who
* wind up in the loo.

Cahier de curieuse personne

ODD WOMAN

Your hair is made of spiders
black with claws
your brow a desert of blond sand
your nose a rippling noise
your teeth are hungry and
your lips are thin
your chin a hill's
sharp-pointed tip
but your eyes are two craters
and lava fills
those fiery spark-strewn chasms of your face
Your eyes are two worlds lost in space.

Cahier de curieuse personne

* Without daring a detailed explication of this whimsical scenario—a canvas, per-
haps?—I would point out only that bird-catchers often hang mirrors from branches to take
advantage of the birds' confusion at seeing their own reflection. As for the title, it may be
no more than the Spanish exclamation "Look!" This would be typical of Deharme's casual
use of a foreign word now and again, though it is tempting (if far fetched) to see it as an
allusion to a story by her younger contemporary, Gisèle Prassinos. Although "Elmira"—
whose imaginary heroine is a fantasy-pigeon called "Mira, ma belle"—was published after
Deharme's collection, it is not impossible that she might have known the work.

Lise Deharme 985

BÉBÉ EST COURAGEUX

En allant prendre mon bain
j'ai vu un petit lapin
qui m'a dit:
"Je vais au lit
car il est bientôt minuit."
Je lui répondis: "Va-t-en
tu vas faire peur à Maman."

TABLE

Deux et deux font quatre
et aussi cinq
si je veux.
Croyez-vous que le Bon Dieu
s'occupe
si un et un font toujours deux?

LES PÂQUERETTES

Les pâquerettes
trop simplettes
sont des petites dames
sans âme.
Elles font des rondes le jeudi
et sont mangées par les brebis
le vendredi.

BABY IS BRAVE

As I went off to take my bath
a little rabbit crossed my path
and he said:
"I'm going to bed,
midnight's coming, just ahead."
So I told the bunny: "Bah!
* Scram before you scare Mamma."

Cahier de curieuse personne,
"Nurseries Tales"

ADDITION

Two and two make four
and five as well
if I want them to.
Do you think God gives a how-d'ye-do
truth to tell
if one and one always make two?

Cahier de curieuse personne,
"Nurseries Tales"

DAISIES

Daisies naive
(would you believe)
are little ladies, but it's droll,
they have no soul.
Thursday is one long roundelay,
then eaten by the sheep are they,
very next day.

Cahier de curieuse personne,
"Nurseries Tales"

* The poet's common misspelling *va-t-en* (instead of the grammatically correct *va-t'en*) is either a simple lapse or an unusually subtle intent: one that would suggest that Bébé, if he were writing rather than speaking—and assuming that he could, at his age—would make the same childish mistake. In any event, I leave it as is.

Lise Deharme 987

LA POULE NOIRE

La poule noire
dans le potager
a crié
comme une enragée.
Les fermiers
sont allés la voir
elle a dit qu'il allait pleuvoir
on ne l'a pas crue lanturlu
et mon beau chapeau est perdu!

LE RAT BLANC

Le rat blanc a été puni
pour avoir mangé dans la nuit
le fromage que sa grand'mère
mettait de côté pour l'hiver.

LE COCHON BLOND

Le cochon blond
aime le jambon
il l'aime
jusqu'à l'indigestion.
Mais ce n'est pas bon
pour lui-même.

THE BLACK HEN

The black hen out
in the garden-patch
gave a wild shout
and thrashed about.
A batch
of farmers went and took a look
she said it was going to rain no doubt
Bah! They shook their heads and that
was why I ruined my pretty hat!

Cahier de curieuse personne,
"Nurseries Tales"

THE WHITE RAT

The white rat's fate was sealed because
one night he took between his jaws
a cheese—the one his grandmamma
had saved for winter... oh la la!

Cahier de curieuse personne,
"Nurseries Tales"

THE BLOND HOG

The hog—a blond—
is overfond
of ham.
He'll gorge and cram
until it makes
him sick, and gives him stomach-aches:
a problem big,
for a pig.

Cahier de curieuse personne,
"Nurseries Tales"

POAIME

Qu'on ne me dise pas toujours:
"Les coqs chantent la naissance du jour."
Les coqs, ça chante toute la nuit
Mais vous, vous dormez
Comme la plupart de mes amis
Alors jamais vous ne les entendez.

LE RÊVE DU PRISONNIER

Dieux! Toutes les portes sont ouvertes!
    Rêvai-je?
Non, tu es éveillé:
Les portes sont ouvertes.
Il suffisait d'ailleurs de les
    pousser.

* POEMOUR

Don't tell me as you always do:
"The cocks crow at the dawn's first peep."
No. The cocks crow the whole night through.
But you? You sleep,
As do most of my lovers. So
It's just that you can never hear them crow.

THE PRISONER'S DREAM

Ye gods! All of the doors are open!
    Did I dream it?
No, you're awake:
The doors are open.
And all you had to do was
†   give a push.

* This poem, with its fancifully misspelled title, and the following one are found in the diary entry for Christmas Eve 1942 in *Les années perdues.*

† The understandable prisoner's dream recalls the ironically comical denouement of Alphone Allais's celebrated story "La nuit blanche d'un hussard rouge," published in 1887 and in frequent collections of his works thereafter.

Lise Deharme 991

Louise de Vilmorin (1902–1969)

The birth date usually given for the novelist and poet Louise Lévesque de Vilmorin, granddaughter of a noted botanist reputed to have been a descendant of Felípe II of Spain, is 1902, though some sources suggest 1912, and at least one, splitting the difference, gives 1906. There is no confusion, however, about where she spent most of her life. With the exception of residences in America and Europe (especially Hungary), she was for years one of the reigning figures of the Paris intelligentsia. Eventually, her *salon bleu* (blue salon) at Verrières-le-Buisson, near Versailles—whose color crops up frequently in her verse—became the gathering place for an impressive company of luminaries in the world of mid-century art, music, letters, and film. (A number of her novels were adapted for the screen, and many of her poems were set to music by such prominent composers as Poulenc, Milhaud, Auric, and others.) René Clair, Max Ophuls, Bernard Buffet, Anaïs Nin, Zizi Jeanmaire, the multi-talented Leo Ferré... The catalogue is long and varied. And those who shared the culinary delights of her celebrated pot-au-feu in the elegance of the seventeenth-century château that had been in her family since 1815 enjoyed no less the art of conversation for which she was famous.

Perhaps the chronological uncertainty of Vilmorin's birth was the result of no more than a coquettish desire to lie about her age. A much-sought-after beauty, she followed in the age-old footsteps of many another icon of age-defying feminine French allure. One thinks of the almost legendary Ninon de Lenclos and the irrepressible Fanny de Beauharnais (see pp. 425–75), and, no less, of the contemporary Coco Chanel, whom Vilmorin knew and whose often mendacious confidences she revealed in her memoirs. Youth, after all, has always been a desirable commodity for the "femme fatale." And it was precisely by that epithet that the young (and, later, young*ish)* Louise de Vilmorin was often described, thanks to her amours, official and unofficial.

Those who have read any of her dozen novels, published between 1934 and 1967—perhaps best known among them, *Madame de* *** (1951), *Histoire d'aimer* (1955), *La lettre dans un taxi* (1958), and *Migraine* (1959)—might find this description a trifle disillusioning and even jarring. Not that they do not trace adventures (im)properly filled with carnality, spousal deceit, and such, but because they do so in the most refined of tones and in a style whose purity of language and psychological intimacy recall classically constructed narratives (with an actual beginning, middle, and end, no less!) the likes of the prototypical *La Princesse de Clèves* (1678) and *Adolphe* (1816). One hardly imagines that the author's reserved, elegantly told tales, however steamy their subjects, would be the work of a vamp or a seductive siren, as Jean Chalon paints her.[1]

But Vilmorin was, indeed, not one to shrink from amorous liaison. Twice mistress to Malraux—once in the 1930s and, more seriously, in the 1960s—she had had her fling too with Saint-Exupéry, meeting him in 1918 and becoming officially his fiancée in 1923, albeit for only a few months. (Perhaps the title of her verse collection *Fiançailles pour rire*, of 1939, was an allusion to this "make-believe engagement.") Other names, too, would pepper her career. She was, for example, twice the "other woman" in love triangles involving the romanesque Hungarian countess Maria Anna Paula Ferdinandine von Wurmbrand-Stuppach—known to the Parisian social register as Etti Plesch: once in 1937, when she married Count Paul Pálffy ab Erdöd, and again, seven years later, when the errant husband in question was another Hungarian count, Tamas Esterházy von Galantha... Vilmorin's travels to Hungary were apparently not mere tourist excursions. She had also had the time, a few years earlier, to marry an American, Henry Leigh-Hunt, and live with him long enough in Las Vegas to present him with three daughters, finally divorcing him in 1933 when he refused to move to France.

Escapades, however, did not keep her from writing—indeed, may have inspired—her novels, her two collections of posthumous memoirs, *Promenades et autres rencontres* (2000) and *Intimités* (2001), or her three collections of poems (plus one published posthumously in 1972). Nor did they prevent her receiving the Grand Prix littéraire de Monaco in 1955 for her (strictly literary) accomplishments to that point in her career. And when she died in 1969 at the family estate, she left an enviable literary *œuvre* and a romantic reputation no doubt envied too by many.

Less "profound" a poet than many others, though not without a serious side, Louise de Vilmorin cultivated, especially in her later work, a light-hearted verse similar in spirit if not in style to that of Lise Deharme (see pp. 976–91), and reflective of the wordplay and linguistic frivolity that no doubt entertained her admiring guests.[2] The nineteen short (and ultra-short) poems translated here, many of which are included in the volume *Poèmes*, represent all four of her collections.

NOTES

1. See Jean Chalon, *Florence et Louise les magnifiques: Florence Jay-Gould et Louise de Vilmorin*, pp. 99–163.

2. For other biographical sources, see Jean Bothorel, *Louise, ou La vie de Louise de Vilmorin*; Albertine Gentou, *Louise de Vilmorin: "Si vous me connaissiez..."*; and the *Essai sur Louise de Vilmorin* by one of her four brothers, André de Vilmorin, in the series "Poètes d'aujourd'hui," devoted (with supposed objectivity) to her life and work.

L'étoile de mes vœux file un coton d'ennui
Tandis que l'araignée condamnée aux présages
Sur ton ombre brisée, oh! profil de mes nuits,
Prend l'ombre d'un baiser rapporté de voyage.

FLEURS

Fleurs promises, fleurs tenues dans tes bras,
Fleurs sorties des parenthèses d'un pas,
   Qui t'apportait ces fleurs l'hiver
   Saupoudrées du sable des mers?
Sable de tes baisers, fleurs des amours fanées
Les beaux yeux sont de cendre et dans la cheminée
   Un cœur enrubanné de plaintes
   Brûle avec ses images saintes.

LA SOLITUDE EST VERTE

Chasseresse ou dévote ou porteuse de dons
La solitude est verte en des landes hantées
Comme chansons du vent aux provinces chantées
Comme le souvenir lié à l'abandon.

La solitude est verte.

Verte comme verveine au parfum jardinier
Comme mousse crépue au bord de la fontaine
Et comme le poisson messager des sirènes,
Verte comme la science au front de l'écolier.

La solitude est verte.

My wished-on star spins a glum thread, unravels,
* While the night spider—doom's unwitting sign—
Captures a shadow-kiss brought from my travels,
In your shade's tatters, oh! night shadows mine.

Fiançailles pour rire

FLOWERS

Flowers he promised, flowers in armfuls, these,
Flowers sprung from a stride's parentheses,
    Who brought those winter flowers to you,
    Strewn with sea-sand? Your kisses, too,
Sand-strewn, flowers of loves dead, withered, gone...
Lovely eyes turn to ash, and, lying on
    The hearth, a heart ribboned in sighs
    Burns with its holy icons, dies.

Fiançailles pour rire

SOLITUDE'S GREEN

Bearer of gifts or prude or huntress, she:
Solitude's green in haunted heath far-flung,
Like songs in rustic provinces wind-sung,
Like wild abandon joined to memory.

    Solitude's green.

Green, now, like garden-balmed vervain, and now
Like crinkling mosses by the fountain, and
Like herald fish dear to the mermaid band;
Green, like the knowledge on the student's brow.

    Solitude's green.

* The poet seems to be alluding here, somewhat obscurely, to the French superstition that a spider seen in the evening portends hope, unlike the morning spider, an omen of trouble: "Araignée le matin, chagrin, araignée le soir, espoir." Also, I have tried to preserve the wordplay on the common expression "filer un mauvais coton" (to be in a bad way—literally, "to spin a bad thread").

Louise de Vilmorin 995

Verte comme la pomme en sa simplicité,
Comme la grenouille, cœur glacé des vacances,
Verte comme tes yeux de désobéissance,
Verte comme l'exil où l'amour m'a jeté.

La solitude est verte.

––––––––––

ADIEUX

Les mots sont dits, les jeux sont faits
Toutes couleurs toutes mesures,
Le danger cueille son bouquet,
Aux falaises de l'aventure
Je ne reviendrai plus jamais.

Adieu chapeau de Capitaine
Adieu gais écheveaux du vent,
Astre du Nord, étoile vaine,
Un baiser est au firmament
Des jardins où je me promène.

Adieu bateaux au jour défaits,
L'heure attendue est bien venue,
L'amour me choisit mes secrets.
A la tour des peines perdues
Je ne monterai plus jamais.

––––––––––

Souvenir et plaisir ne font pas bon ménage,
Vois déferler les pleurs au revers des beaux jours,
Vois au flot du regret la parure baignée,
L'écharpe de minuit de sanglots imprégnée,
Vois le baiser qui cherche à rejoindre l'amour
Et l'amour s'enivrer de nos larmes sauvages.

Green, like the apple's stark simplicity,
Like the frog, frozen heart of emptinesses;
Green, like your gaze that never acquiesces,
Green, like the exile where love banished me.

      Solitude's green.

Le sable du sablier

FAREWELLS

The chips are down, we've said our say—
Chips of all sizes, shapes, and hues—
Danger goes picking its bouquet,
Adventure's cliffs, hear my adieus:
Nevermore shall I pass this way.

Farewell to seadog's cap, and you,
Gay tangles of the wind, goodbye,
Farewell to you, vain Northstar, too,
A kiss shines in the garden sky—
The garden paths I amble through.

Farewell boats disarrayed by day,
At last, now comes the longed-for hour,
Love plumbs my secrets for its prey.
Futile, life's pains, too high the tower:
Nevermore shall I climb this way.

Le sable du sablier

Pleasure and recollection, it appears,
Don't get on well: witness the undersides
Of pleasant days, tear-strewn; the bauble swathed
In longing's flood; the midnight scarf, sob-bathed;
The kiss that longs to find where love still hides;
And love grown drunk on our ferocious tears.

Le sable du sablier

Louise de Vilmorin 997

LES MARCHES

Monterai-je encore souvent ces marches vertes?
Monterai-je souvent pensant toujours à toi
Ces marches conduisant à ma chambre déserte?
Referai-je toujours la route d'autrefois?

SIESTE

Quand le soleil ogre de feu
Aura dévoré les nuages
Et roulera dans son lit bleu,
Mettez à l'abri vos images.

Profils que le cœur élima
Jusqu'à n'en laisser que l'hostie.
Couple dont l'accord s'imprima
Sur la fleur d'amour investie.

Linge, avalanche de désir,
Linceul du baiser souvenir
Et source liant leur partage.

De l'étang des demi-remords
Ne tirez pas vos personnages:
Le soleil en ferait des morts.

Aidez-moi doux Seigneur et j'oublierai la plage
Et le ciel sur la mer et la mer à mes pieds,
Et les villes la nuit et mon joli village
Et les regards d'amour et mon amour dernier.
Faites l'obscurité, doux Seigneur, dans ma cage,
J'ai fait peur à mon âme et mon être insensé
Ne peut se résigner aux rigueurs du courage:
Il aimait le plaisir, il veut recommencer.

THE STAIRCASE

Shall I climb youth's green staircase, tireless?
Shall I, thinking of you, forgetting never,
Keep climbing to my bedroom's emptiness?
Shall I retrace yesterday's path forever?

Le sable du sablier

SIESTA

When the fire-breathing ogre-sun
Rolls in his bed of blue, when he
Gobbles the clouds up, every one,
Best you safekeep each memory.

Silhouettes that your heart pared, trimmed
Down to only a sacred host.
Couple in tune, whose concord limned
Its shape onto love's flower, engrossed.

Sheets, avalanche of passions, winding-
Sheet of the kiss remembered, binding
Two fleeting beings in harmony.

Don't dredge up, from the swamp of your
Half-guilt, your players; let them be:
The sun would strike them dead, for sure.

L'alphabet des aveux, "Poèmes"

Help me, sweet Lord, and I will vow to clear
My mind of beach, and sky above the sea,
And sea's expanse, and nighttime towns, that dear
Village of mine, those looks cast lovingly,
And my last love. Sweet Lord, let darkness here
Surround my cage; my frightened soul fears me,
And all my foolish being will not give ear
To bold heart's harsh demands: it reveled free,

Louise de Vilmorin 999

Aidez-moi, doux Seigneur, à vaincre ces images
Dont mon sang obstiné ravive les couleurs.
Le repentir m'appelle aux confins de mon âge
Pour remettre en vos mains mon rosaire de pleurs.

———————

PASSIONNÉMENT

Je l'aime un peu, beaucoup, passionnément,
Un peu c'est rare et beaucoup tout le temps.
Passionnément est dans tout mouvement:
Il est caché sous cet: *un peu,* bien sage
Et dans: *beaucoup* il bat sous mon corsage.
Passionnément ne dort pas davantage
Que mon amour aux pieds de mon amant
Et que ma lèvre en baisant son visage.

———————

LES CHÂTEAUX

Que la chance vienne ou s'écarte
    Les beaux châteaux
Ne sont que des châteaux de cartes
    De casino.
    Quand la main passe
Les beaux châteaux changent de mains
    Et dans leurs glaces
Se mire en passant l'incertain.

Would still. Help me, sweet Lord, make disappear
Those blood-whipped memories of vivid hue.
Age would have me repent of yesteryear,
And give my tear-strung rosary to you.

L'alphabet des aveux, "Poèmes"

———————

PASSIONATELY

I love him somewhat, lots, passionately:
Somewhat is little, *lots* won't let me be.
*   *Passionately* commands each inch of me.
He lurks beneath that *somewhat,* self-possessed,
And in that *lots* he beats beneath my breast.
Passionately knows no more sleep or rest
Than love, before my love, on bended knee,
Or lips against his lips, tenderly pressed.

L'alphabet des aveux, "Poèmes"

———————

CHÂTEAUX

Whether good fortune go or come,
      Our fine châteaux
Are nothing but card-castles from
      Some *casino.*
      With each new hand
They change hands too: reflected, we
      Pass by, look, and
Mirror our own uncertainty.

L'alphabet des aveux, "Poèmes"

* In this adaptation of the French version of the "he loves me, he loves me not" daisy
divination, the poet leaves no room for the feared *pas du tout* (not at all).

INVITATION

Ouvert par le soleil qui le dore et s'y mire
Le maïs nous invite à manger son sourire.

OÙ SONT TES LETTRES?

L'automne, ah, c'est déjà l'automne,
Où sont tes lettres du mois d'août?
Tes mots ne sont plus à personne.
L'été mourut d'un billet doux.

PIERROT

Sur les monts de la lune aux cascades d'opale
Pierrot boit la liqueur qui le rendit si pâle.

LA LEÇON

Récitez-moi votre leçon:
"L'oiseau se prend à l'hameçon,
Le poisson s'apprivoise et chante.
Le papillon est une plante.
L'Eté ramène les grands froids."
Je vous l'ai redit mille fois.

INVITATION

Sun gilds the yawning corn, reflects therein,
As it invites us to consume its grin.

L'alphabet des aveux, "Fantaisies"

WHERE ARE YOUR LETTERS?

Ah, autumn, come so soon? But how?
Where did your August letters go?
Your words belong to no one now:
A billet-doux laid summer low.

L'alphabet des aveux, "Fantaisies"

PIERROT

On moon-mounts' opaline cascades, Pierrot
Quaffs the liqueur that paled his visage so.

L'alphabet des aveux, "Fantaisies"

THE LESSON

Recite the lesson you've been taught:
"The bird is on a fishhook caught,
The fish is tamed and chirps its chants.
The butterfly's one of the plants.
The Summer brings cold to our climes."
I've told you so a thousand times.

L'alphabet des aveux, "Fantaisies"

Un de mes amis me raconte
Sans éprouver la moindre honte
Qu'il prend le conseil de son chien
Quand il écrit à sa maîtresse.
Elle ne se doute de rien
Et, dit-il, sans délicatesse:
"Mon chien et moi nous rions bien."

MAI

Aujourd'hui dans ma vie encore un jour de mai
Encore un inconstant que les aubes font naître
Et que la nuit emporte en disant: "Plus jamais
Tu ne verras ce jour que tu voulais connaître."

Aujourd'hui dans ma vie encore un soir de mai
Trop troublant et trop bleu trépassant sur la terre
Sans que j'aie rien donné de ce que je remets
Aux mains de mes amours où tremblent mes prières.

Sous un arc-en-ciel un canapé bleu
Dans une plaine bleue. Au loin la route
Qui serait bleue, et puis un arbre bleu
Et sur le canapé nous deux sans doute.

Without the slightest shame thereat,
A friend of mine has told me that,
When he writes to his mistress, he
Writes what his dog suggests he say.
But unsuspecting, quite, is she;
And says the tactless popinjay:
"My dog and I chuckle with glee."

*   *L'alphabet des aveux,* "7 1 9 13 et 3"

MAY

Another May morn in my life today,
Another fickle day, of dawn new-born,
One that the night, too soon, will whisk away,
Saying: "You'll see no more this longed-for morn."

Another May eve in my life today,
Too blue, too troubling, falling through the air
And dying; for, too long did I delay
Gracing my hands with love, trembling with prayer.

Solitude, ô mon éléphant

Under a rainbow, in a meadow, blue,
A blue divan. The road, far off, would be
Blue also, and likewise a tree, blue too.
And on the divan, we two, probably.

Solitude, ô mon éléphant

---

   * The title of the brief section that concludes *L'alphabet des aveux*—a collection that revels in wordplay, holorhyme, and even palindrome—is typical of Vilmorin's playful vein. Pronounced aloud, the numeric "7 1 9 13 et 3" produces the statement: "C'est un œuf très étroit" (It's a very narrow egg), though I would not venture a guess as to the significance of that observation or its relevance to the poems in question.

En naviguant une eau d'avril,
L'aiguille vive à mon corsage,
L'aiguille vive et blanc le fil
Pour rebroder mon personnage,

J'ai vu les enfants des marais
Revêtus d'enfance éternelle
Jouer dans les jardins défaits
Sous de bleus bosquets d'hirondelles.

LA JACINTHE

  La jacinthe
Bleue et raide en son parfum
Fleurit mes regrets défunts
  Et mes plaintes.

Je ne porterai plus les bijoux du hasard,
Diadème imprudent, bague mésalliée,
Mais, don de ton accueil, l'iris de ton regard
Et, pavois du repos au jour de mon départ,
Une jacinthe bleue à ma gorge liée.

―――――

Sailing an April watershed,
Stitching my bodice, filigreeing,
Stitching and stitching, white the thread
To reembroider all my being,

I saw the children of the swamp,
Clad in eternal childhood-hour,
In run-down gardens, run and romp
Beneath blue-vaulted swallow bowers.

Solitude, ô mon éléphant

―――――

THE HYACINTH

    Blue, the crisp scents
Of hyacinth adorn
My dead regrets, forlorn,
    And my laments.

No more will I wear jewel castaways,
Diadems brash, rings of the tawdriest.
Only your welcome-gift, your iris-gaze
And—bunting for our passion's parting days—
A hyacinth, blue, pinned fast to my breast.

Solitude, ô mon éléphant

Louise de Vilmorin 1007

Andrée Sodenkamp (1906–2004)

Few, if any, of the poets in this volume received as many prizes for their poetry as did [Maud-]Andrée Sodenkamp. Some eleven, at least. Nor was her admirable longevity the reason, affording her all the more time to win them. Universally admired, this dean of modern Belgian poets filled her decades-long career with collection upon collection of poetry that not only stands out sharply visual in color and tableau, but also that begs, as all real poetry should do, not simply to be looked at on the printed page but to be heard. And heard in all its vigorous yet flexible measures, its musical and not unyieldingly rigid rhymes, precursors, in their occasional freedoms, of her later-life free verse. Unlike some poets who espouse formlessness out of necessity—like some abstract painters who abhor the respresentational in art because they cannot master it—she had given ample proof of the excellence of her formal craft before putting it gently and respectfully aside.

Sodenkamp's is a poetry that is not simply a self-absorbed vehicle for the poet's own emotions, but rather a corpus replete with dramatis personae, often drawn from history: Cleopatra, Salome, et al., in all their panoply and dramatic array. Or even semi-personified places, like her lush native Brabant. As her compatriot Liliane Wouters has said, herself one of Belgium's most gifted poets and dramatists, and represented in these pages as well (see pp. 1086–1115): "Sodenkamp's poems are replete with characters. It is even surprising that she has never attempted the theater."[1] Indeed, Sodenkamp's verse presents not only "sumptuous" harmonies—the word springs to the pen of Wouters and many others—but also, and especially, evocative mini-scenes rich in color, flowers, and light—the decors and costumes of the theater too, with all their attendant baubles and props, reminiscent of a Flemish interior. What's more, they seem totally unlabored. And, whether or not they were, in fact, the result of hard work—what poet does not have to give a tug or a tuck to a line on occasion?—they always succeed at least in giving the impression of total spontaneity, as if each line, flowing effortlessly in the best romantic tradition, were necessary and predestined, the only one that could possibly be called upon to clothe the poetic exigencies of the moment.

In an ideal world ruled by equity and balance, Sodenkamp's longevity might be seen as a kind of compensation for the sadness of her early childhood. Born in the Saint-Josse-ten-Noode section of Brussels on January 18, 1906,[2] she lost her Dutch father in 1913 and her mother, a suicide, a scant week later. Hardly an auspicious beginning, even for a future poet. Brought up by her grandparents and her mother's brother, while studying to become a teacher she would lose her uncle-guardian as well in 1918, to the ravages of war. Sodenkamp spent a decade teaching at the Institut Gatti and the Lycée d'état de La Louvière before becoming, in 1936, a professor of literature and history at the Athénée in Gembloux, where the municipal library today bears her name. She was appointed inspector of public libraries in 1959. Her marriage at age thirty-eight to Camille Libotte lasted until his death in 1987, reflecting the couple's solidly burgher values.

Sodenkamp did not publish her first volume, *Des oiseaux à tes lèvres,* until 1950, and her second, *Sainte terre,* recipient of the Prix Renée Vivien, until four years later. After that she continued her productive and distinguished career, proving with her most recent collection, *C'était une nuit comme une autre* (1991)—recipient of the Prix de la Sabam—that her capacities and remarkable gifts refused to be diminished by age. She died on January 27, 2004.[3]

The ten translations that follow, most of which are reproduced in *Poèmes choisis,* indicate their original provenance: *Les dieux obscurs* (1958), *Femmes des longs matins* (1965), *Le fête debout* (1973), and *Choix* (1980).

NOTES

1. Liliane Wouters, preface to *Poèmes choisis,* a volume that also includes a perceptive appreciation by the eminent poet Charles Norac.

2. Robert Frickx and Michel Joiret, in *La poésie française de Belgique de 1950 à nos jours,* give the year of her birth as 1904, an oversight I suspect. They also theorize that the Gypsy origin of one of her grandmothers may have influenced her "creative vitality and love of song" (p. 227), though their logic escapes me.

3. For a summary chronology of her life and works, see *Poèmes choisis,* which cites also some of the anthologies in which her poetry has appeared, as well as a number of critical opinions (pp. 245–60). Marie-Claire d'Orbaix's entry in Anne-Marie Trekker and Pierre Vander Straeten, *Cent auteurs: Anthologie de littérature française de Belgique,* pp. 401–4, is also most informative, as are several collections of her works. Among them, Marcel Thiry and Roger Brucher's *Andrée Sodenkamp* (1973) is readily available, as is Sodenkamp's anthology *Choix.*

MON CORPS

Mon corps, mon compagnon, ma bête et ma faiblesse,
L'âme vous aime fort et se souvient de vous.
Je n'ai longtemps vécu qu'au seuil de vos caresses.
Nous allons, doucement, vous mener jusqu'au bout.

PLAINTE

J'ai de rapides soirs encombrés de corbeaux.
La mort donne du bec contre moi et s'amuse.
Suis-je comme ces rois trop aimés des oiseaux
Et de pierre déjà au flanc de leur église?

Je ne suis belle, hélas, qu'en mes légers matins
Quand le jardin se lève, ardent, sous ma paupière,
Qu'il entre dans la chambre avec ses pieds de thym
Et que je crois avoir dormi avec la terre.

FEMMES DES LONGS MATINS

A Louis Aragon

Femmes des longs matins, mes belles amoureuses
Dont le nom s'attardait à la bouche des morts
Qui faisiez du malheur une brûlante rose
Et déchiriez le temps entre vos ongles d'or.

Body mine—comrade, weakness, beast—ah, yes!
My soul loves you, remembers you, dear friend.
Long I lived on the sill of your caress;
Now will I ease you in, to reach your end.

Les dieux obscurs

LAMENT

Quick-passing eves are mine, with crows encumbered.
Death pecks me with its beak, enjoys its pranks.
Am I like kings, now, loved by birds unnumbered,
Sculpted in stone, along their churches' flanks?

Ah! Dawn alone—airy-light—finds me fair
When flower-patch wakes and, in my eye, glows bright,
And, in my room, thyme-footed, creeping there,
Makes me feel that I bedded earth last night.

Les dieux obscurs

WOMEN OF LONG-DRAWN MORNINGS

† *For Louis Aragon*

Women of long-drawn mornings, beauties you,
Whose names dwell yet on dead men's lips, and whose
Nails of gold ripped and clawed at time, and who
‡ Made of despair and woe a burning rose.

---

* This poem should not be confused with an earlier poem with the same title published in *Sainte terre* (1954).

† Louis Aragon (1907–1982) was one of the leading members of the surrealist movement and a prominent poet of the Resistance during World War II.

‡ My less-than-perfect rhyme echoes the poet's two similar liberties in this poem (*amoureuses/roses, ombre/tombes*), a poetic license in which she often indulges.

Andrée Sodenkamp 1011

Est-ce la Nonne ardente et que Juan oublie
Ou dans ses jupons fous, l'innocente Manon,
Cléopâtre tapie au creux des pierreries
Qui retient son amant, au poing, comme un faucon?

Voici celle qui vint de la France en Ecosse,
Eblouie comme l'aigle au soleil des plaisirs,
L'abeille qui foudroie en son plein ciel des noces
Et met le goût du sang aux saveurs du désir.

Nous sommes belles par vos seins levés dans l'ombre
Par vos hanches donnant le merveilleux danger
Et dans l'odeur d'amour ouverte sur vos tombes
Nous régnons sur l'amant qui a les yeux fermés.

―――――――

TES CALMES MAINS SUR TOI

Je jalouse ce soir le ventre de ta mère
Qui a pu te garder bien plus longtemps que moi.
Comme le paysan après son tour de terre.
Dors en paix, mon gisant, tes calmes mains sur toi.

Demain je cacherai mes seins de pécheresse
Sous ma robe d'épouse en t'apportant le jour.
Et dans tes yeux de juste, oublieux des caresses.
Je reverrai l'ennui qui vient après l'amour.

Is it the Nun, craving her Don Juan, fled?
Or Manon, simple, petticoats awry?
Or Cleopatra, swathed in gems outspread,
* Clutching her love, poised falcon, loath to fly?

Here, she who left for Scotland from our France,
Awed, like the eagle, by sun's pleasures graced,
Like bee, who in her wedding-sky's expanse,
† Strikes, and gives lust's delight blood's bitter taste.

Fair are we, with your shadowed breasts upturning,
With your flanks that entrap and tyrannize;
And, in love's scent above your tombs, the yearning
Lover bows to your power, and shuts his eyes.

Femmes des longs matins

HANDS CALM POISED

I envy so, this night, your mother's womb
That kept you hers much longer than could I!
Sleep—hands calm poised, like form carved on a tomb—
Like peasant, when he puts his labor by.

Tomorrow I shall hide my sinner's breast
Beneath my wifely garb, bring you the dawn,
And, in your proper glance, now uncaressed,
See the ennui that follows love anon.

Femmes des longs matins

* The three beauties evoked in this quatrain are Doña Ines, a character in the Don Juan tale originally framed by Spanish playwright Tirso de Molina in *El burlador de Sevilla* (1630) and which subsequently led a life of its own in literature and music; Manon Lescaut, the really not-so-innocent heroine of the Abbé Prévost's sentimental novel of degrading passion by that name (1731); and, of course, the Egyptian temptress Cleopatra, who figures several other times in the poet's work.

† The reference is, clearly, to Mary Stuart, Queen of Scots (1542–1587), who was briefly queen of France (1559–1560) as consort of François II. Upon his death she returned to Scotland and married the ill-fated Lord Darnley, in whose murder she was later allegedly implicated.

Andrée Sodenkamp 1013

JE SUIS DU TEMPS

A Maurice Carême

Je suis du temps des lents et vieux romans d'amour,
Des Grands Meaulnes poussant des portes solennelles.
On se mangeait le cœur en guettant sur la tour
Un pays balancé de bois et d'hirondelles.

C'étaient les temps heureux des grandes fautes tendres,
Des confessionnaux pleins de voix murmurées
Et de chagrins si beaux qu'on ne pouvait attendre
Pour les souffrir déjà de n'être plus aimée.

BRABANT

Que cette terre est belle où les jours ont le temps.
Ma province de l'herbe et de la femme ronde.
Avec ses champs épais, son modeste printemps
Et ce lait bleu de chaux dont il repeint le monde.

La plaine est une mer qui ne sait où aller
Quand le flot des vergers roule sa blanche écume.
C'est le pays de l'aube en longue liberté.
L'immense blé commence à bouger dans la brume...

MY TIME

*   *For Maurice Carême*

My time was when love novels were in flower—
† Long, *Le Grand Meaulnes*, and such—when, solemnly,
Doors came ajar, and, swaying on the tower,
Woodland and swallow stirred heart's misery.

Those were the gentle times of tender sin,
Confessionals that many a whisper bore,
And woes so sweet that we could not begin
To wait the pain of being loved no more.

Femmes des longs matins

BRABANT

How beautiful my land, where days have time:
Province of grass, plump woman, modest spring,
Land of lush meadows, and of that blue lime
That it goes painting over everything.

The plain spreads like a great purposeless sea
When orchard-froth rolls white in turns and twists.
Province of endless dawn, endlessly free.
Vast, the grain stirs to life beneath the mists...

‡   *Femmes des longs matins*

* Maurice Carême (1899–1978) was a prominent French-language Belgian poet. Born in Wavre, he drew much of his inspiration from his Walloon countryside; his home in the Brussels suburb of Anderlicht became a museum dedicated to his name.

† *Le Grand Meaulnes* was the only novel of author Henri-Alban Fournier, known as Alain-Fournier (1886–1914).

‡ This encomium to the poet's Belgian province and its fertile countryside originally appeared in the collection *Femmes des longs matins* under the rubric "Tu penses à des pays" (You think of countries), a line inspired by Rilke.

Andrée Sodenkamp 1015

LES REINES MORTES

Salomé qui portiez de foudroyantes robes
Et tendiez un léger et vague corps en fleur
Vers la bouche lippue et les langueurs d'Hérode,
Que les roses du sang brillent sur votre cœur.

Et vous Marie qu'on voit humblement meurtrière
En vos châteaux d'Ecosse, endormant quelque époux,
Que j'aimerais voler votre jeune lumière
Quand vous veniez de France, ignorant tout de vous.

Parce que j'ai cherché la forme d'air et d'eau
Et les parfums dormant sur la reine d'Egypte
Qui décidait de Rome en ouvrant son manteau,
J'ai gardé cette lèvre ardente et ces yeux tristes.

MAI

Tu gonflais en riant ta douce gorge nue,
Jeune fille de mai si longue sous ta tresse.
Je devins ce jour-là, te suivant dans la rue,
Amoureuse soudain de ma vieille jeunesse.

J'ai eu ce mouvement qui joue avec la taille,
Cet oiseau vif du sein si léger à porter
Et dans ton ventre étroit préparé aux semailles
J'ai su comment battait ta jeune faim d'aimer.

THE DEAD QUEENS

Salome, light of body in full flower,
Who offered up your ever-shifting poses
To Herod's languid-lipped, lascivious glower,
Ah, how your heart shines with the blood of roses.

*   And Mary, queen, soft-spoken murderess
Of some Scot-castled spouse; you, from a France
That knew you oh so little, even less!
Would I owned your youth's lightsome elegance.

Because I sought the airy, fluid form
† Of Egypt's queen, who, bathed in fragrance, slept,
‡ And, gown spread wide, had sealed the fate of Rome,
Those burning lips and sad eyes have I kept.

§   *Femmes des longs matins*

MAY

Laughing, you swelled your fair décolletée,
May lass, long-drawn of limb, beneath your tresses.
And, as I followed close behind, that day,
I loved at once all my old youth's excesses.

I felt that birdlike flutter round your waist,
Your breast; that hunger in the slimness of
Your belly, made for seeding; sensed your taste
And your embracing appetite for love.

La fête debout

* Again, the reference is to Mary Queen of Scots (see p. 1013n).

† Cleopatra seems to have fascinated Sodenkamp; see "Women of Long-Drawn Mornings" above and the poem entitled "Cléopâtre" in *Les dieux obscurs* (1958).

‡ My slant rhyme echoes the poet's two similar assonances in this poem (*robes/Hérode, Egypte/tristes*), a not uncommon liberty in her work.

§ This is one of a dozen of the forty-two poems in the collection *Femmes des longs matins* not included in *Poèmes choisis*.

Andrée Sodenkamp 1017

LE PRINTEMPS DE VAN GOGH

Printemps bleu de froid de Van Gogh
Où claque des dents le bonheur.
Trois fois viendra chanter le coq.
La toile peinte sent la fleur.

Des bleus, des verts à en pleurer.
Le monde est à l'envers du sombre.
Avril blanchit son linge au pré
Dans un brouillard d'oiseaux à fondre.

Qu'importe le mois qui se moque
S'il se laisse prendre au pinceau.
Dans la pauvre âme de Van Gogh,
Au moins, ce jour-là, il fit beau.

Je ne veux plus de lune à dessiner mes lèvres,
De robes à ouvrir et de beaux yeux qu'on peint
Et ce plaisir plus vain et plus vif que le lièvre
Qui fuit en nous laissant sa chaleur sur les mains.

Je ne veux que l'oubli et ce malheur si tendre
Bercé comme l'enfant parmi le blé nouveau
J'ai peur de ces lilas dont l'odeur va m'attendre
Quand ma jeune vieillesse ira vers les oiseaux.

THE SPRINGTIME OF VAN GOGH

Oh, cold blue springtime of Van Gogh,
Teeth chattering in happy mood.
* Three times the cock will come and crow.
Canvas, fragrantly flower-hued.

Blues, greens, enough to weep! The world
Shuns all that's dark and somber there.
April's wash, in the field unfurled;
And birds, dissolving, fog the air.

Who cares what month mocks him, if, lo!
It lets itself be painted thus!
Ah! In the poor soul of Van Gogh
That day, at least, shone glorious.

La fête debout

---

† I want no more moon now to trace my lips,
Revealing gowns, eyes painted opulent,
Or that vain joy, swifter than hare that skips
And flits, leaving our hands warm with its scent.

I want only forgetfulness, that tender
Woe, like a babe midst new grain's lullaby.
I fear these lilacs, lest I should surrender
My aging youth, as toward the birds I fly.

* It is not without a little guilt that I yield to the common mispronunciation of the celebrated painter's name, one that the French original pleasantly avoids.

† Originally one of an unpublished group entitled "La harde," this poem was subsequently included in the published collections *Choix* (1980) and *Poèmes choisis* (1998).

Andrée Sodenkamp 1019

Anne-Marie Kegels (1912–1994)

When Anne-Marie Kegels (née Camet), born in Gascony, near Agen, in 1912, realized that she and her husband were to leave Brussels for the Ardenne, she faced with a certain trepidation the prospect of quitting the cosmopolitan capital that had become her home. Years later, her preface to the collection *Les doigts verts* (1967), "Paroles pour l'Ardenne" (Words for the Ardenne)—a touching apostrophe to her future town of Arlon, a stone's throw from the Luxembourg border—reveals the anxiety of a young woman who, married at nineteen and a mother at twenty-seven, and already uprooted once, saw herself about to leave "a river of faces . . . palpitating with life" to confront a new existence in a small town "that seemed only an absurd dot on the map," totally unknown to her, and whose doubtless shortcomings she could only imagine. Soon, however, the joys of the passing seasons won her over, and the devotion to the beauties and wonders of nature that she had brought with her from her native Gascony—a legacy from her generations of wine-grower ancestors—found itself easily transplanted to the soil of her new surroundings.

She brought with her as well her devotion to poetry, early instilled in her by a literature-loving grandmother and a grandfather who enjoyed regaling the family with evening recitations of Occitan verse. Despite that early love, her own first collection of poems, *Douze poèmes de l'année* (1950), did not appear until she was thirty-eight. Apparently worth waiting for, it was the recipient of the Prix Théophile Briant. Two successive collections, *Rien que vivre* (1951) and *Chant de la sourde joie* (1956), were prestigiously honored as well; the former with the Prix Renée Vivien and the latter with the Prix Gérard de Nerval. One can assume that, to some extent at least, her native poetic gifts were encouraged by her literary friendships with the many writers who had disabused her of her fears of an artistically sterile Belgian hinterland; especially writers like the prolific Camille Biver and Pierre Nothomb. (It was, in fact, in grateful memory of the latter that she would pen the abovementioned preface.)

Kegels's verse, respectful of the French prosodic tradition but more and more daring in the liberties of assonance and "free-ish" verse as her career progressed, is not only imbued with the nature that was so much a part of her life and the calm acceptance of the passage of time that is its inexorable concomitant. No less typical is her observation of, and concern for, small, everyday objects, inanimate and animate, reminiscent of her close contemporary Eugène Guillevic but without his lapidary concision: a chair, a bird, hands, a loaf of bread, a statue, an embankment under the sensual weight of a peasant-girl asleep... It is a poetry that one reads with the joy of discovery, always struck by the realization of just how vast and boundless the stuff of poetry can be. And how lovingly and musically it can be transformed by the alchemy of a truly gifted poet.

When Anne-Marie Kegels died in 1994, she left behind nine collections of verse, the last published in 1978, and all a telling tribute to her late-blooming gifts. A volume of her *Poèmes choisis,* edited by Guy Goffette, had appeared in 1990.[1] Four of her major collections are represented in the twenty-two translations that follow, with a final one that does not belong to any of them.

NOTE

1. For biographical and bibliographical details, see, among other studies, Frédéric Kiesel, *Anne-Marie Kegels,* and Louis Daubier's concise but perceptive entry in Anne-Marie Trekker and Pierre Vander Straeten, *Cent auteurs,* pp. 229–31. For more general works, see Robert Frickx and Michel Joiret, *La poésie française de Belgique de 1950 à nos jours,* pp. 232–33; and Renée Linkhorn and Judy Cochran, *Belgian Women Poets,* pp. 59–75.

LA CHAISE

La chaise qui fut branche, résonance
        d'ailes à venir
et qui maintenant n'a que le silence
        pour se souvenir,
la chaise hantée de volante neige,
        de vent, de soleil,
s'étonnant d'avoir été prise au piège
        d'un fixe sommeil,
cherche à s'éveiller, à fuir de la chambre.
        —Je l'entends, la nuit,
gémir à tâtons et toute se tendre
        vers l'ancien pays...

Ce murmure d'eau et de branche,
ces gestes vifs, doux et fuyants,
la vie entière qui se penche
et se redresse, au fil du temps.

La route longue, chaotique.
Les mains sans lampe ni secours.
Quelque insaisissable musique
pour les songes de chaque jour.

La tête enfin, la tête folle
qui fait un soir ce vœu léger:
étouffer toutes les paroles,
atteindre à l'immobilité.

THE CHAIR

The chair, who was a branch once, echoing
     the sounds of wings to come,
and who, to do all her remembering,
     has but a silence glum;
the chair, haunted by thoughts of sun, of wind,
     of flying snow, asleep,
but wondering how it happened so, chagrined,
     trapped in a slumber deep,
tries to awake, escape, to flee my room.
     —At night, I hear her, when,
* groping her way, she moans, yearns, through the gloom,
     for her old home again...

Rien que vivre

Murmuring water, murmuring bough,
gestures—some slow, or sharp, or sly—
a life entire, now bowing, now
rising again, as time flows by.

Long the road, and chaotic. Hands
without a lamp or help to guide you.
Music that no one understands
for daydreams rising up inside you.

And then the head, the foolish head...
Silly its wish one night: ah yes,
to choke back all the words unsaid
and reach ideal motionlessness.

Rien que vivre

* Although I attempt to be as formally faithful to my originals as appropriate, I do not follow the poet in her use of an unorthodox rhyme (*chambre/tendre*), as occasionally occurs in her work.

Anne-Marie Kegels 1023

Peut-être seras-tu cette femme dernière.

Tu forceras la porte avec tant de lumière
dans les bras, que l'aimé enfin te connaîtra.
Il étendra ses mains, doucement te dira
de cette voix du soir qu'assourdit le mystère:
"C'est toi que j'ai cherchée aux chemins de la terre.
Oh! viens que je te touche..." Et tu t'avanceras
tremblante, toute simple et riche de tes bras,
et l'immense clarté que tu auras conquise
en marchant sans pleurer sous le gel et la bise
se répandra sur lui. Alors il te verra
et fera de sa main un tel adieu, là-bas,
à celles d'autrefois qui étaient filles d'ombre
que tu resplendiras de joie—et que le nombre
des baisers à venir s'éveillera soudain
et viendra te toucher les épaules, les seins,
d'un grand pressentiment, pur comme une prière...

Peut-être seras-tu cette femme dernière
qui restera en lui et qu'il espérait tant
pour boire à son regard la défaite du temps
et pour fonder en elle une saison profonde
pleine de chants, d'appels, et d'ailes sur le monde.

NUIT

Quand les chauves-souris te cousent
à grands points d'ombre et de tiédeur
de quel seigneur es-tu l'épouse?
Je sais que tu marches sans heurts
les hanches pleines du mystère
d'avoir étouffé la lumière.
Tantôt là-bas, si noire et nue,
toute bruissante devenue
tu t'es roulée au long des pentes
où dorment les reines des prés.

Perhaps you'll be the last one he has sought.

You'll burst into the room, your arms so fraught
with light that he, so loved, will suddenly
know that, at last, it's you he seeks. And he
will hold his hands out to you and begin
to speak to you tenderly, softly, in
that mystery-shrouded voice of night: "My love!
You are the one I'm always thinking of,
and traveling the earth to find! Come here
and let me touch you!..." And you will draw near,
rich in the fullness of your arms, and cast—
trembling, naïve—upon him that bright, vast
splendor you captured while, time and again,
tearless, you trudged the windswept frost. And then,
with his "Farewell, amen!" to all of those
shadowy wenches of his past, there grows
a sum of kisses yet to come, firm pressed
about your back, your neck, your glowing breast,
like a great omen, of pure prayer wrought.

Perhaps you'll be the last one he has sought,
there to remain in him... And, in his eyes,
his hope to let you drink up time's demise,
build you a worthier time: on wings unfurled,
to spread song, joyous shout, over the world.

Rien que vivre

NIGHT

When the bats sew you up with wide
and looping, tepid-shadowed stitch,
of what fine lord are you the bride?
I see you ambling on—no hitch,
no halt—hips full of mystery
of how you stifled, utterly—
the light of day. Just now, out there,
with your hushed rustle, black and bare,
you rolled along the slopes where sleep
the wildflower pinks. Mad lover, you!

Anne-Marie Kegels 1025

O folle, amoureuse imprudente,
maintenant les doigts de l'été
sont imprimés sur tes épaules.
Et loin de toutes les paroles,
renversées au cou de minuit,
mille femmes volent ton cri.

MAINS

Touchez longtemps ce qui se touche,
l'écorce, l'eau, l'herbe, la bouche,
avec l'ardeur au creux des doigts
touchez le chaud, touchez le froid,
pour en faire votre aventure
touchez la mer et la voilure,
le mont, la plaine au cri de blé.
Un soir touchez vos doigts usés
comme un drap où les corps roulèrent.
Touchez enfin—noces dernières—
aux feux assourdis du couchant
vos souvenirs mêlés au vent.

L'ÉTANG

Parfois, dans mon sommeil, je rencontre un étang
qui sort de sa torpeur comme un fleuve déborde.
Il m'entraîne avec lui. Dans un rapide exode
je renverse, je couvre et sans fin je m'étends.
J'efface les talus avec des eaux sauvages,
j'emporte les roseaux, je noie des paysages,
je couche dans mes bras des foins échevelés.
Les oiseaux de la mer viennent nous regarder.

The summer's fingertips sink deep
into your back. Far from the slew
of empty words long said, there, pressed
supine against the midnight's breast,
a myriad women likewise lie,
groaning, stealing the sounds you sigh.

Chants de la sourde joie

HANDS

Touch with a touch that lolls and lingers
everything you can touch, with fingers'
deep-cupped desire, touch water, grass,
mouth, bark, hot, cold, let come to pass,
with all you touch, your destiny,
yes, touch the rigging and the sea,
the mountain and the meadow, plain
resounding with the shout of grain.
Then, one night, touch your fingers, crumpled
like a sheet—bedding lying rumpled
where bodies turned and tossed. And, for
one final wedding, touch still more:
the sunset's fires, muted flames, these
tousled and windswept memories.

Chants de la sourde joie

THE SPRING

At times, asleep, I come upon a spring
that, like an overflowing stream, will throw
* its torpor off, drag me along. We go
coursing in headlong flight, and everything
I touch will topple, fall, as everywhere
my untamed torrent spreads. Banks, slopes once there
are there no more. I bear away reeds, grasses,
tousled hay, drown the plain where my flood passes.

* Here, again, I do not follow the poet in her use of a questionable rhyme, *déborde/exode.*

Anne-Marie Kegels 1027

La plaine disparaît. Nous tuons la lumière.
Quand le matin revient me percer les paupières,
je demeure longtemps à retrouver mes yeux
et à les ramener, par des vols hasardeux,
vers la solide terre où tremblent mes journées
de ruisselante nuit encor toutes mouillées.

———————

L'OISEAU

Ce sang qui vole,
ce cœur flottant,
la parabole
contre le vent,
c'est un oiseau.
Jailli de terre
le voici haut
dans la lumière.
Et mes yeux nus
contre la vitre
ne savent plus
quel toit m'abrite
ni qui m'appelle.
Ecartelée,
je suis restée
prise à ses ailes.

———————

À LA MÉMOIRE DE CATHERINE FAULN

A pas légers de somnambule
elle a quitté le bruit du sang...
Recouverte de crépuscule,
on ne sait où elle descend,

The seabirds come to watch. Light dims and dies...
When morning dawns, piercing my lids, my eyes
waver, unsure, long hesitating, though
I try to swoop them toward the ground below,
solid again; yet, in the trembling light,
my days will quiver, ever wet with night.

Chants de la sourde joie

THE BIRD

Heart flowing free,
blood flying high,
trajectory
on windswept sky...
What is it? Just
a bird in flight,
borne on a gust
up to the light.
My place? In vain
my naked eyes,
against the pane,
try to surmise...
Who calls me, sings?...
Torn limb from limb,
I follow him,
caught in his wings.

Chants de la sourde joie

---

* IN MEMORY OF CATHERINE FAULN

With a sleepwalker's tread—deft, light—
she left blood's murmurings behind...
Clothed in the dusky almost-night
she goes—who knows where?—clear of mind,

---

* Catherine Fauln, born the same year as the poet (1912), died in 1951, leaving three privately published collections: *Fenêtre sur le paradis* (1946), *Chants pour la statue* (1948), and *Les éphémères*, of which only three copies were printed. Five examples of her modest work appear in Jeanine Moulin, *Huit siècles de poésie féminine*, pp. 308–11.

Anne-Marie Kegels 1029

prudemment, avec ses yeux larges.
On ignore quelle est sa charge
de blé d'amour au creux des reins
et quel été trahi la blesse.
Ne tentez pas une caresse,
elle vous brûlerait les mains.
Il ne faut pas baiser ses traces.
Nul ne sait où elle a passé.
En courant elle a trébuché
au bord fulgurant de l'espace.

RIVE

Tu glisseras vers moi sur une barque noire.
Tu me découvriras à l'ombre des osiers,
printanière, glacée, dans les cercles de moire
qui viendront de ta rame au frisson de mes pieds.

Un chasseur attardé, tirant la sauvagine,
déchirera le soir mais je ne crierai pas.
Je tiendrai le silence heureux sur ma poitrine.
Tu toucheras la rive et nous aborderas.

Je mettrai à ton cou mes bras de longue peine.
Les herbes nous diront leur goût d'asile amer.
Nous tremblerons, roulés dans ton manteau de laine.
Ta barque détachée ira droit à la mer.

STATUE

C'est en vain que les roses sourdent
à ses pieds, comme une lueur.
Elle est aveugle et elle est sourde.
Ignorante de nos rumeurs
elle s'obstine à faire un geste
qu'elle ne peut jamais finir.
La seule chaleur qui lui reste
c'est un rayon qui va mourir

eyes wide. And none can say what load
of loving grain lies deep bestowed
within her loins, what summer stands
betrayed, wreaking its ire on her.
Don't chance a soft caress: you'll stir
her wrath, her fire will burn your hands.
Don't kiss her path: a merry chase
she leads, we know not where... She slipped
away and, as she ran, she tripped
over the blazing edge of space.

Chants de la sourde joie

SHORE

You'll come gliding toward me, on a black barque,
and find me, fresh and chill as early spring,
in the reeds' shade, as rings, shimmering dark,
born of your oar, reach my feet, shivering.

A fowler, tarrying late, will, with his blast,
sunder the evening. Silent will I stand.
I'll clutch the happy calm and hold it fast.
Approaching me, your barque will touch the land.

My longing arms will hug you by and by.
Bitter, the reeds will lull our secrecy.
Trembling, wrapped in your cloak of wool, we'll lie.
Adrift, the barque will float out to the sea.

Haute vigne

STATUE

In vain the roses grow, entwined
about her feet, glow, glistening.
For she is deaf and she is blind.
Unmindful of our murmuring,
she stands striking a stubborn pose:
a gesture timeless, endless quite.
And the sole warmth her body knows
is a slight, dying ray of light

Anne-Marie Kegels 1031

et qui pour un instant se pose
comme un passereau dans son cou.
Je songe à la métamorphose
qui délivrerait ses genoux.
Et quand au ciel l'ombre dérive
je viens parfois furtivement
toucher les pieds de la captive
et les dénouer dans le vent.

LA MARE

L'eau pauvre, la boue et les ronces,
un pré bourru pour s'y cacher,
c'était la mare sans réponse
à ceux qui venaient s'y pencher.

Mais je ne sais par quelle grâce,
quel amour délivré du mal,
je voyais briller à sa place,
chaque soir, un étang royal.

COLLINE

Le vent met son bras
autour de sa taille.
Elle rit tout bas
au creux des broussailles.

Ni vigne, ni blé.
Nul soc ne l'offense.
C'est la seule danse
des génévriers.

that settles briefly, gingerly,
sparrow-like, on her neck's form, flees...
I muse on how, were she to be
transformed, free, she would flex her knees
at last. And when the shadows, from
the sky, go spreading, sometimes I
furtively to the victim come,
unbind her feet, and let her fly...

Haute vigne

――――――――

THE POND

Foul water, muck, a brambled plot
of field to hide in, muddy pit...
Such was the pond that answered not
those who leaned low to question it.

Nor do I know by what pure love,
what grace, I saw, casting its light
and gleaming bright in place thereof,
a royal pool, night after night.

Haute vigne

――――――――

HILL

Wind's arm round her waist,
she stands as she stood,
laughing low, embraced
* in the briarwood.

No vine, no grain; hers,
no plow plunged askance,
Nothing but the dance
of the junipers.

* Though it does not appear that the poet's change of rhyme scheme beween this qua-
train and the rest (*abab/abba*) was aesthetically motivated, I follow her lead.

Anne-Marie Kegels 1033

Depuis trois cents ans
livrée aux couleuvres,
elle n'a pour œuvre
que terreaux dormants,

sentes soleilleuses
dans les éboulis
—sous un vaste bruit
d'ailes ombrageuses.

————————

Le pain a brillé sur ma table
avant de m'être retiré.
J'ai touché son corps adorable
et j'ai mordu l'âme du blé
dans sa plus douce chair de mie.
Jours repliés, fêtes finies,
je puis rire de ma famine.
Au plus secret de ma poitrine
court dans l'ombre, peine sans bruit,
mon sang à jamais ébloui.

————————

CONVALESCENTE

On la voit remonter la sente
—souffle court—d'un ravin de nuit.

Ne lui parlez jamais des plantes,
ni des lichens qu'elle cueillit
au loin de vos talus solaires.
Ils ont brûlé ses yeux, ses doigts.
Et chaque soir on aperçoit,
contre ses tempes, ses paupières,
tendre, tenace, vénéneux,
le halo de leur pollen bleu.

Mere serpent-prey, she:
three hundred years deep
in her mouldering sleep,
lying peacefully.

Sunlit passagings,
pebble-scattered ground
under a vast sound:
shadow-spreading wings.

Haute vigne

———————

The loaf shone on my table, whole,
before they wrested it from me.
I felt its flesh, bit of its soul
of tender wheat, adoringly.
Days packed away, feasts done at last,
I can laugh at my famine past.
Now, deep within my bosom, where
all lies in utter secret, there
flows in the shadow, pounding low,
my blood, awed by its afterglow.

Haute vigne

———————

CONVALESCENT

One sees her struggle, hears her pants
as she climbs up the night's ravine.

Don't speak to her about the plants,
mosses, she's picked, betwixt, between,
far from your sunlight's grassy crest.
They've burned her fingertips, her eyes;
and every night one can surmise
against her lids, her temples, pressed,
tender, tenacious—poisonous too—
their pollen in a haze of blue.

Haute vigne

DORMEUR

Baigné d'oubli, lourd comme pierre,
avec ce vol sous tes paupières
        d'oiseaux soumis,
ô quel feu d'ombre te consume?
Quel étroit sillon te résume
        au creux du lit?

Je te regarde, taciturne.
Renversé sous ton faix de lune,
        souffle prudent,
tu fais le sûr apprentissage
d'un air léger, brumeux, sans âge
        privé du temps.

Je porterai mes ans ainsi qu'un chaud butin.
J'aurai mon juste poids de jours frappés de songe.
Face à l'eau des miroirs que sonde le matin
je laisserai blanchir mes cheveux sans mensonge.

Dans mes yeux s'ouvriront encore les sentiers
où ma jeunesse allait, droite comme une reine.
Où s'est-elle enlisée? On a vu son soulier
meurtri près du cresson qui ronge la fontaine.

Je ne dirai jamais si je pleure sa mort.
J'aurai les bras trop lourds d'épis et de branchages.
Que peut faire l'assaut de tous les vents du Nord?
Nul ne m'arrachera mes récoltes sauvages.

Si ma gerbe est d'épeautre emmêlé de chardons
c'est que j'ai tout cueilli, doigts brûlants, au passage.
Qu'un unique terreau m'accorde le pardon
des faims que j'exauçai tout au long de mon âge.

SLEEPER

Heavy as stone, bathed in a deep
forgetfulness; lids pressed, in sleep,
      on tame birds, fled;
what shadow-flame consumes you thus?
What furrow fits you, congruous,
      tight in your bed?

Silent, your breath... Beneath the pack
of moonbeams bundled on your back,
      I watch you there,
doing your staunch apprenticing
to weightless, timeless, drearying,
      and ageless air.

Haute vigne

I'll wear my years like a warm prize, proud-borne.
Of dream-struck days, I'll bear the weight, just right.
Before the mirrors' waters, that the morn
plumbs deep, I'll let my hair, untouched, turn white.

In my eyes, still, those paths will take shape, where
my youth, straight as a queen, went wandering.
What swamp engulfed her? Her slipper lay there,
limp, by the watercress that gnaws the spring.

I'll never say if I lament her death.
Too full of grains and boughs my arms will be.
Why should I fear the North Winds' savage breath?
No one will wrench my wanton crops from me.

Cows' grass and brambles, my bouquet: my burning
fingers picked all I passed. May one lone hill
of mouldering earth forgive me now the yearning
that all my days I hastened to fulfill.

Haute vigne

Anne-Marie Kegels 1037

Ils ont dit: c'est la mauvaise herbe.
Ses racines mordent profond.
Moi je louangeais sa foison
son entêtement, sa superbe.

Ils ont dit: c'est l'herbe ennemie.
J'ai regardé de près sa tige.
Aucune arme. Le seul prodige
d'une dure sève éblouie.

Ils ont dit: c'est l'herbe coupable.
Nous l'arracherons sans arrêt.
Moi mon amour vous souriait,
vaste chiendent intarissable.

CLAIRIÈRE

Elle est posée au creux des bois
comme une jonquille plus grande
et aux quatre vents fait l'offrande
de la lumière qu'elle boit.

Midi la roule dans son lit.
Des faons sourcilleux la traversent.
Elle ébroue au gré des averses
sa robe de millepertuis.

Des abeilles lourdes de miel
emportent son goût de genièvre.
On l'aperçoit qui se soulève
et qui émigre au creux du ciel.

They said: "They're weeds, no more, no less.
Their roots bite deep into the ground."
Myself, I watched them thrive, abound,
and praised their haughty stubbornness.

They said: "They're weeds, the enemy."
I looked close at their stems. No arms.
Only a dazzling sap that charms
with a relentless energy.

They said: "They're weeds, what rack they're wielding.
We'll rip them out, again, again..."
But my love smiled upon you then,
you, couch grass, spreading vast, unyielding.

Les doigts verts

_____

CLEARING

She lies in woodland greenery
like a great jonquil bright, sunlit,
that drinks the light then offers it
up to the four winds, solemnly.

Noon coddles, beds her. Fawns cavort,
aloof, about her, to and fro.
And, as the rain's whims come and go,
she shakes her gown of St. John's wort.

Honeybees, laden, bear on high
her taste of juniper. And there,
one seems to see it in the air,
rising, settling within the sky.

Les doigts verts

PAROLES DU TALUS

Quand la fille des foins, soûle de trop d'arômes,
a besoin de sommeil, je fais signe à son corps.
Je m'arrondis pour elle et mets contre ses paumes
mon versant préservé des offenses du Nord.

J'aime sentir sur moi sa taille renversée.
Ses cheveux apaisés m'accordent leur tiédeur.
Je vois sur son corsage une verte araignée
marcher à pas furtifs à l'endroit de son cœur.

Moi je ne bouge pas. Elle dort et je veille.
Je ne jalouse plus l'arbre au geste si beau.
Sur mon flanc herbager où son cou s'ensoleille
cette fille épandue est mon fruit sans défaut.

CROCUS

Pour Hélène

C'est demain qu'un doigt vert écartera le sol.
Le merle en sifflera un couplet un peu fol.

Un crocus tâtonnant, sous l'arbre encore chauve
va hisser vers le jour sa robe jaune ou mauve.

O première couleur exacte au rendez-vous,
le jardin vous fera briller sur ses genoux.

Nous entendrons l'hiver s'enfuir dans l'air mouillé.
Mais rien ne bougera, qu'un crocus réveillé.

WHAT THE EMBANKMENT SAID

When, drunk on smells, surfeited overmuch,
the hay-lass yearns to sleep, then, beckoning,
I arch my back for her and, to her touch,
offer my slope, safe from the North Wind's sting.

I love to feel her body gently pressed
against me, feel her hair's calm warmth. I see
a spider, shaded green, upon her breast,
crawl toward her heart, gingerly, furtively.

She sleeps. I lie awake, silent and still.
The grace-limbed tree inspires no envious awe.
Spread on my fodder flank she shines her fill
of sunlight, she, my fruit without a flaw.

Les doigts verts

CROCUS

For Hélène

A finger, green, tomorrow will poke up through.
Blackbird will trill his praise in notes askew.

Beneath a tree, still bare, a crocus, shy,
will hitch her skirt—mauve, yellow—toward the sky.

O year's first hue, spring's never-tardy sign,
there, on the garden's lap, once more you'll shine.

In the moist air we'll hear winter's leavetaking.
All will lie still, all but a crocus, waking.

Les doigts verts

LES FEUX

Le mauve des lilas s'est glissé dans l'aster.
Septembre a soupiré que des brumes l'étranglent.
Une inquiète pâleur se traîne, tourne l'angle
de la maison frileuse au bord des feux déserts.

Les feux ne mûriront qu'aux soirées de Novembre.
Ils rougiront alors, tels grenades d'été.
Nous aurons le reflet des tisons éclatés
sur nos fronts fascinés et sur nos mains de cendre.

Appuyés aux carreaux, des vents pleins de rancœur,
supplieront qu'on les laisse entrer par les jointures.
Mais sereinement sourds, derrière les tentures,
les feux seront le lieu plénier de la douceur.

DES FLAMMES

Cette année-là
l'hiver fut un loup

On le vit bondir sur le village
le rouler dans la neige

Sur chaque vitre
s'étoilèrent ses griffes
brilla son œil rouge

tandis que dans les âtres
des flammes dévouées
s'exténuaient pour les vivants.

THE FIRES

The lilac's mauves into the asters seep.
September sighs: fog chokes her, makes her ill.
An anxious pallor lolls about the chill
walls of the house. The fires, untended, sleep.

The fires will not burn bright until November's
nights. Then, like summer's pomegranates, they
will light our spellbound brows, our hands, ash-gray,
with the reflection of the crackling embers.

Pressing the panes, winds full of rancor might
beg entry through the cracks. But then, unhearing,
behind the drapes, serenely calm-appearing,
the fires will be the seat of sweet delight.

Les doigts verts

* FLAMES

That year
the winter was a wolf

We saw it lunging at the town
rolling it in the snow

On every pane
its star-claws sparkled
its red eye glistened

and meanwhile on the hearths
flames all but spent
faithfully labored for the living.

* Previously unpublished, this typical winter tableau in uncharacteristic free verse first
appeared in Anne-Marie Trekker and Pierre Vander Straeten, *Cent auteurs*, p. 232.

Anne-Marie Kegels 1043

Sabine Sicaud (1913–1928)

Death, never an even-handed antagonist, seems especially capricious in his deal-
ings with our poets. Supremely liberal with an Andrée Sodenkamp, he was tragi-
cally close-fisted with an Elisa Mercœur (see pp. 641–51), and even more so with
the precocious Sabine Sicaud. Born in Villeneuve-sur-Lot on February 23, 1913,
Sabine began scribbling poems, we are told, on her doctor grandfather's me-
dicinal prospectuses. An unfortunate irony when one considers that none of
the remedies called upon to cure her untractable and painful malady a decade
later did any good whatever... She would die on July 12, 1928, after much suffer-
ing, alleviated by only sporadic remissions, during which she would continue
to write the poetry that, along with the ministrations of her devoted family, her
books, and the rich imagination that would let her travel the world over, offered
her a small measure of relief.

When, in 1924, at the age of eleven, Sabine submitted a poem for Le Jasmin
d'Argent—a local competition founded a few years before to promote Gascon
literary talent—the judge, Marcel Prévost, of the Académie française, suspected
a hoax. He was disabused only when he met Sabine, who improvised a poem
for him virtually on the spot. She not only received a silver medal but also went
on, the following year, to win several awards at the venerable Jeux floraux de
France and—more important still—the admiration of its famous judges, the
academician Jean Richepin and the poet Anna de Noailles (see pp. 834–57). A
signal honor for anyone, but unheard of for a twelve-year-old. The comtesse
de Noailles would express her admiration in a preface to Sabine's only collec-
tion to appear during her brief life: the twenty-nine Poèmes d'enfant (1926). In
it, the eminent countess admired the poetic grace with which a mere child, for
all her inexperience, was able to avoid the pitfalls lying before any poet's inspi-
ration; an inspiration that, for young Sabine, personified the flora and fauna of
the intimate natural world about her and the often whimsical products of her
fertile musings.

When François Millepierres published the Poèmes de Sabine Sicaud in 1958,
on the thirtieth anniversary of her death, he gave once more to readers, for
whom she was little more than a name, if that, the opportunity to encounter her
charm in vivo. And when Odile Ayral-Clause, in 1996, brought her more recently
before the public in Le rêve inachevé, Robert Sabatier would, in his preface, echo
the earlier praises, admiring Sabine's "mischievous view of the world" and the
originality of a technique untrammeled by oversophistication, that had much to
teach her poet elders, male and female alike.[1] Sabatier went on to wonder—as
must we all—how much more she might have written, and to suggest, a little

cynically, that, cut down as a child, she would not, at least, suffer the contamination to which "literature" might have exposed her.

What might she have become? Would she have reined in her verse—a curious mélange, in equal doses, of formal, blank, and free? Or would she have followed the current of her time along the demanding but deceptively simple-appearing path of poetic liberty? Would she, in fact, even have continued to write? Would physical cure have deprived her of her need to do so? Would she, Rimbaud-like, let poetry go hang, to be ignored as a childish pastime, or, like that more recent prodigy of the 1950s, Minou Drouet, dissolve into the little-read footnotes of literary history? Whatever the answer, Sabine's work remains: her *vita*, indeed *brevis*, but her *ars*, deservedly *longa*.[2]

Though exact chronology of Sabine's poems is virtually impossible to determine, the following translations, except as indicated in the notes, are presented in the order adopted in *Le rêve inachevé*.

NOTES

1. *Sabine Sicaud: Le rêve inachevé*, ed. Ayral-Clause, p. 5.

2. See further the collections edited by Millepierres and Ayral-Clause. *Poèmes d'enfant* has long been unavailable.

LA CHÈVRE

L'herbe est si fraîche, ce matin,
Que son velours tendre nous hante
Son velours neuf qui sent la menthe,
Le jeune fenouil et le thym.

La vache s'étire, gourmande,
Vers le champ de trèfle voisin.
Tous les verts bordent le chemin
Du vert acide au vert amande.

Mais c'est un velours trop soigné
Qui s'aligne entre les clôtures...
Dans les ronces, à l'aventure,
La chèvre aime s'égratigner.

Elle aime le vert des broussailles
Où l'ombre devient fauve un peu,
Et ce vert d'arbres presque bleus
Que tous les vents d'orage assaillent.

C'est bien au-delà des sillons
Et des vergers gorgés de sèves,
Que les clochettes de son rêve
Eparpillent leurs carillons...

Parfois, un glas les accompagne...
Mais il fait beau, c'est le matin!
Chevrette de Monsieur Seguin
Ne regardez pas la montagne...

THE GOAT

Cool is the grass this morning; our
Sense yields to its smooth redolence,
Like velvet, tender mid the scents
Of mint, and thyme, and fennel flower.

The glutton cow yearns toward the clover.
Greens—acid-tart and almond green,
And all the shades that lie between—
Follow the path, border it over.

Too tender and too neat, alas,
To please the goat, penned in. For she
Would much prefer to saunter free
And scratch against the prickly grass.

She loves the brambles' green, unfenced,
Where shadows cast a tawny hue;
The green of trees, turned almost blue,
That storm winds howl and pound against.

Far from these furrows, wandering on;
Far from the sap-rich orchards these;
The dream-bells of her reveries
Sprinkle their tinkling carillon...

At times a knell too fills the air,
*   Though fair the morning... Ah! Daudet's
Little goat! Please, I pray you gaze
Not on the mountaintop out there...

* The reference is to Alphonse Daudet's well-known story "La chèvre de Monsieur
Seguin," from his *Lettres de mon moulin* (1869), in which a foolhardy goat, yearning for the
freedom of the mountain, comes to grief despite her courageous battle against a wolf.

Sabine Sicaud 1047

PREMIÈRES FEUILLES

Vous vous tendez vers moi, vertes petites mains des arbres,
Vertes petites mains des arbres du chemin.
Pendant que les vieux murs un peu plus se délabrent,
Que les vieilles maisons montrent leurs plaies,
Vous vous tendez vers moi, bourgeons des haies,
Verts petits doigts.

Petits doigts en coquilles,
Petits doigts jeunes, lumineux, pressés de vivre,
Par-dessus les vieux murs vous vous tendez vers nous.
Le vieux mur dit: "Gare au vent fou,
Gare au soleil trop vif, gare aux nuits qui scintillent,
Gare à la chèvre, à la chenille,
Gare à la vie, ô petits doigts!"

Verts petits doigts griffus, bourrus et tendres,
Vous sentez bien pourquoi
Les vieux murs, ce matin, ont la voix de Cassandre.
Petits doigts en papier de soie,
Petits doigts de velours ou d'émail qui chatoie,
Vous savez bien pourquoi
Vous n'écouterez pas les murs couleur de cendre...

Frêles éventails verts, mains du prochain été,
Nous sentons bien pourquoi vous n'écoutez
Ni les vieux murs, ni les toits qui s'affaissent;
Nous savons bien pourquoi
Par-dessus les vieux murs, de tous vos petits doigts,
Vous faites signe à la jeunesse.

CARTE POSTALE

Quand l'anémone rouge et les jacinthes bleues
Fleurissent les parcs d'Angleterre,
Une petite fille en robe rouge ou bleue
Descend les escaliers de pierre.

FIRST LEAVES

You reach your little tree-green hands to me,
Little green hands of trees lined orderly.
The old walls crumble, wounds are seen
Scarring the aging houses, yet you reach
Your hedge-hands to my fingers, each to each.
Your little fingers green.

Little shell-fingers, young,
Luminous, eager, hurrying to grow...
You reach over the old walls spread below.
An old wall says: "Beware wild gusts, beware
The sun, burning unstrung.
Beware the night twinkling the air.
Beware the goat, the caterpillar's tongue...
Beware life, little fingers green!"

Fingers, like rough or tender claws this morning,
How well you know what those walls mean.
Cassandra-voiced, they warn you. But what for?
Tissue-like fingers, or
Velveted, or enameled, shimmering green—
How well you know why you ignore
Those ashen-colored walls and all their warning...

Frail little fans of green,
Hands of next summer's heat,
How well we know why you eschew
Those crumbling roofs and the old walls effete:
Over the walls, it's youth that you
Are reaching to...

POSTCARD

English parks lush with flowers overgrown—
Red hyacinths and blue anemones...
In dress of blue or red, like these,
Little girl coming down the steps of stone...

Sabine Sicaud 1049

De green, les parterres, le lierre,
Les beaux arbres jamais taillés
Et les sous-bois pleins de jacinthes...

En robe rouge ou bleue—anémone ou jacinthe—
Une petite fille est peinte
Dans le printemps vert et mouillé
De la vieille Angleterre.

———————

Quand j'habitais Florence avec tous mes parents,
Ma mère, ma grand-mère et l'arrière grand-mère
Aux longs cheveux d'argent,
J'aimais tant les iris de nos jardins toscans
Et le parfum de leur terre légère...

Ah! le printemps, depuis, n'est plus un vrai printemps!

Il n'a plus la couleur des vitraux, vos couleurs,
Sainte-Marie-des Fleurs,
Et celles de l'Arno
Sous les ponts recourbés où passait Béatrice.

Le soleil qui baignait les salles des Offices
N'a plus cet or subtil de matins déjà chauds
Le long des murs anciens et des champs de repos.

Les rossignols, depuis, ont tous une voix triste
Et l'aube qui persiste
A l'ombre des cyprès, je ne la connais plus.

Nos jardins d'autrefois, nous les avons perdus.

flowerbeds, ivy, unpruned trees,
Hyacinths in the underbrush... And green...
Green everywhere, and everything...

In dress of blue or red—like these
Hyacinths and anemones—
Little girl pictured... Lovely scene:
Olde England, green and wet with spring.

———————

When I lived off in Florence with my kin—
Mother, Nana, Great-grandmama as well,
With her long, silver hair—there, in
Our Tuscan gardens, how I loved the spell
Cast by the iris, and earth's airy smell...

Ah! Spring, since then, is not what spring had been!

It wears no more your stained-glass colors, O
Santa Maria dei Fiori, nor
The Arno's, whose arched bridges bore
* The steps where Beatrice used to go.

The sun that once bathed the Ufizzi's halls
In subtle morning gold warms us no more
Along the leisure fields and ancient walls.

Since then, the nightingale sings a sad song
And dawning daylight seems all wrong,
Trying to pierce the cypress-shade somehow.

Yesterday's gardens... No, we've lost them now.

* "Beatrice" here should best be given four syllables, as in Italian. But even if anglicized,
it can be made to scan. Let the reader decide.

CHEMINS DU NORD

Lorsque "je pâlissais au nom de Vancouver"
et que j'étais du Nord,
trop de froid traversait ma pelisse d'hiver
et mon bonnet de bêtes mortes.
Mes frères chassaient les oursons
jusqu'au fond des grottes de fées;
du sang parlait sous leurs trophées,
les Tomtes se cachaient, le vent hurlait aux portes
et la glace barrait les fjords
lorsque j'étais du Nord.
Murs blancs du froid, prison.
Je ne voyais jamais passer Nils Holgerson.

Selma, Selma, pourquoi m'aviez-vous oubliée?
Il fallait naître à Morbacka, le jour de Pâques.
Je savais bien pourtant que j'étais conviée...

LE CHEMIN DES VEUVES

Veuves—tant de veuves si veuves
avec ce nom créé pour elles,
avec ce noir comme une preuve.

Pauvre veuve. On dit: pauvre veuve,
et c'est le malheur en série.
Ah! c'est un Dieu sourd que l'on prie.

* NORTHLAND PATHS

† Back when "the name Vancouver turned me pale,"
I was a Northerner:
the winter chill pierced my pelt cape; the gale
blew through my cap of dead-beast fur.
My brothers, deep in fairy grottoes, were
hunting for bear cubs. Eloquent,
beneath their trophies, blood lay spent;
the Goblins hid away; the winds rose, fell,
growled at the doors... Again, again...
Ice closed the fjords up tight, back when
I was a Northerner:
walls white with cold, a jail... And I
never did see Nils Holgerson fly by.

Ah! You forgot me, Selma! Why, pray tell?
Would I were born at Morbacka, on Easter Day.
I know I was invited though!... Oh well...

WIDOWS' PATH

Widows well-widowed... So many stood
with that name made for them alone,
with that black, proof of widowhood.

Poor widow. Yes, that's what we say,
poor widow, woes strung one by one.
Ah! God is deaf to those who pray.

---

* This Nordic fantasy is, apparently, a testimony to the child poet's admiration for the Swedish novelist Selma Lagerlöf (1858–1940), born in the village of Morbacka (line 15), and for her often supernatural folkloric tales. The one specifically referred to (line 13), *The Wonderful Adventures of Nils Holgerson* (1906), recounts the travels of a mischievous child-turned-dwarf, who flies from Sweden to Lapland on the back of his farmyard goose.

† This quotation had successfully eluded many efforts to explain it. Odile Ayral-Clause has shown, however, that, rather than merely being evidence of young Sabine's passion for geography, attested to by François Millepierres in his preface to *Les Poèmes de Sabine Sicaud* (pp. 13–14)—and abetted by the irresistible rhyme "Vancouver/hiver"—it alludes to a poem by Marcel Thiry, "Toi qui pâlis au nom de Vancouver" (see *Le rêve inachevé*, p. 64n3).

Veuve jeune, belle peut-être,
ou vieille et seule un soir de vent.
Ah! cet arbre sous la fenêtre...

On allait dehors deux ensemble.
On savait bien peu l'un de l'autre
mais la prière des Apôtres
brûlait peut-être dans le vent.

Quai désert. Havre dévasté.
Qui peut dire de quel moment
on est veuf pour l'éternité?

———————

LE CHEMIN DE SABLE

Ne pas se rappeler en suivant ce chemin...
Ne pas se rappeler... Je te donnais la main.
Nos pas étaient semblables,
Nos ombres s'accordaient devant nous sur le sable,
Nous regardions très loin ou tout près, simplement.
L'air sentait ce qu'il sent en ce moment.
Le vent ne venait pas de l'Océan. De là
Ni d'ailleurs. Pas de vent. Pas de nuage. Un pin
Dont le jumeau fut coupé dans le temps
Etait seul. Nous parlions ou nous ne parlions pas.
Nous passions, mais si sûrs de la belle heure stable!
Ne te retourne pas sur le chemin de sable.

Widow, young, perhaps lovely still,
or lonely, old, some windy night.
Ah! that tree by the window sill...

Together we would take the air.
We knew each other little, though
the words of the Apostles' prayer
seemed to burn in the windy night.

Abandoned wharf. Harbor laid low,
laid waste. Who knows what moment we
* are widowed for all eternity?

---

† THE PATH OF SAND

Not to remember as we trod the sand...
Not to remember... I gave you my hand.
Our shadows' single tread
Blended as one, went trotting on ahead.
We looked off in the distance, or close by
Now and again. The air smelled then as I
Can smell it now. No Ocean wind... A dead
Calm, not a breeze from anywhere. The sky,
Cloudless. And there, a pine that, once upon
A time, was two, but that now stood alone,
Its twin chopped down. And on we walked, and on
We talked—or didn't—sure that we would own
That hour fair, hold it ever in our hands!
Don't stop to look back when you walk the sands.

    * Without following her liberties exactly, I have tried to preserve the effect of Sabine's unorthodox, even nonexistent, rhymes, in spite of (or perhaps because of) which her verse achieves a remarkable and simple musicality.

    † This poem and the one following are not included in *Le rêve inachevé* and are reproduced from *Les poèmes de Sabine Sicaud*.

Sabine Sicaud 1055

LE CHEMIN DU MOULIN

Embranchement. Le moulin me fait signe.
Ce n'est pas un moulin à vent
Mais ses ailes battent dans l'eau secrètement
Et ses canards sont blancs comme des cygnes.
Ses colombes ont l'air du Saint-Esprit. Son porche
A l'air de précéder une église. Au couchant
Sa fenêtre à meneaux flambe comme une torche.
Il n'a pas d'autre nom que le Moulin, pour le passant.

LE CHEMIN DE L'AMOUR

Amour, mon cher Amour, je te sais près de moi
Avec ton beau visage.
Si tu changes de nom, d'accent, de cœur et d'âge,
Ton visage du moins ne me trompera pas.
Les yeux de ton visage, Amour, ont près de moi
La clarté patiente des étoiles.
De la nuit, de la mer, des îles sans escales,
Je ne crains rien si tu m'as reconnue.
Mon Amour, de bien loin, pour toi, je suis venue
Peut-être. Et nous irons Dieu sait où maintenant?
Depuis quand cherchais-tu mon ombre évanouie?
Quand t'avais-je perdu? Dans quelle vie?
Et qu'oserait le ciel contre nous maintenant?

LA VIEILLE FEMME DE LA LUNE

On a beaucoup parlé dans la chambre, ce soir.
Couché, bordé, la lune entrant par la fenêtre,
On évoque à travers un somnolent bien-être,
La vieille qui, là-haut, porte son fagot noir.

Fork in the road. The mill beckons to me.
It's not a windmill, but its wings
Shimmer the water with mute flutterings
And ducks as white as swans, doves that could be,
Each one, the Holy Ghost... Its little porch's
Space seems a church-front. Sunset, and the sky,
Torch-like, flares in its mullioned panes—flames, scorches...
"The Mill"... Its only name known to the passerby.

THE PATH OF LOVE

Love, dearest Love, I know you're next to me,
So fair of face. You may
Change your name, age, your heart, the way
You speak... But your face cannot faithless be.
Those eyes that light your face, Love, next to me,
Shine, patient as the stars. If you but nod,
I fear no night, vast seas, bleak isles... For you,
I've come, Love, from afar, perhaps. Whereto
Do we go now, we two? Good God,
Who knows? How long have you been searching now
To find my shadow, vanished in thin air?
When did I lose you, Love? In what life? Where?
And how can heaven dare to undo us now?

THE OLD WOMAN IN THE MOON

Tucked in... Tonight a lot of bedroom chatter...
The moon slips through the window; on her back
The old crone hauls her sheaves of firewood, black,
As in a drowsing calm we wonder at her.

* Included in neither published collection, this poem is one of a number of *inédits* in
the possession of Odile Ayral-Clause, which she has been good enough to share with me.

Qu'elle doit être lasse et qu'on voudrait connaître
Le crime pour lequel nous pouvons tous la voir
Au long des claires nuits cheminer sans espoir!

Pauvre vieille si vieille, est-ce un vol de bois mort
Qui courbe son vieux dos sur la planète ronde?
Elle a très froid, qui sait, quand le vent souffle fort.
Va-t-elle donc marcher jusqu'à la fin du monde?

Et pourquoi dans le ciel la traîner jusqu'au jour!
On dort... Nous fermerons les yeux à double tour...
Lune, laisse-la donc s'asseoir une seconde.

———————

LA GROTTE DES LÉPREUX

Vallée du Gavaudun

Ne me parlez ni de la tour,
Ni des belles ruines rousses,
Ni de cette vivante housse
De feuillages en demi-jour.

La gorge est trop fraîche et trop verte;
La rivière, comme un serpent,
S'y tord, à peine découverte
Sous trop d'herbe où reste en suspens
Le mystère des forêts vierges.

Ne me parlez ni de l'auberge,
Ni des écrevisses qu'on prend
Dans la mousse et les capillaires.

Je n'ai vu, de ce coin de terre,
Ni la paix du soir transparent,
Ni celle des crêtes désertes.

How weary she must be beneath her pack!
What crime was hers, that—hopeless, till the crack
Of dawn—she roams the night? What was the matter?

Poor soul, so old! Was it her theft? Was it
For some dead twigs that she bows, bending low
* On planet round? And when the chill gusts blow,
Must she plod on, eternal, infinite?

Why drag her through the sky till day's first light?
Sleep, now... We close our eyes and lock them tight.
Moon, let the poor thing sit and rest a bit.

THE LEPERS' GROTTO

†   *The Gavaudun Valley*

Don't talk to me about its tower,
About its ruins reddening,
About its foliage blanketing
In shade the dim-lit leafy bower.

The gorge is all too cool, too green.
The stream goes trickling, snakes its course
Between the rocks, twists, scarcely seen—
Too thick the grass!—where forest gorse
Holds its breath's virgin mystery.

Don't talk about its inn to me,
About the river's moss and fern,
And crayfish caught at every turn.

Twilight's transparent peace was not
What I saw in this calm sojourn,
Nor the high crests that time forgot.

---

* Sophisticated beyond her years, the poet would seem to be making a reference—gender-deformed in accordance with the usual French feminization of the moon—to the biblical story of the man who was punished by God for gathering firewood on the Sabbath (Num.15:32–36). His identification with the moon is found in a number of folkloric variations, and, with the addition of a dog, it explains an allusion in *Midsummer Night's Dream*, in the lines of the prologue to the Pyramus and Thisbe sequence: "This man with lantern, dog, and bush of thorns presenteth moonshine."

† Gavaudun, in the southwestern *département* of Lot-et-Garonne, was—and still is—a tourist resort known for its picturesque gorges and grottoes.

Mais, barrant le ciel, deux roch'ers
Tout à coup si nus, écorchés,
Avec plusieurs bouches ouvertes!

Vers ces bouches noires, clamant
On ne sait quelle horreur ancienne,
Savez-vous si, furtivement,
De pauvres âmes ne reviennent?

Où sont-ils, où sont-ils, mon Dieu,
Ces parias vêtus de rouge
Qui, là-haut, guettaient les soirs bleus
Par les trous béants de ce bouge?

Grotte des Lépreux, seuil maudit
Au bord de la falaise ocreuse...
Il faudrait qu'on ne m'eût pas dit
Quel frisson traversait jadis
Ce décor de feuilles heureuses...

UN MÉDECIN?

Un médecin? Mais alors qu'il soit beau!
Très beau. D'une beauté non pas majestueuse,
Mais jeune, saine, alerte, heureuse!
Qu'il parle de plein air, non pas trop haut,
Mais assez pour que du soleil entre avec lui.

Qu'il sache rire—tant d'ennui
Bâille aux quatre coins de la chambre—
Et qu'il sache te faire rire, toi, souffrant
De ta souffrance et du mal de Décembre.

Décembre gris, Décembre gris, Noël errant
Sous un ciel de plomb et de cendre.
Un médecin doit bien savoir
D'où ce gris mortel peut descendre?

Qu'il soit gai pour vaincre le soir
Et les fantômes de la fièvre—
Qu'il dise les mots qu'on attend
Ou qu'on les devine à ses lèvres.

No. There against the sky I saw,
Suddenly, two cliffs—rocks spread bare,
Ragged—with many a yawning jaw.

To those black mouths, wailing with their
Who-knows-what age-old baleful yearning,
Don't ghosts come back? Aren't you aware
Of poor souls furtively returning?

Where are they? Where, my God, those souls,
Pariahs clad in red, and who,
Up there, peered at the skies of blue
Through that hell-haunt's wide-gaping holes?

The Lepers' Grotto! Cursed threshold
Into the cliffs' ochre recesses...
How I wish I had not been told
What shudders racked, in days of old,
This realm of leafy lovelinesses...

A DOCTOR?

A doctor? Well, at least let him be fair,
Good-looking! But not all haughtily so.
Healthy, young, spirits high... Voice low—
To talk about the out-of-doors, fresh air—
Just loud enough to bring some sunlight in.

Let him know how to laugh—chagrin
Yawns in the corners of this sickroom, fills
It full—and how to make you laugh, poor thing,
Sick with your sickness and December ills.

December! Gray!... Christmas, meandering
Beneath a lead-and-ashen sky.
All of that dead December gray, descending...
Oughtn't a doctor know the "whence," the "why"?

Let him be bright and gay at daylight's ending,
Rout fever's ghosts and night's unrest.
Let him tell us what we would like to hear:
Comforting words, spoken aloud or guessed.

Qu'il soit gai, qu'il soit bien portant,
(Ne faut-il croire à l'équilibre
Qui doit redevenir le nôtre, aux membres libres,
A l'esprit jouant sans efforts?)
Qu'il soit bien portant, qu'il soit fort—sans insolence,
Avec douceur, contre le sort...
Il nous faut tant de confiance!

Qu'il aime ce que j'aime—J'ai besoin
Qu'il ait cet art de tout comprendre
Et de s'intéresser, non pas de loin,
Mais en ami tout proche, à ce qui m'intéresse.

Qu'il soit bon—nous voulons une indulgence tendre
Pour accepter notre révolte ou nos faiblesses.

De la science? Il en aura, n'en doutez point,
S'il est ce que je dis, ce que j'exige.

Mais exiger cela, c'est, vous le voyez bien,
Leur demander, quand ils n'y peuvent rien,
Quelque chose comme un prodige!

Lequel, parmi vos diplômés,
Ressemble au médecin qu'espère le malade?
Lequel, dans tout ce gris tenace, épais, maussade,
Sera celui que moi je vois, les yeux fermés?...
.   .   .   .
Ou bien, alors, prenons-le contrefait,
Cagneux, pointu, perclus, minable;
Qu'il flotte en ses effets
Comme un épouvantail—et semble inguérissable
Des pires maux, connus ou inconnus!

Prenons-le blême et vieux, que son crâne soit nu,
Ses yeux rougis, sa lèvre amère—
Et que rien ne paraisse au monde plus précaire,
Plus laid, plus rechigné que cet être vivant,

Let him be bright and gay, full of good cheer.
Give him good health. (Oughtn't he make us see
A picture of the vigor that will be
Our own when, free of mind and cured of limb,
We will be strong and healthy too, like him?)
Give him good health and strength, defense
Against fate's blows, but gentle, not
Arrogant toward our woes and human lot...
Oh how we need to feel his confidence!

Let him like what I like: I must
Know that he has that art of comprehending
All my concerns, but as a friend I trust,
Not just some distant somebody, pretending.

Let him be kind and good, indulgent for
The feelings of revolt our weakness breeds.

Knowledge? Science? Of course! To suit my needs,
He must have oh so much, and even more!

But fruitless are the cures at their command!
I fear that my demands would take
At least a miracle for my poor sake!

And so, in all this deep, gray devastation,
In all your doctor-titled band,
Is there one like the one I hope for, and
The one I see in my imagination?
. . . .
If not, let's have one squat, unfit—
One who, knock-kneed and crippled, nasty, vile,
Clings to his clothing, swims in it,
Scarecrow-like, and who suffers all the while
From all the fatal ills known and unknown!

Let's have one old, bald, pale, down to the bone,
Eyes rimmed with red, lips wizened, cold—
Such that no one could be, if truth be told,
Uglier or more nearly dead than he—

Afin que, chaque jour, l'apercevant
Comme un défi, parmi les fleurs venant d'éclore,
Nous pensions, rassurés, soulagés, fiers un peu
De nous sentir si forts par contraste: "Grand Dieu!
Qu'il doit être savant pour vivre encore!"

———————

Filliou, quand je serai guérie,
Je ne veux voir que des choses très belles...

De somptueuses fleurs, toujours fleuries;
Des paysages qui toujours se renouvellent,
Des couchers de soleil miraculeux, des villes
Pleines de palais blancs, de ponts, de campaniles
Et de lumières scintillantes... Des visages
Très beaux, très gais; des danses
Comme dans ces ballets auxquels je pense,
Interprétés par Jean Borlin. Je veux des plages
Au décor de féerie,
Avec des étrangers sportifs aux noms de princes
Des étrangères en souliers de pierreries
Et de splendides chiens neigeux aux jambes minces.

Je veux, frôlés de Rolls silencieuses,
De longs trottoirs de velours blond. Terrasses,
Orchestres bourdonnant de musiques heureuses...
Vois-tu, Filliou, le Carnaval qui passe?
La Riviera débordante de roses?
J'ai besoin de ne voir un instant que ces choses
Quand je serai guérie!

So that, each day, on his arrival, we
See him—midst flowers fresh-blooming on the sill—
Defy death! and think, with a sigh, somewhat
Proud to look well compared to him: "God! But
What skill he must have, to be living still!"

(unfinished)

---

* Once I've been cured, Filliou,
I'll want to see nothing but pretty things...

Luxurious flowers in endless blossomings,
Landscapes forever fresh and new,
Sunsets miraculous, bell-towers, white
Palaces, bridges, sparkling in the light...
Beautiful faces, bright and gay,
Dancers I only dream about today—
† Like Jean Borlin leaping his *entrechats*...
And oh, the beaches!... Ah,
Yes! That's what I'm going to long to see,
Beaches graced with a fairy touch,
And muscled strangers—Princes Such-and-Such—
Ladies with jeweled slippers, finery,
Splendid dogs, lean of leg and white as snow...

I'll want long promenades, plush and blond, where,
With voices hushed, Rolls Royces come and go.
Terraces, orchestras abuzz with their
Beautiful music... Carnaval, Filliou!
The rose-strewn Côte d'Azur... See?... Rest assured,
One glance is all I'll need! Just one will do,
For me to see those lovely things,
Once I've been cured!

* "Filliou" was Sabine's and her brother's pet name for their mother.
† Jean Borlin (or Börlin) was a ballet celebrity of the period, famous for his choreography of Cocteau's *Les mariés de la Tour Eiffel,* which had premiered on June 18, 1921, with music by Milhaud, Poulenc, and other members of "Les Six." He was one of many contemporary personalities immortalized in posters by the caricaturist Steinlen, which Sabine might well have seen.

J'aurai ce châle aux éclatantes broderies
Qui fait songer aux courses espagnoles,
Des cheveux courts en auréole
Comme Maë Murray, des yeux qui rient,
Un teint de cuivre et l'air, non pas d'être guérie,
Mais de n'avoir jamais connu de maladie!

J'aurai tous les parfums, "les plus rares qui soient,"
Une chambre moderne aux nuances hardies,
Une piscine rouge et des coussins de soie
Un peu cubistes. J'ai besoin de fantaisie...

J'ai besoin de sorbets et de liqueurs glacées,
De fruits craquants, de raisins doux, d'amandes fraîches.
Peut-être d'ambroisie...
Ou simplement de mordre au cœur neuf d'une pêche?

J'ai besoin d'oublier tant de sombres pensées,
Tant de bols de tisane et d'heures accablantes!
Il me faudra, vois-tu, des choses si vivantes
Et si belles, Filliou... si belles ou si gaies!

Nul ne sait à quel point nous sommes fatiguées,
Toutes deux, de ce gris de la tapisserie,
De l'armoire immobile et de ces noires baies
Que le laurier nous tend derrière la fenêtre.

Tant de voyages, dis, de pays à connaître,
De choses qu'on rêvait, qui pourront être
Quand je serai guérie...

———————

Vous parler? Non. Je ne peux pas.
Je préfère souffrir comme une plante,
Comme l'oiseau qui ne dit rien sur le tilleul.
Ils attendent. C'est bien. Puisqu'ils ne sont pas las
D'attendre, j'attendrai, de cette même attente.

I'll wear that brilliant-spangled cape that brings
To mind a rash torero, and my hair
* Will halo round my head, Mae Murray style,
Cut short. My eyes will wear a twinkling smile,
My fair skin will be bronze-tinged, with an air
Of health, without an inkling anywhere
Of that cruel illness that stalked me a while!

I'll have perfumes, "the rarest one can buy."
A room with brash motifs, a red-tiled pool,
Cushions of silk with cubist shapes. For I
Yearn for a life where fantasy's the rule...

I'll yearn for sorbets, iced liqueurs, and cool
Almonds, crisp fruit, grapes succulent and sweet.
Ambrosia too, perhaps, to eat?
Or simply sink my teeth into a peach?

I'll yearn to cast out somber thoughts, forget
All those depressing moments, banish each
And every hot *tisane!* I'll want to let
Nothing but living things into my life:
Beautiful, happy, living things, Filliou!

For no one knows how tired we are, we two,
Of this gray-papered room, dull-furnitured,
The laurel-berries, black, beyond the sill.

So many countries, travels, pleasure-rife,
Dreams only dreamt, that soon I will fulfil
Once I've been cured...

———————

To speak, to tell you? No, I can't.
I'd rather bear my suffering like a bird—
Perched silent in the linden tree, unheard—
Or even waiting, like a patient plant...
Waiting... Yes, like them I wait patiently.

* After gaining fame as a dancer, Mae Murray—"The Girl with the Bee Stung Lips"—
went on to be featured in the Ziegfeld Follies, eventually starring in silent films opposite
such leading men as John Gilbert and Rudolf Valentino. Unfortunately, her voice was not
as pleasant as her looks, and the advent of the talkies gradually ended her career. Sabine's
reference to her "short hair" is curious. She is usually pictured with rather full, wavy locks.

Ils souffrent seuls. On doit apprendre à souffrir seul.
Je ne veux pas d'indifférents prêts à sourire
Ni d'amis gémissants. Que nul ne vienne.

La plante ne dit rien. L'oiseau se tait. Que dire?
Cette douleur est seule au monde, quoi qu'on veuille.
Elle n'est pas celle des autres, c'est la mienne.
Une feuille a son mal qu'ignore l'autre feuille.
Et le mal de l'oiseau, l'autre oiseau n'en sait rien.

On ne sait pas. On ne sait pas. Qui se ressemble?
Et se ressemblât-on, qu'importe. Il me convient
De n'entendre ce soir nulle parole vaine.
J'attends—comme le font derrière la fenêtre
Le vieil arbre sans geste et le pinson muet...
Une goutte d'eau pure, un peu de vent, qui sait?
Qu'attendent-ils? Nous l'attendrons ensemble.
Le soleil leur a dit qu'il reviendrait, peut-être...

Alone, they suffer. We must learn to bear
Our pain alone. Let no friend come bestow
A hypocritic smile or moan on me.

Mute is the plant; the bird, still. What is there
For them to say? Like it or not, this woe
Of mine is all my own. No others share it.
One leaf's distress, one bird's, will always be
Unknown to others. Bird and leaf must bear it.

Unknown... Unknown... Are others like us? No.
And, if they were, what would it matter? Here,
Tonight, I have no wish to listen to
A lot of chatter... So let time elapse...
Mute as the finch, still as the old tree near
My window, I wait... For a drop of dew?
A breeze? Who knows? We'll wait together though.
The sun promised them to return, perhaps...

Lucienne Desnoues (1921–2004)

Rare would be the poet from whose works Nature, in one form or another—along with Love, Death, and the all-embracing cliché "Life"!—would be completely absent. Even Baudelaire, who professed utter scorn for Nature, and who refused to "go into raptures over a vegetable," tips his hat obliquely to it on occasion. We have seen it inspire in varying degrees and different scenarios the poets presented thus far in these pages. For Lucienne Desnoues, however, it is almost an obsession: the nature of her native Ile-de-France, of her adopted Belgium, of the Provence to which she returned after the death of her husband in 1986 . . . Other subjects will attract her from time to time—she is too much the poet to be completely single-minded—but even a glance at a few of the titles of her dozen verse collections reveals her intense devotion to it: *Jardin délivré* (1947), *Les racines* (1952), *La fraîche* (1959),[1] *Le compotier* (1982).

But for all the near-single-mindedness of her inspiration, nourished by her admiration for Jean Giono and Jules Supervielle, the variety of Desnoues's poetic expression is nonetheless impressive. Whether she is word-painting the simplicity and rugged strength of peasant life or the copious rustic larder, the fertile soil that invites the hands to plunge deep within it, or the many brief tableaux of her favorite icon, the owl—to which, in fact, one of her collections is entirely devoted—the same underlying inspiration dominates: Her love of the bounty and vigor that nature imparts and that suffuse all its creatures, and that require little sophistication of soul to appreciate or complexity of vocabulary to sing. Hers is a direct, almost transparent poetry, "old-fashioned" in its refusal to adhere to obscurantist aesthetics of the moment. Indeed, she readily acknowledges her adherence to the values of the past—her professed *passéisme*—suggesting, in the preface to her *Anthologie personnelle* (a collection of her own favorite poems written between 1947 and 1997), that "to look one's own time squarely in the eye and shun its imperatives is a way of being truly a part of one's time."

Whether one accepts the logic of her premise or not, it is clear that she makes no excuses for staunchly maintaining those other-age values, social as well as artistic. It is not that she is naively unaware of the incursions that technology has made into the natural world or the damage it has done, and continues to do, in the cause of progress. Far from it. In the same preface she laments, albeit with only a gentle nostalgia, the transformation of the once-bucolic village of Roissy into a bustling town in the shadow of the Aéroport international Charles de Gaulle. And she insists, in a winsome exaggeration, that, while "the feathers of Pegasus go blowing, scattered to the winds by the great turbojets," she prefers to

1070

follow in the tradition of those poets who once used a goose quill "to confront, to nourish, and to enchant the soul." No computer for her, no metamorphosis of words into numbers...

Lucienne Desnoues was born in 1921 in the Val d'Oise village of Saint-Gratien. Her marriage in 1947 to the writer Jean Mogin, whose poet-father Georges Mogin wrote under the pseudonym Norge, let her exchange a legal secretary's career in Paris for life in a prominent literary family in Belgium. It was while living in Brussels that she wrote six of her ten collections of verse as well as two collections of stories, including one for children. Widowed mother of two daughters and grandmother of four, she spent most of her later years quietly in the Vaucluse, in the countryside of Petrarch's and Laura's poetic amours, continuing not only to write but also to participate in the literary life of both her countries until her death in the summer of 2004.[2]

The thirteen poems translated in the following pages are from a variety of Desnoues's collections. Most of them were reprinted in her 1998 *Anthologie personnelle.*

NOTES

1. Henri Sauguet's *Cantate sylvestre* (1974) is based on *La fraîche,* and several of Desnoues's other works have also been set to music.

2. On Desnoues's life and work, see, among many sources, Anne-Françoise Jans, *Lucienne Desnoues*; Gisèle Leibu's entry in Anne-Marie Trekker and Jean-Pierre Vander Straeten, *Cent auteurs,* pp. 131–34; Liliane Wouters and Alain Bosquet, *La poésie francophone de Belgique,* pp. 303–4, Renée Linkhorn and Judy Cochran, *Belgian Women Poets,* pp. 111–23; and Robert Frickx and Michel Joiret, *La poésie française de Belgique de 1950 à nos jours,* pp. 229–32.

LE PREMIER FESTIN

Noire, noire et noire olive,
Bel œil, bel œil langoureux,
Oignon frais, tomate vive
Et toi l'ail couveur de feu,

Les melons et la tomate
Si bien tournés pour la main,
Et les poivrons écarlates,
Et les piments de carmin,

Aubergine violette,
Figue au gousset éclaté,
Luisez mes joyaux en fête
Dans les coffres de l'été.

Le thym maigre se régale
De pierraille et de clarté.
Les grillons et les cigales
Chantent la frugalité.

Que mettrons-nous sur la table
Pour le tout premier festin?
Le bolet farci, le râble
Et la fraise au Chambertin?

Non, l'olive nue et pure
Et nus et crus les oignons,
Le fromage sans parure,
L'eau de source et le quignon.

THE FIRST FEAST

Olive black, black, black of flesh,
Fair eye languorous, fair eye yearning,
Bright tomato, onion fresh,
Garlic, you, with fire slow burning,

Melons and tomatoes, all
So well-turned to fit the hand,
And the peppers, big and small,
Ruby-red and scarlet, and

Eggplant of the purplest hue,
Figs that burst their pouch-tight skin:
Shine, you festive jewel-box you,
With my summer's gems within.

Fragile, the thyme feasts upon
Gravel, light, and even less.
* Crickets chirping on and on
Sing a song of frugalness.

What shall be our bill-of-fare
For this first feast? Some *vin fin?*
Fine stuffed mushrooms? Saddle of hare?
† Strawberries dipped in Chambertin?

No! Just olives, pure, pristine,
Simple cheese, unfrilled, unfussed,
Onions—bare, and raw, and green—
Water from the spring, a crust...

La fraîche, "Pierres sèches"

---

* Less entomologically punctilious than the poet, who specifies both *grillons* (crickets) and *cigales* (cicadas), I make do with just the former. No emulators of La Fontaine's famous spendthrift *cigale,* co-heroine of his first fable, variously translated in English versions as "cricket," "cicada," and even "grasshopper," the *cigales* of the present harvest-song seem eager to make up for her shortcoming.

† Chambertin is a variety of wine from the Côte d'Or region of Burgundy. Connoisseurs might take the poet to task for even suggesting that it be drunk with hare, since, in the region, Pommard is the wine of choice with that dish, whereas Chambertin is usually reserved for capon.

Lucienne Desnoues 1073

LA MISE AU MONDE

Quand se dégourdit la petite faune
Des fleurons lovés, larvaires et froids,
Quand le fond des cœurs et le fond des bois
Sont tout pépiants de germes béjaunes,

J'enfonce mes mains dans votre gésine,
Printemps des humus, printemps des forêts.
Sous la mousse intime, au vif du secret
J'agriffe mes doigts parmi les racines.

Les nerfs du printemps, tendons de guitare,
Grondent sous mes doigts, claquent dans mes doigts,
Et leurs sons profonds raniment en moi
Cent mille défunts accoucheurs d'hectares.

Folle sage-femme aux bras pleins de glaise
J'aide l'éternel à se délivrer
Et par le dessous des prés et des prés
J'aide obscurément mes forêts françaises.

LES VIRTUOSES

Approche-toi du cygne si tu oses.
(Le cygne a l'œil tellement venimeux!)
Vois comme au sol platement il se meut.
Pourtant le cygne est un grand virtuose.

THE DELIVERY

When, with a cold and larval blooming, earth
Writhes, from its numbness, gently into life;
When hearts and forest depths ooze, teeming, rife
With peeping, twittering fauna's new-sprung birth;

I plunge my hands into your gravid flesh,
O fertile-humus springtime, woodland spring.
Deep in the clinging moss, coy covering,
About earth's roots, my fingers clasp and mesh.

The spring's nerves—tendons, taut, as if they were
Guitar strings, that I twang, pluck groaningly—
With low-voiced sound, bring back to life in me
* Ten myriads of dead hectare *accoucheurs*.

Mad midwife, clay caked on my arms, my hands,
In the eternal's labor—field to heath
And heath to field—darkly I toil beneath
The soil, and serve my France's forest lands.

March 1956
La fraîche, "La main à la pâte"

THE VIRTUOSI

Draw near the swan, unless you fear to go so
Close (for his glance is oh so venomous!).
See how he hugs the ground, low, languorous.
And yet, the swan is a fine virtuoso.

* Readers unhappy with my arithmetic might note that the etymological meaning of "myriad," ten thousand, amounts to the same hyperbole as the poet's *cent mille* (one hundred thousand). Perhaps they will agree that, no less clinically precise, it is, at least, a little more poetic.

Approche-toi, que vers l'eau il claudique,
Puis qu'il se glisse où le ciel se trempait,
Et le rivage est frappé de respect
Quand il conduit sa nage mélodique.

De hauts nageurs piétinent dans nos foules.
Sans le savoir nous croisons la grandeur.
J'aime songer qu'un grand rêve grondeur
Vient d'occuper l'espace que je foule.
Et ce passant que rien ne te désigne
Fera ce soir mille cœurs s'empresser
En approchant d'un piano glacé
Ses graves mains comme un couple de cygnes.

———

PAUVRE LÉLIAN

Rôdeurs, filous, marlous, soiffards, trognes vilaines
    A votre heure un hibou frôle mon toit.
Son chant est doux et double et trouble comme toi
    Et comme ta chère absinthe, ô Verlaine.

Draw near, and, all at once, you're seeing him
Plod toward the water, where down dipped the sky;
And the shore stands, respectful, awestruck by
* The music of his stately gliding swim.

Such lofty swimmers, too, tread our dense spaces.
Blithely we cross their paths, with grandeur fraught.
I love to muse that some great grumbling thought
Just filled the space that now my footfall traces.
And he—some *type* your glance won't linger on—
Tonight, will cause a thousand hearts to pound
As, to a cold, still piano, he draws round
With two hands, solemn as a brace of swan.

Anthologie personnelle

---

† PAUVRE LÉLIAN

Derelicts, prowlers, pimps, drunks, foul-faced men,
An owl grazes my roof, night's yours alone.
‡ Soft, low, its double-toil-and-trouble moan,
Like you and your dear absinthe, O Verlaine.

Anthologie personnelle

* The original, like my translation, is rather ambiguous here, since it is not clear whether the poet's *nage mélodique* (melodic swimming) refers to the rustling of the water or to sounds produced by the voice of the swan himself. (While some swans—especially the trumpeter swan—do make sounds, at least one variety is completely mute, thus giving rise to the well-known literary and folkloric commonplace, developed at length by Plato in the *Phaedo* [84e and 85a], that the swan sings only at the moment of its death, hence the term "swansong.")

† "Pauvre Lélian" (Poor Lélian) is an anagram of "Paul Verlaine," which the celebrated symbolist poet (1844–1896) adopted, partly in jest, partly as a sincere expression of self-pity for his Decadent excesses, not the least of which was his fondness for absinthe.

‡ I cannot guarantee that the poet had this Shakespearian echo in mind; but, given the surrounding elements that evoke the powers of darkness and mystery—among them, the owl, one of her frequent hallmarks—I would like to assume that she did.

LES SOLEILS ET LE HIBOU

Que redis-tu sur ce faible thème,
Fauve à qui tout soleil est interdit?
Demandes-tu de connaître Midi,
 Ou bien que l'on t'aime, que l'on t'aime?...

HIBOU & PERMANENCE

Ce muezzin plumeux, de sa voix qui défaille,
 Recommande: "N'oubliez pas
Qu'autour du monde, à tout instant, sans une faille,
 On passe de vie à trépas."

UN CRÂNE

Sous ces voûtes ont habité
La raison et les frénésies,
L'espérance, la charité.
Les dieux y furent inventés.
Est-ce Lascaux ou Les Eyzies,
Cet antre si désaffecté
Où le vice eut ses élevages,
La haine ses repas sauvages,
L'amour ses grands feux agités,
Ses longs échos l'éternité,
Le langage ses fourmilières,
L'horreur ses voltigements noirs?
En ce troglodyte manoir
Des voix chantèrent, supplièrent,
Mystérieuses, familières.

SUNS AND THE OWL

Beast forbidden from the suns above you,
What are you asking with that one-note tune?
That you come, somehow, simply to know Noon,
Or that someone love you, someone love you?...

Anthologie personnelle

OWL AND CONTINUITY

"Remember," warns this feathered muezzin, wailing,
    Trembling of voice and short of breath,
"Around the world, ever, and never failing,
    Somebody goes from life to death."

Anthologie personnelle

A SKULL

Reason and rage, hope, *bonhomie,*
Madness and mind all lived inside
This vaulted space. Here, came to be
The gods invented, glorified.
Is this Lascaux, or Les Eyzies? *
This den, this cave unoccupied
Where vice once bred its beasts? This lair
Where hate held savage feasts, and where
Love's flames flared high, impassionedly?
Where echoes of eternity
Pulsed long? Where language grew in fuss
And ant-hill frenzy? Tenebrous
Horrors swirling: troglodyte dwelling,
Voices in song and prayer swelling,
Familiar and mysterious...

* Lascaux and Les Eyzies are sites of prehistoric caves in southwestern France, famous for their wall drawings.

Lucienne Desnoues 1079

Ces lieux ignorent leur passé.
Les occupants n'ont rien laissé.

Sur vos parois bien dénudées,
Occipital et temporaux,
Nul faon, nul mammouth, nul taureau.
Les resplendissantes idées,
Les sombres principes moraux,
Dans cette caverne calcaire
N'ont gravé ni chiffres ni mots,
Ni beaux symboles animaux.
Tous les engins de Jules Verne
Et tous les oiseaux de Rameau,
L'ardente faune de Shakespeare.
De Rodin et du Tintoret
Avec les elfes des forêts
Et les anges et les vampires
Ont hanté ce rupestre empire.

Et de tant d'hôtes repartis,
Rien. Pas le moindre graffiti.

Ignorant of its past, this place:
Those who once dwelt here left no trace.

Over your walls, now stripped and bare—
Temporal and occipital—
No mastodon, bull, fawn is there.
No deep, dark moral principle
Or shining thought has, anywhere
In this bone-cavern, carved or drawn,
For one to look in awe upon,
Numbers, words, figures animal.
And yet, all the fantastical
Jules Verne machines, all Rameau's birds,
All Shakespeare's fauna—passionate words
And ardent souls—Rodin's as well,
* And Tintoretto's: every kind
Of angel, imp, fell vampire hell
And heaven spawned... These one used to find
Lodged in this empire of the mind.

What did they leave, these lodgers all?
Nothing. Wiped clean, the cavern wall.

Anthologie personnelle

* The familiar names in this somewhat whimsical précis-catalogue of human intel-
lectual and artistic accomplishment would seem, to some extent at least, to be determined
by exigencies of rhyme. Perhaps, given the skull image, the Shakespearean reference is
also an echo, intended or otherwise, of the gravedigger scene in *Hamlet*. As for the allu-
sion to "tous les oiseaux de Rameau," the poet is probably referring to the number of the
composer's works inspired in part by birds: among them, the scene entitled "Le ramage
des oiseaux" (The Chirping of the Birds) in his opera-ballet *Le temple de la gloire* (1745), for
which Voltaire provided the libretto, and the extensive use of bird sounds (and, indeed,
other animal noises, including frogs and a donkey), in the satiric opera *Platée* (1745). It is
also worth mentioning here that the French line with which *Jules Verne* seems expected to
rhyme (line 23 of the original) is clearly an oversight, and that the line intended should be
"Dans cette calcaire caverne."

Lucienne Desnoues 1081

L'AU-DELÀ

Le hibou chantait au fond des coudraies
    D'une voix hantée
Comme un pauvre mort qui se souviendrait
    De la volupté.

LES AMANTS

Et les amants s'en furent se cacher
Dans le bourru de la chaude garrigue,
Dans le touffu que nul sourçon n'irrigue,
Dans le griffu qui croque du rocher.
Que ce fut doux, sous les broussins d'yeuses,
Pour baldaquin les bâches du mistral,
Pour matelas le chaos minéral,
Que ce fut doux l'amour minutieuse!
Que ce fut doux, quand le soleil oppresse,
Tout excité d'insectes zélateurs,
Donner au Temps des leçons de lenteur,
Donner à Dieu des leçons de tendresse.

SOIR D'ÉTÉ VILLAGEOIS

    Fraîches touffeurs où nous nous attardons,
Estouffades d'amour à même l'édredon.
L'oiseau des bois lointains souligne vos bouffées
    Avec sa voix de plumes étouffée.

THE HEREAFTER

An owl was hooting in the hazel wood,
    And its low howls would strike
A haunted note, like some poor corpse who could
    Recall what lust was like.

Anthologie personnelle

THE LOVERS

And then the lovers hid; their refuge was
In the gruff underbrush, a scrubwood space,
In the scruff of a dense unwatered place,
In the rough grip of heat's rock-smashing claws.
How sweet it was, beneath the holm oaks, tangled—
The mistral's gusting canvas overhead,
The earth's metallic chaos for their bed—
How sweet it was, that love intense, old-fangled!
How sweet it was, in sun's torrid excesses,
Buzzing with frenzied insect litanies,
To give Time lessons in love's languid ease,
To give God lessons in love's tendernesses.

Anthologie personnelle

VILLAGE SUMMER EVENING

    Whiffs of air, stuffy, sweltering heat,
Welter of quilt-top love, our long retreat...
Stifled, muffled, its ruffled cooings heard
    Each time you puff: a distant bird...

Anthologie personnelle

* The original, in a remarkable counterpoint, plays on both sound—*touffeur* [swelter-
ing heat] / *estouffade* [stew] / *bouffées* [puffs] / *étouffée* [muffled]—and ambiguity: is the *vos
bouffées* addressed to the supposed lover, or simply to the *soir d'été* invoked in the title? I try
to suggest something of both delicious effects, at once simple and complex.

Lucienne Desnoues 1083

HIBOU DE LA PLEINE LUNE

La lune est limpide avec délice. Oh!
D'où vient ce refrain de mauvais augure
Quand le plaisir et la truite fulgurent
Au creux des lits et du lit des ruisseaux?

LES HIBOUX DE VERSAILLES

Et sous vos baldaquins, très grand émir,
    Après musique et patenôtre,
    Par-dessus les buis de Le Nôtre
Vous entendiez le royaume gémir.

L'ESPÉRANCE

Vous, hiboux, ténébreux hiboux, ne voyez pas,
Bien que fils des forêts, que les forêts sont vertes.
Comptez-vous comme nous sur l'éclair du trépas
Pour faire du réel l'entière découverte?

OWL OF THE FULL MOON

Limpid delight, the glowing moon. Ah me!
What is that baleful chant moaned roundabout
The flash of pleasure and the flash of trout,
On bed and riverbed, respectively?

Anthologie personnelle

THE OWLS OF VERSAILLES

Beneath your canopies, O great emir—
    Done the "Our Father's" and the singing—
*   Over Le Nôtre's boxwoods winging,
The groanings of the kingdom reached your ear.

Anthologie personnelle

HOPE

You, owls, sons of the forest, tenebrous,
Who never see the forest greenery,
Do you count on the flash of death, like us,
† To let you see life's stark reality?

Anthologie personnelle

* The elegant gardens of Versailles were the work of Louis XIV's celebrated architect André Le Nôtre (1613–1700). The poet's allusion to owls in the title is even more abstract here than in her other "owl" quatrains, suggesting not specific birds but simply an atmosphere of foreboding and impending revolutionary doom.

† In the preface to *Anthologie personnelle* (p. 11), the poet tells us that it was with this next-to-last poem—the last being a dedication to her two daughters, reprinted from *La fraîche,* one of her earliest collections—that she intentionally closed it, choosing to "clore le défilé sous le soleil de l'Espérance" (end the procession under the sun of Hope). This would tend to give a more optimistic tone to the quatrain, consonant with its title, than the one that it seems, on first reading, to suggest.

Lucienne Desnoues 1085

Liliane Wouters (1930–)

We have already met the name of Liliane Wouters in the foregoing pages (see pp. 1008–9 above). Her extensive knowledge of Franco-Belgian poetry has produced several important anthologies, among them the *Panorama de la poésie française de Belgique* (1976), the authoritative four-volume *La Poésie francophone de Belgique* (1985–1992), with Alain Bosquet—for whom she is one of the three or four major women poets in the history of French verse[1]—and, most recently, *Un siècle de femmes* (2000), with the Belgian poet Yves Namur. To most of her public, however, this imposing figure of modern Belgian letters is known primarily as a playwright and poet, as well as an eminent translator from medieval and modern Flemish, the language that shares her bilingualism.

Wouters was born on February 5, 1930 in Ixelles, Belgium, where she taught school from 1949 to 1990. Her literary career began with three collections of verse: *La marche forcée* (1954), *Le bois sec* (1960), and *Le gel* (1966), winning her a number of awards along the way. The first of these alone won four, among them the Prix Renée Vivien and the prestigious Prix de la Nuit de la Poésie, the jury for which included Jean Cocteau, Pierre Reverdy, Louis Aragon, and other notables. Eventually, Wouters took a leave from poetry in order to devote herself principally to her first love, the theater. (At age thirteen she had already written several school plays for her classmates to perform.) Explaining the contrasting attractions of the two genres, she would later say that while "the poem's quest, like that of the Holy Grail, is in the nature of an esoteric experience, and while its impact is a personal one, the theater stands in direct contact with the world."[2] That contact quickly brought her to the attention of the public. Thanks to plays like the gay-inspired *Vies et morts de Miss Shakespeare* (1979) and the ironic, award-winning comedy *La salle des profs* (1983), which draws on her own teaching experiences, she is today considered one of Belgium's foremost dramatists.

But love of the theater notwithstanding, Wouters's poetic muse, alive and well, refused to be still. In 1983, she published the volume *L'aloès*—the title of the last poem in *Le gel* of some seventeen years before—a selection of poems from her three previous works (including *Le gel* in its entirety), plus over five dozen new poems of a distinctly sensual bent not without lesbian under- and overtones. She gave to this collection the name of the plant known for its slow maturation as well as its soothing properties, a metaphor, it has been suggested, for the gradual development of her middle-year poetic talents. Two other collections, *Parenthèse* (1984) and *Journal du scribe* (1990), followed; and, more recently still, *Le billet de Pascal* (2000), in which she plunges headlong into the realm of free verse. Clearly, her poetic vein is far from exhausted.

Prizes and honors for both her poetry and her theater, and no less for her translations, have continued to crown Wouters's work. She received the Grand Prix de la Poésie de la Maison de Poésie in 1989; the Prix Montaigne in 1995; the Prix Goncourt de la Poésie in 2000; and is a member of both the Académie royale de langue et de littérature française de Belgique and the corresponding Flemish institution. It is a tribute to her importance as a poet that in 1997 a large part of her *œuvre* was made readily accessible in a single collection, *Tous les chemins conduisent à la mer*, with a foreword by the well-known Belgian poet Jean Tordeur, and that another selection, *Changer d'écorce*, chosen from among what she herself considers her representative works, appeared in 2001, with an introduction by Yves Namur and a preface by the novelist and poet Robert Sabatier, of the Académie Goncourt.[3]

The reader will appreciate, even from the following limited selection—a dozen-and-a-half poems from only her first three collections and three from her first "post-hiatus" volume—that Wouters's most characteristic poetry is dense and compact in its virtuosity. Beginning as direct, straightforward, even wryly humorous narrative, it soon developed into a spare and hard-edged verse, almost brittle in the sonorities of its starkly cold tableaux. But it is never rarefied or overly aestheticized. One feels no concessions to an avant-garde modernity for its own sake. And if, as some have rightly observed, some of her early poems read much like the free verse that she would eventually espouse—thanks to the compelling enjambments of *Le gel*, for example—they have no trouble respecting the dictates of French prosody. In so doing, they produce that maximum of tension that is the satisfying result of a freedom restrained by form.

NOTES

1. Cited in Robert Frickx and Michel Joiret, *La poésie française de Belgique de 1950 à nos jours*, p. 226.

2. See Anne-Marie Trekker and Jean-Pierre Vander Straeten, *Cent auteurs*, p. 449.

3. Bio-bibliographical information on Liliane Wouters is a little difficult to come by, because of her almost aggressive defense of her privacy. (See, for example, her terse statement, in Trekker and Vander Straeten, *Cent auteurs*, that "My biography is my own business" [p. 450].) Among the sources, see "Grenier Jane Tony," *Liliane Wouters: Poète, traducteur, dramaturge;* the abovementioned prefatory remarks of Jean Tordeur and Robert Sabatier; the appreciation in Frickx and Joiret, *La poésie française de Belgique*, pp. 225–27; Andrée Sodenkamp's observations in Trekker and Vander Straeten, *Cent auteurs*, pp. 447–50; as well as notes in Renée Linkhorn and Judy Cochran, *Belgian Women Poets*, pp. 227–41.

PÂQUE RUSSE

Alexis Petrovitch est parti pour la foire
      de Nijnii-Novgorod.
Il veut voir Katiouchka qui a des boucles noires
      et les yeux, bleu de fjord.

Le gros marchand de cuirs, avec ses deux pelisses,
      conduit la troïka.
Dans la steppe sans fin son attelage glisse
      de l'Irtych au Volga.

Il traverse l'Oural pour aller voir sa belle.
      Il a quitté l'isba
au poêle de faïence où sur son escabelle
      tricote la baba.

Il voit se dérouler le calme paysage
      de bulbeux clochetons
et de sapins frileux jetant vers les nuages
      leurs Kyrie Eleison.

Il va le long du fleuve où traînent les chaloupes.
      On le dirait songeant.
C'est qu'il a, bien cousu au fond de sa touloupe,
      un petit sac d'argent.

RUSSIAN EASTER

Alexis Petrovich leaves for the fair
　　at Nizhni Novgorod—ah!—
to see Katushka, of the black-curled hair,
* 　　eyes blue as mountain *voda.*

† Off to the Volga from the Irtysh riding,
　　wrapped in his double fur,
the fat pelt-merchant in his troika gliding
　　treks the vast steppe toward her.

Over the Urals to the *dyevushka!*
　　Left in the *izba,* sitting
‡ by porcelain oven, his old *gospozha*
　　is tending to her knitting.

The tranquil landscape, onion-domed, flies by
　　before his eager gaze,
and shivering firs raise to the clouded sky
　　their host of Kyries

Passing the sleepy sloops that sail the river,
　　he seems to dream, his loins
wool-warmed. Sewn in his vest, something to give her:
　　a little sack of coins.

---

* The poet's rhyming of *fjord* with *Novgorod,* is something of a stretch, but one that sets the whimsical tone for her poem. Not wanting to duplicate her near-rhyme, and being as hard-pressed to find a good one in English, I take a leaf from her book and at least try to maintain the whimsy. The Russian noun transliterated as *voda* means "water," and the reader probably recalls that Nizhni Novgorod—in central Russia, on the Volga east of Moscow, and rebaptized Gorki for a time—was long celebrated for its fair.

† The Irtysh is a long river rising in the Altay Mountains of western Mongolia, flowing northwest and emptying, in the far north of western Siberia, into the Gulf of Ob. It is clear from the scenario that the hero, living by that body of water, travels southwest in his peregrination, across the Urals.

‡ Three Russian words, two of which I take the liberty of introducing into the text in a shameless quest for rhymes, mean, respectively, "young girl," "hut," and "woman." The last of the three replaces the original *baba* (old woman), more familiar to American readers in its diminutive form, *babushka* (grandmother).

Liliane Wouters 1089

Les roubles en tintant réchauffent la poitrine
    du négociant rassis.
A Nijnii-Novgorod, il doit, le gros barine,
    jouer au cœur transi.

Son nez, pourpre de froid, séduira-t-il la belle?
    Il sait, le vieux matou,
qu'un diadème d'or décide les rebelles
    mieux que cent billets doux.

Le voici débarqué sur le terrain de foire
    où popes et moujiks
discutent les produits venus de la mer Noire
    sous l'œil des pomiestchiks.

Alexis Petrovitch veut réchauffer sa couche
    avec le tendre corps
de Katia Dimitrov, qui aura ces babouches
    et ces lourds anneaux d'or.

Mais elle dit: Va-t'en avec tes deux touloupes
    retourne vers l'isba.
En longeant le grand fleuve où rêvent les chaloupes,
    va-t'en chez ta baba.

Je ne pourrais dormir un œil sur ta sacoche
    l'autre sur ton cou sec
et j'aime mieux Boris qui tourne en vain ses poches
    pour trouver un kopek.

Car il a des yeux noirs et quand ses mains caressent
    la guitare ou mon front
on dirait qu'un oiseau dans le jardin se blesse
    ou que mon cœur se rompt.

A la prochaine Pâque on lèvera l'icône
    sur nos doigts réunis.
Alexis Petrovitch avec ton rire jaune
    que viens-tu faire ici?

The jingling rubles warm the bosom of
        our merchant ripe with passion.
In Nizhni Novgorod how he shall love
        in lordliest of fashion!

The old fox knows—nose purple from the cold—
        that many a fine love letter
fails to win stubborn belles, but that, with gold
        and such, one does much better.

Now, at last, Nizhni Novgorod! The fair's
        expanse before him lies.
Muzhiks and priests haggle for Black Sea wares
        before rich bourgeois' eyes.

Alexis Petrovich would warm his bed
        with Katia Dimitrov.
Slippered in gold she'll be, arms heavy-spread
        with bangles too thereof.

"Be off," says she, "you and your double fur,
        back to your vile *izba.*
Return, past sleepy sloops, O *voyageur,*
        to your old *gospozha!*

"I would not sleep with one eye on your pack,
        one on your withered neck.
Boris I love, though he squeezes his sack
        in vain for one kopek!

"Black are his eyes, and when he strokes my brow
        or his guitar, I ache
like a poor wounded bird, and some would vow
        they can hear my heart break.

"The saint will bless our rings, Easter next year,
        me and my other half.
Alexis Petrovich, what brings you here,
        you and your nasty laugh?"

---

* The poet seems to have erred here in not giving Katia (or Katushka) her appropriate patronymic, namely "Dimitrovna," but I am happy to follow her lead, rhymes being hard to come by.

Je m'en vais, je m'en vais, répond le gros barine.
    Et la neige tombait
pendant qu'il étouffait les coups de sa poitrine
    en serrant le harnais.

Il repasse l'Oural, il rentre en sa demeure,
    près du golfe d'Obi.
Sa baba lui demande: Où étais-tu à l'heure
    où le fleuve a grossi?

A Nijnii-Novgorod, et j'ai vu la tzarine
    (elle était tout en or).
Elle m'a dit pour toi: Saluez Catherine
    qui vous espère au Nord.

La baba est contente, et Alexis se couche
    sur le haut poële blanc.
Il rêve qu'on l'embrasse et ce n'est qu'une mouche
    qu'il avale en ronflant.

Alexis Petrovitch, avec tes deux pelisses
    reprends la troïka
sous les clochers bulbeux, dessous la neige glisse
    en buvant ta vodka.

La Pâque reviendra. Tu es vieux, tu es bête!
    Dans la rivière Irtych
va pêcher des poissons, va pêcher pour la fête,
    Alexis Petrovitch.

NAISSANCE DU POÈME

Mon corps s'écartera pour le laisser jaillir:
    après neuf mois de peines,
la mère voit soudain son ventre tressaillir
    pour la douleur prochaine.

O souffle! c'est l'effort de mon fragile enfant
    qui lutte pour son être.
Me déchirant pour lui, je l'aide et je défends
    son faible corps à naître.

Our portly gent cried: "Nu! I'll go! I'll go!"
        tugged on the reins to quell
the pounding in his breast. Meanwhile the snow
        about the landscape fell.

Over the Urals he trekked home again—
        his Gulf of Ob' abode:
"And where were you?" his *baba* asks, "just when
        the river overflowed?"

"In Nizhni Novgorod. Her Majesty
        greets you (all gold-bedecked)
and sends to Catherine, waiting here for me,
        her homage and respect."

Happy is she. Alexis climbs the high
        white oven, sleeps... There follows
a dream: his lips are kissed... But it's a fly
        that, as he snores, he swallows.

Fur-wrapped, Alexis Petrovich, go riding,
        drawn by your horses three.
Beneath the onion-domes, snow-swept, go gliding,
        with vodka flowing free.

Easter will come again, foolish old man.
        Go fish the Irtysh, rich
in fish. Fetch for the feast all that you can,
        Alexis Petrovich.

                                        La marche forcée

BIRTH OF THE POEM

My limbs will spread, my body will deliver:
        after nine months hard spent,
at last the mother sees her belly quiver
        for the pain imminent.

O breath! my fragile offspring's quickening,
        its struggle and its strife...
My body torn, I strain to help, to bring
        its feeble being to life.

Sans forme ni couleur, il m'a déjà tout pris
    c'est moi qui le modèle
en lui prêtant mon corps, et mon sang le nourrit.
    Croissant, il m'écartèle.

Dans un demi-sommeil, on me l'arrache enfin.
    Je trouve son visage
le même que j'ai vu tracé par le burin
    depuis le fond des âges.

Mon double, mon écho, poème en devenir
    avec ta voix étrange
serais-tu pas le Dieu, qu'un soir pour m'endormir
    me promettait un ange?

On a conté Yseult la blonde
et Juliette à son balcon.
Les plus belles amours du monde
apportent pleurs et trahisons.

Lorsque je songe à Cléopâtre
qui s'en alla par le venin,
plutôt qu'aimer au coin de l'âtre
dans le couvent, j'irais nonnain.

Je dormirais toujours seulette
sous quatre doubles édredons,
plutôt que d'être bergerette
et de danser le rigodon.

Amour profane en ses caresses
nous prend le cœur, et puis s'en vont
au vent d'hiver, galants, promesses.
Adieu Lisette, adieu Manon.

Oui c'est toujours la même chose
pourtant chacun veut voir comment
de la Noël aux Pâques closes
amour s'en va, revient et ment.

Mine is the shape, the color, that I give
         form it whole, at length:
wrought of my flesh, sucking my blood to live.
         Growing, it saps my strength.

Then, in a half-sleep, ripped from me at last:
         and on its face, its features,
I find engraved that look that time long past
         has traced on all its creatures.

Echo, my double, poem in the becoming:
         strange-voiced, might you not be
that god some angel, one night, while benumbing
         me to sleep, promised me?

La marche forcée

They tell about Iseult the blonde
and Juliet on her balcony.
The loveliest loves the world has spawned
bring only tears and treachery.

When Cleopatra springs to mind—
she by the venomous asp undone—
by cozy fireside ill inclined
to love, I'd sooner be a nun.

I'd rather sleep companionless
under four double quilts alone,
sooner than be a shepherdess
and dance to shepherd's toot and drone.

Fleshly love wins our hearts, however
fickle and false our cavaliers:
gone with the winter wind forever!
Farewell Lisette, Manon, poor dears.

Yes, all the same I fear are they,
Yet still we watch to see, between
* Christmas and Quasimodo's Day,
how love comes, lies, and quits the scene.

  * The French *Pâques closes* refers to the Sunday after Easter, known in English as Low
Sunday, honoring the pseudo-saint Quasimodo.

Et qui l'a vu hoche la tête
"Quand vous saurez autant que moi,"
Mais Chaperon est toujours prête
à rencontrer le loup du bois.

Montre d'abord sa patte blanche.
La bobinette alors a chu.
Conte fleurette et puis se penche.
Il faisait noir, je n'ai rien vu.

On m'attendait l'autre semaine
dans un moutier de bonnes sœurs.
Mais en courant la prétentaine
dans le ruisseau, j'ai vu mon cœur.

Ce n'est point là grain de nonnette
à dormir seul sous l'édredon.
J'ai trouvé mieux qu'une cornette
et j'ai dansé le rigodon.

———————

Le choc de mes pensers toujours contradictoires
heurte mon front plus fort qu'un gantelet de fer.
La honte que je bus persiste en ma mémoire
et je la sens brûler aux pôles de ma chair.

O corps! Temple du nerf! Entrailles, faims muettes!
Le cri que j'ai poussé prolonge encor en moi
ce lancinant écho que mon esprit rejette.
Raison, je ne veux plus m'éteindre sous tes lois.

Faux chevalier traînant mon inutile armure,
j'attends que me provoque en outrancier duel
la bête qui, de nuit, me tend sa paume dure.
Elle a mordu mon front de son baiser cruel.

And those who've seen it nod: "Ah so!
If you knew what I know..." But then
Red Riding Hood gets set to go
and find the Big Bad Wolf again.

Holds out his paw—the hypocrite!
* Open, the latch swings free. His best
sweet nothings purrs, bends low. But it
was dark and so I missed the rest...

Last week the nuns expected me
to join their holy band, but I
saw my heart, brookside, floating free
as I went gayly gadding by.

Under four quilts alone to sleep
is not the habit I would own.
I threw the nuns' coif on the heap
and danced to shepherd's toot and drone.

La marche forcée

My thoughts clash, clang, constant antagonists,
punch my brow like an iron fist. My soul
and mind recall shame past, and it persists,
searing, burning my body, pole to pole.

My flesh! Nerve's temple! Silent hungers, guts!
My scream still lingers long within me, draws,
throbbing, its echo that my soul rebuts.
Reason, I'll not be stifled by your laws.

Dragging my useless armor, would-be knight,
I wait now for the beast nocturnal, this
creature rough-clawed who goads me to the fight,
beast that once bit my brow with savage kiss.

* The original "la bobinette a chu" literally means "the doorlatch fell," and I assume it
to imply that the couple moved inside. But I may be misinterpreting here, since *bobinette*
is also a dice game, and the expression could conceivably suggest something like "the die
was cast."

Liliane Wouters 1097

Mais vous, cher suzerain, si peu féal je semble
prenez en pitié douce un cœur trop indécis
pour qu'au tournoi de mort, si mon épaule tremble
j'ose croiser le fer sans implorer merci.

————————

Plages et goémons que savez-vous de moi?
Forme vivante, forme où le soleil pénètre.
Buvez à lents frissons l'azur où je décrois.
Ce n'est qu'un vin mortel qui a saoûlé mon être.
Plages et goémons, que savez-vous des temps?
Et toi dont la présence a su doubler ma vie,
Amour que je souhaite et fuis au même instant,
la plus humaine part, la plus inassouvie,
c'est toi qui l'as reçue. Elle est sans lendemain.
Nous sommes tous les deux enfants de ce royaume
où la plus douce fleur saura brûler nos mains.
Prends garde à ce qui dort en tes fragiles paumes.
L'amour que je te porte est plus que moi mortel.
J'ai parfumé d'encens une ombre périssable:
si quelque jour la mer emporte mon autel
c'est qu'il était bâti sur de stériles sables.

Pareil exactement à ce que j'ai rêvé
tu gis sous mes regards, tel un archange triste,
ô toi mon autre corps, et je vois s'aviver
l'ombre cernant tes yeux où l'horizon persiste.
Si loin de moi, toujours; si proche aussi, pourtant.
Ensemble nous allons où vont les créatures
roulant comme galets sur le gravat des temps,
roulant comme galets à l'origine obscure.

————————

VERSETS DE L'ÉCHELLE

L'Echelle de Jacob se dresse devant moi.
        J'y vois monter des anges.
J'en vois d'autres descendre et ne puis faire un choix.
        Ma pierre est sur la fange.

But if, dear lord, I seem not every inch
your liege, pity a heart in doubt ensnared,
so that, duelling with death, though my arm flinch,
I dare cross swords and not beg to be spared.

La marche forcée

———————

Beaches, seaweed, what can you know of me?
Living shape, form pierced, run through by the sun...
Drink, in slow gasps, the blue that gradually
does me in—deadly wine!—drunk and undone...
Beaches, seaweed, what can you know of time?
And you, whose being made of my one a two,
Love that I flee yet yearn for, Love sublime,
most human part, most unfulfilled, it's you
who own it now. With no tomorrows though.
Children, we two, both from that realm wherein
the softest flower might burn our hands. And so
beware yours, fragile, and what sleeps therein.
My love for you more mortal is than I.
I've strewn my incense where mere shadow stands:
If the sea sweeps my shrine, the reason why
is that I've built it on the barren sands.

Just as I dreamt, I see you lying there,
sad angel-double mine, and I see spring
to life the shade around your eyes, dark, where
the far horizon is still mirroring.
So near, and yet ever so far from me...
Together we go where those creatures go,
rolling like pebbles over time's debris,
rolling, rolling from where we'll never know.

La marche forcée

———————

VERSICLES ON THE LADDER

Before me rises Jacob's Ladder. I
        see angels as they climb
some up some down. I cannot choose, for my
        stone stands here in the slime.

Liliane Wouters 1099

Je reste dans la boue et veux jouer avec.
　　　　Revienne la tempête
pour que déborde enfin ce cœur devenu sec
　　　　où logent quatre bêtes.

L'une est le grand Morholt et l'autre le dragon,
　　　　l'une est le Minotaure.
La quatrième, un ver, ne porte pas de nom.
　　　　C'est lui qui me dévore.

L'une est le monde, et l'autre était jadis l'enfer.
　　　　L'une est ma chair mort-née.
La quatrième, c'est moi-même, c'est le fer
　　　　qui tourne dans la plaie.

L'Echelle de Jacob se dresse devant moi.
　　　　J'y vois une lumière.
Descendre ou bien monter? Je ne puis faire un choix
　　　　et reste sur la pierre.

SOUFFLE

Souffle à moi petite haleine
de court débit d'humble sort
Ménage ton feu ta peine
ne prends pas ton plein essor

Je n'ai que toi Je n'existe
que par ton chaud va et vient
Au fil des heures persiste
à respirer mon seul bien

I wallow in the mire, would play with it.
    Let the winds' tempest roar,
blow my heart overflowing, dry, where sit
    my bestial creatures four.

* One is the great Morholt, another is
    a dragon, number three,
the Minotaur, the last, a worm. And his
    it is to glut on me.

One is the world, the second once was hell.
    The third, my flesh, stillborn.
The fourth, my being entire, whose dagger fell
    twists in my wound, slashed, torn.

Before me rises Jacob's Ladder. I
    see it now brighter grown.
Climb up? Climb down? I cannot choose, and my
    feet stand here on the stone.

La marche forcée

BREATH

Humble little breath of mine
spare your efforts' fire I pray
Plan no grandiose design
to take wing and fly away

You are all I have   I live
by your tepid in-and-out
Hour by hour cease not to give
what I cannot live without

Le bois sec, "Naître pour mourir"

---

* Unlike the well-known adolescent-eating Minotaur of Greek mythology in the following lines, half-man, half-bull, the Irish giant Morholt was a human creature of the Celtic tradition. It was after subduing him in combat that Tristan won the fair Iseult, supposedly for King Mark, but, by accident of a fateful potion, for himself.

Liliane Wouters 1101

LA CORDE RAIDE

Je n'ai plus les pieds sur la terre
Où je vais nul ne me suivra
Je retourne au lieu solitaire
d'où le souffle un jour me tira

Au sommet dont j'eus connaissance
avant que mon âme prît corps
Au pays d'avant la naissance
où je peux marcher sans mon corps

Que les heures passent J'avance
sur la corde raide au tournant
d'un futur qui déjà commence
d'un passé qui fut maintenant

Est-ce vie Est-ce mort Les hommes
parlent dans un rêve éveillé
Si tu veux sortir de ton somme
près de moi demeure à veiller

Ainsi de l'eau souterraine
dont nous surprend le cristal
Sombres argiles moraines
furent son pays natal

Qu'elle ait traversé les boues
ou reflété la blancheur
toujours au creux de ma joue
je sens la même fraîcheur

Dans la pure transparence
du verre qui t'a fêté
dis-nous miroir où commence
l'ombre où finit la clarté

THE TIGHTROPE

My feet no longer touch the ground
Where I go none will follow   I
am once more for that lone land bound
whence some day on a breath I'll fly

That peak I used to know back when
my soul was not yet clothed a-fresh
That land before birth where again
I'll go about without my flesh

As hours go passing one by one
I walk a tightrope in between
a future that has now begun
a past that has already been

Is it life   Is it death   Men seem
to talk in waking reverie
If you would quit your sleep your dream
then come and lie awake by me

Le bois sec, "Naître pour mourir"

Like pure waters that amaze
awe us springing from the earth
Somber mirky glacial clays
were the country of its birth

Whether through the muck it rise
or white's clear reflection be
on my sunken cheeks it lies
and feels fresh and cool to me

In the flattering glassy glare
tell us mirror crystalline
where does shadow end and where
does reality begin

Le bois sec, "La lampe et le miroir"

———————

Mon âme était jadis comme une lampe
Je ne sens plus sa flamme sa chaleur
Le sang qui bat à l'ombre de mes tempes
de quel sommeil est-il avant-coureur

Je suis vivante et pourtant je n'existe
plus qu'à demi Le feu paraît éteint
Autour de soi brouillant toutes les pistes
l'esprit se cache où nulle chair n'atteint

Je me regarde et sans me reconnaître
je me demande où cela va finir
et si je suis en passe de renaître
ou seulement plus proche de mourir

———————

Visible ton haleine, tes pupilles
trop largement ouvertes. C'est le jour
qui les dilate, c'est pour toi que brille
ce blanc total.

                J'entre dans le séjour
sans larmes. Tout liquide y prend des pierres
le poids, l'éternité. Pleurs solennels!
Douceur niée avec l'eau! Tes paupières
connaîtront, lourdes, le pouvoir du sel.

———————

Tant de couches végétales:
mols repos, lits entr'ouverts,
herbes heureuses, pétales
innocents. Votre univers

My soul was like a lamp   Now it grows cold
and I lie unwarmed by its flame   What sleep
is this that my blood heralds uncontrolled
pounding within my temples shadowed deep

Still do I live and yet my body feels
half-alive little more   Near-dead the fire
My spirit covers up its tracks conceals
itself far from the flesh's least desire

I look upon myself but what I see
I cannot recognize for all my trying
Where will this end   Am I about to be
reborn or only closer now to dying

                   Le bois sec, "La lampe et le miroir"

Your breath's visible puff, your pupils too
dilated by the light. This whiteness pure,
utterly white and shining there for you
and you alone.

          I come into this dour
tearless realm. Any liquid here takes on
the weight of stone, eternal. Solemn sighs!
Everything soft and wet, rejected, gone!
And salt will press down, heavy, on your eyes.

                         Le gel, "Le gel"

Couches vegetal deep-spread
round about: grasses content,
pallet soft, sly-beckoning bed,
petals blithely innocent.

* I do not take the liberty of altering the original here, though I think the poet mistakenly supposes that increased light dilates the pupils. Anyone who has a cat will realize that quite the opposite is true, and that the pupils constrict as the light grows brighter, dilating as it dims.

                         Liliane Wouters 1105

m'échappe à jamais. Les brises
ont fui, le gel est venu.
Capitale son emprise,
pétrifié le monde nu.

———————

Vierge l'espace devant moi mais d'une
virginité seconde. Etat cruel.
Quand les couteaux de l'âme au rituel
de la saison obéissent, chacune
des lames tranche dans le vif. Or quel
grand purificateur des bois sonores
fige les chants d'oiseaux, détruit la flore,
immole tout mensonge à son autel?

———————

Inaltérable, unique, après la sombre
splendeur du feu, après le dévorant
désir, l'acier, le fer polaire, prend
visage et s'illumine. D'ombre en ombre
j'errais, fuyant le brasier. Voici que
mon corps se fige. Halte rude, gel!
(Dès autrefois, un monument de sel
ceignit le front des ruines) Toi musique
propre au silence, rythme intérieur,
que je perçoive dans la note unique,
dans l'inhumaine matité, un chant
presque fatal. Et que, sous le tranchant
des lames, sous la glace, à roche fendre,
je puisse enfin mon âme faire entendre.

Lost, your universe. The freeze
lays its chill grip everywhere.
Fled, the softly gentle breeze,
turned to stone, the world now bare.

Le gel, "Le gel"

———————

Virgin the space before me, but not quite:
say, of renewed virginity. Cruel state.
When the soul's daggers, with blades profligate,
obey again the season's yearly rite,
each of them plunges deep. Who is that great
cleanser of the resounding woods, who will
freeze the birds' song, who will the flora kill,
and falsehood on his altar immolate?

Le gel, "Le gel"

———————

Changeless, unique, after the fire's outspent
dark splendor; after, too, the yearning lust,
then frigid steel and arctic iron must
take form and shine. From shade to shade I went
wandering, fleeing the glowing brazier. Here
and now my whole being stands congealed. Rude halt,
hard freeze! (Time was, a monument of salt
enwreathed the ruins' brow.) You, music drear
* and fit for silence, inner rhythms, let
me hear, in the one note, in its dull, blear
inhumanness, a chanting deathlike sound.
Let me, over the ice-imprisoned ground,
beneath the sharp-edged blades' relentless cold,
finally reveal myself, stark, naked-souled.

Le gel, "Le gel"

---

* Curiously, the poet, usually punctilious in matters of form, offers no rhyming line in
the original, and I follow her lead.

Liliane Wouters 1107

Pour qui le bouc émissaire,
l'holocauste? Libations
innommables: les viscères
prescrites, le nécessaire
appareil d'incantation!
Souille l'offrande, lacère
la victime. Sois sincère
jusqu'à la profanation.

Corps balancé de la rive
au fleuve, corps tout entier
privé de soi et qu'on prive
des autres, mort sans quartier.

Qui connut l'ardeur brûlante
de ton sang, qui partagea
tes soleils, ton ombre, tente
de les oublier déjà.

Ai-je demandé à naître?
Ai-je accepté de mourir?
Vivre, serait-ce promettre
d'aller, sans plus revenir?

Sans moi, je reçus la vie.
Sans moi, j'y dois renoncer.
Je refuse qu'on me nie
après m'avoir prononcé.

———————

Whose, the suffering scapegoat here,
*   sacrifice and divination?
Why the solemn rite austere:
entrails, wine, and all the gear
proper for an invocation!
Foul the sacrosanct oblation,
hack the victim! Be sincere
even unto desecration.

Le gel, "Le gel"

———————

Body from the river's shore
chucked and flung into the water,
body robbed of self and, more,
robbed of others: dead, no quarter.

Those who shared the passion-fire
of your blood, that so beset them
with your suns, your shade, desire
now already to forget them.

Le gel, "Escales"

———————

Did I ask to be born, to live?
Did I agree to die, be gone?
Is life a promise that we give
not to come back once we pass on?

To live, I really had no say.
To die, I'll have none, not a whit.
No! Don't you spirit life away
once you pronounced me into it.

Le gel, "Escales"

* The poet uses the French cognate *holocauste* in its original etymological sense of "sacrifice," not in the more common meaning that it has acquired in modern times.

Liliane Wouters 1109

Instant qui dors sous l'écorce
du temps mortel, qui t'efforces
d'en sortir, instant parfait,
l'éternité qui t'a fait
s'abîme en toi, s'y dégage
du réseau des jours, des âges,
l'éternité qui te prend
tel qu'en toi-même te rend.
Là, je suis vivante, intacte,
invulnérable, mes actes
sans passé, sans avenir,
vont enfin m'appartenir.

Quatre mille jours,
Quatre mille jours, quatre mille nuits,
Nous avons partagé le lit, la table,
Bu aux mêmes fontaines, tiré l'eau des mêmes puits
—Et l'eau n'était pas toujours claire mais
Transparentes étaient nos mains.

Nos mains, nos yeux et notre cœur commun.
Où est-il à présent? Il a cessé de battre.
Quatre mille levers de lune, quatre
Mille nuits sans savoir ce que veut dire "seul."

A présent je le sais. Je me trouve à l'extrême
Pointe de mon chagrin, où l'on n'est plus que soi,
Désespérément soi enfermé en soi-même.

Instant, who sleep beneath the peel
of mortal time, instant ideal
and perfect, who struggle to free
yourself, but that eternity
that wrought you gets sucked deep inside
your being, freed from the time and tide
of days enmeshed in ages' net,
eternity that holds you, yet
would give you back yourself. There I
live, stout and strong, intact, and my
deeds, without future, without past,
will be my own, mine, at long last.

Le gel, "L'aloès"

Four thousand days
Four thousand days, four thousand nights,
We shared one bed, one table, drank
From the same fountains, drew from the same wells—
The water wasn't always clear, but sights
Shone bright through our transparent hands.

Our hands, our eyes, the heart we shared.
Where is it now? It beats no more.
Four thousand risings of the moon, yes, four
Thousand nights when "alone" was meaningless.

I know its meaning now. I sprawl beyond
My being, on the sharp tip of my chagrin,
Where, desperate, oneself closes one within.

L'aloès, "Etat provisoire" ("Etat")

*

* The group of poems in *L'aloès* from which this and the following texts are taken is
entitled "Etat provisoire" and is divided into two sections, "Etat" and "Provisoire." The
present poem is from the former. It is a good example of the path toward free verse that
Wouters was following at this point in her career.

Liliane Wouters 1111

LA FILLE D'AMSTERDAM

Elle avait dit: "En Amsterdam
Nous ne vivrons qu'une aventure.
Je n'y laisserai pas mon âme.
Amour toujours jamais ne dure."

Hélas! Je ne la croyais pas.
Sous les pignons à cols, à cloches,
Quand se mêlaient nos mains, nos pas,
Quand j'espérais, dur comme roche.

L'eau verte suivant son chemin
Aurait dû me dire: "Tout passe."
Mais je ne sentais que sa main
Serrant la mienne dans l'impasse.

Amsterdam suait ses bordels
Et ses putains aux cuisses fortes
Tandis que je marchais près d'elle
Sans présager nos amours mortes.

Peine plus dure que le dam
Et sel des larmes que je pleure,
Pour cette fille d'Amsterdam
Que ne donnerais-je à cette heure?

Les cloches de Saint-Nicolas,
Le quai aux plantes, les dix mille
Pilotis de la gare et la
Rivière Amstel, avec ses îles.

C'était un jour du mois de mai.
Elle me disait: "Rien ne dure."
Moi, je pensais que je l'aimais
Beaucoup trop pour une aventure.

THE GIRL FROM AMSTERDAM

She said: "In Amsterdam we'll play
Life's game—it's just an escapade.
But I won't give my soul away.
Love never lasts long, I'm afraid..."

I didn't take her seriously.
Beneath the fancy-gabled, sloping
Roofs, as in single lockstep we
Locked hands... Ah! How hard I kept hoping...

I should have heard the brackish brine
Warn, with its flow: "Nothing comes back!"
No. I felt but her hand on mine,
Pressing, there in the cul-de-sac.

Amsterdam's brothels stood there, stinking,
Sweating, with thick-thighed whores, as I
Sauntered beside her, never thinking
How soon our love must lifeless lie.

Harsher my woe, more bitter am
I now than each and every tear
I cry... That girl from Amsterdam...
What wouldn't I give to have her here?

* Saint-Nicholas's bells, dock spanned
With plants, ten thousand sunken piles
Spread out beneath the landing, and
The River Amstel's many isles...

It was a day in May. My Dutch
Girl said: "Nothing lasts, I'm afraid."
And I thought that I loved her much
Too much for just an escapade.

L'aloès, "Etat provisoire" ("Etat")

---

* The reference is to the Russian Orthodox church of Saint Nicholas of Myra.

Liliane Wouters 1113

    Grain de sable sur la plage,
    Dans l'océan goutte d'eau,
Rien n'est à toi. Sauf l'usage
Provisoire de ta peau.

Grain of sand beside the sea,
Drop of water in the tide,
Nothing yours... Except your hide
To use temporarily.

*

L'aloès, "Etat provisoire" ("Provisoire")

---

* Concerning the source of this curiously formatted quatrain, see p. 1111n.

Albertine Sarrazin (1937–1967)

As with a panoply of French writers from Villon to Genet, the twin stars of literary talent and dubious moral inclinations presided over the birth of the novelist-poet known as Albertine Sarrazin. Indeed, she was only one of a number of lesser-known French women whose writing talents seem to have been brought into focus by their imprisonment...[1] But if, for many readers, the attraction of Sarrazin's work lies in the prison surroundings and the social marginalization in which much of it was conceived, for most, her *œuvre* is a stirring proof of the artistic vigor with which the human spirit can win out against most negative odds.

She was born in Algiers in 1937 to a Spanish housemaid of fifteen, a mother whom she was never to know but whose absence always tormented her. Adopted as an infant, she was taken to Aix-en-Provence to begin a turbulent existence as the problem child of no-less-problem parents. (Recent research has established that her biological father and her adoptive father, a military doctor, were actually one and the same.)[2] Her early years were one long cycle of misbehavior and mistreatment, punishment and abuse. Raped by an uncle at the age of ten, she had little reason to respect the strictures of the society in which she grew up, and was eventually confined to a reform school in Marseille to continue the studies for which she had—despite her problems—shown a marked ability. The day of her *baccalauréat* exam, however, she clearly preferred freedom to a diploma, and made her escape, finding her way to Paris. There she would lead the vagabond life of the street, supporting herself by prostitution even while reading avidly and continuing faithfully to keep a journal that she had begun several years before.

In 1953, Sarrazin and a lesbian accomplice were imprisoned after a failed holdup attempt. It was during her stay at the prison in Fresnes, and subsequently at a less restrictive institution in Doullens, that she penned a number of her poems. But loss of liberty did not agree with her free spirit, and she took the opportunity, on April 19, 1957, of jumping some thirty feet to freedom, breaking a bone in her foot in the process. Complications from that injury would eventually lead to her death. But in the shorter term, it resulted in much of the only happiness life would offer her. Rescued by a passer-by, one Julien Sarrazin, she was taken under his wing and became his lawful spouse two years later. It was not until 1964, however, that the couple would actually live together, each pursuing over the intervening years lives of petty crime, imprisonment, and sporadic escapes.

During these several prison stays, Albertine indulged her eloquent, if earthy, talent to compose two first-person novels, *L'astragale* and *La cavale,* richly psychological narratives born of her (mis)adventures and her unfulfilled yearnings, and had already begun, like many a gifted social pariah, to attract the attention of the respected literary establishment. When she and Julien finally settled down, first in the Cévennes and later in Montpellier, Sarrazin, to her surprise, had become something of a celebrity. Her two novels (smuggled in bits and pieces out of prison), as well as a third, *La traversière* (1966), were published by Jean-Paul Pauvert. Probably "not for her beautiful eyes," as the French say, but more than likely because he foresaw her budding cult status and smelled the profit it would bring.[3]

Though Sarrazin has faded somewhat into the background, remembered today more for her prison journals than for her other works, that cult flourished for a time, especially just after her death. Ironically, the success that could have been hers eluded her finally when, on July 10, 1967, a botched operation ended her life at the height of her celebrity. Her devoted husband sued the negligent clinic and won. But his only real consolation came as the result of his establishing a (short-lived) publishing house for her unpublished writings, and in seeing a number of honors paid to her ill-starred talent.[4]

Sarrazin would surely have been both bemused and amused to find her novels studied in the schools—not reform schools either!—and to see her poems—brash, energetic, and cynical as herself—take their place in anthologies. Her poems were published in three collections—*Romans, lettres et poèmes* (1967), *Poèmes* (1969), and *Lettres et poèmes* (1971), the first of which, the definitive edition of her *œuvre,* has a preface by the novelist Hervé Bazin. The seven translated here, whose prosodic regularity clashes strikingly with their fractured syntax and intentional inelegance of tone, are taken from that volume.

NOTES

1. Elissa Gelfand, *Imagination in Confinement: Women's Writings from French Prisons.* A section of this study, whose author has written widely on Sarrazin, is devoted to her (see pp. 214–38).

2. See Jacques Layani, *Albertine Sarrazin, une vie,* pp. 24–25.

3. It was at this time, too, that *L'astragale* was made into a film (1969), starring Marlène Joubert.

4. For several earlier studies, interpretive as well as biographical, of this engaging, colorful, and troubled author, see also Josane Duranteau, *Albertine Sarrazin* (one of the volumes published by Albertine's husband); Margaret Crosland, *Women of Iron and Velvet: French Women Writers After George Sand,* pp. 171–79; and Benjamin Lambert, *La cavale: Mémoire d'Albertine.*

Le soleil voudrait saigner sans arrêt
Il coupe mon corps de longues aiguilles
Mais l'aube naîtra d'ici partirai
Un jour n'est pas loin nous reconnaîtrons
Ta voix franchit en liberté mes grilles
Tes cheveux encor dansent tes chansons
Je voudrais tant dire et ne parle pas
Car la nuit est froide où sans fin tu brilles
Chut j'écoute en moi l'écho de tes pas

O mémoire dis-moi pourquoi
Même la beauté m'est amère
Pourquoi l'amour n'est plus le roi.
Pourquoi la terre est notre mère
Le pollen rose au cœur des fleurs
Les yeux voilés de ma déesse
Ont maintenant saveur de pleurs
De cultes morts je suis prêtresse
Obsession du souvenir
Berceuse lancinante et tendre
Mon âme veut redevenir
Mon âme lasse de l'entendre

Il y a des mois que j'écoute
Les nuits et les minuits tomber
Et les camions dérober
La grande vitesse à la route
Et grogner l'heureuse dormeuse
Et manger la prison les vers

The sun would bleed me nonstop no reprieve
It cuts with its long needles pierces me
But dawn will rise newborn I'll take my leave
A day is not far off we'll know it when
Your voice comes through my cell bars bounding free
Your hair dances your songs again again
So much to say but I don't say a thing
For night is cold where you shine endlessly
Shhh let me hear your steps keep echoing

Memory tell me why what for
Is beauty bitter to my eye
And why is love the king no more
And why is earth our mother why
Pink pollen deep within the flowers
Goddess eyes veiled all taste of tears
Priestess obsessed I wield the powers
Of cults now dead my yesteryears
Lullaby tender aching pain
Drones in my head relentlessly
My soul yearns to become again
† My soul tired of its melody

For months I've heard the nightfalls rumbling
Midnights too and I've heard the hum
Of trucks whose speed is pilfered from
The roads I've heard that woman grumbling
Whom sleep has blessed and heard worms trying
To eat the prison wall by wall

* Although the verb *saigner* (to bleed), which can be used transitively or intransitively, has no object expressed in the original, I think the following line suggests that a "me" is implied, and I take the liberty of including one.

† This poem and the following one were apparently written while Sarrazin was imprisoned at the Fresnes penitentiary in 1954–1955 after she and another young woman attempted to hold up a Paris dress shop, whose owner was shot and wounded by the accomplice. See Albertine Sarrazin, *Lettres et poèmes*, ed. Jean-Jacques Pauvert, p. 15.

Printemps étés automnes hivers
Pour moi n'ont aucune berceuse
Car je suis inutile et belle
En ce lit où l'on n'est plus qu'un
Lasse de ma peau sans parfum
Que pâlit cette ombre cruelle
La nuit crisse et froisse des choses
Par le carreau que j'ai cassé
Où s'engouffre l'air du passé
Tourbillonnant en mille poses
C'est le drap frais le dessin mièvre
Léchant aux murs le reposoir
C'est la voix maternelle un soir
Où l'on criait parmi la fièvre
Le grand jeu d'amant et maîtresse
Fut bien pire que celui-là
C'est lui pourtant qui reste là
Car je suis nue et sans caresse
Maix veux dormir ceci annule
Les précédents Ah m'évader
Dans les pavots ne plus compter
Les pas de cellule en cellule

————————

Paris aux yeux tristes
Ciel inimité
En vain tourmenté
Des méchants artistes

Comme alors la reine
Je cours sans souliers
Aux blancs escaliers
Qu'a noyés la Seine

Richesse complète
Avoir mon tombeau
Au fin fond de l'eau
Où Paris reflète

Winters springs summers autumns all
Have done for me no lullabying
Unused my beauty lies alone
Here in this bed useless and doomed
To wallow weary unperfumed
In the cruel shadows where I've grown
Sallow and now the window-pane
I broke screeches as through the crack
Rumpled scenes of the past gust back
Blustering on the wind again
And posing in a thousand ways
Cool sheet that mawkish art that licks
The wall-surrounded crucifix
Cries one night through a feverish haze
Motherly voice love's give-and-take
The worst and yet the scene I keep
Beside me as I yearn to sleep
Bare unembraced Ah how I ache
To slip away in sleep to dwell
Among the poppies and ignore
Those things and all the rest no more
To count the steps from cell to cell

Paris sad of eye
And the vain attacks
Of poor artist hacks
On her peerless sky

And like the queen then
I run barefoot right
To those steps washed white
And drowned by the Seine

What wealth what perfection
In this grave to sleep
Where shines on the deep
Paris's reflection

Albertine Sarrazin 1121

Ton pied bute et rôde
Par la chambre chaude
Où l'aube maraude
L'adieu sans pleurer
A l'heure d'errer
Dans Paris doré

Moi très peu bavarde
Au lit qui me garde
Moi qui nous regarde
Pauvres cœurs cachés
Toujours arrachés
Vers d'autres péchés

Lorsque je n'aurai plus les saxophones noirs
Je volerai la danse aux échos des kermesses
Lorsque sur le compte d'un conte de jeunesse
J'offrirai la tournée aux tendres au revoirs

Lorsque j'aurai un peu reniflé les printemps
Et tendu cette main qu'épelle la justice
Et de l'autre en riant dans le fauve calice
Lorsque j'aurai lavé les pieds joueurs du temps

Lorsque s'affranchira la terre en paradis
Je languirai pourtant les ivresses finales
Lorsque j'irai m'étendre aux genoux des étoiles
Lorsque j'oublierai la soif et l'oasis

Your foot pokes here and there
In the warm bedroom where
Dawn prowls the morning air
Goodbye with tearless eyes
To roam where Paris lies
Under goldening skies

And me close-lipped in my
Bed I still lie and I
Watch us as by and by
Two hidden hearts done in
Wrenched from where they had been
Move on to some new sin

_____

When my black saxophones are out of songs
I'll steal dance echoes from some village fair
When for some youthful tale's details I share
The wealth and buy a round for sweet so longs

When I have sniffed a bit more spring and I'm
Through spelling justice with this hand outspread
And this one in the chalice tawny red
Laughing washing my feet gamblers with time

When earth freed dwells the heavens' blessèd spaces
I'll languish in my one last drunk good-bye
When by the stars' knees supplicant I lie
* When I forget the thirst and the oasis

* For the perceptive reader who would balk at my rhyming "oasis" with "places," let me point out that Sarrazin's equivalent is no less imperfect: *paradis* and *oasis* rhyme only for the eye, but definitely not for the ear.

Lorsque tu t'en reviens aux gens
C'est toujours un lit qu'ils te donnent
Les logeuses et les patronnes
Les médecins et les amants
Du berceau tout enguirlandé
Jusqu'à la couche mortuaire
C'est bien le pucier ma chère
Le meuble le plus demandé

Bed's what they always offer you
When you come back into their lives
The landladies the owners' wives
The doctors and the lovers too
From cradle with flowers wreathing it
To final funerary bier
Of all our furniture my dear
The fleabag is the favorite

Selected Bibliography

This bibliography is just what it purports to be: selective. But that should not be taken to imply anything about the quality of the many works left unselected. If this were primarily a research study (what academe likes to call a "scholarly work"), I would have felt obliged to be more exhaustively (and, be it said, more exhaustingly) inclusive. As it is, in addition to a listing of useful general works—encyclopedias and literary histories dealing with women authors—readers of these poems and translations will find the provenance of the originals, various other noteworthy published works of each poet, and a representative, and reasonably up-to-date, sampling of biographical and aesthetic appreciations, as well as other secondary sources referred to in the notes. For some of the poets, such sources are scarce, and—when they exist at all—hard to come by, and I have, on occasion, had to turn to encyclopedia entries in the pious hope that the information they present is accurate. For others, conversely, there is a staggering amount of scholarship, and I have been obliged to pick and choose from among an embarrassment of riches. Except in a small number of cases, I have limited such choice to book-length works, thus omitting many worthy and pertinent articles of often specialized interest, whose inclusion would have greatly expanded the size of this already extensive undertaking. Indeed, few of our almost five dozen poets would not be well served by more detailed individual study, both "scholarly" and aesthetic. Perhaps there are readers who will be encouraged to provide it.

Ackermann, Louise. *Contes en vers.* N.p., 1855

———. *Contes et poésies.* Paris: Hachette, 1863.

———. *Pensées d'un solitaire.* Paris: A. Lemerre, 1883.

———. *Poésies.* Paris: A. Lemerre, 1874.

Adam, Antoine. *Histoire de la literature française au XVIIe siècle.* Paris: Editions mondiales, 1962.

Aelian, Claudius. *An English Translation of Claudius Aelianus' "Varia Historia."* Edited and translated by Diane Ostrom Johnson. Lewiston, N.Y.: Edwin Mellen Press, 1997.

Altmann, Barbara K., and Deborah L. McGrady. *Christine de Pizan: A Casebook.* New York: Routledge, 2003.

Ambrière, Francis. *Le Siècle des Valmore: Marceline Desbordes-Valmore et les siens.* Paris: Seuil, 1987.

Amer, Sahar. *Esope au féminin: Marie de France et la politique de l'interculturalité.* Amsterdam: Rodopi, 1999.

Anthologie de la poésie française, XVIIIe siècle. Bibliothèque de la Pléiade. Paris: Gallimard, 2000.

Ardouin, Paul. *Maurice Scève, Pernette du Guillet, Louise Labé: L'amour à Lyon au temps de la Renaissance.* Paris: A. G. Nizet, 1981.

————. *Pernette du Guillet: L'heureuse renaissance*. Paris: A. G. Nizet, 1991.

Arnaud-Duc, Nicole. "Les contradictions du droit." In *Histoire des femmes en Occident*, vol. 4: *Le XIXe siècle*, ed. Geneviève Fraisse and Michelle Perrot, 109. Paris: Plon, 1991.

Aronson, Nicole. *Mademoiselle de Scudéry*. Boston: Twayne, 1978.

Baale-Uittenbosch, Alexandrina E. M. *Les poétesses dolentes du romantisme*. Haarlem: De Erven F. Bohn, 1928.

Babois, Marguerite-Victoire. *Elégies et poésies diverses*. Paris: Le Normant, 1810. 3d rev. ed. 2 vols. Paris: Nepveu, 1828.

————. *Elégies*. Paris: F. Didot, 1805.

————. *Epîtres aux romantiques*. Paris: Dezanche, 1830.

Baker, Deborah Lesko. *The Subject of Desire: Petrarchan Poetics and the Female Voice in Louise Labé*. West Lafayette, Ind.: Purdue University Press, 1996.

Banville, Théodore de. *Camées parisiens (deuxième série)*. 4 vols. Paris: R. Pinceborde, 1866.

Barbey d'Aurevilly, Jules. "Madame Ackermann." *Le constitutionnel*, April 28, 1873. In *Les œuvres et les hommes*, 2d ser., vol. 11: *Les poètes*, 157–72. Paris: Lemerre, 1889. Reprint, Geneva: Slatkine, 1989.

————. "Madame de Girardin: *Œuvres complètes—les poésies*," *Le Pays*, March 29, 1862.

Barnes, Julian. *Something to Declare: Essays on France*. New York: Knopf, 2002.

Barnet, Marie-Claire. *La femme cent sexes ou les genres communicants: Deharme, Mansour, Prassinos*. New York: P. Lang, 1998.

————. "To Lise Deharme's Lighthouse: *Le phare de Neuilly*, a Forgotten Surrealist Review." *French Studies*, July 2003.

Barney, Natalie Clifford. *Nouvelles pensées de l'Amazone*. Paris: Mercure de France, 1939.

————. *Pensées d'une Amazone*. Paris: Emile-Paul frères, 1920.

————. *Poems & poèmes: Autres alliances*. Paris: Emile-Paul frères; New York: George H. Doran, 1920.

————. *Quelques portraits-sonnets de femmes*. Paris: Société d'Editions littéraires et artistiques, 1900.

Baudelaire, Charles. "Marceline Desbordes-Valmore." Under the rubric "Réflexions sur quelques-uns de mes contemporains" in *Œuvres complètes*, ed. Claude Pichois, 2: 145–49. Bibliothèque de la Pléiade. Paris: Gallimard, 1975–76.

Baum, Richard. *Recherches sur les œuvres attribuées à Marie de France*. Heidelberg: C. Winter, 1968.

Beauharnais, Fanny de. *Mélanges de poésies fugitives et de prose sans conséquence, par Madame la comtesse de ****. Amsterdam; Paris: Delalain, 1776.

Beauvoir, Simone de. *Le deuxième sexe*. 2 vols. 1949. Reprint. Paris: Gallimard, 1976. Translated by H. M. Parshley as *The Second Sex* (New York: Knopf, 1957).

Beizer, Janet. *Ventriloquized Bodies: Narratives of Hysteria in Nineteenth-Century France*. Ithaca, N.Y.: Cornell University Press, 1994.

Bénétrix, Paul. *Les femmes troubadours: Notes d'histoire littéraire.* Agen: V. Lenthéric, 1889.

Benet's Reader's Encyclopedia. 4th ed. Edited by Bruce Murphy. New York: HarperCollins, 1996.

Benstock, Shari. *Women of the Left Bank.* Austin: University of Texas Press, 1986.

Berdou d'Aas, Bernard. *Jeanne III d'Albret: Chronique, 1528–1572.* Biarritz: Atlantica, 2002.

Bergmann, H., L. Cahen, H.-G. Ibels, L. de La Laurencie, J. Letaconnoux, D. Mornet, J.-J. Olivier, and M. Rouff. *La vie parisienne au XVIIIe siècle: Leçons faites à l'Ecole des hautes études sociales.* Bibliothèque générale des sciences sociales, 49. Paris: F. Alcan, 1914.

Beriot-Salvadore, Evelyn. *Les femmes dans la société française de la Renaissance.* Geneva: Droz, 1990.

Bernard, Catherine. *Œuvres.* Edited by Franco Piva. 2 vols. Fasano: Schena; Paris: Nizet, 1993–99.

Bernier, Claudine. "Anne-Marie Kegels ou les chants de la sourde joie." *Revue générale* 131, 6–7 (June–July 1996): 33–41.

Bertaut, Jules. *La littérature feminine d'aujourd'hui.* Paris: Librairie des Annales politiques et littéraires, 1909.

Biographie universelle, ancienne et moderne. Edited by J. F. and L. G. Michaud. Paris: Michaud frères, 1811–62.

Bishop, Michael. "La poésie féminine contemporaine en France." In *French and Francophone Women, 16th–21st Centuries: Essays on Literature, Culture, and Society with Bibliographical and Media Resources,* special issue of *Women in French Studies,* ed. Catherine Montfort and Marie-Christine Koop, October 2002: 110–22.

———. *Women's Poetry in France, 1965–1995: A Bilingual Anthology.* Winston-Salem, N.C.: Wake Forest University Press, 1997.

Bloch, R. Howard. *The Anonymous Marie de France.* Chicago: University of Chicago Press, 2003.

Blois, Robert de. *L'Enseignement des princes.* In *Robert de Blois, son œuvre didactique et narrative,* ed. John Fox. Paris: Nizet 1950.

The Bloomsbury Guide to Women's Literature. Edited by Claire Buck. New York: Prentice-Hall General Reference, 1992.

Blum, Léon. "L'œuvre poétique de Madame de Noailles." *Revue de Paris,* January 15, 1908. Reprinted in *L'Œuvre de Léon Blum,* vol. 2: *1905–1914,* 407–24. Paris: Albin-Michel, 1962.

Bogin, Meg [Magda]. *The Women Troubadours.* New York: Norton, 1980.

Bondy, François de. *Une femme d'esprit en 1830: Madame de Girardin.* Paris: P. Lafitte 1928.

Bonnefoy, Yves. "Marceline Desbordes-Valmore." Preface to Marceline Desbordes-Valmore, *Poésies,* 7–34. Paris: Gallimard, 1983. Reprinted in Bonnefoy, *La vérité de parole,* 9–39. Paris: Mercure de France, 1988.

Borely, Marthe. *L'émouvante destinée d'Anna de Noailles.* Paris: Albert, 1939.

Boschian-Campaner, Catherine. *Georges Périn, poète messin.* Paris: Messène, 1999.

Bothorel, Jean. *Louise, ou la vie de Louise de Vilmorin.* Paris: B. Grasset, 1993.

Boutin, Aimée. "Marceline Desbordes-Valmore and the Sorority of Poets." *Women in French Studies* 9 (2001): 165–80.

———. *Maternal Echoes: The Poetry of Marceline Desbordes-Valmore and Alphonse de Lamartine.* Newark: University of Delaware Press; London: Associated University Presses, 2001.

Boutin, Aimée, and Adrianna M. Paliyenko. "Nineteenth-Century French Women Poets: An Exceptional Legacy." In *French and Francophone Women, 16th–21st Centuries: Essays on Literature, Culture, and Society with Bibliographical and Media Resources,* special issue of *Women in French Studies,* ed. Catherine Montfort and Marie-Christine Koop, October 2002: 77–109.

Bouvelot-Ulrich, Paule. *Le lyrisme d'Amélie Murat.* Moulins: Marmousets, 1984.

Brée, Germaine. *Women Writers in France: Variations on a Theme.* New Brunswick, N.J.: Rutgers University Press, 1973.

Briquet, Fortunée B. *Dictionnaire historique, littéraire et bibliographique des Françaises et des étrangères naturalisées en France . . . depuis la Monarchie jusqu'à nos jours.* Paris: Gillé, 1804. Facsimile reprint. Paris: Indigo & Côté-femme, 1997.

Broche, François. *Anna de Noailles: Un mystère en pleine lumière.* Biographies sans masque. Paris: Robert Laffont, 1989.

Broglie, Gabriel de. *Madame de Genlis.* Paris: Perrin, 1985.

Bronfen, Elisabeth. *Over Her Dead Body: Death, Femininity and the Aesthetic.* New York: Routledge, 1992.

Brown-Grant, Rosalind. *Christine de Pizan and the Moral Defence of Women: Reading Beyond Gender.* New York: Cambridge University Press, 1999.

Bruckner, Matilda Tomaryn, Laurie Shepard, and Sarah White, eds. *The Songs of the Women Troubadours.* New York: Garland, 2000.

Brun, Charles. *Renée Vivien.* Paris: E. Sansot, 1911.

Bryson, David. *Queen Jeanne and the Promised Land: Dynasty, Homeland, Religion and Violence in 16th-Century France.* Boston: Brill, 1999.

Buche, Joseph, "Pernette du Guillet et la *Délie* de Maurice Scève." In *Mélanges de philologie offerts à Ferdinand Brunot.* Paris: Société nouvelle de librairie et d'édition, 1904.

Burgess, Glyn S. *Marie de France: An Analytical Bibliography.* London: Grant & Cutler, 1977.

———. *Marie de France: An Analytical Bibliography. Supplement.* London: Grant & Cutler, 1986.

Burnat-Provins, Marguerite. *Le livre pour toi.* Paris: Editions Seghers, 1963.

Cambridge Companion to Medieval Women's Writing. Edited by Carolyn Dinshaw and David Wallace. Cambridge: Cambridge University Press, 2003.

Cameron, Keith. *Louise Labé: Renaissance Poet and Feminist.* New York: Berg, 1990.

Cardinal, Agnès, Dorothy Goldman, and Judith Hattaway. *Women's Writing on the First World War*. New York: Oxford University Press, 1999.

Cardonne-Arlyck, Elisabeth. "'Un néant follement attifé': Modernité de Renée Vivien et Catherine Pozzi." *L'esprit créateur* 37, 4 (Winter 1997): 106–24.

Cave, Terence. *Devotional Poetry in France, c. 1570–1613*. London: Cambridge University Press, 1969.

Chalon, Jean, *Florence et Louise les magnifiques: Florence Jay-Gould et Louise de Vilmorin*. Monaco: Rocher, 1987.

———. *Portrait d'une séductrice*. Paris: Stock, 1976. Translated by Carol Barko as *Portrait of a Seductress: The World of Natalie Barney* (New York: Crown, 1979).

Champdor, Albert. *Louise Labé: Son œuvre et son temps*. Trévoux: Editions de Trévoux, 1981.

Champion, Pierre. *Histoire poétique du XVe siècle*. Paris: E. Champion, 1923.

Charbonnel, J[ean Ferval]-Roger. "La renaissance du paganisme." *Akadémos* 1 (January 1909): 32.

Chéron, Elisabeth-Sophie. *Essay de Pseaumes et cantiques, mis en vers*. Paris: Michael Brunet, 1694.

Cholakian, Patricia F., and Rouben C. Cholakian. *Marguerite de Navarre: Mother of the Renaissance*. New York: Columbia University Press, 2006.

Cocteau, Jean. *La comtesse de Noailles oui et non*. Paris: Perrin, 1963.

Coignard, Gabrielle de. *Œuvres chrétiennes de feue dame Gabrielle de Coignard*. Edited by Colette H. Winn. Geneva: Droz, 1995.

———. *Spiritual Sonnets*. Edited and translated by Melanie E. Gregg. Chicago: University of Chicago Press, 2004.

Colet, Louise. *Ce qu'on rêve an aimant*. Paris: Librairie nouvelle, 1854.

———. *Les fleurs du midi*. Paris: Dumont, 1836.

———. *Lui: Roman contemporain*. Paris: Librairie nouvelle, A. Bourdilliat, 1860.

———. *Poésies complètes*. Paris: Charles Gosselin, 1844.

Collado, Mélanie E. *Colette, Lucie Delarue-Mardrus, Marcelle Tinayre: Emancipation et résignation*. Paris: l'Harmattan, 2003.

Columbia Dictionary of Modern European Literature. 2d ed. Edited by Jean-Albert Bede and William B. Edgerton. New York: Columbia University Press, 1980.

Continuum Dictionary of Women's Biography. Edited by Jennifer S. Uglow. New York: Continuum, 1989.

Cooper, Clarissa Burnham. *Women Poets of the Twentieth Century in France. A Critical Biography*. New York: King's Crown Press, 1943.

Cosnier, Colette. *Marie Pape-Carpantier*. Paris: Fayard, 2003.

Cottrell, Robert D. *The Grammar of Silence: A Reading of Marguerite de Navarre's Poetry*. Washington, D.C.: Catholic University of America Press, 1986.

Cousin, Victor. *La société française au XVIIe siècle d'après "Le grand Cyrus" de Mlle Scudéry*. Paris: Perrin, 1886.

Craveri, Benedetta. *The Age of Conversation.* Translated by Theresa Waugh. New York: New York Review Books, 2005.

Croguennoc, Sylvie. "Renée Vivien ou la religion de la musique." *Romantisme: Revue du dix-neuvième siècle* 17, 57 (1987): 89–100.

Crosland, Margaret. *Women of Iron and Velvet: French Women Writers After George Sand.* New York: Taplinger, 1976.

Cuénin, Micheline. *Madame de Villedieu (Marie-Catherine Desjardins, 1640–1683).* Lille: H. Champion, 1979.

D'Albret, Jeanne. *Mémoires et poésies de Jeanne d'Albret.* Edited by Alphonse de Ruble. Paris: Paul, Huart & Guillemin, 1893.

Danahy, Michael. "Marceline Desbordes-Valmore and the Engendered Canon." *Yale French Studies* 75 (1988): 129–47.

Dauguet, Marie. *A travers le voile.* Paris: E. Sanso 1902.

———. *Ce n'est rien, c'est la vie.* Paris: R. Chiberre, 1924.

———. *Clartés.* Paris: Librairie E. Sansot, 1907.

———. *La naissance du poète.* Paris: E. Sansot, 1897.

———. *Par l'amour.* Paris: Mercure de France, 1904.

———. *Paroles du vent.* Paris: 1904.

———. *Les pastorales.* Paris: E. Sansot, 1908.

Le débat sur "Le roman de la rose." Edited by Eric Hicks. 1977. Reprint. Geneva: Slatkine, 1996. Texts of Christine de Pizan et al. in Latin and Old French, with French translation.

Deharme, Lise. *Les années perdues, journal, 1939–1949.* Paris: Plon, 1961.

———. *Cahier de curieuse personne.* Paris: Editions des Cahiers libres, 1933.

———. *Farouche à quatre feuilles.* Paris: Grasset, 1954.

Delarue-Mardrus, Lucie. *L'ange et les pervers.* Paris: J. Ferenczi et fils, 1930.

———. *Ferveur.* Paris: Editions de La Revue blanche, 1902.

———. *Figure de proue.* Paris: Charpentier, 1908.

———. *Mes mémoires.* Paris: Gallimard, 1938.

———. *Nos secrètes amours.* Paris: Les Isles, 1951.

———. *Les sept douleurs d'octobre.* Paris: J. Ferenczi et fils, 1930.

Delzangles, Fernand. *Biographies et morceaux choisis d'écrivains d'Auvergne.* Aurillac: Poirier-Bottreau, 1933.

Demerson, Guy, ed. *Louise Labé: Les voix du lyrisme.* Paris: CNRS, 1990.

Dépillier, Mady, *Louise Labé: La première féministe.* Nice: Losange, 2002.

Desbordes-Valmore, Marceline. *Huit femmes.* 2 vols. Paris: Chlendowski, 1845.

———. *Les œuvres poétiques.* Edited by Marc Bertrand. Grenoble: Presses universitaires de Grenoble, 1973.

———. *Poésies.* Paris: Gallimard, 1983.

———. *Poésies inédites.* Geneva: Jules Fick, 1860.

———. *Textes choisis.* Translated by Marc Bertrand. Nîmes: HB Editions, 2002.

———. *Les veillées des Antilles.* 2 vols. Paris: F. Louis, 1821.

Descaves, Lucien. *La vie amoureuse de Marceline Desbordes-Valmore.* Paris: Flammarion, 1925.

——. *La vie douloureuse de Marceline Desbordes-Valmore.* Paris: Editions d'art et de littérature, 1910.

Desessarts, Nicolas Toussaint Lemoyne. *Les siècles littéraires de la France.* Paris: Chez l'auteur, 1800–1803.

Deshoulières, Antoinette. *Poésies de Madame Deshoulières.* Paris: Sebastien Mabre-Cramoisy, 1688.

——. *Poésies de Madame et Mademoiselle Deshoulières.* Brussels: Veuve Foppens, 1740.

Desnos, Robert. *La ménagerie de Tristan; Le parterre d'Hyacinthe.* Reprinted in *Chantefables, chantefleurs.* Paris: Grûnd, 2000.

Desnoues, Lucienne. *Anthologie personnelle.* Arles: Actes Sud, 1998.

——. *Le compotier.* Paris: Editions Ouvrières, 1982.

——. *Dans l'éclair d'une truite.* Cercy-la-Tour: Gérard Oberlé, 1991.

——. *Fantaisies autour du trèfle.* Hyères: Les Cahiers de Garlaban, 1992.

——. *La fraîche.* Paris: Gallimard, 1959.

——. *L'herbier naïf.* Cercy-la-Tour: Gérard Oberlé, 1994.

——. *Jardin délivré.* Paris Editions Raisons d'être, 1947.

——. *Un obscur paradis.* Cercy-la-Tour: Gérard Oberlé, 1998.

——. *Les ors,* pref. Marcel Thiry. Paris: Seghers, 1966.

——. *La plume d'oie.* Brussels: Jacques Antoine, 1971.

——. *Quatrains pour crier avec les hiboux.* Cercy-la-Tour: Gérard Oberlé, 1984.

——. *Les racines.* Paris: Editions Raisons d'être, 1952.

Des Roches, Madeleine, and Catherine des Roches. *From Mother and Daughter: Poems, Letters, and Dialogues of Les Dames des Roches.* Edited and translated by Anne R. Larsen. Chicago: University of Chicago Press, 2006.

——. *Les missives.* Edited by Anne R. Larsen. Geneva: Droz, 1999.

——. *La puce de Madame des Roches.* 1582. Paris: D. Jouaust, 1868.

——. *Les œuvres.* Edited by Anne R. Larsen. Geneva: Droz, 1993.

——. *Les secondes œuvres.* Edited by Anne R. Larsen. Geneva: Droz, 1998.

Dijkstra, Bram. *Idols of Perversity: Fantasies of Feminine Evil in Fin-de-Siècle Culture.* New York: Oxford University Press, 1986.

Diller, George. *Les dames des Roches: Etude sur la vie littéraire à Poitiers dans la deuxième moitié du XVIe siècle.* Paris: E. Droz, 1936.

Du Bellay, Joachim. *Œuvres françoises de Joachim du Bellay, gentilhomme angevin.* Paris: Frédéric Morel, 1573.

Du Bos, Charles. *La comtesse de Noailles et le climat du génie.* Paris: La Table Ronde, 1949.

Du Fresnois, André. "Réflexions sur la literature feminine." *Akadémos* 10 (October 15, 1909): 503–13.

Du Guillet, Pernette. *Rymes.* 1545. Edited by Victor E. Graham. Geneva: Droz, 1968.

Dupin de Saint-André, Fanny. *Madame Pape-Carpantier.* Paris: Fischbacher, 1894.

Duranteau, Josane. *Albertine Sarrazin.* Paris: Sarrazin, 1971.

Encyclopedia of Continental Women Writers. Edited by Katharina M. Wilson. 2 vols. New York: Garland, 1991.

Engelking, Tama Lea. "Anna de Noailles Oui et Non: The Countess, the Critics and *la poésie féminine.*" *Women's Studies* 23 (1994): 95–110.

———. "The Literary Friendships of Natalie Clifford Barney: The Case of Lucie Delarue-Mardrus." *Women in French Studies* 7 (1999): 100–16.

———. "A Voice of Her Own: Gérard d'Houville's Thread and Literary Tradition." *Women in French Studies* 9 (2001): 28–39.

The Feminist Encyclopedia of French Literature. Edited by Eva Martin Sartori. Westport, Conn.: Greenwood Press, 1999.

Fénelon, François de Salignac de La Mothe. *Le traité de l'éducation des filles.* Paris, 1687.

Ferguson, Gary. "The Feminisation of Devotion: Gabrielle de Coignard, Anne de Marquets, and François de Sales." In *Women's Writing in the French Renaissance: Proceedings of the Fifth Cambridge French Renaissance Colloquium, 7–9 July 1997,* ed. Philip Ford and Gillian Jondorf, 187–206. Cambridge: Cambridge French Colloquia, 1999.

———. *Mirroring Belief: Marguerite de Navarre's Devotional Poetry.* Edinburgh: Edinburgh University Press, 1992.

Feugère, Léon. *Les femmes poètes au XVIe siècle.* Paris: Didier, 1860.

Finch, Alison. *Women Writing in Nineteenth-Century France.* Cambridge: Cambridge University Press, 2000.

Flaminio, Marc'Antonio. *Les divines poésies de Marc Antoine Flaminius, contenant diverses prières, méditations, hymnes et actions de grâce à Dieu, mises en françois, avec le latin respondant l'un à l'autre, avec plusieurs sonnets et cantiques ou chansons spirituelles pour louer Dieu.* Translated by Anne de Marquets. Paris: Nicolas Chesneau, 1568. A printing of the following year bears a slightly altered title.

Flat, Paul. *Nos femmes de lettres.* Paris: Perrin, 1909.

Fontainas, André. *Tableau de la poésie française d'aujourd'hui.* Paris: La Nouvelle Revue Critique, 1931.

Forhand, Kate Langdon. *The Political Theory of Christine de Pizan.* Burlington, Vt.: Ashgate, 2002.

Foster, Jeanette H. *Sex Variant Women in Literature.* New York: Vantage Press, 1956.

French Culture, 1900–1975. Edited by Catharine Savage Brosman. *Dictionary of Twentieth-Century Culture,* vol. 2. Detroit: Gale Research, 1995.

French Novelists Since 1960. Edited by Catharine Savage Brosman. *Dictionary of Literary Biography,* vol. 83. Detroit: Gale Research, 1989.

French Women Writers: A Bio-bibliographical Source Book. Edited by Eva Martin Sartori and Dorothy Wynne Zimmerman. New York: Greenwood Press, 1991.

Frickx, Robert, and Michel Joiret, *La poésie française de Belgique de 1950 à nos jours.* Paris: F. Nathan, 1977.

Galli-Pellegrini, Rosa. "Le courage de le dire: Les rêveries végétales dans la poésie d'Anna de Noailles." *Travaux de Littérature* 9 (1996): 217–28.

La Guadeloupe secrète de Marceline Desbordes-Valmore. Pointe-à-Pitre, Guadeloupe: Musée Saint-John Perse, 2003.

Gauthier, Xavière. *La vierge rouge: Biographie de Louise Michel.* Paris: Editions de Paris, 1999.

Gay and Lesbian Literature. Edited by Sharon Malinowski. Detroit: St. James Press, 1993.

Gelbart, Nina Rattner. *Feminine and Oppositional Journalism in Old Regime France.* Berkeley: University of California Press, 1987.

Gelfand, Elissa D. "Albertine Sarrazin: The Confined Imagination." *L'esprit créateur* 19, 2 (Summer 1979): 47–57.

———. *Imagination in Confinement: Women's Writings from French Prisons.* Ithaca, N.Y.: Cornell University Press, 1983.

Genlis, Stéphanie-Félicité de. *Herbier moral, ou Recueil de fables nouvelles, et autres poésies fugitives.* Paris: Maradan, 1801.

Gentou, Albertine. *Louise de Vilmorin: "Si vous me connaissiez ..."* Paris: Perrin, 1998.

Gérard, Rosemonde. *Un bon petit diable.* Paris: Charpentier & Fasquelle, 1912.

———. *Les muses françaises.* Paris: Charpentier, 1948.

———. *Les pipeaux.* Paris: Alphonse Lemerre, 1889.

———. *Rien que des chansons.* Paris: Charpentier, 1939.

———. *La vie amoureuse de Madame de Genlis.* Paris: E. Flammarion, 1926.

Germain, André. *De Proust à Dada.* Paris: Editions du Sagittaire, 1924.

———. *Renée Vivien.* Paris: G. Crès, 1917.

Gertz, Sunhee Kim. *Echoes and Reflections: Memory and Memorials in Ovid and Marie de France.* New York: Rodopi, 2003.

Giacchetti, Claudine. *Delphine de Girardin, la muse de juillet.* Paris: l'Harmattan, 2004.

Girardin, Delphine Gay de. *L'école des journalistes.* Paris: Dumont, 1840.

———. *Essais poétiques.* Paris: Gaultier-Laguionie, 1824.

———. *Une femme qui déteste son mari.* Paris: M. Lévy, 1856.

———. *Lettres parisiennes.* Paris: Charpentier, 1843.

———. *Nouveaux essais poétiques.* Paris: Urbain Canel, 1825.

———. *Œuvres complètes.* Paris: Plon, 1860–61.

———. *Poésies complètes.* Paris: Charpentier, 1842.

Giraudon, Liliane, and Henri Deluy. *Poésies en France depuis 1960: 29 femmes. Une anthologie.* Collection Versus. Paris: Stock, 1994.

Godenne, René. *Les romans de Mademoiselle de Scudéry.* Geneva: Droz, 1983.

Goodman, Dena. *The Republic of Letters: A Cultural History of the French Enlightenment.* Ithaca, N.Y.: Cornell University Press, 1994.

Gossot, Emile. *Madame Marie Pape-Carpantier: Sa vie et son œuvre.* Paris: Hachette, 1890; 2d ed., 1894.

Gouges, Olympe de. *Ecrits politiques, 1788–1791.* Edited by Olivier Blanc. 2 vols. Paris: Côté femmes, 1993.

Gourmont, Jean de. *Muses d'aujourd'hui: Essai de physiologie poétique.* Paris: Mercure de France, 1910.

Grand, Serge, and Micheline Bood. *L'indomptable Louise Colet.* Paris: P. Horay, 1986.

Gray, Francine DuPlessix. *Rage and Fire: A Life of Louise Colet, Pioneer Feminist, Literary Star, Flaubert's Muse.* New York: Simon & Schuster, 1994.

Great Women Writers. Edited by Frank M. Magill. New York: Holt, 1994.

Greenberg, Wendy. *Uncanonical Women: Feminine Voice in French Poetry.* Atlanta: Rodopi, 1999.

"Grenier Jane Tony" [Emile Kesteman, Andrée Sodenkamp, Mireille Dabée, Alain Carré]. *Liliane Wouters: Poète, traducteur, dramaturge.* Brussels: Emile Kesteman, 1983.

Guibert, Elisabeth. *Poésies diverses.* Reprint. Nice: Centaure, 1973.

La guirlande des muses françaises de Marceline Valmore à Marie Noël. Edited by Yves-Gérard Le Dantec. Paris: Emile Paul, 1948.

Hammond, Mason. "Notes on the Words and Music Used in Harvard's Commencement Ceremonies." *Harvard Library Bulletin* 26, 3 (July 1978).

Harmand, Jean-Baptiste. *Madame de Genlis, sa vie intime et politique.* Paris: Perrin, 1912.

Harry, Myriam. *Mon amie Lucie Delarue-Mardrus.* Paris: Ariane, 1946.

Hart, Kathleen. *Revolution and Women's Autobiography in Nineteenth-Century France.* New York: Rodopi, 2004.

Hartig, Franz de Paula Anton, Graf von. *Lettres sur la France, l'Angleterre et l'Italie.* Geneva, 1785.

Héritier, Jean. *Essai de critique contemporaine. Première série.* Paris: R. Chiberre, 1923.

Higonnet-Dugua, Elisabeth. *Anna de Noailles, cœur innombrable: Biographie, correspondance.* Paris: Michel de Maule, 1989.

Histoire des femmes en Occident. Vol. 4: *Le XIXe siècle.* Edited by Geneviève Fraisse and Michelle Perrot. Paris: Plon, 1991.

Histoire littéraire de la France. Edited by Pierre Abraham, Roland Desné, et al. 6 vols. Paris: Editions sociales, 1965–82.

Holmes, Diana. *French Women's Writing, 1848–1994.* Atlantic Highlands, N.J.: Athlone Press, 1996.

Holmes, Urban T., Jr. *A History of Old French Literature from the Origins to 1300.* Rev. ed. New York: Russell & Russell, 1962.

Homans, Margaret. *Women Writers and Poetic Identity: Dorothy Wordsworth, Emily Brontë, and Emily Dickinson.* Princeton, N.J.: Princeton University Press, 1980.

Houville, Gérard d'. *Clowns.* Abbeville: F. Paillart, 1925.

———. *Enfantines et amoureuses.* Paris: Editions de la Nouvelle France, 1946.

———. *L'inconstante.* Paris: Calmann-Lévy, 1903.

———. *Jeune fille.* Paris: A. Fayard, 1916.

———. *Les poésies de Gérard d'Houville.* Paris: B. Grasset, 1931.

———. *La vie amoureuse de la Belle Hélène.* Paris: E. Flammarion, 1928.

———. *La vie amoureuse de l'Impératrice Joséphine*. Paris: Flammarion, 1925.

———. *Vingt poèmes*. Paris: E. Champion, 1925.

Huchon, Mireille. *Louise Labé: Une créature de papier*. Geneva: Droz, 2006.

Jans, Anne-Françoise. *Lucienne Desnoues*. Brussels: Didier Hatier, 1986.

Jardillier, Robert. "La musique dans l'œuvre de la comtesse de Noailles." *Revue musicale* 112 (February 1931): 97–124.

Jasenas, Eliana. *Marceline Desbordes-Valmore devant la critique*. Geneva: Droz, 1962.

Jay, Karla. *The Amazon and the Page: Natalie Clifford Barney and Renée Vivien*. Bloomington: Indiana University Press, 1988.

Jenson, Deborah. "Gender and the Aesthetic of 'Le Mal': Louise Ackermann's *Poésies philosophiques*, 1871." *Nineteenth-Century French Studies* 23, 1–2 (Fall–Winter 1994–95): 175–93.

———. "Louise Ackermann's Monstrous Nature." *Symposium* 53, 4 (Winter 2000): 234–48.

Johnson, Barbara, *The Feminist Difference: Literature, Psychoanalysis, Race, and Gender*. Cambridge, Mass.: Harvard University Press, 2000.

———. "Gender and Poetry: Charles Baudelaire and Marceline Desbordes-Valmore." In *Displacements: Women, Tradition, Literatures in French*, ed. Nancy Miller and Joan de Jean, 163–81. Baltimore: Johns Hopkins University Press, 1991.

———. "The Lady in the Lake." In *A New History of French Literature*, ed. Denis Hollier, 630. Cambridge, Mass.: Harvard University Press, 1989.

Jones, Ann Rosalind. *The Currency of Eros: Women's Love Lyrics in Europe, 1540–1620*. Bloomington: Indiana University Press, 1990.

Kaplan, Edward. "The Voices of Marceline Desbordes-Valmore." *French Forum* 22, 3 (1997): 261–77.

Kegels, Anne-Marie. *Chant de la sourde joie*. Lyon: Les Ecrivains réunis, 1955. Reprint. Paris: Editions de la Revue Moderne, 1956.

———. *Les chemins sont en feu*. Mortemart: René Rougerie, 1973.

———. *Les doigts verts*. Brussels: André de Rache, 1967.

———. *Douze poèmes pour une année*. Brussels: Cahiers de l'Hypogriffe, 1950.

———. *Haute vigne*. Brussels: Verseau, 1962.

———. *Lumière adverse: Poèmes*. Brussels: André de Rache, 1970.

———. *Poèmes choisis*. Edited by Guy Goffette. Brussels: Académie royale de langue et littérature françaises, 1990.

———. *Porter l'orage*. Brussels: André de Rache, 1978.

———. *Rien que vivre: Poèmes*. Dison: A l'enseigne du Plomb-qui-Fond, 1951.

Keller-Rahbe, Edwige, ed. *Madame de Villedieu romancière: Nouvelles perspectives de recherches*. Lyon: Presses universitaires de Lyon, 2004.

Kennedy, Angus J. *Christine de Pizan: A Bibliographical Guide*. London: Grant & Cutler, 1984.

Kennedy, Fraser. *Ornament and Silence: Essays on Women's Lives*. New York: Knopf, 1996.

Kiesel, Frédéric. *Anne-Marie Kegels*. Brussels: P. de Méyére, 1974.

Labé, Louise. *Complete Works*. Edited and and translated by Edith R. Farrell. Troy, N.Y.: Whitston, 1986.

———. *Œuvres complètes*. Edited by François Rigolot. Paris: Flammarion, 1986.

Laborde, Alice M. *L'œuvre de Madame de Genlis*. Paris: A.-G. Nizet, 1966.

Lacher, Walter. *L'amour et le divin: Marceline Desbordes-Valmore, Anna de Noailles, David-Herbert Lawrence, Charles Morgan*. Geneva: Perret-Gentil, 1962.

La Férandière, Marie-Amable de. *Œuvres de madame la marquise de la Fer . . .* Paris: Colnet, 1806. 2d rev. ed. Janot & Cotelle, 1816.

La Fontaine, Jean de. *The Complete Fables of Jean de La Fontaine*. Translated by Norman R. Shapiro. Urbana: University of Illinois Press, 2007.

———. *Fifty Fables of La Fontaine*. Translated by Norman R. Shapiro. Urbana: University of Illinois Press, 1985.

Lalande, Rosalind Decker. *A Labor of Love: Critical Reflections on the Writings of Marie-Catherine Desjardins (Mme de Villedieu)*. Madison, N.J.: Fairleigh Dickinson University Press, 2000.

Lambert, Benjamin, *La cavale: Mémoire d'Albertine*. Paris: Nizet, 1994.

Landry, Diane. *Le dialogue chez Louise Labé et Catherine des Roches*. Montréal: Université du Québec, 2000.

[Laporte, Joseph de]. *Histoire littéraire de femmes françaises, ou lettres historiques et critiques*. 5 vols. Paris: Lacombe, 1789.

Larnac, Jean. *La comtesse de Noailles: Sa vie, son œuvre*. Paris: Editions du Sagittaire, 1931.

———. *Histoire de la littérature féminine en France*. Paris: Editions Kra, 1929.

La Rochefoucauld, Edmée de. *Anna de Noailles*. Paris: Editions universitaires, 1956.

La Salle de Rochemaure, Louis-Félix, duc de, and René Lavaud. *Les troubadours cantaliens*. 3 vols. Aurillac: Imprimerie moderne, 1910.

Lassère, Madeleine. *Delphine de Girardin: Journaliste et femme de lettres au temps du romantisme*. Paris: Perrin, 2003.

Lasserre, Pierre. "La littérature feminine." *L'Action française: Organe du nationalisme integral*, February 9, 1909.

La Suze, Henriette de Coligny, comtesse de. *Recueil de pièces galantes, en prose et en vers, de madame la comtesse de La Suze, et de monsieur Pelisson. Augmenté de plusieurs pièces nouvelles de divers auteurs*. Trévoux: Imprimerie de S.A.S., 1725

L'Aubespine, Madeleine de. *Les chansons de Callianthe, fille de Ronsard*. Edited by Roger Sorg. Paris: L. Pinchon, 1926.

Laubier, Marie de. *Marie de Régnier, muse et poète de la belle époque*. Paris: Bibliothèque nationale de France, 2004.

Layani, Jaques. *Albertine Sarrazin: Une vie*. Paris: Ecriture, 2001.

Lazard, Madeleine, *Louise Labé, Lyonnaise*. Paris: Fayard, 2004.

Le Dantec, Yves. *Renée Vivien, femme damnée, femme sauvée*. Aix-en-Provence: Editions du Feu, 1930.

Le Hir, Marie-Pierre, and Dana Strand. *French Cultural Studies: Criticism at the Crossroads.* Albany: State University of New York Press, 2000.

Lejeune, Paule. *Louise Michel l'indomptable.* Reprint. Paris: l'Harmattan, 2002.

Le Sourd, Auguste. *Recherches sur Jacques et Marie de Romieu, poète vivarois.* Villefranche, 1934.

Letexier, Gérard. *Madame de Villedieu (1640–1683): Une chroniqueuse aux origines de La Princesse de Clèves.* Paris: Lettres modernes Minard, 2002.

Linkhorn, Renée. "Les écrivaines francophones de Belgique au XXᵉ siècle." In *French and Francophone Women, 16th–21st Centuries: Essays on Literature, Culture, and Society with Bibliographical and Media Resources,* special issue of *Women in French Studies,* ed. Catherine Montfort and Marie-Christine Koop, October 2002: 153–81.

Linkhorn, Renée, and Judy Cochran, *Belgian Women Poets.* New York: P. Lang, 2000.

Une littérature de la conscience: Paul Gadenne, Georges Perros, Henri Thomas, Louise de Vilmorin. Rennes: Part Commune, 2001.

Lloyd, Rosemary. "Baudelaire, Marceline Desbordes-Valmore et la fraternité des poètes." *Bulletin baudelairien* 26 (December 1991): 65–74.

Lorenz, Paul. *Sapho 1900, Renée Vivien.* Paris: Julliard, 1977.

Loubens, Emile. *Madame Pape-Carpantier: Sa vie et ses ouvrages.* Paris: Duval, 1879.

Maclellan, Nic. *Louise Michel.* New York: Ocean Press, 2004.

Magnan, André. *Dossier Voltaire en Prusse: 1750–1753.* Studies on Voltaire and the Eighteenth Century, 244. Oxford: Voltaire Foundation, 1986.

Magne, Emile. *Madame de la Suze et la société précieuse.* Paris: Société du Mercure de France, 1908.

Makward, Christiane P., Madeleine Cottenet-Hage, et al., eds. *Dictionnaire littéraire des femmes de langue française: De Marie de France à Marie Ndiaye.* Paris: Karthala, 1996.

Le mal dans l'imaginaire littéraire français. Edited by Myriam Watthée-Delmotte and Metka Zupančič. Paris: l'Harmattan; Orléans, Canada: Editions David, 1998.

Mallarmé, Stéphane. "Le tombeau d'Edgar Poë," In *Œuvres complètes,* 38. Bibliothèque de la Pléiade. Paris: Gallimard, 1998.

Malo, Henri. *Une muse et sa mère.* Paris: Emile-Paul frères, 1924.

Marchand, Alfred. *Poètes et penseurs.* Paris: Fischbacher, 1892.

Maréchal, Chantal A. *The Reception and Transmission of the Works of Marie de France, 1774–1974.* Lewiston, N.Y.: Edwin Mellen Press, 2003.

———, ed. *In Quest of Marie de France, a Twelfth-century Poet.* Lewiston, N.Y.: Edwin Mellen Press, 1992.

Marie de France. *L'espurgatoire Seint Patriz of Marie de France: An Old-French Poem of the Twelfth Century.* Edited by Thomas Atkinson Jenkins. Philadelphia: A. J. Ferris, 1894. Reprint. Chicago: University of Chicago Press, 1903.

———. *Expurgatoire seint Patriz.* Edited and translated into modern French by Yolande de Pontfarcy. Louvain: Peeters, 1995.

———. *Fabeln der Marie de France.* Edited by Karl Warnke. Halle: Niemeyer, 1898.

————. *Les fables.* Edited by Charles Brucker. Louvain: Peeters, 1991. Paris: Livre de Poche, 1995.

————. *Fables.* Edited by Alfred Ewert and Ronald C. Johnson. Oxford: Blackwell, 1942.

————. *Fables.* Edited and translated by Harriet Spiegel. Toronto: University of Toronto Press, 1994.

————. *Les lais.* Edited by Jeanne Lods. Paris: Champion, 1959.

————. *Les lais.* Edited by Alexandre Micha. Paris: Flammarion, 1994.

————. *Les lais.* Edited by Jean Rychner. Paris: H. Champion, 1966.

————. *Les lais.* Edited by Karl Warnke. Paris: Librairie générale française, 1990. Originally published as *Die Lais der Marie de France* (Halle: Niemeyer, 1924).

————. *Les lais.* Edited and translated by Laurence Harf-Lancner. Paris: Livre de Poche, 1990.

————. *Lais.* Edited by Alfred Ewert. 1944. Reprint. New York: B. Blackwell, 1960.

————. *The Lais.* Edited and translated by Glyn S. Burgess and Keith Busby. 1986. 2nd ed. New York: Penguin Books, 1999.

————. *The Lais.* Edited and translated by Robert Hanning and Joan Ferrante. 1978. Reprint. Durham, N.C.: Labyrinth Press, 1982.

————. *Saint Patrick's Purgatory: A Poem by Marie de France.* Translated by Michael J. Curley. Binghamton, N.Y.: Center for Medieval and Early Renaissance Texts, 1993.

Marks, Elaine. "1929. Jean Larnac Publishes a *Histoire de la littérature féminine en France.*" In *A New History of French Literature,* 887–91. Cambridge, Mass.: Harvard University Press, 1989.

Marquets, Anne de. *Sonets, prières et devises en forme de pasquins pour l'assemblée de messieurs les prélates et docteurs, tenue à Poissy.* Paris: Veuve G. Morel, 1562.

————. *Sonets spirituels de feue très-vertueuse et très-docte Dame Sr. Anne de Marquets, religieuse à Poissy, sur les dimanches et principales solennitez de l'année.* Paris: Claude Morel, 1605.

————. *Sonets spirituels.* Edited by Gary Ferguson. Geneva: Droz, 1997.

————. See also under Flaminio, Marc'Antonio, above.

Marquiset, Alfred. *Les Bas-bleus du premier Empire.* Paris: Champion, 1913.

Marzouki, Afifa, *Amable Tastu, une poétesse à l'époque romantique.* Tunis: Université de Tunis, 1997.

Masson, Georges-Armand. *La comtesse de Noailles, son œuvre, portrait et autographe: Document pour l'histoire de la littérature française.* Célébrités d'aujourd'hui. Paris: Carnet-Critique, 1922.

Maurras, Charles. *L'avenir de l'intelligence.* Paris: A Fontemoing, 1905. Reprint. Paris: Flammarion, 1972.

————. *Romantisme et révolution.* Paris: Nouvelle librairie nationale, 1922.

————. "Le romantisme féminin: Allégorie du sentiment désordonné," *Minerva,* May 1, 1903. Reprinted in *L'avenir de l'intelligence* (1905), 145–234.

Medieval Women Writers. Edited by Katharina M. Wilson. Athens, Ga.: University of Georgia Press, 1984.

Ménard, Auguste-Louis. *La Fontaine et Mme de Villedieu, les Fables galantes présentées à Louis XIV le jour de sa fête, essai de restitution à La Fontaine.* Paris: Chavaray frères, 1882.

Mercœur, Elisa. *Œuvres complètes.* 3 vols. Paris: Pommeret & Guenot, 1843.

Mervaud, Christiana. *Voltaire et Frédéric II: Une dramaturgie des Lumières, 1736–1778.* Studies on Voltaire and the Eighteenth Century, 234. Oxford: Voltaire Foundation, 1985.

Michaud, Stéphane. "Idolâtries: Représentations artistiques et littéraires." In *Histoire des femmes en Occident*, vol. 4: *Le XIXe siècle*, ed. Geneviève Fraisse and Michelle Perrot, 125. Paris: Plon, 1991.

Michel, Louise. *A travers la vie et la mort.* Edited by Daniel Armogathe. Paris: F. Maspero, 1982.

———. *Mémoires.* Paris: F. Roy, 1886.

———. *The Red Virgin: Memoirs of Louise Michel.* Edited and translated by Bullitt Lowry and Elizabeth Ellington Gunter. Tuscaloosa: University of Alabama Press, 1981.

Michelet, Jules. *La femme.* 1859. Paris: Flammarion, 1981.

Mignot-Ogliastri, Claude. *Anna de Noailles, une amie de la princesse Edmond de Polignac.* Paris: Méridiens-Klincksieck, 1986.

Mirecourt, Eugène de. *Madame de Girardin (Delphine Gay).* Paris: G. Havard, 1855.

Modern French Poets. Edited by Jean-François Leroux. *Dictionary of Literary Biography*, vol. 258. Detroit: Gale Group, 2002.

Modern Poets of France: A Bilingual Anthology. Edited and translated by Louis Simpson. Brownsville, Ore.: Story Line Press, 1997.

Montanclos, Marie-Emilie Maryon, baronne de Princen. *Œuvres diverses de Madame de Montanclos.* 2 vols. Grenoble: J. L. A. Giroud, 1790.

———. *Robert-le-bossu, ou les Trois soeurs, vaudeville en 1 acte.* 1798. Paris: Barba, 1802.

Montfort, Eugène de, ed. *Vingt-cinq ans de littérature.* 2 vols. Paris: Librairie de France, 1920–29.

Moore, Mary B. *Desiring Voices: Women Sonneteers and Petrarchism.* Carbondale: Southern Illinois University Press, 2000.

Morgan, Cheryl A. "The Death of a Poet: Delphine Gay's Romantic Makeover." *Symposium* 53, 4 (Winter 2000): 249–60.

Moroy, Elie. *La littérature féminine définie par les femmes écrivains.* Geneva: Semaine à Genève, 1931.

Morrissette, Bruce. *The Life and Works of Marie-Catherine Desjardins.* Saint Louis: Washington University Press, 1947.

Moulin, Jeanine. *Christine de Pisan.* Paris: Seghers, 1962.

———. *Huit siècles de poésie féminine.* Paris: Seghers, 1975, 1981.

———, ed. *La poésie féminine.* Vol. 1: *Du XIIe au XIXe siècle*; vol. 2: *Epoque moderne.* Paris: Seghers, 1963–66.

Murat, Amélie. *La chant de la vie.* Saint-Félicien-en-Vivarais: "Au Pigeonnier," 1935.

———. *D'un cœur fervent.* Paris: E. Sansot, 1908.

———. *Le livre de poésie.* Paris: E. Sansot, 1912.

———. *Passion.* Paris: Garnier, 1929.

———. *Le rosaire de Jeanne.* Aurillac: U.S.H.A., 1933.

———. *Vivre encore.* Uzès: Editions de la Cigale, 1937.

Navarre, Marguerite de [Marguerite, queen, consort of Henry II, king of Navarre].
  Chansons spirituelles. Edited by Georges Dottin. Geneva: Droz, 1971.

———. *Les dernières poésies de Marguerite de Navarre.* Edited by Abel Lefranc. Paris:
  A. Colin, 1896.

———. *Les prisons.* Edited and translated by Claire Lynch Wade. Bilingual edition.
  New York: P. Lang, 1989.

———. *The Prisons.* Translated by Hilda Dale. Reading, England: Whiteknights Press,
  1989.

———. See also under *Poésies du roi François Ier, de Louise de Savoie, duchesse
  d'Angoulême, de Marguerite, reine de Navarre . . .* below.

Niderst, Alain. *Mademoiselle de Scudéry, Paul Pellisson et leur monde.* Paris: Presses
  universitaires de France, 1976.

Nineteenth-Century French Poets. Edited by Robert Beum. *Dictionary of Literary
  Biography,* vol. 217. Detroit: Gale Group, 2000.

Nizet, Marie. *Le Capitaine Vampire.* Paris: Auguste Ghio, 1877 [1879?].

———. *Pour Axel.* Brussels: La Vie intellectuelle, 1923.

Noailles, Anna de. *Le cœur innombrable.* Paris: Calmann-Lévy, 1901.

———. *Derniers vers et poèmes d'enfance.* Paris: Grasset, 1934.

———. *Les éblouissements.* Paris: Calmann-Lévy, 1907.

———. *Les forces éternelles.* Paris: Fayard, 1920.

———. *L'honneur de souffrir.* Paris: Grasset, 1927.

———. *Le livre de ma vie.* Paris: Hachette, 1932.

———. *L'ombre des jours.* Paris: Calmann-Lévy, 1902.

———. *Poème de l'amour.* Paris: Fayard, 1924.

———. Preface to *Le Jardin des roses,* by Saâdi, trans. Franz Toussaint, xiii–xxxiv. 1912.
  Rev. ed. Paris: H. Piazza, 1965.

———. *Quatre douzaines de fleurs de prunus. I, Abricotiers, amandiers, pêchers.* With
  photographs by Alain Mazeran. Paris: Florès, 2002.

———. *Les vivants et les morts.* Paris: Fayard, 1913.

Nochlin, Linda. "Why Have There Been No Great Women Artists?" In *Art and Sexual
  Politics: Women's Liberation, Women Artists, and Art History,* ed. Thomas B. Hess
  and Elizabeth C. Baker, 5. New York: Macmillan [1971], 1973.

Olin, Norma Ireland. *Index to Women of the World from Ancient to Modern Times:
  Biographies and Portraits.* Westwood, Mass.: F. W. Faxon, 1970.

Orléans, Charles d'. *Les poésies du duc Charles d'Orléans.* Edited by Aimé-Louis
  Champollion-Figeac. Paris: J. Belin-Leprieur & Colomb de Batines, 1842.

Oxford Companion to French Literature. Edited by Sir Paul Harvey and J. E. Heseltine.
  Oxford: Clarendon Press, 1959.

Paden, William D., ed. *The Voice of the Trobairitz: Perspectives on the Women Troubadours*. Philadelphia: University of Pennsylvania Press, 1989.

Paliyenko, Adrianna M. "Is a Woman Poet Born or Made? Discourse of Maternity in Louisa Siefert and Louise Ackermann." *L'esprit créateur* 29, 2 (Summer 1999): 52–63.

———. "(Re)Placing Women in French Poetic History: The Romantic Legacy." *Symposium* 53, 4 (Winter 2000): 261–82.

Pape-Carpantier, Marie. *Préludes*. Paris: Perrotin, 1841.

Parnasse des dames. Edited by Edmé Billardon Sauvigny. 5 vols. Paris: Ruault, 1773.

Paulin, Louisa. *Florilège poétique*. Edited by Théodore Briant, Georges Bouquet, and Pierre Menanteau. Blainville-sur-mer: L'Amitié par le livre, 1957.

———. *Poèmes*. Albi: Editions de la Revue du Tarn, 1969.

———. *Rythmes et cadences*. Albi: Editions du Languedoc, 1947.

———. *Sorgas*. Toulouse: Privat, 1940.

Pauphilet, Albert. *Poètes et romanciers du Moyen Age*. Paris: Gallimard, 1952.

Pellisson, Maurice. *Les hommes de lettres au XVIIIe siècle*. Paris: A. Colin, 1911.

The Penguin Book of Women Poets. Edited by Carol Cosman, Joan Keefe, Kathleen Weaver, et al. New York: Viking Press, 1978.

Perche, Louis de. *Anna de Noailles*. Paris: P. Seghers, 1964.

Périn, Cécile. *Bretagne*. Paris: Le Divan, 1951.

———. *Les captives*. Paris: E. Sansot, 1919.

———. *Dicté par une ombre*. Paris: Le Divan, 1934.

———. *D'une chambre ouverte sur le ciel*. Paris: Le Divan, 1953.

———. *La féerie provençale*. Paris: Le Divan, 1930.

———. *Mélodies*. Paris: Ophrys, 1943.

———. *Paroles à l'enfant*. Paris: Le Divan, 1954.

———. *Vivre*. Editions de la Revue littéraire de Paris et de Champagne, 1906.

Perrin, Marie, *Renée Vivien, le corps exsangue: De l'anorexie mentale à la création littéraire*. Paris: l'Harmattan, 2003.

Perry, Catherine. "Flagorneur ou ébloui? Proust lecteur d'Anna de Noailles." *Bulletin Marcel Proust* 49 (1999): 37–53.

———. "In the Wake of Decadence: Anna de Noailles's Revaluation of Nature and the Feminine." In *Women of the* Belle Epoque / *Les Femmes de la Belle Epoque*, ed. Jean-François Fourny and Elisabeth Cardonne-Arlyck, *L'esprit créateur* 37 (Winter 1997): 94–105.

———. *Persephone Unbound: Dionysian Aesthetics in the Work of Anna de Noailles*. Lewisburg, Pa.: Bucknell University Press; London: Associated University Presses, 2003.

Peyramaure, Michel. *Fille de la colère: Le roman de Louise Michel*. Paris: R. Laffont, 2003.

Peyre, Henri. *French Novelists of Today*. New York: Oxford University Press, 1967.

Pizan, Christine de. *La cité des dames*. Translated by Thérèse Moreau and Eric Hicks. Paris: Stock, 2000.

———. *Livre de la cité des dames*. Translated by Earl Jeffrey Richards. New York: Persea Books, 1982.

———. *Livre des fais et bonnes meurs du Sage Roy Charles V*. Edited by Eric Hicks and Thérèse Moreau. Paris: Stock, 1997.

———. *The Love Debate Poems of Christine de Pizan*. Edited by Barbara K. Altmann. Gainesville: University Press of Florida, 1998.

———. *Œuvres poétiques de Christine de Pisan*. Edited by Maurice Roy. 3 vols. Paris: Firmin Didot, 1886–96.

———. *Poésies d'amour: Poèmes*. Paris: Aumage, 2003.

———. *Selected Writings of Christine de Pizan: New Translations, Criticism*. Edited by Renate Blumenfeld-Kosinski. New York: Norton, 1997.

———. *Writings of Christine de Pizan*. Edited by Charity Cannon Willard. New York: Persea Books, 1994.

———. See also under *Le débat sur "Le roman de la rose"* above.

Planté, Christine. "Marceline Desbordes-Valmore: Ni poésie féminine, ni poésie féministe." *French Literature Series* 16 (1989): 78–93.

———. *La petite sœur de Balzac: Essai sur la femme auteur*. Paris: Seuil, 1989.

———, ed. *Femmes poètes du XIXᵉ siècle: Une anthologie*. Lyon: Presses universitaires de Lyon, 1998.

Plat, Hélène, *Lucie Delarue-Mardrus: Une femme de lettres des années folles*. Paris: Grasset, 1994.

Poésies choisies de messieurs Corneille. Bensserade. De Scudéry. Boisrobert. Sarrasin. Desmarests. Bertaud . . . et plusieurs autres. Paris: Charles de Sercy, 1653. The "Recueil de Sercy."

Poésies du roi François Ier, de Louise de Savoie, duchesse d'Angoulême, de Marguerite, reine de Navarre, et correspondance intime du roi avec Diane de Poitiers et plusieurs autres dames de la cour. Edited by Aimé-Louis Champollion-Figeac. Paris: Imprimerie royale, 1847.

Poignault, Rémy, ed. *Présence de l'antiquité grecque et romaine au XXe siècle*. Tours: Centre André Piganiol, 2002.

Poullain de La Barre, François. *De l'éducation des dames*. Paris: J. Du Puis, 1674.

———. *De l'égalité des deux sexes*. Paris: J. Du Puis, 1673.

———. *De l'excellence des hommes*. Paris: J. Du Puis, 1673.

———. *François Poullain de La Barre's Three Cartesian Feminist Treatises*. Edited by Marcelle Maistre Welch. Translated by Vivien Bosley. Chicago: University of Chicago Press, 2002.

Pourrat, Henri. *La veillée de novembre*. Uzès: Editions de la Cigale, 1937.

Proust, Marcel. *A la recherche du temps perdu*. Vol. 4: *Le temps retrouvé*. Edited by Yves Tadié. Bibliothèque de la Pléiade. Paris: Gallimard, 1989.

———. *By Way of Sainte-Beuve*. Translated by Sylvia Townsend Warner. London: Chatto & Windus, 1958.

———. *Contre Sainte-Beuve*. Paris: Gallimard, Folio, 1997.

———. "*Les éblouissements* par la comtesse de Noailles." *Le Figaro, Supplément littéraire,* June 15, 1907. Reprinted in *Essais et articles,* ed. Pierre Clarac and Yves Sandre, 229–41. 1971. Paris: Gallimard, 1994.

———. "La vicomtesse Gaspard de Réveillon." In *Jean Santeuil,* 2: 304–13. Paris: Gallimard, 1952.

Quennell, Peter, ed. *Genius in the Drawing-Room: The Literary Salon in the Nineteenth and Twentieth Centuries.* London: Weidenfeld & Nicolson, 1980.

Quérard, Joseph-Marie. *La France littéraire.* Paris: Maisonneuve & Larose, 1964.

Quillet, Jeannine. *De Charles V à Christine de Pizan.* Paris: Champion, 2004.

Rachilde [Marguerite Eymery]. *Pourquoi je ne suis pas féministe.* Paris: Editions de France, 1928.

Rathery, Edmé-Jacques-Benoît, and [?] Boutron. *Mademoiselle de Scudéry, sa vie et sa correspondance, avec un choix de ses poésies.* 1873. Reprint. Geneva: Slatkine, 1971.

Raymond, Marcel, *L'influence de Ronsard sur la poésie française (1550–1585).* Paris: H. Champion, 1927. Reprint. Geneva: Droz, 1965.

Raynaud, Gaston. *Rondeaux et autres poésies du XVe siècle.* Société des anciens textes français. Paris: Didot, 1889.

"Recueil de Sercy." See *Poésies choisies de messieurs Corneille* [etc.] above.

Ribeyreix, Christine. *Louise Michel: Quand l'aurore se lèvera.* Périgueux: La Lauze, 2002.

Rodriguez, Suzanne. *Wild Heart, a Life: Natalie Clifford Barney's Journey from Victorian America to Belle Epoque Paris.* New York: Ecco, 2002.

Roelker, Nancy Lyman. *Queen of Navarre: Jeanne d'Albret (1528–1572).* Cambridge, Mass.: Harvard University Press, 1968.

Romieu, Marie de. *Les premières œuvres poétiques.* Edited by André Winandy. Geneva: Droz, 1972.

Rostand, Jean. Preface to *Choix de poésies,* by Anna de Noailles, 7–15. Paris: Bernard Grasset, 1976.

Sainctonge, Louise-Geneviève Gillot de. *Circé, tragédie.* Paris: Christophe Ballard, 1694.

———. *Didon, tragédie.* Paris: Christophe Ballard, 1693.

———. *Histoire secrète de Dom Antoine, roi du Portugal.* Paris: Jean Guignard, 1696.

———. *Poésies diverses de madame de Sainctonge.* Dijon: A. de Fay, 1714.

———. *Poésies galantes.* Paris: Jean Guignard, 1696.

Sainte-Beuve, Charles-Augustin. "Madame Emile de Girardin." February 17, 1851. *Causeries du lundi,* 3: 384–406. Paris: Garnier Frères, 1855.

———. "Madame Tastu." 1835. In *Portraits contemporains,* 1: 381–96. Paris: Didier, 1855.

———. *Panorama de la littérature française de Marguerite de Navarre aux frères Goncourt: Portraits et causeries.* Edited by Michel Brix et al. Paris: Livre de poche, 2004.

———. *Portraits contemporains.* Paris: Didier, 1847.

———. *Portraits de femmes.* Paris: Garnier frères, 1843. Reprint. Paris: Gallimard, 1998.

Sarrazin, Albertine. *L'astragale.* Paris: J.-J. Pauvert, 1965.

———. *La cavale.* Paris: J.-J. Pauvert, 1965.

———. *Lettres et poèmes.* Paris: J.-J. Pauvert, 1971.

———. *Poèmes.* Paris: J.-J. Pauvert, 1969.

———. *Romans, lettres et poèmes.* Paris: J.-J. Pauvert, 1967.

———. *La traversière.* Paris: J.-J. Pauvert, 1966.

Sartre, Jean-Paul. *"Huis-clos": Suivi de "Les mouches."* Paris: Gallimard, 1947.

Saulnier, Verdun Louis. *Etude sur Pernette du Guillet et ses "Rymes."* Extrait de la *Bibliothèque d'Humanisme et Renaissance* 4 (1944): 8, no. 2.

Sauvage, Cécile. *L'âme en bourgeon.* Paris: Steff, 1955.

———. *Œuvres de Cécile Sauvage.* Paris: Mercure de France, 1929. Reproduces, in addition to fragments and prose works, the collections *Tandis que la terre tourne, L'âme en bourgeon, Mélancolie, Fumées, Le vallon,* and the incomplete *Primevère.*

———. *Tandis que la terre tourne.* Paris: Mercure de France, 1910.

———. *Le vallon.* Paris: Mercure de France, 1913.

Scève, Maurice. *Délie: Object de plus haulte vertu.* 1544. Edited by Eugène Parturier. Paris: Nizet, 1987. Edited by Françoise Joukovsky. Paris: Dunod, 1996.

Schneider, Marcel. *Histoire de la littérature fantastique en France.* Paris: Fayard, 1985.

Schopenhauer, Arthur. "On Women." In *Parerga and Paralipomena: Schopenhauer: Selections,* ed. De Witt H. Parker, 434–47. New York: Charles Scribner's Sons, 1928.

Schultz, Gretchen. *The Gendered Lyric: Subjectivity and Difference in Nineteenth-Century French Poetry.* West Lafayette, Ind.: Purdue University Press, 1999.

Scudéry, Madeleine de. *Artamène, ou Le grand Cyrus.* Paris: Augustin Courbé, 1649–53. Reprint. Geneva: Slatkine, 1972.

———. *Clélie: Histoire romaine.* Paris: Augustin Courbé, 1654–61. Reprint. Geneva: Slatkine, 1973.

———. *Clélie: Histoire romaine, seconde partie.* Paris: Champion, 2002.

———. *Mathilde.* Translated by Nathalie Grande. Paris: Champion, 2002.

———. *Poésies choisies.* 3 vols. Paris: Charles de Sercy, 1653–58.

———. *Selected Letters, Orations, and Rhetorical Dialogues.* Translated by Jane Donawerth and Julie Strongson. Chicago: University of Chicago Press, 2004.

Séché, Alphonse. *Les muses françaises: Anthologie des femmes poètes (1200 à 1891).* Paris: Louis-Michaud, 1908.

Segrais, Marie-Madeleine Joliveau de. *Fables nouvelles en vers, suivies de quelques poèmes.* Paris: Cordier & Legras, 1801. 3d rev. ed. Paris: Janet & Cotelle, 1814.

Seiler, Sister Mary Hilarine. *Anne de Marquets, poétesse religieuse du XVIe siècle.* Washington, D.C.: Catholic University of America Press, 1931.

Shapiro, Norman R., trans. *The Comedy of Eros: Medieval French Guides to the Art of Love.* 1971. 2d ed. Notes and commentaries by James B. Wadsworth and Betsy Bowden. Urbana: University of Illinois Press, 1997.

———, trans. *The Complete Fables of Jean de La Fontaine.* Urbana: University of Illinois Press, 2007.

———, trans. *Fables from Old French.* Middletown, Conn.: Wesleyan University Press, 1988.

———, trans. *The Fabulists French: Verse Fables of Nine Centuries*. Urbana: University of Illinois Press, 1978.

———, trans. *Fifty Fables of La Fontaine*. Urbana: University of Illinois Press, 1985, 1997.

———, trans. *One Hundred and One Poems of Paul Verlaine*. Chicago: University of Chicago Press, 1999.

Sicaud, Sabine. *Poèmes d'enfant*. Poitiers: Cahiers de France, 1926.

———. *Les Poèmes de Sabine Sicaud*. Edited by François Millepierres. Paris: Stock, 1958.

———. *Sabine Sicaud: Le rêve inachevé*. Edited by Odile Ayral-Clause. Bordeaux: Les Dossiers d'Aquitaine, 1996.

Slama, Béatrice. "De la 'littérature féminine' à 'l'écrire femme': Différence et institution." *Littérature* 44 (December 1981): 51–71.

———. "Où vont les sexes? Figures romanesque et fantasmes 'fin de siècle,'" *Europe: Revue littéraire mensuelle* 69 (December 1991): 27–37.

Smarr, Janet. *Joining the Conversations: Dialogues by Renaissance Women*. Ann Arbor: University of Michigan Press, 2004.

Sodenkamp, Andrée. *Arrivederci Italia*. Brussels: André de Rache, 1965.

———. *Autour de moi-même*. Brussels: André de Rache, 1976.

———. *C'est au feu que je pardonne*. Brussels: André de Rache, 1976.

———. *C'était une nuit comme une autre*. Amay, Belgium: Maison de la Poésie d'Amay, 1991.

———. *Choix*. Brussels: André de Rache, 1980.

———. *Des oiseaux à tes lèvres*. Charleroi: Héraldy, 1950.

———. *Les dieux obscurs: Poèmes*. Brussels: Georges Houyoux, 1958.

———. *Femmes des longs matins: Poèmes*. Brussels: André de Rache, 1965.

———. *La fête debout*. Brussels: André de Rache, 1973.

———. *Poèmes*. Paris: Gallimard, 1970.

———. *Poèmes choisis*. Brussels: Académie royale de langue et littérature françaises, 1998.

———. *Sainte terre*. Paris: Librairie les Lettres, 1954.

Sommers, Paula. *Celestial Ladders: Readings in Marguerite de Navarre's Poetry of Spiritual Ascent*. Geneva: Droz, 1989.

Sorrell, Martin, ed. and trans. *Elles: A Bilingual Anthology of Modern French Poetry by Women*. Exeter, England: University of Exeter Press, 1995.

Souhami, Diana. *Wild Girls: Natalie Barney and Romaine Brooks*. London: Weidenfeld & Nicolson, 2004.

Stantchéva, Roumiana. "Anna de Noailles et l'orgueil du choix." *Euresis: Cahiers roumains d'études littéraires* 1–2 (1993): 39–43.

Stanton, Domna C., ed. *The Defiant Muse: French Feminist Poems from the Middle Ages to the Present. A Bilingual Anthology*. New York: Feminist Press, 1986.

Steele, Stephen. "Le 'Cruel Silence' autour de Louisa Paulin, poète provenço-français." *Romance Notes* 37, 2 (Winter 1997): 193–97.

Stephenson, Barbara. *The Power and Patronage of Marguerite de Navarre*. Burlington, Vt.: Ashgate, 2003.

Stivale, Charles J. "Louise Michel's Poetry of Existence and Revolt." *Tulsa Studies in Women's Literature* 5, 1 (Spring 1986): 41–61.

Tastu, Amable. *Poésies*. Paris: A. Dupont, 1826.

———. *Poésies complètes*. Paris: Didier, 1858.

———. *Poésies nouvelles*. Paris: Denain & Delamare, 1838.

Testut, Charles. *Les échos*. New Orleans: H. Méridier, 1849.

Théïs, Constance-Marie de, princesse de Salm-Reifferscheid-Dyck. [writing as Constance D. T. Pipelet] *Epître aux femmes*. Paris: Desenne, 1797.

———. *Œuvres complètes de madame la princesse C. de S. D.* 4 vols. Paris: F. Didot, 1841–42.

———. *Poésies*. Paris: F. Didot, 1811, 1814.

Theobald, John Richmond, ed. and trans. *The Lost Wine: Seven Centuries of French into English Lyrical Poetry*. La Jolla, Calif.: Green Tiger Press, 1980.

Thibaut IV. *Chansons de Thibaut IV, comte de Champagne et de Brie, roi de Navarre*. Reims: P. Regnier, 1851.

Thiry, Marcel, and Roger Brucher, eds. *Andrée Sodenkamp*. Collection Poètes actuels. Paris: Formes et langages, 1973.

Thomas, Edith. *Louise Michel*. Translated by Penelope Williams. Montréal: Black Rose Books, 1980.

Trekker, Anne-Marie, and Pierre Vander Straeten, eds. *Cent auteurs: Anthologie de littérature française de Belgique*. Nivelles, Belgium: Editions de la Francité, 1982.

Turgeon, Frederick King. "Fanny de Beauharnais." Ph.D. diss., Harvard University, 1929.

Van Bever, Adolphe. *Les poètes du terroir*. Paris: C. Delagrave, 1909.

Van Dam, Francis. "Andrée Sodenkamp et Anne-Marie Derèse: L'incessant partage." *Le Langage et l'Homme* 27, 2–3 (June–September 1992): 195–204.

Verlaine, Paul. "Art poétique." In *Anthologie de la poésie française: XVIIIe siècle, XIXe siècle, XXe siècle*, ed. Martine Bercot, Michel Collot, and Catriona Seth, 734–44. Paris: Gallimard, 2000.

———. *Les poètes maudits*. 1884. Reprint. Edited by Michel Décaudin. Paris: Société d'Edition d'enseignement supérieur, 1982.

Vigny, Alfred de. *Œuvres poétiques*. Edited by Jacques-Philippe Saint-Gérand. Paris: Garnier-Flammarion, 1978.

———. *Poèmes antiques et modernes*. Paris: E. Flammarion, 1826.

Villedieu, Marie-Catherine Desjardins de. *The Disorders of Love*. Translated and Annotated by Arthur Flannigan Saint-Aubin. Birmingham, Ala.: Summa Publications, 1995.

———. *Fables, ou Histoires allégoriques*. Paris: Claude Barbin, 1670.

———. *Œuvres meslées par Madame de Villedieu*. Paris: Claude Barbin, 1664–74.

Vilmorin, André de. *Essai sur Louise de Vilmorin*. Paris: P. Seghers, 1962.

Vilmorin, Louise de. *L'alphabet des aveux.* Paris: NRF, 1954.

———. *Fiançailles pour rire.* Paris: Gallimard, 1939.

———. *Intimités.* Paris: Le Promeneur, 2001.

———. *Poèmes.* Paris: Gallimard, 1970.

———. *Promenades et autres rencontres.* Paris: Le Promeneur, 2000.

———. *Le sable du sablier.* Paris: Gallimard, 1945.

———. *Solitude, ô mon éléphant.* Paris: Gallimard, 1972.

Vincent, Patrick. *The Romantic Poetess: European Culture, Politics and Gender, 1820–1840.* Becoming Modern Series. Hanover, N.H.: University Press of New England, 2004.

Vivien, Renée [Pauline Mary Tarn]. *Cendres et poussières: Poèmes.* 1902. Edited by Hubert Juin. Paris: R. Deforges, 1977.

———. *Etudes et préludes.* Paris: A. Lemerre, 1901.

———. *Evocations.* Paris: A. Lemerre, 1903. 2d ed. 1905.

———. *Lettres de Renée Vivien à Kérimé.* Edited by Jean Leproux. Aigues-Vives: HB Editions, 1998.

———. *Poèmes de Renée Vivien.* Paris: A. Lemerre, 1923–24.

———. *Sapho.* Paris: A. Lemerre, 1903.

Walton, Whitney. *Eve's Proud Descendants: Four Women Writers and Republican Politics in Nineteenth-Century France.* Stanford, Calif.: Stanford University Press, 2000.

Weiss, Andrea. *Paris Was a Woman.* London; San Francisco: Pandora, 1995.

Who's Who in Lesbian and Gay Writing. Edited by Gabriele Griffin. London: Routledge, 2002.

Wickes, George. *The Amazon of Letters: The Life and Loves of Natalie Barney.* New York: Putnam, 1976.

Willard, Charity Cannon. *Christine de Pisan: Her Life and Works.* New York: Persea Books, 1984.

Wilwerth, Evelyne. *Visages de la littérature féminine.* Brussels: Mardaga, 1987.

Women Writers of Great Britain and Europe: An Encyclopedia. Edited by Katharina M. Wilson, Paul Schlueter, and June Schlueter. New York: Garland, 1997.

Women Writers of the Renaissance and Reformation. Edited by Katharina M. Wilson. Athens, Ga.: University of Georgia Press, 1987.

Wouters, Liliane. *L'aloès.* Paris: Luneau Ascot, 1983.

———. *Le billet de Pascal.* Echternach, Luxembourg: Editions Phi, 2000.

———. *Le bois sec.* Paris: Gallimard, 1960.

———. *Changer d'écorce.* Tournai, Belgium: Renaissance du livre, 2001.

———. *Le gel.* Paris: Seghers, 1966.

———. *Journal du scribe.* Brussels: Les Eperonniers, 1990.

———. *La marche forcée.* Brussels: Editions des artistes, 1954.

———. *Parenthèse.* St. Laurent du Pont: Atelier d'Art, 1984.

———. *Tous les chemins conduisent à la mer.* Brussels: Les Eperonniers, 1997.

———, ed. *Panorama de la poésie française de Belgique.* Brussels: Jacques Antoine, 1976.

Wouters, Liliane, and Alain Bosquet, eds. *La poésie francophone de Belgique.* 4 vols. Brussels: Traces, 1985–92.

Wouters, Liliane, and Yves Namur, eds. *Le siècle des femmes.* Brussels: Les Eperonniers, 2000.

———, eds. *Un siècle de femmes.* Echternach, Luxembourg: Editions Phi, 2000.

Writings by Pre-Revolutionary French Women. Edited by Anne R. Larsen and Colette H. Winn. New York: Garland, 2000.

Wyndham, Violet Leverson. *Madame de Genlis: A Biography.* London: André Deutsch, 1958.

Yenal, Edith. *Christine de Pizan: A Bibliography of Writings by Her and About Her.* Metuchen, N.J.: Scarecrow Press, 1989.

Index of Authors

Index of French Titles and First Lines

Index of English First Lines

My doll, with her glazed porcelain eyes,
797

My eyes, fearing too many a tear to shed,
165

My feet no longer touch the ground, 1103

My life seems duller, I confess, 853

My limbs will spread, my body will
deliver, 1093

My lord, throughout the strife of civil
war, 177

My love, come yet again this night, 87

My love, I would not leave you so. It will,
741

My lovely cat, scornful, remote, 815

My lyre, they chide, is much too gay, 697

My portrait by Nanteuil: ah, 'tis, 285

My shepherd—black, gold—like striped
flag, goes leaping, 815

My son, no wealth have I with which, 75

My soul was like a lamp Now it grows
cold, 1105

My thanks, ye comely *demoiselles,* 607

My thoughts clash, clang, constant
antagonists, 1097

My time grows short, and great my soul's
desire—, 119

My time was when love novels were in
flower—, 1015

My verse is slight, my Muse is slight no
less, 255

My wished-on star spins a glum thread,
unravels, 995

Naught can you do, the fort is won, 89

Neither his thoughts, winging from
distant skies, 737

Neither the dazzling dawn beyond the
high, 851

Neither the green fields' flowering gaiety,
239

Neither Ulysses nor one shrewder might,
143

Never had I a notion that you might, 185

Never have I drunk from that spring
profane, 233

Nevermore, never, O my heart, may you,
223

Niobe am I: pity my despair, 193

No, dear Philinte, I must remain, 445

No, I am loath to offer you, 395

No, you shall not have my bouquet, 575

No day I spend but that I burn, 305

No longer is there any need that I, 125

No one has yet, nor will one ever, 675

No one seek I to love or pity me, 593

No peace I find, nor know war's bale and
bane, 253

No remedy I seek, in my defense, 125

No sooner do I, yearning, take my rest,
149

Nostalgic night, shivering, peters out,
897

Nothing you think of but your sheep, 565

Not to remember as we trod the sand,
1055

November blooms on rose trees of our
May, 895

Now, at last, I perceive the truth: ah, yes!,
117

Now comes the autumn, harsh,
voluptuous, 733

O beauteous hand that bends my Liege's
bow, 203

O Beauty, fatal gift of Heaven!, 461

O breeze blown from the South, come
drink the snow, 959

O captive Zion, prisoner pent, 363

October's and November's twilights, gray,
927

O days' dreams and nights' labor,
mystery, 813

O Earth! Here, in your shadowed breast,
so lonely, 823

O fair brown eyes, looks that aloof
remain, 143

Off he goes begging in his costume gray,
245

Off in the evening darkness shall we go,
899

"You, caterpillar vile, what good are you?" 413

You, owls, sons of the forest, tenebrous, 1085

You grow and I decline; you glow, 669

You hear no more those hillside voices sing, 893

You know not yet what joy it is to see, 371

You lifeless things, nature's most lowly! Why, 313

You live on the weather; on, 863

You'll always love me!... So it goes, 973

You'll come gliding toward me, on a black barque, 1031

You lure me not with all your charms, O fair, 289

You need but make a move and Europe quakes, 279

Young friend, in this your tender age, 493

You pause before the fragrant grave where lies, 823

Your art is well above my own, by far, 387

Your breath's visible puff, your pupils too, 1105

You reach your little tree-green hands to me, 1049

Your foot pokes here and there, 1123

Your hair is made of spiders, 985

Your heart between two creatures fair is split, 289

Your heart offered itself intact to me, 805

Your hearts are hot as embers' breath, 719

Your wounded pride, obstinately, 883

You say I write because Their Highnesses, 191

You scorn the rules of friendship, written, 407

You spend your leisure hours in that discreet, 871

Youth's graces, in their flight—oh, well I know!—, 559

You who proclaimed yourself our liberator, 545

You won my heart and swore by Love that you, 291

Credits

The translator and publisher are grateful for permission to use copyrighted material by the poets listed below. Every effort has been made to trace copyright holders, but if any have been inadvertently overlooked the publisher will be pleased to make the necessary arrangements at the first opportunity.

Poems from *Ferveur* and *La figure de proue* by Lucie Delarue-Mardrus. Reproduced by permission of Editions Bernard Grasset, Paris.

Poems by Lise Deharme. Reproduced by permission of Sophie Deharme.

Poems from *Anthologie personnelle* by Lucienne Desnoues. Reproduced by permission of Actes Sud, Arles.

Poems from *Les pipeaux* by Rosemonde Gérard. Reproduced by permission of Editions Bernard Grasset, Paris.

Poems from *Les poésies* by Gérard d'Houville. Reproduced by permission of Editions Bernard Grasset, Paris.

Poems by Anne-Marie Kegels. Reproduced by permission of Eliane Barnich-Kegels.

Poems by Louisa Paulin. Reproduced by permission of the Fédération de Sociétés intellectuelles du Tarn.

Poems by Cécile Périn. Reproduced by permission of Lise Jamati.

Poems from *Œuvres: Romans, lettres et poèmes* by Albertine Sarrazin. © 1967 Jean-Jacques Pauvert; © 2000 Jean-Jacques Pauvert, Département de la Librairie Arthème Fayard. Reproduced by permission.

Poems by Andrée Sodenkamp. Reproduced by permission of the Académie royale de Langue et de Littérature françaises.

Poems from *Fiançailles pour rire, Le sable du sablier,* and *Solitude, ô mon éléphant* by Louise de Vilmorin. © Editions Gallimard, Paris. Reproduced by permission.

Poems from *La marche forcée, Le bois sec, Le gel,* and *L'aloès* by Liliane Wouters. © 2004 SABAM Belgium. Reproduced by permission.